THE OXFORD HANDBOOK OF

LINGUISTIC
FIELDWORK

OXFORD HANDBOOKS IN LINGUISTICS
RECENTLY PUBLISHED IN THE SERIES

THE OXFORD HANDBOOK OF

LINGUISTIC FIELDWORK

Edited by

NICHOLAS THIEBERGER

OXFORD
UNIVERSITY PRESS

OXFORD
UNIVERSITY PRESS

Great Clarendon Street, Oxford, OX2 6DP,
United Kingdom

Oxford University Press is a department of the University of Oxford.
It furthers the University's objective of excellence in research, scholarship,
and education by publishing worldwide. Oxford is a registered trade mark of
Oxford University Press in the UK and in certain other countries

© editorial matter and organization Nicholas Thieberger 2012
© chapters their several authors 2012

The moral rights of the authors have been asserted

First published 2012
First published in paperback 2014

Impression: 1

All rights reserved. No part of this publication may be reproduced, stored in
a retrieval system, or transmitted, in any form or by any means, without the
prior permission in writing of Oxford University Press, or as expressly permitted
by law, by licence or under terms agreed with the appropriate reprographics
rights organization. Enquiries concerning reproduction outside the scope of the
above should be sent to the Rights Department, Oxford University Press, at the
address above

You must not circulate this work in any other form
and you must impose this same condition on any acquirer

Published in the United States of America by Oxford University Press
198 Madison Avenue, New York, NY 10016, United States of America

British Library Cataloguing in Publication Data

Data available

ISBN 978–0–19–957188–8 (Hbk.)
ISBN 978–0–19–968981–1 (Pbk.)

Printed and bound by
CPI Group (UK) Ltd, Croydon, CR0 4YY

Links to third party websites are provided by Oxford in good faith and
for information only. Oxford disclaims any responsibility for the materials
contained in any third party website referenced in this work.

CONTENTS

PART III COLLABORATING WITH OTHER DISCIPLINES

PART IV COLLABORATING WITH THE COMMUNITY

Notes on Contributors

Chie Adachi is a PhD candidate in Linguistics at the University of Edinburgh. Currently, she works on Japanese complimenting behaviour within the framework of (interactional) sociolinguistics for her PhD project. She is interested in how young Japanese speakers socially and linguistically construct the speech act of complimenting. She is also interested in the gendered nature of this speech act. Her study at Edinburgh is fully funded by the Ministry of Education, Japan, for three years.

Linda Barwick (Associate Professor, University of Sydney) is Director of PARADISEC, the Pacific and Regional Archive for Digital Sources in Endangered Cultures, established in 2003 by several Australian universities with support from the Australian Research Council. An ethnomusicologist with fieldwork experience in Australia, Italy, and the Philippines, she is interested in using digital technologies to extend access to research results by collaborating communities. Recent song documentation projects jointly undertaken with linguists include the Murriny Patha song project, the Western Arnhem Land song project, and the Iwaidja Project. Her publications include multimedia CDs and web resources produced in collaboration with singers and communities.

Andrea L. Berez is currently finishing her doctoral dissertation in the Department of Linguistics at the University of California, Santa Barbara. She is primarily a documentary and descriptive linguist specializing in Ahtna, an endangered Athabascan language spoken in south central Alaska. Her linguistic interests include geographic cognition, intonation, polysynthesis, and discourse, and she has been active in promoting and developing the technological infrastructure for language documentation and archiving.

Marc Chemillier is Director of Studies at the EHESS in Paris (School for Advanced Studies in Social Sciences). He received a PhD in Computer Science and also has degrees in Mathematics, Musicology, Philosophy, and Anthropology. He has conducted fieldwork among the Nzakara of Central African Republic to study their harp music, and in Madagascar to work on the ethnomathematics of divination. His main interests focus on the modelling of elaborated knowledge developed in oral tradition, thus associating fieldwork for the ethnographic recording of data and digital technologies for the modelling aspect of his approach. His recent research deals with musical knowledge and improvisation in collaboration with

IRCAM in Paris (Institute for Research and Coordination Acoustic/Music). He is the author of *Les Mathématiques naturelles* (2007).

Barry Conn is a Principal Research Scientist at the National Herbarium of New South Wales, Royal Botanic Gardens Sydney, and is an Associate Professor at the University of Sydney. He is a plant systematist with interests in the phylogeny of the Lamiaceae, Loganiaceae, and Urticaceae, and has published more than 190 research papers in scientific journals. Dr Conn has undertaken field studies throughout Australia and has worked extensively in the tropical forests of Indonesia and Papua New Guinea. He has maintained strong interests in electronic data, and has assisted with the development of international standards for the storage and transfer of electronic natural history database records.

Laurent Dousset is an anthropologist specializing in Australian Aboriginal cultures, and has recently also engaged in fieldwork in Vanuatu. His main interests are kinship and social organization, social transformations, and issues of landownership. Currently associate professor at EHESS (the School for Advanced Social Studies, Paris and Marseilles), he is director of CREDO (the Centre for Research and Documentation on Oceania, Marseilles) and has published numerous scientific papers on various issues in Aboriginal Australia. He also published two books, *Assimilating Identities* (Oceania Monograph, 2005) and *Mythes, Missiles et Cannibales* (Société des Océanistes, 2011).

Nicholas Evans is Professor of Linguistics at the Australian National University. He is a field linguist with wide expertise in language documentation and typology. After decades of work on Australian Aboriginal languages (especially Kayardild, Dalabon, Iwaidja, and Bininj Gun-wok), he has recently begun work on Papuan languages in Southern New Guinea, particularly Nen. He has published grammars of Kayardild and Bininj Gun-wok, dictionaries of Kayardild and Dalabon, and over 100 papers on a wide range of linguistic topics. In addition to scientific work, he has been extensively involved in returning his expertise to indigenous communities through vernacular-language educational materials, court interpreting, land and sea rights work, and cultural interpreting for indigenous artists.

Jarita Holbrook (Near Eastern Studies, University of Arizona) is the author of *Following the Stars*, a study of modern stellar navigation, and editor of *African Cultural Astronomy* (2008). Her research on humans and their relationship to the sky includes studies of indigenous people, the general public, and professional astronomers. She is currently working on a book investigating academic programs focused on increasing the number of minority astronomy doctorates. Currently, she is the youngest chair of the Historical Astronomy Division of the American Astronomical Society and the first African-American Vice President of the European Cultural Astronomy Society (SEAC).

Pierre Lemonnier is a Director of Research at CNRS (CREDO, Marseilles). After field research (1978–82) among the various Anga peoples of Papua New Guinea, he chose the Ankave valley for long-term anthropological fieldwork. He has published books on the anthropology of technics, *Elements for an Anthropology of Technology* (1992), *Technological Choices: Transformation in Material Cultures since the Neolithic* (1993), and on Melanesia, *Guerres et festins: paix, échanges et compétition dans les Highlands de Nouvelle-Guinée* (1990), and *Le Sabbat des lucioles* (2006), which deals with witchcraft and mourning among the Ankave. His current research is about the rôle of objects in Anga rituals.

Monica Macaulay is Professor of Linguistics at the University of Wisconsin-Madison, and specializes in the morphology of American Indian languages. She has worked on Mixtec, Chinantec, Karuk, and Menominee. She is currently involved with language revitalization projects with the Menominee and the Potawatomi, creating dictionaries of both. She is also co-founder of the Women in Linguistics Mentoring Alliance, a book reviews editor for the Linguist List, and a past member of the LSA Executive Committee. She is the author of *Surviving Linguistics: A Guide for Graduate Students*, now in its second edition.

Asifa Majid is a Senior Research Fellow at the Max Planck Institute for Psycholinguistics. Her work is interdisciplinary, combining standardized experimental methods, in-depth linguistic analysis, and ethnographically informed description. This coordinated approach has been used to study space, event representation, and most recently perception and emotion. Representative works include *Cutting and Breaking: A Crosslinguistic Perspective*, co-edited with Melissa Bowerman, and *The Senses in Language and Culture*, co-edited with Stephen C. Levinson.

Anna Margetts has been conducting fieldwork in Papua New Guinea with the Saliba-Logea language community since 1995, and is the chief investigator in the Saliba-Logea documentation project within the DoBeS (Dokumentation Bedrohter Sprachen/Documentation of Endangered Languages) program. She has published on topics including transitivity and three-participant events, serialization, language change, linguistic documentation, and research methodology. Her research interests include the morphosyntax of Oceanic languages, the interface between pragmatics and grammar, the analysis of spoken language, language typology, and documentary linguistics. She is a Senior Lecturer in Linguistics at Monash University in Melbourne.

Andrew Margetts is a member of the Saliba-Logea documentation team funded by DoBeS (Dokumentation Bedrohter Sprachen/Documentation of Endangered Languages), and has been developing the project's database, linking the text collection with associated information. He maintains the project data flow from raw recordings to annotated texts, and has created an online Transcriber-Toolbox converter.

His interests include database methodology and animations for linguistic stimuli. He has published on using Toolbox with media files, and is currently developing a browser based tool for displaying and querying Toolbox lexicon data. He spent several years in Papua New Guinea working as a volunteer.

David M. Mark is a SUNY Distinguished Professor of Geography at the University at Buffalo (UB), where he is the director of the Buffalo site of the National Centre for Geographic Information and Analysis (NCGIA). He also is a member of UB's Centre for Cognitive Science. He completed his PhD in Geography at Simon Fraser University in 1977, and joined the University at Buffalo in 1981. He has written or co-authored more than 230 publications and has edited five books. His research interests include cultural differences in geographic conceptualization, geographic cognition and language, geographic ontology, and geographic information science.

Will McClatchey grew up on the White Mountain Reservation in Arizona, then completed high school in Oregon. He earned BSc degrees in Anthropology and Pharmacy from Oregon State University. While working as a pharmacist he earned an MSc in Ethnobotany from Brigham Young University and a PhD in Botany (Evolutionary Biology) from the University of Florida. His MSc and PhD research was conducted in the southwest Pacific region. He is currently the Director of Research at the Botanical Research Institute of Texas, where he addresses hypotheses about evolution of humans and artificial ecosystems, and production of traditional alcoholic beverages.

Miriam Meyerhoff is Professor of Linguistics at the University of Auckland. She is interested in how synchronic language variation feeds into language change, especially in creole speech communities. She is also interested in the relationship between language variation and ideologies about language. She has undertaken sociolinguistic fieldwork in varied locations and social settings. She is the author of *Introducing Sociolinguistics* and is the co-editor of *The Handbook of Language and Gender, The Routledge Sociolinguistics Reader,* and the Creole Language Library.

Ulrike Mosel is Professor of General Linguistics at the University of Kiel. After gaining her PhD in Semitic languages at the University of Munich (1974), she started researching South Pacific languages and became an expert in collaborative fieldwork. Her books include *Tolai Syntax* (1984), *Samoan Reference Grammar* (1992, with Even Hovdhaugen), and *Say it in Samoan* (1997, with Ainslie So'o). Currently she is working on the documentation of the Teop language of Bougainville, Papua New Guinea. Together with Christian Lehmann, Hans-Jürgen Sasse, and Jan Wirrer, she initiated the DoBeS (Dokumentation Bedrohter Sprachen) language documentation program funded by the Volkswagen Foundation.

Golnaz Nanbakhsh received a BA degree in English and Language Literature in 2002, and an MSc degree in Applied Linguistics from the University of Edinburgh in 2005, where she continued her studies as a PhD student in Sociolinguistics. Her research looks at the interplay of linguistic and sociolinguistic norms of politeness portrayed with Persian address system. She is interested in the analysis of language and social interaction, specifically the intersection of language, culture, and society, using spontaneous interactions. Since September 2010 she has been a faculty member of Islamic and Middle Eastern Studies at the University of Edinburgh.

David Nash is Honorary Visiting Fellow in Linguistics, School of Language Studies, The Australian National University. He has published on Australian languages over the last three decades, including co-editing *Language in Native Title* (2002) and *Forty Years On: Ken Hale and Australian Languages* (2001), and has been a consultant for a number of claims to traditional land in Australia. He continues to be involved in the mapping of sites in the country of the Warlpiri and their neighbours in central Australia.

Paul Newman received his BA and MA from the University of Pennsylvania and his PhD (Linguistics) from the University of California, Los Angeles. He has held academic positions at Yale, Bayero University (Nigeria), University of Leiden (Netherlands), and Indiana University, where he is Distinguished Professor Emeritus. He has published eighteen books and over 100 articles and reviews. He is regarded as the world's leading authority on the Hausa language. Newman is also a lawyer (JD, *summa cum laude*, Indiana University). He was copyright specialist at the University of Michigan and Fulbright professor in law at the University of Haifa. He was formerly Special Counsel to the LSA.

Carolyn O'Meara is an assistant professor and researcher in the Seminario de Lenguas Indígenas within the Instituto de Investigaciones Filológicas at the Universidad Nacional Autónoma de México in Mexico City. She received her PhD in Linguistics from the University at Buffalo in 2010. She has been conducting fieldwork in El Desemboque, Sonora, Mexico, with the Seri people since 2004. Her interests include landscape classification (e.g. ethnophysiography/landscape ethnoecology) and semantics, including spatial reference and lexical semantics. She is currently extending her work on landscape classification in Seri to the larger domain of the structure of the nominal lexicon in Seri.

Nancy Pollock has retired from her position as Senior Lecturer in Anthropology and the later position as Acting Director of Development Studies at Victoria University of Wellington, New Zealand. Her research work on food security, health issues, and dietary change is derived from initial work in the Marshall Islands. This work was the basis for many publications on food issues, including *These Roots Remain*, and *Social Aspects of Obesity*, co-edited with Igor de Garine. She has worked on Nuclear Claims for Compensation post-Bravo in 1954, and also on Nauruan claims for compensation for the effects of mining phosphate on Nauru. She is currently completing a book on the social impact of mining on Nauru.

Keren Rice is University Professor and Canada Research Chair in Linguistics and Aboriginal Studies at the University of Toronto. She studies the Dene (Slavey) language of Canada's Northwest Territories, and has written on fieldwork and on ethics in linguistic fieldwork.

Mandana Seyfeddinipur is a senior research fellow and the director of the Endangered Languages Documentation Programme of the Hans Rausing Endangered Languages Project at the School for Oriental and African Studies (SOAS). Her main research interest is the visual mode of language, especially gestures, language use, and the psychology of language. She has worked on Azerbijanian and Iranian gesture use, and on the integration of disfluent speech and gesture.

Jane Simpson is Chair of Indigenous Linguistics, School of Language Studies, The Australian National University. She has studied Australian Indigenous languages for more than three decades, acted as a consultant on land claims, and co-edited *The Land is a Map: Placenames of Indigenous Origin in Australia* (2002) and *Children's Language and Multilingualism: Indigenous Language Use at Home and School* (2008).

David Stea received a BSc (hons) in Mechanical/Aeronautical Engineering from what is now Carnegie-Mellon University, an MSc in Psychology from the University of New Mexico, and a PhD in Psychology from Stanford University. He is Professor Emeritus of Geography and International Studies, Texas State University, San Marcos, and Research Associate, Centre for Global Justice (Mexico). A co-founder of the field of environmental psychology, his research interests include spatial cognition, map learning in young children, participatory planning with Indigenous peoples, and sustainable development. He has written several books, including *Image and Environment, Maps in Minds, Environmental Mapping*, and *Placemaking*.

Anna Strycharz is a PhD student at the University of Edinburgh. Her research interests focus around language variation and change in Japanese, especially in the area of honorifics in the dialect of Osaka. She has lived, worked, and conducted fieldwork in Japan.

Nicholas Thieberger wrote a grammar of South Efate (central Vanuatu) arising out of a media corpus he built in the course of his fieldwork. In 2003 he helped establish the digital archive PARADISEC (paradisec.org.au) and is a co-director the Resource Network for Linguistic Diversity (RNLD). He is interested in developments in e-humanities methods and their potential to improve research practice, and he is now developing methods for creation of reusable data sets from fieldwork on previously unrecorded languages. He taught in the Department of Linguistics at the University of Hawai'i at Mānoa and is now an Australian Research Council QEII Fellow at the University of Melbourne.

Andrew Turk has degrees in Surveying, Applied Science (Cartography), and Arts (Psychology Honours and Philosophy major), and a PhD. In the 1970s and early 1980s he worked for the Australian Government producing topographic maps. In 1983 he commenced research at Melbourne University into design of tactual maps and graphics for visually impaired persons. From 1993 he has worked at Murdoch University teaching and researching social aspects of ICT and working with Indigenous communities in Western Australia. His current research and publications concentrate on ethnophysiography (cultural/linguistic aspects of conceptions of landscape and place).

INTRODUCTION

NICHOLAS THIEBERGER

1.1 WHY ANOTHER HANDBOOK OF FIELDWORK METHODS?

Linguists engaging in fieldwork have traditionally focused on a grammatical analysis of a language that may never before have been subjected to this kind of scrutiny. With increased awareness of the number of endangered languages (see Evans 2010, or Harrison 2010) has come a stronger emphasis on recording a range of material while in the field, also giving rise to language documentation as a distinct methodology within linguistics. This recognition of the loss of linguistic diversity has led to support for the ongoing use of these languages and the production of records of as many different aspects of the language as possible. At the same time the development of new technological approaches to language recording allows us to record more and to create richer textual annotations of recorded media than we could in the past. Linguists are in a position to record much more than narratives and example sentences, but need guidance once the topics of discussion go beyond everyday expertise.

We can characterize the new methods and tools associated with language documentation as forming a new paradigm of research. This paradigm focuses on collaboration with speakers and on the interdisciplinary nature of knowledge systems, of which language is one part. A further focus is on primary data as the warrant for analytical claims, and emphasizes replicability of the analysis resulting in such claims. From this new paradigm flows the need to create reusable primary data, and to provide for its accessibility and longterm curation.

A linguist may be the only outsider to learn and prepare materials in a given language and culture, and so this handbook aims to increase the usefulness of those materials, both in their form and their content. The form of records can depend on the quality of recordings made in the field and this can vary considerably depending on the type of equipment used, the expertise of the user, and the environment in which the recordings are made. The ability to keep track of the various outputs of fieldwork (recordings, transcripts, fieldnotes, images, texts, analyses, dictionary and so on) requires planning and an explicit methodology. Advice on optimizing both the form and content of field material is provided in this volume.

Sanjek (1990) discusses the transformation of primary ethnographic data into 'analysis', a topic that has occupied many anthropologists but not so many linguists. Linguists typically operate in a framework that starts from a set of data and applies a method that originates most recently in the structuralism of Saussure and Sapir—described in a number of fieldguides and manuals (surveyed by Mosel in Chapter 3 of this volume). While this method begins with data collection, the data is soon relegated to what Marcus (2009: 22) calls a 'present absence'—it is claimed as the basis for the conclusions provided in a grammatical description, but is not provided to allow verification of those claims. There has been an interpretive leap from linguistic fieldwork to analysis that has been described as using 'inductive generalizations' but which has not presented primary data together with the analysis, thus weakening the claims that can be made and not allowing reanalysis of the generalizations arrived at by the fieldworker. As advocated in various chapters in this collection, data can (and should) now be more central to linguistic analysis, and, if it is curated appropriately, can be reused in ways not originally planned for by the fieldworker, so that we can 'anticipate a future need to know something that cannot be defined in the present' (Strathern 2004: 7).

The focus on documenting endangered languages can be likened to salvage anthropology, which has been criticized as an attempt to capture some authentic version of a culture before it is 'tainted' by contact with other cultures. It is the case that the project of language documentation includes recording aspects of a range of human knowledge systems that exist without the influence of metropolitan languages, or perhaps in cases where such influence is not yet as complete as it is likely to be. The particularities of each language provide insights into the range of possible diversity of human expression, and it is often in the discourse of monolingual speakers of a generation before extensive shift to a metropolitan language that these particularities are still to be found. Lest this be construed as a defence of the appropriation of indigenous knowledge (see §16.4 of Turk et al. in Chapter 16 of this volume) I should make clear that a major motivation for the methods promoted in this handbook is to create accessible records of a language which are typically the ones sought by speakers (and their descendants) when they become aware of the changes occurring in their language.

Documentation is most urgent where the language may cease being spoken, but even in a large population of speakers a decline in the variety of speech genres or registers is a motivation for recording as broad a range of language performance as possible. We therefore need to record as diverse a range of people and as diverse a range of topics as we can. If we take the broader project of linguistic fieldwork to be a deeper understanding of human knowledge systems and societies, then it makes sense that we create material from our own research in forms that colleagues from other disciplines can use. As Evans (Chapter 8 below) puts it, 'undocumented languages contain too much information to be wasted on linguists alone'. This suggests that we need assistance with interdisciplinary topics not normally covered in linguistic field guides as they have been constructed up to now. A number of books provide advice on the kind of linguistic structures that can be expected based on typological surveys (e.g. Comrie and Smith 1977; Payne 1997; Shopen 2007). Most such guides offer sample wordlists and sentences for elicitation (e.g. Bouquiaux and Thomas 1976; 1992; Samarin 1967). Some go further and briefly discuss issues around preparation for fieldwork (e.g. Abbi 2001; Bowern 2008; Chelliah and de Reuse 2010; Crowley 2007; Vaux and Cooper 1999). Some are quite brief (e.g. Bartis 2002), some bound in a theory that makes them unusable (e.g. the tagmemics of Longacre 1964), and some are so detailed that it is difficult to find relevant information (e.g. Bouquiaux and Thomas 1976; 1992). Rather than producing yet another guide in the same tradition as those listed here, this handbook takes a different approach.

Linguistic fieldwork can result in more than just a description of the grammar of a language, it can also record cultural information that provides new insights into local knowledge systems. The problem for a linguist is that they cannot possibly be prepared for every topic that could arise in the course of fieldwork. As a result, either opportunities to explore such topics may be lost or the records produced may not be as useful to others as they could be. What would a musicologist like to see included in the recording of a performance? What would a botanist like to know about a plant's use and how it has been identified? Which constellation of stars is it that features in a particular traditional story? Of course, once we start down the road of trying to explain the world we could go in many directions. An early example (but by no means the earliest: see Urry 1972 for a summary of the literature) of just such a guide to anthropological issues— *Notes and Queries* (Royal Anthropological Institute of Great Britain and Ireland 1951) (produced in six editions between 1839 and 1951)—ran through a vast list of topics under four broad headings (Physical Anthropology; Social Anthropology; Material Culture; Field Antiquities) that could be used by colonial officials to collect primary records. These prompts provided the basis for many of the records produced by early observers, most of whom who were untrained in ethnographic methods.

1.2 THE CHAPTERS IN THIS HANDBOOK

The twenty chapters in this volume aim to support the creation of better records from fieldwork, both for linguistic research and for other purposes—especially for the use of speakers of the language being studied or their descendants with an interest in the range of topics described here, and for specialists in these areas. In general, chapters in this volume should be seen as a point of entry to the topic under discussion. Authors have often provided a guide to further reading that covers key relevant literature.

While collaborative fieldwork is desirable and productive (see Yamada 2007 and Evans, Chapter 8 below), it can also be logistically tricky to organize. In the absence of specialists, what can a lone researcher do when topics go beyond their expertise? It is clearly impossible in one book to cover all the information that a fieldworker may encounter in their field location, even more so when our focus is not confined to a particular geographic or linguistic region.

This volume aims to be geographically inclusive, with contributors who work in the Americas (Berez, Chemillier, Macauley, Mark, O'Meara, Rice, Stea, Turk), Africa (Chemillier, Holbrook, Newman), Asia (Adachi, Nanbakhsh, Majid, McClatchey, Seyfeddinipur, Strycharz), Europe (Barwick), the Pacific (Conn, Evans, Lemonnier, Margetts and Margetts, Meyerhoff, Mosel, Pollock, Thieberger), and Australia (Barwick, Dousset, Evans, Mark, Nash, Simpson, Thieberger, Turk). For fieldwork guides specifically focused on particular geographic regions, see Abbi (2001) for India, Dai Qingxia, Luo Rendi, and Wang Feng (2009) and Heimer and Thøgersen (2006) for China, Steinhoff, Bestor, and Lyon-Bestor (2003) for Japan, Wurm (1967) and Sutton and Walsh (1979) for Australia.

1.2.1 Data collection and management

The first section of the volume deals with data collection and management. It is all too common for researchers to be sent into the field with no training at all in the use of equipment, with the result that their vital primary data is not as useful as it could have been. Central to the project of language documentation is the creation of records, and our reliance on fragile technologies to do this requires care and attention to detail. As a number of chapters (e.g. Chemillier, Majid, Meyerhoff et al., Seyfeddinipur) reiterate, a recording is often the only way of analysing an event that occurs too quickly for human observers to fully appreciate. It is highly desirable to record dynamic performances in order to study them, and to then ensure that these recordings provide the basis for claims made about the performances and the language. In Chapter 1, **Anna Margetts and Andrew Margetts** outline techniques and equipment for making the best quality recordings in the field and include a discussion of what characteristics to look for in your field kit (recorders, microphones and peripheral equipment), and what sort of power sources to consider when planning a fieldtrip.

Asifa Majid (Chapter 2) discusses experimental field elicitation techniques, how to design activities to encourage speakers to use particular conceptual categories and how to produce non-linguistic stimuli for elicitation as a means of exploring semantics. She describes how to administer various versions of the well-known Max Planck Institute materials, and how to interpret the results.

There have been a number of guides to linguistic fieldwork. **Ulrike Mosel** (Chapter 3) distils from a survey of this existing work the key points relevant to modern fieldwork and provides 'a guide to the guides', pointing out their pros and cons on a range of aspects of fieldwork methods, including various kinds of elicitation, text collection, and the development of a representative corpus. She emphasizes the need for linguists to know what is typologically expected for the target language and notes that non-linguistic researchers can still make an important contribution by making recordings with the help of speakers.

Nicholas Thieberger and Andrea L. Berez (Chapter 4) provide a guide to managing fieldwork data, from fieldnotes and recordings through transcription and annotation to analysis. They liken the creation of good fieldwork records to building a house with firm foundations, allowing subsequent extensions secure in the knowledge that the initial work can support them. Dealing with general principles as well as the specifics of data conversion, they discuss the underlying issues related to separating the form of data from its content, and the importance of preparing field material for posterity, both for our own reuse of it in our ongoing study of the language, and for the people we record.

1.2.2. Recording performance

The second group of papers focuses on performance of various kinds. **Miriam Meyerhoff, Chie Adachi, Golnaz Nanbakhsh and Anna Strycharz** (Chapter 5) present methods (including questionnaires, observation, and structured interviews) for determining variation within speech communities. Such variation may be based on characteristics like gender and power, and the authors explore ways in which field researchers may discover speakers' ideologies about and attitudes to language and society and how they use language for social and interpersonal purposes.

Mandana Seyfeddinipur (Chapter 6) guides us through the need to include gestures in our understanding of human communication, pointing out that there are no known societies in which gesture does not play a role. She provides an overview of the range of functions associated with gesture, the dimensions in which cultures differ in their gesture use, and describes ways in which gestures may give insights into cognitive diversity, as they have been shown to correlate with language-specific categories (like directional terms, or time references using gestures). From that theoretical base, the chapter describes how to include gestures in language documentation, with suggestions for both what to record and how to record it.

Fieldworkers are often in a position to observe musical performance and the types of questions they could ask and the ways in which they can record these are the topic of **Linda Barwick**'s Chapter 7. Recordings of songs are valued within the community and can be used to pass on traditions via new technologies. As pointed out also in Evans's chapter, new domains of vocabulary can emerge from the study of song texts as can insights into archaic forms of language preserved in song. Barwick also gives advice on technical and practical requirements for a good musical documentation and how these might differ from language documentation.

1.2.3 Collaborating with other disciplines

In the next section of the handbook, 'Collaborating with other disciplines', chapters deal with collaboration, that most desirable but elusive state of working with experts from other disciplinary backgrounds in order to benefit each other's research program and to enrich it with novel insights. An example of such relationships is discussed by **Nicholas Evans** (Chapter 8), working with anthropologists and musicologists to create richer records of Iwaidja that allow them all to explore details of cultural categorizations not previously apparent to any of them working individually. Such details include trirelational kinterms, distinctive verbs of wearing for different parts of the body, and previously unattested gender prefixes with lexicalized verbs. While this chapter points out the benefits of collaboration, the next chapters assume that the linguist is on their own in the field and so provide advice about ways in which a range of topics can be addressed by linguists.

Encountering systems of kinship and understanding their implications for everyday behaviour can take some time for the novice fieldworker, and **Laurent Dousset** (Chapter 9) provides a guide to notions of social organization and kinship and then to kinship terminologies. Forms of social organization based entirely or mainly in kinship have rules that prescribe who can marry whom, who can talk to whom, who is responsible for certain ceremonial duties, and for other more symbolic aspects of social reality. Understanding these rules will also facilitate one's own work by clarifying forms of one's own relationships that may not otherwise have been apparent.

In Chapter 10, **Nancy Pollock** outlines the anthropology of food, noting that various theoretical approaches have dealt with food in economic and nutritional terms in addition to a colonial notion of correct food consumption. She points to the need to observe who is collecting, hunting, and growing food as a means for understanding social organization. Food as an exchange also provides insights into relationships of reciprocity. Research into what is considered good food, what is used for feast occasions, and methods of food production and processing can provide valuable texts on topics that are central to everyday life.

From kinship and an understanding of social relationships as exemplified in the use of food, we move on to two chapters dealing with the broader biological context, first **Barry Conn** (Chapter 11) describes methods for collecting plants, with suggestions for identifying or at least providing informed descriptions of plants. This chapter guides the uninitiated field worker in collecting plant specimens and points out the importance of doing so in order to verify the identification. Copious references are provided covering various plant types and many geographically specific resources. This chapter concludes with a very practical set of notes for the requirements of fieldwork including considering permits required, first aid, the use of GPS to locate specimens, and thinking carefully about your own ability to conduct what may be quite difficult hikes while seeking botanical information.

Focusing more closely on human uses of biological material, **Will McClatchey** (Chapter 12) makes a plea for the involvement of linguists in discovering how biological knowledge is acquired, learned, and controlled. What, if any, are the links between biological and linguistic diversity? How is new biological knowledge learned by migrants into new environments, and how long does it take? What are the systems for classifying plants and animals in the language, and how much are they culturally determined?

From the natural world and its cultural construction we move to an exploration of human artefacts. **Pierre Lemonnier** (Chapter 13) suggests linguists could record technical processes like making bread, weaving and so on and shows that objects and technical processes need to be understood in their cultural context. Similar to Pollock in Chapter 10, Lemonnier reminds us that culture underlies all technical processes, no matter how much they may appear to relate to the purely physical world. His case studies of the Baruya fence and Ankave drum illustrate wonderfully the cultural basis for these two otherwise apparently functional objects.

Understanding how quantification works in another culture can take some background knowledge of the range of possible counting and computational systems, including measurement of time, weight, and distance. **Marc Chemillier** (Chapter 14) describes methods for observing both quantification systems and more complex mathematical algorithms, such as sand drawings and divination games. This work emphasizes the value of experimental tests and observation, as asking speakers how they compute divination tables (illustrated in the chapter) gives a different result to observing their calculation of relationships in the table.

Still in a computational mode, the next chapter provides a crash course in cultural astronomy. **Jarita Holbrook** (Chapter 15) shows how to learn about celestial bodies before arriving in the field. She discusses how the stars and planets have been incorporated into cultural practices, including divination, calculation of seasons, and calendars, and into legends that help to explain their recurring patterns observed by most human societies.

From the cosmological we move to the terrestrial. In the first of two chapters related to indigenous views of geography, **Andrew Turk, David Mark, Carolyn O'Meara, and David Stea** (Chapter 16) describe methods for discovering how landscape is culturally conceptualized. The field of ethnophysiography explores a semantic domain that has not been central to linguistic explorations in the past (although the authors note that it did feature as a domain of study in Voegelin and Voegelin 1957) which asks how landscape is talked about, what features are considered to be distinct, and how they are related to each other.

Focusing on toponymy, **David Nash and Jane Simpson** (Chapter 17) provide examples of placenames and their possible role in analysing the semantic systems of the speech community. Their discussion covers denotation, sense, etymology, and etiology of placenames, as well as connotations, and morphological and grammatical properties. They point out there may be a number of sources for placenames which may, for example, act as mnemonics for an event which is believed to have happened at the place, related to the exploits of ancestral beings.

1.2.4 Collaborating with the community

As the goals of documentation include recording more people in more domains than was previously the case, they also raise new possibilities for ethical concerns, such as consent among a broader group of people, longer fieldwork duration, archiving recorded material, and a greater role for speakers in collaboration and coauthoring of publications. It is common for linguistic field manuals to dive straight into elicitation and analysis, as if selecting and settling into the field location, the establishment of personal relationships, and concerns about ownership of material have already somehow been dealt with elsewhere. In Chapter 18, **Keren Rice** guides us through a range of ethical issues related to fieldwork, summarizing formal codes of ethics and pre-fieldwork institutional ethics approvals, noting that many such processes are intended for medical procedures rather than for cross-cultural humanities research. She provides useful advice on putting your own ethics procedures in place regardless of whether they are formally required or not. Such procedures include informing yourself as fully as possible about the language and about cultural values in your field location to avoid causing unintentional harm.

Tied in to ethical fieldwork practices is the importance of understanding ownership of the material recorded and the need to obtain consent from speakers for whatever use you want to make of the resulting material. These topics are addressed in Chapter 19 by **Paul Newman**, dealing with copyright, moral rights, and intellectual property, and the added complication of the jurisdictions in which each of these may apply. Also important for the production of publicly funded research is the question of access to the outcomes; in addition to copyright, Newman touches on Creative Commons licences and Open Access models for provision of both primary material and published results of analysis.

In the last chapter, **Monica Macaulay** points out that the anthropological literature on fieldwork and its joys and disasters is vast, yet linguists have typically not been introspective about the nature of fieldwork and the difficulties of life in the field. Notable exceptions (some published since Macaulay's article appeared in 2004 are Kulick and Willson's (1995) collection on sexuality in the field, Crowley's (2007) personal account of fieldwork, Besnier's (2009) discussion of the politics of fieldwork, Bowern (2008) on 'fieldwork and identity', and Nagy's (2000) concern at the number of skills required by a fieldworker (theoretician, applied linguist, technical wizard, sociolinguist etc.).

Some subjects that had been planned for inclusion in the present collection had to be omitted for various reasons. These subjects included zoology, the analysis of narrative and folklore, and the collaborative development of materials for revitalization programs from the results of fieldwork. Further relevant topics have already been dealt with recently and did not need to be duplicated here, for example: Maddieson (2001) on field phonetics; Franchetto (2006) on ethnography; Schneider (2011) on second-language learning methods in the field; Kulick and Willson (1995) on sexuality in the field; and the collection of papers on various topics in Gippert, Himmelmann, and Mosel (2006).

The scope of topics addressed in this handbook is wide—it is hoped that each chapter will provide a starting point for exploration of its topic, giving many references to key literature in the area. The field of language documentation is drawing enthusiastic newcomers to linguistics, as well as attracting more established practitioners to engage with new methods. This handbook is offered as a guide to this emerging paradigm.

1.3 ACKNOWLEDGEMENTS

The idea for this volume started at the Australian Linguistic Institute in 2000, where I co-taught a course in language documentation with Margaret Florey.

We discussed the theme of the linguist in the field as a 'one-person orchestra' who needs to collaborate with, or to have input from, specialists in other disciplines. Some time later, Oxford University Press invited a proposal for a volume on linguistic fieldwork and the present collection was begun. Thanks to the OUP team (John Davey, Julia Steer, Chloe Plummer, Jenny Lunsford and Karen Morgan) for their ever helpful advice. Thanks also to Charmaine Green (former president of the Aboriginal Languages Association) for permission to use her painting 'Land & Sky' as cover art.

Each of the chapters was reviewed by up to three readers, and the following list includes both readers and others whose help I am happy to acknowledge here: Aung Si, Peter Austin, Marieanne Ball, Cheryl Bartlett, Helen Bromhead, James Carson, Barry Conn, Christopher Cox, Cathy Edwards, Cathy Falk, Mike Forman, Jeff Good, Prune Harris, Mark Harvey, John Haviland, Nikolaus Himmelmann, Anthony Jukes, Barb Kelly, Tamara Kohn, Lamont Lindstrom, David MacDougall, Anna Margetts, Camilla Mason, Merrin Mason, Miriam Meyerhoff, Simon Musgrave, Toshihide Nakayama, Daphne Nash, David Nash, Marybeth Nevins, Mary Patterson, Ken Rehg, Keren Rice, Stuart Robinson, Gloria Stillman, Peter Sutton, Andrew Turk, Brigitte Vézina, Fiona Walsh, Gerhard Wiesenfeldt, and David Wilkins.

While working on this volume I held positions at the Department of Linguistics at the University of Hawai'i at Mānoa and at the Department of Linguistics at the University of Melbourne, and was funded by Australian Research Council grants DP0450342 and DP0984419.

PART I

DATA COLLECTION AND MANAGEMENT

CHAPTER 1

....

AUDIO AND VIDEO RECORDING TECHNIQUES FOR LINGUISTIC RESEARCH

....

ANNA MARGETTS
ANDREW MARGETTS

1.1 INTRODUCTION
....

This account of practical issues with audio and video recordings in a fieldwork setting is based on our own experience and on that of friends and colleagues.[1] In addition to some standard recommendations, it includes points learned through

[1] The authors thank Nick Thieberger and two anonymous reviewers for valuable feedback on earlier drafts of this chapter. We also thank the people and communities in Milne Bay Province who have welcomed and supported our work. We would like to acknowledge past financial fieldwork support from the Max Planck Institute for Psycholinguistics in Nijmegen, the Feodor Lynen Program of the Alexander von Humboldt Foundation, and the DoBeS program of the Volkswagen Foundation. We also thank Rick van Viersen, Gerd Klaas, and Paul Trilsbeek at the MPI for past technical advice on field equipment and recording techniques.

mistakes, happy accidents, and trial and error. Comments about specific equipment will be out of date by the time this volume is published. Nevertheless we give specifications for at least some items in the hope that this will help to identify types of equipment we have found worthwhile.

The chapter first addresses some general points about what to record in a field situation, outlines the workflow of data processing, and provides notes on managing equipment. We then discuss audio and video recordings and touch on the question of energy supply and useful auxiliary equipment. Section 1.7 gives links to more information, and the appendix (§1.8) provides suggestions for a basic field equipment kit.

1.1.1 What to record?

The primary purpose of recordings for linguistic research is to record speech in order to analyse the structure of the language, rather than, say, documenting cultural practices, analysing the content of a story, or creating teaching materials. A good database for linguistic analysis should ideally allow for all of these things and be valuable for other parties than linguists, but it is this primary purpose which determines how the data is treated and processed.

The broader and more varied a text collection is, the more representative it will be of the language in terms of its grammar, the use of different registers, speech styles, and so forth. If possible it is therefore good to aim for recordings with a range of speakers, both men and women, speakers from different generations, with different educational background, with a variety of specialist knowledge and different standings in the community. A good text collection also includes a variety of text types. Besides narratives (stories, legends, etc.) and expository texts (e.g. describing how things are done), ideally the collection will include conversations. Conversations do tend to dry up when the recorder is on, they are difficult to transcribe and messy to 'chunk' for text-audio linkage; nevertheless they are worth the effort: there may be a whole range of grammatical features which only show up in conversation. The main point is that variety in the data is good.

One should therefore record 'everything', i.e. as much as possible, anywhere, anytime. For video recordings, having the camera running frequently can help people become used to being filmed, relax a bit and maybe, eventually, stop insisting on wearing their Sunday best as soon as the machine is on. There are two basic set-ups for doing this. The first one is to position the camera somewhere and let it record whatever happens to be within its frame. This can work quite well when people are sitting and chatting. The fieldworker can reposition the camera from time to time to catch different scenes but does not have to stand behind it all the time. The drawback is that there will always be speakers just outside the frame or just too far away from the microphone to be clearly audible. The second possibility is for the fieldworker to be behind the camera as much as possible. This may make for better recordings but speakers are less likely to forget about the camera. A second drawback is that extensive filming can be exhausting. The situation for audio-only recordings is similar if simpler. Having an extra person on the team to handle the recording equipment (and perhaps other technical tasks as well) is extremely helpful, particularly for video work. In this case one person can concentrate on the content (negotiating with the speakers) and the other on the context (wrestling with the lighting and acoustics).

While it is good when people relax and forget about the machine, this increases the chance that they will say or do things they may not want to have recorded, transcribed, or played in public. It is the responsibility of the researcher to be sensitive to such situations and, if this is called for, to delete parts of the recording.

Speakers sometimes prefer to plan and discuss what they will say during a recording because they want to deliver a polished performance. If speakers agree, such preparatory discussions should also be recorded. These sessions often constitute the most interesting data, as they can provide naturalistic conversational interaction and also useful supporting information that may be missing in the 'official' version.

Every recording should start with a spoken statement of some basic metadata: an ID for the recording or tape, the date, location, language, and the name of the principal speakers. If the content to be recorded is known, this should be stated too. All of this is vital information and not necessarily easy to reconstruct if omitted at this stage.

1.1.2 Workflow

The workflow, which for linguistic analysis would start with the video or audio recording and end with an annotated text-audio/video-linked database, goes through a number of stages which may involve different people (see also Thieberger and Berez, Chapter 4 below). The steps typically include making the recording, capturing, or copying recordings to a computer,[2] identifying and cutting sessions, transcoding media files to open and common formats, chunking sessions into units (such as intonation units, pause units, or intonational sentences: see e.g. DuBois 1991; Edwards and Lampert 1993; Edwards 2003; Himmelmann 2006b), transcribing,

---

[2] If the source audio/video is in analog format the first step of the workflow will have to be digitizing the analog data. The website of the DoBeS Program (http://www.mpi.nl/DOBES/audio-video) provides some useful practical information on digitizing and capturing.

interlinearizing, and translating the text. The less familiar the researchers are with the language, the more of these steps require input from native speakers. An ideal workflow would be efficient in terms of the equipment and the software programs involved, and would avoid double handling of data (such as creating handwritten transcriptions which are later typed). An ideal workflow would also allow for at least some of the data to be fully processed during the fieldtrip (simply because that is where the native speakers' input is available). Such a workflow relies on transcriptions being typed directly on the computer, but where power supply is limited this can be a problem. Moreover, it may not be culturally appropriate, or safe, to even use a computer in the field. In any case it is good practice to plan for an alternative workflow which does not rely on the computer for every step and which includes backup options if major equipment items fail (as they will because of heat, dust, humidity, ants, and that sugary cup of tea spilled into the keyboard). Such a workflow may comprise transcriptions which are handwritten by speakers at the field site and then typed by the researcher during a weekend in the next town with proper power supply.

1.1.3 Keeping equipment working

Keeping equipment working in the field is a challenge. The main enemies are moisture, humidity, dirt, dust, and temperature extremes. Waterproof containers are a basic requirement; if they are insulated, padded, and rigid, so much the better.

Silica gel helps to keep things dry. Equipment items should be kept in individual, airtight bags or containers, or with as little air as possible and each with a small pack of silica gel crystals.[3] The crystals absorb and bind the moisture in the remaining air. The crystals need to be dried regularly, for example in a pot over the fire. Dry crystals are typically blue and turn purple/pink as they become saturated.

Cold as well as heat can be an issue, affecting, for example, battery function. A reliable guide to equipment storage is to avoid locations that would be uncomfortable to humans—consider shade, ventilation, and ambient temperature. In extremely hot conditions, evaporative cooling can be useful. It works by placing a damp cloth over the container or waterproof bag in which the equipment is stored. The evaporating water cools the surface underneath.

If you know that the equipment will be exposed to extreme conditions, then weigh up the specifications carefully. For instance, it is possible to obtain waterproof video cameras quite cheaply; however, you will have to accept compromises in the recording quality.

---

[3] Simple waterproof sacks with fold-over openings, as sold in camping shops, are a good solution.

1.2 AUDIO RECORDINGS

Audio recordings constitute the core data for linguistic work (other than the study of sign languages) and for many purposes they are sufficient. But equally, in many contexts the addition of video is preferable or even necessary, particularly if the corpus aims to document more than just the language. With audio-only recordings it is especially important to record basic metadata about each session, because there are no visual clues to the identity of the speakers and the recording location or date. The following observations on audio recording techniques, standards, and ancillary equipment (e.g. microphones and headphones) hold for both audio-only and audiovisual recordings. Issues specific to video are discussed further in §1.3.

There are many different equipment settings that can become relevant depending on the circumstances, and we recommend taking equipment manuals to the field, at least as electronic documents.

1.2.1 Things to consider

It is becoming a standard assumption in linguistic research that data analysis involves direct access to the audio data and not just to a transcription. One should be in a position to verify, improve, or correct transcriptions at any time by checking the audio file (see Ochs 1979; Margetts 2009; Thieberger 2009: 402). For this to be possible, a linguistic text database needs to incorporate text–audio linking. This means that the audio (and possibly the video) which corresponds to a text chunk is accessible by a mouse click (the record for each chunk contains start and end time-code data) and this requires digital media files. So, if the master recording is analog it will need to be digitized. If the master recording is on digital tape, the tape needs to be captured to disk. Digitizing and capturing are both very time-consuming processes compared with simply copying a digital file (as is the case with solid-state recorders). These are points which may influence the choice of equipment.

1.2.1.1 Recording resolutions

High-resolution, non-compressed audio recordings are a good and practicable goal. They are a requirement for analysing phonetics, since compressed recordings severely compromise the acoustic quality of the data. In principle the data should be able to support such analysis even if the collector has no personal interest in phonetic research. Recordings should ideally be lasting records of a language, and be available and suitable for all kinds of different analyses and uses for future researchers and community members. This is of particular importance if the language is under threat. For such reasons non-compressed audio is the archiving standard for most language archives. This does not mean that all recordings need to have the same high quality, as long as a good proportion does. Section 1.2.2.1(iii) below provides some comments on the place for lower-resolution recorders.

1.2.1.2 Background noise

One must often choose between a noisier but naturalistic setting and a quieter but maybe less relaxed recording situation. The first might seem richer, but it is easy to underestimate the deleterious effect of background noise. There may also be a choice between recording with background noise or not recording at all. These are not easy decisions to make, but it does not necessarily hold that any recording is better than none. Making a recording in which the speaker is simply inaudible is useless, and may be worse than not recording because the speaker may not be happy to repeat the session.

Sources of problematic background noise include rain (particularly on tin roofs), wind, surf, animals (chickens!), and engines of all kinds. Humming insects right next to the microphone can also be surprisingly noisy.[4] It may be worth waiting for the rain to stop, or looking for a house with a less resonant roof or a place further away from the beach or generator. A good wind gag (or wind screen) for the microphone is essential whenever you record outdoors. Even one made on the spot with foam or fur or other fluffy material can help. Electrical interference can also be a source of noise; we briefly address this in §§1.2.2.2(i) and 1.4.1.

Test how intrusive the background noise is by recording a sample of speech at the beginning of each session and then replaying with headphones to check it. This entails trying to understand or transcribe what is being said without visual clues (such as the speaker's face or gestures which may help one's understanding in the speech situation but which may not be available during transcription).

The type and especially the position of the microphone will make a big difference in noisy recording situations. The closer the microphone is to the speaker's mouth, the better the chance that the speech will be clear and audible. Lapel microphones can be very good in this respect. Highly directional microphones can also be helpful in that they focus on a sound source (but they can be problematic too: see the discussion in §1.2.2.2 below).

1.2.1.3 Audio levels

Balancing input levels before starting a recording should be a routine task (assuming the equipment allows for such balancing—and high quality recorders and cameras will). Such 'balancing' entails setting the recording level as high as possible

---

[4] Insects can be attracted to microphones if they are sticky or smelly, so keep them clean.

while preventing the loudest passages reaching the upper limit and so introducing distortion or clipping: this is a subjective and challenging task. As well as making an initial check, ideally one would also continue to monitor the input levels and the degree of background noise while recording, since conditions can easily change without it being readily apparent to the naked ear, but this can be hard to manage for one person. It is wise to become familiar with the idiosyncrasies of the equipment settings before going to the field.

1.2.2 Equipment

Recording quality has to be the first criterion for choosing equipment. Other considerations are power consumption, weight/bulk, ruggedness, and expense. One further consideration is the question of who will be using the equipment. If machines will be used by the speech community, it is worth investigating what type of equipment people are already familiar with. It is also helpful to consider how easy it would be for a novice to use a particular machine. For example, some recorders have only two or three buttons to regulate a whole range of functions through various combinations. This can make it much harder to learn to use them because the commands are not linked to individual buttons. It is also good to remember that many common symbols that may appear on buttons or on a display are not particularly iconic and require some background in the history of western material culture (e.g. the camera icon which indicates the recording setting on most cameras looks nothing like modern video cameras).

1.2.2.1 *Recording equipment*

We recommend using machines which can record non-compressed digital audio in a non-proprietary format,[5] but we also refer to some other options. This standard essentially implies making high-resolution (16 bit/44 kHz or better) uncompressed PCM[6] recordings stored as wav files (Windows) or aiff files (Mac).[7] Countless alternatives exist, all of which have their strengths. Compressed but very high-quality (i.e. 'lossless compression') formats exist both in proprietary (e.g. Apple lossless) and open (e.g. FLAC) forms. Similarly, 'lossy' formats can be proprietary (e.g. the ubiquitous MP3) or open (e.g. AAC, intended as a successor to MP3).

---

[5] Proprietary format specifications are typically not publically available and may be subject to patents and other measures designed to limit access to their design. They may also require usage fees or licence payments, and their future support is not guaranteed.

[6] PCM: pulse-code modulation. A digital representation of an analog signal.

[7] wav: Waveform Audio File Format; aiff: Audio Interchange File Format. They are very similar container formats for raw PCM audio and both are compatible with Windows, Macintosh, and Linux operating systems.

Arguments can be made for all these formats (not least on the grounds of file size, which translates to portability and availability over the internet). Sometimes the proprietary formats are the most efficient (quality vs. size) and/or the most common (at present). However, they can leave your data stranded if at some point the format is no longer supported. We have already discussed why any kind of audio file compression is generally not a good thing. So regardless of the temptations, non-compressed, non-proprietary PCM files remain the safe standard for primary recordings. It is always possible to make alternative versions of these using different codecs[8] for special purposes such as streaming over the web.

(i) Solid-state recorders. Solid-state recorders record directly to flash memory (internal, on removable media, or both) rather than to tape or disk. They comprise a huge range from humble and tiny MP3 devices (perhaps embedded in your phone) to studio quality, not particularly portable, mixing decks. The subset under discussion here are those that are compact enough for the field and also record in uncompressed PCM format. Early models tended to be bulky, heavy, expensive, and power-hungry. Today there are smaller, lighter, energy-efficient models, and a solid-state audio recorder makes a good primary recording device.

There is a plethora of ever-changing options regarding performance and features, but perhaps the most important distinction lies between those models that accept external professional quality microphones (usually via some combination of $\frac{1}{4}$ in. TRS or XLR jacks)[9] and those that do not. A further distinction can be made between those that support 'phantom powered' microphones and those that do not (see §1.2.2.2(ii) below). Since many good microphones require such power, this ability extends the range of equipment compatible with the machine. Even if microphones do not require phantom power, having suitable TRS and/or XLR jacks is desirable—our marvellously useful wireless microphones, for example, are self-powered but they use XLR connectors.

A machine that does not accept external microphones at all (or which does so poorly—it is worth searching online for user reviews on this topic) cannot be wholeheartedly recommended for linguistic fieldwork, since there are simply too

---

[8] Codec: originally coder-decoder, now more often compressor-decompressor. A hardware or software device now commonly associated with the conversion of one digital signal format to another, often involving a change in compression characteristics.

[9] TRS: Tip, Ring, Sleeve. The most common form of audio jack, cylindrical and compact, found in various diameters and configurations (e.g. mono, stereo, and balanced mono). The ¼in. (6.3mm) size is the original and largest and tends to be found in more professional applications.
XLR: Cannon X, Latch, Rubber. A relatively bulky but reliable plug/socket system used mainly in professional audio/video equipment. Typically but not necessarily comprising three pins/holes within a larger cylinder. (Although XLR refers only to the connection type, it is often used as a synonym for the professional, balanced audio system, e.g. 'XLR microphone' implying a balanced microphone. This is unfortunate, since TRS and other connectors can also be part of a balanced system. See §1.2.2.2 (i) for discussion of balanced audio.)

many situations where the ability to use an external microphone is important, if for no other reason than to control the effect of background noise, as mentioned earlier. While this is less of a problem with solid-state audio recorders than with video cameras (because with audio-only it is generally easier to place the recording apparatus close to the speaker), it is still a major factor. We will discuss this further in §1.2.2.2(i).

Apart from the specifications regarding microphones, the differences between recorder models come down largely to rather subjective matters like ergonomics and perceived durability. A quantitative exception to this is the 'noise floor' characteristic, i.e. the background signal created by the device itself. It is very important to minimize this for quiet recording situations.[10] Handling the equipment during recording (e.g. to change settings) may also create noise which will be recorded (a solution might be a remote control).[11]

In an era of convergence (phones as computers, computers as phones and so forth), it is worth keeping an open mind on what functions a particular device can support. A particularly interesting new development in solid-state audio recorders is the incorporation of a basic video camera (so far only in the 'Zoom Q3'). This rather reverses the balance found in cheaper video cameras (i.e. good-quality optics but scant regard for audio capability—discussed further in §1.3.2.5). Although no substitute for a good quality video/audio setup, such a recorder may provide a satisfactory solution for situations where good quality filming is not possible but where a video record would still be valuable for context.

Perhaps in due course manufacturers will also think of adding GPS logging to audio recorders (as they have for some still and video cameras). Such a capability would be well worth employing, since it would provide location metadata which can be difficult to reconstruct for audio-only recordings.

(ii) Direct to computer. In general we would not recommend recording straight to the computer in the field, for both practical and technical reasons. A computer is more vulnerable than the average recorder and is likely to consume more power. Furthermore a typical PC will not have a built-in sound card of adequate quality. Although it is possible to upgrade this, internally or externally, this represents additional expense that could have been better spent on a dedicated recorder.

Nevertheless there are several situations where such a solution might make sense. Perhaps all recordings will take place in controlled indoor environments with AC power; or perhaps it is only feasible to carry a computer and a microphone. Another scenario where recording directly into the computer can make sense is

---

[10] This might be relevant if e.g. a project includes recordings of faint naturalistic sounds like bird calls.
[11] E.g. some 'Zoom' models reportedly are sensitive even to touching the body of the recorder.

where simplicity of the workflow is important. For example, when working with community members to produce audio materials (e.g. as teaching materials or talking books), it may be helpful if all processes are done on the same machine because you can edit sections on the spot by recording over them directly. Another reason could be if you wanted an uninterrupted recording whose file size will be too large for the recording device's memory. However, be aware that any long uninterrupted recording runs some risks. Depending on the equipment, the audio file may not be written to disk until you press stop, so if your equipment crashes halfway though you will lose it all.

There are two satisfactory options for direct recording. The better option is to use a USB pre-amplifier to bridge between a professional microphone and the computer. The simpler one is to use a special USB microphone—a type marketed principally for podcasting—which incorporates the necessary circuitry.[12] (Such microphones can only be used for direct input to the computer; they do not work for other recording devices.) Some solid-state recorders can also be used as a USB microphone (the 'Zoom H2' is an example), although in this scenario it is hard to see the benefit of making field recordings to a computer rather than to the recorder unit itself.

(iii) **Compressed digital and older recording technology.** There may still be a place for machines which record compressed digital audio or use older technologies. One legitimate use for such equipment is as a low-energy and/or low-cost backup to the main recorder. The quality will likely be suboptimal but there are some scenarios where they can be useful. Machines for this purpose could be 'MP3', 'dictaphone', MiniDisc, or analog recorders.

Solid-state models are particularly handy as go-everywhere pieces. Just as one should carry a notebook and pencil everywhere, it makes sense to carry a small, inexpensive recording device, just in case.[13] They are ideal for trips away from the main field site where it may be too difficult or precarious to take the master recording machine. Such trips are often the situations where fantastic data comes one's way, such as animated conversations, impromptu singing, traditional speeches, or additional speakers one did not know about. It is great to be able to record when such opportunities arise.

Another scenario is where researchers already have access to older good-quality technology such as DAT or the Sony 'Walkman Professional' compact cassette recorders. There is an economic rationale for this (good equipment at no cost), but even so we do not recommend using such machines as primary recorders

---

[12] E.g. the 'RODE Podcaster' or the 'Samson G-Track'.
[13] Note, however, that there are now such small, inexpensive machines capable of recording to good-quality uncompressed PCM format, e.g. the 'Zoom H1'.

because the data need to be digitized or transferred to disk. (Likewise, existing data on such tapes will need to be converted while this is still possible, i.e. before the equipment disappears altogether.) The cost of this time-consuming and exacting work rather cancels out the savings on the hardware.

Another application for lower-quality recording equipment is its use for hand transcription of recorded data in the field. This is not ideal because, as mentioned, the transcription and the text–audio linkage will become two separate steps in the workflow and this means more work (much more). We recommend this scenario only in cases where the basic transcription cannot be made directly into the computer. We have had good experience both with analog players and with an MP3 player/recorder in situations where there was limited power and the speakers who did the transcriptions had no experience with computers. The MP3 machine even allowed the transcribers to select a chunk of text, which was then replayed as a loop until the section was transcribed. To make this work we transferred compressed versions of the original audio files from the PC.

In another situation, because of limited solar power supply during the rainy season, a colleague created analog tape recordings just for the purpose of transcription by using a battery-run analog cassette tape recorder in parallel to her master recording equipment (which was digital video). This meant she did not have to capture or convert the recordings in the field and speakers could transcribe directly from the tape. She chose analog equipment because speakers were familiar with this technology.

MP3 and MiniDisc (MD) recorders are small, relatively inexpensive, and handy but they record in compressed and sometimes proprietary formats. Moreover, the MiniDisc system, despite being digital, only allows analog transfer to computers (unless one uses specialist equipment). The later Hi-MD recorders can record in lossless PCM, but early models were plagued by encryption and transfer policies (imposed by the manufacturer, Sony) that made it hard to transfer digital recordings to the computer. Although these restrictions have since been eased, Hi-MD technology has effectively been superseded by the solid-state machines discussed above.

A further problem with all MiniDisc models is the possibility of including machine noise (from the disk spinning up intermittently) in recordings if the microphone placement is unfortunate. A similar risk exists with all mechanical recorders (digital video, compact cassette, etc.) as opposed to solid-state flash memory devices. The additional danger with MiniDiscs lies in the fact that because the noise is not constant it might not even be registered as an acoustic hazard before it is too late. MiniDisc recorders, although small, cannot be as miniaturized as some MP3 recorders because of the physical dimensions of the disk itself.

Digital Audio Tape (DAT) recorders record non-compressed data in excellent quality but they have essentially been superseded by solid-state recorders. As with all digital tape formats, DAT recordings need to be transferred to disk in real time before the sessions can be fed into the normal workflow (and note that this is not as straightforward for DAT as for DV tapes).

While the recording quality of high-end analog machines can be very good, the tapes require digitizing. The problem is that this is not easy to do oneself without sacrificing quality. Archiving bureaus use specialized tape decks and computer interfaces to do the best possible job. It can be tempting to create a 'rough' digital copy (so that analysis can begin) using a regular cassette deck and the line-in jack of a PC, either in the field or while waiting for the high-quality version to be processed by a bureau. If you do this, the two different versions, the home-made and the professional one, will differ in their time code. So there is no point in creating text–audio linkage with your home-digitized data. When using analog recorders it is essential to choose high-quality tapes (rather than no-name products) and to avoid tapes longer than 60 minutes; longer tapes tend to be of lower quality.

In summary, we cannot recommend DAT or analog machines as primary recording devices. If you must use them, you need to be aware of the additional steps this creates in your workflow, and we urgently recommend that you transfer all recordings to hard disk as soon as possible. We do not recommend MiniDisc either unless there is no other option. An exception might be made for the Hi-MD version, since it is capable of high-quality PCM recordings that (at least in theory) can be transferred digitally to computer. However, before using this device in the field it should be checked that the resulting files are in an open, editable format.

MP3 and other low-end solid-state recorders (e.g. 'dictaphones', mobile phones, and PDAs) may well have their place in a field kit as long as they are not the main recording device. If you use them, be aware that the recorder's default compression setting is not necessarily the best of which it is capable, so check the settings and choose best recording quality rather than maximal duration.

1.2.2.2 *Microphones*

Microphone technology is a large and complex topic. There are innumerable variables in both internal design and external form. What follows is related principally to field recordings of speech events as opposed to, say, music perfor-mances or other semi-formal scenarios where aspects other than intelligibility of speech might be important (see Barwick, Chapter 7 below on methods for record-ing music).

(i) **General comments and recommendations.** It is best not to rely on built-in microphones. For one thing, there is the risk of recording motor and other internal noise with video tape cameras and other mechanical recorders. This is not a problem with true solid-state recorders which do not have tape motors or hard drives—but remember that cameras of this kind may still have zoom and focus motors. Also, internal microphones have historically not been of equal quality to dedicated external ones. This is less the case today. Indeed, many recent audio recorders, such as the 'Zoom' range, clearly have very carefully designed internal microphones. Regardless, external microphones simply provide more flexibility and potentially better performance than inbuilt ones, especially if they can be used remotely.

Since we recommend external microphones, we need to introduce the topic of 'balanced audio'.[14] This method of connecting devices provides protection against noise created by electrical interference, for example when using long cables between microphone and recorder (as you do when filming). Professional microphones tend to be of the balanced type. There is nothing inherently wrong with a microphone that is not balanced and therefore connects with conventional cable (typically with TRS mini jacks), but in this case long cable runs greatly increase the likelihood of static crackle. The longer the cable, the more crackle. Balanced microphones (typically with XLR connectors) avoid this, but unfortunately the cables required are rather bulky.

While it might seem obvious to take advantage of stereo or surround sound capabilities in a recording device, it is seldom the case with linguistic recordings that this kind of fidelity is required. Certainly a single speaker usually requires only a mono recording. Making mono recordings can be helpful in situations where it might be difficult to determine an optimum recording level (or where there is no time to make the usual pre-recording checks): it is often possible to feed the input of one microphone into both channels and to set each channel to slightly different levels. This gives one the opportunity later to choose the recording that gave the best result in terms of signal distortion.

As already mentioned, a good wind gag is a vital microphone accessory for most fieldwork. This is not the same thing as the piece of foam surrounding the device itself that was probably supplied with the microphone. Such foam sleeves do help in controlled conditions, but they are not adequate for outdoor use. A suitable wind gag will resemble a piece of fur (one nickname for larger gags is 'dead cat') and is generally intended to be used over the supplied foam cover not instead of it.[15] Commercial wind gags are generally superior to homemade ones because

---

[14] Balanced audio is where the connecting cables (e.g. between external microphone and recorder) form a 'balanced signal pair' with equal electrical impedances to each other, to ground and to other components.

[15] Although there is also the opinion that it is better to omit the foam sleeve, the idea being that this creates a better 'still air space' around the microphone proper and so a lower degree of wind noise transmission.

they employ 'acoustically transparent' materials to avoid an overall loss of sound.[16] Most designs are intended for large stand-alone microphones, but there are also models available for lapel types and even for entire camcorders (to shield their internal microphones). Note that no wind gag can be totally effective against strong wind conditions. However, paying attention to the orientation and placement of the microphone (i.e. so that it is shielded from the wind even if the object of the recording is not) can mitigate the problem.

Recording individual speakers. Almost any kind of good quality microphone can be effective when recording just one speaker; the choice becomes more critical when recording a group, as discussed in the next section. Nevertheless we have developed a strong preference: our best recording experiences when recording individual speakers have been with lapel (also called tie-clip or lava-lier) microphones ('Sony ECM-C115/C10') and in particular with radio lapel microphones ('Sony UWP-C1'). In this arrangement (supplied as a package), a lapel microphone is connected by a short cable to a transmitter, and both components are with the speaker. The transmitter can be clipped to a belt, put into a pocket, or simply placed next to the speaker. The third part of the setup is the receiver which is plugged into the recorder as any other microphone would be. The advantages of radio microphones become obvious whenever there has to be some distance between the recorder and the speaker, for example with video recordings.

For one thing, there is no cable between the speaker and the camera over which people may stumble.[17] Cables are always a problem, but especially for systems without balanced connectors (i.e. many microphones and most MP3 recorders, and consumer and prosumer video cameras) for which long runs constitute acoustic hazards as mentioned earlier. Even more importantly, radio microphones allow the speaker to move around freely. This allows a craftsman, gardener, or performer to go about their business while being filmed. We also have good experience with radio microphones for running commentaries. We come back to this in the section on commentaries below.

Radio microphones are quite likely to have professional type connectors such as XLR. In order to use such a microphone on a more basic recorder, some kind of adaptor might be required. This might be either a simple converter lead or a more sophisticated unit providing signal level control, etc. (e.g. 'BeachTek DXA-2S'). The

---

[16] If you choose to make your own wind gag, reasonably acoustically transparent materials are apparently 'gardening fleece' (as used to protect plants from frost) and cloth intended for loudspeaker covers.

[17] When working with a long microphone cable on the ground between camera and speaker, tying the cable to the very bottom of one of the tripod legs reduces the leverage and the risk of making the camera topple if someone pulls on the cable.

latter option is preferred if the recorder lacks such controls, though it is rather expensive.

Radio microphones need not be of the lapel type; they can also be handheld, which can work well for an experienced performer (e.g. a singer or orator). However. for the naïve user (like most of us) a lapel microphone that can be fastened to the clothes near the mouth, and then forgotten, probably works better. (But it requires that people wear some kind of shirt or top to which the microphone can be attached.) We recommend that all lapel microphones—wired or wireless—should be of the omnidirectional type. Unidirectional lapel microphones will, in theory, isolate the speaker's voice from the background better, but if the relation between the mouth and the microphone should change (through slipping or turning of the head) the recording quality will be very poor.

A variation on the lapel microphone is the headset microphone (the 'Voice Technologies VT700' omnidirectional has been highly recommended by a colleague). In this configuration a very small microphone is suspended in front of the mouth by the headset. This arrangement probably gives even better results than the lapel microphone (no rustling shirts!) but is a little more intrusive to wear, and will be more obvious on camera.

Despite our own bias towards radio lapel microphones there are serious drawbacks to both the 'radio' and the 'lapel' aspects that should be mentioned. Regarding the radio technology, electrical interference can be a disastrous problem, particularly if it occurs during an unmonitored session (although we have never experienced this, probably because we operate in remote rural locations). Also, keeping track of the charge state of both the transmitter and receiver elements of a radio set-up is onerous (they are rather hungry); and having to stop a recording to change batteries is far from ideal.

As for the lapel design, it does entail the risk of recording noise generated by the wearer, either due to accidental microphone movement or caused by gestures involving touching the body close to the microphone (e.g. slapping the chest). The first type of risk can be reduced to some extent by careful attachment and the use of a pad and/or wind gag.

A second objection to the lapel type is simply that the recording process can be inhibited by the fact that someone must wear a piece of equipment. If the speaker is reluctant to wear a microphone or if the logistics of attaching the microphone are a problem, a solution might be found by mounting the lapel microphone on a stick as close to the speaker as possible. We feel this still provides an effective way to concentrate on one speaker (and it remains a reasonably discrete and non-threatening object, as microphones go). But of course there will be situations where it is impractical to place anything near to even a single speaker. In such a case some of the scenarios described in the next section might be appropriate.

If only the radio aspect constitutes a problem, wired lapel microphones may be a solution. The range includes both professional, often XLR models (e.g. 'Sony ECM-

44B') and consumer, mini-jack models (e.g. 'Sony ECM-C115' or 'ECM-T6'). The latter type is attractive for secondary or backup devices because they are very small, relatively cheap, and quite modest in their power requirements (though they do still require a battery). However, they are generally best suited to audio-only recordings because of the general requirement with video to place the camera at a distance.[18]

Recording groups of speakers. Documenting activities involving groups of speakers rather than recording one or two speakers may require mobility and switching between speakers or performers. Using lapel or headset microphones means that one has to commit to recording primarily one speaker (or two, if one has a microphone for each channel). If the recorded event includes a lot of verbal interaction by several people who are moving around, then a different arrangement is required. Options include 'table top' microphones (e.g. 'Sony ECM-F8') and the external microphones designed specifically for some consumer video cameras. Table top microphones work well for semi-controlled environments (i.e. indoors). Once again, consumer models are best suited for audio-only recording (because of the problems of long cables).

Regarding gear for cameras, one option is the so-called 'zoom microphone' (e.g. the 'Panasonic VW-VMS2'), a hybrid device in which the balance between directional-mono and wide-stereo input is altered as the lens is zoomed (widest lens angle equates to full stereo). While this option does not produce 'professional' audio, we found that there were situations where it worked well, allowing the camera operator to make ad hoc decisions where to focus and record, and it was definitely better than relying on the camera's inbuilt microphone.[19]

Quite good results can also be achieved by simply mounting one or two radio lapel microphones (or regular balanced XLR microphones with long cables) onto sticks which are either poked into the ground or held by assistants. We recommend taking a simple microphone splitter jack which allows two mono microphones to record simultaneously into the two channels of a typical stereo jack input. If there is only one principal speaker, the second microphone can be directed towards the audience.[20]

Recording with live commentary. There are times when the main purpose of a recording is to capture a primarily non-linguistic (e.g. ceremonial, musical,

---

[18] Such microphones are not balanced and therefore should not be used with long cables. So for video, a professional wired model would be required.

[19] A recent development in consumer/prosumer video cameras is the provision of inbuilt zoom microphones offering, in theory, some kind of surround sound. We suspect that this trend has more to do with marketing than with providing useful audio capability. It is worth noting that the more expensive camera models do not offer this, so it is probably a gimmick.

[20] This splitter will not be required on a machine with professional audio or with an XLR to mini jack adaptor as there should then already be provision for independent input to each channel. But the splitter can be used effectively with lesser equipment, e.g. an MP3 recorder with a couple of basic wired lapel microphones.

sporting) event. In these situations it is worth considering adding a live commentary. The techniques and pitfalls are somewhat different from normal recording.

In the simplest scenario, the camera operator or a person standing next to them might comment on what is being recorded. This is not ideal for several reasons, but it can be appropriate in certain circumstances. For example, when a member of the community films events independently, any observations they make about what is going on enhance the recording in two ways: by adding linguistic data, and by explaining what is happening for people who were not present. This setup will only work satisfactorily if the microphone used can record an audio source close to the camera (i.e. not a zoom or directional microphone trained on what is being filmed, but rather the camera's internal microphone or a wired lapel microphone).

A drawback with this scenario is that the commentator is tied to the camera. As mentioned earlier, one solution is to use radio microphones which allow the speaker to move around freely. For example, we were able to film a soccer match and record a running commentary, including impromptu interviews with the referees, by a speaker who was on the other side of the playing field (see Margetts 2011). Having the commentary made the record of the match more interesting and worthwhile both for the community and for the project.

In theory one can even have two simultaneous, independent commentaries with this method, one for each audio channel, since with the radio microphones the commentators may be at a distance from each other. This might be useful for some events.

A potential problem with commentaries is that in many cases (e.g. a musical performance) the recording of the main event should not be contaminated by the commentary, i.e. it should be possible to turn the commentary off when playing back the recording. Again, a radio microphone can solve this problem by placing the commentator well away from the second microphone which is recording the main event. A drawback with this arrangement is that the audio for the event itself will only be mono, since the other channel is in use for the commentary.[21]

There are other setups apart from radio microphones that will work for recording commentaries without interfering with the primary performance, such as using long XLR cables with a wired microphone (commentator at a distance from camera and performance) and/or using highly directional microphones (camera and commentator at a distance from performance). In any case, commentaries are a good method to acquire additional linguistic data.

---

[21] If it is important to achieve a stereo recording of the event then two recorders could be used. It should be relatively easy to subsequently synchronize the separate recordings, since the audio for the commentary will include the main event in the background.

(ii) Microphone design. There are a number of microphone designs, but the two that concern us most here are the dynamic and the condenser microphone. Most dynamic microphones operate in a similar fashion to a loudspeaker, only in reverse. Generally they do not require external power (although some modern designs do) and are resistant to water, as well as being tough and relatively inexpensive. However, they tend to be bulky and basically come in the design that you need to poke in someone's face. They work well for stage performers.

Condenser microphones (also known as capacitor or electrostatic) are more commonly found in a linguistic field kit, because they tend to be more compact and more varied in design. For example, they come as lapel and table-top microphones and as a miniature type—the electret microphone—which is often found in things like headsets, mobile phones, and computers. Condenser microphones always require a power source of some kind. This can be from batteries or via 'phantom power', where the microphone draws electricity from an external source, generally the recorder itself. In this system, 48 volts DC is supplied through the balanced audio connection itself. One problem is that some microphones which do not use phantom power, and which can actually be damaged by it, also use balanced audio connections (typically XLR). So in general phantom power should be switched off unless you are using a microphone which requires it. Another type of in-line power supply is found in some microphones for computers and portable recorders. These employ a stereo TRS mini-jack, even though the microphone itself is mono: the redundant channel is used to supply power to the microphone.

Battery-powered microphones may have some power-saving mechanisms, but unfortunately they do not turn themselves on or off, adding to the fieldworker's margin for catastrophe. As mentioned, this is especially the case with radio microphones, which require considerable power for both the transmitter and receiver packs.

(iii) Directivity. Many different degrees of directivity exist in microphones. To some extent, different patterns of sensitivity tend to be associated with particular designs and configurations (e.g. small table-top microphones are commonly electret and omnidirectional), but there is a large degree of cross-over. Choosing an unsuitable combination is therefore quite easy.

The omnidirectional pattern has been recommended in this chapter, but there are situations where it is not appropriate, particularly where the microphone cannot always be close to the intended speaker. In situations like this, where the speaker may be drowned out by other voices and noises, uni- and semi-directional microphones are more suitable. At the extreme is the 'shotgun' pattern. Microphones of this type are very directional and are used for example in wildlife recordings, where they can be used at a great distance to capture discrete events.

The very narrowness of their scope makes them tricky to use—the relationship to the speaker must be constantly monitored. Should the speaker or the microphone move during recording, then you risk recording even more rain or surf. Having such a microphone mounted to a video camera in line with the lens (common on professional models) provides a relatively low-maintenance solution, assuming that someone is monitoring the recording through the camera most of the time. Shotgun microphones seem to perform better outdoors than inside, where they can cause phase problems and odd echoes.

Less extreme, semi-directional microphones are the so-called 'cardioid' types. Three distinctions are often made: cardioid, super-cardioid, and hyper-cardioid, in increasing degrees of directivity. These patterns favour sound from the front, without being too narrow. While placement is less critical than for shotgun models, such microphones do still place an onus on the sound engineer (i.e. you) and/or the speaker to maintain a good spatial arrangement. Again, such microphones can be mounted on a camera (and are likely to be the type of microphone supplied with a professional camera). These are the primary micro-phones used by documentary film-makers, presumably because of the useful degree of directivity (especially when mounted on the camera and therefore automatically aligned with the subject). Our experience with this technique was that, for reliable results, the camera had to be closer to the speaker than we generally felt comfortable with, and rather than using a cable to get the micro-phone closer (and then continually monitoring this arrangement) we preferred to use the radio microphones.

(iv) **Mono vs. stereo microphones.** We already mentioned that stereo recording is not particularly relevant for many linguistic field recordings. However, there are clearly applications, such as musical events, where it is desirable. A good solution would be to use the inbuilt microphones of a modern solid-state recorder on such occasions. These often have paired microphone sets crossing over in a so-called 'X/Y' arrangement such that both are on the same axis, avoiding time lag between channels. In some cases there are two sets (i.e. four microphones) with forward- and rear-facing configurations. It is the post-processing of all four channels which can achieve a kind of surround sound. Sometimes the angle between the paired phones can be altered to suit different conditions (e.g. narrower angle for smaller music ensembles). Such microphones provide a point-and-shoot option for producing accurate stereo.

Another workable scenario is to string up a couple of omnidirectional radio microphones in a rough 'stereo' configuration (or, for video, to employ one 'local' radio microphone plus a camera-mounted microphone feeding into separate channels). The result will be more stereo than mono, and might be sufficient to capture the ambience of an event, as well as giving some insurance against disaster in case one of the microphones fails to provide an adequate record.[22]

1.2.2.3 *Headphones*

Headphones are an essential part of a field equipment kit. They are necessary for checking the audio levels before, during, and after recording and for transcription of the data. Earphones, i.e. phones which are plugged into the ear (rather than covering it), are handy because they are small, light, and discreet. They can however be very uncomfortable if they are used for any length of time, and this can become a problem for transcribing. We have good experience with foldable headphones which are quite small, compact, and inexpensive, and more comfortable than earphones in the long run. A kit could contain both: headphones for transcription and earphones for checking audio quality during recording. If you are recording in situations where there is a lot of background noise, consider high-quality headphones which cut out much of the external sound and enable you to focus on what is actually being recorded.

A splitter plug which connects two pairs of headphones and therefore allows two people to listen to a recording is essential when working on a transcription together with a speaker. The alternative is to use loudspeakers, but they consume more power and create a more public work situation. Such a splitter plug may look the same as the microphone splitter but they are not interchangeable.[23]

1.3 VIDEO RECORDINGS

We advocate video recordings as the basic recording method for a number of reasons. Video provides information which is important for certain kinds of linguistic analyses such as gestures and facial expressions but also information about who is speaking, who else is present, orientation and seating arrangement of speakers, recording location, and time of day. In short, video helps greatly to establish the context of a speech event. Only some of this context can be captured by metadata, and that only if such metadata is meticulously recorded and

---

[22] The traditional professional approach to stereo recording is to use two or more mono microphones in strategic locations—something of a black art. Professional stereo microphones also exist, but some are professional enough to consume an entire field budget.

[23] The microphone splitter combines two mono channels (one from each microphone) into one stereo channel. In the case of the headphone splitter, the same stereo signal is delivered to two sets of headphones.

preserved. Also, remembering that in the long run linguists are not the only group interested in the data, it is clear that audio/video is generally superior to audio-only recordings for the documentation of cultural setting and interaction.

The choice of video over audio as the basic recording technique should not, however, be at the expense of the audio quality, and so a good-quality camera is essential.[24] Cameras in the professional range have professional audio inputs, circuits, and controls; cameras in the consumer and prosumer ranges do not. Whatever other bells and whistles they provide (inbuilt GPS, YouTube upload feature, 5.1 surround sound, 'Automatic Smile Shutter', etc.) they do not give serious consideration to audio quality. Even so, a non-professional camera can be a satisfactory backup device provided it can take some kind of external microphone (this may be via a 'hot-shoe' for a dedicated camcorder microphone and/or a TRS mini-jack; but remember that the latter can result in problems with static crackle from longer microphone cables as mentioned in §1.2.2.2(i)). We have had good experiences with a bottom-of-the-range professional camera which had XLR audio (the 'Sony DSR-PDX10P') and which was only marginally more expensive than the top-end consumer model at the time.

Choosing a camera as the master recording device does not mean everything has to be recorded as video. It may not always be possible or appropriate to film, for example because of low light or community/individual sensitivities about what should be filmed. In such cases the camera can simply be used with the lens cap on as a high-quality audio recorder.

Even more than with audio equipment, video cameras have many different settings that can be relevant for recordings and they are capable of a bewildering range of error messages: do take the manuals to the field.

1.3.1 Things to consider

Unlike with current audio recorders, it is still common for good-quality video cameras to record to digital tape rather than to hard disk or flash memory (i.e. solid state). Although this is changing, DV and HDV[25] tape will be around for some

---

[24] This section assumes that the camera is required to fulfill both audio and video functions acceptably. Another scenario is to continue to record audio independently with a dedicated recorder, and to synchronize audio and video tracks in the editing software afterwards. In this case, the observations about camera audio quality do not apply. Audio purists may argue that even professional cameras cannot match professional audio equipment. This is technically true, since the maximum setting for DV recordings is 16bit/48kHz (audio sample size/rate) PCM whereas current solid-state recorders can achieve 24bit/96kHz. However, it is still better than standard CD quality (16bit/44.1kHz) and sufficient for most phonetic analyses.

[25] Most HD tape cameras that will be within budget use the same tape format as conventional Mini-DV/DVCAM. Moreover most are backwards compatible, i.e. they can record in DV as well as HDV quality.

time as a common, affordable recording medium. This raises two important considerations. First, it requires a time-consuming (i.e. real-time) capturing process to transfer the data to disk. Second, one may therefore be tempted to put this task off. But at some point suitable cameras and tape decks will become obsolete and then un-transferred material risks being left unconvertible, so tapes should be captured to disk as soon as practicable.[26]

Hard-drive and solid-state cameras might seem a better option in this respect, but they provide their own hazards in terms of file format, quality, and specification. The problem is that in order to save disk space they typically transcode on the fly to some more compressed format than that used by the standard tape formats, for example to a version of MPEG2 or AVCHD.[27] There is nothing inherently wrong with this (except that these formats often need transcoding again before they can be handled in mainstream non-linear editors, or in other player applications, e.g. ELAN[28]). But, particularly for consumer-range machines, it increases the risk that the data is being recorded in what turns out to be a non-standard, non-popular format/version which will need to be expertly transcoded at some stage to prevent loss of quality and maintain long-term playability. The topic of data conversion and preservation is discussed further in the next section.

1.3.1.1 *Recording resolutions*

Unlike with audio files, the goal of creating uncompressed video is not currently feasible—the quantity of data required is simply too great for standard data storage mechanisms. This is particularly the case with high-definition video which is gradually superseding standard definition. Even compressed video can be a problem: an hour of recording in standard MiniDV format consumes about 13 Gb—too large to be archived on a standard DVD. With newer technology (e.g. single sided Blu-Ray disks can accommodate 25 Gb data) and the increasing affordability of large hard drives, this problem is to some extent diminishing, and there is a case to be made for backup copies being made in the original format. Nevertheless, at present compression is often necessary, at least for delivery of the content, and the aim is to find a format and standard that entails minimum loss of data while remaining open and well supported. We suggest referring to large linguistic archives such as DoBeS or PARADISEC for recommendations.[29] In our project

---

[26] Keep the originals, though: at present tapes are still widely used for archiving because they are in some respects safer and more durable than digital files on e.g. a hard drive or DVD, so it makes sense to preserve the tapes until and unless a more reliable backup technology becomes widely available.

[27] This applies to HDV tape cameras as well, i.e. they too use a version of MPEG2 compression.

[28] ELAN: EUDICO Linguistic Annotator. A powerful and widely used, XML-based, audio/video annotation tool, http://www.lat-mpi.eu/tools/elan/.

[29] DoBeS: Dokumentation Bedrohter Sprachen/Documentation of Endangered Languages, http://www.mpi.nl/DOBES/.

we follow DoBeS specifications (and software guidelines) for creating MPEG2 and MPEG1 versions from DV tapes.

It is important to realize that, although the typical standard-definition video cameras (i.e. MiniDV) create uncompressed linear PCM audio, current high-definition (HD) cameras typically do not. Instead, they record audio in compressed forms (e.g. MPEG1 layer 2, AAC/MPEG4 or Dolby Digital/AC3). This rather speaks against most HD cameras for our purposes if they are intended to also be the main audio recording device.

1.3.1.2 *Filming techniques*

Filming introduces a whole new range of things to get wrong. It is not usually possible, on your own or as a two-person team, to attend to everything, and audio settings should always take priority. But even if the camera has to be on auto-everything, there are a few things one can try to always remember that will improve the results. Ideally no one would go into the field without some basic training in the use of video equipment, preferably given by a film-maker rather than a shop assistant. At the very least you should experiment vigorously before you go.

As with still photography, a flat horizon such as the sea should be a level line. It is easy to overlook this in the heat of the moment and record with the horizon at an angle. Unlike with still photography, it is a major hassle to rotate and crop the result; normally one has to live with the shame.

Even with perfect exposure it is very easy to mar a shot by omitting to use a lens hood of some kind. (Maybe it was not a problem at the start of the session, but then the sun came out...) Amazingly, consumer/prosumer models rarely include a dedicated hood. Perhaps the smaller lenses they use need less shading, or perhaps the manufacturers calculate that most people would rather have a sleeker machine than a clearer image. Professional models always seem to include a hood. If you have one, do use it to keep lens flare[30] and the consequent loss of detail and contrast at bay. If necessary, consider making one out of cardboard; at the very least be aware of the problem.

Lens filters are also invaluable. They are inexpensive and protect against damage to the lens besides filtering out problematic light. The basic type is the UV filter which screens out ultraviolet rays, thus reducing haze effects. Also useful is the polarizing filter. This is adjustable and functions to darken the sky and also to reduce reflections, for example from a water or glass surface (meaning that objects behind the surface can be seen).

PARADISEC: Pacific And Regional Archive for Digital Sources in Endangered Cultures, http://paradisec.org.au/.

[30] Where light from a strong source (either in the image itself or just outside it) 'bleeds' into other areas or causes a haze.

Most video cameras have an external indication that they are recording, typically a red light near the lens. This can be helpful when one is using the remote control to operate the camera, for example, if the researcher has to be in the picture together with the speaker for an elicitation task. However, the red light can also have the drawback of alerting people that the camera is recording and may cause them to modify their behaviour. The camera is likely to have the option of turning the red light off.

(i) Tripods vs. handheld filming. We believe that in most fieldwork settings it should be standard practice to use a tripod for filming. There are several good reasons for this. A handheld camera invariably moves and shakes and this makes for bad recordings. Holding the camera for any length of time is exhausting. Speakers are more likely to relax and forget about the camera if there is not someone constantly behind it.

There is a different school of thought which advocates filming without a tripod. The idea is that people actually relax more with a handheld camera than with a tripod, because after a while they are more aware of the person than of the camera to the extent of not even noticing it any more. From this point of view, one is therefore better off learning to hold a camera steady and level rather than fussing with a tripod.

We think that this approach is probably more appropriate for documentary film-making than for the type of linguistic data collection generally under discussion here. Films are composed of a number of small scenes arranged to tell a story—irregular camera movement can be either edited out or is simply overlooked because of the composite nature of the final production. But for many, if not most, linguistic data samples, long unedited recordings with video matched to audio are the norm, since the point is primarily to capture a speech event. For such recordings, the inevitable camera shake from a handheld recording of an essentially static scene is likely to be very noticeable and distracting. Either way, it is good practice (often suggested by documentary film-makers) that the camera should appear to run as much as possible, particularly at the beginning of a shoot, simply to help people accept the camera as normal.

Typical fieldwork may encompass a range of filming scenarios: some recordings will be static set pieces, others on-the-fly recordings of things that just happen (it may simply be impractical to lug a tripod around while following a speaker who has agreed to demonstrate e.g. traditional gardening or fishing methods). In other words, a decent tripod and good handheld technique can both be recommended.

If you do succeed—by whichever method, fixed camera or handheld—in putting your subjects at ease, do remember that the more likely speakers are to forget that they are being recorded, the more important it is that they can later veto parts of the recording they do not want to have made public.

If one opts for a fixed camera, even a very small, lightweight tripod or propping the camera up on a table is better than nothing. But if the budget allows, a professional camera should be complemented by a sturdy tripod. Such a tripod need not be heavy (though it will be relatively bulky); carbon-fibre models are comparatively light. Apart from the fact that a professional camera tends to be bigger and needs more support than a consumer one, a good tripod with a good head will allow much smoother camera movements. Before filming, the tripod should be leveled (most tripod heads include a bubble level).

If the camera is to be handheld, one should choose the steady-shot option, which compensates to some extent for jerky movements. A hand-grip (of the sort sold for still cameras, e.g. 'Hama' brand) can be very effective for steadying a video camera. The grip can also be used for mounting a microphone away from the camera itself, so reducing its susceptibility to mechanical noise. If most of the recording will be done on the hoof, a small sized 'stabilizer' might be justified: these devices assist a walking camera operator to create smooth footage (e.g. 'Steadicam', 'Glidecam', and 'Blackbird' brands).

(ii) Zooming, panning, and composition. Elaborate camera work is rarely necessary or desirable for decent language recordings. If speakers are stationary, there is little reason to use zooming and panning at all. As tempting as they are, it is good to avoid these manoeuvres; they make recordings look chaotic and unprofessional. Overly active camera work can also cause loss of visual data, such as gestures. When zooming in on the speaker's face or panning to capture other aspects of the recording situation, there is no record of the speaker's hand gestures for that segment (see Seyfeddinipur, Chapter 6 below).

The zoom function should therefore generally be used merely as a tool for composition: frame the speakers intelligently and then stop. Likewise for the camera direction and position: if you do choose to use so called 'developing shots' (i.e. when you zoom or pan during a shot), a good rule of thumb is to keep the image still for at least ten seconds before and after the movement. Also, make all such adjustments slowly ('slow' here means about three times slower than you might think during filming). Zooming and panning typically appears too fast and hectic when reviewing the recording. Remember that most camera movement should be motivated by the subject, not the camera operator, and so in general camera movement should only be required to follow someone and keep them in frame.

Recordings that take place in confined spaces can be very hard to frame—one simply cannot zoom out far enough. The solution is a wide-angle lens. Such a lens is often available for professional cameras, and simply fits over the standard lens. We found this a very worthwhile accessory.

It is nice to get a close-up of the speakers who participated in a recording (which can be used for stills too) and a record of who else was present.[31] But ideally this would be separate from the filming of the linguistic data. To do this one can add a segment at the end of a recording that includes a slow zoom onto the speaker and a slow pan across all the people present.

Active zooming and panning may have a place in the documentation of events and activities where people are moving around and it is hard to capture everything. But even here less is more. A better option is proper editing post recording to create good cuts between scenes. If the budget allows it, a second (possibly lower-grade) camera is useful on such occasions. If two cameras are filming aspects of the same event, the first can do a continuous overview of the scene while the second does close-ups. The two can later be edited together. This is no small undertaking, however.

(iii) Lighting and positioning. This topic is related to composition, but here the emphasis is on achieving optimal exposure and therefore clarity of all the data that the video contains. It is helpful to understand some of the characteristics of camera systems in dealing with the variability of light intensity across an image, and therefore how exposure settings are arrived at and what their limitations are. Knowing this one can then make intelligent choices both with the setup of the scene (discussed here) and with the exposure controls on the camera (discussed below in §1.3.1.3(ii)). We will discuss three points of interest here.

First, it is easier to compensate for too much light in a scene (by using a smaller iris setting and/or a faster shutter speed) than for too little, which can only be done at the cost of a 'noisy' image. So, if possible provide plenty of light.

Second, it is important to realize that any automatic exposure mechanism makes assumptions about the quantity of light in an image. The default setting is to assume that the sum of all the lights and darks makes a neutral grey. For many images this is a reasonable approximation, but it is also commonly inappropriate for typical field-work setups. If, for example, there is a large area of bright sky/sand/snow in the scene, the net effect may be considerably brighter than a neutral grey. The camera's auto-exposure assumption would then be wrong, with the result that all tones will be rendered darker than they should be, and this may well mean a loss of detail in the human face. Most cameras offer various pre-programmed modes ('backlight', 'portraiture', 'beach', etc.) which attempt to do better than the default setting in certain conditions, but their success depends on the operator understanding and remembering to use them. It is safer to learn how to set the exposure manually such that the main point of interest is correctly exposed, and then to always do this.

---

[31] We are not discussing still images here, but it is appropriate and also helpful to have a portrait photo of each speaker who has contributed to the text collection. The photos can help to remember who is who, they make good gifts for speakers, and they can be included in a speaker database or in a publication of recorded texts. Video cameras generally have a setting to take stills.

Third, the problem of incorrect exposure would not be so serious if it were not for the limitations in exposure range of the camera sensor, i.e. the fact that tonal detail is not well captured at the extremes—light and dark—of an image. This means that without efforts to limit the overall tonal range (i.e. contrast) in a scene—usually by brightening the darker areas with artificial lights or reflectors, and perhaps darkening the light areas with screens—some visual information will be lost, and it is not possible to recover this information in post processing.[32]

Since the use of auxiliary lights and other props is probably neither a possible nor desirable option for most fieldworkers, attaining the control of professional film-makers is not a realistic goal: unintentional lens flare, burnt-out highlights, and featureless shadows can all be expected from time to time. But it is possible to minimize, or avoid altogether, such defects impinging on the essential features of a video document by paying attention to the orientation of the scene, as well as to the exposure setting on the camera.

Filming against the light or a bright background—for example the speaker sitting indoors in front of a window—should, but often cannot, be avoided. In this situation, manual exposure on the face or using a pre-programmed backlight option are essential to avoid filming a mere silhouette. This problem is amplified if the person has dark skin. Although an acceptable result regarding the face can be achieved using this method, this is the least satisfactory orientation.

Shooting 'with the light', i.e. having the light source behind the camera, is generally better but does not necessarily solve this problem. If the speaker is sitting in the sun in front of a light-coloured background, such as the wall of a house, the background will reflect the light and still be brighter than the person being filmed; finding a darker background will make a big difference. Also, if the speaker is facing strong light they may squint, be uneasy, and display unflattering facial shadows.

Filming in the shade helps, but can still be problematic. We once filmed a group of speakers sitting comfortably under a tree, but all around there was coral gravel reflecting the sun such that there was no angle where the camera could have avoided a bright background. Again, in such situations the backlight option or manual exposure helps.

An ideal arrangement would be for the speakers to sit at a 45 degree angle to the light, outdoors (where there is generally more light), and positioned in such a way that bright objects, such as walls, reflect light onto the face but are not directly in the background. However, best positioning for image may not be the same as best positioning for audio. Factors such as wind and other sources of noise are arguably more important (discussed in §§1.2.1.2 and 1.2.2.2(i) above).

---

[32] The fact that 'High Dynamic Range' imaging, where an image preserves detail across all tones, requires the merging of several photographs which are identical except for their exposure levels, demonstrates clearly the limitations of the standard image.

1.3.1.3 *Adjusting settings*

As with audio recordings, adjusting the available settings of video cameras can make a major difference to the quality of the recording. The auto settings are not necessarily suitable. A camera should allow controlling for focus, exposure/iris, shutter speed, white balance, and audio input levels. Unfortunately this is not always the case, particularly regarding audio control.

(i) Focus. The ubiquitous auto focus function is very convenient but has a drawback: if something passes through the picture in front of the speaker, the focus will automatically switch to the entity in the foreground; when it has disappeared, the focus will switch back to the speaker, causing moments of blur while the camera refocuses. This can be avoided by only using auto focus to choose the right focus and, once that is set (i.e. on the speaker), by locking the focus in that setting. Alternatively, one can simply operate the camera in manual focus. Auto focus can also be unreliable at low light levels with the camera going in and out of focus, 'hunting' for the right target, so again it is better to make a decision and lock the focus.

(ii) Exposure/iris. Setting the exposure correctly is a subjective and to some extent impossible task. Sometimes the amount of light available, and/or the contrast in the scene, will push the camera's sensor to its limits, resulting in areas that are over- or underexposed. The best that can then be done is to ensure that the speaker's face is adequately exposed. Normally one would want to capture facial expressions and movements of the mouth (which can help, e.g. with phonetic transcriptions).

Setting the exposure manually (by adjusting the iris) is again the preferred option. A reliable technique is to zoom in on the face of a speaker so that it fills the screen, adjust and then lock the exposure, and zoom back out to the appropriate frame for recording the scene. This can be done with the camera on standby; there is no need to record it. If the light changes considerably during filming (e.g. because the sun comes out), the locked exposure can become a problem and will need to be redone.

As mentioned above, cameras generally have preset options for low-light and back-light settings (often employing a 'gain' control which boosts the electronic signal, giving you lighter but more noisy or grainy pictures). These can be used as quick alternatives to manually setting the exposure. Be especially aware that a low-light option sets up the camera to make the most of the available light, but does so at the expense of sensor resolution and/or shutter speed. The result can be very grainy images and/or images with disjointed motion. This might still be better than no image. (The audio recording is unaffected, of course.)

(iii) **Shutter speed.** Unlike exposure, shutter speed rarely has to be adjusted manually for linguistic recordings. An exception could be the filming of some rapid gestures or other significant activity where high shutter speeds would be beneficial. (The difference may not be so apparent in the video itself, but will manifest itself as sharper still frames.) As with all photography, higher shutter speeds require wider exposures (resulting in shallower depth of field, which demands greater focussing accuracy) and/or more light. The optimal shutter speed for normal recording is 50, to maximize light but avoid blurred images.

(iv) **White balance.** Setting the white balance means essentially giving the camera a reference point of what white is, which makes all the other colours correct (and therefore avoids pink or green faces). This has to be redone for every recording session that takes place under different lighting conditions (e.g. moving from indoors to outdoors). Cameras usually have an auto white balance function as well as some preset modes (e.g. for artificial light or a sunny day), but manual calibration, if available, is the most reliable method. It is also a simple and quick process, requiring only a white surface, such as a sheet of paper or a white T-shirt, as a reference which should fill the entire screen during balancing.

(v) **Audio levels.** As mentioned, not all cameras provide adequate audio input controls. All professional models do, but even high-end prosumer ones may be somewhat deficient. A camera may accept external microphone input but still lack manual control for it.

Something to especially watch out for is 'auto-gain', a function on cheaper cameras which continually adjusts audio levels depending on the input at the time. We had this problem with such a camera: when the speaker was talking background noise was low, but whenever they paused the level would reset to the new ambient conditions, amplifying the background noise. The result was normal speech punctuated with crashing surf sounds. Make sure your camera does not have an auto-gain function, or that it can be switched off.

1.3.2 Equipment

The same criteria apply to video equipment as to audio regarding quality vs. other constraints such as budget, weight, and complexity of use. The situation with video is more extreme because of the extra paraphernalia associated with cameras (lenses, tripods, etc.). The reality is that professional film-making is less attainable than professional audio recording. The purpose of using professional equipment and techniques, as far as is reasonable, is simply to create the best possible record.

As for audio recorders, we recommend using cameras that can record audio in uncompressed linear PCM. That rules out solid-state cameras of most grades and formats. We also do not necessarily recommend high-definition tape cameras, even those of professional or semi-professional grade. At present, most high-definition cameras actually offer inferior audio to their standard definition counterparts. The problem is that high definition equates to recording many more pixels per frame, but the storage medium remains essentially the same (HD is recorded on normal MiniDV cassettes). In the competition for data space, the audio quality has been compromised. This will probably improve in the future as data storage technology continues to develop, but in the meantime it cannot be taken for granted that hi-def video means hi-fi audio.

It is also arguable that many so-called high-definition cameras, particularly in the consumer/prosumer range, do not really deliver better video than their standard-definition counterparts. Certainly they will produce the required quantity of pixels, but there are very many other factors that also determine the final image: lens quality, sensor type and size, in-camera signal processing and compression capabilities. In addition, HD playback can be less than smooth on the average laptop, and so, for the time being, we recommend standard-definition over high-definition video cameras.

Regarding camera technology there is debate about whether a CCD or CMOS light sensor is better.[33] In many situations CMOS has begun to displace CCD technology for reasons such as cost of manufacture and power consumption. Our conclusion is that there are so many variables in design and implementation, as well as in other camera components, that an easy comparison is impossible. Different high-end cameras follow different paths to achieving quality. However, clearly 3CCD systems—where three separate CCDs are employed for each of the red, green, and blue light components—are superior to a single CCD system.

The following sections consider camera types in rough order of preference for linguistic fieldwork.

1.3.2.1 Tape cameras (MiniDV, HDV)

The MiniDV camera type has a good track record and that is what we recommend. It produces the required audio formats and quality by default. Eventually both the format and the recording mechanism (i.e. tape) might become obsolete, but that time has not yet come. However, it is becoming hard to buy this type new as HDV becomes the norm. It is worth noting that HDV tape cameras typically offer standard DV as a recording option, in which case non-compressed linear PCM audio is available. A modern tape-based, HD, low-end professional machine, such

---

[33] CCD: charge-coupled device; CMOS: complementary metal-oxide semiconductor. Both refer here to the chips which take the place of the film in a digital camera.

as the 'Sony HVR-A1P', would therefore be a fine main recorder when used with the standard DV rather than the HD setting.[34]

1.3.2.2 Solid-state/hard-drive cameras

Tape as a recording medium is steadily losing ground to disk and flash memory for two good reasons: the time-consuming capturing process is no longer required, and there are fewer moving parts and less weight in the camera. Some models replace the tape with a conventional hard disk, but as the capacities of memory cards have increased (and the prices dropped) the solid-state model is becoming prevalent. This trend is stronger in the consumer range, but also apparent in professional cameras.

The problem with this technology shift is that, at present, there is an unfortunate lack of uniformity regarding recording file formats (compared to MiniDV, which is well established). Therefore extra care should be taken that recordings are created in, or converted to, archivable formats.

(i) **High-definition cameras.** There is no doubt that high-definition video is tempting—the higher screen resolution is hard to dislike. But as mentioned, there are problems, particularly with models which do not offer a recording option with uncompressed audio. Generally, then, this camera type cannot be recommended. This situation will probably change, however: there is already at least one current semi-professional model, the 'JVC GY-HM100', which seriously addresses the audio question by recording uncompressed linear PCM audio alongside the MPEG2-based HD video. This would appear to be a fine camera for the field in every respect, though it is more expensive than the 'Sony HVR-A1P' mentioned above.

(ii) **Standard-definition cameras.** Given the typical problems of solid-state/hard-drive cameras (unconventional formats, lack of uncompressed audio), it is hard to recommend them on the grounds of convenience alone (i.e. not requiring the capturing process) since they provide no better video resolution than a standard tape-based machine. Since they are light, compact, and relatively inexpensive, however, a case can be made for such cameras as auxiliary or backup machines. As noted before, not every recording need be of top technical quality: sometimes having a camera/recorder to hand is the main thing.

---

[34] Secondhand professional cameras such as the 'Sony Z1' or 'PD150' models are also worth considering. Such cameras are designed to be maintained and serviced, and hold up better than the consumer/prosumer types.

1.3.2.3 All-weather cameras

There is also a place for all-weather cameras which are water- and dust-proof and sometimes quite resistant to impact and extremes of temperature. We are not dealing with professional-quality models here but rather with consumer machines (solid-state type) packaged for use at the beach, in the snow, and so forth. They are a safer option for filming in wet conditions such as boat trips. We provided such a camera to speakers to do their own recordings when we were not present and could not help with the maintenance of the equipment in a tropical climate. Some of the community-made recordings we have received from this camera would have been unattainable by an outside researcher.

Such cameras are not particularly expensive, but there is a price to pay in reduced audio/video quality. Critically, they do not allow for external microphones and have rather weak internal ones. This makes them decidedly second-rate as audio recorders. To get the best possible sound the camera must be positioned as close to the speaker as possible (rather than being positioned at a distance and capturing the right frame by zooming in).

For even more challenging conditions, such as filming fishing or hunting activities, there are specialist cameras designed for extreme sports. An example is the 'GoPro HD HERO' range. These small and quite inexpensive cameras are waterproof to 60m and highly shockproof (they can be mounted to surfboards or crash helmets), yet shoot HD video with 48 kHz mono audio.

1.3.2.4 Still cameras

Many cameras designed to take still images can also function as video cameras. There are two broad categories: SLR cameras offering very good HD video in some format, and compact cameras with a lower quality (even if marketed as HD) video mode. For many reasons, only the SLR type can be recommended for primary recordings (e.g. SLRs tend to have better built-in microphones than compact cameras and some models even allow external microphones), but even then only with qualifications.

The main issues with video on SLR cameras are the limited duration of recording and the sound quality. Nevertheless there are some cameras with useful specifications. As an example, the 'Pentax K-7' apparently records up to 25 minutes (or 4 Gb file size) of HD video (720p variety, i.e. 1280 × 720 pixels) with sound. This camera also has a stereo jack for an external microphone (though not XLR). Benefits of such cameras include the compact size of the apparatus (good for cramped indoor situations) and the control over depth of field afforded by the lenses available (which e.g. allow speakers' faces to stand out clearly). So this kind of equipment may work well for many fieldwork settings, especially if complemented by a decent solid-state audio recorder.[35]

1.3.2.5 *Incidental cameras*

We mentioned earlier (§1.2.2.1(i)) the 'Zoom Q3' recorder which includes a video camera for basic QuickTime movies of 640 × 480 pixel resolution at 30fps. Such a device seems almost a gimmick, but could actually provide just the right balance of good audio plus reference video in a small package for on-the-run fieldwork.

The 'Flip' range of pocket sized camcorders are also worth considering as backup or go-everywhere devices. Although these cameras are not optimized for sound, they offer good video in a very compact format. Other devices that could be used to capture really basic audio/video in emergencies include some mobile phones, iPods, PDAs, and webcams.

1.4 ENERGY SUPPLY

1.4.1 Things to consider

Different field sites have very different power constraints. In an urban setting, mains electricity may be regularly available but perhaps likely to suffer power outages or voltage spikes without warning. In this case a good UPS[36]—or just a surge/spike protector—might be the only essential energy supply item to pack. A rural field site may well lack any regular source of electricity, in which case solar- and/or fuel-powered generators will be required along with regulators and storage batteries.

Which of these often heavy and bulky items need to be brought to the field and which can be bought locally will also vary. At our field site we had to bring in solar panels and auxiliary electronics but were able to buy a large truck battery in the nearest town. We needed a big battery because we had several computers, cameras,

---

[35] When choosing a camera, note that the typical LCD screens are all but useless in strong sunlight, so models with no optical viewfinder should be avoided. Manufacturers are beginning to promote digital SLRs as video recorders—e.g. Zoom suggest that their H1 model can be used as an external microphone on such a machine—but it should be remembered that the camera audio quality and controls are likely to be less than ideal: check the specifications.

[36] UPS: Uninterruptible Power Supply. A battery-like device for providing back-up power for a limited period after a power failure; it also protects against spikes and surges. Note, however, that no such equipment protects completely against all electrical hazards, and that the surge protection can wear out if subjected to too large or frequent demands.

and other equipment to run. If one only needs to recharge the recording equipment periodically, one may get away with just a solar panel plus a regulator—so a storage battery is not always required.

Some recording equipment can be run from mains power. Even if the circumstances permit it, we avoid doing this, both to retain flexibility (i.e. so that the machine is not tethered to an outlet) and because with such a power source one may need to look into shielding to prevent interference in the audio.

Equipment, including battery chargers, will be designed to run on regular mains AC power[37] and/or 12 volt DC power. For many field setups the latter will be the only electricity source available. Adaptors for using such a source almost invariably come with a cigarette lighter-type plug (so that they can be used in a car, as with common mobile phone chargers). The most convenient way to connect these to a home-rigged power source is therefore to use the corresponding cigarette lighter sockets (available at any electrical supplies). For wiring these, the centre point is positive (+ve) and the cylindrical sleeve is negative (–ve).

Assuming that some kind of electrical competence, beyond simply attaching a plug to a socket, will be required, it is worth learning a bit about 12/24 volt DC circuits (e.g. from a boat maintenance book). If some ad hoc wiring will be needed (quite likely in the case of solar equipment), make and test the system before going to the field. A basic toolkit, including a multi-meter and soldering iron, will be helpful. Otherwise the power regeneration scheme can easily become the Achilles heel of the operation. Be aware that low-voltage systems can be every bit as deadly as mains AC in certain circumstances (risk of fire due to high currents in small cables, battery explosions from short circuits, etc.).

1.4.2 Equipment

1.4.2.1 *Generators*

Some field sites may provide an irregular power supply via an existing fixed generator. This is characteristic of some mission or trade stations which usually require some kind of power infrastructure. If such power is available, then the main concern is to make sure that the supply does not damage the equipment. Simple precautions include disconnecting equipment before shut-down and only re-establishing connections once the generator has stabilized after startup. A UPS provides further protection both against variability in line quality and inadvertent power outages.

---

[37] Which however may be of the ~ 230 v (e.g. Europe, Australia) or ~ 120 v (e.g. USA, Japan) varieties: check carefully that the equipment will run happily on either (as with most laptop computer power leads), otherwise obtain a suitable step-up or step-down transformer before plugging into an AC source.

It is worth considering connecting a large battery to the generator and charging this as well. This provides some capacity for either running or charging the equipment when the main generator is off. The best arrangement perhaps would be to only use this battery, i.e. never to run equipment directly from a generator. This would obviate the need for a UPS (which, like a battery, is heavy) and provide the best protection for the equipment. Some generators will offer a direct 12V DC outlet; otherwise a transformer type car battery charger would also be needed.

If no fixed generator exists and solar power is not an option, a portable generator running on diesel or petrol will most likely be the next best option. The same precautions should be taken regarding protecting the equipment.

1.4.2.2 *Solar power*

Solar panels are a good option in many situations—they certainly cannot be beaten for quiet operation. However, there are a number of complications.

The first is where to mount them. Obviously sun orientation needs to be considered, but also factors like accessibility, and protection from animals and missiles. We were allowed to mount panels on an iron roof, which was in many ways ideal. Connecting the panels to our battery was tricky, however: long wires are a problem with low-voltage systems because of resistance losses, so we had to find the shortest route and the thickest electrical cable for the job. This is where a multimeter is invaluable, as it allows one to check whether one's non-optimal solution is actually functional or completely useless.

Another complication is the wiring itself. Solar panel generators need voltage regulation and blocking diodes—the former to protect against overcharging, the latter to prevent current running in reverse and draining the battery at night. Some designs have this circuitry built in, but otherwise you must wire-in dedicated components, which should be sized according to panel area (which equates to output current). Getting the balance right between panels, regulators, battery, and equipment takes a bit of calculation. Some of the panel suppliers give rule-of-thumb guides—at least for matching regulators to panels.

Solar panels can be rigid, flexible, or foldable. The rigid type is the most reliable and durable but also the heaviest and most awkward to transport. We have had quite good experience with a flexible model, which could be rolled into a large cylinder that just fitted in a suitcase. It was vulnerable, in that crushing or folding would have ruined it: careful packing and padding was necessary. Foldable types are light, compact, and very tempting but apparently less reliable: several people have reported that the cells failed despite good maintenance.

There are different technologies for creating solar panels. The three best-known types are monocrystalline, polycrystalline, and 'thin film', in descending order of both cost and efficiency. In other words, the monocrystalline type is ideal for on-the-move fieldwork in that a smaller panel can be used but it is also more expensive. There are a few other factors to consider, however. The monocrystalline type is the most fragile, the thin film type the most robust. Also, the thin film type can be found in a flexible laminate form which can be more easily attached to difficult surfaces, and it works better in very hot conditions. Probably the best application for this type would be where a permanent or semi-permanent field station was to be established (e.g. an entire roof could be covered with such panels).

1.4.2.3 *Other power sources*

In some ways a solar power generator is a fairly extreme setup given the unit costs and the fragility and bulk of the components. We have already mentioned the portable petrol/diesel generator as an easy option, but this has obvious drawbacks as well, not least in terms of noise pollution. Two other potential electricity sources should be considered: the opportunistic use of motor vehicle power, and wind generators.

It is not efficient to run a motor vehicle just in order to charge a battery, but should the field trips involve regular long journeys by car, bus, or truck anyway, then there may be a case for using the cigar lighter socket during the journey, to charge either individual equipment pieces or a small 12V battery that can be used as a charging source later (in which case it would be best if this battery is of the 'deep cycle' type that is designed to be completely discharged without harm).[38]

The same technique can, in principle, also be used on a boat (but in this case it is unlikely that a suitable socket will be available, so you may need to add the necessary wiring). Never attach anything directly to the starter battery of a boat unless you want a shipwreck. Instead, charge your equipment or dedicated battery through the running engine.

Depending on the prevailing weather at your field site, small wind generators (e.g. as found on sailing boats) could be more useful than a solar panel and no more expensive, bulky, or complex to set up.

1.4.2.4 *Batteries*

Normally, equipment will be run on batteries for most of the time. These may be internally or externally mounted. If they are internal, then non-removable arrangements should be avoided (i.e. not removable by the user—such as found in iPods): it is essential that batteries can be replaced in the field.

---

[38] Unfortunately, this variety is heavier, dearer, and rarer than the common starter motor battery. Deep-cycle batteries are also recommended for solar generators. However, since they are so much harder to source and since in a well-managed solar setup the battery need not be discharged to damaging levels, we do not think that this type is essential. (Our solution was to buy the biggest truck starter battery we could find locally, make sure it was fully charged before first use, and then monitor its condition regularly.)

Make sure to consider all your equipment needs before setting off. For example, because laptop computers have internal charging circuits and external chargers are not readily available, we needed a special adaptor to power (and therefore recharge) our laptops directly from the truck battery.

Most equipment will allow batteries to be charged by the machine itself, but we recommend not relying on this if possible. It is better to take dedicated chargers for two reasons: it allows equipment to be used with one set of batteries while another set is being charged, and it avoids using the precious machine for such a mundane task. Fortunately, there are universal-type chargers which are readily available from camera shops (e.g. 'Inca' brand), and which are cheap, light, and versatile (one only needs to swap the charging plate to adapt them for different battery types, and they run on both household AC and 12V DC systems).

For video cameras particularly, one should take several high-capacity batteries— and then add another one or two. It is bad enough having to replace tapes or memory cards in the middle of a session without having to swap batteries as well. In our experience, batteries need not be manufacturer-brand items (despite the warnings in the manuals)—we have had no problems using generic units which were about half the price. For such 'clip-on' batteries it is always best to physically remove them when not in use to minimize power drainage. For internal batteries this may not be practical, so remember to always turn the device off after use.

Some equipment will be designed to run on standard batteries, e.g. AA or AAA size. Do not assume that it will run on rechargeable versions—it may or it may not, so check the specs and test. Our radio microphone transmitters and receivers use AA batteries (lots of them!) but refuse to run on rechargeables because the voltage is actually a bit lower than for disposable ones. The discovery of this in the field meant that we suddenly had to source large quantities of good-quality alkaline batteries.

1.5 OTHER EQUIPMENT

A number of electrical devices other than recording and power equipment are likely to find their way into a field kit. The most obvious one is a portable computer. This may be complemented by accessories such as external hard drives, and perhaps a GPS device and digital still camera.

If it will be necessary to capture digital video tape in the field, then a reasonably powerful Notebook/Laptop computer (which includes a Firewire port) will be required. If this is not the case, then a 'Netbook' type computer may be quite adequate and more convenient. This relatively new type of miniature laptop is cheaper, smaller, lighter, and less power-hungry than a conventional machine.

Most models will easily be able to run programs typically used in the field, such as word processors, linguistic databases, and audio/video applications.

All portable computers can benefit from a dedicated laptop stand (or just an external keyboard plus a cardboard box to raise the screen height). This helps prevent strain on the wrists and neck and can make a big difference to your well-being. Foldable, flexible, or laser projection keyboards are available which save space and weight.

Regardless of primary disk capacity, some external storage—hard drive or flash—is required for data transfer and backups. One can pay a considerable premium for 'rugged' USB sticks which are resistant to various calamities, but simply taking the same precautions as with other equipment is probably sufficient. External hard disk drives should be of the (more expensive) portable variety since, as well as being small, they generally do not require their own power source but run off the computer.

If a laptop computer is not available (perhaps it is not advisable to take one to the field at all), another solution for audio-video data backup is a device which combines a card reader with a hard drive (e.g. 'Nexto' or 'HyperDrive' brands).

For reading electronic documents (such as PDF versions of equipment manuals), a better option than the laptop would be an eBook reader. Although this might seem like superfluous expense and baggage, it is much easier to read for any length of time (especially in strong daylight) from these devices than from conventional screens. They are light and compact and are low on energy requirements. Currently not all e-readers are good at dealing with PDF documents however (e.g. they may reduce the font size to something illegible in order to fit a document to the page rather than 'reflowing' the line breaks).

It is becoming commonplace to add precise location information to metadata of language recordings. A GPS[39] device is required for collecting this information. Some cameras now contain built-in GPS capabilities for 'geo-tagging'. Small units that connect directly to the computer via a card slot or USB port are also available. Some of these devices are designed as 'track loggers', i.e. they can continuously monitor and store location against date and time over long periods using very little power. This data can then be downloaded to a computer in various formats (e.g. Google Earth KML). Such a track might help, for example, to define a poorly charted coastline or river, a footpath between settlements, or a property boundary. The best option, however, may be a simple but weatherproof handheld device, as these allow greater flexibility for recording both specific points (e.g. a field recording site) and track information. For transferring data to the computer, models that connect via USB rather than the older serial port are much more convenient.

---

[39] GPS: Global Positioning System. This uses a network of satellites to provide position and time information. GPS receivers vary widely in accuracy, speed of acquiring data, and reliability, i.e. how well they keep track. Typically they are of limited use in overhung situations, e.g. thick forest.

1.6 SUMMARY

The topic of recording techniques and related equipment is complex. The disadvantage of the tremendous technological advances that are being made is that it is seemingly impossible to assess all the available choices between different devices. When it comes to buying equipment, our general advice is to ask fellow researchers (in person or via email lists like RNLD) for their suggestions on specific items. We advocate the use of video recorders as the basic recording device because it makes for a richer documentation. Where this is not appropriate or possible, a high-quality solid-state audio recorder should be the standard. Smaller recorders are also good as go-everywhere pieces, as are small devices with at least limited video capability. In general, external microphones should be the first choice for recordings.

Buy the best equipment you can afford and learn how to use and maintain it at a basic level. At the very least you should know how to adjust audio levels and, for video, to make manual adjustments to exposure and focus. You must also be able to keep the power supply going. Beyond that, you should be able to assess the nature of a recording situation and identify potential problems with noise and lighting so that you can then make the best of it by adjusting settings and arranging the recording setup with a minimum of fuss.

The goal of good-quality recordings is complicated by the many environmental and human variables one must consider. The aim is simply to achieve the best recording quality under the circumstances, not to emulate broadcast standards, and naturally considerations of content (what you record) should take precedence over those of technique (how you record it) as long as you obtain a decent audio quality. In terms of what to record, variety is good—the broader the range of recordings, the richer will be the documentation of the language and culture.

1.7 WHERE TO FIND MORE INFORMATION

We do not supply links here to individual technical equipment. What follows is an eclectic list of sites that people have found useful.

http://www.i.nl/DOBES/audio-video
    Dokumentation Bedrohter Sprachen/Documentation of Endangered Languages: audio and video-related information.

http://www.rnld.org

Resource Network for Linguistic Diversity: the email list includes field recording topics which are summarized in the FAQ pages on the website.

http://bartus.org/akustyk

Bartek Plichta's audio resource which includes his vowel analysis software, equipment reviews, and field recording advice.

http://transom.org

Includes postings about audio recording techniques and tools.

http://www.camcorderinfo.com

Reviews of consumer camcorders.

http://www.video101course.com

http://multimedia.journalism.berkeley.edu/tutorials/video

http://www.film.queensu.ca/250/250HOME.html

Various tutorials and overviews of film making techniques and use of equipment.

1.8 APPENDIX: A BASIC FIELD EQUIPMENT KIT

We provide a list here with some basic requirements for a field kit. The different parts should all be tested and checked for compatibility. This list is not necessarily complete, nor are all items on it mandatory but it provides a starting point.

- solid-state audio recorder
- 4–6 battery packs
- 1 or 2 battery chargers
- 2 microphones
- microphone splitter (to allow for simultaneous use of two microphones)
- 2 headphones (more if several people transcribe in the field)
- headphone splitter
- professional-range video camera
- 4–6 battery packs
- 1 or 2 battery chargers
- tripod, hand grip, and/or camera stabilizer
- portable computer
- 2 battery packs
- 12 Volt power cord
- USB sticks and/or portable external drive and/or card reader with hard drive

- cables (e.g. XLR for microphone to recorder/camera, USB, and/or Firewire for transferring/capturing to computer)
- consumer-range video camera (as backup and for two-camera documentation of events)
- MP3 type small solid-state recorder
- GPS device
- digital still camera
- laptop stand or external keyboard
- eBook reader

- solar panels (or wind generator), plus regulators/blocking diodes to suit type
- car/truck battery, fuses, cable
- multi-meter, soldering iron, other basic electrician's tools

- waterproof bags (at least one for each equipment item)
- silica gel
- bubble-wrap (for padding inside bags)

CHAPTER 2

....

A GUIDE TO STIMULUS-BASED ELICITATION FOR SEMANTIC CATEGORIES

....

ASIFA MAJID

2.1 INTRODUCTION[1]

....

Fieldwork is the collection of primary data outside of the controlled environments of the laboratory or library, and is the province of many scientists: biologists, geologists, anthropologists, as well as linguists (see also Senft 2009). Traditional linguistic fieldwork has relied heavily on elicitation and observation, with a view to producing a grammar, dictionary, and texts. The linguist might use a word list or questionnaire and ask a consultant, 'How do you say X?', probe for grammaticality judgements, or solicit translations. This is often accompanied by mining texts, i.e. narratives by speakers, for naturalistic examples. This sort of data can fruitfully

[1] Thanks to Loretta O'Connor, Niclas Burenhult, Nick Enfield, Gunter Senft, Stephen Levinson, Nick Thieberger, and two anonymous reviewers for thoughtful and critical comments on an earlier version of this chapter. The writing was funded by the Max Planck Gesellschaft.

elucidate lexical and constructional resources within a language, their formal properties, the kinds of expressions that occur, and so on. In recent years, with the widespread availability of cheap and portable recording technology, more and more field workers rely on audio or video recordings. This has made it easier for linguists to include a wider variety of linguistic materials in their repertoire, most notably to encompass everyday conversational data. Recordings make it possible to listen to speakers' utterances again and again, thus improving the quality of final transcripts and making it possible to update and refine analyses. Nevertheless there are limitations to these techniques, especially when it comes to understanding semantics, the topic of this chapter. As a result, there is a move—which has gained new momentum in recent years—towards using non-linguistic stimuli for elicitation as a means of exploring semantics.

The bulk of this chapter sets out a guide to the various stages of constructing a non-linguistic stimulus set in order to investigate semantic categories within a language. This should furnish a novice to this field with some of the key concepts and issues so that they can construct their own study. There are, however, many existing resources already available—off-the-shelf-materials, as it were (see §2.8 below). Stimulus sets have been developed for spatial and event categories, the language of perception and emotion, and more. These materials can be invaluable tools towards fulfilling traditional linguistic fieldwork goals, as well as serving as worked out examples of this approach.

As previously stated, the focus in this chapter is how to use non-linguistic stimuli for a more thorough investigation of local semantic categories. Semantics is at the heart of linguistic description. The field linguist attempts to identify the sound units that convey distinctions in meaning—the lexical and grammatical classes that can be grouped together and distinguished for function, and so on. Individual forms will be provided with glosses in translations. Some will receive fuller descriptions in dictionaries, and ideally will also be contextualized with respect to local cultural practice and knowledge (see Hellwig 2006 and Evans and Sasse 2007 on rich semantic description in linguistic fieldwork). This chapter aims to provide some basic tools and methodology to inform semantic analyses. But the methods discussed are not limited to the exploration of semantics by any means. The 'pear story' (Du Bois 1980) and 'frog story' (Berman and Slobin 1994) studies, which utilized picture and video-based stimuli, have led to key insights into morphosyntactic packaging and discourse construction. Creative use of non-linguistic stimuli could, without doubt, benefit linguistic analysis of most language phenomena.

This chapter also assumes a qualitative orientation to data analysis (§2.6), but the use of stimulus materials does not require such an approach. Stimulus-based elicitation can be used in conjunction with traditional data collection methods to increase the amount of primary linguistic material available and thus provide further information for qualitative description.

Before embarking on the how-to guide, it is worth considering what the benefits of a stimulus-based approach are, and how it overcomes some limitations of conventional methods. Consider traditional field linguistic techniques, for example translation: find a consultant who speaks a contact language and ask them to translate word lists, simple sentences, etc. This can be an effective way to get into the linguistic system, but there are limitations. Using a specific formulation of a statement or word can 'prime' speakers to produce a similar formulation (Pickering and Ferreira 2008), even though it may not be the default, or most natural, within the language. More importantly, much of the juicy semantic detail of the language cannot be elucidated this way. Another method is to mine 'naturalistic' data, i.e. elicited narratives, myths, etc. This is an important source of evidence, but when consulting these sources a term of interest may occur infrequently, or not at all, making it difficult to generalize or extrapolate further about meaning or grammar (Hellwig 2006). Elicitation using questions and acceptability judgements go a step further, but there are notorious difficulties in obtaining and interpreting such judgements. If asked to make grammaticality judgements, for example, speakers may reject sentences that are actually grammatical because they violate some prescriptive norm (Greenbaum and Quirk 1970), or because they are difficult to process (Bever 1970). Repeated questioning can lead to an increase in acceptability judgements for sentences previously thought to be ungrammatical (Dale 1978) as can embedding a sentence in the 'right context' (Bolinger 1968). These same issues plague semantic judgements too. Instead of asking for grammaticality judgements, the field linguist may want to establish whether an interpretation is semantically entailed or only pragmatically implied, whether two forms are synonymous, or whether they are taxonomically or partonomically related, and so on. To disentangle these issues, semantic judgements can be elicited (e.g. Cruse 1986; Lyons 1968). As with grammaticality judgements, these tests rely on native-speaker intuition and are therefore subject to the same sorts of problems. Does the speaker accept a sentence because it is semantically acceptable or because of context and repeated questioning, for example?

Non-linguistic stimuli can avoid these pitfalls. We need not presume meaning equivalence where there is translation equivalence, we no longer wait for a form simply to turn-up in a text, and we can avoid conflating linguistic data with metalinguistic judgements. And there are other advantages. Speaker descriptions of non-linguistic stimuli do not require special training of consultants or specialized knowledge, so data can be collected easily. Knowing precisely what the speaker saw when they produced the description minimizes erroneous interpretations on the part of the analyst, as the exact stimulus can be referred to later in the analysis stage, long after the utterance was produced. And the constant platform of the stimulus enables cross-speaker and cross-language comparison (cf. Berlin and Kay 1969; Levinson, Meira, and The Language and Cognition Group 2003; Majid, Boster, and Bowerman 2008). In the classical study of colour by Berlin

and Kay (1969), a palette of Munsell colour-chips was used to establish the boundaries and foci of colour categories across languages. The standardized colour-space
provides an objective space where indigenous categories can be mapped, and cross-
linguistic equivalence measured (e.g. Kay and Regier 2003; Regier, Kay, and Khetarpal
2007). Of course, non-linguistic stimuli are not without flaws (see §2.7), but used in
concert with traditional methods, the linguist has a much richer, more nuanced and
firmly grounded dataset to inform his or her analyses.

A stimulus-based approach, as laid out in this chapter, will enable the researcher
to access one aspect of meaning, namely the extension. What things in the world
are denoted by which forms in the language? This can feed into an analysis of
intension or sense, the abstract linguistic meaning. Intension is often equated with
the sets of relations which hold between linguistic forms (Cruse 1986: 15–20; Lyons
1968: 427–8), such as semantic relations of synonymy, antonymy, taxonomic
inclusion, contrast, etc. A word's extension is a function of its intension, thus a
study of extension informs our analyses of intension. The extensional array in a
stimulus set serves as an etic metalanguage sometimes referred to as an etic grid
(Levinson and Wilkins 2006:8; Levinson, Meira, and The Language and Cognition
Group 2003: 487; Pike 1967). This is an objective array that makes a criterial
number of discriminations, so that language-specific groupings—the emic
concepts—can be identified. The rest of this chapter provides a guide to creating
such a stimulus-set.

2.2 FORMULATING YOUR RESEARCH QUESTION: SOME THEORETICAL CONSIDERATIONS

The first step towards constructing your stimulus set is to identify your specific
research question. It could be a modest endeavor: perhaps you are investigating the
number system in your field language and you have a singular/dual/paucal/plural
distinction. You wish to know the semantics of the paucal term. Is it, in fact, a
quadral (meaning precisely four)? Does it exclude two? What is the maximum
quantity it includes? Where does the boundary between the paucal and plural lie?
In order to tease apart these questions you could construct a stimulus set of
pictures, depicting differing amounts of various objects and ask participants to
describe them. You could then establish the boundaries of the categories, and
establish whether there was agreement across speakers.

The research question could be grander in scale. Many classical investigations of
how semantic domains are categorized by lexical resources—in studies of colour,
emotion, and folk biology, for example—attempt to quantify the extent to which

there are universally shared or culturally relative categories. If you were to investigate number from a cross-linguistic perspective, then a stimulus set might be built differently than if you were only to investigate the boundaries of a 'paucal' category within one language. For cross-linguistic comparison, you would want to first consult existing resources on what the possible distinctions across multiple languages from different linguistic stock might be, and then be sure to build those into your stimulus set (more on this later). In any case, the first step is to articulate the scope and aim of the investigation.

2.2.1 Do I start with form or function?

There are alternate emphases in formulating a research question. Investigations differ in whether their primary focus is on formal class (e.g. adpositions) or conceptual domain (e.g. space). One approach is to begin with a form-class, or rather a specific form, and track the possible functions it can have. An alternative approach, common to most anthropological and psychological investigations, begins with a conceptual domain and then tracks how that is 'carved up' in different languages. Both approaches can lead to valuable insights about semantic categorization. Nevertheless, it is important to be aware of the underlying assumptions and problems of both the 'bottom-up' approach of beginning with form and the 'top-down' approach of beginning with function.

2.2.2 Beginning 'bottom-up'

The advantage of beginning with form is that the phenomenon of interest is relatively easily delineated and identified—at least within a single language, or related languages. To take an example from Haspelmath (1997), one could conduct a study on the semantics of the Instrumental case in Slavic languages, where the modern day reflexes of the Proto-Slavic forms *-mĭ,*-mi, and so on, were studied. Or we could take a lexical domain and compare cognate terms, for example, the English *break*, German *brechen*, Dutch *breken*, Swedish *bräcka*, etc., all of which spring from the single Proto-Indo-European root *bhreg- (Majid, Gulberg, et al. 2007).

The disadvantages of this approach become clear as soon as we try to scale up to include other languages. What should we count as equivalent forms (Croft 2001; Haspelmath 2007)? Obviously, as we move away from Slavic languages, we are not going to find suffixes that have the precise instantiation of *-mĭ, *-mi, etc. We could, in response, expand the scope and criteria of our investigation. We could simply study Instrumental case across languages. The problem with this is that the definition used to identify 'case' differs from researcher to researcher (see Haspelmath 2007). Even if we could agree on a way to identify the phenomenon of interest, the criteria used to identify Instrumental case in Language A may be difficult to apply or not relevant at all to Language B. Moreover, because a form stands in paradigmatic relation to other forms within a system, comparable forms across languages will not be equivalent since they will stand in different oppositional arrangement to each other (Boas 1911; Saussure 1966[1916]). Finally, this approach fails to capture the affinities between the job done by case in one language and that done by a prepositional adjunct phrase or serial verb construction in another. That is, the same function can be expressed in different forms across languages, and a purely bottom-up approach will miss these interesting points of comparison.

2.2.3 Beginning 'top-down'

In the top-down approach, we begin with a conceptual domain, such as 'colour' or 'body'. This approach has been criticized on various grounds. An often-voiced objection against studying domains such as 'colour' or the 'body' stems from questioning whether the domain actually forms a coherent construct for speakers. Critics point out that there are languages which lack superordinate terms for such domains and suggest therefore there is no universal *concept* for colour or body or whatever (Wierzbicka 2005; 2007). The assumption is that subordinate terms are not deemed to be a cohesive set by speakers, if the superordinate concept is not lexicalized. But this inference relies on two faulty premises. First, it supposes an isomorphism between words and concepts. Lack of a word does not imply lack of a concept. In fact, there is a whole research agenda devoted to uncovering how linguistic semantics and conceptual structure are related—and if our concepts are indeed limited to those which find lexical expression in language. This consequence is accepted grudgingly by some. Wierzbicka (2005: 220) states: 'It is true that the absence of a word does not prove the absence of a concept; but how does one prove the *presence* of a concept for which there is no word?' Non-linguistic behavioural responses, such as sorting pictures or videos, can provide such evidence (see e.g. Boster and Johnson 1989; Khetarpal et al. 2010; Malt et al. 2008). The second faulty premise is that terms do not form a semantic domain without a lexicalized superordinate. Words form a semantic domain if they have related meanings, are deemed similar to one another by speakers (synonymy), or opposites in meaning (antonymy). None of this requires the presence of a lexicalized superordinate. People access information from memory based on the semantic closeness of terms. If I say to you 'cat, sheep, horse... what other things are like this?', you are likely going to respond with 'dog, cow, goat, etc.'. There is a set of related terms here, whether the language has a word for 'animal' or not.

Another line of critique against a top-down approach worries about the neglect of the emic perspective, and lack of attention to language-internal structural considerations. By ignoring structural encoding, it has been argued, non-equivalent objects are being studied: in essence apples are being compared with oranges (see Lucy 1994 for a critique of the work on space, and Lucy 1997 on colour). Lucy argues that it is essential to begin with a structural analysis of the language, that is, first establish that the domain of study forms a coherent category on formal grounds. This is because a crucial component of the meaning of a word is determined by its combinatorial properties: the meaning of A, is determined by what construction A can enter into, and what other words, B, C, D..., enter into that construction, since these provide information about how these terms contrast. In the weak interpretation of Lucy's critique, paying attention to structural facts can reveal meaning components that cannot be discovered otherwise. In the strong interpretation, ignoring structural facts means the analyst is imposing categories that may not exist in the language in the first place: 'Lexical items are grouped together and analysed as a coherent set not because speakers of those languages group them together in a set as revealed, for example, by common grammatical treatment, but because the analyst so groups them' (Lucy 1994: 624).

Lucy (1997) argues that differences in meaning components exist with each difference in formal encoding. While English uses adjectives to express colour, in Kilivila nouns are used,[2] in Chinook particles, and in Samoan verbs (Dixon 1982). Examination of the distributional properties of English colour terms shows that although they are all adjectives they do not form a homogeneous class. For example, we can *blacken (the chimney with soot)* and *whiten (your shirt with detergent)*, but we cannot **yellowen*, **greenen*, or **blueen*. Why should the difference in grammatical encoding of colour categories matter? Because differences in grammatical encoding are associated with differences in meaning components. Nouns, for example, refer to more stable entities than verbs (e.g. Gentner 1982; Hopper and Thompson 1984; Sapir 1921), leading to the proposal that colour terms encoded in verbs encode the notion of change, or 'becoming', whereas colour terms encoded in nouns and particles refer to an intrinsic, unchanging property (Hickerson 1975). On the other hand, although there are associations between form class and meaning entailments, not every form difference results in a meaning difference[3] (Kay 2006). Thus, restrictions in morphosyntactic distributions can be due to grammatical arbitrariness, rather than meaning difference. The larger point made by Lucy nevertheless remains: by ignoring differences in grammatical encoding the analyst can mistakenly conclude that there is a unified construct (of colour, space, parts of the body, etc.), where in fact there is no such coherent category for the native speaker.

---

[2] According to Senft (1986), Kilivila colour words are adjectives.

[3] This is a point that Lucy himself recognizes: 'It has long been taken as a truism in linguistics that meaning and form class are not usually in perfect one-to-one relationship. There will always be exceptional cases because of the historical and situationally contingent nature of linguistic structures' (1994: 649).

While it is clear that one piece of evidence for a unified construct would be a unified encoding in the grammar of a language, other sorts of evidence can demonstrate that a set of terms together form a coherent construct. In Arrernte (a Pama-Nyungan language spoken in Australia), colour terms do not constitute a separate form class, but are part of a much larger set of terms to do with surface properties of objects (e.g. reflectance). Yet in a free word association test (where the consultant is given a word and they have to produce the first word that comes to mind in response), colour terms overwhelmingly elicit other colour terms, and are rarely elicited in response to non-colour terms (data from Wilkins, reported in Kay 2006). This data suggests that this 'close-knit semantic set' forms a coherent construct for speakers of Arrernte, even though they are not formally a class. Similarly, the body can be considered a coherent construct to the extent that speakers conceptually group terminology for the body together, regardless of the formal category the term falls into.

But how small or big can the semantic domain be? Wierzbicka and colleagues have argued that rather than looking for universals of colour, we should look for universals of the higher order concept of 'seeing' (because all languages have a word for seeing). But why stop there? If there is a named higher-order superordinate to 'seeing' (such as 'perceiving'), should we take perception as our domain instead? And if there is another collapsing (e.g. between perception and emotion), then a bigger domain again? On this, I advocate a pragmatic approach of 'fractal domain'. Investigations of subsets of semantic domains, if that is what they are, can nevertheless lead to real insights. For example, some languages include in their basic colour words information about texture or succulence (Conklin 1955; Lucy 1997), thus going beyond the psychophysically defined colour space. But these terms still display comparable restrictions in range over hue and lightness as dedicated colour terms (Kay and Regier 2003). That is, the extension of colour terms in psychophysically defined colour space is similar regardless of whether the term also has a meaning in terms of texture or succulence. Thus constraints on semantic range within a narrowly defined domain (i.e., colour as hue and lightness) have an identifiable structure not predictable from the wider uses and broader senses beyond it.

2.2.4 Summary

There are two different potential starting points for constructing your stimulus set. In one approach, you begin with form and trace possible functions. In the other, you delineate your conceptual domain and examine how it is populated by different forms. Both approaches have problematic aspects. No one study will be able to address all weaknesses. But care can be taken in minimizing these as much as possible. The point is to be conscious of these weaknesses and consider how they may affect your stimulus design and, more importantly, the interpretation of your findings.

2.3 Creating an etic grid

In some domains—such as colour—there is a well-worked-out psychophysical space that can help determine the selection of a stimulus set. But even with an informed array, there are still problems in how exactly to select stimuli. Take colour, for example—the actual number of colours discriminable to the human eye is in the millions, but obviously no study has used all of these in a naming task. Instead, a sub-selection is made of the colour space. In the World Colour Survey (Kay et al. 2009; Berlin and Kay 1969), 330 colour chips were selected that were equally spaced for hue and brightness, while holding saturation constant. Further work has separately examined the role of saturation variation (e.g. Boynton 1997). And, as we saw above, a stimulus space that also included variations in luminance, texture, and reflectance might be better to study how colour is categorized in language (Lucy 1997). Nevertheless, it is impossible to explore all possible dimensions or contrasts at once in a systematic fashion. Thus, it is important to set the priorities and scope of the investigation before constructing your stimuli.

2.3.1 Aren't the domains you can study restricted to concrete ones?

In principle there is no restriction on what domains can be handled using a stimulus-based approach. Recently, within the Language and Cognition group at the Max Planck Institute for Psycholinguistics, we have begun to investigate smells, tastes, and tactile texture using a non-linguistic stimulus-based approach (Majid 2007). There is also no restriction on lexical categories. The same logic and motivation could be used to investigate constructional resources as exemplified by the work of Bohnemeyer and Caelen (1999), Bohnemeyer et al. (2007) on event complexity, and by Evans et al. (2004), and Evans et al. (2011) on reciprocals.

Wierzbicka (2009: 165) critiques the stimulus methodology on the ground that 'the most important things are invisible'. She argues that video clips and other such depictions cannot capture 'human values, moral categories, emotions, intentions, relationships or understandings', that what really matters for some sorts of concepts are motivations and projected outcomes rather than the physical acts themselves. No doubt there are serious challenges in depicting complex psychoso-cial states, but nevertheless there is reason to be optimistic about using a stimulus-based approach. When it comes to the interpretation of even the simplest of depictions, people go beyond the physical and interpret intentions, motivations and projected outcomes. Heider and Simmel (1944), for example, showed American undergraduates very simple cartoons featuring geometrical shapes, such as triangles and circles (see Fig. 2.1). These shapes were depicted as moving using a trick-film method, where the shapes are actually paper cutouts and are placed on a transparent plate. For the illusion of movement the shapes are moved small distances and then snapped at a location. The resulting snapshots are then played as one movie. When participants are shown these simple movies, they describe the movements depicted, not in terms of physical motion, but instead ascribing psychological intentions to the shapes. Most participants describe the video as a love triangle with two of the geometric shapes in an antagonistic relationship to the third, and provide elaborate stories accompanying each of the movement shifts. People also attribute personality traits to the individuals: aggressive, villainous, heroic, defiant, etc.

This type of inferencing is not limited to the American undergraduate. Social psychologists have been using this type of material to study cross-cultural differ-ences in the attribution of causes (e.g. Morris and Peng 1994). Although these studies typically resort to urbanized populations in East Asia who may have familiarity with these sorts of materials anyway, we know from work in our own group that simple animations can also yield rich data from peoples not familiar with video technologies. The Heider and Simmel studies demonstrate that even from the simplest of cues people infer complex social and psychological states, *contra* Wierzbicka. Moving from 2D black-and-white animations with geometric figures to naturalistic video would only increase the possible scenarios that could be depicted.

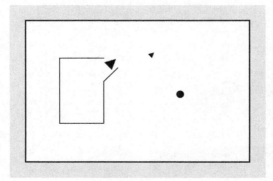

Figure 2.1. Adaptation of a still taken from Heider and Simmel (1944).

2.3.2 What contrasts to build into your stimulus set?

The stimulus space selected will depend on the question being addressed. Is the purpose a typological study? If so, then a first step could be to explore the available literature and identify the relevant cross-linguistic parameters. Another useful arena for potential parameters of relevance can come from language acquisition data. In our work on cutting and breaking events, we looked to developmental data to identify common errors children make in learning cutting and breaking verbs as a way to sketch out possible bordering domains (such as 'opening' and 'peeling'). We hypothesized that confusion errors attested in child verb usage may be the result of perceived similarity between breaking-type events and opening-type events, and that this similarity might also be reflected in cross-linguistic verb semantics (Majid, Bowerman et al. 2007; Majid, Boster, and Bowerman 2008) (see Fig. 2.2). We took a different approach when studying reciprocal constructions. In that investigation, we were led to test whether certain logical parameters (such as temporal organization, simultaneous vs. sequential and cardinality, or dual vs. plural) were of universal relevance (Evans et al. 2004; Majid et al. 2011).

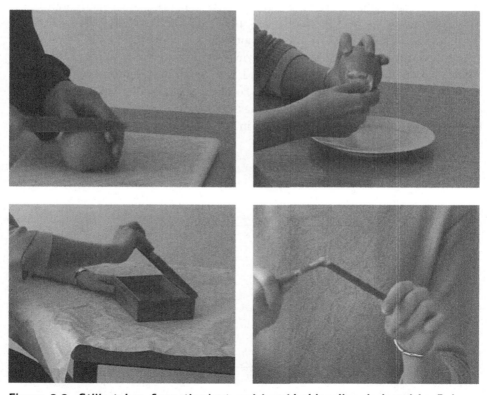

Figure 2.2. Stills taken from the 'cut and break' videoclips designed by Bohne-meyer, Bowerman, and Brown (2001), see also Majid, Bowerman, et al. (2007), and Majid et al. (2008).

The stimulus parameters in that study were thus derived from a theoretical framework, and only indirectly based on attested typological variation.

Is the purpose to investigate a domain within a single language? Here the typological perspective can also be useful, but in addition, consulting your language corpora for potential hypotheses about the domain is invaluable (Hellwig 2006). In addition, you can ask speakers to 'free-list' exemplars from a domain ('Can you tell me all the types of X?'). This can provide possibilities for further investigation. Additional exploratory interviewing and observation beforehand can be productive for identifying relevant contrasts for constructing a stimulus set.

2.3.3 How many stimulus materials should I use?

There is a practical limitation to how many materials you should use. If you are doing a naming task, where consultants describe the materials, then a session with a 60-stimulus set can taken anywhere from 10 minutes to an hour to conduct (depending on how many ancillary questions you ask, and how free you invite your participants to be in their talk—a straight run through without additional questions should take around 15 minutes per participant on average). It is possible to use far larger stimulus sets (cf. the World Colour Survey: Kay et al. 2009), but participants can get bored and distracted, so the quality of data that you elicit may suffer. Also the more time it takes to run a single participant, and the less they enjoy it, the harder it will be to find additional volunteers for that task.

2.3.4 But there will be lots of things you miss!

No single stimulus set will address all of the possible factors of potential relevance to a semantic domain. Human fatigue is only one limiting factor. The larger the stimulus set, the more worrisome the possibility of participants becoming stuck in a response set (e.g. only producing a limited number of responses as a result of priming). So the selection of a stimulus set has to be clearly motivated. And, of course, the results will prompt you to pursue further hypotheses and avenues.

2.4 COLLECTING DATA

2.4.1 I have my stimuli, now what?

Construction of a stimulus set is the first phase, but thinking about how you are going to use your stimuli is just as important. When presented with a pictorial or video stimulus, a person may focus on many different aspects of the materials, and not necessarily the one that is critical for the researcher (Du Bois 1980). Unfamiliar objects and settings may call for commentary, joking, and curious speculations. Field researchers have reported more than once that consultants viewing videos of a woman with short hair were drawn to comment on her gender. Perhaps even more extreme, Segall and colleagues working in the 1960s on the cross-cultural perception of visual illusions reported various indigenous groups commenting more on the white band around the edge of a photograph than the picture depicted therein (Segall, Campbell, and Herskovits 1966). Such descriptions may be interesting in their own right, but more often they are tangential to the aspects of interest. Build into your elicitation task a period of familiarization. Cross-cultural research on the perception of pictorial materials suggests that a brief period of familiarization is sufficient to achieve a coherent interpretation of pictures (Miller 1973).

It is important to ensure that participants are familiarized with pictorial materials so that they can identify objects, especially as objects of a particular type. For example, in the Topological Relations Picture Series (also known as the 'bowped' pictures: Bowerman and Pederson 1992), which has been used to investigate spatial notions such as 'on' and 'in', spatial descriptions can vary either because the indigenous semantic categories are indeed different, or because the consultants misinterpreted the depicted objects and had a different construal of the scene. For example, in Fig. 2.3, if the ground is correctly interpreted as a ring, then a consultant might describe the apple as being 'in', but if they did not recognize the ground and instead interpreted it as a plate, then they might describe it as an 'on' relation instead. A casual inspection of the distribution of responses may lead a researcher to conclude that spatial relations are encoded differently in language X, because Fig. 2.3 was described as 'in' in all other languages but as 'on' within language X. But this would be a wrong conclusion. We simply do not know what speakers in language X would have said had they the appropriate construal in mind. So it is of utmost importance that the researcher reflect before beginning data collection: what am I trying to establish with this data session and how can I ensure that the speakers are oriented towards the relevant contrasts, i.e. those the stimuli are intended to depict?

Figure 2.3. Taken from Bowerman and Pederson (1992).

The specific protocol being used in the elicitation also requires a phase of familiarization. If you are focusing on free spontaneous descriptions, then do not begin with the target stimulus materials straight away. Always include in your set two or three stimulus items that are not designed to test anything in particular, but are there to familiarize the participant with the task and the nature of the materials. Ask consultants to describe these first. Items should share general properties with the task materials (i.e. they are also videos or pictures of the same sort). This helps orient the participant to what it is that you are hoping to get from them. It is an important step, because the kind of description you get can be qualitatively different when the consultant does not know what is expected of them.

2.4.2 What procedures can I use to elicit descriptions?

The simplest method is free description. Show participants the stimuli and ask them to describe the relevant stimulus. You can use the stimulus materials to elicit metalinguistic judgements too. As well as knowing what the most salient description is, you may wish to establish whether another descriptor could be used with that stimulus. This can be useful data but, as discussed in the Introduction, there are limitations to this method of data gathering. To illustrate, Labov (1978) showed speakers line drawings of containers and then asked them either to describe the dishes or to judge whether a drawing could be labelled *cup* or *mug*. He found that the data from free descriptions could be scaled to produce a perfect set of implication hierarchies. But explicit judgements did not show this regularity and were much messier overall (although see Malt et al. 2008 for a case where naming data and judgements do converge to reveal category structure).

It is important, however, not to mix procedures. If you are collecting free descriptions, do not ask explicit metalinguistic questions in the middle of the procedure. By asking for a reflective answer, you change the task from a purely linguistic task to a metalinguistic one, which can encourage strategic responding (see e.g. the discussion in Hellwig 2006). If you want to do both, complete the free description task, and then go back and ask for any metalinguistic judgements later. Always run free description tasks before any metalinguistic tasks, for the same reasons.

Another method to collect language data is to use a 'matching game' (Clark and Wilkes-Gibbs 1986). In this procedure, you have two sets of the non-linguistic stimuli and two participants. One set of materials is given to a 'director', the other set to a 'matcher'. They are screened off from one another so that they cannot see each other's stimuli. The director has to describe the materials one at a time such that the matcher can find the corresponding stimulus in their own set. Since participants are screened from each other, they have to rely purely on the verbal descriptions to complete the task. They can discuss each stimulus as long as they like, until they are both satisfied that they have a match, at which point they set aside that match and move on to the next one. When all stimuli are 'matched', the barrier between the participants is lifted and the consultants can compare their cards to see how many matched. This method will produce rich linguistic responses. The procedure eliminates the researcher from the linguistic interaction, and so speakers are interacting with each other in a free manner, and without having to tailor their language for a non-native speaker. Under this procedure, the speech event is no longer an interview but rather a collaborative endeavor between native speakers. Because the game is the focus, rather than the linguistic response, it is highly unlikely that consultants will be engaging in any kind of metalinguistic responding. So there are advantages to this method over a standard free description paradigm. On the other hand, there are limitations. The responses will not be as standard and therefore it can make interpretation trickier. The practicalities involved may also be difficult: two consultants need to be coordinated, the screen and recording need to be in place, you must monitor the matches/mismatches, etc.

2.4.3 How should I record the responses?

The ideal way to record responses is with an audio or video recording. Trying to note what people are saying while they are saying them is slow, clumsy, and error-prone. It slows down the elicitation process, and in the worst-case scenario participants will produce responses tailored to your activity. They produce simpler formulations because they see that you are struggling to write down what they are saying. Moreover, you have to make on-the-fly decisions about what the relevant response token is. By recording responses, you can later, with reflection, parcel out the bits of the response that are of interest.

2.5 CODING THE DATA

The aim of coding your data is to be able to identify the referential range of the expressions that were used within the task. To do this, you must first transcribe the full responses of consultants, assuming you have recorded responses. You can then identify the constructional resources employed, how the semantic information you are interested in is distributed over the clause, etc. This can be a period to consider whether additional forms or constructions should also be part of the analysis. It is also a useful phase for weeding out responses which were not 'on target', by which I mean that the participant clearly had a different construal in mind than what the stimulus item was designed to elicit. For example, if when working with spatial stimuli the participant reverses the figure and ground relations ('the table is under the cup' rather than 'the cup is on the table'), then this is not a target response. Or if, in describing a colour chip in a colour-naming task, the participant describes the shape, this is not on target. These can be interesting responses in themselves but do not speak to the intended depicted event or object.

In the process of collecting the data, consultants may have volunteered multiple responses, perhaps a first 'spontaneous' response, and then secondary responses. You may also have additional judgements about which other forms could be used, and whether some forms are not applicable. In the process of coding your data, it is important and worthwhile to tag your responses for whether or not they are the first response; whether they are free descriptions or reflective comments; and so on. In the analysis stage, you may want to consider separately each type of response.

2.6 ANALYSING THE DATA

In order to explore the extensional semantics of a form (word, morpheme, construction), you will need to identify all of the stimuli that were described by that particular form. One simple way to do this is to code your data in a spreadsheet. You can create a column which has an ID for each of your stimuli, and alongside this insert your linguistic responses in the next column. A separate column for each speaker is helpful. You can then use the 'sort' function which will enable you to identify all the stimuli that were grouped together with the same term.

Standardized coding and eyeballing your data will get you quite far in figuring out the sorts of situations that call for descriptions of particular types but there are tools to go beyond this. There are a number of multivariate statistical techniques, such as multidimensional scaling, correspondence analysis, and cluster analysis, to name a few, which can be implemented in ordinary statistical packages, such as SPSS, SAS/STAT, or the open source freeware package R. These techniques are becoming increasingly important in the field of cross-linguistic semantic studies (e.g. Croft and Poole 2008; Majid et al. 2008). A comprehensive overview of these techniques is beyond the scope of this chapter, but for a gentle introduction see Grimm and Yarnold (1995).

2.6.1 Why do I need to use statistics?

There are numerous benefits to a statistical approach, but perhaps it is worth briefly outlining the perils of *not* using it. Let's say you have coded your data and have looked over the results, in a procedure akin to that described above. Now you are to examine the sorts of situations that receive a particular description and speculate on what feature of the stimulus may be calling for that form. The danger of relying only on intuition, here, is that people are notoriously prone to seeing correlations where there are none and missing them where they do exist (see Piattelli-Palmarini 1994 for an engaging illustration of all the ways we misjudge data). That is, you may be lured into thinking a feature of the stimulus is important when, in fact, it is not, or overlook something that is vital because you are not oriented towards it. This becomes all the more likely when you are dealing with multiple speaker data, or even multiple languages, and there is variation in precise extensional patterns. A statistical analysis can help in identifying which patterns are robust and reliable, and offer novel perspectives on your data.

There are multiple advantages of a statistical approach. Multivariate techniques can extrapolate more complex (multidimensional) solutions from your data, whereas working by hand will quite likely limit you to much simpler (and possibly only unidimensional) solutions. Most multivariate statistical tools also allow you to graphically represent your findings—a 'semantic map', as it were. These maps visually represent data in a manner that is much easier to absorb than reams of numbers. Finally, these techniques allow for quantification of how accurate a model is to the data, which means that we can assess our degree of confidence in any specific outcome.

2.7 WATCH OUT! PITFALLS AND DANGERS

A standardized stimulus set has numerous advantages. You do not need to wait for the phenomena of interest to turn up in spontaneous speech. You can efficiently map out the range of situations a term or construction applies to. And, in cross-linguistic (or cross-speaker) comparison, you can identify exceptional cases among common patterns for further exploration. However, there are potential pitfalls. The data obtained from a stimulus-based approach is only as good as the methods applied. It is crucial that you are clear and consistent in application of your procedures, coding, and most importantly in your reporting of your findings. This is essential for appropriate interpretation of your data.

More critically, the stimulus-based approach—like any other method of obtaining data—is not flawless. As discussed earlier, you have to be selective in the stimuli you use in any one sitting; the way you ask the question can lead to differences in responses; etc. But more egregious, perhaps, is the potential to overlook the emic perspective entirely. Even restricting ourselves to referential range, it is important to supplement the stimulus-based approach—like the one described here—with an examination of typical referents outside of the confines of the specific stimulus-set. Where else are these forms used? What are the typical foci? (See e.g. Conklin's 1955 classical study on colour.) It is important to explore how these forms are used *outside* the confines of the task to be able to interpret appropriately what they mean *within* the task. The stimulus-based approach does not replace corpus and verbal elicitation methods but supplements them and is supplemented by them. By combining methods, the limits of any one technique are overcome and converging evidence provides more confidence in findings (see e.g. Evans et al. 2011; Levinson and Wilkins 2006; Majid and Bowerman 2007; Majid and Levinson 2011).

2.8 ADDITIONAL RESOURCES

For ready-to-go stimulus materials of the type described above, see the Language and Cognition Field Manuals and Stimulus Materials website, hosted by the Language and Cognition group, Max Planck Institute for Psycholinguistics:
http://fieldmanuals.mpi.nl/
The Pear Story, a short film made at the University of California at Berkeley, is available on:
http://www.linguistics.ucsb.edu/faculty/chafe/pearfilm.htm;
Frog, Where Are You? from the original Mayer (1969) book, as published in the Appendix of Berman and Slobin (1994):
http://childes.psy.cmu.edu/manuals/frog.pdf

CHAPTER 3

....

MORPHOSYNTACTIC ANALYSIS IN THE FIELD: A GUIDE TO THE GUIDES

....

ULRIKE MOSEL

3.1 INTRODUCTION

....

This chapter will focus on existing field guides for morphosyntactic analysis of previously undescribed languages. The first comprehensive modern linguistic field guide was written by Samarin (1967), followed by Bouquiaux and Thomas (1976; 1992), Healey (1975), and Kibrik (1977). Apart from Burling's (1984) small but very useful book, *Learning a Field Language*, there were no fieldwork guides published in the 1980s. Since the early 1990s the rising awareness of the imminent global loss of language diversity, the recognition of linguistic typology as an important discipline of linguistics, and the advances in language recording and processing technology have led to an increasing interest in the documentation of endangered languages and fieldwork methods (Himmelmann 1998; Austin 2003–10; Gippert, Himmelmann, and Mosel 2006). In addition to new fieldwork guides (Abbi 2001; Bowern 2008; Crowley 2007; Newman and Ratliff 2001; Vaux, Cooper, and Tucker 2007), fieldwork manuals and questionnaires are now also published as on-line resources in the internet (see the end of this chapter for links).

These guides have to be distinguished from publications that inform students on the diversity of language structures, or train them through exercises in the analysis of linguistic data (e.g. Kroeger 2005 and Payne 2006). The borderline between these two kinds of text book, however, is not sharp. Bouquiaux and Thomas (1992: 95–173) devote a whole section of their book to 'concepts of linguistic analysis' before they present their questionnaires, while Bowern (2008: 73–106) briefly explains selected areas of the typology of morphosyntactic structures and gives useful recommendations for further study along with her presentation of data gathering methods. Abbi (2001: 115–220), who focuses on fieldwork in India, structures her chapters on morphology and syntax in a similar way. In each section of these chapters she first explains the morphosyntactic characteristics of Indian languages and then makes suggestions about how they can be elicited. Since the Indian languages belong to different, typologically diverse language families (Indo-European, Dravidian, Sino-Tibetan, Austric, and Andamanese), the book is also useful for fieldworkers in other areas of the world.

The following sections will first recommend a number of books that provide basic and specialized information on languages and language structures (§3.2) and then address anthropologists and other non-linguistic researchers who are interested in collecting language data (§3.3) in the course of fieldwork. The next section (§3.4) discusses the interaction of researchers and indigenous consultants, while §3.5 presents an overview of the various methods of collecting data, i.e. language learning and participant observation (§3.5.1), elicitation (§3.5.2), and the collection of texts (§3.5.3). The last section (§3.6) gives a summary of the state of the art. The term morphosyntactic analysis refers in this chapter to the analysis of the structure and meaning of linguistic units from sentence to word level. It does not presuppose any specialized theoretical approach.

Since the collection of data for the morphosyntactic analysis of a previously undescribed language implies that the researcher spends some time in the field, this chapter will not address language surveys and short-term exploratory field trips.

3.2 Obtaining information on Languages and their morphosyntactic structures

More than any other linguistic discipline, fieldwork requires intuition and emotional intelligence, but this does not mean that the prospective fieldworker can neglect the study of general linguistic theories or the findings of linguistic typology, which explores the diversity of language structure. All fieldwork guides emphasize the importance of careful preparation. Here we will distinguish between the essential prerequisites of any kind of linguistic fieldwork (§3.2.1), sources that help fieldworkers to inform themselves on the languages of a particular field site (§3.2.2), and sources that are useful to consult while working on the morphosyntactic analysis of the target language and planning further fieldtrips for supplementary elicitation (§3.2.3).

3.2.1 Basic information on diverse language structures

Many linguistics departments all over the world offer courses on the phonological, grammatical, and semantic analysis of languages from a typological perspective, but there are also departments that focus on linguistic theories and only use secondary sources for examples from 'exotic' (i.e. other than standard European) languages, or departments of regional studies that offer courses on particular languages and cultures without giving the students some background in general linguistics or linguistic typology. It is the latter two groups for whom this section is written. Anthropologists and researchers who are not primarily interested in morphosyntax, but nevertheless want to collect data that are useful for linguists, are referred to §3.3.

Assuming that they have some education in the grammar of English (if not, Biber, Conrad, and Leech 2002, Blake 2008, and McGregor 2009 are recommended for a start), prospective linguistic fieldworkers must be fluent in transcription and skilled in analysing the phonological and grammatical structure of words and sentences of structurally different languages. The more researchers know about the structural diversity of the world's languages, the better they will understand the structure of the target language and the less they will be unconsciously influenced by the contact language or their native language. Good introductions into the theoretical background and the methods of morphosyntactic analysis are found in various students' textbooks. The list below recommends books which also offer ample exercises, and selects those chapters that in my experience are absolutely necessary for a basic training in morphosyntactic analysis.

Morphology:

>   Aronoff and Fudeman 2005 (chs 1–6; suitable for beginners)
>   Bauer 2003 (ch. 1–4, 6; suitable for beginners)
>   Booij 2007 (chs 1–5; difficult for beginners)
>   Haspelmath 2002 (chs 1, 2, 4, 5; difficult for beginners)

Morphology and syntax:

>   Kroeger 2005 (chs 1–8, 10–16)
>   Payne 2006 (chs 1, 2, 4, 5, 7, 8, 10)

3.2.2 Information on the languages of a particular field site

Rice, who has done extensive fieldwork on North American Indian languages recommends: 'As a fieldworker, it is necessary to embrace all sources of material and learn from them, but at the same time to treat them with necessary scepticism' (Rice 2001: 248). This scepticism is especially warranted when the sources you consult are written with a Eurocentric bias and do not recognize the presence of exotic, unexpected features or the absence of familiar standard-European properties that have been believed to be universal, as Gil (2001) demonstrates.

Preliminary information on about 7,000 particular languages and their distribution in the countries of the world is provided by Ethnologue (http: //www.ethnologue. com), while information on the grammatical structure of languages can be obtained from the *World Atlas of Language Structures* (http: //wals.info). This atlas allows you to search for 141 particular language features and 2,650 languages by language name, language family, region, and country. (Haspelmath et al. 2008; reviewed by several authors in the journal *Linguistic Typology* vol. 13, 2009).

Books in which the basic structures of a representative sample of the languages of the world are described are Comrie (1990a–d), Garry and Rubino (2001), and Brown and Ogilvie (2009), surveys are also found in the Cambridge Language Surveys, the Routledge Language Family, and the Curzon Language Family series.

3.2.3 Information on particular morphosyntactic phenomena

Students who plan to write a reference grammar are recommended to consult:

* encyclopedias and handbooks (Booij, Lehmann, and Mugdan 2000 and 2004; Haspelmath et al. 2001; Spencer and Zwicky 2001);
* textbooks on linguistic typology (Comrie 1989; Givón 2001; Shopen 2007; Song 2001; Whaley 1997);
* articles about individual languages in volumes on specific typological topics such as argument structure (Plank 1985), case (Malchukov and Spencer 2008; Plank 1995), complementation (Dixon and Aikhenvald 2006), coordination (Haspelmath 2004), nominal classification (Senft 2000), or valency (Dixon and Aikhenvald 2000);
* the articles in *The World Atlas of Language Structures Online* (Haspelmath et al. 2008).

3.3 RECOMMENDATIONS FOR ANTHROPOLOGISTS AND OTHER NON-LINGUISTIC FIELDWORKERS

Researchers who do not have a background in linguistics can contribute to the study of endangered languages when they learn to understand the language and record, transcribe, and translate samples of spoken language with the help of bilingual native speakers. Burling's small book *Learning a Field Language* (1984) is especially written for researchers who want to learn the language in the field but are not primarily interested in linguistic analysis. He emphasizes 'techniques for learning to understand' and devotes half of his book to this 'neglected aspect of language pedagogy' (p. 6). For both comprehension and production, he recommends that the earliest stages of learning focus on vocabulary and word order without worrying too much about grammatical detail. But the book also offers an excellent, concise description of the essentials of grammar and gives some advice on how learners can advance their grammatical competence (Burling 1984: 55–64, 86–91).

3.4 LINGUISTS AND INDIGENOUS CONSULTANTS

The quality of the data for the morphosyntactic analysis of a previously unresearched language very much depends on the interaction between the researcher and the native speakers the researcher works with in the fieldwork project. In many publications these people are called 'informants' (Abbi 2001: 57; Samarin 1967: 20), but as 'informant' has the connotation of 'informant to the police', other linguists prefer the term 'language helper' (Crowley 2007: 85f.) or 'consultant' (Bowern 2008: 10; Burling 1984). In the context of linguistic fieldwork, it seems useful to distinguish between consultants and local experts. While the consultants directly help the researcher with the collection and processing of field data, the local experts are people like storytellers, fishermen, healers, or architects who are interviewed on their specialized knowledge.

3.4.1 Selection of consultants

Most fieldwork guides contain a section on 'Selection of informants', 'Choosing language helpers', and the like, which lists the qualifications of the ideal consultant (Samarin 1967: 20–44; Kibrik 1977: 54–6; Vaux, Cooper, and Tucker 2007: 6). However, in practice matters can be quite different. The researchers coming as guests to the speech community are neither in a social position to choose people by themselves nor do they know the people well enough to identify their talents. Consequently they have to ask their hosts or the elders of the community to find the right people. These will have different interests and qualifications, so that it is the researchers' task to adapt to their various talents and accordingly train them in tasks they enjoy and can cope with. (Dimmendaal 2001: 58–66; Grinevald 2003: 67–8; Rice 2001: 245–7).

Recommendations like the following are not practicable and may be counter-productive. 'Before hiring the reference speaker, we must test him. One day of work with the candidate will be enough for this purpose' (Bouquiaux and Thomas 1992: 33). Grinevald (2003: 67) warns, 'one should try never to turn away any member of the language community that expresses interest in working on the project . . . one never knows how things will evolve, and what contribution any particular person can make.' Even semi-speakers or non-speakers may be helpful (Evans 2001).

3.4.2 Training of consultants

The training of consultants has several components and very much depends on their educational background, their standing within the language community, the personal relationship between researcher and consultant, and, of course, their talents and interests. As Healey emphasizes, '[a]lthough there are differences of aptitude from helper to helper, it is nevertheless true that good research assistants are not born, they are trained. And giving this training is one of the major responsibilities of the fieldworker' (1975: 347) With respect to collecting data for a grammatical analysis of the language, this means that linguists should explain what needs to be done for which purpose and train the consultants on the job without any kind of patronizing attitude. Rather, the fieldwork project has to be understood as a joint enterprise in which the researchers from outside and the local experts and consultants share their knowledge and treat each other with the utmost respect.

Typically, linguistic field guides mention the possibility of training native speakers as consultants only in passing (Bowern 2008: 200–201; Bouquiaux and Thomas 1992: 34–5; Healey 1975: 347–9; Samarin 1967: 41–4; Vaux et al. 2007: 29) or completely ignore this important aspect of research (Abbi 2001). There is a series of articles on capacity building in various endangered speech communities in Austin (2004). However, guidelines on how to train consultants in the field do not exist yet. Samarin's remark that 'the ultimate goal is to get the informant to think about language as the investigator does' and to answer questions in 'the way he should respond' (Samarin 1967: 41) is misleading (see §3.5.2).

In order to get recordings that are as natural as possible (see Himmelmann 1998 on the 'naturalness' of recordings and Samarin 1967: 56–7 on the notion of 'natural speech'), researchers are recommended to train members of the community to do the recordings themselves without the researchers being present at a place where the speaker feels comfortable.

Literate consultants can be trained in doing preliminary transcriptions (Dixon 2010: 322), and literate and bilingual consultants can also be trained in doing translations. Such transcriptions can be done in any kind of orthography—even inconsistent orthographies may be helpful. However, the transcribers must learn to only write down what the speakers have said and not what, in their opinion, they should have said. Thus all hesitation phenomena, wrong names, code switching, etc. need to be rendered in this preliminary transcription. Transcriptions done by native speakers can be very helpful, especially when they render phonetically reduced and fused forms by their corresponding full forms. They may also reveal the transcriber's metalinguistic intuitions about the morphophonology of the language and the boundaries of linguistic units (Himmelmann 2006b: 254).

If the speakers want the transcriptions to be edited before presenting them to other people, the researchers may give them some advice on how to transform a transcription into a readable text without completely changing its style and adapting it to that of the contact or the written dominant language. Editing texts does not mean rewriting them. Rather, the editors should respect the speaker's way of expression and, for example, remove only those repetitions that are caused by stuttering, or add words and phrases that are absolutely necessary to understand the written text. Nevertheless, some editors will not refrain from changing expressions and will, for example, simplify constructions or make them more complex. Such changes should not be criticized by the researchers but considered as an interesting source for the morphosyntactic analysis of the language, because they show how the same content is expressed by formally different constructions. A parallel corpus of the transcriptions of spoken texts and the corresponding edited versions also provides a new kind of data for the study of the differences between spoken and written language in general. (Bowern 2008: 120–21; Mosel 2006a: 80; 2008; Murray and Rice 1999).

3.5 COLLECTING DATA

The following section reviews a number of fieldwork guides with respect to the methods they recommend for gathering data on the morphology and syntax of the target language. Instead of discussing the strengths and weaknesses of each book in turn, we will scrutinize what they say with respect to the following four kinds of method:

language learning and participant observation;
translational elicitation;
non-translational elicitation;
collection of texts (in the widest sense).

See the chapters in this volume dealing with technology of recording (Margetts and Margetts, Chapter 1), archiving and language data management (Thieberger and Berez, Chapter 4), and experimental elicitation (Majid, Chapter 2).

3.5.1 Language learning

Speech communities differ in their attitudes towards outsiders trying to learn their language. Some might not appreciate the researcher's ambitions to speak their language (Crowley 2007: 157; Hill 2006; Mosel 2006a: 73–4). But if they do, the researcher should try to learn the language because being able to communicate with the people

- is a pleasure and helps to cope with the fieldwork situation;
- contributes towards acceptance by the host community;
- brings the researcher into contact with more people in different situations and consequently allows the researcher to gather a more diversified corpus;
- allows the researcher to collect data by participant observation;
- raises the researcher's awareness of certain constructions, when native speakers correct his or her mistakes;
- allows the researcher to use the target language as the mediator language, which will reduce the danger of interference from the lingua franca. (Abbi 2001: 146; Bowern 2008: 9–10; Crowley 2007: 155; Dimmendaal 2001: 72–3; Everett 2001; Hale 2001: 81–2; Kibrik 1977: 52; Samarin 1967: 49–55).

However, with the exception of Healey (1975) and Burling (1984), language learning methods are not discussed in the literature on linguistic fieldwork.

3.5.2 Elicitation

Elicitation means collecting linguistic data by asking native speakers to produce words, phrases, or sentences that can serve as data for the analysis of a particular linguistic phenomenon. Some authors also speak of 'eliciting' texts, but here the term 'elicitation' will exclusively be used in the narrower sense defined above.

3.5.2.1 Questionnaires

For each elicitation session the researcher should have prepared a list of specific questions that he or she wants to ask the consultant in order to obtain data for hitherto unexplored areas of grammar or to clarify problems that have come up when analysing the results of preceding sessions. The collection of data with the help of questionnaires is not a 'mechanical process', as Kibrik (1977: 51) remarks, but should be guided by hypotheses that are based on the findings of linguistic typology and research into language universals and on the analysis of previously collected data. If the new data contradict a hypothesis, this hypothesis needs to be revised and checked against new data, until 'it predicts the construction of new data the investigator has not yet encountered' (p. 51). This routine of making and testing hypotheses can be equally applied to elicited and textual data, but the literature on linguistic fieldwork and typology only provides questionnaires for elicitation and for analysing and describing the typological profile of the target language:

1. Translational questionnaires consist of lists of words, phrases, and sentences whose translation into the target language is supposed to reveal some grammatical properties of the target language, e.g. '*a chief, the chief, some chiefs, the chiefs, both chiefs, the two chiefs, . . .*' (Tersis 1992: 277).

2. In scenario questionnaires, the questions first describe a particular scenario and then ask for an expression of a particular content that would be grammatically appropriate in the given context. Dahl's 'TMA questionnaire' is of this kind (1985: 198–206). The first question '[Standing in front of a house] The house BE BIG,' means that the interviewee should imagine that he/she is standing in front of a house and makes the statement that the house is big.

3. Grammatical structure questionnaires contain questions about the existence of particular grammatical structures, e.g. 'Does the language make any distinction between direct speech and quoted speech?' or 'Are there adjectives that take arguments? optionally/obligatorily?' (Comrie and Smith 1977). A similar checklist is given by Aikhenvald (2007: 63–4) for the analysis of 'word-formation', while other articles in Shopen (2007) unfortunately lack such lists. For some critical remarks on the questionnaire compiled by Comrie and Smith (1977), see Mosel (2006b).

In comparison to translational questionnaires, scenario questionnaires are less likely to produce data that are influenced by the contact language, especially when they are used in the manner and tone of a casual conversation. The grammatical construction questionnaires cannot directly be used for the elicitation of data, but only serve as a checklist for the design of translational or scenario questionnaires or for the analysis of data that have already been gathered from texts and elicitations. Bowern (2008: 214–18) presents 'a basic morphology/syntax checklist' that is 'loosely based on the *Lingua* Questionnaire by Comrie and Smith 1977,' but it looks more like the table of contents of a particular grammar because it lists the terms of grammatical categories, e.g. 'causatives', 'passives', 'copular clauses', 'auxiliary verbs', without any further comments. This kind of list creates the impression that these categories are universal and can be elicited in any language. But passive constructions are, for example, far from being universal; in her survey of 373 languages, Siewierska (2008) found that 211 languages lack a passive construction.

3.5.2.2 *Kinds of elicitation techniques*

None of the linguistic fieldwork guides systematically describes:

• what kind of questions would trigger what kind of answers;
• what kind of questions would be useful for which area of grammar;

- which areas of grammar would be most efficiently investigated by what kind of questions;
- how different kinds of questions could possibly complement each other.

Samarin (1967: 77) distinguishes between 'translational' and 'non-translational' elicitation, while Bouquiaux and Thomas (1992: 186–397) exclusively rely on translations from the contact language into the target language. Others mix both methods, but often do not explicitly state how the questions are actually to be worded in an interview on a particular grammatical topic, although the way you ask is crucial for the kind of answer you get. In her section on data manipulation, for example, Bowern (2008: 81) simply lists a number of transformations without further comment:

- Turn sentences into questions (and vice versa).
- Manipulate voice and valency possibilities; e.g., active–passive/antipassive . . . (Bowern 2008: 81)

In order to test if the sentences produced by translations, scenario descriptions or sentence manipulations express the intended meaning, the consultant should always be asked for a translation from the target language into the contact language. Ideally such back-translations are not done on the same day.

A third type of elicitation mentioned in fieldwork textbooks is that the researcher constructs sentences in the target language by him- or herself and then asks native speakers for a so-called 'grammaticality judgement', i.e. telling him or her if the sentences sound right (Abbi 2001: 108, 118; Bowern 2008: 76, 78) This method cannot be recommended because the acceptance or rejection of a sentence created by a non-native speaker can be based on various, but not necessarily grammatical, reasons (see Bowern 2008: 78–80; Chelliah 2001: 158–61; Mithun 2001: 48; Samarin 1967: 57; Vaux et al. 2007: 278).

3.5.2.3 Translational elicitation

Linguistic fieldwork on a previously unresearched language starts with the compiling of wordlists in order to investigate the sound system of the language and develop a practical orthography. Most fieldwork manuals recommend the translation of wordlists in the contact language and present a sample in their appendices. These samples contain language specific function words like 'at', 'if', or 'in', or words like 'freeze', 'ice', and 'snow' which are only appropriate for certain regions of the world (Abbi 2001: 244–5; Bowern 2008: 223–4; Kibrik 1977: 99–124; Samarin 1967: 220–23). They therefore need to be modified. Function words like prepositions and conjunctions must be removed, and the list of content words should be adapted to the natural environment and culture of the speech community, as done by Abbi in her wordlist 'for Indian concepts' (2001: 246–7). The manifold problems of translational elicitation which have been identified by several authors, include:

- The consultants may be ashamed when they do not understand the meaning of a word or a construction in the contact language or when they do not remember the translation equivalent in the target language or the concept in question is not expressed by a single word in their language (Bowern 2008: 89; Mosel 2006a: 75).
- The consultant's knowledge of the contact language may not be sufficient to understand all nuances of meaning the linguist wants to have reflected in the translation (Bowern 2008: 89; Chelliah 2001: 157; Samarin 1967: 141).
- The consultant and the researcher speak different varieties of the contact language like Indian and American English (Chelliah 2001: 157).
- The form of the translation may be not idiomatic because of interference from the contact language (Bowern 2008: 85–7; Chelliah 2001: 155).
- If the contact language lacks a grammatical category that exists in the target language, it can hardly be systematically uncovered by translational eliciting (Chelliah 2001: 157).
- In different languages words, grammatical categories and constructions are polysemous in different ways so that there is always the risk that an expression in the contact language or its translation equivalent in the target language are not interpreted in the same way by the researcher and the consultant, especially when the researcher does not describe the context in which the target sentence might be used (Abbi 2001: 88–91; Bowern 2008: 86).

3.5.2.4 *Non-translational elicitation*

Non-translational elicitation does not generally exclude the use of the contact language, but only avoids the direct translation of single sentences from the contact language into the target language. In order to avoid all the flaws of translational elicitation mentioned above, I recommend a non-translational approach even in the initial stage of fieldwork: first explain what the word list is used for, and then ask the consultants to list any words denoting persons, things, actions, and properties of a particular semantic domain that come to their mind or that you suggest (Mosel 2006a: 75–6). Once the words of a particular domain like food and food preparation have been collected, e.g. 'wash', 'peel', 'cook', 'boil', 'potatoes', 'pot', 'water', 'dirty', 'hot', the 'word-to-text technique' (Samarin 1967: 83) can be applied. This technique requires the native speakers to select a few words from the list and compose short meaningful utterances like 'boil the water!', 'dirty potatoes'. These sentences are then translated by the consultant into the contact language, and can later serve as the basis for the following non-translational techniques, each of which is discussed further below.

1. substitution elicitation (Kibrik 1977: 58; Samarin 1987: 115–17);
2. paraphrasing (Kibrik 1977: 58; Samarin 1967: 119);
3. sentence completion (Samarin 1987: 83);

4. eliciting examples (Kibrik 1977: 58);
5. transformational elicitation (Bowern 2008: 81–2; Kibrik 1977: 60);
6. paradigmatic elicitation (Kibrik 1977: 57–8).

1. The **substitution technique** uses phrases and clauses already elicited in the target language as a frame in which a word or a phrase is substituted for another one. If, for example, you want to know how singular and plural are distinguished or whether there is agreement between certain constituents with respect to number, you may take a simple clause with a singular argument and ask, 'What would you say if it is not only one but several X?' In a similar way, a wide range of morphosyntactic phenomena can be investigated, for example:

1. the argument structure of clauses by substituting a verb with various other kinds of verbs that presumably require a different argument structure;
2. gender by substituting nouns denoting males by nouns denoting females and classifiers by using nouns referring to objects of different shapes, sizes, and substances, human beings, and animals as the head of subject and object noun phrases (Abbi 2001: 118, 123);
3. the tense, aspect, and mood marking by adding or substituting temporal or modal adverbs ('today', 'yesterday', 'never', 'always', etc.) or adverbial phrases ('a long time ago', 'in the future', 'for a week', 'in a week', etc.);
4. the person marking on verbs or in the verb complex by substituting nominal subjects and objects with 1st and 2nd person pronouns;
5. complement clauses by substituting a complement taking predicate, for example verbs meaning 'know', 'believe', 'see', 'say', 'want' (Noonan 2007: 149–50).

2. **Paraphrasing** means that the consultants are asked to say 'the same thing in a different way', which may reveal new types of clause structure, if the sentences are 'related by a common meaning and by sharing the fundamental lexical items' (Samarin 1967: 119).

3. With the **sentence completion** technique, the investigator chooses a sentence from the existing corpus, removes parts of it, and asks the consultant to complete the sentence by adding anything that seems appropriate. This technique can, for example, be employed to elicit different types of complement or adverbial clauses, or to investigate the use of tense, aspect, and mood categories in complex sentences (Samarin 1967: 83).

4. The greatest variety of expressions can be elicited by asking the consultants to **create example sentences** for a particular word. Since there is always the danger that created examples sound unnatural, the best results are achieved when two or three native speakers work together. The disadvantage of this method is that the researcher has no control over the kinds of grammatical constructions the native speakers might use. On the other hand, these freely created utterances may reveal unexpected constructions that the researcher would never have thought of.

5. **Transformational elicitation** means that the interviewee is asked to transform one type of construction into another one, e.g. affirmative clauses into negative ones, statements into questions by asking 'what would you say if this was not true?' or 'what would you ask if you did not know that it was X?'

6. The most difficult kind of elicitation is the **elicitation of paradigms**, but it is indispensable for inflecting languages, as even very large corpora do not supply all forms needed for a comprehensive presentation of inflectional paradigms in a reference grammar. I would recommend applying the substitution method first to parts of the paradigm and then, on the basis of the elicited data, explaining to the consultants what a paradigm is. One or the other consultant might then understand the nature of paradigms and be able to construct them by themselves. For example, one could first take a simple clause in the past tense with a 3rd person singular subject from the data, e.g. 'the woman cooked the potatoes', and ask the consultants to substitute 1st and 2nd person singular subjects for 'the woman' to make them aware of the grammatical category of person, then transform the singular arguments into plural arguments to understand how the category of number is formally expressed, and eventually substitute a few other verbs for the verb 'cook'. After several of these past tense paradigms have been completed, one could ask what people would say to express that the woman always, now, or tomorrow would cook potatoes to elicit other tense/aspect categories. Bowern (2008: 89f.) observes that consultants react very differently to paradigm elicitations, and that it might be necessary to do them 'in small batches on different days, combined with other topics'.

3.5.2.5 *Shortcomings of elicitation*

All fieldworkers agree that elicitation is a useful tool to quickly gather data in a controlled way, but that it cannot serve as the sole empirical basis for the grammatical analysis and description of a language. There are two reasons.

First, by definition, elicitation only provides examples of decontextualized isolated sentences, whereas natural speech is always embedded in the context of a particular speech situation. Consequently, elicited examples cannot show how the meaning of linguistic units is shaped by their context. Furthermore, elicitation fails to uncover any structures that only occur in contexts larger than sentences.

Second, elicitation focuses on certain linguistic phenomena the researchers are particularly interested in, so that they run the risk of missing those grammatical categories and constructions they have been unaware of (Chelliah 2001: 156; Gil 2001: 115). Mithun concludes:

But if the research is limited to eliciting translations of English vocabulary and syntactic constructions, collecting grammaticalitys and checking off known typological diagnostics, we may miss what is unexpected about the language under study. In so doing, we risk depriving the speakers' descendants of what is special about their heritage, and we lose opportunities to expand our own theoretical horizons. (2001: 53)

3.5.3 Text collections

Since 'linguistic elicitation is artificial even under the best circumstances' (Samarin 1967: 59), any grammatical analysis and description should in the first place be based on a good text collection, while the elicitation of data should only be used at the very beginning of the project or as a means of filling gaps in the data as they usually occur in inflectional paradigms (Dixon 2010: 321–2; see §3.5.2.4 above). Correspondingly, the examples illustrating grammatical categories and construc- tions in a grammar should as much as possible be quotations of naturally occurring utterances (Bright 2007: 16; Mithun 2007a: 59–60, 62–4; Weber 2007: 200). If the corpus does not provide a simple example to illustrate the grammatical phenome- non in question, the grammarian can resort to an elicited example and supplement it by a quotation from the text corpus.

In view of this central role of text collections, the fieldwork manuals contain surprisingly little information on what constitutes a good text collection and how it can be gathered, why it should cover various genres, and what kind of linguistic data can be found in texts of different genres. The fullest accounts of what constitutes a good corpus and what kind of texts it might contain are given by Samarin (1967: 55–68) and Rivierre (1992: 56–63). In the following I will only discuss the content of conventional text collections and how it relates to the morphological and syntactic analysis of the target language; for the technical aspects of recording see Margetts and Margetts (Chapter 1 above), Austin 2006, Schultze-Berndt 2006, and Seifart 2006; for experimental and stimuli-based tech- niques of recording connected discourse see Majid (Chapter 2 above).

3.5.3.1 *Features of a good corpus*

Samarin discusses 'six of the outstanding features of a good body of data' (Samarin 1967: 55–68). A good corpus is:

1. 'dialectally uniform';
2. 'natural', i.e. produced and accepted by native speakers as 'appropriate under a given set of circumstances';
3. 'varied', i.e. it would ideally cover all varieties of language that can be attributed to (a) the age, (b) sex, and (c) social class or occupation of the speaker, (d) the emotion at the time of speaking, (e) the speed of utterance, and (f) the topic, (g) type, and (h) style of discourse;
4. 'complete' in that 'all the closed classes of linguistic elements are fully accounted for';

5. 'repetitious' in order to facilitate the identification of the distribution and function of particular grammatical elements;
6. 'interesting', i.e. containing authentic genres and telling something about the culture of the speech community.

The native speakers' use of particular grammatical categories and constructions is determined not only by the structural properties of the language but also by the nature of the particular communicative event, because all languages provide for alternative ways of expression and rules for their contextually appropriate selection. For an introduction to the ethnography of speaking, see Hill (2006), Franchetto (2006), Trudgill (2000: 81–104). More detailed accounts are given in specialized textbooks on ethnolinguistics, register, and genre such as Saville-Troike (2003) and Biber and Conrad (2009).

With regard to morphosyntactic analysis, Samarin's requirements for a good corpus imply the following recommendations for gathering textual data. First, for a varied corpus one needs to make recordings of several types of text spoken by different kinds of people, such as traditional narratives (epics, legends, etc.), spontaneous narratives (anecdotes, personal histories, etc.), descriptions of activities, descriptions of objects, conversations, etc. (see §3.5.3.2), and as the corpus should also be repetitious, each genre should be represented several times. Since this ideal text corpus, which also has to include transcriptions and translations of all recordings, cannot be gathered in just a few years, the researchers and the speech community have to be selective and set priorities which are not determined by linguistic criteria, but by the practical necessity of recording first what the community considers as most important. If this, for example, is the traditional oral literature or the description of traditional rituals, the corpus may in the end lack casual conversations. On the other hand, the community may want to prioritize the recording of typical everyday communication as the basis for language revitalization measures. Accordingly, a grammar based on such corpora would not cover the full spectrum of verbal interaction, but nevertheless it can be an excellent grammar as long as it is made clear on what kind of data it is based.

Since the speakers' selection of linguistic forms depends on the kind of speech situation, the sources of all texts have to be described by metadata (Austin 2006: 92–4; Bowern 2008: 56–8; Caprile, Rivierre, and Thomas 1992; Himmelmann 2006a: 11–15; Samarin 1967: 102–4; and Thieberger and Berez, Chapter 4 below). Furthermore, in order to allow future researchers to scrutinize the morphosyntactic analysis, all text examples given in the grammar should be retrievable in the text corpus, and the text corpus itself should be accessible. To date these requirements are only met by a very few grammars, for example Thieberger (2006) and Wegener (2008).

Second, to 'get people talking', some fieldworkers use picture prompts like the frog stories as recommended by Bowern (2008: 116); others are more critical, because what people say when looking at such picture books is neither 'natural' nor 'interesting'. As Foley (2003) demonstrates, it may also differ structurally quite considerably from authentic narratives, and consequently may lead to false generalizations about the grammar of the language.

Third, translated texts of any kind should not be used, unless the researcher is fully aware of translational problems and wants to conduct a specialized investigation on translational interferences from the contact language. Recommendations to use translated material otherwise should not be taken seriously, although they are found in the fieldwork guides. Vaux et al. (2007: 105–7) even suggest inventing texts for an 'informant' to translate and 'tailor the text to fit your own interests as an investigator'. For a critical assessment of the use of Bible translations in morphosyntactic research, see De Vries (2007).

3.5.3.2 *Text types*

Rivierre (1992) presents a classification of text types that are relevant for linguistic fieldwork. He starts with the distinction between texts of the oral tradition 'with their careful, affected and often even archaic style', including the major traditional genres of historical narratives, myths, poems, etc., and 'more spontaneous texts, such as explanations of techniques, biographical accounts and anecdotes, or conversations in quite a different style which is often neglected' (Rivierre 1992: 56). He recommends collecting texts 'while developing the lexicon, proceeding by means of categories' and distinguishes six thematic categories (pp. 59–61):

1. locations and geographical and social environment;
2. plants and animals;
3. social organization;
4. seasonal and non-seasonal activities;
5. life of the individual;
6. technology.

Each of these categories is further subdivided and accompanied by comments on how these themes and subthemes relate to various genres and how the various kinds of texts can be collected.

Rivierre's categorization is also useful for the creation of a corpus for the grammatical analysis of a previously undocumented language because different themes are talked about in different ways and different genres stimulate the use of different grammatical constructions. In other words, the text type—here defined in terms of themes and genres—determines the frequency of certain grammatical constructions. Consequently, the choice of a particular text type can help to avoid artificial elicitation. Here are a few examples from my own research:

• In order to investigate how the use of temporal expressions differs in accounts of habitual activities and narratives of past events, I recorded and analysed the description of how to butcher a rooster, and an anecdote telling how someone butchered a particular rooster.

• Instrumental constructions such as prepositional phrases or applicatives occur quite frequently in procedural texts describing how something is done with certain tools or made from certain materials.

• Narratives focusing on the actions of people usually favour clause structures in which an agentive human participant features as the subject of an active verb. In order to test what kind of constructions the Teop language has to background human agents, I recorded descriptions of plants and what they are used for.

• A convenient text type for the analysis of syntactic behaviour of property words denoting size, colour, and shape are descriptions of fishes, flowers, and fruit.

Text types like procedural texts or the description of plants and fishes may not belong to the traditional genres of the speech community or other kinds of conventionalized language use, but as they reflect the native speakers' linguistic competence and show the expressive power of the language, they can be considered a reliable source for the syntactic analysis of the language.

3.6 SUMMARY AND CONCLUDING REMARKS

Linguistic fieldwork on a previously unresearched language presupposes a good knowledge of linguistic typology or at least of the grammar of a closely related language (§3.2). Without this background knowledge, the researcher will not be able to analyse the data he or she collects, develop new hypotheses, and accordingly prepare new questionnaires while still in the field. Researchers without linguistic training can contribute to the documentation of a language by compiling lists of words and sentences or doing recordings, transcriptions, and translations with the help of bilingual speakers (§3.3).

The success of a fieldwork trip very much depends on how the researchers interact with their indigenous consultants. The more the consultants understand the aims and the methods of the research project, the more they will be interested in cooperation and contribute good data. Ideally they can be trained in some research activities like recording, transcription, and translation (§3.4).

Data on morphosyntactic phenomena can be gathered by various methods of elicitation and by the recording of texts. Elicitation methods can be classified into translational and non-translational elicitation. Since translational elicitation may, as many fieldworkers have observed, lead to unreliable data, the non-translational strategies like substitution, paraphrasing, and transformation are preferred (§3.5.2). For a thorough understanding of the morphosyntax of the target language, fieldworkers record, transcribe, and translate texts as early as possible. This corpus of texts should, if possible, comprise texts of a variety of genres and deal with diverse topics, because the selection of certain grammatical constructions depends on the linguistic and extralinguistic context of the speech event (§3.5.3).

The fieldwork guides discussed in this chapter provide useful information on how to collect various types of data, but they also make evident that the methodology of gathering data for morphosyntactic analyses in the field is still in its infancy.

Websites for further information include:

http://www.ethnologue.com
http://www.ling.udel.edu/pcole/Linguistic_Questionnaires/LinguaQ.htm
http://wals.info
http://projects.chass.utoronto.ca/lingfieldwork

CHAPTER 4

....

LINGUISTIC DATA MANAGEMENT

....

NICHOLAS THIEBERGER
ANDREA L. BEREZ

4.1 INTRODUCTION[1]

....

Documenting a language requires the production of records that will persist and be accessible into the future. If we look at the number of language descriptions for which there is no corresponding accessible primary data, it would seem that creating persistent, well-structured, and citable language records has proven to be a considerable barrier to linguists in the past.[2] This is due, in part, to the lack of advice and training in the use of appropriate methods and tools for recording, transcribing, and analysing linguistic data. This chapter seeks to provide such advice by focusing on the nuts and bolts of the creation and management of sustainable data in the course of linguistic field research, including pre-fieldwork planning and the follow-up archiving, annotation, and analysis of field-collected materials. The approach to data management presented here assumes that it is the

---

[1] Thanks to Christopher Cox and Toshihide Nakayama for their comments as reviewers of this chapter. Thanks also to Laura Berbusse, Tobias Bloyd, and Aaron Waldrip for helpful suggestions.

[2] See Johnston (1995) and Antworth and Valentine (1998) and the other papers (a little dated but still useful) in Lawler and Aristar-Dry (1998) to see how these topics have been part of linguistic discussion for some time.

professional responsibility of linguists to create long-lasting, archivable primary data and to then situate any subsequent analyses in that data.

We advocate the use of appropriate technologies to record, manage, and annotate linguistic data, in order not only to create good records of the languages we study but to also provide access to the data upon which we make generalizations. Good data management includes the use of specific software tools (e.g. Toolbox,[3] Fieldworks,[4] ELAN[5]), but more importantly centres on an understanding of the nature of linguistic data and the way in which the tools we use can interact with the data. Tools will come and go, but our data must remain accessible into the future.[6] We are primarily aiming our discussion here at academic linguists, but we hope that it will be useful to anyone engaged in the many tasks involved in the documentation of underdescribed languages, which may not involve academically trained linguists at all, or may involve linguists who are from the communities in question, for whom 'the field' is in fact home (cf. Crippen 2009).

If we liken our research endeavor to building a house, we can think of planning and managing our data collection as providing the firm foundations on which a solid house is built—that is, one we can live in for many years, and which can grow as we need further renovations and extensions. These extensions are akin to the different ways we will be able to use or present our data in the future, including text collections, various lexicons, and multimedia representations of the language. Some of these outputs we can envisage now, others we cannot. Our foundations need to be built today in a manner that makes our data perpetually extensible.

If, however, we do not build our foundation correctly, there will be little hope for extending our research, and our data may not even serve our immediate purposes without the need for constant reworking. Consider, for example, a dictionary written in Microsoft Word in which the elements (headwords, definitions, part of speech tags, and so on) are differentiated on the page only through formatting conventions (i.e. the use of bold or italic styles) and are not explicitly marked for their status as elements. One cannot easily convert such a dictionary into multiple versions for diverse audiences (say, a reversal of headword language or a learners' or children's dictionary), nor can one automatically link entries to media and so forth (cf. Black and Simons 2009). This is because the elements in the dictionary, not being explicitly identified by use of structural tags of some kind (e.g. the 'backslash' tags of Toolbox, or perhaps XML tags, see below), are not automatically accessible to computational processes. Equally important are our data descriptions; if we do not take a few moments during our field sessions to write simple descriptions

---

[3] http//www.sil.org/computing/toolbox

[4] http://www.sil.org/computing/fieldworks

[5] http://www.lat-mpi.eu/tools/elan

[6] See Bird and Simons (2003) for a detailed discussion of the principles underlying the creation of good linguistic data from fieldwork.

about our collections, their very existence may become unknown—not only to ourselves, but to the speaker communities we work with.

This chapter is not concerned with determining how much data needs to be recorded in the course of fieldwork. Instead, we assume that researchers can decide for themselves how much is adequate for a given situation, and we focus on proper principles for managing the data that is collected. It is of no small concern to see colleagues swamped by masses of recordings, photos, and texts, confused by discussions of which standards to follow and unable to keep track of not only the items in their collection, but also the status of those items (e.g. 'Has this video been transcribed?', 'Has this text been interlinearized?', 'Has this collection of photographs been described?'). The result is that within a short time these colleagues cannot fully access their own collections because of insufficient description of the contents, or because the data is tied to now-defunct software, or even because of permanent data loss from lack of a suitable backup procedure.

In a discussion of the general problem of data 'deluge', Borgman (2007: 6) notes: 'The amount of data produced far exceeds the capabilities of manual techniques for data management.' This has become a truism for computational tasks on the web, and it is also true of the comparatively small datasets created by documentary linguists. If we want to move beyond tedious manual techniques for manipulating our data and make use of far more efficient automatic and global operations, we need to learn how to first prepare *well-formed data* in a predictable structure that conforms to existing standards, so that we can then allow computers to do the rest of the work. After all, handling repetitive (and tedious) tasks quickly and accurately is what computers do best.

Publishing and citing the primary data on which an analysis is based is becoming more common and may soon become a requirement for major research grants (cf. Borgman 2007: 240–41) and submission to journals. Until the late 1980s it was difficult to cite primary data in a linguistic analysis (although Heath's 1984 grammar of Nunggubuyu is a valiant attempt at linking examples to textual sources). Since then, however, only a few grammatical descriptions (e.g. Morey 2004; Thieberger 2006) link the descriptions and analyses of linguistic phenomena to examples from a corpus. The methods described in this chapter build citable corpora and encourage the use of cited data in any resulting analysis, a practice that has been part of lexicographic and corpus-based linguistics for some time (cf. Liberman 2009).

We want to be clear, however, that the goal of this chapter is not to drown field linguists in the virtual ocean of stringent and ever-changing specifications of 'best practice' procedures that our discipline sometimes seems to be swimming in. In this context it is important to bear in mind Voltaire's admonition (Arouet 1877) that 'the best is the enemy of the good'. Bloomfield is quoted as saying, 'each of us should take a vow of celibacy, not teach, and dedicate the entirety of our summers to fieldwork and our winters to collating and filing our data, year after year' (Hockett 1962). We suggest it would be better for linguists to become more efficient using the methods we advocate, and to still have a life!

This chapter aims to help find the balance between the desire to record and annotate our data to the highest possible standards, and the reality of the time constraints we all work under. In fact, if we take the time to produce well-formed, reusable data, our linguistic analyses will be more convincing, and our production of language materials will become more efficient. The initial outlay of time and effort required to understand the methods and tools for good data management may seem high, but the investment will pay off in the end.

This chapter is organized as follows. The remainder of §4.1 provides some basics about data and metadata, as well as an overview of the workflow for creating well-formed data. In §4.2 we outline the planning required before setting off on fieldwork, including preparing to use (or not use) technology in the field and making contact with an archive. The data management tasks you will face, including file naming, care for fieldnotes, metadata collection and storage, regular expressions, time-aligned transcription and interlinearization, and the use of lexical databases, are discussed in §4.3. For those who are not so technically oriented, we suggest skipping §4.3.3.1 to §4.3.4. In §4.4 we discuss the broader advantages of creating well-formed field data for linguistics as a discipline, and §4.5 contains concluding remarks.

4.1.1 What is data?

Linguistic data arise from a range of techniques that straddle traditional humanities and scientific methodologies, from field-based observation to corpus data to experimentation. For this chapter, 'data' is considered to be the material that results from fieldwork, which may include: primary observational notes, recordings, and transcripts; derived or secondary material such as lexical databases and annotated texts; and tertiary material, in the form of analytical writing, published collections of texts, or dictionaries. In addition, fieldwork results in elicited data: elicitation is always a part of fieldwork, and many linguists also use questionnaires and experimental field methods (see Majid's Chapter 2 above). All of these types of data and their associated metadata (see below) together make up the larger documentary corpus. Like the house with solid foundations, a documentary corpus grows and changes over time and is continually updated as we collect more recordings, refine our annotations, and publish more analyses.

4.1.2 What is metadata?

Simply stated, *metadata* is one set of data that describes another set of data. In terms of linguistic field data, your metadata is your catalogue of 'what you have'—a list, stored in a relational database or a spreadsheet, of all the important bits of information that describe each recording, transcript, photograph, and notebook in your corpus. Keeping accurate, up-to-date metadata is crucial, because without it, you very soon lose track of the details of the items in your collection (try to remember the contents of a recording you made last year to see how important a brief description is). You would not know, for instance, if recording x predates or postdates recording y, or if photograph p is of mountain m or mountain n, or if recording z has been transcribed yet, or if WAV file w was originally on cassette.

You may think that you can keep track of all of this information in your head—and indeed, you may be able to—but consider what would happen if others wanted to access your collection, perhaps when you are back home after summer fieldwork, or after your retirement or death. Without a catalogue of metadata, there would be no way for anyone else to know what your corpus contains, or the conditions under which it was collected.

Fortunately, there are two widely accepted metadata systems for linguistic material that can guide fieldworkers in which bits of information to collect as part of a catalogue. These are the standards provided by Open Language Archives Community[7] (OLAC) (see below) and the ISLE MetaData Initiative[8] (IMDI). You should not feel limited to just the fields provided by either one. Since you may want to collect types of information that neither system requires, you can build your catalogue so that it can export to a form that can be used by any archive.

4.1.3 Form and content

Critical to the goals of this chapter is the distinction between the *form* of the presentation of data and its *content* (cf. Black and Simons 2009). The content of data should be constructed, or *marked*, in such a way that it is possible to derive many different presentation forms. A simple example of this is shown in Fig. 4.1. Two different kinds of markup are shown: in (a), a form-driven markup like HTML (the encoding used on the World Wide Web), and in (b), a content-driven markup.

In this example the presentation of the data is the same for both, but the mechanism by which this presentation happens is different. In (a), the bold type would be rendered directly from the strictly presentational <b> (bold) tag, whereas in (b), the data would be processed through a stylesheet that assigns different styles to different tags (in this case, everything marked as <sentence>, <header>, and <adj> are bolded). Without a structural identification of a word as being, for example, an adjective, there is no way to quickly change the presentation form of just one kind of element (e.g. so that the adjective *grumpy* is italicized instead of bolded), nor is there any way to search for structurally different elements, e.g. headers only. Imagine having to comb through a 10,000-entry lexicon, entry by entry, just to make a minor format adjustment that could instead be accomplished with a single click or a couple of keystrokes.

---

[7] http://www.language-archives.org
[8] http://www.mpi.nl/IMDI/documents/documents.html

(a) Form-driven markup (in HTML)

      Marked data: <b>This is a sentence.</b>

      Presentation: **This is a sentence.**

      Marked data: <b>Chapter1</b>
                                   He was <b>grumpy</b> about being left out.

      Presentation: **Chapter 1**
                                   He was **grumpy** about being left out.

(b) Content-driven markup

      Marked data: <sentence>This is a sentence.</sentence>

      Presentation: **This is a sentence.**

      Marked data: <header>Chapter 1</header>
                                   He was <adj>grumpy</adj> about being left out.

      Presentation: **Chapter 1**
                                   He was **grumpy** about being left out.

Figure 4.1. Form-driven versus content-driven markup.

A more relevant example is that of a dictionary project. A single well-structured lexical database can give rise to a number of different presentation formats: on paper, on-line, with linked sound files and images, just as a simple wordlist, with reverse-language indices, and so forth. These many presentations of dictionaries are possible if contents of the elements (lexemes, glosses, definitions, example sentences, etc.) are described with, for example, backslash[9] field markers, rather than just with formatting information. Similarly, texts have logical structures: they usually include an orthographic representation of the spoken words, a morphemic parse, a morpheme gloss, and a free gloss as shown in the example of a Toolbox text fragment in Fig. 4.2, where each line is marked by a code (e.g. \tx = text; \mr = morphemes; \mg = morphemic glosses; \fg = free gloss). Describing or marking the content of these structures in our data allows various presentation formats to be generated for different audiences.

Structuring linguistic data by content allows it to be arranged and rearranged in new ways, providing visualization of relationships within the data. Such visualization allows new generalizations to be made, and also helps ensure consistency in the data. For example, being able to sort a lexicon on various fields puts similar types of information

---

[9] So-called 'backslash' codes or standard field markers are a simple way to delimit fields in a text document. MDF, or Multi-Dictionary Formatter, is the system used by Toolbox to create dictionaries as styled RTF documents from a structured Toolbox file (cf. http://www.sil.org/computing/shoebox/mdf.html), and it provides a set of over 100 standard 'backslash' codes.

```
\id       061: 005

\aud      AHT-MP-20100305-Session.wav 02: 19.320-02: 21.780

\tx    Ga    łdu'    ben    yii    taghił'aa.

\mr    ga    łdu'    ben    yii    ta-    ghi-    ł-    'aa

\mg    DEM   FOC    lake   in     water  ASP    CLF   linear.extend

\fg       'As for that one (river), it flows into the lake.'
```

Figure 4.2. Structure of interlinear glossed texts.

next to each other which can also be useful for creation of topical lists where the lexicon is sorted by semantic field rather than just alphabetically. Mistakes, such as duplicate entries or typos, are more easily located when such sorting is carried out.

4.1.4 Reuse of field data

Reuse of our field recordings and research outputs is central to the methodology advocated here. We need to be able to reuse our own field materials in our analysis of the language, and also ensure that others can access them in the future. It is increasingly common for linguists to deposit primary material with an archive early and then to regularly keep adding to their collection. Once items are archived, any subsequent work—transcribing, annotating, or selecting example sentences for published analyses—can be cited back to an archival file. The archive provides this citability for you, so if you archive your files before you begin your analysis, you allow your research to be embedded within the data (Thieberger 2009) and then to be verified by other researchers with reference to the primary data.

4.1.5 A workflow for well-formed data

Creating well-formed data from linguistic fieldwork entails a workflow like the one in Fig. 4.3. The workflow begins with project planning, which for our purposes includes preparing to use technology in the field and deciding on which file naming and metadata conventions you will use before you make your first recording. (Clearly there is a great deal of non-data-related planning to be done before the first recording can be made, but that is not the focus of this chapter.) After recordings are made and metadata are collected, data must be transcribed and annotated with various software tools, and then used for analysis and in representation of the language via print or multimedia. Note that depositing materials in an archive is carried out at every phase of the procedure.

Because you will subject your data to a number of processes, there is always a risk that some parts of it may be lost along the way if the outputs of one software tool do not align exactly with the input requirements of the next tool in the workflow. For example, importing a time-aligned transcript from ELAN (see §4.3.5) into Toolbox for interlinearization may result in some extra fields appearing in Toolbox. These fields correspond to the original ELAN data categories, but are not necessary for the Toolbox interlinearization process. You must take care, then, that you do not delete these extra fields so that they will still be present when you re-import the data into ELAN.

Another significant problem that arises from using a variety of tools in a workflow is that the exports of one tool may not be in a format that fits into the import routine of the next tool in the workflow. For example, time-alignment software (e.g. ELAN or Transcriber) typically produces a native XML file which can be exported to a number of interchange formats, but none of these can be opened *directly* in, say, Toolbox or Fieldworks (although more import and export formats are being added to these tools regularly, so this may become less of a problem over

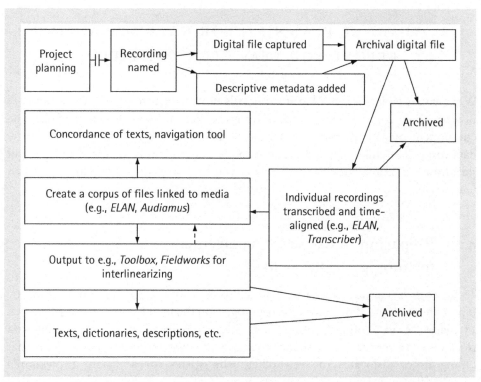

Figure 4.3. Typical workflow resulting in well-formed linguistic data (adapted from Thieberger 2004).

time). A useful way of converting text into new formats is to use regular expression functions as discussed in §4.3.4.

A final potential problem with workflows is that you need to keep track of which parts of your corpus have undergone which steps, with the risk that you may end up with different versions of the same file on your hard disk. If this happens, you may accidentally edit two different versions of the same file and subsequently have to use a 'compare documents' function to keep all of the edits you have made. For this reason it is also helpful to keep *administrative* metadata (which describes your processing of the data) to track items through the steps in your workflow, as well as *descriptive* metadata (descriptions of the data itself) to describe the items.

Care on your part and an awareness of what is lost and what is gained by the use of a particular tool can mitigate all these dangers. Understanding what the various tasks along the workflow involve can make your life easier, and will also determine what tools are applicable at each stage of the workflow.

4.2 ADVANCE PLANNING FOR DATA MANAGEMENT BEFORE YOU LEAVE FOR THE FIELD

While you are planning the logistical details of your upcoming fieldwork (and see Bowern 2008: 222 or Fox[10] for lists of things to take and do before departing), one component of your preparation should be planning for the management of the data you will be collecting in the field. Some advance planning before you leave will save time and effort later and will ensure you have a good strategy in place when you arrive.

4.2.1 Preparing to use data management technology in the field

Technology has always been a part of fieldwork. Clifford (1990: 63) notes that the typewriter, once used by many anthropologists in the field (he cites Clifford Geertz, Margaret Mead, Colin Turnbull, and Gregory Bateson as examples), allowed researchers to reorder and enhance the day's handwritten notes. He suggests that typing notes dislocates the researcher, who writes for a distant professional

---

[10] http://www.stanford.edu/~popolvuh/field-checklist.htm

readership, from the field: 'Facing the typewriter each night means engaging these 'others', or alter egos. No wonder the typewriter or the pen or the notebook can sometimes take on a fetishistic aura' (Clifford 1990: 64).

The fetishizing of technology is not surprising, nor is it necessarily a problem. We adopt the best tools for the job at hand, and typewriters have given way to laptops, which are now commonly taken to the field, as are various handheld devices, e.g. PalmPilots (cf. Gibbon 2006), iPods, iPads, and the like. If you can use a computer in your fieldwork situation, it can help you stay organized and allow you to query data that may otherwise have to await your return.

The use of computers for managing field data could be seen as exemplifying the technological distance between the linguist and the people we work with in the field. Carrying costly equipment in a cash-poor community is incongruous and potentially dangerous (if you are likely to provide a target for theft). This is something that you need to seriously consider before departing for fieldwork; trust your knowledge of the field location to guide what you think it is appropriate to take with you (cheap netbooks are quite inconspicuous, and it's not the end of the world if they break). Unlike lugging a typewriter into the field, the laptop, recorder, camera, GPS, and video camera are not so robust and need special care (see Margetts and Margetts, Chapter 1 above, on recording). You may decide that a laptop is not going to survive your field environment, but that you will access a computer in a nearby location where you can organize your material away from the field.

Digital data is very fragile, so avoiding its loss has to be integral to your planning. Ironically, analog cassette tapes are in some sense hardier than digital files: a tape kept in a dry, temperature-stable filing cabinet can usually be played again a decade later, but digital files stored on a hard disk are unlikely to last that long. Also, accidents can happen—your field materials could be burned, flooded, eaten, stolen, or lost, despite your best efforts to keep your data backed up. Backing up your digital files can be done in one of several ways depending on the details of your field situation. Taking an extra external hard drive or two with you and copying your files to them on a regular basis is a good solution (one author who works in a region that is prone to forest fires takes two external hard drives to the field, copies files to both of them daily, and stores one in her cabin and the other in her car). You may also investigate online storage that can be accessed when you have an internet connection, perhaps on a regular visit to a town if that is an option. If you are not bringing a laptop to the field and plan to use multiple memory[11] cards to hold your recordings, a USB 'On-The-Go' (OTG)[12] storage

---

[11] Memory cards of various kinds are used in many portable devices like digital recorders and cameras.

[12] OTG USB devices are those that can act as hosts to other USB devices and also interact with a computer; in this case, a device to which you can upload files from your recorder's SD card for storage until you can transfer them to a computer.

device is a compact solution for backing up those recordings (but leave the original recordings on the memory cards during your trip so that you have multiple copies, rather than reusing the cards).

Having sufficient power to run the equipment is no small undertaking if there is no electricity supply in your field site. Choosing devices that run on ordinary batteries makes life easier, and chargers that run off car batteries, generators, or solar panels are also an option (see McGill and Salffner n.d. and Honeyman and Robinson 2007 on the use of solar power and portable generators for fieldwork, and also Margetts and Margetts, Chapter 1 above).

4.2.2 Archiving: plan for it now

A major difference between the newer methods in language documentation and those that preceded them is the use of digital media. As pointed out above, digital data has no proven longevity, and format changes can potentially lead to orphaned data that can no longer be read by available software. Therefore, the sooner your data can be stored in a dedicated repository, with trained staff and an institutional commitment to protect and migrate your data, the better. A proper archive will describe your data adequately, assign persistent identifiers, and share data in several locations to ensure its long-term accessibility. Archiving is an essential part of any language documentation work in which a major motivation is to create an enduring record of the language. Unfortunately, your computer is not an archive. An external hard drive, as crucial as it is for day-to-day backup, is not an archive, nor is a website from which you make multimedia files available for download.

Many people think of archiving as the last step in a research program, to be done years after the fieldwork is complete, after everything has been transcribed and mined in service of analysis—essentially, something to be done after we are 'finished' with the data. Here, we advocate the exact opposite: data should be archived immediately and often (subject, of course, to your having resolved any ethical issues that may have arisen about what you recorded, and whether the speakers have agreed to have their recordings archived—see Rice, Chapter 18 below, for further discussion of ethical issues).

It is quite possible—and becoming increasingly common—to archive recordings periodically from the field as they are collected. Then, whenever you finish a transcription, archive it. When you write up an analysis, archive it. As your lexical database grows, archive it. If you make a children's book from your data, archive it. Think of your archived collection as another backup of your entire corpus, only this one is stored in a remote offsite location and maintained by professionals. If the idea of sending your data to another location before it is ready to be made available to the general public makes you uncomfortable, you can temporarily restrict access to certain parts of your collection.[13]

Establishing a relationship with an archive before you leave for the field ensures that the staff can work with you from the beginning of your project to secure the long-term preservation of your collection. Finding out what kind of metadata and file naming conventions the archive uses is a good idea, because this will guide how you set up your metadata database. Be sure to keep track of the information the archive requires, as well as any extra information that you will find helpful that is not necessarily requested by the archive. You can also make some arrangements for regular deposits of your data from the field, either via direct upload to the archive or by mailing DVDs or a small hard drive.

Example of the use of methods advocated in this chapter

Scenario 1
Having established my field location and the relationships with the people I will be working with, I am now in the process of eliciting and recording information. I set off for a story-telling session with my backpack of equipment (video and still cameras, audio recorder, headphones, tripod, and microphone) and my notebook. The speaker has already completed a consent form and I have taken their photo to include in future presentations of stories they have told. After a cup of tea and a chat they are ready to start. I do my best to ensure that there is no background noise and that the lighting is appropriate, then set up the tripod, video, and audio recorder. I put on the headphones, then start the recording by saying the date, place, and name of the speaker. They then tell their story and I take notes of contextual information that may be relevant, like the direction they are facing, or gestures they use to help in communicating the story. When they are done they may want to retell parts of the story or explain aspects of it, and I will try to record that information as well. Afterwards, I note the name of the file assigned by the recording device. If the location of the recording is not easily described with a place name, then I would also have a geographic reference from a GPS and that would be part of the metadata for the recording.

---

[13] Temporarily restricting access may also be necessary if your recordings include sections with local gossip or other content that a speaker subsequently requests to have suppressed. Given the problem of 'data deluge', this necessary work can become more and more onerous as the collection grows, and is not a task that current digital tools provide much help in automating. Restricting access to all primary materials contributed to the archive until they can be reviewed and edited offers an immediate solution to issues of preservation and privacy, but it does not necessarily address the bottleneck created by this kind of review, and potentially poses difficulties for later open access. Furthermore, it could be controversial to archive language materials outside of the speaker communities involved in documentation, especially in cases where past research relationships have contributed little of appreciable benefit to the speaker communities involved, or even proven hurtful in the treatment of language materials which may have been removed from those communities. This is a matter that often requires more discussion between all partners in documentation to arrive at a solution that ensures long-term preservation while respecting the concerns of all involved.

I employ a speaker of the language to transcribe recordings, using exercise books to write the language and a translation. These books are then scanned for ease of access and will be typed when I return from the field.

My notebooks are the primary source of information about this recording session, and when I can get to a computer, I enter that information (e.g. speaker name, place and date of recording) into a database, with the key field of the record being the name of the media item. Later, as I proceed with my analysis of the language, the name of the transcript of the media will be entered, or at least, the fact that it has been completed would be checked off in the database. Then, when I extract a text from that transcript for interlinearization, I note the identifier of the text in the database too.

4.3 MANAGING YOUR DATA

If you work in a location with electricity, much of your initial data management will be done in the field on a daily basis as you collect recordings, including naming your files appropriately, recording the associated metadata in your database, creating backup copies and preparing files for archiving. If there is no electricity in your field site, you will want to take care of data management at the soonest possible opportunity, either on a visit to a town or immediately upon returning home. Be vigilant and resist the temptation to do it later, as it is too easy to lose track of what you have collected. It is useful to audio record simple details of who is speaking, where, and when at the beginning of the recording session; if you forget, you can add it at the end of the recording.

4.3.1 File naming and persistent identification

File names are critically important, and, while a seemingly trivial matter, the failure to plan properly for file names can wreak havoc with your data organization. Each file that you create has to be named in a way that lets you find it later. The names have to be unique—i.e. you should avoid having one directory with file 1, file 2, file 3, etc., and another directory with exactly the same file names in it. If those files are ever removed from their original directory (and they surely will be), there will be no way to trace their provenance.

You may be tempted to use the default file names assigned by your equipment; for example, your digital recorder may name files with something like STE-001, and your camera may assign names like IMG_0086. As a first step, you can always make note of the default name in your notebook, but be sure to rename it and record the correct metadata to them as soon as you can. These default file names may not be

ERK20080304FBHuntingStory.wav
ERK: ISO-639-3 language code for South Efate
20080304: recording date (4th of March 2008)
FB: speaker's initials
Hunting: genre of text
Story: type of text

Figure 4.4. Example of semantic file naming.

unique, especially if you are using multiple recording devices or if your device recycles file names upon download.[14]

There are several strategies you can choose from when you are deciding on your file naming convention. Some people prefer semantic file names, which carry a great deal of information, as in Fig. 4.4. The file name, shown in the top line, includes several meaningful chunks, including a language code, the date of recording, the speaker's initials, and a brief description of the contents. One advantage of this system is obvious: you can easily see basic information as you look through your directory of files. Another advantage is that your computer will sort your files depending on how you order the information in the file name (in this case, by language first, then by recording date, then by speaker). A disadvantage of this strategy is that the names are rather long and can be difficult to read. Another disadvantage is that this system may not coincide with your archive's naming system. When you deposit your files you will need to assign each file an archive-appropriate name. This strategy for file naming is also a bit redundant: all the information contained in the file name will also be repeated in separate fields in your metadata catalogue. Nevertheless this system is useful for browsing your directories.

Another approach is to include most metadata only in your catalogue, and assign relatively simple unique file names that include only a minimum of meaningful information. An example would be *2011001.wav*, for the first recording made in 2011. This approach is easier to read and a bit less redundant in terms of record-keeping, but the file name may still need to be converted for deposit in an archive.

A third approach is to simply adopt the file naming convention that your archive requires, for example *ALB01-001-A.wav* for an item held in PARADISEC. This file name carries little meaningful information beyond the depositor's initials and the

---

[14] A temporary solution might be to append the date, such that IMG_0086 could become 20110102IMG_0086 (for 2 January 2011).

order of creation, but it is the least redundant method and will require no conversion upon deposit.

In the end, the choice of a naming convention is up to your preferences, but consistency is key and, more importantly, a file's name must be permanent once it is assigned. Take care with hyphens and underscores (and other non-alphanumeric characters), as these may be 'reserved' characters in some archives and will need to be converted later. To ensure the greatest legibility and persistence of your file names it is still best to use ASCII characters, although Unicode may become more acceptable in the near future. Be consistent in using upper and lower case—for some computer systems upper- and lower-case characters are treated equally, but in others they are not.

The names you assign to your files can be used by the archive and, together with their address, will provide a persistent identifier, i.e. a name that will allow the file to be located now and into the future. Persistent identifiers may include a URL, but remember that websites alone cannot provide persistence of location unless they have adopted conventions like those offered by Digital Object Identifiers[15] or Handles,[16] which are both services that allow permanent names to be applied, via a redirection service, to impermanent addresses.

4.3.2 Handwritten fieldnotes and headnotes in digital language documentation

Since long before the age of digital language documentation, handwritten notes have been integral to linguistic fieldwork. Even in the current age of widespread awareness of the advantages of digital documentation, much day-to-day practice by field linguists is still based on analog procedures. Many linguists consider pen-on-paper to be the best method for preliminary elicitation and analysis; some field sites have no reliable power source, or perhaps using a computer in some locations would be obtrusive. Regardless of your reason for making handwritten notes, it is important to stay organized. You can use paper notebooks of whatever size you find convenient (or, in extreme need, scraps of paper that are conveniently to hand, or even, as in the case of one report, a coconut that was inscribed with a precious example: cf. Crowley 2007: 107). Whenever possible, use acid-free paper and pens with waterproof, archival-quality ink. Researchers working in damp, rainy, or flood-prone areas might try waterproof all-weather notebooks.

In addition to being an obvious source of primary data, written fieldnotes also provide contextual information for recorded media, including the place, date, and participants, as well as any observations you want to note about the recorded performance itself. Much of the process of linguistic discovery is embedded in these

---

[15] http://www.doi.org/   [16] http://www.handle.net/

notebooks in the form of ethnographic notes, thoughts, and early errors, and in fact the left-to-right, top-to-bottom format of western notebooks itself provides important temporal information about the fieldwork session.

Written notes are further supplemented by 'headnotes' (Ottenberg 1990: 144), which include the memories the researcher has that continue to enrich their analysis over time. Headnotes and written notes are, says Ottenberg, in constant dialog: 'only after their author is dead do written notes become primary, for the headnotes are gone' (p. 147). The ability to access the primary data in digital form facilitates this dialog, bringing new forms of interpretation to bear on the collection over time due to the ease of access provided by files in a digital format.

While the interpretive and creative application of the researcher's experience results in more than can be reduced to the data objects stored in an archive, without those objects the linguistic analysis lacks an authoritative base. Fieldnotes, like recordings, should be scanned as part of your regular backup routine and archived as images. You can also type up your written notes to make them electronically searchable, allowing you to reflect on what you have written, add to it, and formulate new questions.

4.3.3 Your metadata catalogue

Simply amassing a number of digital files will not give you access to the material in them, just as a bookshop with thousands of uncatalogued books does not make information easy to find. The metadata that you provided for items in your own collection as they were created can later be uploaded to an archive's catalogue. These metadata will also make it easier for you to work with your own collection in your continuing analysis of the language.

An up-to-date metadata catalogue is a key component of your documentary corpus. Even if you have chosen a file-naming convention that captures a lot of information, you still need to keep a digital catalogue. Initially you are likely to be creating metadata in your paper notebooks, jotting down the name of a speaker or the object being photographed, the date, the location, and so on, and then keying this information into your catalogue at the earliest opportunity. Ask your archive what metadata they require for deposit, and you can also add other information that is important to your particular situation.

4.3.3.1 Relational databases

A relational database is a good choice for a catalogue, and in this section we discuss how one can be conceptualized (but we refer readers to other sources for the details of using any particular database management system (DBMS), like Filemaker Pro, MS Access, or OpenOffice.org Base). If you do not know how to build a relational database, you can still keep well-organized metadata in a spreadsheet, but you should be aware that a spreadsheet has some limitations. For instance, you will need to enter identical information multiple times, and there is no easy mechanism for enforcing consistency, whereas a DBMS can constrain entries to a fixed list, using dropdown menus to assist in data entry. For these reasons you may wish to make the leap from a spreadsheet to a relational database when you have time to learn how to use one (Harrington 2009 is an excellent introductory guide), or adapt an existing relational database to suit your needs. As with all digital files, periodically backing up your catalogue to a readable text format is good insurance against losing your catalogue in the event that someday the DBMS software is no longer supported.

Relational databases provide ways of linking related but conceptually different kinds of data, such as information regarding recordings, transcripts, and people that are part of your fieldwork project, as shown in Fig. 4.5. In your database, each *record* relates to an *item* in your collection. An item can be whatever you select it to be, perhaps a recording session that lasted two hours of which there are photos and video and audio, all of which can be summarized in one database record. On the other hand, you may want to list each recording as an item, each with a unique name and with a catalogue record devoted to it. This would allow you to find information at a level lower than the session. Sample catalogue files in various formats are available from archiving projects (see e.g. Arbil,[17] IMDI,[18] PARADI-SEC[19]) to help you decide. We hope that in the near future we will have access to more user-friendly metadata entry tools such as Saymore[20] and Fieldhelper,[21] which promise to use drag-and-drop functions for metadata entry.

Everyone has different ways of working, but we all need to keep track of some basic kinds of information, such as information about media recordings, about people, about transcripts and texts, and about lexica. A DBMS stores similar kinds of information together in *tables*, and then establishes *relationships* between tables so that you should (in theory) never need to enter the same piece of information twice, thus saving time and eliminating chances of typos. The links between tables in a DBMS work by using *keys*, a unique identifier for each record in the database.

To illustrate this, consider Fig. 4.5. A metadata database will have a table that keeps track of your **recordings**. You will want to store a number of different pieces of information about each one, e.g. the file name, the date recorded, the equipment used, the location of the recording, a summary description of the contents, and the length. At the same time, the DBMS can also establish a unique identifier, or key, for each recording (here, Recording_ID).

To understand how relations between tables work, imagine you also want to keep track of your **transcripts**, which are related to, but separate from, the recordings

[17] http://www.lat-mpi.eu/tools/arbil/
[18] http://www.mpi.nl/IMDI/
[19] http://www.paradisec.org.au/downloads.html
[20] http://saymore.palaso.org/
[21] http://www.fieldhelper.org/

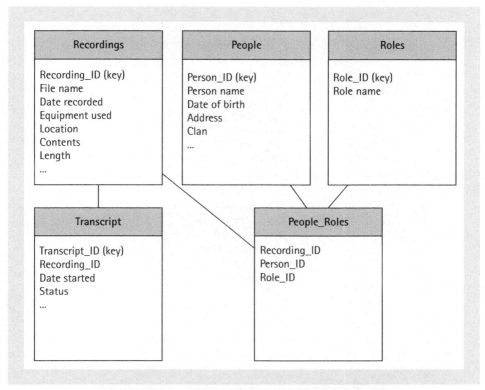

Figure 4.5. A simple relational database for fieldwork metadata.

they transcribe. You can keep information about your transcripts, like the start date and the status (in progress, finished, etc.), in another table. Notice in Fig. 4.6 that the transcripts table not only contains the unique identifier, or key, for each transcript, but also references the key of each associated recording. Including in one table the key from another table establishes the relation between the two tables.

A more complex example is that of tracking the various **people** who are associated with the items in your collection, with information like their names, their dates of birth, their clans, etc., and their **roles**. People can have roles as speakers, linguists, transcribers, singers, and so on; furthermore, a single person may hold multiple roles across your collection, and particular roles will most certainly be filled by different people for different items.

Rather than listing all the people associated with a particular recording and their roles within the recordings table, it is more efficient to have a separate table with all of the people involved in the project, and another table listing all the possible roles people can hold. A third table, known as a 'composite table' (or 'link table'), then lists **person–role** pairings (each by their key), and the key of the recording with which each

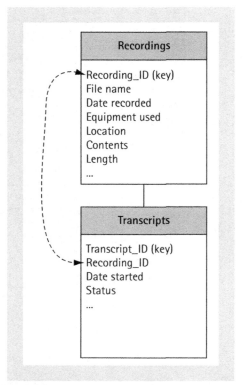

Figure 4.6. Establishing the relation between tables using keys.

person–role pairing is associated. This means that the names of speakers will only appear once and so you do not risk entering variations on the same name into your catalogue, thereby making it impossible to search on all references to one person. Using a database can allow you to query your data in complex ways (e.g. 'Who are the speakers for whom I have completed transcripts of their recordings?', 'What are the different roles that person *p* held in my collection between 2005 and 2010?').

Your catalogue could also include tables listing photographs, interlinearized texts, or geographic data. As long as your metadata catalogue conforms to a few basic principles, it should be possible to export textual data from it into in an archive's catalogue. These principles include using appropriate file names, including only one kind of information in each field of your catalogue database, and using standard forms where possible, e.g. ISO standards for dates[22] (YYYY-MM-DD), country names,[23] and language names.[24]

[22] ISO 8601, http://www.iso.org/iso/ue_detail?csnumber=40874
[23] ISO 3166, http://www.iso.org/iso/country_codes.htm
[24] ISO 639, http://www.sil.org/iso639-3/codes.asp

Open Language Archives Community (OLAC) metadata

The most commonly used open-access metadata system is Dublin Core,[25] with a set of fifteen terms that form the basis of most library catalogues, as well as the Open Archives Initiative.[26] If we want our material to be locatable via international search mechanisms, then all we need to do is to prepare our metadata in a form that they can read. Luckily, OLAC provides a ready-made set of terms that can be the minimum or at least the core of a description of items in our collection. OLAC provides services that aggregate catalogues from cooperating archives and create a set of webpages listing what is available, not only in each archive, but also providing a dynamic page showing what is available in all archives for each of the world's languages, updated every eight hours.

There seems to be some confusion over the use of OLAC metadata. It is not, and was never designed to be, an exhaustive set of terms for describing linguistic data. Your catalogue can have much more information in it than just that provided by the OLAC terms. The key consideration is that if you take the OLAC terms into account in your archive's system, then you can participate in a global information system about the world's languages.

4.3.4 Regular expressions

A consequence of a workflow using different software tools is that data needs to be converted from the output format of one tool to the input format of another tool without losing any of the data in the process. Textual conversions can be achieved by using *regular expressions* (also known as 'regex'), which are sophisticated search-and-replace routines. Regular expressions can save you a great deal of time, and it is well worth at least learning what they can do, even if you don't want to learn how to use them yourself. Basic information is easily found on the web,[27] Friedl (2006) is a useful reference, and Gries (2009: 68–99, 105–72) provides good instruction on using regular expressions in linguistic contexts. You can always find someone to help you with regular expressions if you do not feel confident creating them yourself.

Three examples of the power of regular expressions are given below. Fig. 4.7 shows how regular expressions can be used to convert the tab-delimited output from Transcriber software in (a) into the structured text that Toolbox software requires, shown in (b). While the change could be done with a single regular expression, we have split it into two steps for illustrative purposes.

Step 1 finds the first tab stop, then inserts '\as' (the MDF field marker indicating the time code for start of the audio clip) at the beginning of the line and replaces the first tab stop with a carriage return and '\ae' (for the time code of the end of the

[25] http://dublincore.org/

[26] http://www.openarchives.org

[27] http://en.wikipedia.org/wiki/Regular_expression, http://www.regular-expressions.info/, or http://etext.virginia.edu/services/helpsheets/unix/regex.html.

(a) Output from Transcriber (timecodes followed by the relevant text)

78.813 [TAB] 83.083 [TAB] apu motu nigmam upregi.., rutrau wesi go rapolak

(b) Converted into Toolbox format

\as 78.813

\ae 83.083

\tx apu motu nigmam upregi.., rutrau wesi go

Step 1	Find: \r([^\t]+)\t *(carriage return followed by any non-tab characters followed by a tab)*	Replace with: \r\\as \1\r\\ae *(carriage return followed by \ as and the characters in parentheses in the find expression followed by a carriage return and \ae)*
	78.813 [TAB] 83.083 [TAB] apu motu nigmam upregi.., rutrau wesi go	\as 78.813 \ae 83.083 [TAB] apu motu nigmam upregi.., rutrau wesi go
Step 2	Find: \r(\\ae [^\t]+)\t *(carriage return followed by \ae and by any non-tab characters followed by a tab)*	Replace with: \r\1\r\\tx *(carriage return followed by the characters in parentheses in the find expression followed by a carriage return and \tx)*
	\ae 83.083 [TAB] apu motu nigmam upregi.., rutrau wesi go	\as 78.813 \ae 83.083 \tx apu motu nigmam upregi.., rutrau wesi go

Figure 4.7. Example of a text (a) and its derived form (b), arrived at by use of regular expression search-and-replace routines.

audio clip). The second step finds the next tab stop and replaces it with a carriage return and the MDF text field marker '\tx'.

A second example of the use of regular expressions is the conversion of a dictionary made in a word processor into computationally tractable files, ready to be used in specialized lexicographic software. Fig. 4.8 shows an unstructured Microsoft Word document with a regular pattern of headwords preceded by an asterisk and followed by a definition in italics.[28] Using a regular expression in the

---

[28] This example is from Clark (2009).

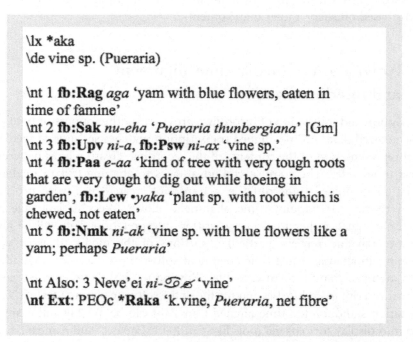

\lx *aka *vine sp. (Pueraria)*

1 **Rag** *aga* 'yam with blue flowers, eaten in time of famine'
2 **Sak** *nu-eha* '*Pueraria thunbergiana*' [Gm]
3 **Upv** *ni-a*, **Psw** *ni-ax* 'vine sp.'
4 **Paa** *e-aa* 'kind of tree with very tough roots that are very tough to dig out while hoeing in garden', **Lew** •*yaka* 'plant sp. with root which is chewed, not eaten'
5 **Nmk** *ni-ak* 'vine sp. with blue flowers like a yam; perhaps *Pueraria*'

Also: 3 Neve'ei *ni-ꟸ* 'vine'
Ext: PEOc ***Raka** 'k.vine, *Pueraria*, net fibre'

***ali=ali**
walk about, move around

Figure 4.8. Limited regular expression search in MS Word, inserting '\lx' before each headword in a document.

\lx *aka
\de vine sp. (Pueraria)

\nt 1 **fb:Rag** *aga* 'yam with blue flowers, eaten in time of famine'
\nt 2 **fb:Sak** *nu-eha* '*Pueraria thunbergiana*' [Gm]
\nt 3 **fb:Upv** *ni-a*, **fb:Psw** *ni-ax* 'vine sp.'
\nt 4 **fb:Paa** *e-aa* 'kind of tree with very tough roots that are very tough to dig out while hoeing in garden', **fb:Lew** •*yaka* 'plant sp. with root which is chewed, not eaten'
\nt 5 **fb:Nmk** *ni-ak* 'vine sp. with blue flowers like a yam; perhaps *Pueraria*'

\nt Also: 3 Neve'ei *ni-ꟸ* 'vine'
\nt Ext: PEOc ***Raka** 'k.vine, *Pueraria*, net fibre'

Figure 4.9. Second insertion of codes into a document on the way to structuring all elements.

Word find-and-replace window locates a carriage return followed by an asterisk and inserts '\lx' as a field marker identifying the headword, as has been done for *aka.

Eventually, more codes can be inserted, as shown in Fig. 4.9, where the '\de' and '\nt' fields have been added. Ultimately, all elements of the entries will be explicitly coded, rather than relying on formatting to imply structure.

As a third example of the use of regular expressions, imagine you have a corpus for which you need to quantify the occurrence of a particular word token expressed as a proportion of the total number of tokens in the corpus. However, the corpus also includes coding in angle brackets for, say, syntactic roles (e.g. <sub> for subject, <prd> for predicate), which you need to exclude from the text count. Using an ordinary find-and-replace tool will not locate all of these items at once (you would need to search for each of them individually). With a regular expression search you can locate all patterns of the form 'three characters enclosed in angle brackets' with the regular expression of the form < . . . >, where a full stop or period represents 'any character except return', thus looking for three such characters inside angle brackets.

MS Word has a very weak form of regular expression search. There are a number of tools with fully-featured regular expression functions, including OpenOffice. org, Text Wrangler (Mac), EditPad Pro (Windows), and regexxer (Linux). Regular expressions can swap the order of items in a text, and insert and change regular patterns based on shape rather than content.

4.3.5 Annotation of media: time alignment and interlinearization

Transcription and translation of recordings provides another opportunity to create well-structured data. A time-aligned transcription matches sections of media to a textual representation of the contents of the recording, creating links between the two via time codes. There are several advantages to aligning text to media over creating an unaligned transcript (i.e. a transcript created in a word processor). From a research standpoint, time alignment allows access to language as an audiovisual signal, rather than just a written interpretation. You will be able to quickly search and retrieve particular portions of the media to assist you in developing an analysis. Most time alignment software produces an XML file that is both archivable and human-readable, allowing the link between the recording and the transcript to endure beyond the life of the software used to create it. From a presentation standpoint, a time-aligned transcript can be quickly and easily converted into display formats via tools like CuPED,[29] Eopas,[30] and Annex/Trova.[31]

[29] http://sweet.artsrn.ualberta.ca/cdcox/cuped/
[30] http://www.eopas.org
[31] http://www.lat-mpi.eu/tools/annex/

There are several software options available for time alignment designed for documentary linguistic use, including ELAN,[32] Transcriber,[33] and EXMARaLDA.[34] When choosing software, things to look for are:

(i) flexibility—does the tool support multiple speakers, overlapping speech, and hierarchical relationships between tiers for interlinearization, comments, or annotation of gesture?

(ii) interoperability—do the tool's import and export options allow easy conversion between the other tools in your workflow, like a lexical database or a text editor?

(iii) archivability—does the tool produce a well-documented XML file?[35]

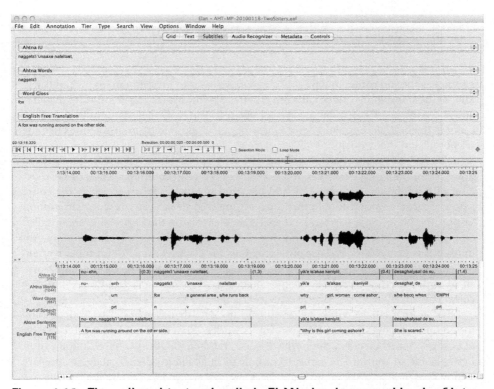

Figure 4.10. Time-aligned text and audio in ELAN, showing several levels of inter-linearization: intonation units, words, word glosses, parts of speech, normative sentences, and free translations.

---

[32] http://www.lat-mpi.eu/tools/elan/

[33] http://trans.sourceforge.net/en/presentation.php

[34] http://www.exmaralda.org/en_index.html

[35] It is best to avoid the less desirable commercial transcription software options targeted to the legal and medical professions.

Once you have produced time-aligned transcripts of the recordings, the next step is to further annotate the transcripts as interlinear glossed text (IGT), adding additional information like morphemic parsing and glosses of words and morphemes. Interlinearization tools that are tied to a lexical database (Fieldworks and Toolbox) are advantageous because they lend consistency and speed—entries are constrained to ensure they are consistent with those already in the database, and as the database grows, interlinearization becomes more and more automatic. It is essential, however, that the time codes from the time-aligned transcript be preserved so that the resulting IGT will still relate to the media. You can choose to bring your fully interlinearized text back into your time-aligned transcript (in essence making a 'round trip' with the data), or not. Fig. 4.10 shows a transcript that was time-aligned in ELAN, then

---

Example of the use of methods advocated in this chapter

Scenario 2

As soon as the sun comes up, my consultant drives over to my cabin in his pickup truck, knocks the snow off his boots, and comes in to sit by the heater and enjoy a cup of coffee and share the latest gossip before getting down to work. We have determined that my cabin is the best place to work, as it is warm, quiet, and free from distractions like the telephone and the television.

Today we are working on transcribing a legacy recording from the 1980s that has been digitized but never transcribed. On my desk are my laptop computer, a pair of speakers, a set of headphones, my notebook and pen, and my digital recorder. I play the entire legacy recording once through, then turn on my recorder to capture the transcription session and play the old narrative sentence by sentence from the ELAN software installed on my laptop. I have already started using ELAN to chunk the recording into intonation units, but as we work today, I use my laptop only for playback, and not for transcription. My consultant repeats the sentences back to me slowly and then provides translations, all of which I quickly scribble in my notebook. We work for a few hours until my consultant tires.

After another cup of coffee, he leaves, and my data management tasks begin. I copy the audio recording I made of the morning's work session onto my laptop, record a bit of post hoc verbal metadata about the session, and then join the two in an audio editor. I give the file an appropriate name, record the metadata in my digital catalogue, prepare a copy for sending to the archive, and back everything up on to external hard drives. I also jot down the relevant metadata on notebook pages containing my transcription. If my catalogue is ever lost, the pages can be rematched to their associated recordings.

Later that afternoon I use the handwritten notes in conjunction with the recording of the morning session to digitally transcribe the legacy text in ELAN. I then export it to Fieldworks, where I simultaneously create consistent multi-tier IGT and populate my growing lexical database. Once IGT is complete, I export the data back to ELAN to create the final time-aligned transcription. The transcript and the Fieldworks database are also prepared for archiving, entered into my metadata catalogue, and backed up locally. I scan my notebook pages monthly, and also mail DVDs of all my archival data to the overseas archive I am working with.

exported to Fieldworks for interlinearization, and then reimported into ELAN, taking advantage of ELAN's hierarchical tier structure for establishing parent–child relationships between the levels of IGT (see Berez 2007; Hellwig and Van Uytvanck 2007).

4.3.6 Lexical databases

Creating a lexical database, rather than writing a dictionary in a word processor, will allow you to build dictionaries of various kinds, including topical lists, reversals or finderlists, simple wordlists or a more fully featured dictionary. All of this will be derived from a single set of lexical data, and this set can also be built from the texts that you interlinearize, with each word in the texts being cross-checked against the lexical database. This is the work that can be done using software like Toolbox or Fieldworks. In the lexical database you can keep track of items associated with the headword, like images, sounds, or videos, and the link to these items can later be developed for whatever delivery mechanism you need to use. For example, you may want to have all headwords in the dictionary spoken and available as media in a web browser. To do this, you would first have prepared a list of headwords that would be read and recorded by a speaker of the language. The same list can then be time-aligned with the media which will give you a citable media reference for each word. These word-by-word references can then be sorted and joined to your lexicon, and the form of the link (e.g. an HTML hyperlink) can be made as needed, using the headword as the key that links the sound and the lexical entry in the database.

4.4 ADVANTAGES OF WELL-FORMED DATA IN ANALYSIS, PUBLICATION, AND PRESENTATION

Interaction with field recordings via their aligned transcripts allows the transcripts to improve as your understanding of the language grows. As an example, the first author's research language, South Efate, has two phonologically similar pronouns, *ga* '3SG'and *gaŋ* '2SG.POS', that need to be carefully distinguished, because in preverbal position the latter in fact acts as a benefactive. In the early versions of the South Efate transcripts, the distinction between pronouns was not always made correctly because of the difficulty of hearing the final velar nasal in *gaŋ*. As the author's knowledge of the language—and his awareness of the benefactive forms—grew, he was able to easily return to the primary recordings and look for discrepancies in the transcript. By having well-structured data, he was able to improve the transcription and confirm the analysis of benefactives in South Efate.

A well-formed corpus allows us to seek answers to linguistic questions that are difficult to ask when data is limited to what can be expressed on the printed page. Much of language structure that is embodied in phenomena like intonation, tempo, and stress, is observable only acoustically; certain aspects of spontaneous language use like disfluencies, gesture, and speaker overlap are difficult to represent on paper. Even the best transcription systems—for example, ToBI (Beckman and Hirschberg 1994), Discourse Transcription (Du Bois et al. 1992; 1993), Conversation Analysis (Schegloff 2007)—are only substitutes for direct observation. Being able to cite archived, time-aligned examples of the phenomenon you describe in your publications by their permanent handles, down to the level of the clause, word, or even segment, allows others to confirm, challenge, and build on your claims. Well-formed data is a powerful tool for research and publication, allowing linguistics as a discipline to participate in the practice of open data that has long been an ethos of scientific inquiry.[36]

The possibilities for multimedia presentation of language material are enticing, and linguists have long recognized the value of dynamic media in capturing and representing the dynamism of language. When multimedia software was first developed sufficiently, a number of projects like CD-based talking dictionaries immediately took advantage of the ability to link text to audio or video as a pedagogical and presentational tool. Unfortunately, many of these early projects had very limited lives. As the software they were built in aged, they became unplayable. Even worse, in some cases, producing the multimedia CDs was the primary goal of the language project, so the data has become effectively lost.

A better objective is to build well-formed, archival data from fieldwork, and then to derive delivery forms of the media from that base. These delivery forms can be on-line or local or paper-based, but they all benefit from being derived from well-structured underlying data. Time-aligned transcripts, with their links to specific points in their associated media, will allow you to install an iTunes jukebox in a local school (see also Barwick §7.3.4.1 below), or develop a simple Flash presentation online or on CD. Well-structured lexical databases will allow you to deliver targeted topical dictionaries on paper or over the web.

4.5 CONCLUSION

An often-voiced objection to the types of processes described in this chapter is that they take too much time. It is true that time-aligned transcriptions and interlinearized texts take some effort to construct, but we can liken it to building a house that has strong foundations. Once the initial effort has been made, the resulting house is able

---

[36] http://en.wikipedia.org/wiki/Open_science_data

to withstand the elements and the passage of time, unlike a shack that is blown over by the first storm. Similarly, a well-constructed set of data will provide ongoing access, allowing you to ask new questions of it and to keep interacting with the primary material for a deeper analysis of the language. There is a great return on this initial investment of effort in creating an accessible and reusable corpus, especially if you will continue working with the same data over a long period of time. Furthermore, there is an ethical responsibility to prepare the data that we have recorded so that it can be located, accessed, and reused by those recorded or their descendants.

It is indisputable that there is more to research on a previously undescribed language than just the recorded data. The headnotes, the associated memories, and contextualization of the research that remain in the head of the researcher continue to inform their analysis. Similarly, the body of material recorded can only ever be a partial glimpse of a language that will continue to change over time. Nevertheless, the records we create will be invaluable for many purposes, and many more than we have planned for in our own research.

Creating good archival data can allow various derived forms that can be improved over time relatively easily. Rather than having to labour over formatting complex documents by hand, automatic processes can be applied to generate diverse outputs periodically as the underlying data is improved or as the analysis develops.

Finally, while the technologies we use will change, the underlying principles described in this chapter should provide some guidance in choosing new tools and methods from those that will appear in future. There is no question that linguistic fieldwork practice needs to change, and that future language descriptions will have to include recorded examples, cited in the analysis, with an underlying corpus that is archived and described in the course of the analysis. By adopting the methods described in this chapter, linguists will be building more detailed and accessible records of the world's languages.

4.6 Sources of further advice

New technologies and methods associated with them are becoming available all the time. To keep up with options for tools or methods to use in your fieldwork, you should subscribe to appropriate mailing lists such as the Resource Network for Linguistic Diversity[37] or read blogs such as Endangered Languages and Cultures.[38]

---

[37] http://www.rnld.org   [38] http://paradisec.org.au/blog

The SOAS Online Resources for Endangered Languages[39] (OREL) links to many useful sites. Another key source of information is the EMELD[40] site. There are also mailing lists specific to each of the tools discussed in this chapter, and this is likely to be the case for any new tools that appear in future. Useful references on topics around fieldwork and data management include Chelliah and de Reuse (2010: 197–225), Austin (2006), and Bowern (2008: especially ch. 4 on data management and archiving, and ch. 13 on working with existing and historical field materials which covers issues not dealt with in this chapter).

---

[39] http://www.hrelp.org/languages/resources/orel/tech.html   [40] http://emeld.org

PART II

RECORDING
PERFORMANCE

CHAPTER 5

SOCIOLINGUISTIC FIELDWORK

MIRIAM MEYERHOFF

CHIE ADACHI

GOLNAZ NANBAKHSH

ANNA STRYCHARZ

5.1 INTRODUCTION

It is challenging to provide an account of methods associated with sociolinguistic fieldwork, as the field of sociolinguistics is extremely heterogeneous. Researchers who identify as sociolinguists may be asking questions about the relationship between language and power (e.g. 'What kinds of honorific forms does this group of speakers use when addressing or referring to some other group of speakers?'—cf. Okamoto 1997). They may equally be interested in the functions of and structural constraints on switches between different languages or dialects in a polylectal speech community ('What does the switch from stylized Asian English to local vernacular forms signify in the speech of British teenagers?'—cf. Rampton 2005). Or they may be concerned with identifying and accounting for the distribution of the different variants that realize a linguistic variable in a speech community ('In what linguistic contexts do speakers reduce the final consonant in words like [wɛst] and [dɹægd]? Do all groups of speakers reduce the cluster equally often?'—Guy 1980).

The latter approach is associated with the work of William Labov (1972a; 1972b; 2001), and generally uses quantitative methods at some point in the analysis. It is often referred to as 'quantitative' or 'variationist sociolinguistics', and for many people this study of synchronic variation in a speech community as a window on the diachronic processes of language change epitomizes the field. The tendency for 'variationist' to describe the methods of data collection and analysis associated with Labovian social dialect work is perhaps unfortunate: arguably, at some level all the sociolinguistic research questions outlined above are concerned with variation in how people use language to social and interpersonal effect.

Sociolinguists have always been heavily influenced by anthropology, not least in their methods, and this means that a lot of sociolinguistic research reports qualitative results, in addition to the quantitative results of the Labovian social dialect survey. Researchers adopting this synthetic approach (e.g. Eckert 2000; Sankoff and Blondeau 2007; Mendoza-Denton 2008) argue that it enhances the explanatory power of their accounts of variation. In this chapter we will review two of the dominant approaches in sociolinguistic fieldwork: the sociolinguistic interview and participant observation. This dichotomy is an idealization, but it is a useful heuristic around which to structure the chapter.

Since many of the methodological issues that sociolinguists have to deal with in their fieldwork overlap with those of any other linguist, we will not review all technical and procedural aspects of sociolinguistic fieldwork (see instead the chapters by Rice (18), Thieberger and Berez (4), and Margetts and Margetts (1) in this volume).

5.2 KEY CONCEPTS

We have already implicitly defined sociolinguistics as a field of research concerned with the study of how language is used in social interactions and in different social contexts. The motivation for focusing on language in its varied contexts of use lies in the conviction that there are limits to what can be elicited through direct questioning of speakers about what they believe is 'good' or 'casual' language, or about their awareness of when one linguistic code is preferred over another. Crucially, at the point of variation that is below the level of conscious awareness or below the level of social stereotyping, speakers' intuitions fail to capture the entirety of their competence. Example 1 illustrates this: Nanbakhsh's direct question about the use of the 2nd person pronouns *to* (intimate) and *šoma* (deferential) elicits the conventional [±respect] meaning of the pronouns, and some insights in how *šoma* functions within an individual's larger habitus (Bourdieu 1990). But in none of her direct questioning did any of the Persian speakers show any awareness of an unconventional but widely used strategy that combines the deferential *šoma* with the subject–verb agreement marking associated with the intimate 2nd person singular pronoun *to* (Nanbakhsh 2010).

(1) Direct questioning about deference norms and the use of plural pronouns in Teheran Persian (Nanbakhsh 2010)[1]

Yasmina: female, 22-year-old university student

Golnaz:

be	*næzære*	*šoma*	*forme*	*khætabiye jam*		*mafhume ehteram*	
prep	opinion	2PL	form	address	PL	meaning respect	
ra	*mi-resun-æd?*						
OM	DUR-send-3SG						

'In your opinion does the plural address form convey respect?'

Yasmina:

Na,	*ehteram*	*fægæt*	*ke*	*be*	*formez*	*khætabi*	
no	respect	only	emphatic	prep	form	address	
nist	*be*	*næhveye*	*bærkhord*	*æst,*	*momkene*	*šoma*	*khatabešun*
be.NEG	prep	manner	behave	is	possible	2PL	address.2PL
konim	*vali*	*ræftare*	*zænændeyi daste*		*bašim*	*ya*	*bæræx.*
do.1PL	but	manner	repulsive have		be.3PL	or	contrary

'No, respect is not only indexed with the forms of address per se but may also be constrained with the stance the individual takes in the use of that form in the interaction. We may address someone with the deferential address pronoun (*šoma*) while being repulsive or rude to them or vice versa, (i.e. respect may also be shown with the use of the informal address pronoun (*to*) but with a polite manner).'

In addition, sociolinguists have repeatedly established that speakers use very different forms when they provide citation forms of speech than they do when speaking casually in conversation (discussed further below). So eliciting individual sentences or asking people to read aloud or to introspect on their linguistic practices all provide a lopsided picture of how language is actually used.

As a consequence, an important goal in sociolinguistics is to obtain 'natural speech', that is, how people use language in ordinary, everyday interactions with all the variability that this entails, since the full range of variability is missed by other methods.[2] However, the notion of naturalness is relative: sociolinguists are always subject to the 'observer's paradox' (Labov 1972a)—the inescapable fact that speakers are more aware of what they are saying and how they are talking as soon as you begin recording them (Meyerhoff 2006: 38 points out the analogy with

---

[1] The list of abbreviations appears in §5.8 at the end of the chapter.

[2] This is not at odds with Goffman's (1959) contention that all social acts are in some sense staged. It means the sociolinguist is most interested in those stagings that are representations of an unmonitored or informal persona.

Heisenberg's uncertainty principle). In this respect, if maximally natural speech is how people talk when no recording is taking place, then this is impossible to capture ethically. Different methods for mitigating the effects of the observer's paradox in sociolinguistic fieldwork are discussed shortly.

It is, of course, necessary to constrain the scope of any study of language in use. In the variationist tradition, this is referred to as the sociolinguistic variable and generally denotes some unit of linguistic structure that is realized by two or more semantically equivalent variants—e.g. the variable (t, d) is realized as a final apical stop in the consonant cluster or is absent in [wɛst] and [dɹægd], above. By convention, variationists use parentheses to refer to the abstract linguistic variable—in this case, they would represent the alternation between either [t] or [d] in a coda cluster and the absence of an apical stop as (t, d).

Variables can also occur at the level of morphosyntax, for example the alternation between the presence or absence of BE in copula and auxiliary positions (cf. Meyerhoff and Walker 2007). Because of the requirement for semantic equivalence, it is more problematic to adapt this paradigm to the study of lexical alternates, e.g. *better* and *improved* may be functionally and referentially equivalent or they may not (such variation is perhaps better studied through genre or corpus-based methods). As noted above, it is possible to conceptualize the alternation between different codes as a similar kind of variation, but because it is impossible to define all and only the places where a code-switch can occur (as we can with a final consonant cluster, or the verb BE), this kind of sociolinguistic fieldwork is not associated with the terms and methods of variationist social dialectology.

What distinguishes sociolinguistic and anthropological linguistic fieldwork from other linguistic research is the search for socially meaningful units that co-occur with specific linguistic forms, routines, or practices. In other words, in addition to the dependent linguistic variable, sociolinguists are concerned with the study of independent social variables which may be more or less powerful constraints on the distribution of the linguistic variation they are studying.

Here is the first place where the traditions of participant observation in anthropology and ethnomethodology may articulate with the social science methods of variationist studies. Although many sociolinguistic studies examine the effect of a relatively small set of social variables on the linguistic features of interest—principally gender, age, social class, and ethnicity—these were never intended to be programmatic. Good sociolinguistic fieldwork deals with independent social variables that emerge through participant observation of socially cohesive subsets of speakers (Briggs 1986; Cameron et al. 1992 argue for the importance and feasibility of sociolinguistic fieldwork *with*, not just *on*, groups of speakers). Sometimes these social groups only emerge as socially meaningful in the course of the research; sometimes they can be recognized as socially meaningful quite quickly even by an outsider. Sociolinguistic terminology differentiates between meaningful social groups of different sizes and constitutions. The meaningfulness of some groups is identifiable through shared practices ('communities of practice': Eckert and Mcconnell-Ginet 1992), shared patterns of association ('social networks': Dubois and Horvath 1999; Milroy and Gordon 2003) or shared abstract patterns of variation ('speech communities': Labov 1972a).

Researchers define speech communities in different ways, some of which focus more on internal, subjective perceptions of commonality and some of which focus more on objectively (and externally) observed patterns of commonality (cf. Labov 1972a; Corder 1973; Duranti 1997). We will use 'speech community' as a very general cover term:

A 'speech community' is any socially meaningful grouping of speakers whose direct and indirect interactions with each other contribute to the maintenance, establishment or contestation of a social order recognizable to the speakers or the researcher.

This definition is useful because it identifies some important issues for sociolinguistic fieldwork. These include:

- Contact between speakers may be direct or indirect (i.e. we need not restrict ourselves to only people who are aware of co-membership).
- Interactions may have very different linguistic outcomes (i.e. we are not concerned with debates over whether community is constituted through consensus or competition)—these differences in outcome are the object of sociolinguistic study (i.e. sociolinguistics attempts not only to document and describe variation in language use, but to relate patterns of language to social dynamics such as the exercise of power or what it means for something to be 'innovative' or 'conservative').
- Language use can be related in an orderly and systematic manner to features of the social setting that the speakers orient to (i.e. the formal linguist's notion of 'free variation' ignores linguistic or social systematicity in the variable use of different linguistic forms).

The focus on patterns of language use often leads sociolinguists to collect their own data, and in the following sections we will discuss in more detail some of the methods used. But it is important to realize that some sociolinguistic questions can be asked and answered using freely available sources of data. The media provides an excellent source of language in use, without the access issues (see below) that sometimes go along with collecting discourse from private domains. The internet has increased enormously sociolinguists' potential datasets in the last decades. Generally, a minimal amount of social information is required about a speaker to enable sociolinguists to explore social correlates of variation (e.g. sex, approximate age, and general social class/occupation). This may not always be available for data on the internet (or other forms of media). However, if research questions don't require too much knowledge about who is producing the data and under what circumstances, the internet can be a useful tool for exploring some basic descriptive questions about language variation and language use (e.g. Herring 1996; Androutsopoulos 2006). Even some questions about social groups and variation can be explored by targeting subject-specific blogs or user groups. YouTube has recently increased greatly the accessibility of lesser-known languages for armchair sociolinguistic fieldwork (Wrobel forthcoming).

Having outlined some of the key concepts underlying work in sociolinguistics, we turn to more practical matters. In the next section, we look at practical issues associated with getting started. We then discuss the structure of the classic sociolinguistic interview and explain how the observer's paradox can be addressed within this kind of fieldwork methodology. We then discuss the use of group recordings as another means for addressing the observer's paradox, and finally, we discuss methods for enriching sociolinguistic fieldwork that borrow more from the anthropological tradition of participant observation.

5.3 SETTING THE STAGE AND GETTING STARTED

5.3.1 Establishing an ethical framework for your research

Like a physician, first, do no harm (as also noted by Rice in Chapter 18 below). For sociolinguists, this means framing research in an ethos of respect and a recognition of the debt owed to the speakers who invite us into their lives long enough to study language in use. Rickford (1997), Wolfram (1998), and Cameron et al. (1992) all focus on what linguists can and should give back to the community they are working with. Wolfram's 'principle of linguistic gratuity' (1998: 273) and Cameron et al.'s argument that good research will actively include the interests of the community both emphasize the moral obligation sociolinguists have to ensure that research engages with and involves the people whose language we are studying. Moreover, as the debates surrounding Ebonics in the United States demonstrated, sociolinguists should be aware of the manner in which their research feeds into public discourses about the language varieties being investigated (Rickford and Rickford 2000; Baugh 2000).

Professional associations such as the British Association for Applied Linguistics (BAAL)[3] and the American Anthropological Association (AAA)[4] offer extended

---

[3] http://www.baal.org.uk/about_goodpractice.htm

[4] http://www.aaanet.org/stmts/ethstmnt.htm, see also more extensive resources at http://www.aaanet.org/committees/ethics/ethics.htm

guidelines for ethical research, and all sociolinguists should be conversant with at least one such set of guidelines (see Rice's Chapter 18 below). This is not only imperative for the conduct of their own research; it can be strategically important too. Such guidelines often provide advice for longer-term research relationships and those where the subjects and the researcher know each other well. They may be more appropriate for sociolinguists than research guidelines set down by medical or psychological associations, which are designed with experimental research in mind. There is a lot of variability in how institutional research review boards (IRBs) or human research ethics boards operate: it may be useful to be able to situate sociolinguistic work within its appropriate academic tradition when applying for research permission.

For example, written consent forms (a common feature of IRBs) may be a good way of ensuring that participants are aware of the general purpose of the research and are reassured that the data will be used solely for research (see Johnstone 2000; see also Newman, Chapter 19 below). But in some cases, personal introductions and verbal guarantees may be more appropriate (e.g. Gafaranga 2007). Paradoxically, the conventional IRB insistence on signed consent forms may clash with speakers' desire for anonymity. This was true for Nanbakhsh's (2010) work in Teheran. People only felt at liberty to talk freely about social change since the 1979 Revolution if they had personal trust in her ability to guard their privacy. Moreover, in this case signed consent is what puts the consultants in danger by creating a paper trail that leads directly back to them if the researcher's materials are confiscated.

The primary purpose of getting consent (whether written or verbal) is to ensure that participants: (i) are aware of the general purpose of the research; (ii) are reassured that the data will not be used for any other purpose but research; and (iii) know they can withdraw their consent at any time if they wish.

5.3.2 Making contacts: planning an overall approach

A number of introductory texts in sociolinguistics outline methods by which researchers have successfully made contacts and been able to begin research within a community (see Milroy and Gordon 2003; Tagliamonte 2006 for social dialect research; Johnstone 2000 for qualitative research; Schleef and Meyerhoff 2010 outline many basic questions for smaller, e.g. student term paper, projects). Tagliamonte (2006) takes a rather extreme methodological position, urging the use of only community 'insiders' for making contacts and for doing the interviews, as she argues this elicits the most vernacular forms of speech.

In general, a flexible and pragmatic approach works best. If, for example, you are interested in how younger speakers use language, you will find your target participants in the institutional context of a school. Indeed, a lot of sociolinguistic research has examined teenagers by first making contacts in schools (e.g. Heath 1983; Eckert 2000; Kerswill and Williams 2000; Mendoza-Denton 2008; though Cheshire 1982 actively sought out teenagers who were *not* going to school) or through after-school clubs/activity classes. However, if the research question is more concerned with how age and gender interact, and how they affect use of language across the lifespan, a broader spectrum of the speech community (e.g. families) where there is a mixed range of age and gender will need to be recorded (Sankoff 2004; Blondeau 2001).

A common first step is to contact people that you know, such as your family and friends, or people you work with who have ties to the community you want to study (cf. Tagliamonte 2006: 20–35). If your initial contacts introduce you to other people, you have the start of a snowball sample (sometimes called 'friend of a friend' networking). Milroy (1980) and Milroy and Gordon (2003) discuss this method in more detail. Labov's work (1972b) with members of street gangs represents the earliest systematic study of language variation through social networks. In this approach it is best to prepare brief questionnaires (whether administered verbally or in writing) for personal information. This is a useful way of categorizing and finding out more about participants whom you have little or no acquaintance with.

Familiarity between the researcher and the participants also has an impact on the patterns of language use that the study will record. Cukor-Avila and Bailey (2001) explore the effect of a familiar interviewer on how people talk, noting that speakers use more vernacular features in conversations recorded with someone they are familiar with, and that general familiarity of the interlocutors seems to have more of an effect on the likelihood that non-standard or vernacular features will be elicited than shared ethnicity alone does (cf. Rickford and McNair-Knox 1994).

5.3.3 Beyond 'friend of a friend'

Aside from being introduced to someone via a friend (or a friend of a friend), it is possible to gain entry to a community through organized groups such as societies, clubs, and churches. You can distribute an email to the club's email list (e.g. 'Participation in research required') or ask for volunteers through community bulletin boards but, in our experience, this produces a very low response rate unless you are already an active member of the club or community group. It helps to think creatively and brainstorm with friends, drawing on their ideas and networks, if your target community seems hard to crack into.

5.3.4 Some comments about sociolinguistic fieldwork in institutional settings

If your aim is to collect data from institutional contexts such as schools and service encounters, you may need to undergo thorough checks of your probity and trustworthiness. These can take a long time (maybe months), so your fieldwork plans need to reflect this. Regulations governing access to institutions like schools or other groups that may be deemed 'at risk' (as the phrase goes in the UK) will vary depending on where you are, so you must seek advice locally. Because gaining access to institutional settings can be slow or problematic, it is advisable to have backup plans in case permission is not granted.

If you need the approval of a ministry or governmental organization prior to conducting your research, it is wise to inquire how other researchers have dealt with such issues. Contact with local universities and/or research institutes before fieldwork starts and good relations with these groups once fieldwork is under way can be helpful too. In addition to familiarizing you with ongoing research and establishing valuable communication channels which can secure ongoing progress in the field, it can help shape a social position for the sociolinguist within the local norms of research culture.

5.3.5 Cultural constraints on making contacts

Feagin (2004) discusses some of the problems that arise when the fieldworker is a foreigner, of different ethnicity, or not a native speaker of the language; these factors can have an effect on how likely people will be to make time for an interview, how they will construct or understand the fieldwork relationship (Briggs 1986), and how much a researcher can infer from patterns of language use that they observe.

On the other hand, doing fieldwork as an outsider can be an advantage. Hazen's (2000) fieldwork in a small town in North Carolina was facilitated in several ways by his liminal status. Because he had married into the community, he had family networks he could tap into, but as an outsider he was not as well acquainted with the speech community as his in-laws, and this also allowed him to assume the role of a 'student', asking questions that only an outsider could ask. Sociolinguistic fieldwork requires the researcher to accept some form of social role, and very often hybrid or new identities enable successful study of language use (Hazen 2000).

As noted above, a sociolinguist's preparation for going into the field (like any other linguist's) requires research into the community and the larger social and cultural context in which fieldwork will take place. In some places, rather conservative ideologies about the role of research and researchers can represent a further obstacle to undertaking sociolinguistic fieldwork. Haeri (1994; 2003) discusses some of the challenges of positioning yourself as a researcher in this sort of cultural context, and reviews some of the techniques by which she overcame outsider status (and some inflexible limits on who she could do fieldwork with) in Egypt.

5.4 THE SOCIOLINGUISTIC INTERVIEW AND ADDRESSING THE OBSERVER'S PARADOX

5.4.1 What is a sociolinguistic interview?

One of the most common ways of gathering natural spoken data is the so-called 'sociolinguistic interview'. This method was developed and later modified by William Labov in his Martha's Vineyard and New York studies (1972a), and has since been used in various forms, by a number of researchers.

The classic sociolinguistic interview consists of four parts: (i) reading a list of minimal pairs, (ii) reading a list of words in isolation, (iii) reading a short narrative, and (iv) talking with the interviewer.

The first three parts are not what we would consider natural or casual speech—the purpose of the various reading tasks is to elicit a wide range of speech styles (defining 'style' is the subject of an entire sub-field in sociolinguistics: see Coupland 2007; Jaffe 2009; Meyerhoff 2006). When combined with free conversation, these tasks are treated as forming a continuum in terms of the amount of attention speakers are paying to their speech. This in turn provides one source of indirect evidence about the social meaning of different patterns and preferences.

Different types of speech can also be found in the conversational part of the interview. 'Careful' and 'casual' speech are typically characterized by changes in topic (e.g. talk about childhood memories tends to be more 'casual' than 'careful'), and addressee (addressing a third person, e.g. a child or another family member, is more 'casual', while addressing the interviewer is more 'careful'). Labov (2001) explores the impact of different topics within the interview in more detail. Thus, a sociolinguistic interview structured with some or all of these different activities elicits a continuum of styles for every speaker.

5.4.2 How many speakers is 'enough'?

Usually sociolinguists who intend to do quantitative analyses of variation try to collect corpora that sample (relatively) evenly across the most relevant social categories in the community where they are working. It's hard to give one answer to 'How many speakers is enough?' because it depends on two things: what linguistic features you are interested in investigating, and what kinds of generalizations you hope to be able to make in the end.

For example, some phonetic features occur very frequently, and you can obtain a lot of data that is linguistically quite rich in even a relatively small sample of speakers. If the researcher's primary interest is to be able to make generalizations about linguistic structure, a small sample will probably suffice. Conversely, some syntactic variables occur rarely, and hardly at all in interview contexts. For instance, interviewees seldom question an interviewer, so a study of spontaneous interrogatives is unlikely to be well served by recordings of one-on-one sociolinguistic interviews. Recording multi-party conversations among friends and family members is likely to be a more useful source of data. Another strategy for ensuring that plenty of tokens of a low-frequency linguistic feature are collected is to record a large number of speakers for as long as possible. It is common for sociolinguists to repeatedly record the same people (repeat interviewing or recording is another means for reducing the observer's paradox, since speakers tend to be more relaxed in later encounters with recording equipment).

If you want to be able to generalize about the trends or preferences among groups of speakers, it is useful to have five or six speakers that fit into each of your target social categories. So if your primary interest is whether or not there is a change taking place in the speech community, a sample of speakers stratified by age is needed. Typically, sociolinguistic fieldwork will involve recording five or six younger, five or six middle-aged, and five or six older speakers. However, if the primary interest of the project is level of education (perhaps it is hypothesized that certain variants are used as markers of prestige or authority), the research might involve recording five or six speakers with primary education (or less), the same number with secondary education, and the same again with some post-secondary.

Of course, if the research questions hypothesize that there is an interaction between age and level of education, then the number of people that have to be recorded increases factorially. For example, to ask the question 'Do people with more education in today's community (i.e. younger speakers) talk like people with less education in the past (i.e. older speakers)?' requires a structured sample of five or six speakers in each of subgroup representing those intersections, i.e. six younger primary educated; six middle-aged primary educated; six older primary educated, etc. If gender is added into the picture (e.g. 'Do younger men with more education in today's community talk like men with less education in the past?'), then the sample size needs to be even larger, e.g. $2 \times 3 \times 2$ (education, age, gender).

5.4.3 Overcoming the 'observer's paradox'

The observer's paradox is triggered in an interview situation by: (i) the presence of someone in the role of fieldworker, (ii) the presence of the recording device, and (iii) the task itself. For these reasons, sociolinguistic fieldwork uses several methods for mitigating the effects of the observer's paradox in an interview. These include modifying the number of people in an interview, the kinds of topics discussed, and the activity.

Fieldwork frequently attempts to avoid the formality of a one-to-one interview by increasing the number of interviewees. In fieldwork in Osaka, Strycharz (2011) usually invited more than one person to participate in a conversation. This meant there was more interaction between participants themselves rather than between the interviewer and the participants, and hence more casual speech. This was perhaps particularly important since Strycharz is an obvious outsider to the community, and (though fluent) is a non-native speaker of Japanese. Since Strycharz (2011) explores how and when Osaka speakers use Standard Japanese vs. Osaka Japanese honorifics, it was extremely important to elicit casual, ingroup conversation (there is a strong expectation that speakers will use Standard Japanese in formal and outgroup contexts).

(2) More casual speech elicited in answer to an interview question in a multiparty conversation

A = Anna (interviewer, outsider); M = Mayuko, S = Shun. Both girls are co-workers in a kindergarten, talking about another co-worker, who clearly is known for saying one thing and doing another. Note switch from Standard Japanese *da* when replying to Anna, to local Osaka Japanese *ya* when talking to each other.

A:	*Y-sensei*	*wa*	*donna*	*hito?*					
	Y-teacher	NOM.	what kind	person					
M:	*Kekko*	*ii*	*sensei*	*da*	*to*	*omou.*	*Ashita*		*mo*
	Fairly	good	teacher	SJ.COP	that	think	Tomorrow		too
	kuru	*tte*	*yutteta=*						
	come	QUOT	say.PROGR.PAST						
S:	*=Konai*		*to*		*omou*	*yo*			
	Come.NEG		that		think	SFP			
M:	*Eee nande?*		*Kuru*		*tte*	*iihatta*		*no ni=*	
	why		Come		QUOT	say.OJ.RH.PAST		even though	
S:	*=ma*		*iihattan*		*ya*	*kedo=*			
	well		say.OJ.RH.PAST		OJ.COP	but			
M:	*=ma*	*sou*	*ya*	*na*	*iu*	*koto*	*to*	*suru*	*koto*	*to*	*hahaha*
	well	so	OJ.COP	OJ.SFP	say	thing	and	do	thing	and	(laugh)
S:	*so*	*ya*	*na* ...						
	so	OJ.COP	OJ.SFP						
A:	What kind of person is Mrs. Y?								

M: I think she's quite a good teacher. She is coming tomorrow as well=
S: =I don't think she'll come
M: why? She said she'd come=
S: =well, she said but=
M: =well, yeah, the things she says and the things she does hahaha
S: that's right . . .

In Example 2, evidence that conversation with a friend rather than an interviewer produces more casual norms can be seen in Mayuko's switch from Standard Japanese *da* (when replying to Anna) to the local Osaka Japanese *ya* (when talking to Shun, and Shun's reciprocal use of *ya*). Other cues that the young women are more relaxed in their conversation include the latching between Shun and Mayuko's turns, their rapid setup of shared knowledge (e.g. Shun 'Well, she said, but' Mayuko 'Well, yeah, the things she says and the things she does'), and the fact that Mayuko doesn't need to finish the proposition opened by 'the things she says and the things she does' for Shun to agree with her. These are all cues of a close and casual relationship (cf. Wenger's 1998 cues for identifying co-membership in a community of practice).

Another strategy for addressing the observer's paradox in interviews is to increase the number of interviewers. This may seem counterintuitive, but Wolfram (1998) reports that the dynamics of a recording session can be changed in a very natural way by having two interviewers—for example, it reframes the event as two friends or a couple having a conversation not an interview. Wolfram suggests that the presence of two interviewers also allows the conversation to naturally develop with a wider range of ideas and topics.

A third strategy involves removing the interviewer altogether. This has the benefit of minimizing the effect of outsider presence, but it also means we have no control over the recording. In research on adolescent speech in Glasgow, Macaulay (2002) recorded pairs of same-sex adolescents without an interviewer present. This seems like a good cross between the sociolinguistic interview and a natural conversation—the setting was quiet and the conversations were somewhat structured, so a lot of data could be gathered quickly from a range of speakers. At the same time, leaving the teenagers to talk on their own produced more relaxed conversations than a classic interview might have (perhaps especially an interview with an older academic). Fieldwork that is based on group recordings where the sociolinguist is more or less removed from the flow of conversation has its own methodological issues, which we discuss in more detail shortly.

5.4.4 Questions: what to ask, how to ask?

The questions we ask are, of course, a crucial part in conducting a good sociolinguistic interview. Since the interview should resemble as much as possible a natural conversation, the interviewer has to keep in mind that he or she is not only a fieldworker and a researcher, but also a speaker and a hearer in a conversation. Tagliamonte (2006: 39) suggests three tricks that will improve an interview: (i) volunteer your own experiences, (ii) react and respond when new issues arise, and (iii) follow the conversation wherever your interviewee wishes to take you. Since this is what we normally do when having a conversation over coffee, these are skills that most people already have in some measure.

The questions we ask are an important factor in establishing the interaction as casual, but they are also key to getting the interviewees talking. There are some questions that are likely to be suitable for most people in any community (family, childhood, dreams, etc.), but there are other questions whose appropriateness will depend greatly on where and whom you are interviewing.

Some topics have proved to be better for eliciting more natural speech. These include topics where speakers can get emotionally involved, for example when talking about their childhood or life history, and this topic has the added advantage of eliciting information about a speaker's biography which may be very useful for adding a qualitative interpretive component to any subsequent analysis. Storytelling recalling personal experiences has also proven to be a great way of eliciting casual speech.

One question that is by now famous in its own right is the 'danger of death' question: 'Have you ever been in a situation where you nearly lost your life? When you thought this is *it*?' Answers to this question usually require some emotional engagement, and it may trigger stories with an abundance of vernacular features (Labov 1972a; 1984). However, it does not necessarily work in all speech communities and for all individuals. Milroy and Gordon (2003) review a couple of studies where the 'danger of death' question seemed unsuitable for various reasons. In a North Carolina study (Butters 2000), the question was often commented on as being 'too scary', and some interviewees refused to answer it, while in Milroy and Milroy's (1978) study in Belfast during the Troubles, the question was treated with minimal emotional involvement, and usually answered in a dry, matter-of-fact way. One of the speakers who contributed to the Bequia corpus (Meyerhoff and Walker 2007) started to cry after answering this question, a telling reminder that good interviewers need to have a wide range of social skills (including knowing how and when to conclude an interview).

In addition, what makes a successful interview topic may be very particular to the community being investigated. The most emotional (and also fun) stretches of speech in Strycharz's (2011) Osaka fieldwork were provoked by questions about the differences between Osaka and Tokyo. Due to the long-standing rivalry between the two cities, people in Osaka for the most part are not very fond of Tokyo, and they are willing to talk about the numerous differences between the two cities and their inhabitants, recollecting funny encounters and misunderstandings between them and Tokyoites.

The precise topics of a sociolinguistic interview will therefore be flexible; its main goal is to uncover areas of interest which speakers feel comfortable talking about. So a good approach is to be observant and act as we normally do in conversations with people we don't know well (or indeed don't know at all). Having some kind of structure prepared is important, but it is perhaps even more important to be flexible and willing to change the plan.

5.4.5 Setting and roles

One of the issues arising from gathering data by means of an interview is precisely that—the fact that we are 'conducting an interview'. For instance, in a classic interview, it is rare to elicit questions *from* the interviewee—that's simply not part of the interviewee role. The interviewer might therefore have to come up with a way to counterbalance the dynamic that may be automatically introduced when we set up an interview.

One good way to counterbalance this is to put oneself in the position of a learner (as in Hazen 2000; see also Labov 1984, and Briggs 1986, who discusses the fact that interviewees may perceive the interaction as one of apprentice/expert). Paying attention to the information obtained feeds into the next question, and being genuinely interested in the interviewee helps to build a less distant relationship than might otherwise be associated with interviewer/interviewee.

5.4.6 Disclosure in fieldwork

Problematizing the role of the researcher in sociolinguistic fieldwork raises questions about how much people should be told about the purposes and goals of the research. Schilling-Estes (2007) argues that researchers do not have to explain in detail what they are studying and why they are studying it. There are at least two reasons for this. First, unless you think you can explain linguistics and sociolinguistics in a wholly non-technical and inclusive way, explanations about vowel raising, object deletion, or the social construction of identity through code-switching may not be terribly informative to the people you are working with, and might be best saved for other audiences (see Barnes 1980 and Besnier 2009 on the problematic notion of 'informed consent').

Second, detailed explanation at the outset of a project about what sociolinguistic features are the target of investigation may bias speakers' performance (consciously or unconsciously). For instance, suppose you are interested in the speech act of complimenting, and you tell people you want to observe as many compliments as possible. They might consciously try to produce as many compliments as possible to assist your research or, conversely, they might try to avoid using them because they are self-conscious. Any compliments generated under those circumstances may offer interesting insights into who stereotypically makes compliments, and about what, but they won't necessarily offer more subtle insights into how compliments oil the social wheels of daily interaction that less monitored tokens of compliments might offer. Likewise, if you are interested in the alternation between local dialect forms of Japanese honorifics and the Standard Japanese forms, telling people this may heighten speakers' awareness of the contrast, pushing them to use more forms of one or the other than they might ordinarily use.

5.4.7 Practicalities of an interview: how long, how much, how many?

Opinions vary when it comes to deciding how long the interview should be. Labov (1984) suggests that it should last from one to two hours, but again it will depend on the research question. Most pronunciation features (e.g. whether people say *dat* or *that*) are far more frequent than grammatical features (e.g. relative clauses and negation), or discourse routines (e.g. compliments and topicalization). If you're interested in syntactic and discourse features (and even some phonological features are comparatively rare—Schleef and Meyerhoff 2010), even a two-hour recording might not provide a lot of data. Milroy and Gordon (2003: 63) suggest that 'certain speech phenomena may be difficult or even impossible to study using interviews'. For example, some of the phenomena sociolinguists are interested in (e.g. style-shifting and code-switching) emerge during extended everyday social interaction or are shaped by potentially idiosyncratic relationships among the speakers.

When interviewing someone for the first time there will inevitably be a fair amount of formality; in the course of a well-conducted interview it can disappear, or at least be minimized. Some studies have documented a shift towards more frequent use of vernacular features over time (hence, differences between the end of the interview and the beginning: Douglas-Cowie 1978; Coupland 2007). How long it takes for this familiarity effect to come into play is unclear—it probably depends on the individuals, but generally it is more than a matter of minutes. Some sociolinguists prefer to conduct subsequent interviews with the same person. Extended contact and repeated recordings over a period of time create the potential for more unselfconscious talk than a one-off interview can. For this reason, many sociolinguists adopt anthropologists' longitudinal engagement with the people they are recording (e.g. Mendoza-Denton 2008, whose recordings of the same young women span years). Repeat interviews have the added benefit of more background information about the speakers, and the integration of the interviewer as a familiar guest. Cukor-Avila and Bailey's (2001) fieldwork in the same small town has been going on for decades and they demonstrate that the familiarity of the interviewer has a major effect on speakers' use of local vernacular features.

Having considered the sociolinguistic interview as a fieldwork methodology, and introduced some of the methods for addressing the observer's paradox in the interview, we turn to an alternative fieldwork model: interviews with groups of speakers.

5.5 GROUP RECORDINGS: NATURAL INTERACTION AND LANGUAGE SOCIALIZATION

As we have noted already, recording people in small group interactions is another way of addressing the observer's paradox and of obtaining more naturalistic, spontaneous speech. Group recordings may reduce some of the awkwardness associated with overt recording, as they allow the speakers to self-select topics and self-select who speaks when. Participants may also feel more relaxed with familiar faces. This method has been used since the inception of sociolinguistics—Labov et al.'s (1968) study in South Harlem involved interviewing groups of friends, and more recent sociolinguistic work influenced by the traditions of ethnography continues to use it. This is particularly true of researchers interested in the process by which social meaning is assigned to variation in highly local interactions, sometimes conceptualized in the framework of communities of practice (Wenger 1998; Eckert and McConnell-Ginet 1992; Bucholtz 1999; Mallinson and Childs 2007).

Indeed, some research questions can *only* be answered by recording self-selecting groups of speakers that reflect everyday patterns of interaction. For example, language socialization (how children acquire the norms of their speech community in context) is best studied by observing multiple, familiar interactants—something that is not really feasible to study through interviews. Schieffelin (1990) and Ochs (1992) (cf. Schieffelin and Ochs 1986; Ochs and Taylor 1995) have led this research field for some time—Schieffelin's (1990) work on the linguistic socialization of Kaluli children (in Papua New Guinea) has been especially influential (cf. Makihara 2005; Garrett 2005; Riley 2007). This approach to sociolinguistic fieldwork documents how children learn to use language and acquire socially loaded linguistic routines (this methodological approach is shared by ethnomethodologists and many sociologists, e.g. Goffman 1971; Drew and Heritage 1992). In Kaluli society, for example, use of the phrase ɛlɛma ('say like this') is an important routine in socializing children, but these corrections of a child's prior formulation are most likely to occur in everyday speech. Socialization is clearly a process that takes place over a considerable period of time (perhaps throughout the lifespan), so sociolinguistic work of this nature involves not only group recordings but extended periods in the field.

Another area of (socio)linguistic interest that rewards study of a range of naturally occurring speech events in the speech community is the effects of language contact. It is certainly possible to document instances of code-switching and individual features that suggest contact-induced change in the semi-formal speech of interviews (either sociolinguistic interviews or radio), but arguably the study of variation provides a more subtle picture of how contact effects take hold among speakers and how they diffuse through a language and a community. That is, by studying recordings of people's everyday chat, we can document how switches from e.g. Rapanui to Spanish and vice versa have interpersonal and social functions—constructing speakers as competent members of the community, or softening teasing between interlocutors (Makihara 2004; cf. Blom and Gumperz 1972).

Furthermore, there is a growing body of evidence documenting how language contact may have an impact on the realization of sociolinguistic variables across languages or varieties. For example, Buchstaller and D'Arcy (2009) explore the similarity and differences in constraints on the use of quotative *be like* in different varieties of English. Meyerhoff (2009) evaluates arguments for and against the transfer of variation from substrate languages into the creole Bislama. A number of articles in Meyerhoff and Nagy (2008) test hypotheses of contact-induced change in individual speakers' performance or in a speech community as a whole by comparing the details of variation in input varieties and output varieties (Blondeau and Nagy 2008).

This work documents the manner in which induced change diffuses through a linguistic system and through a speech community, thereby addressing questions of linguistic and sociolinguistic importance. It is simply not possible to elicit this kind of detail through direct question and answer routines (typical of traditional fieldwork), partly because the patterns involve differences in probabilities across different word classes, phonological contexts or social situations that they only emerge in a large corpus of everyday speech.

A final reason for favouring extended recordings in everyday interaction is that it can be difficult (if not impossible) to interpret the interactional meaning of some speech events without close and lengthy association with a community. Where the fieldworker is not a native speaker (or internal member of the speech community or smaller community of practice), a clear role as learner (see above) is required. For instance, if a researcher is interested in the function of specific speech acts, extensive observation within the community is needed. Adachi (2011) explores what counts as a 'compliment' in spontaneous Japanese conversation. To do this, she recorded extensively—in more than forty hours of multiparty recordings, she found only 369 tokens of exchanges that seem to function as compliments.

In addition, to categorize exchanges as compliments required developing a sense of what prior associations a compliment conjures up and what expectations it generates for the future (cf. Ochs's 1992 notions of 'retextualization' and 'pretextualization' in talk). In some cases, knowledge about the particular participants was needed. In Example 3, it would have been impossible for Adachi (2011) to categorize Kenji's and Ichiro's comments as compliments if she didn't know that Momoko is in fact very petite in a community where petiteness is valued.

(3) Knowing the participants enables a better sociolinguistic analysis (Adachi, 2011).

Ichiro (male) and Momoko (female) are fourth-year university students. Kenji is a master's student. Ichiro comments on Momoko's sugar- and cream-laden coffee drink.

Ichiro:	*Sore*	*meccha*	*karada*	*ni*	*wari:*	*ken,*	*zettai.*
	that	very	body	for	bad	because	certainly

Momoko:	*Debu*	*no*	*moto*	*desyo.*
	fat	GEN	source	COP

Ichiro:	*Debu...,*	*debu*	*no*	*syouchou*	*yo.*
	fat	fat	GEN	symbol	SFP

Kenji:	*Iya,*	*Momoko-san*	*mou*	*chotto*	*debu*	*ni*	*natte*
	no	M.HON	more	a little	fat	GOAL	become
	mo	*iin*	*ja*	*nai*	*yo.*		
	even.if	okay	COP	NEG	SFP		

Ichiro:	*Momoko-san,*	*Momoko-san,*	*Momoko-san*	*ne:*
	M.-HON	M.-HON	M.HON	SFP
	chikinnanban	*kuttotte*	*mo*	*ne:*
	fried chicken	eat.PRGR	even.if	SFP
	gari	*no*	*syouchou*	*dan*	*ne.*
	skinny	GEN	symbol	COP	SFP

Ichiro:	That must be so bad for you.
Momoko:	The source of being fat.
Ichiro:	The epitome of ... being fat.
Kenji:	But Momoko-san, you could be a little fatter [you could put some more weight], couldn't you?
Ichiro:	Momoko-san, Momoko-san, even if Momoko-san eats deep fried chicken, she epitomizes being skinny.

5.5.1 Things to keep in mind: what you lose on the swings, you may gain on the roundabouts

We have reviewed some of the merits of group recordings for mitigating the observer's paradox. However, researchers should also bear in mind issues that are raised by collecting data in group recordings. These are not necessarily problems, but they are considerations to bear in mind when selecting methods for sociolinguistic fieldwork.

The dynamic nature of group recordings means the researcher is unlikely to retain control over the structure and topics of the recording. For example, suppose you were interested in the linguistic routines speakers favour when they are negating or denying events—you may have to record a lot of spontaneous conversation before you find many examples of what you're looking for (unsurprisingly, people spend more time talking about things that *have* happened or they expect will happen than they spend talking about things that have *not* happened or that they anticipate will not happen). Moreover, the examples of negation and denial that you do serendipitously record may come from a very skewed subgroup of speakers or a particular subset of topics. If that skewing is likely to cause problems for the kinds of generalizations, you may be hoping to make (e.g. whether a change is in progress in how negation is expressed in that community), or if your time is limited, it might be expedient to use targeted questions in something more like a conventional interview that are likely to elicit negation. For example, questions like 'Have you ever been blamed for something you didn't do?' or 'Have you ever felt pressured to do something you didn't want to do?' may be more likely than ordinary everyday conversation to elicit discussion of non-events.[5] The trade-off between losing control of the interaction and obtaining more naturalistic data should be a principled and informed decision that determines whether a researcher will use group recordings as the primary means of data collection.

There are also technical issues that sociolinguists need to bear in mind if they allow the speakers themselves to take control of recording interactions: recording quality may be compromised. If there are more people in an interaction, and if the conversation is very casual, there is likely to be lots of overlapping speech. This may make it difficult to identify every participant accurately, and it may be harder to transcribe everything that everyone says. This may be even harder if the researcher was not present when the recording took place. If someone else is deputed to make a recording, it is a very good idea to meet with them shortly afterwards in order for the deputee to go through the recording in real time, identifying speakers and the general topics being discussed.

An additional consideration, if someone else is deputed to make recordings, is the time needed to train them. They need to be as aware as a trained sociolinguist about what situations to avoid (e.g. conditions with background noise from a television or air conditioner, or feedback created by having a microphone too close to other electrical equipment) and about the ethics of fieldwork. Individual microphones for each participant may alleviate problems with speakers being

---

[5] Similarly, for low-frequency phonetic variables, a common strategy for eliciting a minimum of tokens from every speaker is to use what's called a 'semantic differential' question which asks speakers to focus on the differences between two words. Suppose you are interested in the realization of the diphthong in POOR and TOUR (which is the least frequent syllable nucleus in English), you could ask people 'What's the difference between being *poor* and *well off*?'

different distances from a central microphone (Labov 1984), but this is not always practical. (We include a short checklist of factors to consider when undertaking sociolinguistic recordings as Appendix 1 in §5.7.)

Another thing to remember is that groups have their own dynamics. Some people in groups are more quiet and some people are more loquacious. So recording in a small group doesn't guarantee that you will get good quality data from a lot more people. Labov et al. (1968) found that some people who were very quiet in group recordings talked freely in individual interviews. And the quiet people may not always be the group outsiders:

In our South Harlem studies, the most extreme example was Jesse H., who never spoke a word in two group sessions. Yet Jesse was well known to be a person of consequence, who others turned to for advice, and in individual interviews he talked freely and at great length. (Labov 1984: 49).

People often come and go in the less structured context of group or walkabout recordings, and while it may be possible to find out some basic demographic information about participants (e.g. age, gender, social class, occupation, and education), other aspects of their social identities may be impossible to retrieve. These may include speakers' attitudes towards economic and social mobility (cf. Hazen 2002; Meyerhoff and Walker 2007), the communities of practice that individuals participate in regularly (Eckert and McConnell-Ginet 1992; Bucholtz 1999; Meyerhoff 2001; Mendoza-Denton 2008), and many other identities particular to those speakers. Equally, some researchers may want specific data about the nature of the interactions recorded, such as who was sitting where, how participants made eye-contact, and what clothing they were wearing. Some of this data can be provided by video recording, but video is not always feasible or desirable (e.g. in Iran, videoing family conversations may be problematic because women often don't wear head scarves at home but they are expected to wear them in the presence of non-intimates, who might view the video).

Outside the lab it is hard to better the classic anthropological method of taking notes based on what you have personally seen and experienced in the field, typically known as participant observation. The photographs in Fig. 5.1 show the complex positioning and movement of speakers in the university common room where Adachi (2011) undertook some of her fieldwork. This placement and positioning needs to be noted independently if the sociolinguistic fieldwork is not based on video data.

5.5.2 Ethics and the question of surreptitious recording

We have discussed in some detail ways of dealing with the compromises that the observer's paradox forces us into. Readers might ask: why not hide the recording device and simply not tell people that we are recording them? Wouldn't this

Figure 5.1. Photos of positioning of speakers recorded in a university common room at lunchtime as researcher aide memoire. Recording equipment is centre foreground in top photograph.

capture the most naturalistic and spontaneous data? The answer to this is quite simple: it is completely unethical to record people's conversations and interactions without their informed consent. It is a tremendous breach of personal trust and professional standards (see also Rice, Chapter 18 below).

Students often ask whether it is acceptable to make secret recordings if the subjects have given you blanket permission in advance to record them at some unspecified time. This is also ethically unwise. In our experience, it is clear that people continue to subliminally monitor their speech when it's being recorded, even if they seem to be speaking in a wholly relaxed and casual manner. For example, socially or politically dangerous topics may be avoided. In addition, speakers should at any time be able to withdraw all or part of what they say, even if they have given permission to record. But even family and friends may find it face-threatening to contact a researcher afterwards and ask that certain parts of a recording be excised from a project. We should not compound these difficulties by having made surreptitious recordings, which under any circumstances is not good research ethics. Finally, in many places it is simply illegal to undertake surreptitious recording. For all these reasons, surreptitious recordings are never approved in any form of research.

Rice (Chapter 18 below) deals with research ethics in more detail, so we will simply note here the steps usually taken to ensure there is informed consent when recordings of spontaneous speech in public spaces are being collected. Adachi's (2011) fieldwork included recordings in a student common room at the university where she studied as an undergraduate in Japan. One of Adachi's former professors announced her research to all the students in the department prior to her arrival. She subsequently also explained to all the department students that she was going to be conducting recordings at lunchtime in the common room. Finally, on the days when she was actually recording, she put up a note in the room indicating that recording was in progress—this had her name and contact information on it. People who did not want to be recorded could avoid coming into the room as long as the notice was up. Hewitt, McCloughan, and McKinstry (2009) went through a similar process when recording interactions at the reception desks of doctors' surgeries. In this case, recording equipment was turned off when people did not want to be recorded.

5.5.3 Other methods for fieldwork with groups

In this section, we summarize some of the other ways group recordings can be organized.

5.5.3.1 *Group interviews (structured or semi-structured)*

Group interviews can be conducted in much the same way as the classic sociolinguistic interview discussed above. Researchers can prepare specific questions in advance, moving on to the next one when participants don't self-select for further discussion. A semi-structured interview allows the researcher to offer topics that participants can talk about and lead them to have more dynamic discussions between themselves. This method is widely used in language attitude research, qualitative sociolinguistics and quantitative sociolinguistics (Milroy and Gordon 2003). Researchers may remain detached from the interaction with the participants or they may participate fully where they feel this will facilitate conversation.

Another type of interview is the 'playback interview' in which the researcher (whether s/he is a member of the recorded interaction or not) plays back parts of a recording to the participants and asks them to comment on the interactions selected. This method was pioneered by Gumperz (1982), and was the successful basis for Tannen's (1984) study of the conversational dynamics of an extended dinner party. This kind of fieldwork is particularly suitable for researchers interested in the points of convergence and divergence in participants' subjective interpretations of events.

5.5.3.2 *'Free-style'⁶ conversational recordings*

Subject to the ethical considerations reviewed earlier, sociolinguistic fieldwork can be a little more unstructured still. Macaulay (2002) set up a conversation between teenagers (giving them some suggested topics but leaving the room himself) with a recorder running. In some cases, speakers have been asked to record all of their interactions for a whole day (Hindle 1979; Coupland 1984; Holmes 2006). This is a particularly good way of identifying how a single speaker modifies their speech in different contexts and with different interlocutors.

5.5.3.3 *Audio/video recordings*

Group recordings can be conducted with either audio or video recorders. The most beneficial method will depend on what kind of sociolinguistic questions you have. Video recordings can help overcome some or the problems associated with an absent researcher, as video may clarify who is talking to whom (it can't solve all such problems unless you have multiple cameras focused in different directions to capture everyone's gaze). Non-verbal cues may also provide information that's useful in analysing the give and take of conversational interaction. However, audio (at present) is still easier to use if a speaker is undertaking day long free-style recordings.

---

⁶ The term 'free style' to describe this kind of recording as opposed to interview-based recordings was (we believe) coined by Agata Daleszńyska (2011). In the absence of any other widely accepted term to describe these yet, we follow her practice.

5.6 CONCLUSION

In this chapter, we have reviewed some of the basic issues associated with undertaking sociolinguistic fieldwork. We started with an overview of some key terms in sociolinguistics (including 'speech community', 'sociolinguistic variable', and 'sociolinguistics' itself), and we discussed how these notions influence the methods of sociolinguists. We examined in detail the methods of the classic (Labovian) sociolinguistic interview, the rationale behind its structure and methods, and indicated some of its advantages and disadvantages depending on (a) the nature of the linguistic phenomenon being investigated, (b) the kinds of research questions being asked about the relationship between society and language use. We considered also the techniques employed in search of vernacular speech, within the context of an interview and variations on the one-to-one interview format, including group recordings. We explored the intersection between sociolinguistic fieldwork and ethnographic traditions in anthropology and sociology, especially the shared interests in documenting everyday and unmonitored speech as a window on speakers' ideologies about and attitudes to language, society, and their interlocutors.

5.7 APPENDIX 1. TECHNICAL TIPS FOR
SUCCESSFUL GROUP RECORDINGS

These apply to all recording contexts, but are essential for successful group recordings (see also Margetts and Margetts, Chapter 1 above).
Checklist

1. What kind(s) of device(s) are most suitable for your research (what microphone, what recording devices)?
   You might want to use small and unobtrusive recording devices to set participants at ease. If you are asking people to carry around a recording device, you will want a light but sturdy one.
2. Does the equipment work?
   Check all your equipment prior to a recording session to see if it is all working. Do a test recording and check the sound quality in a similar setting to the one where you are going to record.
3. Was the recording session successful?
   Check the quality of every recording soon after every session.
   Label the file carefully and clearly.

4. Did the recording work? Save your sound or video files, and make a backup (or two) straightaway.

   Never underestimate the importance of backups. Ensure you have a safe copy of important information about each sound file, e.g. who it involves, where they were, when they were having the conversation.

5. Are you being responsible to your participants?

   Data that includes any individual's private information should not be available to anyone other than you. It is standard practice to use pseudonyms (or initials or speaker codes) when processing, saving, and reporting on data unless an individual has specifically asked to be identified in your work.

5.8 APPENDIX 2. LIST OF ABBREVIATIONS USED IN THE EXAMPLES:

1	1st person
2	2nd person
3	3rd person
COP	copula
GEN	genitive case (particle)
GOAL	goal marker
HON	honorific (title, suffix)
NEG	negative, negation
OJ	Osaka Japanese
OM	object marker
PAST	past tense
PL	plural
PROGR	progressive
PREP	preposition
QUOT	quotative
RH	referent honorific suffix
SFP	sentence-final particle
SG	singular
SJ	Standard Japanese
=	latching utterances

CHAPTER 6

REASONS FOR DOCUMENTING GESTURES AND SUGGESTIONS FOR HOW TO GO ABOUT IT

MANDANA SEYFEDDINIPUR

6.1 INTRODUCTION[1]

Using gestures, the hand and arm movements speakers make when talking, seems to be a universal feature of human communication. So far there has been no report of a culture that does not gesture. But our knowledge about the cultural diversity of gesture use within linguistic practices is limited, even though gestures are an integral part of those practices. In order to describe linguistic patterns and regularities of language use, understanding gesture is indispensable.

[1] I would like to thank David Wilkins, Anna Margetts, Nick Thieberger, Birgit Hellwig, Adam Kendon, and two anonymous reviewers for valuable comments and suggestions.

Kendon (1986a) shows how gesture is relevant for many areas of study (see also Kendon 2007). This chapter is intended as an introduction to the whys and hows of gesture documentation for linguistic fieldworkers. It will provide an overview of the multifaceted phenomenon of gesture, and an insight into how gesture interacts with language, cognition, and culture. Different aspects of gestures—like their semiotic properties, their multiple functions in conversation, and the cognitive linkage between gesture and speech—will be introduced. This introduction is far from a comprehensive account of the complex phenomenon, but should heighten attention and awareness of a central aspect of human communicative behaviour.

The term 'gesture' has been used for many different phenomena, from facial expressions to making a verbal compliment. For the purpose of this chapter we will use the term 'gesture' to refer only to the hand and arm movements speakers make when they communicate. This excludes other non-verbal behaviours like gaze, head movements, and eyebrow flashes. Note that this is an arbitrary decision, which reduces the breadth of bodily expression to one set of articulators. The gaze, the face, the head, the body, and the hands form an orchestrated whole together with speech, and manual actions are not necessarily the dominant component of visual bodily action in utterance.

We also exclude behaviours like blushing, self-grooming, straightening clothing, or actions like smoking or giving something to someone. The rationale behind this second class of exclusions follows Kendon (2004a: 15), who defines gestures among other features based on how observers treat gestural actions since they are 'directly perceived as being under the guidance of the observed person's voluntary control and being done for the purpose of expression rather than in the service of some practical aim' (see Wilkins 2006 for a critical review of this analytical position).

The interest in gesture reaches back to the ancient Greeks (for an overview of the history of gesture studies see Bremmer and Roodenburg 1991; Kendon 1982; 2004a). And although in recent years the study of gesture has become more and more prominent, gestures have been mostly studied in western societies (for exceptions see e.g. Barakat 1976; Brookes 2005; Creider 1977; Enfield 2009; Green 2009; Haviland 1993; Kita and Essegbey 2001; Le Guen 2011; Sherzer 1991; 1993; Sparhawk 1981; Streeck 1993; 1994; Wilkins 2003).

This chapter provides an overview of some basic aspects of gesture, demonstrating how crucial it is to consider gestures as an integral part of language documentation. Section 6.4 provides some practical advice on how to go about including gestures in language documentation.

6.2 GESTURE BASICS

Following the definition above, gestures, just like words, communicate information. With gestures, speakers may indicate a location, depict the shape or the size of an object, or show how an object moves. A speaker might enact how someone threw a ball and then point to where the ball was thrown. Speakers also do interactive work with their gestures like rejecting, denying, negating, offering, giving, and comparing. Speakers can use gesture to mark discourse structure and to regulate the coordination between speakers in conversation. Communities have repertoires of gestures that are like words and that are used with and without speech (for classifications of gestures see Bavelas et al. 1992; Efron 1941/1972; Ekman and Friesen 1969; McNeill 1992; Müller 1998, Wundt 1973[1921]; and see Kendon 2004a for a comparative discussion).

Conventionalized gestures, like 'thumbs up', have been termed 'symbolic gestures' (Efron 1941/1972), 'emblems' (Ekman and Friesen 1969) or 'quotable gestures' (Kendon 1988a; 1992). They can be used independently of speech and can have different meanings in different cultures (Morris et al. 1979). Members of a community can quote them and provide verbal glosses for them. Their form–meaning relationship is stable and subject to standards of well-formedness. Changing one feature of the gesture's form changes the meaning. In Britain, the 'victory' gesture is made with the index and middle finger extended and spread to form a 'V' shape, with the palm turned outwards. If the orientation of the palm is changed by turning it so that the back of the hand faces the recipients, it loses this meaning. It may become an insult when combined with motion component of moving the V up rapidly.

Several dictionary-like lists have been published documenting the meanings expressed by gestures for different cultures (see Kendon 1981; 1984b for a discussion, and for methodological problems see Collett 2004). Context-of-use studies have shown how certain quotable gestures make reference to central cultural concepts of special importance in a given culture (Sherzer 1991; Brookes 2004; 2005; Kendon 2004a).

6.2.1 Semantic interaction

Gestures are coordinated semantically and temporally, and this close coordination has, among other features, led to the view that the two forms of expression are guided under a single aim (Kendon 2004a; McNeill 1992). The following exemplifies how speech and gesture interact at different linguistic levels in the creation of meaning. The relationship between gesture and speech is complex, and speakers have a variety of ways to combine the information expressed in the modalities. Gesture can be the main carrier of information, or it can add and further specify aspects of the referent that is being talked about (Kendon 2004a; Lascaridis and Stone 2009).

Speakers combine words and gestures into gesture–speech ensembles (Kendon 2004a) or composite signals (Clark 1996). The components of the ensemble differ in their core semiotic properties. Consider someone describing how she threw a ball and smashed a window. While she says *and then I threw this ball*, she lifts her hand next to her head as if holding a ball the size of tennis ball or baseball in her hand and then moves the hand fast forward, extending her arm. With her hand shape she shows the size of the ball and with the movement she enacts how she threw the ball and the direction in which she threw the ball. The information displayed in gesture specifies aspects of the event that are underspecified in the speech portion of her utterance.

Gestures are also used to depict abstract concepts. Imagine someone talking about an argument he had with a friend. He says *and the argument went on and on and on*. The gesture co-occurring with *went on and on and on* depicts the abstract concept of an ongoing duration visually in multiple circular motions. These gestures are representational in that they depict an abstract entity. In this meta-phoric process, an abstract domain (temporal continuity of the arguing event) is represented in terms of a concrete domain (physically repeated circling motion of hands) (Calbris 1990; Cienki and Müller 2008; McNeill 1992).

While in the above examples speech and gesture provide different types of semantic information about an event, gesture can also become the main carrier of information. Speakers may index their gesture with spoken deictics as in utterances like *she held it like this*, followed by a gesture (Streeck 1993; 1994). These gestures can be, for example, pantomimes of actions someone performed, or they can be elaborate depictions of the shape of an object. This kind of relationship can also be observed in pointing gestures accompanied by demonstratives like *here, there*. Without the gesture the recognition of the proposition remains incomplete.

Speakers may use gesture to express something that is socially unspeakable or that should not be overheard, and speakers also substitute words with gestures when they deploy a gesture in the verbal slot of a word not being articulated. Slama-Cazacu (1976) calls these 'mixed syntax'. She reports a case in which a director is talking about spotlight number 5 on a balustrade. He tells an electrician *Five balcony* and the makes a gesture as if switching on the light. The gesture here is basically a substitute for the verb.

In short, in utterances composed of speech and gesture, both modalities con-tribute to overall utterance interpretation. The relationship between gesture and speech is complex and speakers have a variety of ways to combine the information expressed in the modalities.

6.2.2 Gesture and pragmatics

Gestures, as semantic entities, are also used for pragmatic effect. Speakers can use gesture to assist the listener in interpreting how the verbal part of the utterance should be interpreted. A speaker who deploys a 'quotation mark' gesture during a specific part of the verbal part of an utterance provides the recipient with the information that an utterance is a quote, or should not be taken literally. While many cultures have repertoires of these gestures, their usage for pragmatic effects has rarely been studied (but see Kendon 1995; 2004a for a classification and also Müller 2004; Neumann 2004; Seyfeddinipur 2004; Streeck 2009b; Weinreich 1992).

Figure 6.1. Finger bunch hand shape.

In contrast to gestures that show, for example, how something moved, gestures can also mark the 'speech act' or interactional move an utterance performs in conversation, like asking a question or offering information. In Italy, the *grappolo* hand shape (see Fig. 6.1) is deployed in a gesture that functions as a marker for a certain kind of question (Kendon 1992; 1995; Poggi 1983). In this function of the 'finger bunch', the hand moves upwards and inwards towards the speaker multiple times. This gesture is used 'when a speaker asks a question about something because he is surprised, annoyed or puzzled by it, or when he is testing another's knowledge of something' (Kendon 2004a: 231–2).

Speakers also use gesture to mark the focus of verbal elements. Seyfeddinipur (2004) describes a gesture sequence with discourse structuring usage observed in Persian speakers marking the topic comment structure of the co-occurring verbal utterance (see Kendon 1995; 2004a: 233–6 for Italian). The sequence is a combination of two hand shapes marking the topic–comment structure of the spoken part of the utterance. In the example, first the speaker has the right hand closed to a fist with the tip of the index finger and the tip of the thumb touching each other and forming an oval shape. Then the speaker opens the gesture; the index finger and thumb get extended while the other fingers remain curled, the so-called Pistolhand (as a consultant called the gesture). The speaker performs this gesture sequence—Ring–Pistolhand—in synchrony with the topic—comment structure of his unfolding verbal utterance. The Ring gesture is synchronized with the topic part of the verbal utterance and the Pistolhand with the comment part of the utterance, i.e. the verb complex (see Fig. 6.2).

| Ring | hold | Pistolhand | hold | Ring | Pistolhand |
taze hawapejma (1s) tu Iran pejda shode bood jani si chel sal pish as in ma hawapejma nadide boodim ke
recently airplane   in Iran   visible became was   meaning thirty forty years before that we airplane   not-seen were
recently airplanes had appeared in Iran meaning that thirty forty years before that we had never seen an airplane

Figure 6.2. Example of a gesture combination with discourse structuring or parsing function. Straight lines between gesture names mark duration of the gestural configuration; hold means that the hand is held still.

Little is known about the kinds of repertoires and the different uses and pragmatic effects these gestures can have, and how the cultural environment shapes such repertoires.

6.2.3 Interactional organization

Gesture and speech also interact in the organization of the conversation itself. Studies in the tradition of Conversation Analysis have shown how speakers temporally organize their gestures to regulate the interaction.

In a conversation, speakers coordinate their activities in a systematic way. If speakers are interrupted while gesturing, they can freeze their gesture and hold the hand in the air, signalling that they want the floor back (Schegloff 1984; Goodwin 1986). Addressees can yield the floor by lifting the hand, and they can display that they are giving up this intent by dropping the hand again. And listeners can gesture without interrupting the speaker but still indicating how they are taking what the other is saying. It is clear already on this coarse-grained level of observation that gesture is used to organize turn-taking.

Gestures can foreshadow what will be said or done next, which enables addressees to foresee points in time when the turn of the speaker may end and they can take over, so that a gapless switch of speakers is possible (Sacks, Schegloff, and Jefferson 1974; Schegloff 1980; 1984; Streeck 1995; 2009a; 2009b; Mondada 2007). So, for example, when a speaker begins a turn with a counting gesture (e.g. thumb is extended while the other fingers are curled and palm is up), the addressee can infer that the speaker will list something in their upcoming talk. Also, when a speaker encounter problems in finding a word, gesture can play a role in coordinating the conversation during the search (Fornel 1991; Goodwin and Goodwin 1986; Hayashi 2003; Schlegel 1998).

As shown above, speakers use gesture to express semantic and pragmatic information and to coordinate the interaction. Note that a single gesture can simultaneously perform semantic, pragmatic, and interactional functions in an utterance—these functions are not mutually exclusive.

6.2.3.1 Integrated systems for expression

Within language communities, certain domains of expression like numerals or demonstratives have a set of gestural conventions for expression. In gestural convention, hand shape, movement, orientation, or location become associated with specific semantic features. These then can become organized into a set of systematic oppositions for a broader semantic domain. As initially described by Foster (1948) for Tzintzuntzan (see Wilkins 2006), then later by Zavala (2000) for speakers of Akatek (a Mayan language spoken in the Cuchumatan Mountains of Guatemala), a gestural classificatory system is parallel to the classifier system in the spoken language. When Akatek speakers measure objects *in absentia* with gesture, the orientation and the hand shape of the gesture changes depending on whether the referent is, for example, a plant, a bird, a child, or a serpent. If and how this gestural system interacts with the verbal classificatory system is not known.

For Arrernte, a central Australian (Pama-Nyungan) language, Wilkins (1999; 2003) describes a fully integrated speech–gesture system in the domain of demonstrative expression. Arrernte speakers combine gesture and demonstratives into what Wilkins (1999: 30) calls 'composite demonstrative signals' that differ from those known in European languages. Speech and gesture are combined to express different kinds of information that only together provide the basis for a proper recognition of the location of the intended referent (for other conventions on pointing, see Kendon and Versante 2003 for Neapolitan area of southern Italy; for Laos see also Enfield, Kita, and de Ruiter 2007; for pointing in Zinacantán Tzotzil see Haviland 2003). Wilkins (1999) not only shows that pointing, which is often claimed to be universal, is governed by cultural conventions but also that for Arrernte a description of the demonstrative system will remain incomplete and misleading if the gestural component is excluded.

6.2.4 When gesture is organized into a linguistic system itself

Speakers also use gesture to communicate when speech is not possible because of environmental circumstances like distance or loudness or sociocultural circumstances like taboos or cultural practices that prohibit speech. Given the circumstances, 'alternate kinesic codes' (Kendon 2004a) are developed, which can be observed in stock exchanges, sports (baseball, diving), or in guiding the actions of a crane driver (Brun 1969). While the domains of expression and the level and complexity of codification in such kinesic codes are restricted in the above-mentioned examples, there are also more complex systems. Sawmill workers in British Columbia, due to the specific technicalities of the work and the loud environment, developed a gesture system not only to coordinate work flow issues but also to communicate about private matters (Meissner and Philpott 1975).

Members of some religious orders that observe a rule of silence (e.g. Cistercians, Cluniacs, Trappists) are able to communicate for long stretches of time through the use of a limited number of gestures (Barakat 1975; Kendon 1990; Stokoe 1987; Umiker-Sebeok and Sebeok 1987). Kendon suggests that contextual circumstances influence strongly how such systems develop and become elaborated.

The restricted gesture systems described above can become elaborated to what Kendon (2004a) calls 'alternate sign languages'. They are used as an alternative to speech. The Plains Indians of North America used a sign language as a means of communication between tribes that did not share a mutually intelligible spoken language (Farnell 1995; Mallery 1987[1880]; Taylor 1978). Such alternate sign languages have also been described for Indigenous Australians of central Australia (Kendon 1988b). For example, among the Warlpiri of Central Australia, bereaved women traditionally observe a speaking taboo (Kendon 1984a; 1986b; 1988b), and communicate via an alternate sign language.

The systems described above are developed by hearing people who have access to spoken language. Deaf people with no access to spoken language create full-fledged sign languages (for an overview see of the circumstances and the languages created, see Meir et al. 2010). Sign languages demand their own documentary tools, but gesture can also be found in sign language (Liddell and Metzger 1998; Emmorey 2002; Johnston et al. 2007; Kendon 2008).

6.3 CULTURAL DIFFERENCES IN GESTURE

Many aspects of gesture are shaped by cultural conventions, but systematic comparative studies are sparse (for an overview see Kita 2009). Kita suggests four factors influencing gestural behaviour at different levels: conventions on form–meaning associations; pragmatics of communication; language; and cognition.

Cultural conventions on the semiotic structure of gestures determine the size and the content of the repertoire of quotable gestures like the thumbs-up gestures in a given culture (Efron 1941/1972; Kendon 2004b). Pointing, often assumed to be universal and quite simple, is shaped by conventions, and these conventions have to be acquired. Such form–meaning conventions apply to the type of pointing: whether to use lip pointing or the hands, which fingers to point with, and what hand shape and orientation to use (Kita 2003).

Pragmatic conventions on gesture use can be based on considerations of politeness. In the Ewe-speaking region of southeastern Ghana, speakers restrict the way they point because of a left hand use taboo (Kita and Essegbey 2001). When giving route directions, speakers take a conventional respect position with the left hand held behind the back, while the right hand is used for pointing even when pointing to the left. Speakers only use the left for pointing when it is accompanied by the use of the right hand, which is not considered rude.

Other dimensions of gesture like the size of gestural repertoires, the types of gestures, or the extension of gestures are influenced by cultural patterns of interaction, as Kendon suggests (2004a). The first systematic cross-cultural study on gesture was conducted by Efron (a student of Boas) in the late 1930s (Efron 1941/1972). He refuted prevalent Nazi theories stating that gestural behaviour is determined by genetic characteristics of different races by investigating the how gestural practices changed across generations of Italian and Eastern European Jewish immigrants to New York. Efron showed that Eastern European and Sicilian Jewish immigrants to New York differed in their gestural practices from each other, while the second-generation immigrants had assimilated their gestural behaviour in terms of size, number, and types used.

Cross-cultural differences have also been shown for the number and type of hand shapes used in gesticulation and the amount of gestures accompanying speech phrases (e.g. Kendon 2004b on British vs. Neapolitan speakers).

Differences in gesture rate have rarely been demonstrated, although one of the most prevalent beliefs about gesture is that some cultures gesture more than others. Taiwanese mothers when playing with their children produced almost three times more gestures than American mothers. Goldin-Meadow and Saltzmann (2000) suggest this is because they have a stronger interest in instructing their children.

A comparative study of Spanish and German speakers found differences not in the amount of gesturing but in the use of gesture space (Müller 1998). While the Germans gestured mostly from the wrist, the Spanish speakers gestured mostly from the elbow and the shoulder (see also Efron 1941/1972 and Kendon 2004b). It has been suggested that more expansive gestures may be perceived as more prominent, and that this may lead to the idea that certain cultures gesture more than others (Müller 1998; Kita 2009; and see Kendon 2004b for methodological consideration of assessing gesture rates).

Many factors may be responsible for the described differences. Kendon (2004a; 2004b) suggests that the 'communicative ecology' of a given culture has to be taken into account to understand the cross-cultural differences.

6.3.1 Linguistic diversity

There are cross-cultural differences in what kind of information speakers of different languages express in speech and gesture when talking about the same event. In Japanese, for example, the action of swinging cannot easily be expressed in one word as in English. Speakers often use simple verbs like 'go' that do not encode the arc trajectory of the motion. When Japanese speakers describe a swing event they could, in theory, compensate in gesture for this lack of information in their vocabulary by displaying the arc trajectory visually. While Japanese speakers combined speech and gesture in this way, Kita and Özyürek (2003) also found a tendency for them to actually perform gestures that move in a straight line. English speakers, in contrast, who can readily express the shape of the trajectory with the word *swing*, also depict the arc trajectory in their gestures. So gesture does not always compensate for, but often parallels, linguistic packaging. This suggests that the form of the gesture can be influenced by the way information is expressed in a specific language.

The same seems to be true for syntactic structuring (Kita et al. 2007). In Turkish, the way an object moves (manner) and the path of motion are usually expressed in two separate clauses. When Turkish speakers express how something rolled down a hill, they make a rotating movement when they say 'it rolled', followed by a straight, slightly downward movement as they say and 'it went down'. In contrast, English speakers mostly conflate manner and path information in one gesture by making a rotational movement downwards while they say *it rolled down*. The information expressed in gesture is adapted to the way information is expressed in a specific language.

Kita (2009) suggests that these differences are a reflection of diversity in 'thinking-for-speaking' (Slobin 1996). It appears that certain aspects of linguistic typology in sentence packaging and lexicalization may have consequences for the structure of co-speech gesture.

6.3.2 Cognitive diversity

There are cross-cultural differences in how spatial information is conceptualized and expressed, and this kind of cognitive diversity is also reflected in gesture. When speakers express location and directions, they differ in how they anchor spatial relationships (Levinson and Wilkins 2006). Guugu Yimithirr speakers of Hopevale in Queensland anchor spatial relationships at all levels of scale with regard to the cardinal directions. Haviland (1993) reports two instances in which a Guugu Yimithirr speaker is describing how his boat flipped in a storm. The first time he is facing west. While he says, 'The boat was lifted up and starting to turn', he brings up his arms with the palms facing him and rotates them in a flipping motion forward from east to west. Two years later the speaker tells the same story in a different location facing north. He brings up his hands with the palms facing each other and rotates them again in a flipping motion from east to west (clockwise). The directionality of the flipping motion matched the absolute orientation of the incident, and the speaker modified his gesture to preserve the absolute orientation of the turning of the boat.

There are also cross-cultural differences in how an abstract concept like time is represented in gesture. Time tends to be represented in concrete spatial terms. So concepts like past and future are expressed in English by metaphorical expressions like *the event is ahead of us* or *the event is behind us*, mapping the temporal relations onto the sagittal axis, which passes from the front to rear of the body (Boroditsky 2000). There are cultures that reverse the directionality. Nunez and Sweetser (2006) report that speakers of Aymara (Chilean Andes), when talking about the future, often use expressions containing the word 'back' and they often use the word 'front' when talking about the past. Accordingly, especially older speakers with limited Spanish would gesture forward to represent an event in the past while they gestured backward to represent that something will happen in the future. In contrast, French speakers, for whom the future is ahead and the past is behind, gesture forward for the future and backward for the past (Calbris 1990; see also Kita, Danziger, and Stolz 2001 for a comparison between Mopan and Yucatec, Mexico; Boroditsky and Gaby 2010 for the use of cardinal directions in the expression of time in the Australian Aboriginal community of Pormpuraaw).

The way speakers think about space or the way they map temporal relations onto space is reflected in gestural representation. Comparative systematic studies are needed to gain a better understanding of how metaphorical mappings in gesture and speech take place.

6.3.3 Summary

Gesture is an integral part of the linguistic practices of a given speech community. The practices are manifold, and extend from communicative events like ritual speech and monologs to conversations. In everyday interaction, speakers use gesture–speech ensembles to express diverse types of meaning, including referential meaning. Gestures can be used to mark focal elements of the discourse or to provide an interpretation framework for the verbal part of the utterance, and they are used to organize the conversation. Speech and gesture together form composite signals (Clark 1996) that have to be taken into account in order to fully understand and describe certain domains of linguistic expression. When speech is not possible, gestures are used to form kinesic systems for communication.

Cultural differences shape many aspects of gesture, like the repertoire, the size, the content, orientation, the types, the use in context, and so on. Linguistic, cognitive, and social factors underlie these variations. To gain a broader understanding of how cultural differences in gestural behaviour emerge, it is necessary to study gesture in its various contexts of use.

6.4 How to start including gesture in documentation

It may at first seem daunting to include another modality in the documentation of language. But the documentation of the role of gesture in language use and of how the gestural system and the verbal system interact in communication can easily draw upon methods and techniques already established for language documentation. The work of a researcher studying gesture does not drastically differ from the work of a descriptive linguist documenting and describing a hitherto undescribed language. Gestures, like any sign, have different aspects—form, meaning, and context—that can be analysed and described. To enable such descriptions, a minimal approach can be taken by ensuring that the recordings of spoken language is of a quality which allows for (at least some) analysis of gestures at a later stage. This involves using video as the basic recording tool and following certain standards for the filming—such as framing the picture so that it minimally includes the speaker's head and upper body rather than only the face or the hands (see below for more detail). A second more elaborate step is to expand the corpus compilation by including recordings of topics and genres which are gesture-prominent. This minimal approach may be all that can be managed by a researcher whose focus is on other matters.

This section provides an introduction to such a minimal approach—namely, how to go about including gestures in language documentation, in terms both of what to record and how to record, and of how to minimally annotate to make the data accessible.

6.4.1 What to record

A first guiding question for the documentation of gesture is: how do speakers coordinate their verbal and gestural resources in everyday interactions? To answer this question, a starting point is to add to the corpus a variety of topics, and a range of different communicative events (i.e. different text types), which can approach the known range of gesture types (see Seifart 2008 for methods of corpus compilation). Different speakers should be recorded producing the same types of text to control for speaker variability in gesturing.

The fundamental basis is to record gestures in everyday interaction. The tradition of Hymes' (1974) ethnography of speaking can provide a framework for the dimensions and types that should be taken into account (Himmelmann 1998; Hill 2006; Seifart 2008). A guiding view is that using language is a form of joint action (Clark 1996) in which speakers are solving coordination problems by using their expressive resources in different ways. For example, how do speakers draw the attention of their interlocutor to a certain entity in a given situation? Depending on the context, a speaker may use a pointing gesture to direct the attention of the interlocutors to a certain location in conjunction with a demonstrative or they may use a description (like *X is in the kitchen*). Observing these practices and focusing on bodily deployment provides a basis for noticing the role gestural expression may play in a community.

Note that, as an outsider, one is not equipped with the cultural knowledge of the conventions regarding the form–function relation of gestures, as Wilkins (1999;

2006) points out. Community members should be involved in data elicitation and analysis (see Wilkins 2003 for a detailed methodological description).

A starting point is to record situations in which speakers talk about topics that are rich in spatial content, like route directions (Where is x? How do you get to y?) and spatial descriptions (How did the village/area look 50 years ago? What changed and how?). In such situations, speakers are likely to use pointing gestures to indicate locations and they lay out spatial relations with their gestures.

Topics that are rich in spatial content and are very likely to yield a variety of gestures can also be elicited in storytelling. Also, procedural texts about (for example) how artefacts or foods are prepared and used, or how certain rituals take place, typically contain gestures depicting shape, size, use, and concrete aspects of an object or action, and may also contain gestural representations of abstract features like the order of events. This type of discourse can also be recorded in instructional context when a teacher instructs a novice.

Topics dealing with abstract relationships like time (past and future), or kinship (Enfield 2009) are also promising for evoking gesture behaviours. Sometimes sessions set up for some other purpose, such as consultants engaged in discussion within elicitation or translation sessions, can provide interesting data on the use of metaphorical gestures when they (for example) discuss syntactic structures, making them visible through their gestures (Mittelberg 2002).

Gestures with pragmatic function, like structuring the discourse or marking the speech act of an utterance, are most likely to be observed in animated discussions about issues the community cares about and where members may be in disagreement. Political discussions and negotiations often are situations where speakers use these gestures, which may also depict abstract relations (Cienki and Müller 2008).

Gestures can be also elicited in more directed elicitations. Tasks that have proven useful in gesture elicitation are picture book descriptions (e.g. the Frog Story, cf. Berman and Slobin 1994) and cartoon narrations (the Tweety and Sylvester cartoon, cf. McNeill 1992; Road Runner, cf. Bavelas et al. 1992). Using picture books or cartoons has the advantage that the data collected can potentially be compared systematically cross-culturally. Cartoons are rich in motion events of different types (rolling down a hill, entering, exiting). Because of the relatively static nature of picture books, retelling may or may not be successful in eliciting gesture.

More focused gesture elicitation tools have been developed for motion events (e.g. the Tomato man movie: Özyürek et al. 2008) and for spatial reference (see Majid, Chapter 2 above). However, as mentioned above, the applicability of the stimuli depends on the familiarity of a given community with such materials and tasks, and so some stimuli and tasks may not be appropriate for the cultural context, or for use with certain members of the community.

For those who are more interested in undertaking gesture studies, some examples in the literature of gesture research by field linguists are Enfield (2009), Green (2009), Haviland (1993), Kita et al. (2001), Kita and Essegbey (2001), Le Guen

(2011), Sherzer (1991), Wilkins (1999). See also Goodwin (1986) and Kendon (2004a).

6.4.2 How to record

Gesture, just like speech, is a fleeting phenomenon. Because of its ephemeral nature, certain aspects are impossible to catch by casual observation alone. The temporal unfolding over time of the gesture form, its trajectory of motion, and its synchrony with specific elements in speech can only be captured systematically by video. Video recording, however, can be problematic for ethical reasons (Rice, Chapter 18 below), is technically challenging (Margetts and Margetts, Chapter 1 above), and speakers may alter their behaviour in the presence of a recording device.

Video need not only be shot by the fieldworker, but may in fact be better collected by trained community members. Having community members video record interactions can also provide insights into what they consider important in the interactions (for uses of video in documentation, see Ashmore 2008).

In any case, there are some guidelines for recording which best facilitate later analyses of gesture speech interaction. An ideal recording frames the conversational situation with the speakers' upper bodies, with at least an arm-length space around their head. If possible, in framing the span of the interlocutors' space, it is best to overcompensate so that the maximum breadth of possible movement (assuming fixed position) is taken into account. The camera should be positioned at 9 o'clock or frontal, and angled slightly down from eye level of the speakers. With such a framing of the speakers, we can observe the hand shapes and movements along with facial expressions, gaze, and eyebrow and head movements. This is important because these all tend to form elements in an orchestrated whole.

An obvious problem for this setup is that the way speakers are oriented towards each other depends on cultural as well as situational restrictions. In many places it is not very natural to have two or more people side by side facing the camera rather than each other, and any artificial composition placing the speakers in culturally unnatural positions should be avoided. So we always have to find a compromise, such as framing only the main speaker in this way while the other speakers' faces may not be fully visible.

Ideally, the social space created by the interlocutors (including all interlocutors and not just a single speaker) should be recorded. This is because the verbal and gestural behaviour of speakers is contingent on the behaviour of their interlocutors, where they are located, whether they look or not, whether they backchannel their understanding or not, etc. (Schegloff 1984; Streeck 1994; Goodwin 1986). Speakers in some cultures are known to orient their gestures and the direction of movement depending on the location of the interlocutors (Özyürek 2002). In addition, for Canadian English-speaking college students, it was found that speakers' gestures are more pronounced and better articulated when the speaker thinks the recipient does not have prior knowledge of what the speaker is talking about: when the information to be conveyed is not yet in common ground, gestures are more elaborated and complex (Gerwing and Bavelas 2005).

A framing including all interlocutors may not be possible for communities who employ a communal broadcast model of talk (see Walsh 1991; 1997 for Aboriginal communities) rather than a dyadic or face-to-face model of talk. In such a situation, the social space of interlocutors should be framed such that the main actors are captured by the recording.

The video should be coupled with high-quality audio recording. Hence the choice of the right microphones and their placement is crucial (Margetts and Margetts, Chapter 1 above). Only this combination of video and audio data allows us to analyse the way speakers coordinate gesture and speech and other modalities like gaze or head movement. Field notes should include metadata details like identity of the speaker(s) and their relationship to each other, time and location of the recording, and type of speech event.

To obtain good data, the recording setup should be thought through and if possible prepared in advance. This includes choosing the position of the camera and finding a compromise between obtaining good recording quality and minimizing intrusiveness. Setting up in advance has the advantage that sound and picture are adjusted to the location and that one can start the recording beforehand without having to adjust the camera later on. The camera should be fixed on a tripod or placed on a steady straight surface to avoid jittery images; moving the camera in the middle of the recording should be avoided. The less one has to handle the camera during the recording session and in the presence of the consultants, the better. Fiddling with the camera attracts the attention of the people being recorded to the recording device and may lead to very controlled behaviour (Labov 1972a; for a discussion see Himmelmann 1998). Adjusting the camera, for example for panning and zooming, during a recording should be avoided also because there is a high risk of missing crucial parts of the interaction. Static continuous shots are recommended.

If one chooses to prepare a recording as suggested here, this involves two steps. The first step is to film the recording location itself, i.e. where the speakers will be located and what surrounds them. This constitutes important metadata that may be required for the analysis. In addition, a map of the location can be drawn, including again the position of the speakers and the objects or landmarks surrounding them. This may make it possible to analyse the location to which someone is pointing and/or how gestures are oriented spatially (Haviland 1993; Levinson and Wilkins 2006; Kita et al. 2001; LeGuen 2011).

In the second step, the camera is zoomed in to frame the interactional space. In staged communicative events, typically one or two speakers are present and the scene is relatively easy to frame. But natural situations pose a challenge for the recording, since the number of participants and their spatial arrangement change over time. When there are multiple interlocutors, ideally all of them should be recorded. This may be difficult when the participants are located too far apart for the camera to capture them all. Depending on the camera's lens (a wide-angle lens can capture a wider space), the camera needs to be moved further away, but increased distance from the speakers reduces the detail visible in the recordings (such as facial expressions) and potentially also the sound quality, depending on the recording setup and equipment. One way of handling such a situation is to focus the camera on the most active interlocutors and disregard the more distant overhearers who are not actively participating. Even when the focus is on gesture, the intelligibility of the speech should never be compromised. As mentioned above, speech and gesture need to be analysed together to assess meaning and function, and unintelligible speech minimizes the amount of specific information that can be taken from the recording.

One way of being relatively unobtrusive is to set up the camera and leave it running without attending to it (it can help to switch off the little red light that indicates that the camera is running). Speakers, who must be informed about the recording in advance, are more likely to forget or at least not focus on the fact that they are being recorded (for ethical issues that need to be addressed before recording speakers, see the chapters by Rice and Newman, Chapters 18 and 19 below).

6.5 BASIC ANNOTATION OF GESTURE

As discussed in §6.2, researchers studying gesture investigate the coordination of speech and gesture to answer questions concerning the forms and functions of gestural deployment, to determine the role of gesture in communication, and to explore what gesture reveals about cognition. A basic and minimal annotation of gesture consists of marking the periods of time in which the hands are gesturing. This type of basic annotation enables the analyst to locate the stretches in the video which are relevant for gesture analysis, and can be used to assess the time speakers spend gesturing. To identify gesture in the movement stream, the basic structure of gesture has to be taken into account.

Gestural movement can be segmented into four distinct phases (Kita, van Gijn, and van der Hulst 1998; McNeill 1992; Kendon 2004a): preparation, stroke, hold, and retraction. Consider a speaker describing how a ball rolled down a hill by making a spiral movement downwards with the extended index finger. First the hand is lifted from the lap to chest height. This phase is the preparation: the hand is brought into the starting position for the stroke. The stroke then consists of the hand moving downward in a spiralling movement. The stroke is the only obligatory phase of a gesture, and it can be characterized as the most articulated phase during which the most force is exerted. A stroke can be preceded or followed by a hold (pre-stroke or post-stroke), a static phase in which the hand is held still in a position. The phase during which the hand is moved back into rest position is the retraction. A stroke can be static or dynamic, with meaning being expressed through a static configuration (e.g. when size or extension is indicated) or through motion (rotating movement downward). Note that this established segmentation scheme mixes formal (hold) and functional categories (preparation, stroke, retraction). To circumvent this problem one, can distinguish in the annotation between static and dynamic strokes.

The phases can be distinguished based on changes in the direction of movement and changes in the speed of motion (acceleration or deceleration) and changes in the articulation of the motion (e.g. tension of the hand, directedness of motion). The segmentation of the movement into discrete phases can be accomplished by looking at the video frame by frame to see when the points of change occur. When the starting and the end points are determined, the stretch can be tagged and categorized (for a discussion of how to determining moments of transition systematically, see Seyfeddinipur 2006).

The time speakers spend gesturing is the basic gesture unit (Kendon 2004a). This is when the speaker moves his hands away from a rest position (e.g. lap) or an activity (e.g. cutting, smoking) and begins to gesticulate until the hands return to a different activity again.

For multimedia annotation, software like ELAN[2] or ANVIL[3] should be used. These annotation tools allow setting up multiple tiers for different levels of annotation as in a musical score. In each tier a different type of annotation can be provided which is time aligned with the video (see Fig. 6.3). Relevant phases in which the speaker gestures can be marked based on a frame-by-frame inspection of the video. Once a period is identified, it can be tagged and replayed.

For each hand, one tier should be set up, and the times during which gesturing occurs should be marked for each hand. During such a gesture unit, the speaker may use multiple gestures, and the next level of annotation for a more detailed analysis entails a breakdown of the stream of gestural movements into gesture strokes, the semantic nucleus of gestures. This level of annotation can be pursued when the researcher has a clearer idea of which gestures are of particular interest.

For those interested in how gesture can be described in terms of form features, it can be briefly mentioned that four parameters are taken into account: hand shape, orientation, movement, and location (Stokoe 1960). It should also be pointed out that there is as yet no conventional transcription system for the form of a gesture and its temporal unfolding. For some examples of how different researchers

[2] www.mpi.nl/tools
[3] http://www.anvil-software.de/users.html

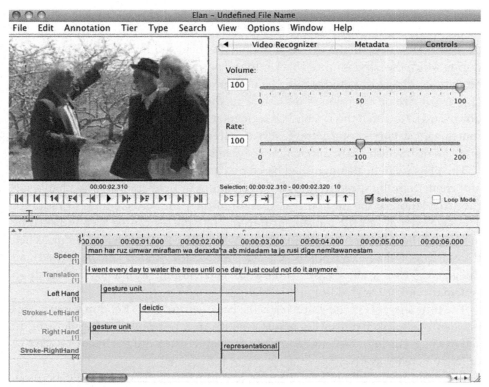

Figure 6.3. ELAN screen. Example for a simple tier set up for basic gesture annotation. Note that the stroke tier for the left and right hand is inserted for those who are interested in more detailed annotation.

transpose the temporal unfolding of the movement in relation to the speech into a graphical representation, see Duncan's annotation and coding procedure described in McNeill 2005; see also Kendon 2004a: 362; Calbris 1990; Mittelberg 2007.

6.6 SUMMARY

The first aim of this chapter was to show why gesture documentation is an important part of language documentation. The second aim was to describe the methodological issues, the procedures, and the results of gesture documentation within language documentation. A minimal approach to the documentation and later analyses of gestural practices has been suggested. This approach requires the researcher to follow certain recording standards, and to broaden the corpus compilation by including recordings of a range topics and genres which are likely to evoke different types of gestures. A further step is making the video recordings accessible for later analyses by annotating the parts of the video in which speakers are found to be gesturing. This minimal approach should be possible as part of a fieldworker's normal recording and transcribing activities. The result, a record of gestural practices of a language community, is invaluable.

Much more can be said about the relevance of gesture in the study and documentation of communicative practices, the methods of data collection and analyses. This chapter provides a first overview of the approaches and the methods used in the study of gesture in communication, culture, and cognition. Gesture is an understudied phenomenon, despite its tight linkage with speech and its complex role in human communication. Accounts of gestural deployment in different cultures are still sparse, especially compared to the descriptions and documentations available for the verbal component of language. Gesture is integral to a better understanding of the use and the interaction of the expressive resources speakers have at their disposal, and of how these shape communicative practices.

CHAPTER 7

INCLUDING MUSIC AND THE TEMPORAL ARTS IN LANGUAGE DOCUMENTATION

LINDA BARWICK

7.1 INTRODUCTION

This chapter is intended for linguistic researchers preparing to undertake field-work, probably documenting one of the world's many small or endangered languages. Recognizing that linguists have their own priorities and methodologies in language documentation and description, I will advance reasons for including in your corpus the song and/or instrumental music that you are almost certain to encounter in the course of your fieldwork. I start by providing an overview of current thinking about the nature and significance of human musical capacities and the commonly encountered types, context, and significance of music, especially in relation to language. Since research funding usually precludes having a musicologist tag along in the original fieldwork, I will suggest some topics for discussion that would be of interest to musicologists, and make some suggestions for what is needed on a practical level to make your recordings useful to musicologists at a later date. I comment on the technical and practical requirements for a good musical documentation and how these might differ from language documentation, and also provide some suggestions on a workflow for field production of musical recordings for community use. Examples taken from my own fieldwork are intended to provide food for thought, and not to imply that music and dance traditions in other societies are necessarily structured in comparable ways.

7.2 MUSIC, LANGUAGE, AND HUMAN DIVERSITY

The human inventiveness that underlies the production and development of language, music, and other communicative modes draws on various innate cognitive capacities for communication that are framed in human sociality (Cross 2008; Sperber and Hirschfeld 1999). Like language, music is taught, learnt, and performed through human interaction. The same arguments advanced for documentation and preservation of the world's linguistic diversity (Grenoble and Whaley 1998) can be applied to musical diversity (Marett 2010; Marett and Barwick 2003). The following survey of the nature and importance of human musicality is intended to provide a framework for the linguistic researcher to understand some ways in which musical and linguistic capacities may differ, and the consequences of this difference for documentation.

7.2.1 Human musicality

Patterned sequences of speech, sound, and movement in the temporal arts of poetry, song, music, and dance are found in every human society. Cognitive psychologists and evolutionary biologists have theorized that this enables group synchrony, thus conferring evolutionary advantage (Cross 2003: 380). Much early work by cognitive psychologists on human musical capacities was tied to western conceptions of music and musical practices, and used western music in its experimental design. It is now acknowledged that non-western musics need to be taken into greater consideration in the field of evolutionary psychology (Cross 2007: 662; Fitch 2006: 206; McDermott and Hauser 2006: 113).

Although some have suggested that in evolutionary terms music can be characterized as 'auditory cheesecake' (Pinker 1997: 534) or 'non-adaptive pleasure-seeking behaviour' (Huron 2001), arising as a side-product of other more important faculties such as language, other researchers have argued that music may have played a key role in enabling the development of human cultures everywhere, and that certain aspects of musicality may have been the target of natural selection (Cross 2009; Huron 2001; McDermott and Hauser 2005). Fitch points out that different components of music capacity may have different evolutionary histories:

music integrates a wide variety of domains (cognitive, emotional, perceptual, motor, ...), may serve a variety of functions (mother-infant bonding, mate choice, group cohesion ...) and may share key components with other systems like language or speech. (Fitch 2006: 174)

The idea that music is a 'universal language' is widespread in western societies, but ethnomusicologists have been deeply wary (Campbell 1997; Harwood 1976) and have generally resisted attempts to define universals in music, stressing the need to understand each music system on its own terms, and pointing to the lack of comparable in-depth knowledge about music in many of the world's societies (Nettl 2000). In recent years, prompted in part by an interest in music by evolutionary psychology and in part by a perceived vanishing of traditional musical cultures in response to pressures from the global music industry (Mâche 2000: 475), there has been some renewed willingness by ethnomusicologists to consider questions of universals. The primary stumbling block to this notion is that, although musical behaviours are ubiquitous, they are heterogeneous, and it is very difficult to arrive at a satisfactory definition of 'music'. Ethnomusicologists and musicologists have generally adopted very broad definitions such as 'humanly organized sound' (Blacking 1973). Others have pointed out that the very heterogeneity of musical expression points to its productiveness as a human capacity. Even though it is difficult if not impossible to arrive at a defining list of features of music that occur in all possible instances of it, all known human societies have cultural practices that can be called musical.

Nevertheless, '[w]hat any non-Western culture conceives of and practises as music may have features that do not map onto Western musical practices in any straightforward way' (Cross 2007: 652). For example, in Pitjantjatjara,[1] one of the Western Desert languages of Australia, the word *inma* encompasses not only music, but ceremony, accompanying dance, body painting, and ritual paraphernalia (Barwick 2000; Ellis 1985: 70–71). This is consistent with Cross's suggestion that since 'the concept of music is amalgamated with that of dance in many—perhaps the majority of—cultures' it would be 'parsimonious to treat music and dance as intrinsically related or simply as different manifestations of the same phenomenon' (Cross 2007: 654). Accordingly, much of what I have to say about music inevitably addresses associated movement, although this chapter will not focus on movement and dance dimensions of ethnographic documentation (those interested will find useful discussion and references in Hanna 2001). Even though not all individuals within a society are musical, and humans may not be the only species to exhibit

---

[1] Language code ISO 639-3 pjt

apparently musical behaviour, 'it seems that humans have an innate drive to make and enjoy music and that they are predisposed to make music with certain features' (McDermott and Hauser 2005).

One human capacity that underlies the social function of music to facilitate group cohesion is entrainment, 'the coordination in time of one participant's behaviours with those of another' (Cross 2007: 15; see also Clayton, Sager, and Will 2005). Interestingly, entrainment of movement to music is not confined to humans, but is also found in various species of birds and other creatures who engage in vocal mimicry, suggesting that the capacity for vocal mimicry, necessary in humans for language learning, is a prerequisite to musical entrainment (Schachner et al. 2009). Attention to periodicity in the form of a sustained musical pulse and period correction mechanisms are two key traits that appear to be both human-specific and music-specific (Bispham 2006). Neuroscientists have shown that the basal ganglia, a brain structure involved in perceptually 'keeping the beat', are also involved in the coordination of patterned movement (Patel 2006: 101). While the human capacity for entrainment of movement to aural periodicity appears to be automatic, entrainment of movement to visual cues is much less successful (Patel et al. 2005). Other research has suggested that music may facilitate group bonding and mood regulation through physiological effects arising from the release of oxytocin (see Huron 2001).

In a series of papers, Ian Cross has argued that music's underspecification of referential meaning also fosters group cohesion by means of what he terms 'floating intentionality' in the 'numerous social situations in which unambiguous reference in communicative acts is not a desideratum as it may precipitate conflict in attitudes or actions' (Cross 2007: 655).[2] He sees music's 'semantic indeterminacy', together with the 'guarantee of cooperativity' offered by entrainment (in group singing and dancing activities), as enabling its social powers to develop and sustain a sense of shared action and intention, and argues that music stands in a comple-mentary relationship with language as part of the 'human communicative toolkit' (Cross 2009: 192).

The ethnomusicologist Bruno Nettl has made the following suggestions for things that all musical utterances have in common:

There is a more or less clearly marked beginning and ending. There is some redundancy, some repetition, balanced by some variety, articulated through rhythmic, melodic, textural means... The musical utterance consists of smaller units which are fairly well marked, and

---

[2] Enfield has argued that the role of inference in semantics means that differing interpretations are perhaps more frequent than commonly supposed even in language. He hypothesizes that 'lower frequency words will show greater variation in meaning across speakers', and that 'because the usage contexts of these words are less varied, speakers will have been deprived of the chance to rigorously test ongoing hypotheses' (Enfield 2007: 7).

for which one may substitute others from a given cultural repertory in order to produce new utterances. (Nettl 1983: 39)

He goes on to enumerate various other ubiquitous or very common features of music. Some apparently universal features of music—such as prosodic chunking, octave generalization and transposability, the tendency for stepwise movements between discrete scale steps, the use of unequal intervals within a scale, descending contours at the end of a phrase—seem to stem from cognitive processing and memorization capacities shared with language (Harwood 1976). Other common features—such as music's association with dance, speech, and religious behaviour, the musical specialist, the valuing of innovation and the exceptional (Nettl 1983: 40–41)—stem from music's social role. The very heterogeneity of musical phenomena and mutability of music-making practices can be seen as domain-specific effects and manifestations of broader human cognitive abilities to create culture (Sperber and Hirschfield 1999), what Cross has termed 'the human capacity for culture'. One of the things that makes artefacts like language and music 'cultural' is that they are 'transmissible by non-genetic means' (Cross 2008: 148). Harwood's observation that 'the process of understanding and engaging in musical behaviour may be more universal than the content of musical knowledge or action' (1976: 523) points to commonalities of function and process in music-learning and music-making.

As many have observed, in several dimensions music and language are 'poles of a continuum rather than existing as categorically discrete phenomena' (Cross 2003: 109). As already mentioned, production and perception of both music and language depend on shared human capacities. Cognitive and neurological studies tell us that although there is considerable overlap in brain processing, there are some specific areas of the brain that appear to be dedicated to musical perception and production (Peretz and Zatorre 2005).

Fitch has proposed a list of 'design features' for music in relation to language that sees them as similar in complexity, generativity, the fact that they are culturally transmitted and that both are transposable in pitch (i.e. a melody or speech intonation pattern is recognizably the same when transposed to a higher or lower pitch). He proposes that music differs from language in having discrete pitches (as opposed to the continuously variable pitch of speech) and isochrony (a regular periodic pulse that provides a point of reference for other temporal features) (Fitch 2006: 178–9). To these may be added music's fostering of simultaneous action in performance, rather than asynchronous interaction as in language (Cross 2007: 654).

Song, the most commonly encountered form of music, integrates music and language, but there are no objective criteria for distinguishing 'song' from 'chant' or 'intoned speech' (Nettl 1983: 39) other than an increasing tendency for quantization of pitch and/or duration as we move along the continuum towards 'song'.

Poetry and other verbal genres that are not sung typically share three further distinguishing 'design features' that Fitch attributes to music rather than language: they typically occur in specific performance contexts, they may consist of a repertoire of discrete repeatable pieces, and they tend to be what Fitch terms 'a-referentially expressive' (equating to Cross's 'floating intentionality' already mentioned) (Fitch 2006: 179–80). The language of song, like the language of poetry, is frequently oblique, cryptic, and emotionally moving (Juslin and Laukka 2003; Walsh 2007). In many cases, poetry and the verbal arts, like music and song, may be measured isochronously and performed in synchrony by multiple participants, meaning that in some key respects they resemble music.

7.3 MUSIC IN LANGUAGE DOCUMENTATION

Although music and song are not directly mentioned in some of the foundational texts of documentary linguistics, sung musical genres may be indirectly referenced by such titles as 'ritual speech event' or 'litany' (Himmelmann 1998: 179) or 'verbal art' (Woodbury 2003: 47). Documenting musical events when they occur (and when invited) falls squarely within language documentation's brief to be diverse and representative of as wide a range of language use as possible: 'documenters take advantage of any opportunity to record, videotape, or otherwise document instances of language use' (Woodbury 2003: 48). As form/meaning units, songs should be 'included in any complete language description' (Turpin and Stebbins 2010: 1). Because of music's ability to 'transform experience' (Mcallester 1971: 380), its integration into other realms of human activity (Cross 2007: 658), and its association with pleasure (Blood and Zatorre 2001), it is likely to be highly valued by collaborators within the speech community (Barwick 2006). Not all societies have instrumental music genres separate from vocal music (e.g. the traditional musical genres of Aboriginal Australia consist entirely of vocal music, some with instrumental accompaniment, but no genres of purely instrumental music). If present, instrumental music is likely to be valued just as highly by community collaborators as vocal music and dance.

Documenting music, dance, and the verbal arts may also yield interesting data for language documentation, suggest new directions of linguistic inquiry, or fill in gaps. For example, in documenting Iwaidja *Jurtbirrk* love songs, new domains of emotional vocabulary emerged, and the songs' frequent use of the first and second persons and directionals filled in some missing slots in Iwaidja verb paradigms that had proven next to impossible to elicit directly (Barwick, Birch, and Evans 2007; Evans, Chapter 8 below).

Because of the likely significance for participants, working on song and music can be a great way to build relationships with collaborators and produce tangible outputs from your project in the form of CDs or videos of performances. In Wadeye, Northern Territory, the iTunes database we helped to create in the Wadeye Library and Knowledge Centre to provide a community access point to research results from various song documentation projects has been the most accessed collection in the library (Barwick et al. 2005; Nakata and Langton 2005). Song and music recordings may be used as a point of reference for future tradition bearers (Marett et al. 2006), and the emotional power of hearing the voice of deceased family members is often remarked on by users of archival recordings.

The efforts of communities and language documenters to record and document musical events may also contribute to an important record of human diversity. 'Many practices testifying to . . . cultural diversity . . . are no longer available outside the archives where our taperecorders have allowed us to freeze their images' (Mâche 2000: 475). The provision of secure archiving for recordings of music and dance may be an important motivation for community collaborators interested in music and dance.

It is clearly impossible to predict exactly the content, structure, and social and contextual meanings of the music and dance in any society. Linguists preparing for their first field trip may wish to prepare themselves by consulting previous research to ascertain whether there are any existing descriptions of performance genres in the area. Even so, because of the high value typically given to innovation and creativity in musical expression, the musical pieces and dances performed are likely to change over time, as new composers and performers make their contributions.

It is, however, possible to make some generalizations as to the types of contexts in which music can be expected to occur. Crucially, the interactive nature of musical behaviour means that it is likely to occur in interpersonal contexts. The use of music in caregiver/infant interactions, including lullabies and children's songs, appears to be ubiquitous in human societies (Trehub 2003), as does its use in entertainment, courtship, and religious or ritual occasions (Cross 2007).

Recording in any of these domains is likely to involve issues of privacy and/or intellectual property. Music, songs, dances, and poetry are defined as 'works' under international copyright law (see Newman, Chapter 19 below), and researchers have an ethical responsibility to acknowledge the moral and legal rights of musicians and performers under both traditional and international law, and to align our research and archiving methodologies to support and not interfere with traditional means of knowledge maintenance and transmission (Janke and Quiggin 2006; Seeger 1992; 2001; 2005).

It is advisable to record information about who has rights and interests in music, preferably before making any recording. Bear in mind that traditional law may classify rights and ownership in quite different ways from western knowledge institutions. For example, in some Australian song traditions, only the song owner or ceremonial leader has the authority to explain a song, although others may well be entitled to sing it and to have a say in whether or not it is documented (Ellis and Barwick 1988; Marett et al. 2006). Taking advice on these matters is likely to provide some lively conversations, as well as helping you to manage your data and any future publication of it appropriately.

7.3.1 Documenting song texts

With knowledge of the language, linguists are in an excellent position to work on song texts, but as I have discussed elsewhere (Barwick 2006), there are some common pitfalls. It may be necessary to work with a group of people rather than a single individual in documentation of song texts. It is advisable to be alert to different interpretations and not to assume that there is a single correct form or interpretation of a song text (Walsh 2010) (see Meyerhoff et al., Chapter 5 above for a discussion of variation in language performance). It is very common for repetition patterns or special song words to be omitted during spoken elicitation of song texts. There may also be elements of improvisation or allowable change between performances of the same song. Phonetic changes, sometimes apparently deliberate, are common and numerous other features of song language have been documented by linguists and musicologists (Dixon 1980; Hercus and Koch 1995; Koch and Turpin 2008; Marett 2000; Turpin and Stebbins 2010; Walsh 2007). In Australia, it is not uncommon for songs to include words in several different languages (e.g. one Murriny Patha *Malgarrin* song our team documented as part of the Murriny Patha Song project contains words in the Kimberley languages Djaru and Gija, as well as English: Barwick et al. 2006). Other songs may include or even entirely consist of words in 'spirit' languages (Marett 2000; O'Keeffe 2010), as is the case in the Mawng *Inyjalarrku* repertory of David Manmurulu (Apted 2010; Manmurulu et al. 2008). It has often been suggested that the metrical stability of some song and poetic forms may lead to the preservation of archaic words or linguistic forms, but song-specific phonetic changes and the frequently cryptic and allusive semantics may make it very difficult to isolate and identify such archaic forms (Koch and Turpin 2008; Turpin 2005; 2007a; 2007b; Walsh 2007).

7.3.2 Suggestions for discussions about music

Linguistic documentation can be invaluable to musicology, and more broadly to studies of human diversity, because of the opportunity to interact directly with tradition bearers in their own language in recording discourse about music and allied performance arts. Here are some suggested areas for discussion, many of which arise from or relate to the points previously mentioned.

- definitions of music (does it include movement/dance, other verbal arts?)
- music/dance terminology (for genres, instruments, parts of songs (e.g. musical phrases), vocal quality/timbre, tempo, rhythm, melody/tune)
- how musical traditions are taught and maintained (is there a formal apprenticeship? are there children's songs? who has the right to learn and teach a given repertory?)
- social dimensions of music-making (who performs music? are social groupings such as gender differentiated by genre or musical practices?)
- general discussions about music and its social significance
- interviews with practitioners about how they learnt music and their activities as musicians
- ideas about music origins (where does music come from?)
- emotional connotations of music (e.g. is there an idea of happy, sad or angry music? what characteristics are associated with emotions?)
- range of music/dance performance occasions
- cultural histories or narratives about music or that include music
- relationship of musical genres to linguistic genres (narrative, poetry, etc).
- change in musical performances over time (how is music performance different now from in the past?)

7.3.3 Technical recommendations for field documentation of music

In most technical respects, recommendations for the recording of musical events accord with the standard recommendations for linguistic recording (see Margetts and Margetts, Chapter 1 above). Further information about ethnomusicological methods and practices can be found in several volumes (Barz and Cooley 1997; Myers 1992; Post 2004; Topp Fargion 2001). There are some additional technical recommendations that are necessitated by the nature of musical performances or the likely uses of the recordings.

First, music requires high-quality microphones. Get to know your microphone and its capabilities well before your field trip (Kolovos 2010; Nathan 2004). Mono microphones, especially miniaturized lapel microphones often recommended for linguistic research, are usually targeted at the frequencies of the spoken voice at 50–15,000hz (Stevens 1998; Sundberg 1987), which means they cannot capture some of the high harmonics that give timbral character to a voice or instrument. To record music, prefer a microphone with a good frequency response over the range of 20hz–20,000hz (check the specification sheet of your microphone).

Because of the group dimension of musical performances, you will need stereo to be able to separate out different performers, and you will also need some directionality to cut out extraneous background noise from audiences and so on. For all-round flexibility in field recording, I recommend the use of a good single-point stereo condenser microphone of the cardioid (semi-directional) type, with XLR connectors and a good wind protection system if you will be recording outdoors. Wind noise can completely spoil a recording, rendering it difficult to work with and even, at worst, unusable.

Placement of your microphone is crucial: for vocal music, make sure it is positioned near enough to the singer to capture the vocal part precisely, but also aim to capture the overall texture of the performance, so that all singers or instrumentalists are included in the field of the microphone (better microphones allow you to select the angle of capture according to the size and distribution of the group). Sometimes you may need to adjust the position of your microphone during a performance (e.g. if the performing group moves). If this proves absolutely necessary, try to do it between items, not during, because you will introduce noise.

On the sound-recording device, record at the best quality available (on a digital device, a minimum of 16-bit, 44.1khz is recommended). Pay careful attention to setting levels. Too low, and background noise will become obtrusive; too high, and you risk clipping and distortion of the signal. Unfortunately, many cheap recording devices do not allow you the option of turning off any automatic level control (also referred to as automatic volume control or AVC) on the recording device. Avoiding AVC is essential for musical performances, where there may be large variations in dynamic range. For example, in some of the Aboriginal music genres I deal with, it is normal for a song item to start with just didjeridu and voice, and for much louder clapsticks to enter partway through the song. AVC will boost volume levels (and any background noise) to the maximum allowable during the early quieter section, but when the clapsticks enter, the relative volume of the voice drops away very quickly, making it much more difficult to hear and transcribe. For this music, I set the levels in advance to accommodate the clapsticks, so that each sound source remains at a similar dynamic level throughout the recording. Resist the temptation to adjust levels during a piece, but if you must do so, do it very gradually. It is almost impossible for later sound engineering to compensate for the variations in levels introduced by AVC or tinkering by the operator, meaning that recordings will be unsuitable for reuse for professional quality CD publication or for use in a video soundtrack.

It is important to record complete items wherever possible. Since it may be difficult to predict the beginning of an item, the best idea is to turn the recorder on at the beginning of a musical event and leave it running unless asked not to. You can later edit the recording to excerpt the individual items if required for docu-mentation or reuse. Discussions between items are often of considerable interest, and can provide important context to the performance (Walsh 2007).

Because musical performances typically have a group dimension (multiple performers, dancers, or engaged listeners), there are good reasons to use video. Video documentation can help with later documentation of participants and their roles, and is the only effective way of documenting entrainment through movement and group coordination to music, including but not limited to dance (Johnson and Snyder 1999; Sklar 2000). Video can also be invaluable for documenting instrumental technique and for clarifying song text transcription in cases where the audio recording is unclear. Unfortunately for the would-be video documenter, in the tropics many performances take place at night, meaning that the quality of video is likely to be poor and perhaps not suitable for archiving.

Dealing with video data in the field situation can be rather difficult because of the large file sizes and the time needed for ingestion of the video data into usable formats for annotation and archiving. Although some video cameras record uncompressed audio, it can also be time-consuming to extract the audio from the video files. If power consumption is an issue in your fieldwork, a more effective use of resources may be to record audio alongside the video, because audio files are comparatively quicker and easier to copy, excerpt, and annotate in the field. In this situation it may be a good idea to call on research collaborators to assist with operation of the two recording devices, because it is difficult to do justice to recording of what may be a one-off event if your attention is distracted by monitoring two recording devices. It can be best to save editing of the video until you are in a situation where you have access to the necessary time and processing power, and plan to work on annotation and documentation at a later stage, or even in a subsequent trip.

When recording movement and dance, it can be useful to document the performance space by use of a sketch diagram and perhaps photos from different angles. Movement annotation systems like Laban and Benesh operate at the level of the complete body, so while close-up shots may be useful for fine details, most of your video footage should include the whole body (Guest 1989), and at least some of it should include the whole performance group including audience participation in order to document entrainment.

7.3.4 Music production for local access

The following section deals with some methods and workflows developed for providing local access to music recordings in several song documentation projects in northern Australia. This method is only suitable for public music that community members have agreed to share at a community level. Most of the procedures described can be implemented in the course of the fieldwork trip. While my description refers to some specific technologies and implementations, the functions described may well be achievable using different software tools and formats. This account focuses on audio editing and production, because of the issues I have already described in managing video in the field.

7.3.4.1 *Setting up and using a music database for local access*

For local access in communities I have used the free iTunes software, which allows for adding metadata, managing, and sharing music files (Barwick et al. 2005; Barwick and Thieberger 2006; Braue 2004). I have found that this is very quick and easy to set up, although its limitations in metadata management and linking to other digital objects such as images and texts mean that it is no substitute for specialist data and metadata management tools. In most cases a suitable computer was already present in the community in the local library, language centre, council, school, or arts centre. From this local repository community members could then select their own preferred songs for listening or burning to CD.

7.3.4.2 *Digital recording of music*

Like most researchers, I now record directly in uncompressed digital audio formats, using a minimum of 24-bit 48khz audio (the audio quality standard adopted by the sound archive of the Australian Institute of Aboriginal and Torres Strait Islander studies, where I usually deposit my recordings). As soon as possible after recording I transfer the file to the hard drive of my computer using USB or firewire connection, name it according to our project conventions, and write a backup copy of the complete recorded file to CD or DVD as well as an external hard drive. Our project filenaming conventions use a reversed date system, and contain some information about recordist and sequence, which assists in local file management on our computer systems during fieldwork. For example, the filename 20110824LB2.wav would be the second file recorded by me on 24 August 2011.

7.3.4.3 *Excerpting music items*

An hour-long musical recording of Murriny Patha *djanba* songs, for example, would typically contain 15–30 song items of about a minute's duration, interspersed with discussion by the performers. Using a sound-editing application I open the file and insert markers at the beginning and end of each song item, leaving about 3 seconds before and after to ensure there is a complete item. I label the song items according to sequence in the file (e.g. 20110824LB2-03 indicates the third song item contained within the master file), and then use the application's 'split file' command to create new excerpt files, having first set the export file format to CD-audio quality (16-bit, 44.1khz), which enables the files to be opened and annotated in most standard transcription and annotation software, as well as providing optimal quality when burning to CD from within iTunes. In this case I am mainly interested in the musical excerpts, which I now import into iTunes. I usually undertake basic mastering and organization of the music database on my own laptop, and then transfer the music files to an iTunes enabled computer.

7.3.4.4 Adding basic metadata

Inside the iTunes library, select the imported files, and add standard metadata such as the name of the session, the date and the recordist, the performers, and other relevant information that allows the music to be findable using locally relevant categories. (For example, I use the iTunes 'group' field for language name, and the 'genre' field for the repertory name.) I usually reserve the Comments field for identifying the specific song text, if known. Most Murriny Patha *Djanba* songs have known composers and fixed texts, so I may add composer and lyrics information if already known. I then create a playlist from the selected files, which are then available to be shared by listening, burning CDs, or adding to portable music players.

Playlists can also be useful for selecting and ordering particular song items for later use in elicitation sessions (e.g. working with the composer and others to transcribe and translate the song text). If playing back from the iTunes host computer, metadata can be added quickly to the iTunes database itself. In other situations, our research teams have transferred such playlists to an iTunes-compatible portable music player for use with low-power portable speakers in elicitation settings where computer use is difficult.

7.3.4.5 Wider publication of research recordings

Once your music collection has been documented, you and your community collaborators may be interested in producing a CD for local or commercial distribution (Barwick, Birch, et al. 2005; Garde and Djimarr 2007; Papulu Apparr-kari Aboriginal Language and Culture Centre and Barwick 2000). Not only does this provide a good means of local distribution and publicity for your project, it can also contribute to community development by developing a wider public profile for performance groups (Marett et al. 2006). If looking to publish music recordings, it will be necessary to liaise with publishing companies to ensure appropriate legal and financial arrangements to protect copyright and other intellectual property rights, as well as working with sound engineers and designers to produce a professional-quality multimedia package. One advantage of publishing recordings in this way is facilitation of reuse and reference to the relevant song items in research in a way that acknowledges and protects the rights of the creators.

7.3.4.6 Web delivery of music

Many commercial music publishers, such as the world music specialist Smithsonian folkways (http://www.folkways.si.edu/), now use internet services to advertise and distribute musical tracks, both for commercial use and through on-line educational services sold by subscription to libraries and universities. The standard availability of web browsers on new computers and the integration of audiovisual media streaming and off-line operation capabilities into emerging web standards and technologies such as HTML5 (Hickson 2011) means that web applications may be an attractive way of presenting multimedia research content such as music collections for community use as well as researcher use. Even when internet connections are intermittent or very slow, it may be possible to set up a web application to operate in off-line mode. In 2009–10, the Murriny Patha song project group in conjunction with the Wadeye Aboriginal Languages Centre built on the recordings and information collected by the project to develop a web database illustrated by song texts with interlinear glossing and contextual information presented alongside streaming audio files (Barwick et al. 2010). In this implementation, in which there were up to thirty performance tokens of the same song text, it proved too time-consuming to link the song texts to each individual sound file; but we have previously used ELAN to produce timecoding for presentation of glossed song texts in systems such as EOPAS, the Ethno-ER online presentation and annotation system (Schroeter and Thieberger 2006). Such initiatives are quite time-consuming, and depend on the availability of resources and much effort in collaboration from community members and researchers.

7.4 CONCLUSION

Since musical behaviour is so widespread, so dear to human hearts, and so closely allied to language and other communicative codes, linguistic fieldworkers are urged to take advantage of opportunities to work with their community collaborators to record and document music and dance when feasible. The results will be of potential interest not only to musicologists, but also to researchers in allied disciplines such as cognitive psychology and neuroscience interested in understanding human diversity in this important expressive dimension.

PART III

COLLABORATING WITH OTHER DISCIPLINES

CHAPTER 8

....

ANYTHING CAN HAPPEN

THE VERB LEXICON AND INTERDISCIPLINARY FIELDWORK

....

NICHOLAS EVANS

8.1 INTRODUCTION[1]

....

The centrality of language in human life means we cannot document any language without understanding all the spheres of knowledge it is used to talk about. Equally, undocumented languages contain too much information to be wasted on linguists alone. As the medium through which the whole fabric of traditional knowledge about everything in the world is transmitted, the importance of these languages stretches out in the direction of many fields of enquiry, from ethnoecology to comparative jurisprudence to deep history to the study of musical and

[1] I would like to thank all of those who have helped me understand Iwaidja, either as speakers or as fellow outsider-investigators: Kim Akerman, †Reuben Arramunika, Linda Barwick, Archie Brown, Bruce Birch, Murray Garde, Illyjilly, †Rae Kirribuk, Ronald Lamilami, Khaki Marrala, †David ('Cookie') Minyimak, Ruth Singer, Amos Teo, †Charlie Wardaga, †Joy Williams, †Brian Yambikbik, and †Mary Yarmirr, as well as two anonymous reviewers of an earlier version of this chapter.

verbal art. Linguists, then, have a responsibility not just to their own field but to all areas of scholarship concerned with the almost infinite varieties of human creativity, and we abrogate this responsibility if we do not seek to follow our documentation of the languages we study down all these lanes and byways of orally transmitted lore.

But, as we struggle to learn a field language and talk to the people who speak it about what matters in their lives, we quickly become aware of how narrow are the boundaries of our knowledge. Whether we fail to identify a local plant or animal species, can't figure out how to describe special ways of tying up roof thatch, or ask dumb questions about mystifying ethnographic details, we risk foreshortening our investigations because—in the words of Ralph Bulmer's Kalam teacher who explained why they hadn't bothered to give him the sort of nuanced terminology for rocks which they had for plants—'why should we waste our time telling you something you couldn't possibly understand?'[2]

One of the appeals of fieldwork is that we get the opportunity to develop interests in many new subjects, from botany through ethnography to thatch-making.[3] But few linguists reach the point where we are able to really penetrate to the heart of all these fields, and in practice the best way to extend our documentary coverage is through some form of interdisciplinary fieldwork. The linguist can then work in concert with experts who can pose the right questions to engage the deep knowledge that speakers have of particular areas. The same Kalam people who had fobbed Bulmer off with a single word, purportedly for all kinds of rock, readily gave his geologist colleague John Chappell a long and nuanced list, because 'your friend's questions showed that he does know about rocks'.

Some form of interdisciplinary collaboration in fieldwork, then, is essential to coaxing out a full encyclopedic coverage of the fine-grained categorizations of its culture and environment which any language contains. In this chapter I show how this can happen in practice, drawing on the efforts of myself and a number of colleagues to document an Australian Aboriginal language, Iwaidja.

To put scientific flesh on the procedural bones of my argument, I will use a specific semantic problem to integrate the case studies I will use in this chapter: the problem of recording a detailed verb vocabulary. In the rest of this section I briefly sketch a range of approaches to interdisciplinary fieldwork, and then give relevant background on the Iwaidja language documentation project. In §8.2 I consider the general problem posed by event-denoting expressions—typically realized as

---

[2] Diamond (1991); Evans (2010: 111).

[3] See Franchetto (2006) for an excellent overview of the main ethnographic issues that linguists should attend to in language documentation, and Haviland (2006) on analytic and elicitation techniques for documenting lexical knowledge.

verbs—for semantic typology. In §8.3 I set up three particular grammatico-seman-tic problems posed by the verb lexicon in Iwaidja: the unusually high proportion of verbs in the lexicon, the analytic difficulties posed by a degenerate and partially fossilized system of double argument agreement across (originally) five genders, and the large number of long and (at least initially) apparently unanalysable verb stems. In §8.4 I illustrate how interdisciplinary fieldwork taking in a range of other disciplines or contingencies driving particular types of data collection—material culture, musicology, linguistic anthropology, art, medical expressions, tidal terms—ended up serendipitously providing data that allowed us to make progress with the problems set up in §8.3. Finally, I draw together these threads into a conclusion in §8.5.

8.1.1 Strategies for interdisciplinary fieldwork

Interdisciplinary fieldwork involving linguists can take many forms, including:

(a) the 'expedition strategy', where a large group are all present in the fieldsite for a lengthy period of time;[4]

(b) the 'partner strategy', where a couple carry out long-term fieldwork in a community, one specializing in language and the other in some other issue (e.g. ethnobotany, kinship);

(c) the 'guest expert' strategy, where a linguist engages in long-term fieldwork in a community, bringing in a range of disciplinary specialists for dedicated shorter-term investigation of particular topics (e.g. botany, material culture, music) in the company of the linguist;

(d) the 'long-haul team' strategy, where an investigator specializing in one field then places one or more students who can deal with other topics—an example being the team established by anthropologist Ralph Bulmer, initially recruiting linguist Bruce Biggs and subsequently linguist Andy Pawley, though this team also made notable use of trained native speakers like Saem Majnep and shorter-term guest experts like biologist John Dumbacher and geologist John Chappell.

Each of these strategies (and many other hybrid possibilities) has its own advantages and disadvantages. The choice between them in a particular case will depend on many factors, such as who is available, what funding support can be obtained, personality of the linguist, and so forth, so I will not adjudicate on the relative merits of these strategies here. I do believe, though, that in all cases it is

---

[4] A famous example being the Cambridge Anthropological Expedition to the Torres Strait, led by Alfred Cort Haddon, in 1898, which produced a 6-volume report covering most ethnographic topics, including language.

crucial that the linguist have enough 'solo time' in the course of their investigations that they can immerse themself in the language and deal directly with its speakers on a one-to-one basis. Otherwise they will find it difficult to acquire the fluency and internalized understanding of the language that is their single greatest research asset. And it is this fluency in the language that allows the field researcher to be a true participant observer, which remains the best way of ensuring that it is the speech community's own practice and expertise, rather than the question-agendas of outside experts, which find their way into a fully rounded understanding of the language.

The advantages of interdisciplinary fieldwork are most obvious in the way it can extend the detailed lexicon of targeted areas—botanical terms with the botanist, rock types with the geologist, terms for spear or personal adornment types with the material culture specialist, and so forth.

The history of interdisciplinary collaboration in field linguistics goes back a long way. An early and particularly illustrious case was the work of Fray Bernardino de Sahagún on Aztec in the mid-sixteenth century in compiling the General History of the Things of New Spain, also known as the Florentine Codex, and arguably the world's first proper ethnography. Originally this was written down in Aztec, then translated into Spanish, and now it is available in English as well (Sahagún 1970), thanks to the translation by Dibble and Anderson. Sahagún's team of Aztec scribes enlisted the expertise of local chiefs and leaders, as well as painters able to portray customs and costumes, enabling him to record a vast panorama covering just about every facet of life from religion to marriage arrangements to the appropriate ways of dealing with errant youths. Revealingly, Sahagún regarded the whole sixteen-volume masterpiece as 'a dragnet to bring in all the words of the language with their meaning'.

A danger of exclusively emphasizing this motivation, however, is that some field linguists simply do not see the compiling of a comprehensive lexicon as part of their core interests—or, at best, see it as a chore rather than a research priority. For this reason, in this chapter I will concentrate on the advantages that inter-disciplinary fieldwork can bring to our understanding of the workings of a central grammatical domain outside the specialist areas being directly investi-gated—event descriptors, typically verbs, that describe what can happen within a given word-world. These are not generally the primary target of investigation by interdisciplinary partners, but from the linguist's point of view are a central and puzzling part of the grammar-lexicon interface. I will show how the investigation of the verb lexicon can be advanced on many fronts, in large part to the rich data thrown up as a by-product of interdisciplinary work in other, targeted domains.

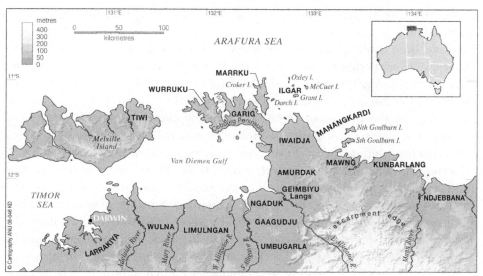

Map 8.1. Location of Iwaidja in northern Australia

8.1.2 The Iwaidja language documentation project

The series of case studies in this chapter will draw on my experiences carrying out interdisciplinary fieldwork on Iwaidja (see Map 8.1), a non-Pama-Nyungan language of Croker Island and the Cobourg Peninsula, Arnhem Land, Northern Territory (Evans 2000a), now spoken by perhaps 150 people, though fewer than 30 still command the full richness of the language. Iwaidja speakers dwell in a region of great multilingualism, with an ideology that ties land to clan identity to distinctive linguistic varieties (see Evans 2010: 5–9).

Typically, Iwaidja speakers also know the closely related language Mawng[5] from Goulburn Island (Capell and Hinch 1970; Singer 2007), the language Bininj Gun-wok[6] (Evans 2003) from the Gunwinyguan family to the south which serves as a regional and ceremonial lingua franca, English, and—among the older people, though most such people have passed away in the last few years—one or more of the highly endangered other languages of the region (Ilgar, Amurdak). Though Iwaidja speakers have now adopted many of the material trappings of Western culture—motorboats, cars, houses, videos—traditional ceremonial life remains strong, drawing in the wide network of relationships of intermarriage and other

---

[5] Earlier spelt Maung.
[6] Also spelt Bininj Kun-wok, depending on which dialect's orthography is being used.

kin ties that link people across scores of clans and dozens of languages in Western Arnhem Land.

I have been working on this language, on and off, since the early 1990s. Throughout that period I have interacted with various types of other investigator. Early on in my engagement with the language, my non-linguist colleagues were lawyers and anthropologists during the preparation of the Croker Island Native Title claim in the mid-1990s.[7] This involved the checking of vocabulary in a number of domains, particularly kinship, social structure, land and sea ownership, and terms for hunting and traditional food-divisions. Later, from 2003 to 2007, I led a language documentation project, funded by the Volkswagenstiftung's DoBeS program[8] and set up on an explicitly interdisciplinary basis. In addition to the two linguists—namely myself and Bruce Birch, who was our anchor-man in the field—this project involved three primary guest fieldworkers: musicologist Linda Barwick, material culture specialist Kim Akerman, and linguistic anthropologist Murray Garde. Each of these guest fieldworkers made two or more short fieldtrips to Croker Island and its surrounds, accompanied by Birch and/or myself. During these trips we carried out detailed investigations of their areas of interest, resulting in products such as recordings of song series (see Barwick et al. 2005; Barwick, Birch, and Evans 2007) and inventories of material culture (see Akerman 2007). The project was also able to enlist the skills of art historian and photographer Sabine Hoeng, who has now begun a PhD on the history of art in the region but also worked with Birch on the compilation of several posters for community use showing traditional knowledge of shellfish, fish, and plants (Birch et al. 2005; 2006a; 2006b; 2007) and in the preparation of a medical phrase book to assist visiting medical personnel (Marrala et al. 2008). We also brought in a range of biologists from the Northern Territory museum who were able to assist with plant, shellfish, fish, and turtle identifications.

8.2 THE ELUSIVE VERB LEXICON

Marianne Mithun (2007b: 32) has pointed out: 'The process of elicitation does tend to reap many more nouns than verbs.' There are many reasons for the difficulty of eliciting verb vocabulary. They include the greater complexity

---

[7] See Evans (2002a) for an account of the role of linguist in this claim.

[8] *Yiwarruj, yinyman, radbiyi lda mali: Iwaidja and Other Endangered Languages of the Cobourg Peninsula (Australia) in their Cultural Context.* Funded from 2003 to 2007 by the Volkswagen Foundation's DoBeS program. I would like to take this occasion to express my gratitude to the Volkswagen Foundation for their far-sighted and generous support of this research.

involved in showing visual prompts for events rather than entities, and the fact that many investigators (e.g. taxonomic biologists) don't tend to think of asking for them. But perhaps most important is the fact that they are likely to be the most cross-linguistically variable part of a language's vocabulary in terms of denotation. This makes it difficult to know in advance what to ask for on the basis of previously studied languages. To make matters worse, the fact that so many grammatical problems are intimately tied up with the grammatical and semantic structure of verbs means that falling short on your event lexicon can hold you back from understanding central architectural issues in the grammar you are dealing with.

As an initial example, consider the rich set of terms in Bininj Gun-wok and other Central Arnhem languages for macropods—kangaroos and wallabies. Some dialects of Bininj Gun-wok—Gun-djeihmi and Kunwinjku—are spoken not far to the south of Iwaidja in Kakadu National Park, and partly due to this, work by biologists and anthropologists interested in Western Arnhem Land flora and fauna had assembled fairly comprehensive species lists by the mid 1980s (Altman 1981; Chaloupka and Giuliani 1984; Russell-Smith 1985). These included terms for all macropod species living in the area, including distinct terms for adult males, adult females, and young. For the antilopine wallaroo (Macropus antilopinus), for example, there are the terms *karndakidj* (adult male), *karndayh* (adult female), and *djamunbuk* (juvenile), as well as *kalaba* for an exceptionally large adult male. And for the agile wallaby (Macropus agilis) the adult male is *warradjangkal* or *kornobolo*, the adult female is *merlbbe*, and the juvenile is *nakornborrh* (there is also a baby term, *nanjid*). The existence of such triple sets is familiar from English sets like *stallion/mare/foal* and *stag/doe/fawn*.

What these lists did not pick up, however, was the existence of an additional set of verbal terms for the distinctive hopping or gait of most macropod types, which extends in most cases to distinctive verbs for the male and female gaits. A subset of these terms is given in (1):

(1) Mayali macropod terms (subset)

barrk	male black wallaroo	*Macropus bernardus*
djugerre	female black wallaroo	
murlbardme	hop (of black wallaroo)	
garndagidj	male antilopine wallaroo	*Macropus antilopinus*
mawudme	hop (of male antilopine wallaroo)	
garndalbburru	female antilopine wallaroo	
djalwahme	hop (of female antilopine wallaroo)	
gornobbolo	male agile wallaby	*Macropus agilis*
merlbbe	female agile wallaby	
lurlhlurlme	hop (of agile wallaby)	

Though documentation of the animal names was almost complete by the mid-1980s, the existence and extent of the hopping verb set did not begin to get comprehensive documentation until the late 1990s, thanks to Murray Garde's very thorough participant-observation-based fieldwork. This included substantial involvement in hunting trips where remarks about gait turned out to be a crucial step in identifying macropod types. In this case the initial identification of the noun terms had been carried out by teams working in close collaboration with biologists, while the verb terms came later through more purely linguistic work. This example illustrates, incidentally, the importance of participant observation in throwing up material that may be overlooked in elicitation or lines of questioning that draw on disciplinary expert's beliefs about preexisting categories. But my main point at this stage is to illustrate that there was a significant time-lag between recording the nominal and the verbal terms in the same vocabulary domain.

Before continuing, it is worth spelling out three key assumptions about language documentation, and in fact about linguistic fieldwork more generally:

(a) It aims for as complete, accurate, and emic[9] lexical coverage as possible.
(b) Not all domains are equally easy to elicit.
(c) Ease of elicitation will reflect, among other things:
  • The 'exhibitability' of stimuli, e.g. by ostensive elicitation (pointing at body parts, or colouring them in to show their extent on a drawing of a body[10]) or by showing pictures of birds, or playing recordings of bird or frog calls.
  • The degree of isomorphism to contact language(s), in the case of translational elicitation. No great semantic harm is done if an English speaker gets the German or Russian words *Bruder* or *brat* by asking for the translation of 'brother', but if I do this for Kayardild[11] I will likely end up with one or more inexact translations: *thabuju* (older brother; male speaker), *duujinda* (younger brother; male speaker), or *kularrinda* (brother of female speaker, but also sister of male speaker).
  • Word class can affect the ease of semantic determination. The simpler a word's morphological possibilities, the easier it will be to obtain, and it is also easier to identify the semantic contribution of the lexical stem and disentangle it from the contributions of a range of inflectional material. Since verbs tend to be the morphologically most complex part of a language's lexicon, this adds an additional layer of difficulty to their relative non-exhibitability.

---

[9] I.e. it captures the language's concepts on their own terms, as far as possible, rather than simply seeking translation equivalents from some contact language.

[10] See Enfield, Kita, and de Ruiter (2006) for the advantages of this technique in discovering unexpected 'cuts' in the extent of body part terms.

[11] Kayardild is another Aboriginal language, not related to Iwaidja except at the deepest level, and spoken many hundreds of km to the east, in what is effectively a different social universe, though it shares significant principles of kinship semantics with Iwaidja. See Evans (1995).

- High-frequency lexical items are easier to detect and define. Excerption from text material is one of the best checks on what a word means, so the more frequently it occurs the more reliable the data is.

Verbs can be difficult to elicit and understand for all but the last of the above reasons. They are hard to exhibit (try imitating the hopping of a female rock wallaby!), generally show limited isomorphism across languages, and belong to a word class that tends to have more complicated morphology than others. But interdisciplinary investigations have the potential to ramp up the likelihood of occurrence of particular verbs in particular domains, thus getting the frequency factor on side, or at least condensing enough discussion on particular topics to give them a chance of showing up in the corpus.

8.3 Verbs in the Iwaidja lexicon: three issues

the set of nouns in a language is always much larger than the set of verbs (Foley 1986: 113)

In this section I discuss three special problems posed for the analysis of Iwaidja grammar and vocabulary by the way it organizes its verb lexicon. This will set the scene for the case studies that I will discuss in §8.4, where I show how particular discoveries thrown up as a by-product of interdisciplinary fieldwork have helped us make progress with these three problems.

8.3.1. Lexicalization in a verby language

Iwaidja is a very 'verby' language—verbs are around 40 per cent of the lexicon, roughly around the same figure as for nouns. Compare this with English, where the ratio of nouns to verbs is greater than 5:1 on some counts (Chang et al. 2002), or with another Australian language, Kayardild, where nouns outnumber verbs by more than 2:1 (figures calculated from Evans 1992), or with languages like Kalam which are normally described as having barely 100 verb lexemes[12]—of which as few

---

[12] As opposed to complex coverb + verb collocations, of which there are thousands, raising the question of what the relevant unit is for comparison, but the figures given above have been widely quoted.

as 15 account for 89 per cent of verb occurrences in text, and 35 for 98.6 per cent of all verb tokens (Pawley 1993: 87).

It has sometimes been asserted that polysynthetic languages encode a greater proportion of their lexicon by verbs than is the case in other languages (Sasse 1988; Mithun 1996). Iwaidja, however, is not a polysynthetic language, although it is definitely head-marking. Verbs agree with up to two arguments by prefix, and have some other verbal morphology (basically for direction and TAM). But they do not show the exuberant growth of applicatives, adverbial affixes, and open sets of incorporable nominals that are found in the polysynthetic languages like Bininj Gun-wok which border them to their south. In this sense, it would be misleading to see the proportion of the total lexicon represented by verbs as directly proportional to the degree of morphological complexity in the verb, since Bininj Gun-wok has more complex verbs but they take up a smaller proportion of the lexicon (around 27 per cent, against 62 per cent for nouns)[13]. (And indeed, before we can test how well the correlation holds between verbal synthesis and the percentage of verbs in the lexicon, we need to get reliable figures on the number of verbal lexemes in the languages in the sample, which we can then cross-tabulate against other typological measures—emphasizing the need to make sure we get good coverage of the verbal lexicon.)

There could be a number of reasons for the swelling of the verbal lexicon in a language like Iwaidja:

(a) Concepts represented by nouns in other languages are represented by verbs instead, with scant change to the actual semantics.
(b) The defining features of holophrastic situations are construed differently, with more of an emphasis on event characteristics than entity characteristics.
(c) Situations are often described using highly specific denotations that incorporate reference to entities as well as processes.
(d) Some kinship relations may be characterized by verbal expressions, particularly in situations that are sensitive to speaker-addressee relations promoting a number of circumlocutions.

We shall see in §8.4.1 that each of these reasons plays a role in boosting some part of the Iwaidja verb lexicon.

8.3.2 A degenerate gender agreement system on the verb?

The ancestor language, proto-Iwaidjan, had a system of five genders (masculine, feminine, vegetable, neuter, land, and liquids[14])—still preserved in Mawng. Verbs

---

[13] Figures calculated from Garde's (1997) electronic dictionary of the Kuninjku dialect.
[14] This is the term used by Singer (2007) for the corresponding gender in Mawng; etymologically it corresponds to the *ku/kun*-marked gender in many other north Australian languages.

agreed with both subjects and objects in gender. However, in Mawng around 35 per cent of verb lexemes have the gender of one or both morphological argument positions fixed in a system of 'lexicalised agreement' (Singer 2007), indicating that the agreement system built in a lot of 'pseudo-arguments'—something like expletive *it* in English *he carked it*,[15] but with more choices for gender and argument position (Evans 2007).

On the basis of material available in the mid-1990s, I concluded (Evans 1998), that Iwaidja had generalized one gender (the neuter) at the expense of all others, retains traces of some others in some verbs with lexicalized agreement (vegetable and land and liquids objects and intransitive subjects, and feminine and masculine transitive subjects with neuter objects), but only a small minority of possible combinations are exemplified. We shall see below that a more extensive sampling of the verb lexicon unearths evidence for a much wider range of combinations.

8.3.3 Morphological opacity of verb stems

Two shortish grammars of Iwaidja had been published before the DoBeS project began—Capell (1962) and Pym and Larrimore (1979). Neither mentions anything about the internal structure of the verb stem, for the good reason that recurring elements are very difficult to find. As a language learner it can be difficult to master large numbers of long stems without any evident internal logic of composition.

Verb stems are long, and lack obvious segmentability once inflectional and derivational suffixes have been peeled off:

(2a)[16] ŋanalʳauɟarama   iwaca
      nganaldaharrama   Iwaja
      'I will speak Iwaidja'
      ŋa- '1sg.intrans.subject', -na 'irrealis': leaving *lʳauɟarama* 'talk'

(2b) ŋatpalʳakpuɭiwakpancilʳin
      ngadbaldakburliwakbanjildin

---

[15] As in 'He'd always bragged about carking it before he hit twenty. When he turned twenty, he escalated the date of his demise to twenty-five' (Kathy Lette 1989: 86). Wiktionary defines this term as 'Australian, New Zealand slang for "to die"', and suggests *cark* may derive from *carcass*. Sarah Barrett (p.c.) suggests the etymology might go back further, to an obsolete West Country dialect word *quark*, meaning the noise someone makes when being strangled, found e.g. in the name of a Somerset house, Quarkhill, built close to a crossroads where the notorious Judge Jeffrey hanged several people involved in the Monmouth rebellion in the 17th century.

[16] At this early stage of the chapter I give examples using both IPA symbols and the practical orthography, which includes many digraphs; later in the paper I will simply use the practical orthography. I will also refrain from interlinearizing examples in these early sections, to encourage the reader to analyse their way into the language. The lʳ (ld in practical orthography) represents a lateral with flapped release.

'we two are going to have a yarn'
Inflectional and derivational elements:
ŋat- '1ˢᵗ plural exclusive', pa- 'irrealis', -kpa 'dual', -ncilʳi- 'reciprocal',
-n 'non-past', leaving lʳakbuɭiwa 'have a yarn'

In these two verbs, it is tempting to posit an initial lʳa or lʳak ∼ lʳas meaning 'word' or 'mouth' or 'tongue'—cf. the Bininj Gun-wok verb *wokdi* 'speak', which can be decomposed into the noun root *wok* 'language' and the verb *di* 'stand'. But there is little evidence for such a morpheme, except in these forms. The Iwaidja noun for 'word, language' is iɲman, the nominal root for 'tongue' is ŋaṛalk. The only glimmer of possible cognacy is the root lʳakbiṛic for 'mouth; lips', which looks like it might be an old compound containing lʳak as its first element, but the correspondence is less clear than one would wish.

The difficulty of decomposing verb stems in Iwaidja contrasts starkly with the situation in Bininj Gun-wok just to its south. Consider how you say 'he has a headache' in the two languages. In Iwaidja (2), the verb stem ŋaʈpanpu (*ngart-banbu*) simply means 'have headache' or, more carefully, 'OBJ has a headache', lit. 'it headaches him', since the verb takes an experiencer object (Evans 2004). It is likely that this verb contains a segment *pu* 'strike' etymologically, but there are no evident recurrences of a morpheme ŋaʈpan in the corpus, and the root for 'head' is the unrelated -waɰyaɭ.

(3)   ɺiŋaʈpanpun
Iw   ri-ngartbanbu-n
      3sg.m.A>3sg.f.O -head.aches-NPst
      'She/He has a headache.'[17]

In Bininj Gun-wok, by contrast, most verb lexemes readily yield to segmentation into crisply defined morphemes (3). There are practically no morphophonemic changes, and almost every element is attested elsewhere as the sole lexical morpheme in a word, so that its meaning can be easily isolated and its contribution to the verbal lexeme identified.

(4)   *ka-kodj-ngarrkme-ø*   [cf. *kun-kodj* // √*ngarrkme* // *ka-ngarrkme-ø*]
BGW   3sgSubj-head-suffer-NPst   IV-head   suffer   3sgSubj-suffer-NPst
      'He has a headache.'   'head'   'suffer'   'He suffered'

Morpheme identification basically depends on the presence of multiple combinations. Would a larger corpus reveal recurrent elements that would allow us to segment such verbs? We return to this question in the next section.

---

[17] Non-standard glosses are: A (transitive subject), f (feminine) m (masculine), NPst (non-past), O (object), ve (vegetable gender). Noun classes (Bininj Gun-wok): IV (basically neuter).

8.4 Some examples of interdisciplinary fieldwork in the Iwaidja project and of how they built up the verb lexicon

Having posed the three analytic problems in the preceding section—all unsolved at the time we began the Volkswagen project—I will now go through each of them, bringing in data largely gathered as a result of various interdisciplinary inquiries, and show how the rich haul of verb lexemes that these threw up as a by-product have helped us to furnish answers.

8.4.1 Semantics of verbal expressions

Some explanation is required if the proportion of the lexicon made up of nouns and verbs varies radically from one language to another (cf. §8.3.1, 'Lexicalization in a verby language'). As it turns out, the verbiness of the Iwaidja lexicon seems to reflect a number of logically distinct factors, corresponding to the questions posed in §8.3.1, which I now examine one at a time.

8.4.1.1 Are concepts represented by nouns in other languages represented in Iwaidja by verbs instead or as well as nouns?

An affirmative answer to this question implies that, for some concepts at least, the meaning expressed by the sign is independent of its combinatorics, i.e. of whether it is a noun or a verb.

One part of the Iwaidja lexicon gives a clear 'yes' answer to this question: the kinship vocabulary. Alongside 'normal' nominal kin terms like *bunyi* 'father, father's brother' and *makamaka* '(paternal) aunt', Iwaidja has verbal kin terms like *mardyarrwun* 'be father or father's sibling of; be first-generation ascending patrilineal relative of' (see Evans 2000b; 2006a). These take the senior kin as their subject, and the junior kin as their object, and make explicit the fact that kinship terms are relational, two-place predicates. Note in passing that the English verb 'to father' is not a good parallel, for a variety of reasons: (a) it focusses on the act of begetting rather than the kinship relation; (b) it cannot be used with female subjects in the way *mardyarrwun* can in a word like *nganngamardyarrwun* 'my paternal aunt, lit. (the female such that) she is (like a) father to me'; (c) it does not generalize to other kin, so there is no English verb 'to paternal grandfather' comparable to the Iwaidja verb *ldakbaminy*.

The semantic difference between nominal and verbal kin terms in Iwaidja is slight. It boils down to two main points:

(a) Kinship verbs have a wider range of referents—e.g. the verb *mardyarrwun* can have a man (father or father's brother) or a woman (father's sister) as subject, whereas the noun *bunyi* can only have a man as its referent. This is a general characteristic of kinship verbs that sometimes contrasts with kinship nouns but not always (e.g. in the grandparent generation both nouns and verbs span cross-sex sibling links), and it is not hard to find examples of kinship nouns in other Australian languages that exhibit comparable semantic ranges (e.g. in Kayardild the word *kajakaja* 'daddy' can also be used to refer to one's father's sister).

(b) Kinship verbs are always 'downward pointing', i.e. they have meanings like 'be older sibling to', 'be father to', or 'be grandparent to', but never 'be younger sibling to' or 'be child of'—though inflected verbs can achieve such reference by forming relative clauses off their objects: 'the one such that I am older sibling to her' for 'my younger sister'. By contrast, there are many nouns that designate kin relations from the junior perspective, such as *ngawiny* 'child of man'. This restriction to downward-pointing terms is unusual in systems of nominal kin terms, both cross-linguistically and in Australia, but is attested for Somali (Serzisko 1983).

Looking at the overall differences between nominal and verbal kin terms, then, they exist but are rather trivial and do not reflect different 'cuts' in the world. Rather, they are an economization of the verbal lexicon that takes advantage of two features of their inflectional potential which allow the number of lexemes to be reduced. The existence of a gender distinction for subject prefixes allows the difference between e.g. 'father' and 'paternal aunt' to be expressed inflectionally rather than by a different root (cf. *rimardyarrwun* 'his/her father', *ri-* 'he > him/her', *kamardyarrwun* 'his/her paternal aunt', *ka-* 'she > him/her'), and the possibility of forming referring expressions off either the subject or object allows either the senior or the junior kin term to be taken as referent, again allowing the system to get away with having just downward-pointing roots: *nganimardyarrwun* 'my father', lit. 'the one such that he is father to me' vs. *abardyarrwun* 'my son', lit. 'the one such that I am father to him'. For the realm of kinship, then, the decision about whether to encode as noun or verb does not appear to result in a significantly different conceptual structure.

8.4.1.2 *Are holophrastic situations construed differently, with more of an emphasis on process than entities, at least in some cases?*

I demonstrate the affirmative answer to this question for Iwaidja by consideration of two semantic domains: clothing/wearing, and tides.

(i) **Clothing terms vs. wearing verbs.** One of our goals in the Iwaidja project was to elicit a detailed material culture inventory together with a set of material culture terms, including terms for items of clothing and body decoration. As part of preparation for our first joint field trip, Kim Akerman prepared a set of photographs showing all known material culture items of the region, on the basis of museum collections: note that these showed objects in isolation, without any person using or wearing them. Akerman, Birch, and I then showed these photos to Iwaidja speakers to elicit the terms for these objects, where still known. In many cases, verbs rather than nouns were preferred as responses to these photos:

(a) Photos of bracelets or arm bangles were described by the verb *dangkardakbung*, lit. '(s)he wears it on his/her arm', though the reference to a particular person implied by the English term is misleading,[18] so that a better translation might be '(something that) one wears on one's arm'. Further questioning revealed that this term could also refer to a watch. (There is in fact a nominal term, *barnda* 'bangle', which eventually came up, but this was not the first term given.)

(b) Loincloth: *wilakbin* 'he wears it tied around his loins'. No directly corresponding nominal term was provided, though the Kunwinjku loanword *manburrba* 'cloth' is often used to denote a sarong.

(c) Belt: the term *ruwurlakbang* 'he has it around his waist' was volunteered. Again, there appears to be no corresponding general nominal term, though the term *kurlawurr* can be used with the more specific meaning of 'ceremonial tasselled belt'.

(d) Headband: the term *kardakbin* '(s)he wears it around his forehead'[19] was used. Again there is no corresponding general nominal term, though there is a term *marraldaka* which refers to 'ceremonial headgear'.

(e) Necklace: speakers volunteered the term *barluriny* 'he has it tied around his neck'; this could also refer to someone with a hangman's noose around their neck. There is no corresponding nominal term.

In all of these cases, then, the favoured and sometimes the only construal was in terms of the action of putting on or wearing, rather than the entity itself. Though wearing verbs are known for some other languages of the world (e.g. Korean, Japanese), they had not previously been reported for Australian languages. Moreover, none of these had been recorded in the Pym and Larrimore draft dictionary (containing 1,605 entries) which was the only record of Iwaidja vocabulary before

---

[18] Cf. Evans (2002b) on the fact that pronominal affixes in many head-marking languages need not be anaphoric.

[19] Incidentally, this term then allowed us to understand the composition of the term for a detachable harpoon head, *kardakbikbin* (with iterative right reduplication of *-kbi*), which can be seen to be a metaphor based on the way the rope of the detachable harpoon head is wound around the head of the harpoon shaft)

the project—nor had Bruce Birch or myself recorded any of these forms before the joint field trip with Kim Akerman. (The two joint field trips with Akerman threw up many additional verbal terms which space prevents me going into here. One of the reasons was that, as a craftsman himself, his first engagement with any new item of material culture was to start trying to replicate the processes of manufacture and use, which he knew about from being able to make similar objects. Iwaidja speakers—in every case accomplished craftsmen or craftswomen themselves—responded to Akerman's craft expertise immediately and began to demonstrate relevant techniques or tricks, throwing up further vocabulary (cf. Birch 2006).)

(ii) Tide terms. The phasal, processual nature of tides does not prevent them from being lexicalized as nouns in English (then combinable with verbs like 'come in/up' or 'go out'). However, Iwaidja uses verbs for all tide terms, as in (5). This suggests that Iwaidja construes tides as processes (e.g. of the sea moving over the sea bottom/beach) rather than as the time at which a particular point is reached, indicated by the etymology of English *tide* as meaning 'time', as the Dutch and German cognates (*tijd, Zeit*) still do.

(5)   *Ma-na-nga-yambu-ng*   *kuburr.*
       3veO-FUT-3fA-tide.be.full-NPst   tomorrow
       'The tide will be really full tomorrow.'

A sample list of Iwaidja tide verbs is given in (6) below. Note that some of these terms employ 'frozen' gender prefixes for subject and/or object (given here in square brackets), a topic I defer until §8.4.2.

(6)   *ldakbarlarlan* 'tide come in'
       ldakirrinirra 'tide come in gradually'
       ldawurtin 'tide come up'
       [inyju-]urdurrikun 'come in, of neap tide'
       [manga-]yambung 'be king tide, be really full tide'
       ijbalmalbakbakbany karlda 'tide be right out, of low spring tide'
       yaburnalkan 'tide go out'
       awunduhulmurndanymin 'be full tide'
       arawurdin mambal 'be spring tide'

A few of these terms were already known from Pym and Larrimore's draft dictionary.[20] Birch had begun collecting some of these terms during the first phases of the

---

[20] Pym and Larrimore had listed them as nouns: the part of speech categorization used in their electronic dictionary didn't allow for deverbal nouns, and in any case some of the lexicalized prefixes can throw analysts off the track here. In their sketch grammar of Iwaidja, Pym and Larrimore (1979: 58–9) include a brief discussion of problematic lexemes which take verbal morphology but which 'are used as nouns with their own meaning', such as *rimuni* 'thunder' (lit. 'he hits it') and *wurtiyin manyij* 'sunset' (lit. 'the sun dives into the water'), though they do not extend this discussion to tide terms.

DoBeS project, but again, it was only when Akerman joined us for joint fieldwork that most of the set emerged—in this case not because they are material culture items, but because of his experience doing other fieldwork (oriented to maritime technology) with other Aboriginal groups (e.g. Bardi) in areas with prominent tidal variation.

8.4.1.3 Are situations often described using highly specific denotations that incorporate reference to entities as well as processes?

A third aspect of Iwaidja's lexical style is the large number of verbs which have 'semantically inherent arguments', i.e. entities which must be included in the semantic representation of the verb's meaning but which do not form syntactically visible arguments (and which would not normally be represented by NPs in clauses containing these verbs).

This is most evident in the many verb classes which incorporate reference to a body part:

(a) Wearing verbs (see §8.4.1.2(i) above), e.g. 'wear on arm or wrist'. As mentioned above, these terms were almost all gathered during joint fieldtrips with Kim Akerman to work on material culture.

(b) Washing verbs, e.g. *wudbinybun* 'wash face', *yijbalwinybukbun* 'wash hands', *(d)angkadbinybun* 'wash arms', *ngartbinybun* 'wash hair', *ldahalwinybun* 'wash feet', *ldakbalwinybun* 'wash lips'; these terms were gathered in the course of regular fieldwork.

(c) tying up verbs, e.g. *angkadburang* 'tie (turtle) up by front fin', *angkarrakbun* 'tie armlet on arm'; these terms were gathered during regular fieldwork.

(d) Posture verbs, e.g. *wartbalman* 'lie with forearm across or resting on forehead', gathered during regular fieldwork.

(e) Pain verbs, e.g. *ambudbunya* 'have a burning pain in one's chest', *ambudbarrki* 'have a sharp pain in one's chest', *ambudbanbun* 'have a biting pain in one's chest'. Most lexemes in this set were elicited by Sabine Hoeng during preparation of an Iwaidja medical phrase book to help visiting medical personnel communicate with Iwaidja-speaking patients.

(f) Painting verbs, e.g. *wudbirrawukbun* 'paint face', *amburrardbanjin* 'paint chest', *ngarndalmirrawun* 'paint wall of shelter'. Most of these lexemes were elicited by Sabine Hoeng while investigating art vocabulary on a spin-off project on Aboriginal artists of the Cobourg region.

These examples show there is a clear 'semplate' or 'semantic template' (Burenhult and Levinson 2008b) for characterizing actions in terms of involved body part loci,

---

However, the ability of such terms to inflect for future tense (5), as well as the full panoply of verbal inflections (subject, object, direction), clearly marks them as verbs.

i.e. for specifying the body part which the action is directed at or affects. I return to the importance of this for the morphological analysis of Iwaidja verbs in §8.4.3.

8.4.1.4 Are there situations where verbal expressions get drawn upon, apparently as circumlocutions indexing the social context of the utterance?

All the examples so far have focussed on the denotational aspect of meaning. However, contextual aspects—by which lexical choice indexes aspects of the situation of utterance, particularly the relationships between speaker and hearer—may also play a key role in shaping lexical and grammatical structures.

In many Australian languages this insight is particularly evident in the formulation of kinship expressions, which are shaped not just by the relation between the 'anchor' or propositus and the referent, but by the adjudication between, and recognition of, the fact that the referent may be kin to both speaker and addressee. The question of which speech act participant to choose as anchor may be pragmatically delicate, so much so that many languages have developed expressions that simultaneously relate the referent to both participants, through various formulations, or otherwise obscure the choice.

Consider the expression 'Mary's aunt Joan': 'Mary' is the anchor and Joan is the referent, with the two-place logical relation 'aunt_of X,Y' holding between them: producing such an expression in English is straightforward. Now imagine you are Mary, and that I am your mother, with Joan being my sister. In English I have a range of alternatives: I could refer to her as 'auntie Joan' or 'your auntie Joan', taking your perspective implicitly or explicitly, and leaving my own relationship to her (and you) out of explicit account. I could also refer to her as 'sis' or 'sister Joan', though this would sound pragmatically odd, largely because it is unusual for senior speakers to adopt their own perspective over that of their juniors. But what is not available to me in the grammar or lexicon of English, or of other European languages, is a way of referring to her from both perspectives at once, with a term that means something like 'the one who is your (maternal) aunt and my sister, me being your mother' (about the nearest would be to say 'our Joan', but this would then omit any overt kin term).

Methods for recording kin terms through the so-called 'genealogical method' pioneered by W. H. R. Rivers (1910), and employed during the famously interdisciplinary Cambridge Expedition to the Torres Strait, project this English downplaying of contextual factors into the elicitation of kinship terms, by not treating speaker-addressee kinship relations as one of the factors that needs to be investigated within the domain of kinship terminology.

Since the early 1980s Australianists have uncovered a number of languages whose systems of kinship terminology do index speaker-addressee, i.e. interactional, relations through systems of so-called 'triangular' or 'trirelational' terms—see e.g. Laughren (1982), McConvell (1982), Merlan (1989), Garde (2002), and Evans (2003). Lea (2004) has reported a very similar system in the Amazonian language Mēbêngôkre. One object of our research was therefore to see whether Iwaidja had such a system, and if so to document the relevant lexical terms. Note also, before continuing, that in some circumstances it is possible to represent the 'triangle' of kin reference in context through a two-place verb: this is straightforward if one relation is siblinghood (e.g. 'our mother', where speaker and addressee are both children of the same mother) but can also be achieved, more obliquely, by appealing to other shared properties (e.g. both being in the same lineage) that can be reflected in conventionalized terms, as we shall see with the term *arrambadbi* below.

Even knowing what to look for, though, does not necessarily make it easier to find: asking speakers of Aboriginal languages if they have terms that mean things like 'the one who is my daughter and your mother' never, in my experience, turn up the sort of lexical items one is looking for. Initially (in our 2004 field season), we therefore adopted a strategy that built on linguistic anthropologist Murray Garde's own expertise in the very elaborated trirelational system of Bininj Gun-wok, known in that language as Kun-derbi, Gun-dembui, and other dialect-specific variants. Since most Iwaidja speakers also speak excellent Bininj Gun-wok, it was possible for him to work by giving examples of Kun-derbi terms and asking speakers how they would express them in Iwaidja—and in fact it turns out that Iwaidja does have a number of such terms, in a register known in Iwaidja as *kundeybi*.

The name of this register is a clear Bininj Gun-wok loan, though the actual terms within it are all indigenous to Iwaidja. Once we had a few examples, speakers then got the hang of our line of enquiry and began to furnish other items. (Note, methodologically, that in effect this took the expertise that Garde had developed in another mutually known language of the region through participant observation, then proceeded to use it as an initial source for translation-based elicitation, but where the elicitation language is much closer in structure to the target language than English is. Later on, as Birch developed fluency in Iwaidja, new Kundeybi terms have turned up through direct participant observation in Iwaidja.)

Of the seven Kundeybi terms that were collected by late 2008, two are verbal in form.

The form *arrambadbi* is used precisely in the Mary-and-Joan scenario outlined above: it would be used by a woman speaking to her daughter about someone who is the speaker's sister and the addressee's (maternal) aunt. Analytically, it combines a vowel-harmonized[21] form of the prefix *arrumb(u)-* 'he/she/they > us' with the

---

[21] It is not currently clear why the second vowel gets harmonized in this word, but it may reflect ongoing conventionalization of the word as a gestalt—which would of course lead to it ultimately

verb root *adbi* 'find', thus in this context '(the one such that [someone (to wit, my mother)]) found (conceived) us (i.e. myself and her [and on to you in the next generation])'.[22] Other prefixal combinations with this verb are also possible.

The second verbal form, *yarrunan*, is used by a woman to someone she calls *ngawiny* 'patrichild; child through the male line, i.e. brother's child for a woman's speaker', in referring to someone else she calls *ngawiny*, who would therefore be a sibling of the addressee. Formally, this combines the prefix *yarrun-* 'you singular > us; you plural > me, us' with the verb root *an* 'spear'; at present the motivation for this locution is not understood.

Two general points arise from these examples. First, the role of a linguistic anthropologist (Garde) in the team was crucial in breaking into this problem—for the dual reasons that (a) by his disciplinary training he took an approach that did not bracket out the contribution of interaction to verbal formulation, and (b) prolonged participant observation while learning to speak a related language fluently enabled him to understand a system that can easily slip by unnoticed if one takes a denotationally focussed inquiry as starting point. Later this was followed up by Birch, who, as the investigator who spent most time in the field and has gained the most fluency in the language, was best placed to apply participant-observational methods in Iwaidja itself.

Second, there are interesting reasons why verbal terms seem to play an important role in the system of triangular kin terms. Partly this seems to follow from the fact that verbs can index referent sets (subject and object), which combined with the subset-reference principle mentioned above allows relationships to be constructed as reflecting a common standpoint on the referent. But they also seem to reflect a method of describing kin relationships that uses abstract metaphorical extensions of verbal terms ('find', 'spear') to construct the rather ineffable shared relationships that can then be expressed as holding with respect to the referent, jointly, between both speaker and addressee.

---

becoming a deverbal noun, rather than a verb proper. For the moment its treatment as a verb (albeit with the above irregularity) is warranted by the existence of other prefixed forms (*kudnadbi*, *yadnadbi*, etc.) which behave regularly in terms of their verbal prefixes.

[22] The fact that the inclusive/exclusive distinction is neutralized in objects of transitive combinations nicely allows an implicit extension from 'found us <exclusive>' i.e. my sister and me, to 'found us <inclusive>', i.e. my sister, me, and on to you in the next generation. Note also that the technique of referring to one member of a subset by a prefix denoting the superset is widely used in kinship expressions—e.g. *awunbani*, lit. 'they two sit (i.e. live together)' can refer either to a pair (husband and wife) or, using the subset reference method, to just one member of the pair, i.e. 'the one such that they two live together'. If anything, it is even more widespread in *kundeybi* expressions, where it achieves an appropriate balance of vagueness and inclusiveness.

8.4.2 Lexicalized gender agreement

As mentioned in §8.3.2, when we began the DoBeS project it appeared that Iwaidja had jettisoned most of the morphology associated with a five-way gender contrast in proto-Iwaidjan, and still preserved in Mawng. However, a number of obscure verbs—again mostly thrown up by interdisciplinary fieldwork—have shown that far more of the proto-Iwaidjan gender agreement prefixes on verbs have survived than we originally thought. These relics are difficult to detect, however, because of the highly lexicalized and non-productive nature of some parts of the Iwaidja prefix paradigms.

Often these are limited to a single verb—what Singer (2007) has called 'lexicalized verb agreement', rather like a verb + noun idiom (*kick the bucket*) except that the fixed element is a pronominal prefix of fixed gender, rather than a noun (see §8.3.2). To get an impression of what has happened with Iwaidja, imagine that English had just kept *he* and *she* as 3rd person subject pronouns (shedding *it* and *they*) and just kept *'m* as object pronoun—except that a few verbs can only use *it* as subject, regardless of the referent, and a few others can only use *'m* as object, again regardless of the referent.

If there is just a single verb with a particular prefixal combination, of course, segmentation is difficult to justify since there are no recurring partials, which then makes it hard to demonstrate whether the word should be treated as a verb rather than a deverbal nominal. Luckily, however, the issue can usually be clinched by seeing if there is a future form, since the future prefix *-(a)na-* is generally placed between prefix and root.

To illustrate, here are three examples of previously unattested gender prefixes with lexicalized verbs.

8.4.2.1 ang- *as intransitive subject*

In Mawng, this gender form denotes what Singer (2007) called the 'land and liquids' gender. Pym and Larrimore (1979) refer to this prefix occurring in the object slot of a score or so of transitive verbs generally associated with 'earth' or 'ground', but do not mention the possibility that it can also represent intransitive subjects.

However, a (so far unique) example of this came up during the musicological part of the project, which brought in the collaboration of Linda Barwick. In one of David Minyimak's songs in the *Jurtbirrk* genre (see Barwick et al. 2005; Barwick et al. 2007), he uses the verb *angmarranguldin* (segmentable as *ang-* plus *-marranguldin*). Interpretive discussion of this verb with a range of speakers, and elicitation of further contexts, showed that it refers to particular meteorological conditions (e.g. lightning, wind) that bring back memories associated with a place from which sensory cues are transmitted by the weather conditions. Examples would be the smell of a wind changing as one sits on a beach, or the sight of a place burning after being struck by lightning. The semantic motivation for the *ang-* prefix on this verb appears to be that it is the place or 'country' that is the source of the emotion felt by some affected person—a feeling summed up in the title of Xavier Herbert's novel *Poor fellow My Country*. As discussed in Barwick et al. (2007), many Iwaidja terms for the subtler nuances of the emotional palette appear rarely if ever in normal language but turn up with much higher frequency in the poetic register of song language, tuned as it is to feeling and interiority.

8.4.2.2 manga- *[vegetable object + feminine subject]*

Earlier work, since Pym and Larrimore (1979), had isolated both a vegetable object prefix *ma-* and a feminine transitive subject prefix *nga-* in restricted contexts: for example, the *nga-* prefix only turns up in a tiny corner of the paradigm, for the combination '3sg feminine subject acting upon 3sg object'.[23]

From these forms one would predict the existence of a form *manga-*: 3sg. femA>3veg.O; normal morpheme order is OA—if both are 3rd person. But the non-productive nature of the Iwaidja verb paradigm means that many theoretically possible combinations appear simply not to occur: normally, for example, if one puts a feminine subject with a verb taking a *ma-*object this would be expressed not with *manga-* but with *mambu-*, which etymologically is *maN-* (3fem object with a nasal object marker that has elsewhere disappeared) and *bu-* (3pl subject marker)

Mawng attests this combination, e.g. in the verb *ma-nga-niking* 'she is carrying (it: vegetable) firewood' (Singer 2007: 99), and I had tried making up verbs using this combination, but had met with no success, except for people saying things like 'sounds like you're trying to speak Mawng, but it would be wrong in Mawng anyway!'

When intensive questioning by Kim Akerman about tide terms extended our vocabulary in that domain, however, a word with just this prefix turned up: *mangayambung* (7) means '(it is) a king tide, a really full tide'. (The etymological motivation for these lexicalized gender prefixes may lie with a conceptualization like 'it (sea/current/wave [fem.] lifts it (seaweed: veg.) high up onto the beach' or some such.)

(7) *ma-nga-yambung*
    3sg.v.O-3sg.f.A-be.high.tide
    'It is a king tide'

On first hearing this term, it was not completely clear that it was a verb, rather than (for example) a noun compounded with the root *manga* 'throat'; but checking

---

[23] And even there it is heavily disguised, with the combination 3sgFemA>3sgO normally appearing on the surface as *ka-*, underlyingly *K-nga-* where *K* represents the hardening effects of a 3sg object on the following consonant (Evans 1998).

revealed a future form *manangayambung* ((6) above) which clinches its verbal status, since the future prefix is restricted to verbs.

So far this is the only word we have recorded with this particular prefix combination.

8.4.2.3 inyju- [feminine object iny- plus allomorph ju- of 3pl transitive subject bu-]

Feminine transitive subjects in *nga-* have been attested for Iwaidja since Pym and Larrimore (1979), as mentioned in the previous section. But until our joint work with Akerman there had been no attested occurrences of the corresponding feminine absolutive prefix *iny-*, known from Mawng and Ilgar. Once again, though, an example popped up in the specialized vocabulary of fire tools: the expression for rubbing or twirling a firestick takes the verb *wu-* 'hit/impact upon' and combines it with an object prefix of form *iny-* (reduced to *ny-* by vowel coalescence after the 1sg transitive subject marker *a-*), as illustrated in (8). Here the etymological motivation for the use of the feminine object marker appears to be the commonly employed sexual symbolism in which a firedrill (conceived as a masculine part) enters and creates heat in a receptacle (conceived as a feminine part), hence 'hit/impact upon (a feminine object)'.

(8) *Ngabi*   *a-ny-bu-n*   *kijbu*
     1sg   1sgA-3femO-hit-NPst   firestick
     'I am rubbing the firestick.'

Again, this is the only word we have recorded with this particular prefix combination.

8.4.2.4 Lexicalized gender agreement: summary

As these three examples illustrate, the atrophy of the inherited proto-Iwaidjan prefix paradigm, which productively combined five subject genders with five object genders,[24] into the reduced Iwaidja prefix paradigm did not wipe out as many cells as previously believed. It now looks as if some cells in the paradigm have managed to survive in combination with just a single verb—a finding of great interest to our understanding of how paradigms wax and wane. But each of the three new cells reported on above only came to light as a result of the sorts of multidisciplinary lexical probing outlined above.

---

[24] Well, almost—there is no evidence from any Iwaidjan language of combinations with any of the 3 non-human genders as transitive subject; see Evans (1998) and, for the Mawng paradigms, Capell and Hinch (1970) and Singer (2007).

8.4.3 Segmentability of verb stems

In §8.3.3 I stressed the difficulty of making sense of the many long, apparently unsegmentable verb stems in Iwaidja. Then, in §8.4.2, I illustrated how subsequent collection of verb vocabulary has revealed that many verb stems have specific body-part locus meanings.

Assembling the verbs discussed in §8.4.2 and sorting them by the body part involved has enabled us to identify many 'corporeal prepounds'—recurring first elements of verbs where a recurring form correlates with a recurring meaning. Here are some examples:

(9) *dangkardakbung* 'wear on arm or wrist'
    angkarrakbun 'tie armlet on arm'
    angkadburang 'tie (turtle) up by front fin'
    (d)[25]*angkadbinybun* 'wash arms' (cf. *winybun/binybun* 'wash')
    Recurring element: *(d)angkad* ∼ *(d)angkard* ∼ *angkarr* 'arm, forefin'

(10) *ambudbunya* 'have a burning pain in one's chest' (cf. *wunya* 'burn')
    ambudbarrki 'have a sharp pain in one's chest'
    ambudbanbun 'have a biting pain in one's chest' (cf. *manbun* 'bite')
    Recurring element: *ambud / amburr* 'chest'

(11) *ldakbalwinybun* 'wash lips' (*winybun* 'wash')
    Residual element: *ldakbal* 'lips, mouth'
    with some additional evidence for *ldak* 'mouth' e.g. *ldakburran* 'have in one's mouth'

For most of these elements the corresponding free-form body part term is formally unrelated: cf. *(d)angkad* 'arm' (9) with the semantically equivalent noun root *mawurr* 'arm'. But for some others it is possible to find resemblant forms: an example is the noun root for 'chest', *amburryak* 'chest', clearly related to the verbal element *ambud-/amburr-* 'chest'.

Likewise the second element is sometimes independently attested as a verb in its own right (e.g. *winybun* 'wash', *wunya* 'burn'), but in many other instances it is not (e.g. *warrki* ∼ *barrki*).

It now appears that a once-productive N_{bp}+V compounding strategy of the Bininj Gun-wok type has become frozen, leaving body part morphemes marooned inside the verb stem. Sound changes have increasingly disguised their form, and introduced formal variation making the signifier harder to parse. At the same time, lexical changes have replaced many of the (presumed) original nominal lexemes with new lexemes unrelated to the prepound form. This is the most likely

---

[25] A small number of Iwaidja verb stems have initial *ds* that are only found with a limited set of pronominal prefixes (basically comprising an initial subject element plus an object element ending in *K*). The most likely historical scenario is that the *d* is original and has been lost in all but this environment (Evans 2006b).

explanation of why the Iwaidja verb-stem structure is so much more opaque than those found in Bininj Gun-wok.

Working from the much larger corpus of verb stems that we have now, thanks in good part to the expansion of specialized lexical forms that interdisciplinary work produced, we have been able to analyse a large number of Iwaidja verb lexemes into the following form (see Teo 2007 for detailed evidence)

(12) Body.part.prepound + stem

This morphological analysis only became possible once we had a large enough verb vocabulary to attest multiple instances of the same prepound. By bringing the morphological verb structure into line with that of its neighbours to the south, it has set the scene for the next stage of comparative research, which will be to compare N+V compounds between Iwaidjan and Gunwinyguan languages.

8.5 CONCLUSION

I have stressed how most of the verbs discussed above came to light through interdisciplinary fieldwork. This is not to say they wouldn't eventually have surfaced anyway, given enough linguist-in-field-years or a large enough corpus, or omniscient lexicographers who know, as Sir James Murray well illustrated when he compiled the *OED*, to ask about everything. But the fact is that, within our own project, it was the interdisciplinary work that was crucial in bringing most of these verbs to light: structures that had not yielded to front-on linguistic attack were prised open through interdisciplinary work that came around the side. At a certain point, of course, once patterns start to emerge we can start to play with them in the way linguists excel at, making up new combinations which we guess might occur. But typically this does not begin to happen until we have at least some combinations to start with.

Returning to semantic typology, a fundamental and still unanswered questions is: are some semantic domains more variable cross-linguistically, and if so which?

It is a good bet that event descriptions are one of the most variably lexicalized domains. Yet we won't be able to test this hunch properly until we have extensive cross-linguistic data for the verb lexicon that is comparable in detail to that for the nominal lexicon. My experience across a range of fieldwork projects is that this is going to depend on a whole range of interdisciplinary collaborations—as varied as the realms of knowledge that any language can represent[26]—which greatly broaden the situations in which language in use can be encountered and noted.

[26] For the sake of narrative unity I confined myself in this paper to data arising from the Iwaidja project. But to broaden the argument using examples from other projects, here are some other examples (all verbs) from interdisciplinary work conducted myself or by close colleagues on other Australian languages: (a) Kayardild verbs I only became aware of under the pressures of doing translation or interpreting in legal contexts: these included the difference between two causatives which I had been fruitlessly trying to elicit for years, but which cropped up when speakers pointed out that I used the wrong one (*yulkaanmarutha* rather than *yulkalutha* for 'make permanent, for ever') in the context of a native title handover claim because 'they're only giving us the paper, then we have to trust that', i.e. the purported causation of permanence was mediated rather than direct. Also through interpreting for lawyers, I discovered a relict applicative suffix -*ri*- as attested in the verb *biyarija* 'paddle [a canoe] with [water supplies]', when a lawyer asked me to ask whether people knew enough about the water supplies available on an island to take baler shells of water with them on their canoes when they visited

(b) another example of specialised vocabulary that only arose from transcriptions of Bininj Gun-wok songs from the Nabarlek song cycle in work with Murray Garde, Allan Marett and Linda Barwick on the Western Arnhem Land Endangered Song Language Project, is the rather gruesome verb *ngalwowme* 'drown out the death cries of someone being killed by making camouflaging noises over the top'

(c) verbs of specific choreographic movements in Murrinh-patha, like *wintjirdum* 'while dancing drop on one knee with one hand up one hand down and head bowed for a moment after that (most likely with a woomera)', that arose during the investigation of Murrinh-patha song texts by a team comprising linguist Michael Walsh and musicologists Linda Barwick and Allan Marett; Walsh suggests that compressed song texts favour the appearance of such words because of they way their brevity allows 'semantic density', like a small dessert or liqueur, highly specific tastes can be processed (Walsh 2007:132).

Examples like these, which could readily be multiplied, emphasise that the cases treated in the present paper are just the tip of a very large iceberg.

CHAPTER 9

UNDERSTANDING HUMAN RELATIONS (KINSHIP SYSTEMS)

LAURENT DOUSSET

9.1 INTRODUCTION

Kungkankatja, minalinkatja was the answer of an elderly man to my question, 'How come you call your cousins as if they were your siblings?', when I expected to hear different words, one for sibling and one for cousin. This episode occurred at a very early moment of my initial fieldwork in the Australian Western Desert; certainly early enough to set the stage for some investigations into the complex nature of people's own (emic) views of the idea of human relationships, while considering them against the structure of universal (etic) typologies of the human family. *Kungkankatja, minalinkatja,* literally 'from a woman, from a man', meant in the context of my question that the children of a woman and those of her brother are to be considered identical. Although I shall not go into the analytical details of this particular example (see Dousset 2003; 2005), it will nevertheless provide us here with some elementary guidelines for the conducting of linguistic investigations into the structure of those human relationships anthropologists call kinship and social organization. As we shall see later in this chapter, such short phrases have the capacity to flatten out pieces of intertwined and complex semantics.

'Kinship and marriage are about the basic facts of life,' Fox once wrote (1996 [1967]:27). 'They are about "birth, and conception, and death", the eternal round that seemed to depress the poet but which excites, among others, the anthropologist.' 'Kinship is a system of social relationships that are expressed in a biological idiom . . . It is best visualised as a mass of networks of relatedness, no two of which are identical, that radiate from each individual,' as another scholar wrote (Tonkinson 1991[1978]: 57). Kinship also appears as a 'huge field of social and mental realities stretching between two poles. One is highly abstract: it concerns kinship terminologies and the marriage principles or rules they implicitly contain or that are associated with them. The other is highly concrete: it concerns individuals and their bodies, bodies marked by the position of the individual in kinship relations' (Godelier 1998: 387).

While many anthropologists would agree today that there are no so-called kin-based societies (Godelier 2004; Dousset 2007)—societies in which kinship provides the overarching ideological domain for social structure and behaviour—they would also argue that in many, if not in most, societies it is an important vehicle of social structure, behaviour, and moral order. Be it landownership and its transmission, behavioural codes, role distribution in ritual contexts, status attribution and its political and economic consequences, etc., the domain of kinship is often involved with considerable effects. The fact that in Euro-American systems of law children usually inherit property from their father and mother is a matter of kinship. The analysis of the domain of human relationships thus involves multiple and intertwined levels of social reality—from the human body to the social and moral order, and from spheres of practice to the domain of the symbolic.

This chapter is limited to pointing out a few central concepts and processes that are elementary in the investigation of human kinship. It is strongly recommended that the reader consult some further readings that are particularly useful, such as Carsten's *Cultures of Relatedness: New Approaches to the Study of Kinship* (2000), Schweitzer's *Dividends of Kinship* (2000), or Stone's *New Directions in Anthropological Kinship* (2001), for contemporary discussions on the kinds of research interesting students of kinship nowadays. Above all, however, I recommend Holy's *Anthropological Perspectives on Kinship* (1996), which is the most comprehensive and open-minded piece of work on the topic I have come across.

For the sake of organizing data collection and analysis, it is useful to split the complexities of kinship into its various constituents from which in-depth analysis can proceed. The chapter is thus divided into three parts. In the first, we will discuss the concept of social organization as distinct from but related to kinship itself. The next part will introduce the reader to the constitutive domains of the study of kinship, which are called 'kinship terminologies'. The use of jargon has been kept to a minimum, but avoiding all of these special terms is neither possible nor helpful. At the first use of each of these terms, their meaning will be briefly explained. The last and shortest part will include some avenues for tying kinship to other and more symbolic and bodily aspects of social reality.

9.2 Social organization and kinship: two distinct but complementary domains

The expression 'social organization', as used by anthropologists, may produce some misunderstanding. It does not cover all that is social and organized. The social universe is indeed organized, since reactions to individual behaviour would otherwise be unpredictable and 'living together' difficult. What the expression 'social organization' covers, generally speaking, are those elements that organize people into locally recognized groups, categories, or classes dividing the social body into more or less distinct entities.

One could have started describing social organization by discussing the notion of the 'family'. The family however, as it is understood in its Euro-American meaning, is neither universal nor inevitable. Among the Na of the Yongning region in China, to quote an extreme example, a mother lives with her brother, both raising the children of the genitor (note that I avoid using the term 'father' here), who himself lives with his own sister. Children most often don't even seem to know who their actual genitor is (Hua 2000).

Instead, the most classic and better-defined examples for the kinds of groups or categories that constitute a social organization are clans and lineages. The Baruya of the Papua New Guinea highlands, counting over 2,000 people living in 17 villages, for example, are organized in 15 clans. One of these clans gave the name to the entire society, the Baruya, which is also the name of an insect the Baruya clan members are not allowed to kill. The red wings of this insect are associated to the 'road of fire' the apical ancestor of the clan took in mythical times when he was sent by the sun down to earth to unite people and to establish the clan. Similar myths exist for each clan whose members recognize a link of kinship to their apical ancestor and each such clan is divided into several 'brother lineages' that refer to the same ancestral origins. Since members of one and the same clan share the same ancestor, it is considered incestuous to marry a spouse from within the clan. The clans of the Baruya society are thus linked to each other through ties of marriage (Godelier 1982; 2004).

A society, tribe, or ethnic group may be divided into a number of groups that are called 'clans' if their apical ancestor is mythical, or 'lineages' if genealogical memory traces ancestry back to one single human being. In many cases, as with the Baruya, the clan with its mythical ancestor is itself divided into several lineages each with their human ancestor. These human ancestors themselves, however, link back to one and the same mythical ancestor. They are brother or sister lineages.

Importantly, membership of these clans or lineages is not determined by ambiguous criteria. It is not a club that you can join or leave as you wish. Membership is determined by explicit rules that belong to the realm of kinship. We may talk of 'patrilineal' clans or lineages if membership is defined through the male line, as is the case with the Baruya. In this case, a father, his sons, his sons' sons, etc. belong to the same clan or lineage. A man's daughter belongs to this clan as well, but since she will marry a man from another clan, her children will follow her husband's line of membership.

Less frequent are so-called 'matrilineal' clans or lineages. In this case, membership follows the female line. A well-known example are the Navajo of North America, who think of kinship in terms of *k'é*. 'My relatives', or *shik'éi*, are the particular ones with whom one shares intense enduring relationships: they are relatives through what is called clans. Birth affiliates a child with her or his mother and the mother's clan, those who came out of the same womb. Birth and clanship are located in space, and clan names derived most likely from place names. While Navajo clans do not hold property in common, members often visit and help each other. '*K'é* and clan relationships are the primary way in which the Navajo people locate themselves in the social universe' (Lamphere 2001: 39).

Summarizing, we can say that a clan or lineage claims a common mythical or historical ancestor, and usually recognizes some shared substance, shared memory, or any other shared background which is used to justify the social body as a corporation. Landownership, residential composition, conflict and its resolution, roles in ritual, and so on are in may cases articulated around membership of such categories and around the opposition or distinction of various such categories within a society or ethnic group.

These groupings (clans or lineages) abide by rules that organize their internal structure and establish the relationships between all the clans of a society (usually marriage rules, as we shall see). Additionally, these clans may be organized around local typologies and representations that need to be understood in order to understand the social structure. The Maisin of Papua New Guinea, studied by Barker (e.g. 2005), know two types of clans, *Kawo* and *Sabu*. They stand in an asymmetrical relationship to each other: the former host so-called Great Men, who are leaders and have the role of taking responsibility in other clans, and the latter do not have such Great Men and so are expected to listen to the advice formulated by the former. In other cases, such as in many Australian Aboriginal or lowland Amazonian groups, clans stand in a more symmetrical relationship to each other. They all claim some shared relationship to history, language, and land and thus constitute together a larger unity (a society, tribe, or ethnic group), but each clan also claims to be descended from one particular ancestral being, has the responsibility for particular sites or stretches of land, and in some cases addresses the others using particular speech etiquettes that mark clan distinction. All clans, on the other hand, are related to each other through the exchange of human beings, since women and men of one clan will marry women and men of other clans. They are linked through the responsibility of performing the necessary ceremonies that will reproduce the shared cosmic and social order, through the exchange of goods, and, sharing a common language, through the exchange of words. Relationships between clans and lineages are relationships of distinctions between groups of people; at the same time, relationships of similitude and exchange, unifying these distinctions within a global social entity such as the ethnic group, the tribe, or the society. The same is true for any other type of social category system.

Indeed, while clan and lineages are widespread and important types of social groupings, they are only two among the many other types of categories that belong to the domain of social organization. Some constitute actual and visible corporations of people and families, while others are limited to the domain of discourse and representation but are nevertheless significant in structuring social space and practice. Importantly, these various category systems are not exclusive of one another, but are in many occasions piled on top of each other or encapsulated, thus building up for every individual several layers of membership (or identity) and several contexts of relational speech etiquettes. 'Patrimoieties' or 'matrimoieties' are other quite common category systems. They divide society into two global entities that stand to each other in a relationship of distinction and exchange as well. In a patrimoiety system, belonging to one or the other moiety is defined through 'patrifiliation' (children belong to their father's group), while in a matrimoiety membership is defined through the female line. In certain contexts, speakers may refer to their moiety, in others to their clan, and in yet others to their lineage, organized around what is called a 'segmentary system', as described for example by Evans-Pritchard (1940) for the Nuer or by Riches (1978) for the Tiv. A moiety may encapsulate clans, which may encapsulate lineages. This system is most visible in conflict situations. Imagine two patrimoieties, each composed of several clans and each clan composed of several lineages. When two people within a lineage are in conflict, only immediate family members may get involved in conflict resolution. However, when two people belonging to different lineages of the same clan are in conflict, then all members of each lineage may get involved. When two members of lineages belonging to different clans but to the same moiety are in conflict, then the entire clan may get involved. Even further, if members of two clans belonging to different patrimoieties are in conflict, all members of the patrimoieties may get involved in conflict resolution. In other words, social categories are mobilized with respect to the difference or level of opposition they involve (level of the lineage, clan, or moiety) in particular contexts and calls for solidarity among their members. What looks quite obvious in conflict resolution points to the existence of more confidential structural differences, such as variations and versions in the mythical narratives between levels of social categories.

In Australia, for example, and where clan or moiety structures exist, each owns a portion of a shared mythical narrative. These narratives, known as songlines belonging to the Dreamtime (the name given to the Australian Aboriginal cosmology), depict the story of mythical figures that were travelling in mythical times over the country, covering often enormous distances across clan and tribal territory, and sometimes even across language groups. These figures shaped the landscape through their travels and are at the origin of natural species and established social rules and laws. Singing the songs, telling the stories, and performing the rituals that link back to these mythical figures is crucial, but can only be undertaken by those people that are responsible for—not necessarily the owner of—the stretch of land on which a particular episode of the mythical story occurred, handing the responsibility for other episodes to neighbouring groups. In these cases, recording the mythical narrative is only possible if the researcher has understood the clan or moiety structure of a society and is thus able to identify the owners, and is thereafter able to reconstruct the songline in its entirety (see also Nash and Simpson, Chapter 17 below).

Moieties themselves may, as in some cases in Aboriginal Australia and lowland Amazonia (Dreyfus 1993), be divided into social categories other than clans and lineages, such as sub-moieties, also called sections. These sections may themselves again be divided into subsections. Sections and subsections divide moieties up in different ways than clans do, but in some cases, such as among certain Northern Australian groups, they may in fact coexist. Sections and subsections reflect the distribution of genealogical relationships between people, in some cases linked to ritual roles. The crucial difference between sections or subsections and clans or lineages is that the former do not reflect visible corporate groups. They are rather abstract divisions of society into nevertheless meaningful entities without people belonging to the same category actually living together, owning land together, or mobilizing systems of conflict resolution. In Central Australia, subsection names are gendered, and are used as terms of address and reference, and sometimes even as personal names. In English, a term of address is *dad* or *daddy*, while its term of reference is *father*. The Pintupi people, for example, use eight root terms to group their people into eight categories, but add a gendered marker to distinguish female from male members of subsections. For example, one of these subsections is *kamarra*; another one is *paltjarri*. As such, however, these words are never used. People use *Tjakamarra* and *Tjapaltjarri* for males and *Nakamarra* and *Napaltjarri* for females. These subsections stand in particular relationships to each other, so that *Tjakamarra* is always the husband of a *Napaltjarri* woman and a *Nakamarra* is the wife of a *Tjapaltjarri* man.

'Generational moieties', also called 'alternate generational levels', are yet another important type of social category system. In many societies, these moieties or levels cut across other social groupings such as clans, lineages, or sections. In such generational moieties, a person's co-generationals (siblings, cousins, etc.), his or her grandparents' co-generationals, and his or her grandchildren's co-generationals are included in one moiety, while a person's parents' co-generationals and his or her children's co-generationals are members of the other moiety. These generational moieties usually have considerable influence on everyday behaviour as well as on ritual activities. People of the same generational moiety are usually behaviourally close and occupy similar roles during ceremonies, while relationships between members of different generational moieties are rather those of avoidance or at least respect. In the Australian Western Desert, these moieties have either relative names or absolute names, and sometimes both. Among the Ngaatjatjarra peoples of the Western Desert, *Ngumpaluru* ('shadeside') and *Tjintultukultul* ('sunside') are the absolute names of these moieties; and *nganantarka* ('us bone') and *tjanamiltjan* ('they flesh') are the relative terms. A person is either *Ngumpaluru* or *Tjintultukultul*, and he considers himself and his co-generationals as being *nganantarka*, while members of the opposite moiety he refers to as *tjanamiltjan*. This person would show some restraint and even avoidance towards members of the other moiety, while generally entertaining relaxed and close relationships with those of his own generational moiety.

Let me sum up the general aspects of social organization before moving on to the domain of kinship itself. Social organization describes the structure which divides a society into distinctive 'sociocentric' and multilayered entities that are at the basis of a multilayered definition of individual social membership. Sociocentric here means that, with the exception of generational moieties, a social category is not the consequence of individual relationships but exists irrespective of people's situation. These entities constitute the sociological contexts of speech, of shared responsibilities, of behavioural patterns, and of ownership and sometimes residence. Depending on the level of the entity people use as their context of speech, they may refer to one and the same person as a brother or sister, as a cousin or as a rival, or even as an enemy. It is common that a person refers to a cousin as a 'brother' when the context of speech is a discourse about clans, since he may conceive the person he refers to to be a member of a 'brother-lineage'.

Membership of these entities is defined by rules of descent, i.e. inheritance through generations following particular rules. These rules, as we shall see, are the foundation of the relationship of distinction between social categories. Bonding these social categories back into a global social unity is generally defined in terms of exchanges, in particular marriage, as will be seen. Both descent and marriage may be considered to belong to the domain of kinship, even though some authors argue that it rather reflects social organization. These discussions are irrelevant in the context of this chapter.

While 'social organization' describes the structure of general social distinctions and is sociocentric, kinship is of the realm of the relationships between particular individuals and is thus 'egocentric'. Kinship and social organization must be distinguished as fields of investigation, since they concern separately observable social realities. However, in most cases, the rules that organize egocentric relationships are de facto constitutive of the more general entities which are the categories of social organization. The remaining part of this chapter will discuss kinship rather than social organization; but let us keep in mind the relationship that exists between the individual aspects of belonging to a group of people through the links of kinship and membership of a social group through the principles of inheritance or descent.

During fieldwork the researcher should pay particular attention to the following issues with regard to social organization:

1. Societies are often divided into social groups who own different and complementary aspects of mythological narratives, for example. It is important to understand what these social groups are and how they relate to each other in order to be able to record complete narratives.
2. Social organization constitutes contexts of speech that may change the semantic value of words, for example calling a cousin 'brother' or an aunt 'mother' if the person is member of a particular social category.
3. The names of these social categories are often significant, and etymological work on these names needs to be undertaken, as the Baruya case illustrates. They may be placenames, names of species, of mythical figures, etc., or they may be gendered (as the Australian case illustrates), or include aspects of relatedness, such as with the Navajo.
4. Sometimes these social categories and their names are important for reconstructing the local history. Historical linguistics is relevant here. Names of social categories can often be reconstructed to their proto-forms in a regional scope and provide some perspectives on diffusion, migration, and loan. For example, the central Australian subsection name *Tjakamarra* can be traced back to the section name *Karimarra* used by other groups hundreds of kilometres to the west.

9.3 THE BASICS OF KINSHIP

Investigation into kinship again means distinguishing different fields of interconnected social realities. These may be summed up as follows: terminological systems; systems of descent and filiation (as already seen); marriage rules; and a connected domain, discussions on shared and transmitted bodily substances. I will discuss each of these individually, since they also reflect the evolution of anthropological investigations into the domain of kinship itself. It is, however, crucial to understand that the separation of these domains is an epistemological artefact and that in social interaction all four play combined roles. Let me start by investigating terminological systems—usually also the first step that the researcher in the domain of kinship studies undertakes in the field.

As we have seen in the introduction to this chapter, kinship is a mass of networks of relatedness which radiate from each individual, and this network expresses itself in a biological idiom (Tonkinson 1991[1978]). The biological idiom we are talking about is a set of words or expressions—kinship terms—that are largely attributed through what Fox (1996) called the basic facts of life: conception and birth. What is meant here is that whatever the local term that stands for 'mother' may be and whatever other relationships or things may be expressed by this term, at its very basis it describes the unique relationship between a person and a woman from whose womb he or she was born. Every language and, in some cases, even every dialect has its own set of such words that distribute the network of relationships around the individual we take as our starting point (called Ego): mother, father, uncle, brother, sister, cousin, and so on. However, the structure of this network or terminological map (the list of categories) is culturally ascribed and unique while also following a few universal rules. 'Categories' of people, sometimes also called 'classes', mean here all possible genealogical positions around Ego. For example, in English, the word 'uncle' designates in fact four categories and not just one: one's mother's brother, one's father's brother, one's mother's sister's husband, and one's father's sister's husband. In other languages and cultures, this may be very different. The terminological map—the list of categories that are locally distinguished— constitutes a terminological system. The number of such basic terminological systems invented by human societies is limited. Indeed, identical or very similar such terminological systems are found in societies as far apart as lowland Amazonia, India, China, Australia, or North America; others are of the same type, as among the Inuit peoples of Northern Canada and the European continent. The existence of a limited number of types of terminological systems makes some prediction possible, though this always needs to be carefully confirmed. It is because of the (incorrect) prediction I made that the sentence *Kungkankatja, minalinkatja* became relevant: they were calling each other brother and sister where, because of some systemic rules derived from these universal terminological systems, I was expecting a term for cousin. Let me now move on to those universal rules and systems.

9.3.1 Kinship terminologies

Terminological systems were the first elements of kinship systems to attract anthropologists' attention, starting with Lewis Morgan's *Systems of Affinity and*

Consanguinity of the Human Family (1997[1871]) as one of the major starting blocks for a new discipline. Morgan, who collected terminological systems through corresponding with people from different parts of the world, concluded that despite the diversity in the ways cultures and languages describe a person's genealogical environment, there are important structural similarities that seem to be systemic. He produced a first typology that has since been amended many times by various anthropologist (e.g. Murdock 1949), but that remains widely in use today. What this typology does is present a few basic ways—today one would say algorithms—of mapping the genealogical grid into classes and terms. Nowadays, anthropologists distinguish five such basic systems they call—unsatisfactorily but explicably from a historical point of view—by the names of the groups in which these systems are supposed to be found: Dravidian, Iroquois, Hawaiian, Sudanese, and Eskimo, with some further subtypes such as Crow, Omaha, Aluridja, etc. I shall now, in a very summary way, present particular features of each of these systems.

The **Dravidian** is a very widespread system. It is found on all continents and among the most diverse cultures, even though it is usually associated with small-scale societies. The main feature of this system is what is called 'bifurcate merging'. Bifurcate merging means that categories are bifurcated one generation above Ego (his or her parent's generation) according to gender, but their children are merged again in Ego's generation. What may here sound complex is in fact a very straightforward procedure of distinguishing fathers, mothers, uncles, and aunts following a different principle from that we find in Euro-American terminologies. Ego (the speaker) distinguishes the 'father' from the 'mother', for which one uses two distinct terms. The father's brother, however, since he is of the same gender as the father, is called 'father' as well. The mother's sister, since she is of the same gender as the mother, is called 'mother'. The father's sister, on the other hand, since she is of a different gender from the speaker's father, is called 'aunt' (or FZ, father's sister). Similarly, the mother's brother, since he is of a different gender from the speaker's mother, is called 'uncle' (or MB, mother's brother). In other words, only the mother's brother is an 'uncle' and only the father's sister is an 'aunt' if we use the English words. This is the basic feature from which all other features are derived in so-called Dravidian systems.

Dravidian terminologies are usually extended in such a way that every person with whom one has a relationship of any kind needs to be addressed or referred to by a kinship term. This extension to people other than close genealogical relations follows a very precise algorithm, always according to the principle of bifurcate merging mentioned above. My mother's mother's sister is a mother's mother, but my father's father's sister is of a distinct class.

The number of classes available to designate all the people in a group, tribe, etc. is obviously limited. For example, in Ego's parents' generation, there are usually only four terms available ('mother', 'father', 'father's sister', and 'mother's brother'), which means that each individual knows many people he or she calls 'mother', 'father', etc. Since your 'mothers' marry people you call 'father', fathers' sisters (FZ) obviously marry mothers' brothers (MB). And since all children of people you call 'mother' or 'father' are obviously your siblings, all children of people you call FZ or MB must be called differently, 'cousins' or, as anthropologists say in this case, cross-cousins. The terms for siblings and for cross-cousins are, in a Dravidian system, all that are available to name people of the same generation as yourself. Since one needs to marry someone of the same generation, and since everyone needs to be positioned in a kin category, and since you cannot marry a sibling for reasons of incest prohibition (see below), all you have left as partners are obviously people from the cross-cousin category, i.e. children of people you call 'uncle' and 'aunt'. Once you understand these principles, you can easily extend them to any other person of the society. If I call someone cross-cousin and this person calls someone else cross-cousin as well, I know that this other person is a sibling of mine: the cross-cousin of a cross-cousin is a sibling, while the cross-cousin of a sibling is a cross-cousin. In other words, Dravidian systems distinguish members of a group, tribe, or society as constituting two egocentric entities: first those that are 'affines', comprising all the people who are potentially or actually in-laws (MB, FZ, cross-cousins etc.) and the rest, whom we may called 'consanguines'. Fig. 9.1 displays a Dravidian system using, for pedagogic reasons, the English terminology. Of course, one needs to replace these words with those used in local languages and dialects.

The **Iroquois** system is a variation of the Dravidian-type terminology. While the Dravidian system is a universal system in the sense that the rules of bifurcation and merging operate in the same way in each generation and at each genealogical distance, and thus allow people to know how they stand to each other without even knowing their actual genealogical relationship (see Dousset 2008), the Iroquois systems limits the automatic extension to close kin only. Again, it is not possible here to go into the details of this system and I refer the reader to Godelier, Trautmann, and Tjon Sie Fat (1998). Let us simply underline the fact that in a Dravidian system cross-cousins of cross-cousins are brothers and sisters for Ego, while in an Iroquois system they remain cross-cousins.

The **Hawaiian** system, also called the generational system, is in some respects the simplest since it distinguishes very few categories. In Ego's parents' generation, all women are called 'mother', and all men are called 'father'. Consequently, all co-generationals, i.e. all the children of people called 'mother' or 'father', are brothers and sisters. It is important to note that Hawaiian systems can again be subdivided into two subsystems, largely because of the universal rule of incest prohibition between brothers and sisters. Because in a Hawaiian system Ego only finds brothers and sisters among co-generationals, and because of this incest prohibition rule, possible spouses for Ego need to be distinguished otherwise than by terminology alone. There are two solutions. The first is to limit the use of terminology to very close kin and to apply a strict rule of exogamy (the necessity

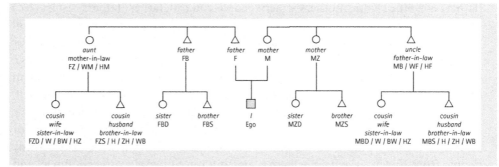

Figure 9.1. A Dravidian system filled with English kin terms. Only very close kin are given in this figure, but it must be remembered that Dravidian terminologies are extended. Triangles stand for males, circles for females. Vertical lines stand for filiation/descent, horizontal lines for siblingship. The line uniting Ego's parents below their figure means they are married. The usual abbreviations used are B (brother), Z (sister), F (father), M (mother), D (daughter), S (son), H (husband) and W (wife). All other kin categories are combinations of these elements. For example, MB (mother's brother) is a matrilateral 'uncle'; his daughter, MBD (mother's brother's daughter), is a matrilateral cross–cousin. Additional abbreviations used by anthropologists are 'y' for younger, such as in yB (younger brother), 'e' for elder, 'm' for a male speaker and 'f' for a female speaker. Older ethnographies often write 'm.s.' for male speaking and 'f.s.' for female speaking.

to marry out into genealogically or spatially distant families). The other solution, when the terminology is used even among genealogically distant kin, is to differentiate the categories of cross-cousins and of siblings as in a Dravidian system, even though before marriage they are all called using the sibling terminology. In the latter solution, the terminology is of the Hawaiian type but marriage rules follow the Dravidian type where cross-cousins are potentially also spouses. The distinction between pre-marriage terminology and post-marriage terminology is relevant here. I will return to this point.

The **Sudanese** system is the most descriptive system. Anthropologists, starting with Morgan, have distinguished classificatory terminologies from descriptive terminologies. Classificatory terminologies denominate with one term several categories or classes of people (such as 'uncle' in the English terminology), while descriptive systems have the characteristic of naming differently every category of kin. The term for cross-cousin in a Dravidian system is typically a classificatory term, while that for MB is a descriptive term (see Fig. 9.1). In fact, it is not possible to distinguish entire systems as being either descriptive or classificatory, since all have some elements of description and some elements of classification. The Eskimo system (and the English terminology is of this type) discussed below, for example, was long considered to be a descriptive system. In fact it has classificatory terms, since the word 'cousin', for example, actually covers four categories of people: matrilateral cross-cousins (MBD/S), matrilateral parallel cousins (MZD/S), patrilateral cross-cousins (FZD/S), and patrilateral parallel cousins (FBD/S). The Sudanese system, though, is one of the most descriptive systems, if not a totally descriptive one. Every single kin category is named using a distinct term.

The **Eskimo** system is found in Europe and, as its name indicates, among the Inuit peoples. Marriage is between genealogically unrelated people, meaning that there is no direct connection between consanguinal and affinal terminology, at least before marriage. The complex distinction between consanguinity and affinity will need to be discussed in more precise ways below. Another characteristic of the Eskimo system is that bifurcation does not occur. 'Uncles' can be found on the father's side as well as on the mother's side.

Crow and **Omaha** are sometimes considered distinct systems. They are, however, more likely to be interpreted as specific variations of the Dravidian system (see Kronenfeld 1991). The particularities of Crow and Omaha systems is that they operate what is called skewing. In certain contexts, a matrilateral cross-cousin is called by the same term as a FZ, and a patrilateral cross-cousin like a MB. In other words, two generations are skewed into one and the same term.

The general system of terminology and its pragmatic usages (and adaptations) in a particular language or dialect can only be determined if the researcher actually records kin terms and their contextualized usages. Besides simply listening to conversations, there exist two basic methods for recording these terminologies. The first is the genealogical method, the second the tabular method. In the genealogical method, the researcher prepares a genealogical sheet (see Fig. 9.1 above) in which are drawn all possible categories starting from an Ego (the speaker): his younger brother, his younger sister, his older brother, his older sister, his father, his mother, his mother's older sister, his mother's younger sister, his mother's older brother, etc. The sheet needs to cover at least five generations: Ego's, his parents', his parent's parent's, his children's, and his children's children's. It is however advised, if possible, to go beyond these five generations. The researcher then sits with an individual, notes the name, the place and date/time of recording, as well as the gender, age, place of residence, social role, etc. of the speaker. It is also useful to write down who else is sitting around and listening, and perhaps contributing to the conversation.

This needs to be undertaken separately with several people, establishing a representative sample covering various characteristics of the speaker: age, gender, social position and role, residence, member of a social category, etc. At least four questions need to be asked of each such person for each of the individual categories drawn on the genealogical sheet: (1) How do you call that person? (2) How do you refer to this person when you talk to someone else? (3) How does this person call you? and (4) How does this person refer to you when talking to another person? Questions 3 and 4 will record what are called the 'reciprocals'. In English, if you are a male, the reciprocal of 'father' is 'son', since this is how your father will call or refer to you.

In some cases it may be difficult to ask direct questions unless one already knows a good deal about the society. In these cases, one needs to use artifice to ask the question. A useful indirect way for obtaining the terms for each position is to work through the genealogical sheet, taking women as the pivotal point. You then ask the following types of questions: What do you call the person from whose womb you came? What do you call another person that came out of the same womb after you and that is a male (younger brother)? You then use the 'marriage' link to get the affinal males: what do you call the man that married (or is living with) the person out of whose womb you came? And so on.

While the genealogical method is a necessary first step, it also has its limits, since it tackles only more or less close kin (those drawn on the genealogical sheet). To extend the analysis of the usage of terminology beyond close kin, the tabular method can be applied. With the tabular method, you prepare one card for each person you interview. Ideally you attach a photograph of the person to the card, since this will greatly enhance the discussions with other people. These cards are numbered so that you can refer to a person through its number. Showing the photographs, you then ask each person how he or she calls and refers to each other person. The results need to be noted in a tabular way: number 5 calls number 93 'younger brother', number 54 calls number 12 'father', etc. You may at a later stage check the reciprocals, as well as elucidate what I call relational triangles (Dousset 2008). They will help to identify which system is at work or to identify situations in which the expected term is not applied: if person A calls person B 'brother', and if person A calls person C 'mother', then person 'B' should be calling person C 'mother' as well, to take the most simple example. If person B does not call person C 'mother', then you need to find out why and in which situations.

What do we need to remember from this brief overview of terminological systems? Here are a few guidelines to help in the recording of terminologies, which is considered to be one of the first steps of inquiry into human social organization and kinship.

1. Recording the kinship terminology and trying to establish which type the researcher is confronted with is one of the first steps. There are several complementary methods for achieving this. One is to use the genealogical method, drawing genealogies and asking what each consultant calls them, and how they refer to them, making sure one works with consultants of both genders, of different ages, status, etc. The second method is the tabular method that allows you to go beyond close kin. Another important method that follows from the two previous ones is contextual observation and recording of how people call or refer to each other in various social situations (among the family, with other clan members, among ritual comrades, etc.). In some cultures, however, people

hardly use kinship terms in everyday interaction; drawing genealogies is sometimes the only means to obtain the terminologies.

It should be noted that real-world systems are never as neat as the theoretical
types described in this chapter. Confronting real-world terminologies with ideal
typical terminologies provides important insights into local representations and
strategies, as our example of *minalinkatja, kungankatja* demonstrates. It is not
sufficient to record all the words believed to belong to the realm of kinship. It is
necessary to record terms with respect to the categories they designate as mapped
against a chart of possible genealogical positions. It is also necessary to distinguish
descriptive terms (those that designate one category only) from those which are
classificatory (designating several categories). For example, there may be a general
category for cross-cousins, but once marriage has occurred with such a cross-
cousin, his or her actual brother may be called differently. In the Western Desert,
cross-cousins are called *watjirra* (classificatory). The actual brother-in-law however, while still a *watjirra*, is also called *marutju* (descriptive).

2. It is thus necessary to record and distinguish kinship terms used between people
   before marriage and after marriage. The same category of people may be called
   differently once marriage is envisaged or has occurred. For example, in the
   Australian Western Desert again, a mother's brother is called *kamuru*, but once
   he is envisaged as a real or potential father-in-law, he will be referred to as
   waputju (wife's father, initiator), since *kamuru* denotes a proximity that is not
   appropriate in the case of in-laws.

3. It is necessary to distinguish terms of reference from terms of address. *Mum* is
   typically a term of address, while *mother* is a term of reference that only in
   certain contexts or certain languages is used as a form of address as well. In
   English, if you address your mother as *Mother*, it does imply a contextual
   connotation that needs to be analysed (emotional distance, aristocracy, not
   taking the mother seriously, astonishment, and so on). Many languages have
   only one term for both reference and address. Additionally, some languages have
   tri-relational terms (cf. Merlan and Heath 1982), for example two people talking
   together about a third related person (myself and my cousin talking about
   another third person), or one person talking about a couple of people (myself
   talking about the couple formed by my grandfather and father).

4. Social, geographical, and discursive contexts of speech may have considerable
   influence on the terms and categories designated. Depending on which social
   category interlocutors stand in with regard to each other and on the social
   context in which they speak or refer to each other, they may use different terms
   or use the same terms differently. In the Australian Western Desert, which has a
   variant of a Dravidian system, for example, people may call each other 'brother'
   (*kurta*) and 'sister' (*tjurtu*) even though they are cross-cousins when the context
   of speech is that of opposing generational moieties, such as during funerals,

which are organized around generational role distribution. In other and more egocentric contexts, however, these same people will call each other 'cross-cousins' (*watjirra*).

5. With the recording of kinship terms and the corresponding categories, there is also the need to record the expected normative behaviour that accompanies the terms. In many languages, the term for 'mother-in-law' is for reference only, since people are not allowed to talk to their mother-in-law. Anthropologists usually distinguish several general types of such normative behaviour: the joking relationship (people are close to each other and may even make sexual allusions or jokes), the avoidance relationship (people are not allowed to talk to each other), the respect relationship (people are allowed to talk to each other but the relationship is asymmetrical, i.e. one gives orders, the other listens; one receives goods, the other gives goods, etc.), and the relationship of reciprocity (people have a symmetrical/equal type of relationship but not as close as that of the joking relationship).

6. Terminologies, as was the case with the names used in social organization, are important in the domain of historical linguistics. Kinship terms are considered relatively stable, and reconstructing proto-words, and through these proto-systems (what was the terminological system in use by the ancestors of the group?), may provide important information on the local and regional history. Kinship terminologies may also be borrowed from neighbouring groups, revealing aspects of intercultural relationships.

9.3.2 Descent and filiation

While terminologies are among the most important elements researchers need to record in the domain of kinship studies, they are not the only aspects concerning the network of relatedness based on a biological idiom. With the emergence of the British structural-functionalist school at the beginning of the twentieth century with scholars such as Malinowski, Radcliffe-Brown, Fortes, and Evans-Pritchard, research increasingly concentrated on the relationship between kinship and political and economic systems. How people were recruited into corporate groups and how these groups also become landowners or land users, for example, became an important aspect of research. Anthropologists were particularly interested in the relationship between social organization as discussed above and kinship, and it was during this period that the notions of lineage and clan received their most comprehensive definitions and articulations. Early on, researchers recognized that these categories' principal mode of recruiting people was the control of descent and the transmission of membership and ownership from one generation to the next. As with systems of terminologies, anthropologists have identified a certain number of types of such modes of transmission which the researcher needs to understand before tackling their linguistic aspects.

Three general types of descent systems have been identified: unilineal, non-unilineal, and mixed systems. In the field, the most visible type is the unilineal system. As the name indicates, unilineal systems trace the process of corporation, inheritance, and transmission through a single line: the father's line or the mother's line. In a patrilineal descent system (the Baruya, for example), membership of a group is inherited through the male line. Children belong to the same group as their father, but to a different group from their mother. In a matrilineal descent system, such as the Navajo, membership of a group is inherited through the female line and children belong to the same group as their mother, but to a different group from their father. In the latter system, the matrilateral uncle (the mother's brother) usually has a very important educational role for his sister's children, and marriage bonds are usually quite weak. It should be evident by now that unilineal systems are those most often found in clans and lineages, and are often also associated with terminologies which distinguish a group of consanguines (one's own lineage) from a group of affines. But this needs to be meticulously investigated, since it is not usually as clear-cut as theory would like to have it.

Among the non-unilineal systems, the most representative is the cognatic descent system. Non-unilineal systems, and in particular cognatic systems, are considered unable to sustain enduring corporate groups. Indeed, in a cognatic descent system, children belong indistinguishably to their mother's group or family and to their father's group or family, or inherit rights and property indistinguishably from their father's side and their mother's side. Hence the general principle of inheritance and transmission does not make it possible to create enduring distinctions between descent groups, since at every generation families or groups are conflated in the children's generation. In practice, however, societies that have a cognatic descent system are able to constitute enduring corporate groups through other mechanisms. In certain parts of Europe, where the cognatic system is the rule, the norm of primogeniture also existed, according to which the first-born male would inherit landownership and constitute, with his close and enlarged family (kindred), a land-based enduring group, he himself transmitting landownership to his eldest son and so on. Younger brothers had to leave the family group or work under the authority of the older brother without ever becoming an owner. Thus, while in theory and in discourses children inherit goods and rights from both their parents' sides, in practice one side may be considered central and the other peripheral, as we shall see below with the concept of 'complementary filiation' and 'double descent'.

Among the mixed systems, the 'ambilineal' one is probably the most difficult to identify, but also very interesting, since it is open to political and economic contextualization and strategies. In an ambilineal system, a person may choose to follow the mother's line or the father's line, depending on opportunities or social pressure. But once he or she has chosen to link up to one or the other side, this choice may not be changed later in life: one is expected to stand by the group or family from which one claims inheritance. In the Australian Western Desert, again, the system at work is very similar to an ambilineal system but, unlike that in Polynesia, where ambilineal groups constitute more or less enduring corporations called 'ramages' (Firth 1957), it has but little consequence in the definition of landownership or membership of distinguishable units.

Another mixed system is 'double descent'. People may trace their descent in different ways depending on what is transmitted or different people may trace descent in different ways. Such is the case among the Mundugumor of Papua New Guinea, where girls and boys do not follow the same rule, girls belonging to their father's group and boys to their mother's. In other societies, such as the Apinayé of Brazil, descent lines are gender-specific: women trace descent matrilineally, men patrilineally (see Holy 1996: 121ff. for a discussion of double descent systems).

The systems at work in the real world are rarely as straightforward and easily identifiable as theory would like them to be. Local descent ideologies are often combinations of different systems, just as was the case with terminologies. More importantly, what we need to concentrate on is the substance of these local systems and the answer to the complex question: What is transmitted or inherited, how is this done and expressed, and what are the reasons (ideologies, representations, symbols . . .) accompanying it? Two complementary investigations are necessary in this respect. Certain elements can be answered and analysed through observation, interviews, and discussions. Who has access to certain resources, on particular land, and not to others? Who constitutes a residential group or a regional group, and which people or families live close to each other or establish particular networks? Who shares what, with whom, and in what circumstances? Who systematically offers goods as presents to whom and what is expected in return? Who looks after each other's children? Which people join together in conflict situations? What happens to a person's body and belongings after death?

The second approach is a more in-depth and systematic way of recording and analysing the semantics and structure of discourse, in which the fieldworker investigates in a semi-directive manner the symbols and representations that constitute the local descent ideology. This investigation should ideally be simultaneous with the recording of genealogies. I will return to this question in the next section, but let me here underline that what is at stake is presenting and analysing indigenous discourses about the constitution of human beings and their environment. These discourses will often, if not always, invoke some principle of inheritance and transmission as a justifying factor of existence in general and of the interlocutor's existence in particular. Within this realm, typical questions the fieldworker may ask are the following. What are the elements that constitute the human body? Which substances of the body have which function or purpose? What is conception of a baby and how does it happen? What happens to the human body once it is lifeless? What, other than flesh and bones, constitutes the human being? How do these other elements penetrate the body? What does the individual share with siblings, parents, neighbours, etc.? How can one see and understand that a person belongs to such and such a group or family? What substances are inherited from one generation to the other? And so on.

These questions may show that certain elements are transmitted through the male line, such as ownership of or access to land, but that others have a different destiny. In many societies, a person's blood, for example, is thought to come from the mother alone and constitutes an element of the individual's identity that diverges from the patrilineal principle of landownership transmission. In such cases, it is useful to distinguish 'descent' from 'filiation'. Descent describes the principles inherent in the transmission of material and immaterial things, rights and duties, over generations. Filiation, on the other hand, is the principle which links a person to his or her immediate parents only. On many occasions, filiation and descent produce similar effects, such as in our example of the transmission of landownership through the patriline. In many other cases however there are additional criteria that establish a relationship to a parent in a different way, without constituting a corporate group, such as is the case with blood inherited from the mother in our example. Fortes (1959) has coined the expression 'complementary filiation' to describe these additional factors and mechanisms.

What do we need to remember from this again too brief overview of systems of descent and filiation? Here are a few guidelines to help in the recording of data.

1. Any social, ethnic, tribal etc. group shares at least three things: a spatial location (even if it is a virtual one as with internet communities), a way of identifying and recruiting its members, and a shared history or memory. Terminologies, as we have seen, structure the social field within the group from an egocentric (a speaker's) point of view. They reflect certain aspects of organization, role distribution, and the circulation of people. Descent and filiation, on the other hand, touch upon the three above-mentioned conditions of social being. They answer questions on how spatial organization is reproduced over generations. They answer questions on how people become and are members of the group and its subgroups, and they are associated to the group's collective history and memory. Very often, patrilineal descent is linked to the existence of clans who each have their own myth of origins.

2. Some aspects of descent and filiation are visible and straightforward; others are hidden, unconscious, and only identifiable through the careful analysis of discourses, symbolism, and ideology with regard to the constitution and composition of the human and the social body.

3. Human beings and, by extension, social groups are made up of substances, be they material or immaterial. The genealogy of these substances, the way they circulate among human beings and groups, the way they are transmitted from one generation to the next or are destroyed, constitute important aspects in the

understanding of the system of descent and filiation in particular, and of the entire group's organization and structure in general. These substances' existence is most often limited to the domain of language and speech, and only rarely and sporadically surfaces in the domain of actual practice.

9.3.3 Alliance and marriage

At the height of descent theory and the interest in descent systems as the constituents of social groups during the first half of the twentieth century, with Lévi-Strauss' work (1967[1947]) a new and complementary investigation into the complexities of human kinship emerged: alliance theory. According to this structuralist theory, society is not (or not solely) made up of principles of belonging (descent and groups), but primarily of principles of exchange. Lévi-Strauss claimed that three types of exchanges characterize the human social realm: exchange of words (language), exchange of goods (the economic domain), and exchange of human beings (marriage). It is only when these three principles of exchange are systematized and functional in a group of human beings that the latter actually constitutes a society with its shared cultural codes. Alliance theorists, as the name indicates, and with them Lévi-Strauss and many other anthropologists, concentrated their research efforts on the domain of the exchange of human beings: marriage. And marriage becomes a system of exchange if it is associated with the obligation of exogamy, i.e. marrying someone from 'outside' your family or group. Brothers and sisters who over generations marry each other will not constitute a society. To do so, Lévi-Strauss explains, we need an incest prohibition which forces people to obtain their spouses from other families.

Before going further, it is necessary to explain the distinction between 'alliance' and 'marriage'. Dumont (1957), another alliance theorist albeit in some respects in disagreement with Lévi-Strauss, has conceptualized the difference in the most systematic way. He talks of alliance (or 'alliance of marriage') when he observes and analyses the repetition of identical marriage types over generations or among co-generationals. Thus marriage is the individual event that happens in a particular place with particular people in a particular context, bringing two people (and families) together with the aim of joining them as spouses and usually future parents. Alliance is the system which reflects a certain regularity in the choice of suitable spouses and describes repetitions of identical marriage types.

Alliance theory distinguishes three of these basic types of marriages. The most basic is called 'direct exchange' or the 'elementary system'. The second type is 'indirect exchange', and the third type is called the 'complex system'. In the direct exchange system, marriages place people and groups in a symmetric relationship.

Females of group A, for example a clan, marry males of group B and females of group B marry males of group A. Group A thus exchanges women or men with group B in a direct and reciprocal way. This exchange system can be linked to the terminological systems mentioned earlier in this chapter. Most often, direct exchange systems occur where the terminology is of the Dravidian or Iroquois type. Let me detail the principles, asking the reader to go back to Fig. 9.1 if necessary, and combine terminology, descent system, and alliance theory in one fictitious example.

Let us say that the descent system is patrilineal and that we have two clans, A and B. Clan A is composed of my father, my father's brother, my father's sister, and other people related through the male line. Clan B is composed of my mother, my mother's brother, my mother's sister, etc. My father, who is from clan A, married my mother from clan B (exogamy). His children thus belong to clan A. In exchange, my mother's brother, who is from clan B, can marry my father's sister, who is from clan A. Their children belong to clan B. Since I can only marry people from clan B (exogamy), I call these children cross-cousins or wife, and not sibling. My children will be of clan A and will marry people from clan B, and so on. What results from direct exchange systems is that a person marries someone he or she calls cross-cousin, and the spouse's sibling is also the sister's or brother's spouse. In practice, as we will see, people only rarely marry their actual cross-cousin but do nevertheless marry a person of the same category.

The second type is the indirect exchange system, which is found in, but is not exclusive to, Crow and Omaha terminologies. Marriage in these cases is either patrilateral or matrilateral: a person can marry a cross-cousin from either the father's side or the mother's side respectively, but not from both. In terms of clans or descent groups, it means that there are at least three exchanging units: clan A marries into clan B, who marries into clan C, who marries back into clan A. The exchange is no longer direct but indirect.

The last and least systemic exchange system is called the complex system. Marriage is here no longer a system of exchange on its own, but merges into other types of exchanges, social structures, and ideologies. An example of a complex system is the modern European system where alliances (repetitions of identical marriages) are very rare, since children of the same family may marry in different ways into the most diverse family backgrounds. Statistically, of course, there are some regularities even among complex systems, but, as already mentioned, they are relevant for social factors other than rules of marriage alone. For example, people of a certain social class tend to marry into the same social class, and people in rural areas tend to marry following strategies that retain the coherence of landownership over time. Complex marriage systems are usually associated with limited, not extensive, terminologies, in which kinship terms are only applied to close or very close kin.

The theories of descent and alliance do not need to be understood as exclusive paradigms but are in fact complementary aspects of similar social and cultural characteristics and practices. Marriage and marriage rules are needed to create more or less stable structures, of which clans and lineages are examples; and clans and lineages are needed if marriage is to be exogamous and link people of different ascent. Descent differentiates and distinguishes people as groups within a society, while marriage upholds the connection between these groups. Data in this respect needs to take into account two distinct explanatory sources: first, actual marriage practices and the choice of partners, and second, discourses about marriage rules. In some cases, practices and discourses may overlap (people actually doing what they say they are supposed to do). In other cases, discourses rather reflect an ideal type of practice which does not happen very often, if at all. Let us look briefly at the main constituents of discourses about marriage rules.

Two types of rules can be expressed in discourses about marriage rules. The first type defines prescriptive practices, the second describes proscriptive marriages. Prescriptive rules are rules that express what one is ordered or supposed to do. They can be characterized as being jural (Leach 1965) or structural (Needham 1973). In a Dravidian terminology with exogamous lineages or clans, the prescription would be to marry a cross-cousin, as we have seen. From Leach's point of view, it is this obligation which creates the clan structure. For Needham, on the other hand, it is the structure of the terminology and of the clan system which, in order to be viable, imposes the prescriptive rule. While I have greatly simplified Leach's and Needham's points of view here, we may nevertheless conclude that this polemic is largely a chicken-and-egg question. In fact, to be operational, a rule needs some collective acceptance (jural) in order to have and to be of structural significance. Obviously, prescriptive rules are not tied merely to terminology and kinship. Consider, for example, India, where one of the prescriptive rules is to marry someone of the same caste. In contrast with proscriptive marriage rules, prescriptive rules point to a class of particular people who are acceptable for marriage. Spouses are prescribed, predefined, and predetermined by their structural position in the system. In addition to prescriptive rules, and particularly in complex systems, proscriptive rules have an important function.

A proscriptive rule defines who cannot be a spouse; it formulates an interdiction. It proceeds by layering these interdictions so as to crystallize what class of people are ideal or acceptable partners. The most elementary proscriptive rule is that of incest prohibition: siblings, parents, and children are in the great majority of cases proscribed as spouses, even though some exceptions of close kin endogamy seem to have existed, such as among European royal families, or even brother–sister marriages among Egyptian pharaohs. The basic incest prohibition rule is frequently extended to other classes of people. We have seen that, in Dravidian or

Iroquois systems, parallel cousins (mother's sister's son, for example) are called by the terms denoting one's siblings. They are hence classified in the same category as oneself and are thus considered to be consanguines and not affines. The fact that it is the actual local words for 'brother' and 'sister' that may be applied to them indeed recalls a process of extending the incest prohibition rule to people other than actual and closely related kin.

Proscriptive marriage rules may also affect criteria other than those of class membership or terminological distinctions. The obligation of exogamy can in fact be applied or interpreted in different ways. It can be genealogical (prohibition from marrying close kin whatever their kin category), terminological (prohibition from marry people whom one calls by certain terms), spatial (e.g. prohibition from marrying people who live in the same village), or social (prohibition from marrying people from certain families, religions, roles, etc.).

In addition to the recording of discourses about marriage and marriage rules, the second source of information lies in marriage practices themselves: who marries whom, in what context, and for what obvious and less obvious reasons? Who organizes the marriage and decides on the suitability of marriage partners? Marriage practice is a far more complex matter to study than are discourses about marriage rules, because it often diverges from discourses for complex and often hidden or obscure reasons. Let me take an example from the Ngaatjatjarra and Ngaanyatjarra people of the Australian Western Desert to illustrate what is meant here.

While their prescriptive marriage rule is a cross-cousin one, there are many proscriptive rules involved as well: spatial exogamy (do not marry someone with whom you live or have lived) and genealogical exogamy (do not marry someone who is genealogically close even if the person is a cross-cousin) are at work. Ideally, the combination of the prescriptive and proscriptive rule could be formulated as follows: people marry a cross-cousin who is at least of the third degree (for example a MMMBDDD) and who is geographically distant. Ngaatjatjarra people also stress the necessity of exchange. It is, in principle at least, an elementary system where a man marries a woman whose brother is also the husband of that man's sister.

Observation and genealogies show, however, that marriages are very rarely an actual exchange of people and that the system cannot be considered to be an elementary one. Each man has several potential partners and ways to find a wife, each of them having particular terms and processes associated with it. First of all, during initiation, the initiator will promise a man his daughter whom Ego will call *pikarta*. This is, according to discourse, the ideal spouse. *Pikarta* is also ideally the sister of the man's sister's husband. In fact, while the man will have a relationship with *pikarta* and her family which resembles that following actual marriage, including the obligations of sharing and hosting etc., he will only very rarely marry this woman. He will in fact be promised a second wife, this time by a potential mother-in-law, just after initiation. This potential wife is called *pam-purlpa's* daughter. But, here again, even though he should marry and engage in an exchange and provide that family with his sister, this will happen only very rarely. Another way of finding a wife is the process called *karlkurnu*. The man provides his potential parents-in-law with presents until they agree to give him their daughter. Many marriages are of this type. The last type, very frequent as well, is called *warngirnu* and is elopement. The young couple simply runs away, not waiting for the parents' approval, and returns to the community once they have a child. Ninety-five per cent of couples are constituted through *karlkurnu* or *warngirnu*, i.e. processes that do not involve the formal exchange of people. One may argue that this shows a weak coincidence between discourse and practice—something that is indeed quite frequent in anthropological studies. In the present case, however, the problem is slightly more complex. It must be remembered that *pikarta* and *pampurlpa's* daughter involve obligations and solidarity between people as if the marriage had actually occurred. Thus, there is no need to actually marry these women: the benefits of alliances are already provided simply through the promise. In marrying someone other than the promised and prescribed partners, the man diversifies his network of relatedness, socially and spatially speaking, and hence secures his position in the network of social and economic obligations and exchange.

What do we need to remember from this again brief overview of marriage and alliance? Here are a few guidelines for recording these elements.

1. Marriages are one of the major ways of maintaining relatedness between families and groups of families. They are regulated by social organization and social strategies in addition to personal affinities. They are an institutionalized way of creating enduring relationships and sometimes corporations. How these particular relationships are enacted in a group or society may in some cases be obscure, in some obvious.

2. Marriage needs to be distinguished from sexual relations. While both are usually structured by some incest prohibitions (which need to be described and documented), they do not respond to the same social impetus. Sexual relations are temporary practices that have no influence on social organization. Marriages, particularly alliances of marriage, on the other hand, create and maintain social corporations.

3. Relationships through marriage—affinal relationships—are not limited to actual marriage. All facets of the various procedures of relatedness creation need to be investigated. These facets may be economic, political, spatial, religious, etc. In most cases they involve particular vocabularies and speech etiquettes.

9.4 STRUCTURE AND SUBSTANCE

Let us now come back to the example quoted at the beginning of this chapter in order to formulate a few concluding remarks. *Kungkankatja, minalinkatja*, literally 'from a woman, from a man', meant, in the context of the question asked, that the children of a woman and those of her brother are to be considered identical. Let us also recall that this happened in a context in which the researcher expected a Dravidian-like terminology, because he had recorded direct exchange-type discourses about the marriage system and because he had constructed terminologies through the genealogical method. Structurally, children from a brother and his sister are cross-cousins, not brothers and sisters. They are what anthropologists call affines (potential or real in-laws), not consanguines. But the definition of consanguinity is cultural. We have seen that there are some universal rules of incest prohibition that denote what kind of people are everywhere (more or less so) considered too close to have sexual relationships or to marry—parents, siblings, and children are among them. However, humans expand the biological idiom of this basic kinship nucleus to include other relatives: aunts, uncles, and their children etc., depending on local rules and norms. Who in this lot is a consanguine, and cannot be married, or not, is a question of local definition according to a local semantic system.

A brother and a sister are, in the example quoted above, locally thought to give birth to children that are identical, that are thus themselves brothers and sisters, and not cross-cousins. They are identical because they are thought to share too many substances. They may have eaten at the same place and of the same food, they may have played together as children and have an extensive shared memory, they were looked after and raised by the same people, they lived at the same places, in the same region, they sat around the same fires. What they share is not so much blood itself, as the term 'consanguine' suggests, but other material and immaterial substances: memory, bodily substances, experiences. Pitt-Rivers (1973) therefore proposed using the term 'consubstantiality' rather than 'consanguinity'. Everywhere people believe they share things—their body, their spirit, or whatever—with other people. The distinction between those with whom one shares something and those with whom one does not is significant and needs to be described. The expressions and explanations that are given for this consubstantiality are crucial in the understanding of social organization, local ideologies, and religious beliefs of the social body in general.

9.5 CONCLUSION

The study of kinship is a study of language, and of a language as it reflects the deep representations that lie beneath a local system of human and social reproduction. This language is made up of rules and norms, of a grammar, made up of rules of descent that define and determine membership and rules of marriage that define exchanges and the network between groups. This language also has a vocabulary made up of kinship terms that are themselves systemic, and of complex nomenclatures of social organization. This language is applied, but often contextually adapted: economic, political, or religious factors play important roles. Bodily substances, experiences, and prerogatives are spelled out in the realm of kinship in ways which, far from appearing to be rules, seem rather an integrated body of social practices and beliefs. It is the researcher's task to identify its elementary constituents and to understand their interaction and interrelation.

CHAPTER 10

THE LANGUAGE OF FOOD

NANCY J. POLLOCK

10.1 INTRODUCTION

Food is a great conversation opener, whether at parties or in an academic forum, and a great topic for gathering data. It is a topic on which most people have a view, whether subjective or objective, implicit or explicit, from the inside or outside. The field of food study exists down the street or in some distant community. An interested fieldworker can gather information from friends, neighbours, in schools, supermarkets, and restaurants, or just about anywhere, asking 'What is your favourite food?' 'What did you last eat?' 'Where did you last eat?' 'Have you seen a programme about food on TV?' 'What did it tell you—what was the message?'

In this chapter we will explore 'languages of food' as they communicate variations of messages about the meanings of food. The local or internal messages, exemplified in this chapter in Marshallese (central Pacific), are contrasted with three external messages: 'civilized eating' as the concern of early outsiders such as missionary wives; economists' approaches largely concerned with production of food; and nutrition education messages about 'good' food. These alternative approaches reflect Douglas's idea that 'every spoken sentence rests on unspoken knowledge for some of its meaning' (1975: 173).

10.2 MEANINGS OF FOOD

Food can have many meanings, whether in the raw ingredients that contribute to a particular dish, in the mode in which those ingredients are assembled, prepared, and cooked, or in the occasions at which it is served. Participants sharing a haggis, for example, bring their own cultural perceptions of the dominant features, including its taste, its history as a gastronomic item, and its place in modern life. Some may question the ingredients, or its value for money, while others may question the taste or the nutritional merits (or demerits) of such a dish. Others may ask questions about the social significance of the dish in Scottish culture, its meanings, and its variations, its place in attracting tourist dollars. What are the key elements in the language of food?

The meanings of foods, particularly unfamiliar ones, bring challenges, some of which seem obvious while others are more obscure. Barthes (1997) frames his psychosocial approach to food consumption as 'a system of communication' analogous to linguistics with constituent units from which a differential system of signification can be reconstructed. The result is 'a veritable grammar of foods' (p. 22). Our introspections into the components of such a 'grammar' lead us to examine the key components that give food meaning. How we interpret food lies in our preconceptions, our biases, and our theoretical approach. The challenge lies in decoding the foods we experience while trying to find a structure that unravels some of the mysteries. As we traverse our own biases of what constitutes an 'edible' item, and thus a food, we begin to identify the differences that appear in another culture's use of 'foodstuffs'. The 'grammar' and variations clarify 'food ways' or what I am discussing here as gastronomies.

I would go further than Barthes, to emphasize the differences in signification of food that are collectively acknowledged rather than those associated 'simply with individual taste' (Barthes 1997: 22). For many communities the emphasis is on sharing food with others; thus tastes are cultivated and gastronomies formulated through household meals or communal events where tastes of individuals must be subordinated to the tastes of others. Tastes that are culturally learned are developed through the choices of foodstuffs, ways of cooking and spicing, and ways of presenting foods that fit into an overarching ideology. Mexican food, for example, differs from Indonesian food, as examples of gastronomies that are identified with particular cultures. Similarly, Dunlop (2008) offers us glimpses of some contrasting features of Chinese gastronomies as differentiated in the different provinces. The language of food is shared within communities, while also expressing unique variations.

In order to focus on significant differences in approaches to food and eating that anthropologists have brought to the fore, I use the concept of gastronomy, as Brillat-Savarin (1970[1825]) elaborated it. His much-quoted epithet 'Tell me what you eat and I will tell you what you are' suggests that food conveys messages that provide identity. It expresses several layers of meaning, whether in its material manifestations, social commitments, or spiritual values. Some foods become formal symbols, for example a roast suckling pig in Tongan rites of feasting, while snacks or sweets may be more informal.

Anthropologists of food have pursued several alternative modes of analyses, borrowed from related disciplines. Initially they focused on food production as it had a place in local economics (Firth 1936), as a political entity (cf. Mintz's 1985 study of sugar), as 'a highly condensed social fact' (Appadurai 1996: 494), or as a set of components such as animal, vegetable, minerals, or carbohydrates, fats, etc. (Jerome 1980).

As an introduction to a range of anthropological studies of food, Belasco (2008) proposes a perspective on a food system through food concepts. These consist of three key elements: identity, convenience, and responsibility, which he derives mainly from an American perspective in order to encourage his students to think beyond food as a material item. I prefer to look at food concepts as they represent the basic values which a household draws on when choosing foods. A gastronomic picture emerges from observations and from questioning people about what they eat and why.

The aim is to compile a broad cultural perspective on the place food holds in social life, and the values so expressed. While Belasco's view of the American food system presents food concepts in terms of three basic elements, other gastronomic approaches underline the variations in the meanings of food that communities share when choosing foods that bring mental or physical satisfaction.

Fisher's (1954) *The Art of Eating* discusses the interactions and bonds between those who produce the food, as well as its many meanings, while *The Gastronomical Me* (Fisher 1997) stresses that the presence of food in the bowl leads to nourishment in the heart and feeds wilder and more insistent hungers. 'We must eat ... There is a communion of more than our bodies when bread is broken and wine drunk' (p. vii). Fisher thus alludes to several layers of meanings and metaphors that anthropologists seek out in order to expand their comprehension of the place of food in society.

There is a wide diversity of symbols attached to food, as well as diverse ways in which food contributes to well-being. The biological is closely intertwined with the psychological and sociological in a gastronomic approach. While early Victorians viewed any matters associated with eating as 'unmentionable', food has emerged from 'the darkness' as a subject of wide debate and media attention. As 'domestic science', taught mainly to female students, it ranked among the 'lesser' sciences. Awareness of the diversity of beliefs and practices associated with food has exposed us to a wide understanding of cultural interactions, and the sense of well-being involving food (Belasco 2008: 3). Thus those writing about the anthropology of food address topics ranging from the politics of food and hunger on a global scale, as set out in the United Nations Millennium Development Goals (2000), to empowering households' access to foods as a step to freedom (Sen 1999), to local ethnographies in which food restrictions are seen to dominate life, for example, in a Papua New Guinea Highland society (Meigs 1984).

An evolutionary interpretation of human history differentiates hunting and gathering as the dominant means of food provisioning from the subsequent stages of sedentary agriculture, plantations, and modern 'grazing' practices, including fast foods. The dominant contrast today lies between those societies that rely largely on growing their own food (subsistence) and those societies that use cash to buy their foods. Both means of access require choices that differentiate and cohere into distinctive gastronomies. Ethnic differences, and local cuisines have emerged, as well as 'slow food' cooking, alongside McDonalds and Coca Cola, as globalizing consumables.

To construct a picture of food consumption and the production criteria that lead to that end, we will illustrate how the language of economics differs from the language of nutrition, and that of social science. Economists have approached food largely through production, as it contributes to concepts such as wealth, capital, and labour. Nutritionists have added medical and chemical analyses to our under-standing of food as more than a biological necessity. Social scientists approach food as it contributes to well-being through the principle of sharing at both the household and community levels, as well as across national boundaries. The stark gastronomic realities for communities considered 'food-poor' reveal a whole range of complex considerations.

All three approaches converge when we consider consumerism, marketing, and globalization and the neologism 'glocalization'. Cuisines, gastronomies, and food cultures all bridge the nature/nurture dichotomy. Anthropologists draw attention to foods/gastronomies as a means of communication shared across communities, whether in the form of mangoes or McDonalds, haggis or sushi, and whether in less-industrialized settings or within Britain, Europe, Asia, or America. The posi-tives of 'good foods' are contrasted with taboos on particular foods, or items deemed unclean, and thus 'inedible' (e.g. Douglas 1982: ch. 4). The material aspects of food are embedded in social values and ideological concepts about well-being.

10.3 Food from an economic perspective

Early anthropologists included their discussions about food within chapters on economics, i.e. how resources regarded as food were produced and exchanged. Authors described how food crops were cultivated, including who was responsible for which tasks, such as planting, weeding, and harvesting, as well as the performance of rituals to increase fertility. Malinowski, an anthropologist teaching at the London School of Economics, devoted *Coral Gardens and their Magic* (1922) to describing how Trobriand people met their food needs through gardening as practised through appeals to the gods.

Political dimensions of food production have emerged strongly as concern mounts about the viability of food production in developing nations. The politics of hunger is based in assessments of food adequacy and food security. Trade imbalances that include a high proportion of food imports, particularly in Pacific societies, have been castigated as leading to a high level of dependence on aid from former colonial powers, i.e. industrialized nations. For those nations who have little to export—whether minerals, industrial manufactures, or cash crops—food imports are considered a drain on their economies. 'Import substitution' messages sought to encourage governments to find ways to increase self-sufficiency, i.e. the amount of foods grown locally. Ironically this reversed history, as many of these nations had been self-sufficient until colonial powers imposed the need to grow cash crops, such as sugar, or coconut for oil, on lands dedicated to subsistence foods. The costs of imported foods over local foods present households with dilemmas of choice. Access to cash presents difficulties in provisioning households.

A Marxist approach to food as it contributes to capital and wealth has helped to broaden anthropologists' views of humanitarian concerns behind trading foods. Labour inputs necessary to produce foods were documented as mainly men's work, whether hunting or growing field crops, with women's work being considered 'domestic' and thus not contributing to the economy. The male bias of 'Man the Hunter' (Lee and DeVore 1968) as distinguished from 'Woman the Gatherer' in early economic literature has since been radically re-evaluated. Such gendered language of labour was vehemently contested in the latter part of the twentieth century, with female anthropologists questioning the biases in the early literature. For example, Weiner's (1976) reevaluation of Malinowski's account fifty years earlier of Trobriand men gaining prestige by filling their yam houses revealed that women's work was equally prestigious. Trobriand women contributed bundles of banana leaves that were essential to kin relationships between those contributing yams. As 'women's work', the banana leaf bundles had been overlooked by Malinowski with his focus on male labour. The cautionary message emerged that women's contributions to the economy, whether in the fields of Ghana or in rice paddies in Southeast Asia, must be taken into account if all dimensions of labour inputs into an economy are to be taken into account.

Anthropologists have also raised concerns about the place of food as a trade item. Early discussions of the complex Kula 'ring' of exchanges of necklaces and armbands, together with food, between several neighbouring Trobriand island societies (e.g. Malinowski 1922) have drawn attention to whether trade for prestige differs fundamentally from trade for wealth. Status achieved by giving away a prestigious object amidst a feast of food may be considered irrational in an economic analysis that stresses accumulation and sale for profit rather than giving. Trading rings such as the Kula and the Potlatch in northwest America have stimulated much debate as to whether they illustrate pre-capitalism, or emerging capitalism, or whether they are economically 'rational'. The question of who profits from such transactions is countered by those who ask whether profit is the dominant value.

Frequent exchanges of food represent dynamics of social relationships that are difficult to assess in strictly economic terms. Contributions to a feast, or a plate of donuts given to auntie's family, meet social obligations, but are difficult to represent in economic terms. The value added accrues at a number of levels as different kinds of reciprocal obligations, whether it involves those donating food to a feast, a woman buying some cabbages from a stall at a marketplace, or a family filling their supermarket trolley. Tracking such food exchanges tells us the values of the foods in terms of the social relationships involved. The 'economy' of any community, whether local or national, would collapse if such exchanges were overlooked.

The values of particular foodstuffs are similarly a matter of concern when assessing poverty. Subsistence activities that provide foods for households from their own lands and with their own labour have been notoriously omitted from assessments of economic well-being. Grain crops are given a monetary value, as they contribute to assessments of Gross Domestic Product—and only five grain types are included (wheat, rice, corn, barley, and rye). Root crops, such as potatoes or taro, and many other foodstuffs are omitted because their monetary contributions are too small. Thus anthropological descriptions of a productive economy differ from economic assessments, as they stress the great variety of foodstuffs and the ways they are used, whereas the economist looks at the proportion of the trade figures attributed to grain crops.

Thus we are faced with a range of alternative views on the adequacy of food supplies for growing populations. Since Malthus (1999[1798]) first suggested in the 1700s that food supplies may not increase as fast as populations, the notion of 'food security' has been added to the language of food. Whether assessments focus on food production or on consumption, our quantification of food output or usage should include both general and particular features. For anthropologists, households consist of both consumers and producers, to which members contribute their labour. Households are enmeshed in an ongoing network of exchanges of foods for both social and economic ends. The adequacy of food production systems to meet community needs is regarded as a step forward to 'freedom' (Sen 1999).

Food poverty and hunger is as much a humanitarian as it is an economic issue. To take steps to improve the poverty situation for large numbers of people around the world, the United Nations has set eight Millennium Development Goals (2000) that encompass a wide range of humanitarian concerns. Food poverty is the first priority, with nations expected to reduce by half by 2015 the number of their people living on less than $1.00 per day. Supporting goals include increasing awareness of women's health issues, political awareness, and education. But without adequate access to food, communities will not be able to achieve the other seven goals.

Food security is a major target in economic development in the new millennium. It is a euphemism for adequacy, for how a nation's political economy is working, or for where a nation stands on any global assessments of comparative standings such as the Human Development Index.[1] Economists such as Stiglitz (2006) underline the need for new directions if national economies are to overcome the limitations that exist on access to food.

10.4 THE NUTRITIONAL LANGUAGE OF FOOD

Nutritionists have their own terms for food, particularly 'good food' and how it contributes to health and well-being. They have introduced concepts such as calories, carbohydrates, and anti-oxidants to the language for talking about food. Their concern is to show the health risks associated with poor food choices and ways of consuming food. They calculate the various elements against standard quantities of each in order to assess levels of inadequacy. They start from a biological perspective on the human body as an organ that requires inputs of food and outputs of energy, with the aim of calculating where supplements are needed to improve intake that will achieve a balanced diet and good health.

An adequate diet is assessed against Recommended Dietary Intakes (RDIs) that have been calculated to achieve the best intake for mid-latitude western consumers. Measurement against these standard figures is based on an adequate caloric intake for men and for women, by age bracket, together with the suggested adequate levels of vitamins, minerals, and anti-oxidants. Nutritionists collect data from their patients/clients in order to calculate an alternative pattern of food intake. Where specific intakes are difficult to assess, an overall programme of less salt, fat, and sugar and more protein is recommended. Transferring those ideas to non-English speaking communities is difficult, in particular where the chemical components of local foods have not yet been analysed. The language of nutrition education is especially difficult for people whose food concepts differ markedly from those in the English-speaking world. A complex dish such as a pizza may have been given a 'standard' composition of elements in an appropriate table of food components, but for any of the side dishes that are served in Chinese gastronomy the ingredients are often very unfamiliar, and have not been analysed. For the Gurage of Ethiopia's

[1] http://hdr.undp.org/en/statistics/indices/

diet of *ensete* bananas (Shack 1966) or taros eaten in Pacific communities (Pollock 1992), there are questions about how to determine the adequacy of their diet. Recommendations to improve such diets require analysis built on 'insider' knowledge.

'Good food' is a local concept embedded in social values as well as in the material aspects of particular foods and their combinations. Those bananas, or taros, or that rice have gained their cultural values within the local gastronomic settings. The food pyramid developed by Euro/American nutritionists places carbohydrates at the base of the pyramid, with protein, particularly meats, at the apex. The tapering nature of the model is also designed to indicate relative amounts of foods, with more vegetables and carbohydrates allowed than meat and eggs. But that model has proved difficult for nutritionists working in communities where food values have their own weightings. For the Inuit, fish and seal blubber dominate their food landscape, while for many other communities, any form of protein is hard to obtain. In urban settings the cost of supermarket meat is beyond the pockets of low-income consumers, so they fill up on rice and potatoes and bread (Pollock, Dixon, and Leota 1996).

The place of meat in these recommended diets is derived from what Smil (2002) refers to as the American 'excessive carnivore' diet. Although the recommended quantities of meat as the main source of protein have been reduced in the last twenty years from 75 grams per person per day to 30 grams, the amounts are still unattainable for two-thirds of the world's population. Not just the meat itself, but the concepts behind meat eating are being challenged: 'man the hunter' has lost many chances to bring home the kill, and with those the prestige and status that used to be given to the 'breadwinner'. Prestige foods in the form of meat, fish, or chicken may be given prime place when guests are present, but such feast occasions are rare. Smil advocates moderation in the amount of meat eaten, and adds environmental concerns, suggesting that of all the meat types, chicken is the most sustainable (Smil 2002). Similarly, Pollan (2006) has demonstrated the inefficiencies of meat production, as the animals consume five times more grains and water than the weight of meat produced.

10.4.1 The meal

Concepts of meals, as the main means of food consumption, have undergone rethinking on two fronts. Not only has it become apparent that affluent westerners set their own eating schedules to fit their work/life situations, but individuals are developing divergent tastes, so that the family meal may no longer meet their needs. Home cooking may be acceptable once in a while, but as households in the western world have reduced the amount of cooking, family dishes and recipes may disappear.

The meal has been transplanted from western gastronomical practices into other parts of the world, but with local variations. One meal a day may be feasible, rather than the nutritionist's recommended three meals a day. In many communities like those in the Pacific, that transplant is recognizable in the terms for meals, food in the morning food at noon, food in the evening (Marshallese *manga in jibon*—'food in the morning' etc.). Previously they ate when food was available, such as when fish came ashore, and waited until the next cooked food appeared. Such irregularity was deemed 'uncivilized' by missionaries, who tried to teach local women 'how to cook' and the 'proper' way to serve food (Pollock 1986). Similarly, English missionaries advised that the meal should consist of meat, potato, and vegetables, with bread and wine added by French arrivals. These ideas were often neither feasible nor acceptable in relation to plenty of local foods. New ideas have been equally difficult when they come from nutritionists using a foreign language. Indigenous nutritionists and dietitians brought up in their local food traditions and undertaking nutrition training have elided the two, so that a food pyramid that contains both local foods alongside western foods has carried the message more successfully (Sio 1995).

Nutritionists have faced difficulties in trying to establish individual intakes when many people eat meals in family settings, where the individual has little choice in the contents of the meal. Elaborate methods of measuring individual portions by weighing them before they are consumed, and assessing any wastage, have proved intrusive, and the results are thus considered unreliable (Pelto, Pelto, and Messer 1989). Data can be collected in this way for only two or three days. Anthropological methods of gathering food data have focused on access to foods as they have been recorded over a year-long cycle. Necessarily, only a limited number of households can be included in such longitudinal approaches, but that is considered preferable to the very short survey method.

One advantage of a year-long study of food is that is that it reveals a wider gastronomic picture. It brings out reasoning behind particular food choices and tastes, as well as rejections of and adjustments to the acceptability of foods. Availability of fuelwood is a key concern that distinguishes cooked food from raw food. Foods such as taro may be inedible in their raw state because of acrid substances; thus ways of cooking in earth ovens have been devised that lessen the demands on fuelwood when this is scarce. Fermented foods may suit local palates whereas they are rejected by those unfamiliar with, for example, rotted corn, or fermented breadfruit or taro. Fermentation may provide additional flavors to bland foods, as well as provisions for seasons when food is short.

The concept of food applies to only some resources, while others are rejected. Those rejections are based on cultural rather than biological concepts. Pork is rejected by many who believe it to be an unclean meat (Harris 1985), while many in Euro/American countries reject horse, dog, and whale for emotional rather than biological reasons. Nutritionists have added to these features by assigning negative values to too much salt, or sugar, or alcohol, giving as their reasoning that they are associated with high risks to health (Coyne, Badcock, and Taylor 1984). But those negative values may be invisible, and thus rejected by those who enjoy their donuts, or their rum. Similarly reducing intake of calories has been a hard message for nutritionists to convey, especially in those communities where large body size has traditionally been valued (Pollock 1995).

Nutritionists and anthropologists continue their dialogue about food and its wider importance, leading to a wider range of ideas for nutrition educators on meal structures, variations in eating, cooking, and gastronomic principles, as well as to new ideas about the links between food and health.

10.5 THE SOCIAL LANGUAGE OF FOOD

The social language of food incorporates not only the material entities of foodstuffs but also the wider place of food in social interactions. Food 'communicates' through a set of categories in which values are embedded. As a code, 'the message [that food] encodes will be found in the pattern of social relationships being expressed. The message is about different degrees of hierarchy, inclusion and exclusion, boundaries and transactions across boundaries' (Douglas 1975: 249). Following Lévi-Strauss's use of binary pairs, such as raw and cooked foods, Douglas draws a contrast between the food categories of meals and drinks as social events, in order to ask whether 'a correspondence is found between a given social structure and the structure of symbols by which it is expressed, the question of consciousness' (p. 251). Alternatively, Barthes argues for:

the (necessary) widening of the very notion of food...as more than a collection of products that can be used for statistical or nutritional studies. It is also at the same time, a system of communication, a body of images, a protocol of usages, situations, and behaviour...Food sums up and transmits a situation; it constitutes an information; it signifies. (Barthes 1997: 21)

The importance of understanding food in its social setting is that it takes us beyond material elements, such as price or chemical components, to discern another layer of categorization. Material objects, whether rice or haggis, embody a range of gastronomic features that include the esteem associated with those foods, the value of labour inputs, the 'proper' foods appropriate to a specific occasion, the ideological principles meeting commitments through sharing, and the panoply of ideological factors behind food sharing.

The many dimensions of food sharing are well illustrated by the multivalence of the Tongan concept of *kainga*. Literally it refers to food (*kai*) for the group (*nga*). But the term is used most frequently to refer to a family group including the space around the household. Tevita Ka'ili (2005) explains the many spaces (*va*) that are alluded to when the term *kainga* is used, whether physical or social spaces. It may refer to a household, or to a church group that shares food and a place to stay, particularly for Tongan groups overseas in California or Maui (p. 101). This multi-layered concept signifies the multitude of ways in which food sharing reinforces social bonds.

Sharing food across national boundaries has increased exponentially around the world in the last forty years (Pollock 2009). As families and individuals establish new communities in metropolitan settings, the foods they share reinforce wider social networks, as they exchange news and ideas and refurbish their national language. Nostalgia for a former way of life is evoked by the tastes and smells of 'home', even if alternative foods, or means of cooking, must be substituted for the 'real thing' (Kolo 1990). Trying to recreate experiences associated with cooking in an earth oven in an urban environment beyond the islands can meet with social disapproval of the new host community—as in suburbs of New Zealand towns, when a Pacific island church group wishes to warm the ties with home through the smell of cooking from an *'umu* (earth oven). The joy of meeting and exchanging news of others is strengthened by familiar tastes and smells, despite the restrictions.

Giving and receiving food, whether to relatives or to strangers, is generally recognized as a mark of positive social encounters. But differences between practices of cooking and eating can also offend, as when cooking smells offend neighbours, or, for example, Japanese were repulsed by the smells from a Maori *hangi* (a feast prepared in an earth oven), prepared by a group of Maori visiting in Japan. The wider significance may be lost in the reaction to an unfamiliar smell or taste. To offer a bear's paw as food to someone with strong conservation values sets up tensions in that relationship that have to be worked through. Misunderstandings through inadequate knowledge of local food ideology can even harm social relationships. When early visitors to the Pacific such as Captain Cook offered some of their prized meat (dried) to their Tahitian noble guests, the honor was misunderstood, since the foods were new to the guests' palates. Similarly, when a visitor to Indonesia is offered durian fruit, she is likely to question the edibility of something that smells so offensive. Learning other people's tastes is part of the social dimension of gastronomic experience.

Foods shared at household meals are cooked and presented in familiar ways. But the protocols of serving food may be unfamiliar to an outsider, as when she is served alone, while the rest of the family waits to eat later; the 'honor' may seem otherwise. The order of foods, whether sweet before savory, or separate foods served in courses, French-style, is passed on through the generations. Shared tastes, perhaps idiosyncratic to particular households, continue over time as well as being modified. A child learns the tastes of different foods from adults and siblings in the household, along with principles that establish certain foods as 'good' foods, or special treats, but then develops their own taste as their experience widens. Chicken and ice cream are no longer the birthday foods they used to be for English children. Instead, a birthday boy may request a party at McDonalds. For some families, a variety of tastes are cultivated in the process of sharing daily meals. For others, access to a variety of foods is limited by availability, whether because of distance from a market or supermarket or other supplier, or because of lack of cash.

Feasts are often occasions at which the range of food available is greater than that used daily in the household. Households may be asked to contribute particular foods, such as specially prepared combination dishes not usually eaten at home. In the Pacific, leaf packets of taro, corned beef, and coconut cream, baked in the earth oven, are offered as 'feast' foods. Similarly, haggis in Scotland used to be a shared communal dish, though now it is available in supermarkets, and even tinned. Thus the foods presented at a feast may be an important signifier of the success of that social event in terms of foods the participants approve of, usually the familiar, and those they consider to be unusual. Sharing ethnic dishes across national boundaries enlarges horizons, as when pizza were first introduced by Italians resident in the United States. But a pizza base topped with bananas and maple syrup indicates adaptation to the new host community.

Religious beliefs can contribute to differentiating 'good' foods from those not to be eaten. All communities select those items from their environment that they consider edible, while rejecting those they deem inedible for various local reasons. Chinese claim they eat anything, a factor that others consider unusual (Chang 1977). While pork is unacceptable to strict Muslims for religious reasons, horse or dog meat is unacceptable to many Europeans for emotional reasons. The association between a particular foodstuff and the ancestors may be a strong reason for not eating it, and for signifying it as a totem. For the Hua community in the Highlands of Papua New Guinea, many rules govern the production, preparation and consumption of their food. According to Meigs (1997), the act of eating connects the Hua to the world, and emphasizes relatedness. They view foods as possessing the vitality and dynamism of living beings, but they also fear certain foods as carrying ill will, or pollution.

Ongoing exchanges of foods between households can be both a social responsibility and a practical exchange. When visiting for any length of time in another community, for example in a Jamaican village, the anthropologist is challenged by the simple need to eat, and thereby faces a complexity of social issues. To understand the relationships expressed by the plate of donuts, or fried fish, that a young girl brings to the door requires many questions. And to return that plate empty is a social offence. The relationships expressed may range from a man's responsibility to ensure his sister is taken care of in a matrilineal society to a wish for a political favour. Food exchanges are the cement of social relationships, whether sharing a family meal or entertaining guests with a banquet in a smart hotel.

To understand the diversity of food concepts, both those expressed and those shared unconsciously, we must go beyond our own biases. What is 'good' food for one community may not be high priority for another. Belasco (2006) has led his students through a process of awakening their minds to five factors they should consider when studying the diversity of American cuisine: 'basic foods, preparation techniques, flavor principles, manners and the food chain' (pp. 16–20). He places beef at the centre of the plate, as he considers protein essential, with starch as a side dish, and vegetables as 'embroidery'. However, when we consider the 'cuisines' or gastronomies of non-American peoples, those categories are highly debatable. For Fijians, taro is their basic, i.e. essential food (*kakana dina* 'food real'), a root starch that satisfies as well as fills, but only when well cooked and eaten with an accompaniment of fish or a piece of coconut and eaten in the company of others. For the Gurage of Ethiopia, *ensete* is their main food (Shack 1997: 127). To identify 'staple' or 'basic' foods we must distinguish outsiders' perspectives from those of insiders. Linguistic clues may help. In the Marshall Islands in the central Pacific, as we learn the language we learn to use a unique possessive adjective for food (*kij-*) and another possessive for drink (*lim-*). Those possessives guide us to what is included in the category 'food'. I learned that Marshallese include cigarettes in their concept of food, using the food possessive *kijo jikka* when talking about cigarettes they are smoking.

The range of food preparation techniques around the world is vast. As Belasco (2006) argues 'humans are creative in devising numerous ways of turning raw foods into cooked foods' (p. 18). From the distinction that Lévi-Strauss drew between the 'raw' and the 'cooked' to separate uncivilized eating from civilized eating, we have come to recognize that the application of heat is only one way to render foods edible; application of lime juice to raw fish (*ceviche* in Mexico) is widely regarded as a form of cooking. And to preparation techniques we must add preservation techniques including salting, or fermenting, or more localized forms such as long cooking (see Pollock 1984 on breadfruit fermentation). Cooking with added spices, or mixing foods, or making bread, all require certain techniques which must meet local flavor principles. Understanding how communities satisfy their particular gastronomic preferences for certain flavors, and reject others, is integral to understanding food concepts, and how food meets social criteria.

Good manners are an integral part of social food rites. Mennell's (1985) historical account of how English and French table manners have changed over time draws our attention to the evolution of criteria of what are considered civilized manners. The gastronomic protocols that govern the use of chopsticks or serving food on a palm leaf, or serving food in the correct hierarchical sequence, are all notable features that send messages about the wider society.

To Belasco's five factors of food concepts we must add the link between food and health that has become so important in recent times. As the Millennium Goals (mentioned earlier) remind us, the ideal of $1.00 a day for accessing food will improve the health status of those in poverty. The hunger concept as addressed by Lappe and Collins's (1986) 'Twelve myths of hunger' reminds us how some deeply entrenched—often ethnocentric—concepts prevent us from understanding how the devastation of world hunger can be addressed. Negative concepts that ban excessive food consumption because of its links with obesity and other non-communicable diseases have been widely addressed from many viewpoints (e.g. Sobal 1999). The links between obesity and desired images of body shape as promoted in Western media suggest that bulimia could now be included as a food concept.

Food metaphors as used by particular language communities underlie the variety of perspectives on the place food plays in society. Appreciating the many levels of those metaphoric uses takes us way beyond food as a material item. Chinese metaphors, widespread for several thousand years, have been written down as aphorisms to guide 'the right way of living' (Chang 1977). In the English-speaking world, bread as the staff of life has been supplanted by notions of 'fast foods' or 'drug foods' (Mintz 1985) or snacks. To decode these in Douglas's terms, we need to study the social language of food.

10.6 Conclusions

Food communicates between people, but in ways as complex as language itself. When we refer to food as a language, we recognize that it carries many meanings that are open to diverse interpretations. Douglas, Lévi-Strauss, and other anthropologists constructed a grammar of food around rules of eating that included table manners, cooked vs. raw foods, and sequences of foods in meals as general structural features. Barthes and others stressed the significations embedded in sharing food. Subsequent studies of the culture of food and gastronomy have shown the diversity of practices and ideologies over and above those regularities, emphasizing the many ways in which food is used to maintain social relationships.

Food is analysed and discussed using very specialized concepts pertinent to specific academic disciplines, such as economics, nutrition, and social science. Foodways are presented either in terms of production output units, such as Gross Domestic Product, or labour inputs to assign a dollar value comparable across nation-states. Alternatively, nutritionists approach gastronomic practices through measures of caloric intake and the chemical elements of food, with such terms featuring in their nutrition education messages suggesting changes to intake in order to improve health. Social scientists present gastronomies as reflections of sharing food that facilitate social relationships. The concepts used by each discipline may differ but the underlying message is similar: that gastronomies are a key element of social communications. The concept of 'good food' has many cultural manifestations that indicate why people choose certain foods over others, and the diversity of tastes that must be met to satisfy the criteria of well-being.

The language of food intertwines the symbols associated with material foodstuffs and the social situations in which communities employ them. A feast or party is socially embellished through the choice of foods on offer. Whether benefits are assessed in terms of the dollars spent, the nutritional value of the foods, or the contributions by fishermen, the success of a social event depends on the right balance of messages conveyed. Foodstuffs, and the gastronomies of which they are a part, have some generally recognizable features which are used in particular cultural context to convey messages of social well-being. They are culturally bounded, and yet tasted beyond those boundaries.

CHAPTER 11

···

BOTANICAL COLLECTING

···

BARRY J. CONN

11.1 INTRODUCTION[1]

···

Since plants are a very important part of the material and cultural heritage of all communities, those who are interested in studying the culture of a people require an understanding of the plants associated with them (Fosberg 1960). To understand plants and their association with the people, it is important to know the identity of the plant species used by them. Knowing the vernacular name of a plant used by a community assists with communication within that community but fails to provide information to a broader group. Furthermore, the information on how this plant is used by other communities remains inaccessible to most researchers. Therefore, it is important to link local plants to their scientific names so that all the information about these plants is available to everyone (Conn 1994). However, the identification of plants is often quite difficult and requires careful examination of the features of the plant and comparison with other previously identified species. Therefore, carefully prepared botanical collections are always required to identify plants

[1] I thank Jeanine Pfeiffer (University of California, Davis, USA) for useful discussions on collaborating with indigenous peoples. Elizabeth Brown (National Herbarium of New South Wales, Sydney, Australia) provided comments on collecting bryophytes. Julisasi Hadiah (Kebun Raya Bogor, Indonesia), Louisa Murray and Andrew Orme (both National Herbarium of New South Wales, Sydney, Australia) commented on the manuscript. Catherine Wardrop (National Herbarium of New South Wales) provided the illustrations.

with certainty. Furthermore, our scientific understanding of the relationship between plants is constantly being revised, particularly as new techniques and data, such as molecular data, are becoming available; the names of many species have been changed to reflect these changes. Therefore, the lodging of botanical collections in scientific herbaria and museums is important for acquiring the currently correct scientific name for a plant. Since each collection will be available for further study at a later stage, the scientific name can be corrected based on modern knowledge, thus ensuring that vernacular names always remained linked to the correct scientific literature.

This chapter provides a brief introduction to the techniques used for collecting botanical specimens that will enable fieldworkers to provide specimens of plants that are adequate for identification and valuable for scientific study.

11.1.1 Botanical identification

Many different types of publications provide information about the diversity of the flora of a region. These publications include:

1. Checklists: a simple list of plants of a specific area. Sometimes these lists are annotated with brief descriptive notes, such as Charters (2003–) and Press, Shrestha, and Sutton (2000–). Local authorities, especially environmental agencies, frequently have unpublished checklists that are often more current than the published lists. These checklists can also be very useful for identifying plants from a specific area. However, a high level of botanical taxonomic knowledge is usually required to use these lists effectively to assist in identification.

2. Field guides: usually provide readily observable features that can be used in the field for distinguishing plants of a specific area, usually with brief descriptions, often with illustrations, of the most common plants of an area (e.g. Balgooy 1997; 1998; 2001; Court 2000). Sometimes field guides are only a list of botanical names and photographs and/or illustrations. However, many popular field guides are excellent (e.g. Harden, McDonald, and Williams 2006; Hutton 2008; Steenis 1949–) and these publications are usually adequate for identifying the plants of a specific region.

3. Floras: descriptions, identification tools (keys), illustrations, and images of plants of a specific area, for example Nee (2004, 2008), Stannard (1995), Steenis (1949–). Recently, more of these floras are readily available via the internet, such as Conn and Damas (2006–), Conn et al. (2004–), Flora of Guianas (1885–), Flora of North America (1993–), Hoch (2000–), Western Australian Herbarium (1998–). eFloras (2009) is an excellent on-line resource that provides a comprehensive listing of electronic floras (e.g. Flora of China 1994; Ulloa Ulloa and Jørgensen 2004) and checklists, as well as other information.

4. Scientific revisions: these are more technical scientific publications than the previous examples and are published in peer-reviewed scientific journals and

books. These publications often deal with larger taxonomic groups, such as a family or genus, frequently dealing with a specific geographic area. They provide the same information as a 'Flora' but usually in more detail and with more precise technical terminology than used in the other forms of publications. However, early scientific publications are often very brief, being little more than a listing with a brief descriptive diagnosis in Latin. All forms of scientific revisions usually require a specialized level of knowledge to use effectively.

There are too many useful publications available to provide a generalized simple list here. However, Frodin (2001) provides an extensive and yet selective annotated bibliography of the principal floras and related works of inventory for vascular plants. The book lists principally specialist publications such as floras, checklists, distribution atlases, systematic iconographies, and enumerations or catalogues. A few popularly oriented books are included. Increasingly, publications that are useful for botanical identification and general information about botanical diversity are becoming available in electronic format, e.g. 'Flora of Australia' (ABRS 1981–), 'Flora of China' (Flora of China 1994–) and 'Flora of Taiwan' (TAI 2003–). Other publications are also available electronically, e.g. the printed version of 'Flora Europaea' (Tutin et al. 1964; 1968; 1972; 1976; 1980; Moore 1993) has been replaced by Walters and Webb (2001). Interactive guides to many plant groups have been specifically developed as CD ROM products (e.g. Agoo et al. 2003; Brooker 2006; Hyland et al. 2003; Jones et al. 2006; Maslin 2001; Schuiteman and Vogel 2001; 2002; 2005; 2006; 2008; Schuiteman et al. 2008; Thiele and Adams 2002).

Since new electronic interactive identification tools are being rapidly developed, regular searching of the internet is strongly encouraged. Specific websites (e.g. Anonymous 2001–) provide current information on their theme. The websites of herbaria are also an excellent resource for links to relevant identification publications (e.g. Missouri Botanic Gardens 2009). Of course, the primary resource should always be the authoritative advice of herbarium staff.

11.1.2 Botanical terminology

The descriptive terminology for plants and their component parts have been developed for the purpose of providing an accurate and complete vocabulary for description, identification, and classification (Radford et al. 1998). The collector requires some knowledge of this terminology so that adequate material and accompanying field notes are provided to assist the identification process and to provide material that is useful for other scientific purposes. For example, a basic understanding of the structure of flower is required if the colour or shape of the parts of a fresh flower are to be described unambiguously for interpretation of the dried material. A glossary of technical terms is usually provided in regional 'Floras' (Conn and Damas 2006–) and in specialized textbooks on plant systematics of taxonomy (Radford et al. 1998–).

A generalized search of the internet will recover several excellent on-line glossaries of botanical terms (e.g. Lyne n.d.; Flora of China n.d.; Wilmé 2002–). However, it is preferable to use the glossary of terms provided in the publication being used for identification purposes. Some otherwise 'standard' terms may be defined slightly differently in various botanical publications. The terminology used in this chapter has been simplified as much as possible, but reference to a botanical glossary may be required. There are a few specialized glossaries that assist with the translation of a botanical term to other languages (e.g. Rossi-Wilcox n.d.).

11.1.3 Collecting equipment

Botanical collecting, especially in remote areas, requires considerable planning before the fieldwork is undertaken. A summary of what should be done to ensure safe and successful field studies is discussed in §11.6. Before starting to collect botanical specimens, the correct equipment is required. The equipment includes: secateurs, hand lens (10× magnification), jeweler's tags, field book, knife, paper and plastic bags (of various sizes to put plant samples in), small clip-lock plastic bags, silica gel (for drying samples quickly if required for molecular studies), plant press, newspaper, cardboard sheets, tissue paper, GPS (Global Positioning System), maps—topographical, road, and any other maps of the area—pencil (preferable) or waterproof or permanent-ink pen.

11.1.4 Using local knowledge

Local knowledge of the landscape (see Turk et al., Chapter 16 below), other natural features including local climate, and an understanding of modifications to the local environment are always valuable. This information may mean the difference between finding a plant and not locating it. Furthermore, since you may need to visit or traverse private land, it is important to obtain permission and assistance from local landowners before undertaking any field activities.

11.2 THE BOTANICAL COLLECTION

The essential aspects of making an adequate plant collection for identification and further scientific study include collecting botanical material that is of adequate size and has required morphological features, and the provision of adequate supplementary information provided by the collector.

The importance of collecting adequate botanical specimens cannot be over-emphasized. Good specimens are always required for accurate identification. The morphological characteristics of good specimens form the basis of continuing scientific research. Although other sources of data are being increasingly utilized, such as molecular data, morphological features remain the primary source of data for communicating species concepts. As our scientific knowledge of taxonomy improves, the identity of good specimens can be re-determined. Since these collections are authenticated vouchers for the original project, the information in that project will remain linked to the most modern taxonomic concepts via these collections.

Although it may be easier to examine an unmounted botanical specimen, normal handling easily damages dried, brittle material. Therefore, herbaria and museums affix these specimens to white mounting cards/sheets. Many of the collections held by these organizations are irreplaceable, and any serious damage would lessen their scientific value. Furthermore, herbaria and museums are custodians of these natural heritage objects on behalf of the citizens of their region. Therefore, it is useful to remember the size of the herbarium sheet that will be used to mount the specimen. Since most herbarium sheets are about 430mm long and 280mm wide (or larger), botanical specimens about 300mm long make suitable specimens of most species.

When possible, collect the entire plant or at least a portion of a plant when it is much large than a typical herbarium sheet. A typical branch or portion of the stem, about 200–300mm long, showing the leaves in position and with flowers and/or fruits (both if possible), should be collected: these are the characteristics that are traditionally used for determining the identity of a plant. If open flowers are not available, then flowers buds should be included. If variation in leaf form is apparent, specimens should include different parts of the same plant to represent this variation. Seeds can be useful in the identification of plants and should be included, if available.

For plants with large leaves or massive fruits, do not limit what makes up the collection because it may be difficult and/or take a great deal of time. It is more important to have a complete, useful specimen than to conform to arbitrary rules (but see below about storage of large specimens).

11.2.1 What to collect

The features most important for identification vary between different plant groups. The major plant groups and some specific requirements for collecting these groups are listed below.

Figure 11.1. Selecting material from a flowering branch for the botanical specimen using secateurs.

11.2.1.1 *Vascular plants*

Vascular plants (also known as 'higher plants') are plants that have specialized tissues (often woody) for conducting water, minerals, and photosynthetic products through the plant. Vascular plants include the ferns, clubmosses, flowering plants, and conifers. There are many useful publications on the collection of vascular plants (see references cited in Taylor 1990). Additional practical advice for working in tropical regions is provided by Hyland (1972), Kajewski (1933), Mori (1984).

(i) Ferns. It is important to make sure that the specimen being collected is fertile (spore-bearing) (Bridson and Forman 1998). The spores are arranged in sporangia which differ in position and appearance in the various groups of ferns. In the majority of ferns the sporangia occur on the margin or on the lower (abaxial) surface of 'leaves' (fronds). Therefore, specimens must include the sporangia (if separate from the fronds), or fertile (spore-bearing) fronds and sterile fronds, as well as part of the rhizome (if present) or base of stem (stipe). For tree ferns, a portion of a fertile frond and the base of the frond stalk bearing scales or hairs must be collected.

(ii) **Herbs.** When dealing with small herbs the entire plant should be collected. Herbs with underground storage organs should be dug up complete with storage organs. However, if the plant is uncommon, make notes on the characteristics of these basal parts, including measurements and drawings, and leave them to shoot again in the following year. This is especially important in the case of orchids and rare species.

(iii) **Grasses.** Grasses and other plants of grass-like habit, such as sedges and rushes, should be collected whole so as to show the rootstock. Grass clumps may be broken up into small tufts of leaves and flowering stalks; two or three of these tufts should make a satisfactory specimen. All soil adhering to the roots should be carefully knocked off or washed away. Grasses are best collected after the flowers have opened, but before fruits are ready to drop. If the grass specimen is longer than the herbarium sheet (see measurements above), it should be bent once, twice or more so as to form a V, N, or M (according to its length) and pressed in this position. Attempts to bend it after it is dry will probably cause it to break. In the case of exceptionally tall grasses, the flowering parts and a piece of the basal parts should be collected, and a note made of the height and habit.

(iv) **Bamboos.** Bamboos are variously woody, temperate, or tropical grasses that have jointed and often hollow stems. They can be identified from sterile material (lacking flowers and fruits); however, reproductive structures have traditionally been used for identification purposes.

The parts of the plant that are essential for identification are discussed in Soderstrom and Young (1983) and Womersley (1969). The features include:

1. Culm sheaths: at least two complete sheaths, from about the fifth node from base of culm ('stem') and several mature sheaths from mid-culm nodes. Attach to each of these sheaths a label that records the node from which they were collected. If too large, then cut or fold as necessary. If a sheath cannot be flattened without fracturing, then roll and do not press. However, it is necessary to protect the fragile apex of the sheath by enclosing the rolled sheath with paper.
2. Leafy twigs: include large and small leaves, both young and old. Since the leaves often begin to 'curl' soon after collecting, it is advisable to press the leaves as quickly as possible.
3. Section of branch: at least one typical section of a branch (15–18cm long) from about half-way along culm.
4. Culm nodes and internodes: a segment of mature-sized culm, including the fourth and fifth nodes above the ground.

5. Rhizome: at least one complete example of the structural unit, preferably two or more units that show the branching habit of the rhizome (the horizontal, usually underground stem that often sends out roots and shoots). Trim off roots.

6. Flowering branches: although rarely present in bamboos, collect enough to show the habit, leaf arrangement and density, and stages of development. Collect fruits if present, making sure they are not lost (during pressing and drying) because they readily detach from the plant.

Photographs, sketches, and additional notes complement the botanical specimen and are extremely helpful when identifying the plant.

(v) Trees and shrubs. As for all plants that are too large to fit onto the herbarium sheet, additional information about the tree or shrub being gathered must be recorded at the time of collection. When collecting trees, the collector's notes should describe the colour and type of bark (e.g. rough, smooth, stringy, or fibrous) and if rough, how far it extends (e.g. over base of trunk only, also on main branches, and/or on fine twigs); sometimes it may be appropriate to collect a wood and bark sample as an ancillary collection. As for other flowering plants, flowers, including flowering buds and fruits, should all be collected if available. Since there may be differences between the types of leaves present on a plant, the collection of adult and juvenile leaves, and sun and shade leaves should be observed and collected if different, or described if any of these cannot be obtained. Since many plants are deciduous, the flowers and fruits may be present when leaves are absent. This should be recorded in the collector's field notes. Each separate stage of the plant's lifecycle can be collected independently and treated as separate specimens, but from the same plant. The bark features may not be as important for the identification of large shrubs, but it is always good practice to record this information at the time of collection.

(vi) Succulents. The tissues of succulents and fleshy plants (e.g. cacti, agaves, aloes, bromeliads) usually contain large amounts of water, and some even tend to retain water during the pressing and drying process. There are several techniques used to overcome this problem (Victor et al. 2004):

1. Remove inner tissue: the specimen can be cut longitudinally or transversely so that the fleshy inner tissues can be removed before pressing. This method is used for *Aloe* species and many species of cacti.

2. Hot water/liquid treatment. Submerge the plant material in very hot water or in methylated spirits, petrol or even vinegar. Prior to submersion, pierce material with a needle to allow ready penetration of liquid.

3. Freezer/microwave: place unpressed material in a freezer for two days and then place in microwave for periods of 5–10 seconds and then check, repeat as necessary until material dried (Leuenberger 1982).

Fleshy flowers can be prepared for pressing and drying by cutting longitudinally, separating the two halves on white card (some prefer moistened gummed paper—Victor et al. 2004), cover with wax paper and enclose in a sheet of newspaper and then press with the remainder of the collection.

There are many excellent references on pressing and drying succulents that should be consulted for detailed information (e.g. De Langhe 1972; Logan 1986; Croat 1985; Griffiths 1907; Jorgensen 1972; MacDougall 1947).

(vii) Plants with large inflorescences or other large parts.

(vii) **Plants with large inflorescences or other large parts.** When collecting plants such as agaves, palms, pandans (Stone 1983), or bananas, the lengths of the flowering and non-flowering parts of the inflorescences and trunk heights should be noted. For plants such as large-leaved palms, cycads, bananas, and aroids, the smallest complete leaf is often many times larger than the standard sheet. There are two collection and storage methods for such plants. One technique is to cut the leaf into numerous (carefully numbered) portions which are attached to multiple herbarium sheets in the herbarium or museum. This has the advantage of not requiring alternative storage areas. Disadvantages include the need for additional documentation, preferably including photographs, and the difficulty of relating the specimen to the living plant. The alternative technique is to collect the entire leaf and to provide special separate storage for such material. The main disadvantages of this technique are that the material is difficult to handle in the field (to press and dry) and greater storage space is required.

(viii) **Bananas.** The collection of giant herbaceous plants, like bananas, some aroids, and heliconias, is always difficult. As for all large plants, it is impossible to collect the entire banana (*Musa*) plant as a herbarium specimen. Photographs, sketches, and extensive detailed notes are essential. Record the following features:

- Pseudostem ('stem'): suckering habit, height, colour, degree of waxiness, colour of exudates (sap), height, and diameter.
- Leaves: held erect or spreading, length and width of lamina (size of leaf blade), length of petiole (stalk of leaf), including leaf colour, waxiness, and markings), margin of sheath (lower part of leaf that more or less surrounds the stem).
- Fruit clusters: banana fruit grow in hanging clusters, with fruit arranged in a 'hand', and several hands form a bunch. Record if the bunches are erect, semi-pendulous, or pendulous, number of hands per bunch, whether hands compact or distant from each other, number of 'fingers' (individual fruits per hand), and whether fingers are close together or distant.

- Fingers: curved upwards or downward, length, diameter, cylindrical or angular at maturity, colour of skin when immature and mature, whether skin peels off mature fingers, colour of pulp surrounding seeds.
- Rachis: the axis of the fruiting bunch. Record if rachis is directly pendulous, slightly S-shaped, or markedly so.
- Male bud: occurs at the end of the rachis. Record shape, size, and colour (photograph and make a drawing). Also record whether or not the bracts overlap each other.

To make adequate herbarium specimens from bananas is extremely difficult, but the best method is to store most material, except for leaf samples, in bottles containing solutions of 70 per cent ethanol or methylated spirit. Removing some of the bracts from female and male flowers assists with the penetration of the preserving liquid.

(ix) **Palms.** When collecting palms it is important to realize that ample time is required to prepare a good herbarium specimen, especially of large tree palms. Since the plant is too large to collect in its entirety, the collection should represent the living plant in such a way that someone else can imagine what the palm looked like from the material that you collected (Dransfield 1986). As for other flowering plants, it is generally not sufficient to collect sterile specimens for the purpose of identification. However, sterile material of rattans (climbing palms) has many useful features for identification purposes in the leaf and leaf sheath (Baker and Dransfield 2006). The features to collect include:

- A section of stem: if stem is slender then take a sample of stem. However, if large, cut off a thin strip of the stem's outer surface.
- Leaf sheath: take an entire sheath and split it down the middle, cut into fragments if very large, representing base and apex (always clearly label all parts).
- Leaf: remove an entire leaf, or if large, then cut into smaller sections representing base of petiole (stalk of leaf), basal part of leaf (often first leaflets) plus apex of petiole, a middle section of leaf with axis (rachis), and then apex. Label all parts carefully. The leaflets from one side of the leaf can be removed if the leaf is very large.
- Inflorescences (arrangement of flowers): if large, then cut inflorescence into sections and provide a basal part, middle, and apical portions.
- Flowers and fruits: good flowers and fruits are required. You may not be able to get both from the same plant. Furthermore, fruits and seeds may be plentiful on the ground. Collect germinating seedlings as these can be useful.
- Rattans (climbing palms): collect the climbing 'tendrils' and record if they arise from the leaf apex or the leaf sheath. Do not attempt to remove the sheath from the stem.

(x) **Aquatic plants.** Generally the entire plant should be collected, if possible. As for terrestrial plants, aquatic vascular plants usually require flowers and mature fruits for identification; others require the rhizomes (e.g. water lilies) and root-stock; since immature and/or submerged leaves are different from mature and/or emergent or floating leaves, these should be collected as well. Remember that aquatic plants will wilt very quickly once removed from the water. Keep them in a bag or bucket with some water at all times until ready for pressing.

Some very small plants, like the floating duckweed (*Lemna*) and floating fern (*Azolla*), do not make very satisfactory pressed and dried specimens, but these can be placed between paper towelling (very absorbent paper) for pressing and drying, to produce reasonable specimens. Plants which contain a lot of mucilage are better pressed between sheets of greaseproof paper (Leach and Osborne 1985). Many publications that provided useful information on collecting aquatic plants (e.g. Haynes 1984; Ceska and Ceska 1986; Fish 1999).

11.2.1.2 Non-vascular plants

Non-vascular plants ('lower plants') are plants that lack specialized vascular tissue. These plants have no true roots, stems, or leaves; however, they often have structures that are superficially similar. Non-vascular plants include two distantly related groups, namely, Bryophytes (Lepp 2008+) and Algae (green algae) (Entwisle and Yee 2000–; Entwisle et al. 1997; Millar 1999–).

(i) Bryophytes (mosses, liverworts, hornworts) and lichens. Bryophytes and lichens should *not be pressed* when collected because the pressing process distorts the form of the plant and destroys some of the critical morphological features.

Detach the specimen from the substrate by hand or by use of a knife blade, taking care to include a narrow layer of soil or bark underneath the plant. Collecting lichens that grow on rocks can be more difficult, and may require some of the rock to be chipped away with a hammer or geological pick.

Place the specimen in a brown paper bag—never use polythene bags. However, remember that some bryophytes, for examples species of peat moss (*Sphagnum*), may contain large amounts of water. Remove as much of the water as possible by gently squeezing prior to placing specimen in paper bag. To make sure that the plants dry quickly, it is usually necessary to open the bags to the air or fan (if available) as much as possible. This is especially true in the wet tropics, where it is often difficult to dry any type of botanical collection. Once the specimen has dried, remove the excess soil and place the specimen back in an envelope and keep in a dry place until ready for despatch to an herbarium for identification.

(ii) Algae.

Freshwater algae Large algae and any attached microalgae can be collected by hand or with a knife, more easily in shallow water than deep. However, the risks associated with tropical waters, such as larvae of parasites, crocodiles, and other predatory animals, strongly indicate the use of various mechanical aids (Fosberg and Sachet 1965). The collection should include at least part of the substrate (e.g. rock, plant, or wood) if possible. When searching for freshwater algae, it is important to search all habitats in the body of water being investigated, including the edge of stones in fast-flowing water, surface of aquatic plants, dam walls, and any floating debris. In running or slightly turbid waters, a simple viewing box made from transparent Perspex enables attached algae to be more easily observed (Entwisle and Yee 2000–). A 10× hand lens is often required to determine if material is fertile. Microscopic floating algae (phytoplankton) can be collected with a mesh net (e.g. with 25–30 μm pores) or, if present in sufficient quantity (i.e. colouring the water), by simply scooping a jar through the water. Water samples can be left overnight allowing the algae to settle and concentrate on bottom of container. Squeezing peat moss (*Sphagnum*) and other mosses, or some aquatic flowering plants is a good way to collect a large number of species (Entwisle and Yee 2000–). Algae growing on soil are difficult to collect and study, many requiring culturing before sufficient materials are available for identification. An understanding of the morphology of freshwater algae is very useful when making collections (e.g. Wehr and Sheath 2003).

In addition to the standard information provided by the collector (see below), the field notes should include information on: whether the water is saline, brackish, or fresh; whether the collection site is terrestrial or a river, stream, or lake; whether the alga is submerged during water level fluctuations or floods; whether the water is muddy or polluted; whether the alga is free-floating or attached, and if the latter, the type of substrate to which it is attached; and the colour, texture, and size of the alga.

Initially, algae can be stored in a container (bucket, jar, bottle, or plastic bag), with some water from the collecting site. The container should be left open or only half filled with liquid; wide, shallow containers are better than narrow, deep jars. For long-term storage, specimens can be preserved in liquid (Entwisle and Yee 2000–; Entwisle et al. 1997), dried, and/or made into a permanent microscope mount. Seek advice from professional phycologists for specific advice and instruction.

Marine algae In general, the collection of marine algae (seaweeds) requires specialist diving skills. However, the collection of littoral algae can be undertaken by most people, with due awareness of the risks inherent within the marine environment. Algae that occur in deeper waters can only be collected by snorkelling and/or scuba diving. Although many collections can be made by hand, tools are generally essential. Collected specimens of different seaweeds should be kept separate while collecting. The specimens need to be fertile (with reproductive structures) because these features are required for identification. These reproductive structures are sometimes visible without a hand lens, because they have different coloration on the seaweeds, either on the surface or on special branches of the thalli (body of the alga) (National Taiwan Museum 2006). In addition, knowing the lifecycle of seaweeds can help with the identification of the species (Millar 1999–) and can assist the collector when selecting appropriate specimens. Hence, it is important to observe and record all details about the form, colours, numbers, substrate, location, and the surrounding environment.

As for freshwater algae, storage and preservation of marine algae require specialized treatment. Therefore, advice from experts should be sought on how to manage the specimens of different algal groups. Freshly collected algae should be kept cool after they are placed in plastic bags or plastic bottles (National Taiwan Museum 2006).

(iii) **Fungi.** When collecting fungi, it is important to place the specimens in a flat-bottomed basket or open box to minimize the amount of damage that may be caused to these delicate specimens. Each collection should be carefully wrapped in newspaper or, especially for the smaller and more delicate species and microfungi, placed in individual containers. Never use polythene bags. For agarics, it is essential to collect the entire 'fruiting body' (what most people think of as a mushroom, puffball, or toadstool), the base of the stipe ('stem'), and the remains (if any) of the cup- or sac-like structure (volva) occurring at the base of the stipe of agarics. A spore-print from at least one specimen of each collection is useful for larger fungi (see Bridson and Forman 1998; Major 1975).

11.2.2 Collecting plant disease specimens

When collecting plant material that appears to be affected by diseases, such as rusts, smuts, leaf spot, galls, cankers, and other diseases, these collections can be pressed and dried (see §11.5). It is important to include a collection of the diseased (host) plant that is adequate for identification. Make sure that as many identifiable stages of the disease are represented by the collection. Since it is important to have some understanding of the possible type of disease affecting the plant, further detailed information should be sought (e.g. Schubert et al. 1999 and literature cited therein).

11.2.3 Collecting living material

Living material may be required for cultivation in botanic gardens and gardens of research institutions (Bridson and Forman 1998). Increasingly, these collections are required for conservation purposes by having a readily available source of viable seeds and/or vegetative material for use in habitat restoration (Offord and North

2009). Cryopreservation of germplasm (seeds, embryos, pollen, and other botani-cal tissue) at −130 to −196 °C in liquid nitrogen is a method of long-term storage of botanical material for conservation purposes (Hamilton et al. 2009). If requested to collect botanical material for cryopreservation, then detailed instruction would need to be provided prior to making the collection. However, as for collecting herbarium specimens, the collection of living plant material from natural commu-nities represents a potential threat to rare species as well as local populations of more common plants. In general, the collection of living material is not encour-aged unless there is an important reason to do so and the person making the collection is adequately proficient in both collecting living material and in main-taining this living material after collection. Note that sale or trade of living material is equally strongly controlled by many regulations. The following are critical points to remember when collecting plants (for further details see §11.6).

- Obtain collecting permits before collecting any material (see §11.6.1) and permission of the landowner before collecting on private land. Report illegal or unauthorized collecting that you encounter to the appropriate authorities.
- If you encounter a plant with which you are not familiar, assume it is rare and refrain from collecting until you have ascertained that it is not rare.
- Collect discriminatingly—even in large populations. Collect only the amount of material you will actually make use of. Care properly for any material you collect —do not let it go to waste.
- Avoid unnecessary damage to sites and their aesthetic values. Avoid frequent visits to the same sites.

If you must collect living plants from natural communities for scientific research, collect in a manner least likely to damage the wild population. Make sure that you understand why the material is required. Although pressed and dried herbarium voucher material can often be prepared with relatively little prior skill, always seek advice and instruction on how to best collect and store the living material.

In order of general preference, collect:

- Seeds, if abundant (see Gunn et al. 2004; Schmidt 2000). For information on how to collect seeds that represent the genetic variation of a species and hence are suitable for long-term storage, see Bridson and Forman (1998), Cochrane et al. (2009), Gunn et al. (2004), Offord and Meagher (2009).
- Cuttings or other plant parts: when plants can be collected and rapidly trans-ported to plant nursery, it is convenient to collect cutting material. Hardwood cuttings of temperate and some tropical shrubs is an inexpensive and simple method for collecting material for propagation. In general, choose shoots with a section of older wood, last season's growth, and a few centimetres long. Soft-wood cuttings are not as resilient (Bridson and Forman 1998). Both types of cuttings should be dispatched as soon as possible by air, wrapped in moist newspaper and enclosed within a padded envelope.

- Whole plants: this collecting technique is required for plants with recalcitrant seeds and/or herbaceous material that are not readily propagated from cuttings. Seedlings should be carefully packed, with moist shredded paper, preferably enclosed in an ethylene absorption plastic bag; a normal plastic bag can be used but should be opened every evening to allow the ethylene to escape, to reduce or avoid damage to the underground parts (roots, runners, or stolons). It is usually essential that cuttings are dispatched by air freight.
- Collect most material: leave behind some reproductive or regenerative parts such as fruits, roots, or rhizomes (Washington Native Plant Society 2007). This is the least satisfactory type of collecting and should be avoided whenever possible.

11.2.4 How much material to collect?

The herbaria and museums are part of an international network of scientists who share botanical specimens, knowledge, and information about the flora of the world. Since no single organization can hope to have scientists who are specialists on the identification and taxonomy of every botanical group, these organizations donate replicate material of their collections to other organizations so that particular experts can provide expert determinations. Therefore, it is important to always collect more than one sample of each collection so that enough material is available as donations. Three to five replicate collections (all with the same collection number) are usually sufficient unless requested otherwise. Of course, this may not be appropriate when collecting rare and vulnerable species.

11.2.5 Label your collections

Each collection and each separate part of a collection should be labelled with a tag (e.g. a jeweler's tag) on which your name and unique collection number is written (preferably in pencil, never in ink that is not waterproof or resistant to methylated spirits, 70 per cent ethanol, or other solutions that may be used to preserve botanical collections). A personal collection-numbering series is worth beginning, even if you do not intend to collect many organisms. A simple numbering series, starting at one (1), is preferable. Once you have started your own collection-numbering series, continue it for all future collections, in numerical order. Avoid the inclusion of the collection date or some other prefix or suffix: these tend to be confusing for others to refer to and frequent errors are made when referring to these collections. The different parts of single gathering (collection), as for collections of large plants, should all be referred to by your name and the same collection number.

11.3 FIELD NOTES AND OBSERVATIONS

The most important rule to following when deciding on what should be recorded at the time of collection is:

If the feature or information is not present on the specimen or is distorted after it has been pressed and dried, then it should be recorded by the collector.

Botanical features that change and so must be recorded include:

- Colours: these often change during the drying process.
- Shape and sizes of fleshy parts: these change dramatically when dried and pressed.
- Features of delicate flowers may become detached and/or lost, or get changed by the pressing and drying process—for example, the shape of complex irregular or zygomorphic flowers, such as orchids, legumes, and labiates, may become very distorted and so difficult to evaluate once dried. These problems can be at least partly overcome if one or two flowers are carefully opened along one side and flattened so that the inner features are displayed.

11.3.1 What to include in your field notes?

- Collector's name(s) and number: always remember to include the names of any local people who assist you with the collection of the specimen. However, remember that the numbering series belongs to the primary collector; the other people are regarded as secondary collectors.
- Date of collection: if you are aware that the flowers of the plant you are collecting do not last for the full day (e.g. some species of *Xyris* and some aquatics), then record the time of collection as well.
- Locality of collection: the descriptive and spatial coordinates of the locality from where the plant was collected. Include:
  - Country.
  - Province/State/Territory—as formally recognized within the country.
  - Districts/SubDistricts—if formally recognized.
  - Special geographic areas—such as Conservation Parks, National Parks and other special reserves.
  - Description of specific locality—e.g. '5km W of Nauti, on road to Aseki'; '300m S of "Resting Place 2" on walking trail to summit of Mt Wilhelm'. Avoid imprecise descriptions of the locality like, 'near Wanang River', 'between Wail and Goroke', 'N of Ciawi'. Remember that the descriptive locality information is often more useful than anything else for relocating the organism.

- Altitude (m) and how measured, plus degree of precision (also in metres).
- Depth (m) and how measured—for aquatic plants, plus degree of precision (metres).
- Latitude and longitude (or geographical coordinates—eastings and northings): these geocodes should describe the locality as accurately as possible so that the collection site and the plant can be re-visited if necessary. The method used to generate the spatial geocode should be provided (e.g. GPS, Map, Gazetteer), the level of uncertainty of the geocode (in metres), and most importantly, the datum used for generating these spatial geocodes (most commonly, the datum for a GPS should now be set to WGS84). If maps are used to generate the geocode, then the map type, scale, map name, and map number should be provided.
- Habitat—a description of the specific habitat, including vegetation structure and composition (e.g. forest type and two or three of the names of the dominant species), substrate—rock and soil type (including name of host plant for climbers, epiphytes, and parasites).
- Habit notes: a description of the appearance of the plant are important for identification; features that may be distorted in the pressing and drying process or are not represented by the specimen collected should be recorded. Comments on the status of the plant at the collection site should indicate whether or not the plant is thought to be naturally occurring or has been introduced, and whether or not the plant is cultivated.
- Vernacular names and plant uses: vernacular names used by the local people (including the name of the language group). The name of the informant as well as his/her language group should be recorded. An audio recording of the vernacular name is preferable, but is rarely done by botanical collectors. If the plant is used by the local people, then this should be recorded, noting which part of the plant and what its uses are.

11.3.2 How useful are photographs for identification?

Photographs never replace the need for good-quality herbarium collections. Photographs and drawings often assist the person identifying a specimen because the images can better represent features of habit, presentation of plant parts, shape, texture, and colour than is provided by the preserved specimen or the collector's notes. However, the specimen is required as an authoritative voucher of the species. Therefore, photographs and drawings should be regarded as secondary and complementary material to the botanical collection.

Photographs of whole plant or parts of the plant may be used to supplement the information included in the notes (a note in the field notebook 'photo taken' is

Collection Type
Wood
Pollinator
Spirit/Wet
Seed
Cutting
Cytological
Spore print
DNA
Photo

Field det.:..

Locality (and Country, State/Province, Region):

Latitude ° ' " N/S Longitude ° ' " E/W

Datum: .... Alt.: .... m Depth: .... m

Accuracy of Lat/Long ...... m

Frequency:

Habitat (incl. vegetation type, dominant species, substrate)

host (if collecting epiphytes/parasites/fungal diseases):

Habit (incl. bark/wood/leaf features):

Flowers (incl. reproductive features of ferns/non-vascular plants):

Fruits (incl. cones of conifers):

General notes:

Local names: ....

Informant (incl. language group): ....

Local uses: ....

Informant (incl. language group): ....

Collector: .... Collection No.: .... Date: ....

Other Collectors: ....

Figure 11.2. A sample page from a collecting field book showing the usual fields of information recorded when collecting botanical specimens. Other possible types of material associated with collection are listed in textbox.

then useful). If additional material (e.g. photographs, separate seeds, wood, and methylated spirit- or ethanol-preserved collection) is also gathered, it should also be numbered with the same collection number as all other parts of the collection.

11.4 Electronic data

Increasingly, computer systems are being used to store and manage biological data. Develop a data field-based system, such as an electronic database or spreadsheet, to record and store botanical collection data. Personal digital assistant (PDA) hand-held computers are also available for direct data entry. Make sure that you enter the information into the data fields (spreadsheet cells) in a consistent manner, according to the data definition of each field/cell. Always be careful with spelling. For information of data exchange standards refer to Conn (1996) and for more recent versions of this standard, refer to HISPID (2007–). Provide these data to the agency receiving your botanical collections. This avoid data processing errors caused by rekeying information, and will make these data part of a much larger national and/or international biodiversity data network.

11.5 Pressing and drying plants

Once the botanical material has been collected, labelled with the collector's name and collecting number, and the field notes have been completed, the next task is to flatten (press) and dry the material as soon as possible (with exceptions discussed above). The selected specimen is inserted into folded newspaper (Fig. 11.3) or into special drying paper with good absorbing properties. If it is not possible to press specimens in the field because of insufficient time or the inaccessibility of the collecting location, then the collections can be sealed within a plastic bag for a short period of time, usually less than one day, without their deteriorating noticeably. In dry conditions, the collections should be moistened with a small amount of water to minimize dehydration. Individual collections can also be rolled in moistened newspaper and sealed in plastic bags for a short time, mostly for less than twelve hours, and then pressed and dried. Botanical specimens should also be kept cool if they are not pressed and dried immediately. However, it should be noted that many plants, particularly some flowers, are not robust enough to survive any delay in pressing. Every effort must be made to ensure that the separate parts of each collection are kept together until they are pressed.

The reasons for pressing and drying botanical material are:

- to preserve the material for future study;
- to prevent wilting and minimize distortion;
- to not only flatten the material so that less space is required for storage, but to protect delicate features that are generally less likely to be damaged in pressed specimens.

Figure 11.3. Plant specimen inserted into folded newspaper or special drying paper with good absorbing properties. All specimens of the collections must be labelled with the collector's name and collection number.

Remember: the drying papers must be inspected and changed regularly, particularly during the first few days of pressing. This is very important in humid environments and for specimens that have a high moisture content.

11.5.1 The plant press

A plant press consists of two strong, rigid lattice frames, made either of wood or of metal that is slightly larger than a standard herbarium sheet (Fig. 11.4). The botanical specimens are enclosed in drying paper. Newspaper is usually used because it is inexpensive, normally plentiful, and has adequate absorptive properties. Place the specimen in one folded sheet of newspaper and then enclose this in another folded sheet of newspaper that covers the opening of the first (Fig. 11.4). In this way, the specimen is more or less held within the two sheets. Corrugated cardboard or metal sheets (Nichols and St John 1918; Stevens 1926) are often used as ventilators to allow airflow across and between the specimens to assist the drying process. The press is usually held together and tightened by two expandable straps or by small ropes (Fig. 11.4). Polyurethane foam is also useful to maintain more or less even pressure on bulky specimens (Chmielewski and Ringius 1986).

Attention should be given to the pressing process: once a specimen is pressed and dried, its overall shape cannot be readily altered without damaging the material. Therefore, position specimens in such a manner so that the different features are clearly visible. Leaves should show both surfaces, so make sure that some leaves have their upper (adaxial) surface showing while the lower (abaxial) surface of other leaves face the opposite way. Likewise, turn some flowers so that both sides are visible when pressed. Spread the lobes of leaves, flowering and fruiting structures, and flower parts so as to show the shape and arrangement of these features more clearly. Arrange each specimen within the press so as to minimize any damage to other collections. Reduce the bulk of specimens with large fruits, thick stems, or underground parts by splitting or cutting away sections. The number of leaves, flowers, and fruits can be reduced if they obscure important features—but always leave sufficient material to make it clear that something has been removed.

A lightweight, temporary alternative to a field press is an A4-size notebook. A more robust temporary press can also be made from interwoven strips of bamboo.

Remember: after twelve to twenty-four hours the specimens in the press should be examined and rearranged if necessary to improve the presentation of the botanical material.

11.5.2 Drying botanical specimens

In dry climates, drying the specimens is usually relatively easy. Artificial heat is usually not required. However, there must be sufficient airflow between the specimens in the press to ensure that the samples dry quickly, otherwise the specimens may become mouldy. Therefore, even in dry environments, the collections should be checked daily and any damp sheets/newspaper should be replaced by dry sheets (Victor et al. 2004). This method is not suitable in the wet humid tropics, where the drying of collections and keeping them dry can be very challenging. Several useful publications suggest excellent solutions to drying specimens in the wet tropics (e.g. Beard 1968; De Wit 1980; Fuller and Barbe 1981). In all instances, the best policy is to

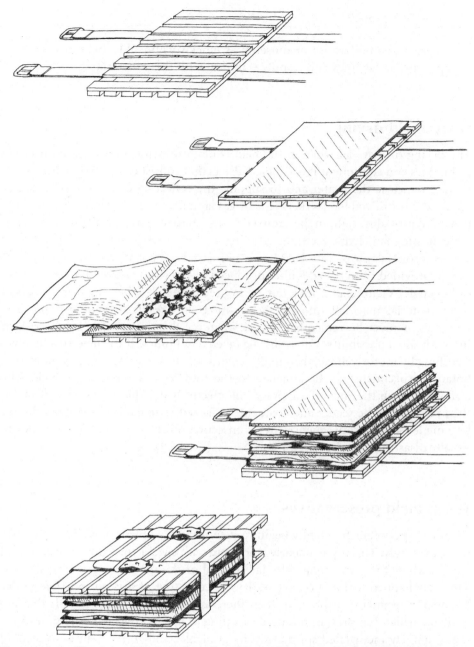

Figure 11.4. Plant specimens being placed in a plant press for drying and pressing. The correct pressing of specimens is very important. The shorter the time between collecting of a specimen and pressing, the better the resulting herbarium specimen. Note: place a cardboard sheet next to the frame of the plant press. Cardboard between the drying sheets surrounding each collection, or between separate specimens of a collection, gives the best results.

get material to a herbarium or museum as quickly as possible, because they have the appropriate facilities and resources to deal with these materials.

11.5.3 Field drying

The drying of material while in the field is often difficult unless the appropriate techniques and equipment is used. Field driers that consist of a source of heat and a frame to enclose the heater and to support the collecting press of specimens are required. Pressurized lamps (kerosene or gas lamps) are very effective and have the benefit of providing light in the camp (Fig. 11.5). If electricity is available, then a hot plate, heating fan (Jenne 1968), or set of light globes makes an effective plant drier (Gates 1950; Hale 1976; Van der Merwe and Grobler 1969; Womersley 1969). Heat can be provided from naked flames produced by gas rings (Halle 1961; Croat 1979) or hot coals (Victor et al. 2004), but are not recommended, because dried pieces of plant material may fall into the heat source and result in a devastating fire. However, it must be remembered that whatever the source of heat, the risk of fire is always a possibility. Care must be taken at all times. If the field trip involves travelling by motor vehicle, then in dry environments, plant presses containing the botanical specimens can be attached to the roof-rack of a moving vehicle. The airflow through the ends of the press will effectively dry the specimens. However, the presses must be secure and frequently checked to make sure that they do not become loose. The consequences of an unsecured press on a travelling vehicle are usually disastrous for the specimens!

11.5.4 Field preservatives

Botanical specimens frequently begin to deteriorate in a plant press if they are not dried promptly. This is particularly a problem with specimens from the wet humid tropics where the leaves frequently fall off and/or the specimens become mouldy. This may happen within a couple of days of collecting. If it is not possible to dry botanical specimens in the field, then there are two preservative liquids that are available which can prevent mould developing in freshly collected botanical specimens, namely methylated spirits (readily available) and 70 per cent ethyl alcohol (with restricted availability). Previously a solution of formaldehyde (known as formalin) was also used, but the previous two liquids are safer to use.

The botanical collections are pressed for up to twelve hours. After this, the specimens are removed from the press, with any damp enclosing newspapers replaced with dry sheets of newspaper. The collections are inserted into a polythene bag or tube (Fig. 11.6). When all the specimens are in the bag or tube (with one end of tube enclosed and sealed with alcohol-resistant tape), add about three average-

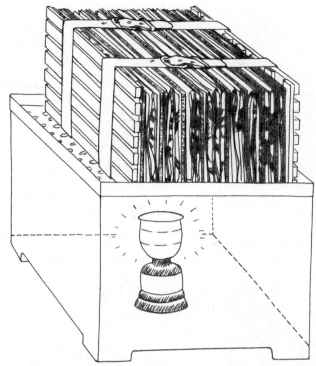

Figure 11.5. A simple plant drier using a pressurized lamp, with plant pressed firmly strapped and placed on one side to allow maximum airflow between the specimens. If the sides of the box/stand enclosing the lamp are of clear plastic, then light is available for other camp activities.

sized cups of methylated spirit or ethyl alcohol solution (Fig. 11.6). Spread the preservative evenly across the open end of specimens, ensuring that sufficient liquid has soaked throughout the material. Since the preservation is effected by the vapor of methylated spirit or ethyl alcohol, it is not necessary that any free liquid be present. Close the open end of tube/bag thoroughly and tie the bundle with a simple crossed string (Figure 11.6) (Womersley 1969).

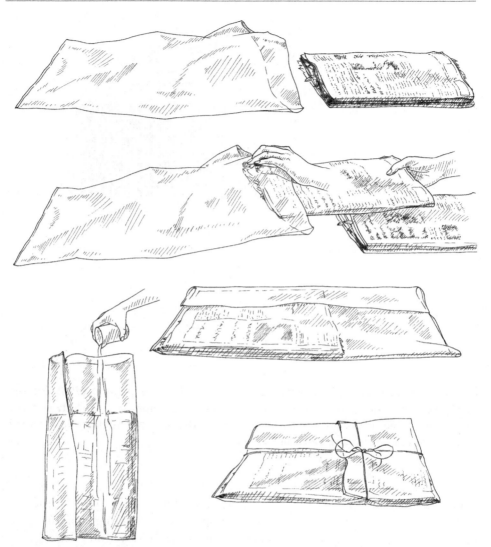

Figure 11.6. Partially pressed specimens can be preserved for later drying by sealing specimens and drying papers in a plastic bag after saturating the papers with methylated spirit or ethyl alcohol. These sealed bags of specimens can usually be kept for two or three months without deterioration. However, the specimens should be sent to a herbarium as soon as possible so that the drying process can be completed.

11.6 WHAT YOU NEED FOR PLANT COLLECTING: PRE-FIELDWORK PLANNING

Botanical collecting in foreign countries, especially in remote areas, requires considerable pre-fieldwork planning to ensure that all the necessary collecting permits and other legal documents have been obtained, appropriate equipment is available, all the personnel have been fully briefed on the social and civil status of the area being visited, and the physical and health risks have been thoroughly assessed. Although some aspects of this planning may not be as necessary when undertaking field studies within the collector's own country, the following points should be considered carefully prior to undertaking any field studies. Cochrane et al. (2009) provide a 'collection checklist' that summarizes important issues to be considered when undertaking botanical collecting.

11.6.1 Plant collecting permit

Most countries are signatories to the International Convention on Biological Diversity (CBD 1993–). Therefore, it is advisable to be fully aware of the laws applicable to the area from which you wish to collect and to obtain the necessary approval and permits. You can usually obtain collecting permits from government departments that are responsible for environment management within the area to be visited. Contact the nearest major herbarium or museum (see Thiers 1997– for contact information) and seek their advice prior to making the collection. Remember, in many countries, separate permits are required for different States or Provinces as well as separate permits for different types of management areas (e.g. conservation parks, national parks, and nature reserves). Finally, remember to obtain permission from local landowners or custodians so that you can undertake field studies on their land.

11.6.1.1 Special permits

Phytosanitary permits will probably be needed when transporting plants across borders of different countries. These permits must be obtained from the country of origin.

The Convention on International Trade in Endangered Species (CITES) legislation regulates and controls the international trade in material obtained from plants considered to be endangered. Remember: scientific material is not exempt from CITES regulations. Therefore, CITES-listed plants require a *CITES export permit* from the country of origin as well as a *CITES import permit* from the authority (herbarium or museum) receiving the material. Since not all botanical authorities are registered as an agency approved to receive CITES material, it is important to verify that your collections are being sent to a herbarium or museum that is legally allowed to receive these specimens.

11.6.2 Pre-planning meeting: field hazard assessment

Possibly the most important aspect of field studies is the recognition, by all members of the field team, of the possible hazards that they are likely to encounter in the field. Careful planning and preparation can avoid many of the potential difficulties of working in remote areas. It is recommended that a 'Field Hazard Assessment' document be completed prior to any fieldwork. A copy of the completed document must be held by the principal organization involved with the work. This document should form the basis of a post-fieldwork evaluation of all aspects of the field study.

The topics and issues that should be covered by this document should include the names of participants, including Team Leader; description of project and area to be visited; dates when field team expected to be at specified localities; and insurance arrangements, especially for non-staff.

11.6.3 Emergency aids and contact schedule

Mobile/cell telephone numbers of all team members must be listed and held by all members of the team. However, since the work is in remote areas, a review of any expected areas of non-coverage is essential. If satellite telephones are to be used (and this is strongly recommended for remote areas), all members of the team need to be trained in their use. Likewise, if a two-way radio is to be used, then all members must be familiar with its operation.

Each member of the team must carry matches (in a water-proof container) or a fire lighting flint, a watch (for estimating time) and/or compass for estimating direction, a small reliable light (head-lamps are usually more convenient), survival blanket (especially recommended in alpine zones or high latitudes), and a whistle (for attracting attention).

11.6.3.1 *Personal Locating Beacons (PLB) and Emergency Position-Indicating Radio Beacons (EPIRBS)*

Emergency or radio beacons are tracking transmitters which aid in the detection and location of boats, aircraft, and people in distress. The basic purpose of the distress emergency beacon is to get people rescued within the first twenty-four hours following a traumatic event, when the majority of survivors can still be saved. Every botanical collecting trip, especially to remote areas, should carry an emergency beacon.

11.6.3.2 Contact arrangements

It is essential that a regular and frequent contact schedule is developed so that emergency rescue authorities can be informed of potential problems if the team fails to make contact at a designated time. The most important safety action is to ensure that people know where you are planning to be and where you actually are so that they can monitor the progress of the fieldwork. Therefore, make sure that there is a reliable contact person that the field team can contact regularly. The primary organization requires agreed emergency procedures and protocols that will be activated when there has been no contact with the field team after a set amount of time.

11.6.3.3 Global positioning systems and maps

A Global Positioning System (GPS) is an instrument that provides spatial coordinates and should be used in conjunction with good maps. A GPS is an excellent way of obtaining accurate coordinates for a locality, but they should not be viewed as a replacement for detailed maps. Always select the best map, at the best scale, for the area that you are visiting. In the event of an emergency, an accurate geocode reference of the team's locality will help rescue agencies to provide rapid assistance.

11.6.3.4 Vehicles to be used, vehicle recovery, and safety equipment

For motor vehicles it is important to list personnel with recovery training or substantive experience; assess physical strain risks for potential recovery tasks; list recovery equipment items being taken, such as gloves, snatch strap, tree strap, chain, shackles, spare tyres.

Other considerations include:

- Boat: record boat registration and ownership; review boat operator licences, radio skills, radio schedules, motor service status, navigational skills and equipment, safety gear, general equipment status—including mandatory certifications.
- Dive equipment and skill (review Divemaster and SCUBA certifications, equipment status—including mandatory certifications, and dive schedules with regard to personnel experience and capabilities.
- On foot: although most of the fieldwork requires considerable amount of time and often involves a considerable distance to be walked, frequently whilst carrying heavy equipment and supplies, there is a tendency not to consider the

risks and hazards associated with this aspect of the work. Review on-track and off-track work expected, with regard to personnel experience, capabilities, and navigational skills/equipment, tree- and rock-fall hazards, and likelihood of danger from animals and poisonous plants).

When working in developing countries and remote communities, the available vehicles (including boats) may not be of a standard that will provide the maximum safety. However, it is still important to ensure that the vehicle, the driver, and the recovery equipment are as good as possible. It is also an excellent opportunity to increase the awareness of general safety issues for within-country agencies if that is required. Well-maintained vehicles are more reliable. It is important to minimize the chances of serious breakdowns, especially in remote areas, as these can seriously impact on the safety of all participants.

11.6.3.5 *First aid training and kits*

Since botanical specimens are often gathered from relatively remote areas, it is important that all members of the field team have training in basic first aid techniques, and that each member always carry a first aid kit that they are familiar with. Knowledge of cardiopulmonary resuscitation and other basic remote area first aid is important. Contact an organization that presents first aid courses in your area for training and more information.

Although you may visit a remote area alone, it is never safe to do so. The field team should consist of a minimum of three people. The skills and limitations of each person should be known to all members of the team to ensure that the fieldwork can be done efficiently and safely.

11.6.3.6 *Medical conditions and personal capabilities*

Within the limits of privacy and with due regard for confidentiality, the field leader must be aware of any medical conditions or physical limitation of all members of the team that may affect the safety of fieldwork. The leader is responsible for providing advice to personnel should a member require medication during field-work. All team members must ensure that they have all of their required personal medications.

It is the leader's responsibility to make adjustments to schedules and tasks to ensure minimal stress on all personnel. Furthermore, the leader should consider the interpersonal dynamics of the team under field conditions and monitor the level of activities and rest periods accordingly.

Medical advice should be sought prior to obtaining antiseptic solutions and med-icines for pain management, antihistamines, anti-emetic medicine for nausea, anti-spasmodic medicine for diarrhoea, and treatment for other medical conditions.

11.6.3.7 *Climatic hazards*

An assessment of the climatic conditions of the area being visited is important. The precautions for dealing with excessive heat, humidity, aridity, cold, and/or wet weather should include having water, protective clothing, sunscreen, amongst other aids. Drinking-quality water should be available, together with water-purifying tablets when relying on local water supplies of unsatisfactory quality.

11.6.4 Working with local communities

The above points have been provided to assist researchers to work in a safe environment, according to the various regulations. However, it is equally important to ensure a respectful, equitable, and mutually beneficial relationship with local community where the field studies are being undertaken. The following suggestions are offered:

1. Plan on a medium- to long-term relationship—although one-off visits are often all that is possible, longer-term collaborations are usually more beneficial to both the researcher and the community.
2. Learn the language—being fluent in a language that allows for communication between yourself and the community is extremely beneficial to essential. Plan ahead—start learning the language at least six months in advance.
3. Obtain at least one extra bilingual dictionary to share with your field research associates if the local language is not fluently spoken by team members.
4. Introduce yourself and your team—it is important to take the time to introduce yourself and your associate researchers to the community so that everyone has some understanding of who is involved with the research program. A introductory photographic album that includes topics of interest, such as photographs of your family, friends, home, garden, and workplace, can be useful.
5. Have copies of your research proposal in the local language—as well as organizing meetings with the local people to explain what you are intending to do while in their area, written proposals allow for people to consider your proposal further after the meeting.
6. Develop a bilingual cooperative agreement/Memorandum of Understanding between yourself and your national counterparts. As part of this process, explain the project at a meeting with local community members. Ensure that women are also informed, either at these meeting or at separate ones, if that is culturally preferable.
7. Purchase additional sets of national and/or local maps to share with the community.
8. Donations and gifts—discuss with the community their needs to ascertain whether or not you can assist. It may be possible to assist a community obtain

funding for a community-based activity. Present any donations in an informal ceremony to institutional representatives, along with an inventoried list of the donations which is signed by the recipients. Do not present donations to individuals. In developing communities, donations of medical supplies for local health clinics or educational supplies for local schools may be welcomed. However, be cautious about providing medical supplies that require greater skills to use than is available within the community.

9. Recruit local community members as field assistants—without discrimination on basis of gender, age, marital status, religion, profession, level of formal education, political affiliation, or sexual orientation.

10. Take photos of community members and distribute them as soon as possible.

11. Translate research results into the local language—make photocopies and distribute widely within the community, inviting comment, and deposit a set of the data with the community.

12. Joint publication with local field assistants: the individuals who provide field assistance and knowledge are rarely included as co-authors of scientific publications. It is always important to consider the significance of their contribution, and to determine if they should be joint authors—or at least fully acknowledged within publications.

CHAPTER 12

....

ETHNOBIOLOGY

BASIC METHODS FOR DOCUMENTING BIOLOGICAL KNOWLEDGE REPRESENTED IN LANGUAGES

....

WILL McCLATCHEY

12.1 INTRODUCTION[1]

....

Ethnobiology methods are undergoing a certain degree of standardization following Martin's (2004) very influential ethnobotany methods book outlining many of the basic field techniques. Translation into Chinese, Spanish, Bahasa Malaysia, and French is evidence of acceptance of this book and its role as a basic tool for learning fundamental techniques. Among its many useful chapters is one on linguistic methods. The descriptions provided in this chapter are intended to build on Martin's procedures, but add recent trends that reflect recent important changes in ethnobiological research. I begin with a discussion of some of the sorts of research ethnobiologists are doing around the globe (which

[1] Thanks to Bruce Hoffman for help with literature sourcing and Kim Bridges, Piet Lincoln, David Reedy, Nat Bletter, Al Chock, and Valerie McClatchey for reading drafts. Thank you to three anonymous reviewers for providing many detailed and helpful comments.

takes place everywhere from modern cities to remote rural forests). This is followed by discussion of some key aspects of the discipline, in order to set the stage for the presentation of five basic field methods that may be applied to collect integrated ethnobiological and linguistic data. The primary purposes of this chapter are to provide encouragement to field linguists considering working with biological materials, and to promote collaboration among scholars, particularly linguists and ethnobiologists.

Ethnobiology is the scientific study of dynamic relationships among peoples, biota, and environments (Salick et al. 2003). This discipline has departed from being descriptive and now attempts to use the full spectrum of scientific methodologies and tools to understand and explain cultural differences and similarities in the knowledge and use of biota and environments (Balée 1994). This methodological shift has taken the discipline well beyond its original inventorying activities (Fox 1953; Diamond 1966; Conklin 1967; Bulmer and Tyler 1968) into an era of the analysis of processes. For example, recent studies have focused on:

- acquisition, distribution, and control of biological knowledge (Berkes and Folke 2001; Zent 2001; 2005; Torre-cuadros and Ross 2003; Zent and López-Zent 2004);
- ongoing management of wild and domesticated natural resources (Posey and Balée 1989; Berkes 1999; Cunningham 2001; Anderson 2005; Ticktin et al. 2006);
- management and conservation of landscapes and biocultural diversity (Sillitoe 1998; Saemane 1999; Maffi 2005; Stepp et al. 2004; Shepard et al. 2004; Lampman 2007; Hoffman 2009); and
- indigenous responses to global climate change (Bridges and McClatchey 2009; Salick et al. 2007; Turner 2009).

In addition, much attention has been paid to intellectual property rights of traditional knowledge holders, and researcher ethics and responsibilities (see Laird 2002). Ethnobiologists are examining topics that cut across the biological and social science disciplines. These have been summarized as: 'knowledge systems [including cognitive research]; medicine, health, and nutrition; ecology, evolution, and systematics; landscapes and global trends; and biocomplexity' (Salick et al. 2003: [3]). Linguistics can benefit not only from recent developments in ethnobiological techniques, but also from the advances in scientific theory being generated in the above research. Obviously this has reciprocal importance: good linguistics research not only aids an ethnobiologist or local people, it may often be a critical contribution in developing scientific and cross-cultural understanding.

An area of past and future research cooperation between linguists and ethnobiologists is a focus on cognitive research. The next section outlines a general understanding of this area by ethnobiologists, and is presented here as a starting point for further discussion and research. This is followed by a section that focuses on basic methodological aspects of ethnobiological research, particularly as they relate to (and may be used by) linguistic researchers. Another view of this research area is seen in the analysis of thirty-four recently conducted ethnobiological studies by Reyes-García et al. (2007). They concluded that there is a 'lack of conceptual consistency and comparable data [that] limit the inferences that can be drawn from empirical analyses of ethnobotanical knowledge' (p. 182). They recommend: 'Future research should 1) validate the consistency of measures of individual ethnobotanical knowledge; 2) analyse the reliability of data generated by the different methods developed so far; and 3) address the relationship between the various dimensions of ethnobotanical knowledge' (p. 182) Their recommendations clearly point to our need to be better aware of methods used by other researchers, and to adopt these when possible in order to generate comparable data sets.

12.1.1 Cognitive research

One of the core areas of research within ethnobiology is the study of human cognition (alternative areas of emphasis include economic, social, legal, and nutritional aspects). While there are many interesting areas within this core, the study of folk or ethnobiological classifications is most germane to this chapter. Berlin (1992) has outlined the essential characteristics of ethnobiological classification systems that most ethnobiological researchers agree are universals. The heart of Berlin's classification consists of nine major 'principles' (Berlin, Breedlove, and Raven 1973) that are cross-cultural and for the most-part comparable (see Dwyer 2005 for an alternative perspective). These are:

1. Nomenclature: In all languages it is possible to isolate linguistically recognized groupings of organisms (taxa) of varying degrees of inclusiveness that have names.
   • Examples at different taxonomic levels are: *animal, bird, raptor, owl, barn owl.*
2. Taxa are further grouped into a small number of classes referred to as taxonomic ethnobiological categories similar in many respects to the taxonomic ranks of globalized science.
   • These categories number no more than six: *unique beginner, life form, intermediate, generic, specific,* and *varietal.*
3. The six ethnobiological categories are arranged hierarchically (as ranks) and taxa assigned to each rank are mutually exclusive.
   • Consider what example we might choose as the archetype for 'plants' or 'animals'? Although we can all identify these, there is not a 'unique' type that is *the* plant or *the* animal that is the 'unique beginner'.
4. Taxa of the same ethnobiological rank usually are at the same taxonomic level in any particular cultural (linguistic) taxonomy.
5. In any system of ethnobotanical or ethnozoological classification, the taxon that occurs as a member of the rank 'unique beginner' (*plant* or *animal*) is not (normally) named with a single, habitual label. This means that people speaking

a particular language often recognize inclusive ranks such as *animals* and can sort a group of things into the that rank, but won't necessarily have a name for the grouping that they have made.

6. There are usually but a handful of taxa that occur as members of the category 'life form', ranging from five to ten, and they include the majority of all named taxa of lesser rank.
   - These life-form taxa are named by linguistic expressions that are lexically analysed as primary lexemes, e.g. *bush, liana, palm, reptile, fern,* and *bird.*

7. The number of generic taxa ranges around 500 in typical folk taxonomies, and most are usually included in one of the life-form taxa.
   - A number of generic taxa may be aberrant, however, and are conceptually seen as unaffiliated (i.e. are not included in any of the life forms). Aberrance may be due to morphological uniqueness and/or economic importance. Examples vary widely between cultures: baobab trees and camels are morphologically unique for many cultures in tropical Africa, while grasses/grain and cattle raised for food are economically important in many Eurasian cultures. Each of these may be generic taxa that are unaffiliated with other generic taxa because of their outstanding or unusual roles in society.
   - Generic taxa are the basic building blocks of any folk taxonomy, are the most salient psychologically, and are likely to be among the first taxa learned by the child, e.g. *dog, taro, oak, banana, ant, clay.*

8. Specific and varietal taxa are less numerous than generic taxa, and occur in small contrast sets typically of two to three members. Varietal taxa are rare in most folk biological taxonomies.
   - Both specific and varietal forms are distinguished from one another in terms of a few, often verbalized characters.
   - Taxa of the specific and varietal rank are commonly labelled by secondary (vs. primary) lexemes, e.g. *three-needle pine, Mexican evening primrose, blue heron.*

9. Intermediate taxa occur as implied members of the category 'intermediate' and usually include taxa of generic rank that have residual characteristics. Residual characteristics are unusual features that distinguish either a monotypic taxon (a weird/unusual sort of thing) or a group that is placed together because of a single (unusual) characteristic. These are not often named but are implied in cultural conversations. However, some can be mentioned.
   - Examples that are named: *spiders, root crops,* and *pigeons.*

The nine principles above are slightly enhanced from the Berlin et al. (1973) outline. For more clarity, see the longer explanation in Martin (2004).

Ralph Bulmer (1974) independently verified and proposed very similar concepts, although Berlin's (1992) theoretical structure is cited by most ethnobiologists. Holman (2005) has verified the generalized, cross-cultural ethnobiological hierarchical folk classification systems for plants and animals showing evidence that they are different from other domains. Holman (2005: 71) states that 'cross-cultural regularities suggest that taxonomic judgements are not entirely determined by culture'.

There is a key assumption implicit in the above that we will accept for the purposes of the balance of this chapter: that cultures are similar enough to be comparable, and that naming and classification systems have not primarily emerged as individual or culture-specific practices but are rather part of generalized human traits. Furthermore, from a biological perspective, we will accept the assumption that taxonomic diversity in the world is discontinuous in its spectrum of characteristic distributions, and that humans are able to recognize discontinuities (see also Turk et al., Chapter 16 below). The result is that humans group like things together in categories as described above using the discontinuities as indicators of domain circumscription. If these assumptions are correct (and some argue that they are not: see Ellen 1996; 2003a; 2003b; 2006; 2007), then comparisons may be made by information learned between individuals and/or groups of people at differing scales (e.g. families, communities, 'cultures', 'languages'). Further, the results then inform us about variations in the human condition and human responses to differing cultural, psychological, physical, and biological environments.

Note that this type of research emphasizes comparisons. Although it is possible to use a non-comparativist approach to research, even non-comparativists must be aware that the results of their work, once published, will be used by comparativists. The danger is that if the research is not framed within a standardized structure, the research will be forced into one, and likely misrepresented. With that in mind, it is probably best to conduct research assuming that the data will be used for comparisons even if that is not the immediate intention.

Modern research in the sister biological discipline of systematics (the study of diversification and relationships of life on earth) provides a clear lesson that relates to the long-term value of these sorts of studies. Systematists are returning to stored biological specimens in herbaria and museums to verify species identities with genetic, anatomical, chemical, and other physical analyses. Studies which generate lists of names/terms must be supported by the deposition of appropriate physical evidence in a secure storage facility. This physical evidence is now a requirement of publication within ethnobiological journals (e.g. Verpoorte 2009). Therefore, modern ethnobiological research increasingly relies upon an evidence-based system that blends quantitative and qualitative data collection (Cook and Prendergast 1995; Alexiades 1996) and analysis in the testing of one or more hypotheses about dynamic relationships between peoples, biota, and environments.

12.1.2 Evidence-based research

Ethnobiological studies, including research on languages, requires evidence. This evidence may be primary/physical, secondary/documentary, or tertiary/observational. While all three of these are important, the first is the most critical. Unfortunately, primary/physical evidence is most often neglected by non-biologists who are doing ethnobiologically-related, ethnographic research.

Primary or physical evidence of language is a sample of the things that people are talking about such as specific birds, plants, insects, rocks, soil, water, or diseases (when samples are collected). These samples are typically stored as catalogued, labelled vouchers in a museum, archive, or other repository designed to maintain them for long periods of time. These facilities also provide appropriate access to scholars and the public so that research results may be verified by others once work has been published.

It is completely understandable that many scholars feel overwhelmed when faced with the need to collect physical samples of evidence from a wide spectrum of things. However, without such evidence, the results of the research are merely hearsay (Bye 1986). Modern science requires verifiability, and this means that other researchers must have a way to check the results by examination of the samples returned from the field site (see Conn, Chapter 11 above, on the collection of samples). In addition, the Biodiversity Assessment of Tropical Island Ecosystems manual (Mueller-Dombois, Bridges, and Daehler 2008) is available in print or for free on-line and includes detailed instructions for non-biologists on how and why to collect a wide range of biological samples. An excellent resource for collection of plants is Womersley (1976), which was specifically prepared for anthropologists and geographers.

Secondary or documentary evidence of language includes photographs and video and audio recordings. These are critical tools for modern ethnobiological researchers, but in most cases they are insufficient for the positive scientific or cultural identification of the items that people are talking about. This is because they cannot record the genetic or other biochemical, morphological, anatomical, viscosity, or the many other physical characteristics that cultural and scientific experts need to assess in order to identify and distinguish samples. However, documentary evidence supplements primary evidence, as it often provides important information about a sample that is lost because of changes that occur due to sampling, decay, or removal from the natural environment.

Tertiary data or observations about a sample are important for establishing the context in which the sample normally resides. The best observations include a combination of etic[2] and emic perspectives and multiple scales from the most immediate/local to the landscape in which the sample resides. For example, a

---

[2] See the introduction to Dousset, Ch. 9 above, for a definition of 'etic' and 'emic'.

collected lizard sample would include observations that note where the lizard was found, such as on a particular named sort of rock outcropping (also sampled), that the collector (scientist or local expert) has said that local experts report that this type of lizard is known to frequent particular forest patches (indicator species sampled), that this type of forest patch is found across a named vegetation zone (indicator species sampled), and that the name of the lizard carries a meaning associated with its use as a food to be consumed in a particular place and time (timing determined within local reckoning). Important types of observational data that have long been recorded by biologists and ethnobiologists that need the help of linguists are the vernacular names and their associations (including metaphorical allusions) and other cultural data recorded on specimen labels associated with primary evidence. Far too many scientists rely too much on the primary evidence to speak for itself, and miss the opportunity to provide critical observations, particularly from emic perspectives.

12.1.3 Comparative ethnobiology

While ethnobiologists consider it desirable to produce data sets that can eventually be comparable in multi-site analyses (Reyes-García et al. 2005), some researchers have conducted comparisons within their data collection and analysis efforts. For example, Nguyen (2006) studied food plant assemblages used by Vietnamese in Vietnam and Hawaii, analysing patterns of evolutionary change in plant constituents as people migrated to new environments. Furthermore, she discussed interconnected roles of botanical and linguistic evidence in understanding human interactions with complex environments (e.g. natural and artificial ecosystems, and other multi-species interactive systems).

12.1.4 Ethnobiology ethics and legal issues

The collection of ethnobiological data, whether it is primary, secondary, or tertiary, has increasingly become the focus of ethical and legal discussions (Laird 2002; see also Rice and Newman, Chapters 18 and 19 below). The most extreme concerns have been fear of bio-piracy, commercialization of traditional knowledge, or the misuse/mismanagement of information that is shared with researchers. Ethical and legal matters are tightly intertwined.

The International Society of Ethnobiology Code of Ethics (2006) is used as a minimal 'framework for decision-making and conduct of ethnobiological research and related activities. The goals are to facilitate ethical conduct and equitable relationships, and foster a commitment to meaningful collaboration and reciprocal responsibility by all parties.' Anyone planning to engage in ethnobiological research should first take the time to read and understand this document (it is published in a number of languages). Among the many concepts of the code of ethics is that of working with people in communities rather than treating them as the subjects of research. Therefore, ethnobiologists, like many linguists, often work and publish with community participants in collaborations, and do not think of or refer to anyone as informants.

12.2 DATA COLLECTION

Ethnobiological research design (Alexiades 1996; Höft, Barik, and Lykke 1999; Martin 2004) typically follows a hypothesis-driven scientific method of evaluation. Five common methods (see below) used by ethnobiologists for the documentation of traditional biological knowledge are likely to be of use in basic linguistic field research settings. These are used to obtain information that is associated with physical evidence. A critical aspect of these methods is that none of them requires that the researcher have more than passing knowledge about the organisms being examined (i.e. they need not be a biologist, although there is a caveat in the final paragraph of this chapter). In each case the actual organisms are the focal point and also serve as the evidence at the conclusion of the study. Local participants and their specifically local perspectives and knowledge are critical to understanding these organisms. These methods are commonly conducted as ethnographic inter-view surveys either within the environment (*in situ*) using biological materials or using fresh, or preserved biological materials away from the environment (*ex situ*) (Thomas et al. 2007).

12.2.1 Free-listing

A common initial approach when working with a participant is to inquire about a category of information (e.g. animals: Nolan et al. 2006; desert plants: Khasbagan and Soyolt 2008; edible mushrooms: Garibay-Orijel et al. 2007; one tree genus: McClatchey et al. 2006; wild foods: Ali-Shtayeh et al. 2008). The result is a list of details, usually names and descriptions. Free-listing may be embedded within a survey that is highly structured (Brosi et al. 2007). Although this may appear to be simple, there are many possible errors to be made in asking poorly considered questions (see Alexiades 1996; McClatchey et al. 2008) that can easily produce useless or misleading results. While it may be desirable when building a dictionary, vocabulary list, etc. to learn 'everything', people seem to sort information into categories, and it is easier to learn from them by beginning with a question such as 'Can we talk about the sorts of birds that you know?' rather than 'Can we discuss everything you know?'

a. Decide upon a set of initial categorical 'free-list' questions, keeping them as simple as possible. These should be broad and simple but not leading questions. (Leading questions provide information that might be desired in possible answers.) The questions should be specific for the desired information and not waste the participant's time with other issues. Appropriate examples are: 'Please list the names of any fish that you catch in lakes but not in streams.' 'Please name as many kinds of fruit (you eat/people eat/animals eat) as you can think of.' 'When you were a child and went to the zoo, what sorts of animals did you see there?' 'What kinds of ingredients does your family use in treatments for coughs and colds?'

b. Each participant (or group of participants) is asked to list his or her answers to one question and their responses are recorded. For some kinds of research the order of the responses is important since what is recalled earlier may be of more importance than what is remembered later. If multiple questions are being asked, it is important that each participant or group be asked the same questions in the same order without other information being provided that would make comparison between participants difficult (in contrast to a free-flow text method, where participants can lead the discussion).

c. After a participant (or group) has finished with the questions, the researcher needs to ask the participant to help to locate and collect evidential examples of each of the responses that were provided. (Note that there is a natural tendency to skip this step if terms have already been identified in the past and recorded in a word list or dictionary. However, it is exceedingly rare that these are supported by physical evidence, it is not unusual for these to be scientifically incorrect, and it is fairly common for names of organisms to refer to more than one scientific taxon and the researcher needs to know which one this participant is talking about. Therefore, collection of physical samples is required to overcome assumptions.)

Since this process is time-consuming, it may require one or more additional interview sessions and take much longer than the free-listing exercise itself. An alternative approach is to complete a set of free-listing exercises with different individuals or groups, compile the composite results, and then, working with a few of the participants, collect the evidence samples. Although this would seem to be more time-efficient, it will still be necessary to take these samples to each of the participants for them to verify their answers; and since some time will have passed, and they were not involved in the collection of the samples, they may not be able to confirm or deny if the samples are representatives of their responses. This presumes that there is little synonymy or taxonomic overlap between individuals/groups, which is the most conservative option. It provides independent confirmation of terms when they are the same across the responses of the sample group, as well as evidence of differences when there is a spectrum of differences within a community of knowledge holders. The choice of using either individual or composite collections largely depends on the ease with which participants are likely to be able to identify the samples that are collected.

12.2.2 Inventory interview

A physical collection of one or more categories of organisms/environmental samples—for instance bees (Mendes dos Santos and Antonini 2008), birds (Boster 1987), crustaceans (Ferreira et al. 2009), fish (Johannes 1981), fungi (Lampman 2007), algae (Ostraff 2006), trees (Jernigan (2006)—is first compiled from a location where the researcher is working. This is then numbered and used as a standardized set of visual (and sometimes olfactory etc.) stimuli for eliciting responses from multiple individuals or groups of participants. Photographs are sometimes used (see Diamond 1991; Nguyen 2003), but there are so many drawbacks that their use is strongly discouraged, particularly because voucher specimens of actual materials will need to be collected as evidence eventually. Cases where photos are actually justified are when organisms are rare, endangered, extinct, or locally unavailable. Photos should not be used as a means to avoid work.

a. A participant (or group of participants) is shown specimens in a specific sequence and asked a set of questions about each one. The questions could be similar to those used in a free list but are often more specific to the details of the specimen being shown. For example, while being shown a specific soil sample (#1) a participant could be asked, 'Does this look familiar? If so, does it have a name? If so, where is this particular substance usually seen? Is it considered useful? If so, what would those uses happen to be?' After recording the responses to the questions, the participant would be shown the next sample (#2) and asked the same questions. Phillips and Gentry (1993a; 1993b) recommend that the minimum data required for inventory interviews are: 'Do you know this . . . ?', 'Do you know a name for this . . . (and if so, what is it?)', and 'Do you use this . . . (and if so, how do you use it)?'

b. The process is repeated with multiple participants (or groups) to produce comparable data sets.

c. With each repetition, additional activities may be conducted using the specimens. For example, specimens may be used in pile sorting exercises to identify Berlin's (1992) hierarchical classifications (Lampman 2007; Mekbib 2007) and, in group or individual follow-up discussions, to determine cryptic classifications (Souza and Begossi 2007). Sorting systems often represent ways in which information is perceived about the world. One way to see more clearly how this

information is perceived is to go beyond the classification by mapping indigenous world views (Davidson-Hunt et al. 2005).

12.2.3 Environmental transect

This has sometimes been called a 'walk in the woods' (Phillips and Gentry 1993a). It
can be a formal survey of a specific area involving repeated examination of a specific
set of organisms in their natural habitat by a group of participants in order to learn
their responses to specific questions (e.g. What are these things called?, Do they have
uses, and if so, what?, Are there things that are usually seen here that are not here
now?, What is this environment called?) There are two variations on this—formal
and informal; often these variations are combined. A formal transect is a specific
pathway that is set out (see below) along which repeated participants may be taken
to collect different perspectives on the same set of environmental stimuli. Informally, a participant may, for example, lead a researcher on a hike through the forest, a
walk through their garden, market, or grocery store, or snorkeling through a reef
pointing out specific biological resources and their names and uses. For informal
transects to be systematically useful and reproducible they may need to be circum-
scribed as area inventories (see §12.4 below).

a. Working with one or more community participants, select a location that meets
   the needs of the project. A suitable site should have the ecological or taxonomic
   diversity that is needed to ask the questions that are planned, or it could be a
   trail/path through a location that needs to be better understood. For example, in
   order to learn about mangrove swamp organisms a boardwalk built for tourists
   might be selected because it allows easy, regular access for elderly participants to
   be able to follow along the same path and see the same locations along the way.
   As another example, a nylon rope could be tied between two poles fixed at
   points in a reef and the reef along the rope used as the transect that is to be
   followed and discussed.
b. Questions are formulated about organisms, ecosystems, contexts, and other
   features that are encountered along the transect. Questions are associated with
   specific points along the transect, although sometimes general questions about
   frequently encountered taxa may be asked at any point along the path.
c. Individual (or groups of) participants are led from a starting point on the
   transect to the finish point and asked questions at a set of points along the way.
   This process is repeated with each participant, recording his or her responses.
d. Samples of the taxa being discussed need to be collected, usually after the last
   interview, since the objective is to collect the sample of the same individual that
   was being observed throughout the process. However, for taxa that are large,
   such as trees, or numerous, such as some insects, it is possible to collect samples
   in advance.

12.2.4 Area inventory

One or more discrete areas—home gardens (Vogl-Lukasser and Vogl 2004), or markets (Nguyen, Wieting, and Doherty 2008), political regions (Pardo-de-Santayana et al. 2007)—or samples of an area—forests (Castaneda and Stepp 2007), or mangrove swamps (Steele 2006)—are inventoried for either a specific category (insects, plants, soil types, ecosystems) or for all categories of knowledge possessed by the participant community managing or interacting with the area. Area inventories are done as rapid assessments (Gavin and Anderson 2005) or as more thorough longer-term analyses (Etkin 1993; Reyes-García et al. 2005).

a. A location is selected, either randomly from within an area type or one that is typical of a particular area type. This is done with someone from the participant community who knows the area categories well. For example, if the objective is to conduct inventories of Puerto Rican markets in New York City, then a Puerto Rican community resident expert in New York City would help to identify a selection of markets that are frequented by members of the Puerto Rican community. A sample of these markets could then be selected at random.

b. The locations are then scouted out and the area boundaries demarcated if they are not already naturally or artificially discrete. Questions are formulated for the area much as they are for an environmental transect, except that the questions may not always be asked in the same order nor at the same location.

c. Participants (individually or in groups) are taken through the area and asked specific questions about the resources within it. It is not unusual for only a small number of participants to be exposed to a single location or (for example) for the location to be explained only by the location owner or manager.

d. Specimens are collected based upon the results of the questions asked. Usually this is done at the time of the interview with the participant directing the process so that the correct samples are collected.

e. At the conclusion the participants are shown the specimens and asked to verify the information associated with them.

12.2.5 Artefact interview

One or more cultural artefacts (e.g. tools, art, clothing, houses) are used as the focus of questions posed to participants usually to learn about such things as the components, history, uses, meanings (Banack 1991; and Lemonnier, Chapter 13 below). Since it is easy for participants to focus on the details of a specific artefact and fail to discuss the general category of the artefact, it is a good idea to have a spectrum of different examples of the same sort of thing present. If a disease complex can be considered as a cultural artefact (albeit an interpreted mental construct rather than a physical articulation), then artefact interviews would also include some kinds of disease-culture-centred research (of disease and its interpretations) that leads to the material basis of remedies (e.g. Balick et al. 2000).

a. For the purposes of an ethnobiological study, questions developed for an interview usually include focus on the material basis of the artefact. The questions should not lead but should rather be simple, such as 'What are the parts of this made from?' Many artefacts are composed of more than one part that is functional in and of itself. As such, these sub-artefacts should be recognized as separate components with their own questions. Some researchers may wish to ask about materials that are used in the production of an artefact but are not physically present in the final product. For example, a tool handle may be sanded with shark-skin during its production but the skin is not present in the final product. An appropriate question could be formulated to elicit this sort of information if desired.

b. At the time of the interview, the participant (or participants) are presented with the artefact(s) and asked the questions in a particular order. The responses are recorded.

c. Following the questions, any materials identified by the participants need to be located and specimens prepared of them. If this process is done with the same participants, they will have identified the materials; if not, the participants need to be shown the specimens in order to verify that what has been collected is the same as they had mentioned in the interview.

d. A special form of artefact interview is a production or reproduction interview wherein a participant or group of participants produces an artefact with the researcher either assisting as a participant in the process or as an observer (see e.g. Cox 1982; Nickum 2008; Rickard and Cox 1984).

12.2.6 Biological evidence

Naturalistic scientists (Atran 1990; 1998) collect almost any sort of evidence. Although it is best to plan for a project by practising how to collect and preserve plants, insects, mushrooms, fish, birds, and soil samples, it is also important to be creative and collect samples when they are realistically available and not be overly concerned about having a perfect sample. At the end of the day, an imperfect sample is better than no sample at all. Common sense should be a good judge about how to collect many samples and what should be collected. For example, preservation in alcohol or drying is often better than storage in water or at environmental temperature because most organisms will decay in the natural environment if left alone. Therefore, by creating an unnatural environment they may be preserved in some fashion. It is not unusual for people within a community to have methods for preserving materials, such as taxidermy, and these should be used when available.

When collecting samples, it is very valuable to collect them in at least triplicate if at all possible; one set for local national deposit, one set for distribution to different international experts for identification, and one set for deposit in another location, either at a different national location or internationally. Sample sets need to all be cross-numbered and labelled the same, so that data determined in one can be shared with the others. The primary set that is deposited locally is evidence that may be accessed by local collaborators and will eventually be the most useful and likely most accessed, so this should be the best set. The set that is distributed to experts will be broken up into separate units with specific items sent to specific experts who are identified as having particular expertise and being likely to identify a particular sample. For example, a beetle expert might be sent all of the beetles, while a humming bird expert might be sent the humming birds for identification. The experts will not send the samples back but will send back identifications and will incorporate the samples into larger international collections. The third collection is basically an insurance policy. Fires, wars, and other things can happen that can result in the loss of, or damage to, a repository. By being placed in a completely different location, the third collection represents a different set that can be used to replace the first if it should become lost or damaged in future.

12.3 DATA ANALYSIS

Each of the methods described is incomplete without leading to an analytical method. The hypothesis, data collection method, and data analysis method all combine to make a complete chain of logic. Results may often be analysed for frequency of mentioned items (Bernard 2002), list length (Brewer 1995), or salience (Smith 1993). Hoffman and Gallaher (2007) have reviewed a range of methods developed for analysing the importance placed on uses of plants and vegetation by people who use them. The same methods should apply to almost any things studied that people interact with from the environment.

12.3.1 Biodiversity

Collection of biodiversity information using participants from local communities and relying on their local expertise rather than on one's external university training is sometimes called 'parataxonomy'. Parataxonomy is being used increasingly to survey areas and to learn about the ethno-species or morpho-species diversity recognized within an area (Pfeiffer and Uril 2003; Janzen 2004; Sillitoe 2007) and to estimate local biological species richness (Oliver and Beattie 1993; Basset et al. 2000; Basset et al. 2004; Jinxiu et al. 2004).

For those who are not biologists, some important points need to be made about the relationships between common/vernacular names (in any language) and scientific names. Scientific names are not magical or more factually correct; they are often derived from common names at one point in the past and now serve as a unifying language around the world for comparative discussions in science. All of these names (scientific or common) circumscribe identifiable units or taxa that people can recognize. When comparing the taxa recognized by one group of people with those recognized by another group they may (a) have about the same circumscription (have the same constituents) or (b) include one considered to be grouping several taxa of the other into a single taxon (a 'lumper'), and thus the other is considered relatively to be dividing one taxon of the first into multiple taxa (a 'splitter'). These divisions are analytically relative to each other and are not based upon a standard other than one's point of reference. This is true not only of folk knowledge but also of scientific species concepts.

12.3.2 Gloss assumptions

Muller and Almedom (2008) have noted the dangers of gloss terms describing traditional foods, and how these may easily come to depict aspects of culture in unrealistic terms. They focused their analysis on the concept of 'famine foods', but a similar examination of almost any rapid interpretation applied by a researcher to describe a complex cultural phenomenon of human interaction with one or more biological organisms or environments will have similar pitfalls. There is not an easy recommendation for dealing with this problem other than to suggest that it is best to gather as much data as possible, with primary data being the best and to apply as much local expertise as possible within the interpretation of results to minimize misrepresentations.

Probably the best advice for those who are non-experts on a subject is to be as clearly descriptive as possible, including both etic and emic observations (see Diamond 1991) and minimal interpretations. For example, if a disease with a certain traditional name appears to be 'breast cancer' but the researcher documenting the term and gloss is not a physician seeing a patient and collecting a specimen to verify this, then it is best *not* to give this as the name, but merely to describe the traditional symptoms of the illness and say nothing about the assumption of breast cancer. The very important reason for not making the assumption is that placing information such as this within a dictionary could lead later to misdiagnoses based upon information that may or may not be true. The same is true for less critical cases, such as naming of birds, plants, soil types, and ecosystems.

A clear description, when joined with physical evidence, can be deciphered by a subsequent expert collaborating scholar, while a bad assumption may not be retracted.

12.4 DISCUSSION

Each of the five methods for the collection of information described here may be used alone or in combination, and each has certain advantages and disadvantages. Free-listing is the most simple and common method, but it is problematic in that it is dependent upon human memories and subsequent ability to find samples of what was being discussed/remembered at an earlier time. However, free-listing can be the most creative because it is not constrained by the physical reality around people and therefore they are able to include examples of taxa that are now extinct, rare, out of season, or otherwise not present but still part of their cultural memory. It is not uncommon for free-listing exercises to result in some data points that lack supporting physical evidence; these problematic data must be either set aside as irreproducible or discussed as suspect. An artefact interview is merely a particular sort of free-listing exercise with a tangible object for the participants to focus their thoughts on. As such, it has similar strengths and weaknesses to be considered.

Inventory interviews, on the other hand, have a high level of reproducibility because the specimens are prepared a priori and therefore none are lacking at the completion of the data collection process. In addition, comparisons between interviews are unambiguous because there is little doubt that the participants were exposed to exactly the same physical stimuli to formulate their response. However, inventory interviews include displays of taxa outside their normal environments and often dried or preserved in ways that make them look less like they do in the natural environment. On the other hand, environmental transects allow for participants to observe taxa within their natural settings or within settings where they are normally encountered by people, and so they may be able to elicit a higher response level than results from an inventory interview. The problem with the environmental transect is that environments do change over time: some organisms move, die, or are damaged by weather. What is seen by one participant may not be the same as what is seen by subsequent participants over a series of days, weeks, or longer. Also, when specimens are collected at the end, they may not be present as they were at times during the interview period. An area interview is a much more formal and larger version of an environmental transect, and suffers from the same strengths and weaknesses, but magnified. However, since there are usually fewer samples taken with an area interview, there is less chance of change over time if the project does not take too long to complete.

Ethnobiological research in many parts of the world has much to offer linguists in the identification of the vocabularies used by people to describe the world around them. Making these descriptions clear does not have to be difficult and, when done in collaboration with experts from other disciplines, should help linguists to feel more confident about the products of their work. As a concluding thought, consider a story (also mentioned by Evans, Chapter 8 above) told about an experience that Ralph Bulmer had with the Kalam in New Guinea (Diamond 1991: 85).

Bulmer, after years of working with the Kalam recording abundant information on plants and animals, recruited a geologist to come with him into the field. The Kalam opened up to the geologist and provided terminology and observations that Bulmer had expected but found difficult to elicit. When he expressed his disappointment that the Kalam had not had these conversations with him, they explained that when he asked about fauna and flora they realized he knew these topics well and was easy to educate. But they found his questions about rocks revealed that he had so little background knowledge that they foresaw a long and difficult process, which they pragmatically sidestepped by denying their geological lore, revealing a minimum of geology words. Had Bulmer selected a different interview technique, perhaps first making a collection of many different sorts of geological samples and then using an inventory interview, he might have had a different experience. But, in this example, the solution to Bulmer's research problem came about through a successful collaboration with an expert in another discipline. The ethnobiologists and other scientists are waiting for the linguists to call.

CHAPTER 13

··

TECHNOLOGY

··

PIERRE LEMONNIER

13.1 INTRODUCTION

··

Several decades were needed for anthropologists to realize that objects produced by humans in society are a social production. Indeed, any given object, be it a battleship, a hammer, or a stone picked up from the ground, is always a product of its fabrication or use, through gestures, skills, and knowledge which may vary from one culture to another. As Mauss stated in his paper on 'the techniques of the body' (2006[1935]: 77–95), this is true of every possible action on the material world. Here he demonstrated that even the most 'natural' actions we perform on *matter* (like walking, swimming, or giving birth) are, always and everywhere, cultural productions. At the same time as it has a physical function, a technique or an object is a component in a system of thought and action which is not particularly 'technical' itself. In effect, the material use to which a given technique or object is put, or the ideas one has about it, may well be related to social strategies, actions, or domains that have nothing to do with a transformation of the material world. Rather, this object or technique may be simultaneously related to non-technical activities. As we shall see, a New Guinea garden fence is by no means only to keep pigs away from sweet potatoes. Similarly, people would agree that, today, sport shoes are as much related to identity and social interaction as designed for jogging.

In other words, techniques are as responsible for producing social ties and types of information as they are for transforming the material world. As sociologists of science and modern technology put it when they refer to a 'seamless sociotechnical network' (Hughes 1986), techniques and objects are embedded in other realms of social actions which we arbitrarily define and name for the sake of social sciences. And because techniques occur in all social actions, it may be incorrect to isolate a domain in human life and production as merely 'technical'. However, while not belittling or forgetting the bulk of human material productions, we can at least loosely decide where techniques start, or how they are conveyed in an action—and, by definition, by an action on matter.

The anthropology of techniques ('technologie culturelle' in the French tradition, and 'material culture studies' in the British tradition) is therefore merely one point of view among others on objects and techniques. It is the one that *not only* asks if an object is an element of a set of 'political', 'religious', 'economic', 'artistic', or other practices and representations, but *also* asks in what way its conception and its material production are characteristic of the human group that manufactures or uses it. Paying attention to the most physical dimension of technical actions is a way to reveal fundamental information about a culture and its social organization or system of thought that is provided by no other anthropological approach.

13.2 TECHNIQUES AS ACTIONS ON THE MATERIAL WORLD: SOME KEY IDEAS

For anyone interested in action on matter, the purpose of an object cannot be understood without the gestures and knowledge needed to put it to use. The term 'operational sequence' (the series of operations to be performed) designates the overall process that leads from a given state of matter to its transformed state. Usually, there is nothing to indicate where an operational sequence begins or ends. Why separate the felling of the trees from the manufacture of the adze making the felling possible; or the making of the drum fashioned from the section of the tree trunk being cut up? These arbitrary divisions depend on the questions asked, but are certainly no reason not to tackle the problem.

The expression 'technical system' is used by Mauss (2007[1947]) in his *Manuel d'ethnographie*, in which, for the purposes of his analysis, the technical system is presented as an isolated aspect of social reality. The notion of a technical system was further developed by the historian Gille, who made it the fundamental concept of his *Histoire des techniques* (1978). As far as ethnographic description is concerned, techniques have a systematic character which can be characterized with three levels of interaction (Lemonnier 1992: 4–11).

On the first level are the components, or elements, that interact with each other in any given technique (understood as a specific action on matter, delineated by the anthropologist, for whatever reason), for example, tying your shoelaces, landing a Boeing 777, or carving chips from a block of wood. These components, or elements, which interact with one another are: the matter being acted on (which can be the body itself when one walks, swims, dances, etc.); tools; gestures; one or several sources of energy; actors; and 'representations'. The components involved in any action aimed at obtaining some material result physically fit together, or are at least more or less mutually compatible in a physical sense. They form a system, in the simplest sense of the term, defined by the fact that a change in one element can lead to the modification of one or more of the others. If heating milk in a saucepan, control of the transformation from cold to boiling is different on an electric plate and on a gas hob. The heat remains when the electric power is cut, whereas it stops almost instantly with a gas cooker.

The term 'representation' deserves special attention, as it is deliberately vague and includes the extremely complicated processes labelled 'skills'—understood as 'care, judgement and dexterity' according to Ingold (1997: 111)—as well as sets of culturally shared ideas about the components comprising a given technique. These skills are part of what anthropologists call 'implicit' or 'tacit knowledge'. This type of knowledge is more of the type 'to know *how*' rather than of the type 'to know *that*' (Varela, Rosh, and Thompson 1993: 208), and it is not restricted to information about how to make the gestures and operations involved in a technical action. It is also made up of particular mental *skills*, for instance, abilities to evaluate a situation in a fraction of a second and to adapt the ongoing technical process to it (Descola 2006: 11).

This 'know how' does not comprise a series of instructions or images listed somewhere in the brain that would constitute a sort of program to be executed. As a result, 'it is not through the transmission of (programmatic forms of rules and representations) that skills are learned, but rather through a mixture of improvisation and imitation in the setting of practice' (Ingold 1997: 111). This 'know how' and skills are embodied and drive actions that are made automatically: for instance, you normally have no consciousness of the many and complex tasks you perform while driving (Bloch 1998: 3–21).

'Actors' and 'energy' are also quite ambiguous terms because, from an emic point of view, some participants and powers in a technical action may belong to what we call the supernatural domain, in which the relationship between means and ends violates western scientific knowledge (to whistle in order to chase the rain away is an example of such a violation).

At a second level, in any one given society and at a given period of time, various techniques are linked with each other in various ways and for various reasons. Here are some examples:

- A technical action depends on the preceding actions: you have to go and cut canes and saplings before you can lash together roof beams for your house; if there are no tires produced and transported to a shop, you cannot get a complete wheel installed on your car; you have to remove the egg's shell before you put it in a frying-pan.

- Different techniques may use the same tool or machine (think about all the situations in which you have to screw or tighten something or pull something out with pliers or pincers); millions of different products can be made by lathes or drilling devices.
- Different techniques can include identical steps (pieces of an operational sequence): whether you build a New Guinea house or a garden fence, you have to fell trees and make planks or posts out of the trunks. Welding sheet metal together is an operation common to many industries.
- Different techniques can rely on the same actors, raw materials, etc.: for instance, the person who welds iron sheets in a car factory during the week is the same one who uses a lawnmower at the weekend or a coffee machine every morning. The raw material that is ordinary salt has innumerable culinary or chemical uses.
- Techniques can result from the embodiment of identical representations in gestures and objects: e.g. knowledge about transformations for clay or iron underlies thousands of technical processes.

In this respect, it is worth noting that Leroi-Gourhan's program on the 'elementary means of action on the matter' (1971[1943]; 1973[1945]) has not yet been seriously documented. Such an elementary means is, for instance 'mixing': whether you are preparing mayonnaise, cement, or orange cordial in a glass of water, you are performing a similar elementary action. How such a universal physical action is actually used by people has never been investigated; nor, as yet, have anthropologists tried to get information on the mental apparatus lying beyond such 'representation' (say, 'adding some kind of liquid to a denser liquid, powder, or solid, gives a paste and homogenizes it, etc.').

At a third level, the ways in which a technique or an object is manufactured, used, or exchanged is linked to practices and thought systems that go well beyond simple material effectiveness. A technical system is therefore always part of the sociocultural whole that includes it. Social representations of techniques include more than the strict domain of action on matter.

As a result, the relationship networks which material actions have with other social acts, or techniques, come from *choices* that are, to a greater extent, at all times, everywhere—even in the case of our most 'modern and rational' techniques—determined by considerations that are in no way technical (Bijker and Law 1992; Latour 1996). For want of a better expression, 'technological choices'—or technological 'options'—emphasize the sorting of possibilities on which the development of a technical system is de facto based, although usually in an unconscious and unintentional way, and they refer both to the process of selection and to its results. The whole problem is to identify where these choices come in; what the logic is behind them; what their consequences are; and so on (Lemonnier 1993a). 'Technical decisions' regarding the building of a metro (Latour 1996), the design of a missile guidance system (McKenzie 1990), or the fencing of gardens rather than pigs in New Guinea (Lemonnier 1993b) do not merely relate to technical actions, but to various ideas, which we label 'political', 'economic', 'gender', 'representations of beauty', etc.

The 'choices' a society adopts, rejects, or modifies in a technical component entail elements that do not serve any material purpose—such as particular ideas about gender relations between the men and women who use the finished object; representations of the relationship between a given material and the cosmos or the gods; political considerations about organizing labour, etc. Such non-technical representations weigh just as heavily as mechanical components in the way an object is thought about and manufactured (or in the way a technique is put to use), its material effectiveness, and even the fate of those who use it (e.g. Schmidt 1996).

Among the Anga people of Papua New Guinea, the use of a given type of tree bark for making capes or loincloths does not result from its affordability in a given ecological zone or specific technical knowledge. Rather, it is correlated to the use women have for this particular raw material: in those groups where women make and wear this type of beaten bark loincloth, it is literally unthinkable that men could use it. Consequently, men ignore the trees in question as a source of raw material for their own capes, using other trees instead (Lemonnier 1984; 1993a: 105–12). What is at stake is gender, and not the botanical adequacy of a raw material.

13.3 ANTHROPOLOGICAL APPROACHES
TO TECHNOLOGY

For years, most studies on how technology interfaces with other social behaviours have dealt either with the *effects* of technological systems on culture and society or with a search for the information human groups *communicate* when making and using artefacts. What social consequences followed the development of the steam engine, or the introduction of steel tools in 'Neolithic' New Guinean societies, or the stirrup in medieval cavalry? These are all questions illustrating this approach. At a general level, Marxist theory proposes the combination of 'productive forces' with 'social relations of production', and has resulted in the best known sociological and economic studies on the two-way interaction between the effects of techniques (and phenomena related to them) and other aspects of cultural and social organization.

The second academic tradition comprises various studies of 'style' by archeologists and anthropologists. Style has mainly been read from artefacts through details of form and decoration as status markers (notably within social hierarchies or gendered positions), with a focus on the identities of groups and individuals, the makers or users of the artefacts.

Although there is still a tendency, primarily in archeology, to correlate stylistic details of artefacts or technical behaviour to the production of 'meaning', many anthropological case studies have demonstrated that technological options have as much bearing on physical dimensions of material culture as on 'style'. As mentioned above, à propos the Metro, missiles, or everyday work in a New Guinea village, the human ability to produce and freely modify technological systems goes beyond formal features that have only unimportant effects on the material world. Technological choices may deeply affect the physical 'function' of an artefact—the quotation marks remind us that style, of course, has its own function.

In the last three decades, the very embedding of techniques in other types of social actions and thoughts have been investigated under two academic labels: 'cultural technology' and 'material culture studies'. 'Cultural technology' has tried to carry on Mauss's 'utopic' (Schlanger 1991; 2006: 147) program of research by paying particular attention to the way things are made and physically used—i.e. by documenting and analysing 'operational sequences' ('chaînes opératoires'), their components, and their variations in space and time; in order to explain how particular aspects of a technical system are linked to some local characteristics of social organization, ritual life, or systems of thought. Examples of this approach can be found in case studies by Gosselain (1999; 2010), Mahias (1993; 2002), Lemonnier (1989; 1993a; 1993b), or Martinelli (1996; 2005), as well as in dozens of papers published in the journal Techniques et culture.

Whereas the theory of 'cultural technology' has been developed by scholars directly influenced by Mauss and by Leroi-Gourhan (1971[1943], 1973[1945], 1993 [1964]), among whom are Balfet (1975; 1991) and Cresswell (1972), material culture studies result from the blending of the anthropology of consumption, initiated by Douglas (Douglas and Isherwood 1979), with an interest in the 'cultural biography of things' (Kopytoff 1986). This approach is somewhat parallel to that of Latour (2005) on the social 'agency' of objects, and is notably illustrated in the Journal of Material Culture. Although dealing with the 'social life of things' (Appadurai 1986), material culture studies have mostly looked at the way objects are involved in various social strategies, identity, and status issues, both in non-industrial societies in the context of modernity, and in the industrial world, often with regard to the consumption of goods (Miller 1995; 2006; Keane 2006a).

In recent years a series of scholars have successfully bridged the gap between material culture studies and cultural technology (e.g. Coupaye 2009; Damon 2008; Douny 2007; Revolon 2007). Simultaneously, attention is now paid in part to the 'embodiment' of particular aspects of local culture, via technical behaviour (body techniques have long been the least developed section in the anthropology of objects and techniques). Such studies show that the engagement of the self and that of the body in technical action is produced by the partial embodiment or internalization of the subjects' interactions with their cultural environment (Ingold 2000; 2004; Warnier 2001; 2007). We are still far from the comparative studies of body techniques which Lévi-Strauss (1987[1950]: xxiii–xiv) asked for almost sixty years ago! But at least the physical engagement of the actor with the material world has now become part of the picture.

Further good news for the anthropology of technology is that real interdisciplinary cooperation is now becoming more common. The old ongoing exchanges between archeology and anthropology are now joined by disciplines such as art history, history of material culture, anthropology of art, cognitive anthropology, primatology, and philosophy which share questions with the anthropology of technology. In particular, many scholars agree to concentrate on the 'agency' or 'materiality' of objects with a growing interest in the role of objects and technical action in non-verbal communication.

Following Gell's (1998) book *Art and Agency*, the 'agency' of objects has become a fashionable idea in anthropology today. Furthermore, Gell's (1996) proposition to blur the border between art objects and utilitarian objects, as well as the unconventional usage of the word 'technology' in his paper on 'technology of enchantment' (1992), are incentives to ask crucial questions about the very nature of objects. However, as Munn (1970) remarked long ago, the idea that objects have an agency of their own is far from new—it was clearly mentioned in that seminal anthropological text, 'The Gift', by Mauss (1954[1923–3]). This 'was concerned with social relationships in which people are bound together through the agency of things and in which, therefore, the things are imbued with notions of persons' (Munn 1970: 141). In other words, to say that objects have some sort of agency is just another way to remind ourselves that material culture can be the object of anthropological investigation. Once this 'agency' is acknowledged, we are beholden to document it, by understanding the relationships tying human beings to material objects. I would add that not only artefacts but also actions on the material world in general should be studied.

By referencing Gell's work, new and good things result in the anthropology of technology, as it makes dozens of scholars ask the same series of questions about artefacts. For instance: in what respect does an 'ordinary' object differ from a seemingly similar artefact, locally considered as a piece of art (or as a ritual object, a relic, etc.)? Is there a difference in the way these various things are produced and physically used? What do people *do* with objects, including 'merely' (if one dare say) building or reinforcing social relations through the use of artefacts? What kind of efficacy do they attribute to the object: a real or imaginary physical action on the material world or an inbuilt power of its own? In what respect does an object lead people to act on one another? Particularly, to evoke Mauss' (1954[1923–4]), Munn's

(1970), and Strathern's (1988) intuitions, how and when is an artefact considered to be a person or an extension of a person? Needless to say, this fundamental question is deeply embedded in our own conceptions of 'person' and 'object' (Keane 2006a).

'Materiality' is another fashionable catch-all term today (Miller 2005). On the one hand, it rightly leads us to ask what it means to invoke the association of social relations and shared ideas with a material object (and I would add, body technique). It also leads us to a hackneyed theme in anthropology: what does 'objectivation' mean? This adds another important question: how is the materiality of things involved in the thoughts and actions of people when they make or manipulate objects? For instance, what do people perceive of their physical characteristics or, as Keane (2006b) would put it, of their 'bundle' of qualities? On the other hand, as Ingold (2007) remarks, understanding the materiality of things implies first and foremost a description of what happens to materials when they are transformed and experienced by those who manipulate them. That is, to 'return to the messy terrain of ethnography' (Miller 2005: 41), and take seriously the 'imperative to get back to material things, and not to surrender physicality and sensuous experience to an exorbitation of language and the sign' (Thomas 1998: 108).

13.4 Two case studies about objects in non-verbal communication

It is one thing to develop theoretical arguments pointing to the importance of the 'agency' of objects, the local ins and outs of 'materiality' or the crucial interaction of bodies with the material world. It is another thing to document these theoretical intuitions in real life, in a real human group. Now is the time for patient and detailed case studies taking into account and investigating the manner by which systems of meaning and actions on matter are organized and enmeshed in human thoughts and actions (e.g. Lemonnier 1993b; 2005; Sillar 1996).

The following ethnographic examples are illustrations of anthropological research paying close attention to making and using artefacts. I have chosen them because they both point to contemporary problems in the study of technology and fit my own interest in this field; but they should be understood as illustrating only one possible way to study technology. In particular, they present a hypothesis about a possible *unnoted* role for objects simultaneously bringing together entire series of thoughts and dealing with several (and various) aspects of the culture and social organization belonging to those who make and use them. In other words, the making and physical usage of some artefacts may be the only way people become aware of key aspects of a system of values and actions. Both case studies are from the Anga people of Papua New Guinea, where I started my anthropological fieldwork in 1978, notably in the study of technology.

13.4.1 A sturdy fence to build social order

The first object I will discuss is an ordinary garden fence observed among the Baruya of Papua New Guinea. Generally in New Guinea, the enclosures surrounding tuber gardens (and those containing sugar cane, bananas, etc.) result from a series of technical choices: rather than enclosing the animals and feeding them intensively, people prefer to protect their crops by enclosing the tuber gardens, while letting the animals forage freely. The women raising the animals then give them a kilo or so of tubers a day (Lemonnier 1993b).

On the whole, this method has been retained by the Anga groups, but on closer observation, several important differences can be seen from group to group. In particular, the observer who visits the valleys on foot is struck by the 'details' of technical function, which are difficult to interpret or even seem quite aberrant. In Ankave villages, for instance, it is rare and even extremely rare to see a completed garden fence, which raises doubts as to their function as garden protection. The Baruya, on the other hand, erect barriers of sharp pointed stakes regularly measuring over 1.5m (up to 2m) in height, something which can seem surprising if one knows that even hungry pigs in New Guinea are hardly noted for their jumping skills, nor do they try to break through far flimsier obstacles ('Chimbu' fences are not even lashed together) (see Fig. 13.1).

These extremely sturdy Baruya fences are as impressive as they are non-'functional'. Comprising three layers of interlaced planks tightly lashed together, they can, when maintained, firmly withstand the onslaught of any pig. My notes indicate that each running meter of fence contains over 50 boards, all painstakingly interwoven and tied together with lianas. This sturdy 'aspect' and the solidity of the oversized garden fences are the result of ten or fifteen men working together clearing a new garden in the forest. The women transport the fence stakes from old gardens in the valley, then gather and burn the underbrush, while the men—especially the garden-'owner's' brothers-in-law and co-initiates—fell trees and build the fences over the course of a week or two. As the tree trunks are turned into boards or sharpened stakes and the fence is assembled, a veritable open-air workshop is on display to the observer.

It is hard, too, not to notice that the fence is one of the occasions when male solidarity is displayed for all to see. In itself, this collective fencing effort is a reaffirmation of certain social relations, between close blood relatives, between brothers-in-law (above all), between co-initiates or between friends. The Baruya's insatiable solidarity stands in opposition to the Ankave's determination that everyone should mind their own business (even if a neighbour is only a few

Figure 13.1. Far from being only a physical means to protect alimentary plants from the pigs, and to delimit family plots, a Baruya fence materializes and demonstrates crucial social relations: those between men and women, between male co-initiates, and between brothers-in-law.

minutes away) and to their strong penchant for long stays in the forest (Bonnemère 1996; Godelier 1986; Lemonnier 2006). When an individual garden is cleared, an Ankave man and his wife take on this forest work alone. Cooperation is almost exclusively the affair of the couple, and even then the husband and the wife carry out complementary tasks. Of course there are some contexts in which cooperation is just as intense among the Ankave as it is among the Baruya, particularly in warfare and male initiations. But for horticulture, hunting, or the manufacture of objects, the Ankave and Baruya worlds are at opposite ends of the spectrum.

Since no characteristic features of gestures, tools, or technical knowledge account for this disparity in the way they organize their work, it must be attributable to other domains of social reality where radically different practices are observed between different Anga groups: namely, initiations, marriage, and ways of working together. This is what a study of cultural technology is able to demonstrate.

Looking at a Baruya fence from a technological point of view—describing the artefact as well as its manufacture, comparing these observations with those from other Anga or New Guinea gardens fences, and placing the particular artefact and its associated technical activities into a comparative study of Anga social organizations at large—reveals that the collective effort of fencing a Baruya garden is a reaffirmation of a certain number of social relations as described earlier. In other words, these impressive ramparts against pigs are not only assigned the concrete task of establishing an impenetrable barrier between pigs and tubers. In them and through them, a whole portion of the Baruya social order is produced, with the emphasis first and foremost on cooperation but also an emphatic display of male solidarity, as a group opposed to the women. Further, there is absolute reciprocal confidence and mutual assistance of the co-initiates, and, lastly, a focus on concordance and collaboration in work between brothers-in-law, who, according to the marriage rule, have 'exchanged' 'sisters'.

What is striking is that these social relations and moral rules, rendered visible and literally embodied by the participants, are precisely those features setting the Northern Anga, Baruya, and also Sambia (Godelier 1986; Herdt 1981) radically apart from their neighbours in the south or the southwest, who in turn are characterized by a spectacularly low level of cooperation. Thus, a garden fence is a way to evoke a series of institutions, actions, and social representations in a non-verbal way.

In this first example, the aspects of a culture are demonstrated in a technical activity. The actual construction of the fence and its mechanical as well as visual sturdiness are often explicitly emphasized in various circumstances: in discourses during male initiations or inside the men's house; each time brothers-in-law comment on their good or bad relationship; each time women are scolded by men. By contrast, in the following case study it is hypothesized that the manufacture and use of the artefact in question is a way to evoke aspects of culture that may not be verbalized. The artefact, a mortuary hand-drum, is used by another Anga group, the Ankave, who live five to seven days' walk away from the Baruya.

13.4.2 A drum that does far more than produce sounds

About once a year, the Ankave, a small group of forest horticulturalists, drive away (completely, they believe), the marauding ghosts of those who have recently died (*pisingen siwi*), during a ceremony called *songen*, named after the drums which are beaten for several nights in a row. These drums look like hourglasses, made of two long, tapered cones joined at the tips and sometimes surmounted by a handle (Bonnemère and Lemonnier 2007: 192–204; see Fig. 13.2).

These *songen* ceremonies are the most visible part of a thought system revolving around vile, man-eating beings, invisible and deeply hostile to humans, known as *ombo'*, which the Ankave hold responsible for most fatal illnesses. The *ombo'* make up a band of invisible cannibals hosted inside seemingly ordinary human beings.

Figure 13.2. Among the Ankave, making and beating the drums that funnel the spirits of the recent dead into another world amalgamates myth, technique, and ritual, and results in the non-verbal communication of a series of key values and aspects of their social organization and system of thought.

The *ombo'* attack, devour, and share between them men, women, and children who are believed to have refused to share things themselves. The obligation to acquiesce to all requests for food or objects is a pillar of Ankave social order of which the *ombo'* are a constant reminder.

According to the Ankave mythology, it is the *ombo'* that humans also have to thank for the *songen* ceremonies, as well as for the masks worn by the drummers and the songs sung during the drumming. It is they who, from the depths of a pond, brought humans the hourglass drums, beaten night after night when it is time to definitively despatch a *pisingen siwi* spirit, and to forget the deceased to whom the ghost belonged. The origin myth of the drums also contains an extraordinary spoken operational sequence, providing a step-by-step explanation of how to make the instrument while underscoring the key aspects of the imaginary device whereby the Ankave dispose of their dead: the origin of the drum skin, made from the skin of a snake-man; and the importance of the 'throat' or middle part of the object (Lemonnier 2005).

The myths also explain that the *ombo'* make endless circuits to the sound of the drumbeat, after men have kept them chained up night after night in our world.

The hourglass drum plays a crucial role in dismissing the spirits of those who have died recently. Drawn in by the arms of the *nowimboxo* mask, the *pisingen siwi* spirit is driven towards the other world by the racket produced by the drum skin, the selfsame din that resounded on either side of the water when the Ankave ancestor discovered this wonderful object. At this point, the spirit of the deceased travels through the two pieces of the instrument. The myths recounting the origin of the *songen* ceremonies have much to say about this: the narrow piece that connects the two chambers of the drum and the python-skin membrane which acts as a gateway to eternity. In other words, an Ankave mortuary hourglass drum is not only a musical instrument, it is primarily a funnel-shaped psychopomp, that is to say the narrow canal whereby the ghost travels from the world of the living to that of the *ombo'*.

Shamans say that these cannibal monsters feed on corpses, killing their victims by inserting objects into their veins or by cutting them, as well as by slashing their liver. Those Ankave people who have had the horrible surprise of identifying an *ombo'* have recognized maternal kinsmen who looked exactly like their uncles or cousins, except for their red eyes and dog-like ears. For the Ankave, a foetus is believed to feed on maternal blood, and everyone agrees that a brother has given to his sister's children the life-giving blood he shares with her. This is one reason why maternal kin always claim they have not received enough gifts to compensate the birth of children who are 'one blood' with them. In the Ankave world-view there is no way to compensate for the blood-life one receives from his maternal kin. And this is the reason why the *ombo'* are like mothers who eat their own children.

But this is not yet the end of the story, as revealed by a contextualizing anthropology of technology. An Ankave mortuary drum is more than a double funnel linking the two sides of the same entity—the Ankave society—with its living and its dead. On the one hand, this artefact does what art or 'images' do, according to various anthropologists. For Wagner, '[a]n image has the power of synthesis: it condenses whole realms of possible ideas and interpretations and allows complex relationships to be perceived and grasped in an instant . . . the power of eliciting [causing to perceive] all sorts of meanings in those who use and hear it' (Wagner 1987: 56).On the other hand, an Ankave drum is neither a piece of art nor merely an image.

To understand an object according to the theory and methods of the anthropology of techniques, one has to consider it within the full complexity of the operational sequences in which it appears, as well as in the systems of thought that refer to it. In the present case, if one considers the drum together with the night ceremony, *and* with the making of the drums, *and* with the operational sequence given in myths, one realizes that it is not the object alone that has what Gell (1996: 37) called 'objectification of complex intentionalities'.

In my view, while using the drums the Ankave are mixing together thoughts and actions belonging to various domains of Ankave culture, social organization, and imagination. Collectively beating the drums is a unique way of putting together myth, ritual action, and material actions, by doing things, and not by simply looking at them (as for an image) or talking about them (as when evaluating art objects). It is because of the drums on which they are focused, and through the material actions by which they are fabricated and used, through contact with the matter—making the drums, beating the drums, singing, waving the 'hands' of the masks, walking in line for hours—that various aspects of Ankave social life are made present to the minds of the participants. These various domains of social action are: the ambiguity of maternal uncles (both cherishing and devouring); the reason shamans have to treat the *ombo'*'s victims and the physical damages to the latter's innards; the necessity of performing *songen* ceremonies to manage mourning; the local representation of life and the overwhelming importance of maternal blood; the origin of the drums, etc.

With regard to the general 'message', 'meaning', or 'social value' that is common to these various instances of social life, these domains are redundant, for they all refer to the idea that you will never be able to repay 'the life your maternal kin gives you, thus, the maternal kin will take it back in the guise of the cannibal *ombo'*'s involvement in mortuary procedures', say the Ankave. It is this same message that is spoken, illustrated, and put into objects and actions in various ways. The drums themselves, making the drums, and thinking about the drums, as well as beating the drums in general, all signal in a non-verbal way the reasons why and when these domains have to be evoked together—when the *ombo'* recapture the life they have given. It is a reminder that some artefacts, ideas, social hierarchies, narratives and gestures have to be thought together. And, most importantly, it evokes the very reasons why they have to be linked.

The difference with the case of the Baruya fence is that the meaning brought to the minds of the participant of a *songen* ceremony cannot be put in words. This particular technical device, a drum used in a ritual context, illustrates these 'implicit non-verbal statements', 'unspeakable truths', as well as the 'blurring of boundaries' (between the living and the dead) that Tuzin (2002) linked with the 'crafting of an illusion' in art objects.

It is worth pointing out that I have not merely hypothesized a vague 'agency' of drums in Ankave culture. Rather, I have explained what that agency is about, and how it works. Also, rather than adding more vehement paragraphs on the necessity of burying all dualisms—nature/culture, spiritual/material, style/function—I have documented two ethnographic cases, paying attention to the actual physical making and using of things in the embedding of meaning and physical actions.

Regarding the two Anga examples above, the new questions that arise are: what are the differences between an art object, a ritual object such as an Ankave drum, and a non-ritual and non-art object like a Baruya fence? The answers to these questions would be established only by careful observation, description, and analyses of artefacts and technical behaviour comprising their whole social context, in the widest sense; and linguistics has a key role to play here.

13.5 LINGUISTICS AND TECHNOLOGY: FIELD QUESTIONS AND METHODS

Besides reflections on the links between the evolution of human ability to develop technical actions on the material world and the origin of language (Leroi-Gourhan 1993[1964]; Ingold 1999), the theoretical relationships between technique and speech that have been studied take several forms, all related to the various ways techniques and objects are associated with 'meaning' or, more generally, some kind of information. But these relationships between linguistics and the anthropological study of technology are paradoxically poorly developed. On the one hand, it is obvious that no technical action can be understood as part of a global social system without paying utmost attention to hours of spontaneous speech or comments on that action; on the other hand, field studies linking the two fields of research are in fact extremely rare.

With the exception of vague and superficial propositions, considering technical actions on matter as some sort of speech, i.e. using language as an analogy to understand some aspects of techniques, has given poor results. For instance, Baudrillard's mention of weird elementary 'technèmes', the combination of which was supposed to characterize artefacts and machines (Baudrillard 1968: 12–13), led nowhere. A technical action (*chaine opératoire*) is not a 'sentence' in which a combination of operations, matter, and actors following some kind of 'grammar' would result in a modification in the material world that, in turn, could be glossed as the 'meaning' of that technical action. More efficiently, most studies have concentrated on the information that techniques and artefacts contain and convey. This information—or 'meaning'—has to be understood both from a wide etic point of view (what do techniques, in their most physical form do in social relationships?) and from an emic point of view (for the people who make and use them, artefacts are markers of some identity; artefacts are inscribed with some information; etc.).

A good reason for this failure to apply some kind of semiotic theory to technical processes derives from the complex aspects of that information and processing that constitute what anthropologists call 'tacit (or implicit) knowledge'. As Bloch (1998: 11) stated, after showing that the operations needed to drive a car 'not only *are* not linguistic but also *must* be non-linguistic if they are to be efficient'. The automation of gestures and mental operations (e.g. what you do in order to overtake another car) that result from a long process of apprenticeship implies that the actors are not (or no longer) conscious of them, and this indirectly makes it hard for the anthropologist trying to grasp them (Mahias 2002: 97–108). Any comment by the actor is welcome, for it may help understand what kind of phenomena are involved, together with the words used to describe the elements put together in a technical process. A good example is Delaporte's (2002) work on the 'herder's eye' in which he explains how Sami herders are able to grasp, in one glance, a set of information which allows them to recognize one particular animal in a herd of several hundred.

From the point of view of the social scientist, by distinguishing one artefact from another by its form, decoration, or characteristics of fabrication, i.e. by studying its 'style', one is able to make hypotheses on the homogeneity, particularities, and inscription in a historical or regional setting of the group of people who produced or used them. As mentioned earlier, this approach is the first step of most archeological research. In anthropology, the deciphering of style has been mostly limited to the marking of identity, following two researchers whose work was influenced by linguistic theory: Bogatyrev (1971[1937]), for whom the folk costume of Moravian Slovakia was a 'sign', and Wobst, who studied the components of the Yugoslav costume as pieces in a process of information exchange (Wobst 1977: 321). Delaporte's work (1988), which is also on costume (that of the Sami), is among the very few studies that envisage the functioning of such a system of signs to identify which are the units used to produce meaning, or what is the nature of the 'meaning' thus produced.

The recent and promising trend in research on technology explores the multiple and diverse manners in which the very materiality of objects and technical actions are part of a system of thought, social relations, and actions. However, a linguistic approach to artefacts *in the making* is extremely rare. Not surprisingly, it was developed by French scholars who were more or less influenced by Haudricourt (1988), who was both a linguist and 'technologue', and by Leroi-Gourhan and his students. In case studies on weaving (Lefébure 1978; Drettas 1980) or the domestic kneading of dough (Virolle-Souibès 1989), a painstaking recording and description of the vocabulary associated with a given technique, as well as a study of the connotations of the terms (their semantic field), allows us to grasp some links between technical acts, what people say about them, and the various activities, symbolic or not, relating to the activity as a whole and to its components.

As we have seen in the Anga cases studies above, some techniques, such as the making of a Baruya garden fence, may be a way to repeat and make tangible some essential aspects of a social system, institutions, shared representations, etc. Others, such as the Ankave mortuary drum and ceremony, evoke and gather aspects of a culture, social organization, and system of thought that may not be verbalized. But these non-verbal ways to evoke key sets of relations (or values) of a given human group cannot be discovered without careful attention to whatever words are uttered about these relations as well as technical actions. If one does not listen to

Baruya men boasting about male cooperation, or to Baruya brothers-in-law having a row because they did not do some work that they should have, there is no way to realize that making a fence is more than making a fence. Similarly, without the words that tell the origin myth of the Ankave drum, or the words that describe the parts of the drum (notably its middle, or 'throat', that swallows the spirits of the recent dead), I have would have had no clue to the complexity of what is going on when people make or beat drums.

13.6 COLLECTING LINGUISTIC DATA ON TECHNIQUES

The collection and analysis of the vocabulary is of crucial importance here: its signification and connotations may reveal links between the technical domain and other domains, as clues to the way the processes in question are represented. As Lefébure (1983) warned, this does not mean that the linguistic structure of the speech about a technique may reveal a concealed technical structure of sorts. But the words in question may reveal how a technical action, its elements, and its social context are represented.

The words to be recorded in the field are those used to qualify the elements of the operational sequences: the matter being transformed, the names of its different states, and particularities of these states according to the actors; the tools and their components, the parts which are named and those which are not; the gestures; the energies; the actors, including the invisible powers at hand—if any. Operations might have their own names, as also might the different steps in a given operation. For example, by noting the phonetic proximity between the name for 'blood clot' and that for a given state of the liquid paste in question, Bonnemère's (1998: 116) study of the preparation of red pandanus fruit's juice is a clue to the fundamental equation made by the Ankave-Anga between that culinary preparation and human blood. There may be also local names for 'know-how', 'skills', 'specialists', etc.

At first, one is overwhelmed by what has to be observed, understood, and recorded with the greatest detail possible in order to be able to understand and explain what is going on in a particular technique observed in a given place at a certain time. In other words, the anthropologist must find some way to be able to see and record which are the gestures, tools, and material put together during each step of an operational sequence. What is the energy used? Who are the actors (and the bystanders)? Are there any comments? What is the duration of each operation? Are these operations named? This is the only way to be able to discover and understand what are the local characteristics of a technique in a particular society.

The more precise the description, the better. Fortunately, modern technologies are of great help to record most of these data.

As explained elsewhere (Lemonnier 1992: 27–30), technical actions are often repetitive, which gives the observer some chance to grasp the characteristics of a given operational sequence. Video recording is an easy way to document technical actions, as long as the researcher remains extremely attentive to what is going on. Back home, it will be too late to ask questions about the action that has been filmed. A good description entails some ability to manipulate simultaneously a pencil, two cameras (photo and video), a stopwatch, and a tape recorder. With some training, this is quite easy. Exhausting, but easy. (See also Margetts and Margetts, Chapter 1 above.)

If possible, one should consider that one description of a given technical sequence is not enough, for the good reason that most of the questions that come to the observer's mind result from differences s/he has noticed between seemingly similar operations. Documenting all sorts of variants is essential here. From one day to another, the same agent may work differently. Two actors may have their own way of doing things, and so on. Observing the same series of technical actions (house-building, basket-making, cooking food, and tens of other mundane or less mundane technical actions), between two neighbouring groups—whatever 'group' means in a given situation—is quite rewarding.

Participant observation deserves a special mention here, for it is not only a way to share people's life and activities; it is also a way to grasp aspects of a technical process that would otherwise escape the anthropologist's observation or the actor's comments. One does not need to be a good potter to describe pottery, but some kind of apprenticeship can be a useful tool in understanding technical processes, allowing the formulation of specific questions. This also gives access to the implicit knowledge mentioned above.

It is important for documenting technical activities and their links to other social spheres of activity to collect descriptions (plural!) of technical activities, including comments at the particular moment of that activity. More generally, it is interesting to know what part of a technical activity is verbalized, never mentioned, or is forbidden to be mentioned. Besides the identification of variants—which really constitute the bulk of the data analysed—the identification of 'strategic operations' (Lemonnier 1992: 21–4) is of importance. These are particular actions or steps in an operational sequence that cannot be delayed or profoundly modified without jeopardizing the whole process at hand. It is interesting to know both what operations are considered to be 'strategic' and how those operations that are crucial from a physical point of view are dealt with. This is of course where technical specialists and social hierarchies may enter the picture.

Neither the objects nor the physical actions of the actors manipulating them say things plainly about the 'meanings' in question, particularly when artefacts lack any decoration. To have people describe in their own words what they are doing is of utmost importance because, on the one hand, they show their personal organi-zation strategies for an operational sequence, and, on the other, they may both emphasize or refrain from commenting particular aspects of the technique (or object) in question.

Therefore, it is only by listening to what people say about these artefacts and technical activities, as well as what they say in any of the activities which are related to them in some way or another, that it is possible to grasp the complex insertion of technical behaviour within various other social logics, including their role in non-verbal communication. Together with a precise understanding of the physical (mechanical etc.) aspects of an artefact, linguistics is a way to enquire into the 'bundle' of qualities (Keane 2006b) within an object which are ready to be 'chosen' by members of a given culture, either to act on the matter in a given way and with a certain efficacy, or to include this artefact or material in a particular system of meaning and/or social relations.

For instance, when the Ankave-Anga of Papua New Guinea use a given plant (cordylines) as fences, territory markers, and key element of sacred sites, they elaborate on one of the inherent qualities of that particular plant, which is its vegetative reproduction. It is plausible that the cordylines used today are the clones of those that grew on an ancestral spot, according to myth. The perception of a particular characteristic of the plant therefore reinforces the veracity of the myth as well as the social efficacy of the artefacts made with the plant.

It is hardly necessary to remark that, in the present state of the anthropology of techniques and objects, no particular approach is more appropriate than another in understanding what people exactly 'do' when they act on the material world. The main challenge, now, is to understand how the phenomena addressed by the various possible approaches are, indeed, linked together within a technical action. Paying attention to the way people 'tell' their techniques is an essential part of this program.

CHAPTER 14

....

FIELDWORK IN ETHNOMATHEMATICS

....

MARC CHEMILLIER

14.1 INTRODUCTION[1]

....

This chapter will focus on the subject of fieldwork research addressing mathematical concepts developed in elaborated traditional knowledge. Its goal is to give advice to fieldworkers from this particular point of view, and to draw their attention to methodological issues with respect to the completeness of data collection during fieldwork and the veracity of the interpretations and analyses subsequent researchers are able to undertake without visiting the field. There is a wide range of activities which might evince mathematical structures such as games (e.g. cat's cradle), kinship structures, poetry, riddles, art and design, music. All belong to the intricate landscape that is ethnomathematics. Their full description involves mathematical concepts taken from various fields such as number theory, geometry, graph theory, algebra, or combinatorics on words. For instance, Stevens (1981) provides a rich collection of two-dimensional patterns from various parts of the world classified according to the crystallographic notions of symmetry. Such a book does not deal with fieldwork, and nothing is said about how to collect such patterns and how native artists conceive them. The same holds for more recent books on a similar subject (see e.g. Horne 2000). Even in works more related to the

[1] The author would like to acknowledge the reviewers for their rich comments which helped to improve this chapter.

'ethno' dimension of ethnomathematics, such as the website *Ethnomathematics in Australia* (Rudder n.d.), the methodology for fieldwork is not dealt with, since these studies are partly motivated by an educational concern about how to teach Western mathematics to Indigenous students. It appears that most of the work in ethnomathematics falls into one of these two categories. Either they are based on existing fieldwork data collection studied by subsequent researchers who have not visited the field, or they are made by fieldworkers working in the particular context of educational activity. As there exist only few studies in ethnomathematics that take account of fieldwork problems, this chapter is restricted to concrete examples, most of them encountered during our fieldwork conducted on the mathematics of divination in Madagascar. It is worth mentioning that many ethnomathematical topics are not covered. Thus the presentation of the Malagasy research takes up a large proportion of this chapter. This is not the place for primary presentation of such a practice and the reader is referred to other papers published elsewhere (Chemillier et al. 2007; Chemillier 2007; 2009). In this chapter I provide some basic definitions to explain the way mathematical concepts are extracted from fieldwork situations.

What is involved in doing mathematics? When playing the cat's cradle game, are the participants doing mathematics or merely engaging in an intricate cultural activity? When we layer western mathematical analyses on the playing of the game, is this 'doing mathematics'? None of these cases corresponds to what we will call 'doing mathematics'. In this chapter, I will refer to the definition of ethnomathematics given by Ascher and Ascher (1986: 125) as 'the study of mathematical ideas of nonliterate peoples'. When someone plays the cat's cradle game, he may only repeat known figures without developing mathematical ideas about them. In the same way, the use of western mathematical concepts to analyse traditional activities does not prove that these activities require mathematical ideas from people doing them (just as the use of symmetry groups in the study of crystal structures does not prove that minerals can have mathematical ideas!). The kind of ideas that we are interested in when doing ethnomathematical fieldwork can be characterized by the following features inspired by Pascal's definition of the 'mathematical mind' (Pascal 2008[1660]: 23). First of all, they are based on principles which are explicit and that one can see fully (e.g. the rules of the Malagasy divination system). Secondly, these principles are removed from ordinary use, and in some cases, there is a shift from reality to abstract speculation by introducing artefacts such as pebbles, notched sticks, knotted cords, seeds (as in the case of Malagasy divination), lines traced on the sand, strings plucked to play music. Note that these artefacts are of no mathematical importance as individual objects, because what is relevant here is their relationship at an abstract level. The third feature of mathematical ideas derived from these principles is that they proceed in a detailed, linear, systematic fashion following a deductive mode of reasoning. As we will see, these three features have direct consequences for fieldwork researchers, in particular with respect to the completeness of their data recording (as Pascal noticed, principles underlying mathematical ideas must be 'plain' and 'palpable').

One must distinguish a mathematical concept and its application. Words for number and for measurement of time, weight, and distance can be involved in mathematical ideas, but they can also be applied to activities not mathematical *per se*. Selling goods at the market place using a weighing machine is business, but it is not mathematics. Words for number and measure are not necessarily organized in a systematic fashion because they are partly determined by practical constraints. For example, traditional measuring methods for short distances took advantage of the practical use of the human body. This gave birth to widespread units such as the foot and the inch (representing the width of a thumb as it is explicit in French, where *pouce* is the translation for both 'inch' and 'thumb'), but these various units were not organized in a logical way. Number words can also have been altered by historical transformations. In French, integers 11–16 are named *onze, douze, treize, quatorze, quinze, seize*, sharing the same suffix *-ze*, whereas 17 is *dix-sept*, without this suffix. This difference is relevant when studying the evolution of the French language from a historical perspective, but it is not relevant from the point of view of mathematicians. In this chapter, we will describe basic mathematical constructions used for number words and measurement units, but we will also point out their practical and historical contingency, which is not relevant in the context of mathematical ideas.

The question of fieldwork in ethnomathematics raises another important issue concerning the relation between language and thought. A famous metaphor by Saussure quoted by Benveniste illustrates their intrinsic link: 'Language can also be compared with a sheet of paper: thought is the front and the sound the back; one cannot cut the front without cutting the back at the same time; likewise in language, one can neither divide sound from thought nor thought from sound' (Benveniste 1971: 45). Nevertheless, ethnomathematical fieldwork brings evidence of the fact that mathematical ideas are sometimes expressed without words and that gestures appear to be a fundamental feature in their development. While one may ask if this is not the case in the development of any ideas, the answer is that the possibility of expressing ideas by means of gestures seems to fit the particular features of what Pascal called the 'mathematical mind' (*esprit de géométrie*) as opposed to the 'intuitive mind' (*esprit de finesse*) (Pascal 2008[1660]: 23). For example, as we will see later in this chapter, it is possible to give a definition of the 'evenness' or the 'oddness' of an integer without saying a single word, by simply moving seeds on a mat. It is much more difficult to do so for holistic notions such as 'beauty' or 'love'. In many cultures all over the world, especially in Africa, a precise system of gestures accompanies the use of number words. It seems obvious in such cases that the recording of language by linguists could efficiently make use of new technological approaches involving more than the simple recording of example words or sentences. This point is dealt with elsewhere in this volume (see above, Seyfeddinipur (Chapter 6) on gesture and Margetts and Margetts (Chapter 1) on recording), but as we will see, it is worth highlighting it with respect to ethnomathematics.

From an ethnomathematical point of view it is useful to make a few observations on the best way to record annotated new media while visiting the field, whether video or computer experiment, in order to make possible afterwards the exploration of their mathematical content. Section two below will be devoted to the question of completeness of data collection during fieldwork, a crucial point in ethnomathematics for checking the consistency of mathematical knowledge embedded in the data. Sections three and four will tackle the question of vernacular lexicons used for numbers and measurement, and we will see that it only partly meet the general goals of an ethnomathematical approach. In section four I discuss the use of measurement terms. The fifth section addresses the question of mathematical operations on approximate quantities (addition, subtraction, comparison) carried out in a society where there are no number words above five. This section focuses on the basic numerical abilities of Munduruku people from Amazonia, and illustrates the use of computer-based fieldwork experiments. The last three sections refer to our research on Malagasy divination, which addresses a more complex traditional knowledge involving elaborated mathematical ideas. First of all, we show how gestures can be used by Indigenous experts as a means of explanation. This case study describes how a diviner explains the distinction between an even and an odd number of seeds. Secondly, we present an experimental task of mental calculation which shows that having a videorecording aids analysis because the transcription of an expert's comments while doing this task reveals afterwards the successive steps of his calculation. In the third example from Madagascar the diviner moves the seeds with his hand in order to execute a complex transformation of a tableau, illustrating a computational rather than explanatory use of gesture. In all these Malagasy examples, I will discuss the vocabulary used by diviners to show that language only makes up a small proportion of the knowledge underlying this complex traditional practice.

14.2 COMPLETENESS AND CONSISTENCY OF DATA COLLECTION DURING FIELDWORK

Some activities in traditional societies seem to rely on a complex set of formal procedures and precise rules that are not easy to describe when doing fieldwork. The development of the field of ethnomathematics has been motivated by the fact that sometimes these sets of rules or procedures appear to have properties of consistency and abstraction which make them close to what we call mathematical ideas, and actually they can be formalized in a mathematical framework. It is crucial to point out that the consistency of such sets of rules cannot be analysed properly if the description of the data lacks some particular element. Ethnologists have to work through every detail of the presentation of the procedures they are studying.

This question goes far beyond the attention to detail that characterizes the work of careful fieldworkers. There is a specific difficulty in the case of ethnomathematics due to the logical dependency linking the completeness of ethnographic data to the consistency of the mathematical knowledge underlying them. Let us take an example to illustrate this point. Traditions of sand drawing in different parts of the world have revealed an interest of native people in a mathematical concept named 'Eulerian path'. It means tracing a figure continuously and covering each line once and only once without lifting the finger from the surface. In order to check that a given path is Eulerian, one has to check that each line is covered 'once and only once' and thus to know exactly how each of them has been traced. As soon as this information is missing for one line, the data are incomplete and the whole mathematical structure becomes unreachable. Fortunately in the case of sand drawing, as we will recall below, we have extant records of these wonderful examples of cultural artefacts. It is not always the case, and one possible reason might be that many anthropologists in the past were limited in their understanding of mathematics. Today, fieldworkers having to record this kind of activity should be advised that the consistency of the described facts must be trusted even when the procedures seem complicated, not to say obscure, because these procedures are probably not at all inconsistent. This applies very well, for instance, to the complex tableaux of seeds used in Malagasy divination that we will study later in this chapter. They are so elaborated that Vérin and Rajaonarimanana (1991: 62) described ethnologists recording the workings of divination as being 'anxious'. As we will see, there exists behind the complexity of divination procedures a strongly consistent mode of thinking.

In his fieldworker's handbook for ethnologists, Mauss noted in 1947:

The most widespread game, reported worldwide, is the string game or cat's cradle. It is one of the most difficult games to describe. The fieldworker should learn how to make every figure so as to be able to reproduce the movements afterwards. It is preferable to use words and sketches to describe the string game since film blurs the figures. To make the sketch indicate the position of the string at each moment and also the direction in which it will be moved so as to pass from one position to the next. The written description will call on a precise vocabulary. (Mauss 2007[1947]: 72)

The string figures of cat's cradle provide a good example of a traditional activity that leads to interesting mathematical problems. In fact how can we characterize the string figures that can be derived from a given one by a combination of simple operations? Some mathematicians have attempted to do so by using elaborated tools called 'knot polynomials' (Stewart 1997; Yamada et al. 1997). From a linguistic point of view, it is possible that in societies where this game is played one can find specific terms used by native people to designate the operations involved in cat's cradle and their combinations into subroutines. For instance, among the Inuit of Pelly Bay in Canada there exist words used for naming different steps of the realization of a figure. The final position is called *ayarauseq*, and various initial positions are called *pauriicoq* or *paurealik*. Even more complex combinations of gestures are named. The word *anitidlugo* has the meaning of a particular subroutine that consists of passing one loop through the other (Vandendriessche 2007: 47).

For such topics involving mathematical ideas in traditional activities that go beyond everyday expertise, it is important to focus on the consistency of the data, as noted earlier, because if they are altered in some way or even incomplete, the formalization of their mathematical content becomes impossible. First of all, fieldworkers have to record the data with the use of appropriate devices such as diagrammatic records. Fortunately, the history of ethnology provides examples of fieldwork conducted by accurate researchers who recorded their data in such a way that their mathematical study has been made possible even a long time afterwards. It is the case for the sand drawings recorded by Bernard Deacon in Vanuatu, as Ascher (1991: 64) notes:

In the 1920s, A. Bernard Deacon studied among the Malekula. With an eye and insight that were especially rare, he collected material that he believed demonstrated mathematical ability and evidence of abstract thought. One of the things he saw as mathematical [...] was 'the amazingly intricate and ingenious' geometrical-figure drawings. He was meticulous in recording about ninety figures, including their exact tracing path.

Let us have a look at the drawing recorded by Deacon reproduced in Fig. 14.1. One can easily recognize the form of a turtle represented on this picture, but there is additional information included in the figure which is very important from our mathematical point of view. All the lines involved in the tracing path have been numbered by Deacon from 1 to 103. Thanks to this crucial information one can have access not only to the form of the drawing but also to the gesture of the native people who produced it. This information allows us to study a particular kind of consistency of the tracing path, which is expressed by the concept of 'Eulerian path'. It appears that most of the sand drawings from Vanuatu are traced in this way. The interest of native people in 'Eulerian path' seems to be shared by different traditions of sand drawing all over the world, not only in Vanuatu but also, for instance, among the Tshokwe of Angola, and it has been studied by various ethnomathematicians (Ascher 1991; Gerdes 1995; 2006).

In Vanuatu an indigenous word is directly related to the tracing path. A figure is called *suon* when the drawing ends at the point from which it began (Ascher

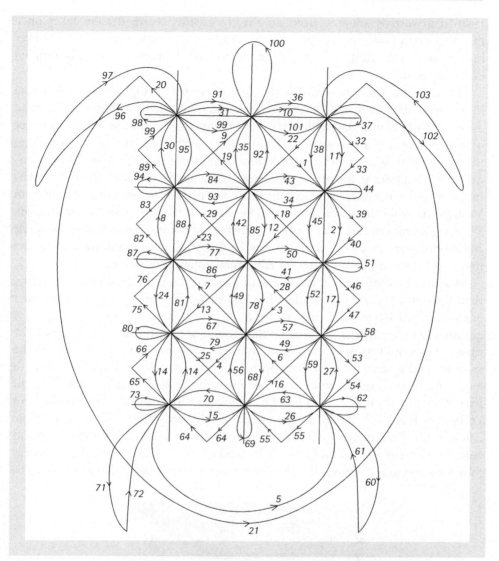

Figure 14.1. Sand drawing from Vanuatu recorded by Deacon (1934). His number-ing of the tracing path shows that each line is covered once and only once in a continuous way, except the jump that occurs between lines 31 and 32 near the head of the turtle.

1991: 45). The word *suon* may have a different meaning in another context, and we will encounter several examples of this type in this chapter. It must be stressed in such cases that the ethnomathematical context gives to the word a new meaning that can be fully understood only when one has a clear understanding of the underlying mathematical procedure. As pointed out by Ascher and Ascher (1986:

126): 'If a word is adopted from an already existing word, it soon takes on a meaning appropriate to its new context. For example, when an English speaker says "a foot" in the context of measurement, no English hearer thinks he is thinking of a body part.'

The fact that Deacon recorded the details of the tracing paths is of crucial importance for the study of the mathematical knowledge embedded in sand drawing. Note that in the particular case of the turtle, the analysis of the sequence of numbers reveals an amazing fact (Chemillier 2002; 2007: 56). Strictly speaking the tracing path is not Eulerian. If you look at it carefully, you will find a discontinuity between lines 31 and 32 (near the head of the turtle). It seems not to be a flaw in the record, since various videos available on the Internet showing people from Vanuatu drawing the turtle always follow the tracing path recorded by Deacon. What is amazing in this case, from a mathematical point of view, is that the turtle could have been traced in a different way, by following Euler's conditions. The fact that it did not remains an unsolved ethnomathematical question.

As soon as a simple detail is missing in the recording of the ethnographic data, then the consistency of the underlying knowledge can be destroyed. In another example taken from our fieldwork on Malagasy divination, Fig. 14.2 shows the gesture of randomly placing seeds on the ground in the process of divination. The diviner takes two fistfuls of seeds from his bag in a random way, and then lumps the seeds into piles on the ground. Then he reduces each pile by deleting the seeds until either one or two are left, and places the remaining seeds in a tableau. On the right part of the picture, the diviner's hand is reducing one pile, and a second pile has not yet been reduced. On the left, some elements have already been placed—a complete column with four entries equal to two, one, two, two, and the beginning of a second column with entries two and one. At the end of the process the final tableau has four rows and four columns, the entries of which can only be one seed or two seeds.

Figure 14.2. Seeds are set up on the ground in Malagasy divination (© 2000 Victor Randrianary). Each randomly chosen pile of seeds is reduced by deleting the seeds two at a time so that at the end only one or two remain.

A fundamental detail is missing in the previous description. When the diviner deletes the seeds of the piles, he does it two at a time with his forefinger and middle finger. It is not very easy to see this on the fixed photograph reproduced in Fig. 14.2, but on the original video from which it has been taken the process is more visible. This detail is of great importance for the consistency of the procedure because it explains why the remaining seeds in each pile can only be one or two seeds. In fact it is a well-known principle of Euclidian division learnt at school that the remainder obtained by dividing an integer is always less than its divisor. This means that the number of possible values for the remainder cannot exceed the value of the divisor. It is precisely the reason why the process of picking up seeds always ends up with one or two seeds, because the diviner picks them up two at a time. Thus in this case the divisor is equal to two and the remainder can only take two values. As we will see later, Malagasy diviners are clearly aware of this mathematical rule, which determines the parity of the number of seeds contained in each fistful that are pulled out of the bag.

14.3 NUMBER WORDS, THEIR MATHEMATICAL CONSTRUCTION, AND THEIR HISTORICAL CONTINGENCY

It is well known that many kinds of numeration systems exist all over the world, which may vary considerably from a few number words to elaborate constructions in which counting extends into the millions. Some societies only have words for 'one', 'two', and a third word signifying 'many'. For example, the Bushmen of South Africa or the communities of the savannah and the tropical forest of South America use very rudimentary numerical systems. We shall discuss later the question of how to describe mathematical abilities in such societies by presenting fieldwork experiments for accessing this kind of ability, a question related to the current debate about Everett's (2005) claim that Pirahã has no number. For the moment, it must be pointed out that numeration systems are developed mainly in relation to practical constraint such as economic need, and that it is obvious in societies in which necessities of life are produced within the community that people do not have to rely on a complex system of counting.

A simple way to represent numbers with sounds is to repeat a simple-sounding event as many times as the value of the number. Actually, this principle is used in the peals of a bell to indicate what time it is. As the value increases, the perception of the corresponding number becomes harder. Thus in languages dealing with numbers not reduced to one, two, and a few positive integer values, the numeration system must involve a grouping of units according to a fixed reference value called a 'base'. Crump noticed that 'the representation of numbers by the single repetition of a simple sound is not to be found in any spoken language' (Crump 1990: 33), highlighting the fact that the construction of number words is not reduced to the simple juxtaposition of units. In most languages, it involves the grouping of units into sets containing a fixed number of elements (the value of the base), and then determining how many such sets can be obtained so that the total amount of units does not exceed the value represented. The representation is thus reduced to two pieces of information: a number of sets and a number of remaining units not grouped into sets. For instance, in the decimal numeration system, the word 'sixty-three' corresponds to the grouping $63 = 6 \times 10 + 3$, which means 'six sets of ten units and three remaining units' ('sixty' and 'three'). This system is called 'decimal' because its base is 10, but in a similar way one can find base-5 systems called 'quinary' or base-20 systems called 'vigesimal'. There exist around the world many systems with different values of the base—10, 5, 20 as previously mentioned, but also 4 or 8, for instance.

Numeration systems can also combine different bases. In such situations, the grouping is first processed with sets containing a number of elements equal to the greater base. The remaining units are then grouped into sets containing a number of elements equal to the next base in decreasing order, and so on. For instance, Zaslavsky noticed that 'counting based on five and twenty, called quinquavigesimal counting, is widespread throughout the world' (1973: 36). Such a system has a word for five; beyond this value, numbers are represented by adding 1, 2, 3, or 4 to combinations of 5, until the secondary base, 20, is reached. Thus twenty-eight is represented by $28 = 1 \times 20 + 1 \times 5 + 3$.

Note that in counting systems where a unique base is defined, there are in fact many grouping sizes which are used, since units are grouped according to the value not only of the base, but also of its square, cube, and successive powers such as 10, 100, 1000 in the decimal system. For instance, the number word for 143 is defined by the decomposition $143 = 1 \times 100 + 4 \times 10 + 3$.

From a linguistic point of view, the construction of number words according to these principles has been analysed by Salzmann (1950), who pointed out three main dimensions. The first is the frame, which consists of a class of elementary numerals (basic words existing in any given language for 1, 2, 3, 4, and so on). The second is the cycle defined by the periodic return of one or several basis terms in the sequence of their successive powers (such as 10, 100, 1000, and so on, in decimal systems) for grouping units to represent numbers. The third is formed by the rules applied to the other two components involving arithmetical operations in order to derive actual patterns of words in the given language, which can express any number used in that language.

The written system of numbers used in western mathematics is called a 'place value system' because the place of a numeral together with its face value determine its meaning. For instance, in 128 the last digit has a value of 8 but the next one does not have a value of 2. Its value is 20 since its place value indicates that it must be multiplied by ten. Thus the digits 1, 2, and 8 in the written representation of 128 correspond to sets of different sizes $128 = 1\times100 + 2\times10 + 8$ in a way that is similar to the grouping of units we have described previously in the oral representation of numbers. As Ascher noticed, there are some similarities between the concepts underlying such a place value system, 'and the cycles and arithmetic relationships that are seen in the number words of many cultures' (Ascher 1991: 23). The main difference is that the mathematical decimal system used for writing numbers in a symbolic form is strongly consistent because the principle of grouping units is applied in a very uniform way which simplifies and enables the progress of arithmetic and calculation, whereas oral systems generally admit exceptions to the rules, or additional rules based on different principles.

For example, in Africa the Yoruba system has an unusual feature because it relies upon subtraction to a very high degree in a way that is similar to some aspects of Roman numerals, as in IX, for instance, which means $10 - 1 = 9$, or to the English reading of time when one says 'twenty (minutes) to three'. Zaslavsky, who studied the system of number words found among the Yoruba, wrote: 'One must be a mathematician to learn this complex system' (Zaslavsky 1973: 204). Some numbers are used as intermediate figures, which means that their successors are calculated as a quantity less than the next higher stage.

The combination of different formulae based on different arithmetic principles can sometimes alter seriously the consistency of the whole system. Lévi-Strauss observed:

As has been emphasized by certain authors, many systems defy all attempts at classification. They make up certain numbers by aggregation and change the formula according to whether the numbers are less than or equal to 10, between 10 and 20, or over 20. Some seemingly identical systems build up the numbers from 6 to 9 and those expressing tens, either by addition or subtraction. (1990[1968]: 336)

French offers a good example of deviance from the base-10 system, which illustrates a change in the formula. For instance, the word for 87 in French is *quatre-vingt-sept* ('four-twenty' and 'seven'), clearly derived from a cyclic pattern with a base of 20. Furthermore, for any number between 80 and 99, the grouping is expressed as a multiple of 20. Thus there are two inconsistent systems that coexist in French: the base-10 decimal system and a base-20 system, probably originating from an older underlying Celtic system. As Crump pointed out: 'The deviant cases often represent lexical survivals' (1990: 36). In fact there is no mathematical reason why French uses a base-10 system for number 60 whereas it uses a base-20 system for number 80. It is not a matter of mathematics, it is a matter of history. There is still a generalization available: that the larger base is used for the larger numbers (and not vice versa). Nevertheless, there is no general and 'palpable' principle able to explain why 60 is not named *trois-vingt* ('three-twenty'); nor is the decimal naming *septante, octante,* and *nonante* used in France for 70, 80, 90 whereas it is in other French-speaking countries (such as Belgium).

14.4 MEASUREMENT OF TIME, WEIGHT, AND DISTANCE IN RELATION TO PRACTICAL CONSTRAINTS

The measurement of time in traditional societies does not necessarily rely on number words. Frequently it is related to the principal activities of the day. Zaslavsky gives examples among the Ankole from Uganda where one talks about 'milking time' (6 a.m., *akasheshe*), 'resting time' (12 noon, *bari omubirago*), 'drawing water time' (1 p.m., *baaza ahamaziba*), 'drinking time' (2 p.m., *amazyo niganywa*) (Zaslavsky 1973: 260). When people in traditional societies reckon time they have to deal with the notion of succession, which implies the possibility of a systematic order based on uniform events. Such events can be of a social nature (natural life cycle between birth and death) or of a physical one (nights and days, seasons). As soon as they return, these events determine a periodic cycle, and its duration can be taken as a reference value for reckoning time. It must be stressed that this value needs not be of a numerical nature. Crump introduces a distinction between linguistic and arithmetical aspects of the measurement of time:

The linguistic system is concerned to name different, and possibly recurrent, points in time, whether these be days, years, or whatever, whereas the arithmetical system measures the lapse of time, again in different units, according to the end in view. The former is characteristic of 'traditional' time, where it is above all important to begin the harvest or observe a festival at the correct time. The latter is pre-eminently an institution of the modern world, in which the use of accurate clocks has enabled time to be equated with other numerical factors, such as distance or money. (Crump 1990: 83)

The events most suitable for the measurement of time are the position of the sun, the moon, the planets, and the stars. The periodic movement of these heavenly bodies in the cosmos is the basis for the reckoning of long time durations. Crump notes: 'This provides the starting point for a system of numeration based on the mathematical theory of congruences, which has been used for counting different units of time—from hours to units comprising several years—in many quite unrelated cultures' (1990: 84). It is not so easy to combine in a consistent way the different periods of the movement of the planets and other heavenly bodies. For instance, as pointed out by Crump, observing the phases of the moon is simple but it is also 'misleading, for any calendar based on it inevitably gets out of step with the seasons' (p. 84). The duration from one full moon to the next appears to be about twenty-nine and a half days, and the solar year is not a multiple of it. Thus the months of the Gregorian calendar are not equal in length, and most of them except February are longer than a true lunar month. Ascher noticed that unlike these various non-congruent cycles, the week is different in kind, because it 'has no intrinsic relationship to any physical cycle; it is, instead, a completely arbitrary grouping of some number of days' (Ascher 2002: 40).

Following these observations, it is not surprising that in many cultures around the world one can find different ways of measuring the periods of time. In Africa, for instance, the Yoruba, Igbo, and Bini of southern Nigeria have a four-day week (Zaslavsky 1973: 64). Among the native people of America, '[t]he numeral type of calendar, in which the series of months or particular months were referred to by means of figures and not descriptive terms, used to be found along a continuous area of the Pacific coast, from the Aleutian Islands and adjacent lands to northern California; inland, the area included part of the River Columbia basin' (Lévi-Strauss 1990[1968]: 338). Some societies between southern Oregon and northern California have a calendar consisting of ten lunar months named after the fingers. In this particular part of America, the total year is the result of the addition of five winter months and five summer months (p. 337).

The fact that time measurement requires the combination of cycles with different periods explains why numerical representations of time generally rely on a multiple base counting system. In the western system of time measurement, 60 is the base for grouping seconds and minutes around the clock, but hours are grouped by 24 according to the duration of the day, and days are grouped by 7 according to the duration of the week. These different bases are combined so that we can perceive durations in an easier way. Let us take an example. Can you perceive the exact duration of 98,745 seconds? You will probably find it a bit difficult, but it should become easier if you represent it as the duration of 'one day three hours twenty-five minutes and forty-five seconds'.

The measurement of weight and distance in societies where there is a need for it makes use of various kinds of auxiliary instruments, such as the ruler for measuring length or the balance for measuring weight. As Crump pointed out, these tools are 'conceptual means by which two different entities can be compared in numerical terms'. For the class to which the measure is applicable, 'this implies that some abstract property is recognized as being common to all members of the class' (Crump 1990: 73). Furthermore, different abstract properties can be linked through the method used for measuring particular aspects of reality. For instance, the area under cultivation 'can be related to time, in terms of the labour input, just as the English acre was originally defined as the area which could be ploughed in a single day' (p. 74).

Let us take an example illustrating a simple but ingenious tool for dividing a given length. In the Solomon Islands, there exist different types of musical wind instruments made of several bamboo tubes called 'panpipes'. Zemp has described the making of this kind of flute:

When cutting new panpipes, the instrument-maker measures octaves not only on two different-sized instruments, but also on pipes of the same instrument. He then either doubles the length of a pipe, or halves it, thus obtaining, respectively, the lower and higher octaves. The instrument-maker then blows simultaneously into the two pipes, to check the accuracy of the tuning by ear. (Zemp 1979: 13)

It is not difficult to double the length of a pipe because you just have to place it in two adjacent positions, but how to 'halve' it? In a film devoted to the making of panpipes, Zemp (1994) reveals the process: the instrument-maker takes a string to measure the length of the pipe, then he joins the two ends of this string and pulls the resulting loop. The length that he obtains is exactly half of the previous one.

Another fascinating activity that led people to measure distances on a much greater scale is the sea travel of navigators from the Central Caroline Islands of the north Pacific. Their ability is known to us thanks to the work of Gladwin (1970). He pointed out the amazing skill developed by each navigator

in judging the speed of his canoe under various conditions of wind, a skill sharpened by long experience, and his attention to the time which has passed as shown by the movement of sun and stars. Strictly speaking, it is not proper even to speak, as I did, of the number of miles the navigator has travelled. In our speech we find it natural to estimate (or measure) distance in arbitrary units. For a Puluwatan the estimate is relative. It is akin to a person walking across a familiar field in the dark. (Gladwin 1970: 184)

There exists a cognitive dimension in this practice that is not of a mathematical nature, since it relies on principles not fully explicit, thus not emanating from the 'mathematical mind'.

14.5 EXPERIMENTAL TASK FOR ACCESSING NON VERBAL NUMERICAL KNOWLEDGE

It is important to point out that the use of language may involve the manipulation of numbers without explicit number words to designate them. In fact, as observed by Schmidl: 'The absence of counting words by no means indicates a lack of counting concepts, since the number concept and the designation for the numbers need not always coincide' (Schmidl 1915: 196, translated by Zaslavsky 1973: 14). Zaslavsky studied African counting systems and observed that standardized gestures often accompany, or even replace, the number words, sometimes in relation to a taboo on counting living creatures (Zaslavsky 1973: 7). In the market-place, for instance, the prices are indicated by moving the fingers. She recorded various systems of gestures by taking a series of photographs (published in Zaslavsky 1973: 243–5, 249–51). Among the Shambaa of northeast Tanzania, some numbers are named on the principle of two equal terms. The number six is named *mutandatu* as the result of adding two equal quantities $6 = 3 + 3$. To illustrate this, she gives a picture of a man showing the last three fingers of his two hands (p. 30). The same holds for eight, which is named *ne na ne* as the result of adding $8 = 4 + 4$. She remarks that during fieldwork, when one has to record properly the gesture involved in the representation of numbers, 'only motion pictures can do justice to this gesture' (p. 241). (See also Seyfeddinipur, Chapter 7 above.)

In many languages all over the world there exists evidence of a former use of gestures for expressing numbers in ancient counting systems. The name for 'five' often comes from the number of fingers on a person's hand. The corresponding word is often the same as 'hand', and in some languages where twenty is used as a base, the name for it is 'man complete', which means 'ten fingers of both hands and ten toes of both feet'. Lévi-Strauss gives examples from Mexico and Central America where twenty is the 'complete number': 'It was referred to by a word meaning "a body" in Yaqui, "a person" in Opata, "a man" in Maya-Quiché and also in Arawak, so that the practice extended also to the northern regions of South America' (Lévi-Strauss 1990[1968]: 336). Note that conversely, the word for 5 can be used to designate the hand as in English, where a 'high five' means a hand gesture that occurs when two people simultaneously raise one hand and push the flat of their palm against the one of their partner. The same holds in Madagascar, where young people sometimes replace the word 'hand' by the world 'five' (*dimy*) in expressions such as '*Raiso ny dimy*', which means 'Let us beat one's hand', that is to say 'Agreed'.

Recent work on the subject of numerical abilities in various cultural contexts tends to prove that sophisticated competence can be present in the absence of a rich lexicon of number words. We will give examples that are interesting for our purpose because they illustrate the use of new technologies in fieldwork research, namely computerized experiments. It concerns numerical cognition in native speakers of Munduruku, a language of the Tupi family from the Para state of Brazil where one can find number words only for the numbers 1 through 5. The research team collected trials in classical arithmetical tasks on a computer, including a chronometric comparison test. With such technologies they were able to test whether competence for numerical operations such as addition or comparison are present in the absence of a well-developed language for numbers (Pica et al. 2004). Later the same team enriched their fieldwork by studying core knowledge of geometry (Dehaene et al. 2006).

The first task consisted in presenting displays of 1 to 15 dots in randomized order, and asking the people in their native language to say how many dots were present. As can be expected due to the limitation of the numerical lexicon, there was little consistency in language use above five. For instance, a response to 13 dots was: 'all the fingers on the hands and then some more'. The word for 5, which can be translated as 'one hand' or 'a handful', was used for 5 but also 6, 7, 8, 9 dots. The authors conclude: 'With the exception of the words for 1 and 2, all numerals were used in relation to a range of approximate quantities rather than to a precise number' (Pica et al. 2004: 500). Furthermore, they remark: 'This response pattern is comparable to the use of round[ed] numbers in Western languages, for instance when we say "10 people" when there are actually 8 or 12.'

This by no means indicates that these peoples are unable to achieve arithmetic operations on approximate numbers. This was established by an approximate addition task, which is thought to be independent of language in western participants. Simple animations on the laptop screen illustrated a physical addition of two large sets of dots into a can. The participants had to approximate the result and compare it to a third set. Munduruku participants had no difficulty in adding and comparing approximate numbers, with a precision identical to that of the French controls (i.e. a group of native speakers of French who were asked to do the same tests).

The question then arose of the ability of Munduruku speakers to manipulate exact numbers. An exact subtraction task was proposed to the participants, who were asked to predict the outcome of a subtraction of a set of dots from a given set (see Fig. 14.3). The displayed animation showed a set of n_1 dots entering the can and another set of n_2 dots coming out of it. The question was: how many dots remain in the can? The initial number of dots n_1, could be up to 8 dots, but the result of the subtraction $n_3 = n_1 - n_2$, was always small enough to be named. Participants responded by pointing to the correct result among three alternatives n_3, (0, 1, or 2 objects left: see Fig. 14.3). It appeared that the Munduruku were close to 100 per cent correct when the initial number was below 4, but their performance decreased sharply as the size of the initial number n_1 increased.

The authors conclude:

Our results shed some light on the issue of the relation between language and arithmetic. They suggest that a basic distinction must be introduced between approximate and exact mental representations of number [. . .]. With approximate quantities, the Munduruku do not behave qualitatively differently from the French controls. They can mentally represent very large numbers of up to 80 dots, far beyond their naming range, and do not confuse number with other variables such as size and density. They also spontaneously apply concepts of addition, subtraction and comparison to these approximate representations. (p. 502)

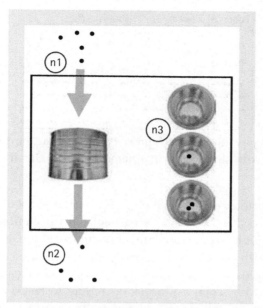

Figure 14.3. Screen display of an exact subtraction task (Pica et al. 2004). The animated picture shows n_1 dots entering the can, then n_2 dots coming out of it. The subject is asked to choose on the right the correct number of dots n_3 remaining in the can.

14.6 GESTURES AS A MEANS OF EXPLANATION FOR MATHEMATICAL CONCEPTS

As there exist numbers without number words, there is also mathematical knowledge without verbalization. We will give examples taken from our fieldwork on Malagasy divination illustrating such situations, and will describe techniques that can be used to access this kind of non-verbal knowledge. As we will see, the fact that this knowledge is not of a verbal nature does not mean that its lexicon is empty, but the meaning of the words of this lexicon cannot be accessed without an understanding of the related knowledge.

The figures used in Malagasy divination are based on one or two seed elements arranged by fours. As each of these four elements can only take two values (one or two seeds), their combination gives $2 \times 2 \times 2 \times 2 = 16$ possible such figures. These are all displayed in Fig. 14.4 with their vernacular name, some of them derived from Arabic terms, since Malagasy divination has its origin in Arabic geomancy (e.g. *tareky* derives from *al-tarîq* meaning 'the way, the pass'). Malagasy diviners group them according to a particular predefined classification. Eight figures are designated princes (*mpanjaka*) while the others are called slaves (*andevo*). This

Princes (*mpanjaka*)								Slaves (*andevo*)							
alokola	*alohotsy*	*adalo*	*alasady*	*adabarà*	*tareky*	*asombola*	*alotsimay*	*alikisy*	*alakarabo*	*alakaosy*	*reniliza*	*alibiavo*	*karija*	*alimizandà*	*alaimora*
•	••	•	•	••	•	••	••	••	•	••	•	••	•	•	••
••	•	••	•	••	•	••	•	••	••	•	••	••	•	•	•
••	••	•	••	•	•	••	•	••	•	•	••	•	•	••	••
•	•	••	••	•	•	••	••	•	•	•	••	••	••	•	••

Figure 14.4. Malagasy divination figures based on one or two seed elements arranged by fours, with their vernacular name and their classification into princes and slaves.

classification into princes and slaves is given Fig. 14.4. If you look carefully at them, you will find that each series shares a particular mathematical property. Before discussing this property, let us elaborate on the practical use of this classification.

In proceeding with the divination, particular figures are set up by randomly choosing piles of seeds, as we saw at the beginning of this chapter, and additional figures are computed by applying formal operations to be explained later. Thereafter, figures obtained in this way are read according to some basic rules related to their predefined classification. A principle for interpreting the randomly generated data given by the seeds is that princes are more powerful than slaves. In her seminal article of 1997 on *sikidy* divination, which is the starting point of our works on the subject, Ascher gives an example of a divination session related to illness that makes use of this relationship (Ascher 1997: 389). When the client appears to be a slave while the illness is a prince, the former is dominated by the latter so that the illness is considered to be serious.

The mathematical criterion that distinguishes princes from slaves among the figures is the evenness of their total number of seeds. It is easy to verify in Fig. 14.4 that princes can have four, six, or eight seeds, each of which is an even number, whereas slaves can have five or seven seeds, each of which is an odd number. During fieldwork it appeared to be difficult to establish such a relationship between the native classification into princes and slaves and the mathematical property of evenness. When asking questions such as: 'What is particular concerning the number of seeds of the princes?', the answer always was: 'They can have four, six, or eight seeds', with no mention of the particular property of evenness shared by these numbers. In fact, how do we express such an abstract concept as evenness? I have made many attempts to do so in the context of fieldwork, but did not succeed until the answer came up in an unexpected way, as we will see.

One day the diviner we were working with put all the princes on the ground and said, 'I will show you something.' The elements of the figures consist of one or two seeds and the diviner grouped the seeds by two in each prince containing isolated seeds. At the end all the princes were reduced to pairs, and he concluded that the result is *tsy ota*. Then he put all the slaves on the ground and grouped the seeds by two in the same way, but as the number of seeds was odd he removed one remaining seed in each of them. He said that the result was *ota*. The English translation for *ota* is 'sin' and *tsy ota* means 'no sin'. The diviner's comment suggests that the grouping procedure succeeded in the case of princes (no sin) because all the isolated seeds have been grouped by two, whereas it failed in the case of slaves.

The diviner's procedure may be considered as a mathematical definition of evenness. In this context the expressions *ota* and *tsy ota* can be translated into the English words 'odd' and 'even' respectively. It is interesting to note that there is a negative connotation associated with the numerical notion of oddness. The same holds in English, where 'odd' can mean bizarre and may also be used to indicate something not paired properly ('an odd glove'). A similar remark can be made in French where the word *impair* ('odd') can be used as a noun with the meaning of a blunder.

It is obvious that in such cases the recording of the mathematical meaning of the terms involves more than the simple recording of example words or sentences. It relies to some degree upon the detailed recording of the corresponding gestures. In this example, the ethnographer is expected to have learnt about the use of the pair of fingers for grouping seeds and noted it by tracing a precise diagram in their notebook, or taking a picture of the seeds as shown in Fig. 14.5. Furthermore, as we

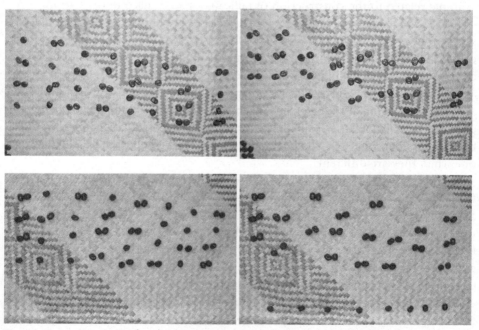

Figure 14.5. Evenness (top) and oddness (bottom) of the number of seeds in each figure (© 2001 Annick Armani). Seeds can be grouped by pairs in (a) and (b), whereas in (c) and (d) one isolated seed remains in each figure.

have pointed out, it was not easy to ask for such an explanation. Actually, when the diviner gave us this explanation for the first time, we were not able to fully understand what he did with the seeds. In this case the video recording was clearly helpful, as we were able to play his gestures back again at night and ask him for the same explanation the next day. This is a simple example showing to some degree that having a video recording of the relevant activity aided analysis. In the next section, the example of a test situation better illustrates the use of video recording an experiment involving computer animation.

14.7 EXPERIMENTAL TASK INDUCING THE VERBALIZATION OF AN ACTION

There are some simple techniques to induce the verbalization of an action. When people are placed in unusual conditions to carry out a task, they have a tendency to talk to themselves while achieving the successive steps of their task. A computer can be the appropriate tool for creating these particular conditions, and here I give an example related to the construction of tableaux of seeds used in divination.

As we have seen, the divination procedure begins with the placing of a tableau of seeds on the ground. The first part of the tableau, called the mother-*sikidy*, consists of four rows and four columns, the elements of which are single or double dots chosen randomly by taking piles of seeds and reducing their content two at a time, as we have described earlier. Then a second part is computed consisting of eight additional columns of four elements each called the 'daughters', placed below the previous ones. They are obtained as the addition of figures according to the rule that adding their one- or two-seed elements gives two when they are identical and one when they are different.

Successive generations of daughters are thus computed, the first ones deriving from the rows and columns of the mother-*sikidy* and the following ones deduced from the preceding. We will denote the eight daughters P_9 to P_{16} according to the position where they are placed in the lower part of the tableau. Fig. 14.6 shows the first three steps of the process. Daughter P_{15} (named *safary*) is computed as the addition of mother-*sikidy* columns P_1 and P_2. Then daughter P_{13} (named *asorità*) is computed as the addition of mother-*sikidy* columns P_3 and P_4. The third step is the computation of second-generation daughter P_{14} (named *saily*), which derives from the two previous ones and is placed between them. In this example, the second-generation daughter P_{14} *saily* contains the figure one, one, two, two resulting from the two neighbouring first-generation daughters P_{13} *asorità* with figure one, one, one, two, and P_{15} *safary* with figure two, two, one, two.

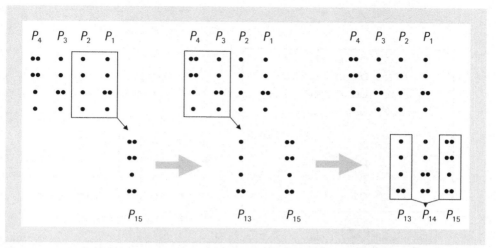

Figure 14.6. First three steps of the computation of daughters denoted P_9 to P_{16} according to their position. Daughters P_{15} (*safary*) and P_{13} (*asorità*) are first computed as the addition of mother-*sikidy* columns, then P_{14} (*saily*) is computed as the addition of its two neighbours.

The whole process involves much more than the computation of first- and second-generation daughters P_{15}, P_{13}, P_{14} derived from the mother-*sikidy* columns. On the left part of the tableau, three more daughters P_{11}, P_9, P_{10} are derived from the mother-*sikidy* rows, which are read from right to left. Daughter P_{11} is derived from the first two rows, followed by P_9 derived from the last two rows, and P_{10} between them results from the addition of both. Then a new-generation daughter P_{12} is placed at the middle (third generation) by adding P_{10} and P_{14}. At last, a fourth-generation one P_{16} is placed at the rightmost position by adding P_{12} and P_r.

During fieldwork we discovered that diviners are able to compute the whole series of eight daughters in a strictly mental way, that is to say by saying the name of the corresponding figures without laying out the seeds. In order to study this mathematical skill we designed a computerized experiment similar to the ones previously described among the Munduruku of Amazonia. A few series of screen displays were prepared showing *sikidy* tableaux where all the daughters were hidden but one. The participant had to check if the visible daughter was correct according to the mother-*sikidy* displayed above it and to press a specific key to answer yes or no (Chemillier 2007; Chemillier et al. 2007). To achieve this unusual task, the diviner began to talk to himself by mentioning all the intermediate operations he was doing in his mind. Fig. 14.7 shows a screen display taken from this experiment with seven hidden figures among the eight daughters, and the corresponding full tableau (further examples are given in Chemillier 2009). The question was whether or not figure one, two, one, two was correct as the third-generation daughter P_{12}. The answer is no, since the correct figure is two,

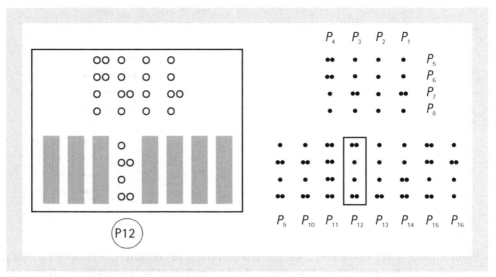

Figure 14.7. Screen display of an experimental task about the mental computation of daughters (on the left). The displayed daughter P_{12} (one, two, one, two) is wrong, since the third–generation daughter should be (two, one, one, two) as shown on the right.

one, one, two as shown Fig. 14.8. In proceeding with the task the diviner first pronounced the following words: '*Alibiavo safary, alasady saily, karija asorità . . .*'. According to the name of the figures (see Fig. 14.5) and the position in the tableau (see Fig. 14.6), this could be translated into: 'figure two, two, one, two at position P_{15}, figure one, one, two, two at position P_{14}, figure one, one, one, two at position P_{13} . . .'.

The diviner's comment proves that in order to check the proposed daughter, he had to compute in his mind some daughters of the older generation as intermediate results. The amazing fact is that he mentioned a second-generation daughter (*saily*, P_{14}) before the first-generation one from which it derives (*asorità*, P_{13}). This is evidence of the fact that the second-generation daughter is computed by the diviner not as the addition of two first-generation daughters but directly from the mother-*sikidy*. Diviners are probably aware of a particular mathematical property. Since P_{15} and P_{13} are obtained by adding respectively the two rightmost and the two leftmost columns of the mother-*sikidy*, then P_{14} is obtained as the sum of the four mother-*sikidy* columns. Thus its four elements are determined by the parity of the mother-*sikidy* rows, which in this case are odd, odd, even, even (or slave, slave, prince, prince in the language of diviners), so that P_{14} contains figure one, one, two, two. The point that must be stressed is that when the diviners were asked about the way they compute the daughter columns, they always answered by referring to the formal definition of the daughters indicated in Fig. 14.6, that is to say P_{14} obtained by the addition of P_{13} and P_{15}, not to the actual computation they achieved in their

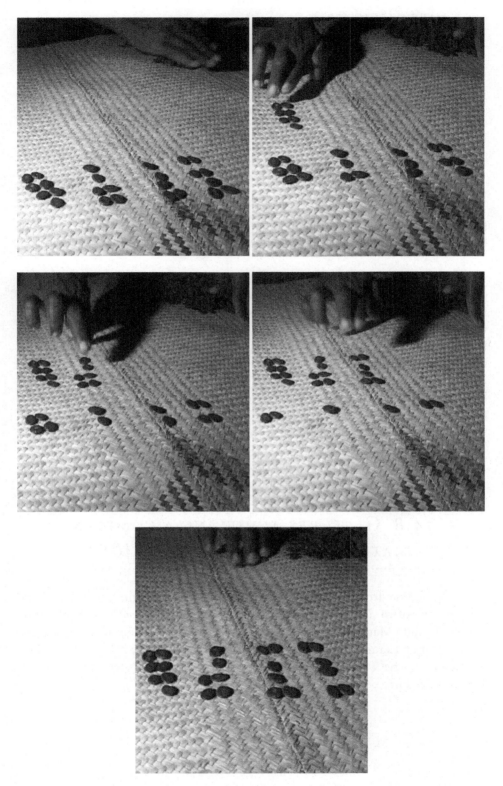

Figure 14.8.(a) Videorecording of the successive steps of a transformation of the mother-*sikidy* by exchanging rows and columns (© Victor Randrianary).

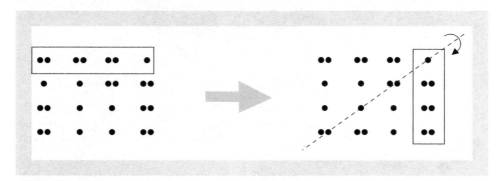

Figure 14.8.(b) As shown in the diagram above, the transformation is a reflection by the second diagonal starting from the top right.

mind. From a linguistic point of view, it appears that the simple recording of verbal explanations given by the native expert fails to access this kind of knowledge. We have designed various experimental tasks of this kind when at base between two fieldwork trips with the help of two cognitive psychologists involved in the project, Denis Jacquet and Marc Zabalia. Such experiments can easily be used and adapted in the field, since they are based on simple software environments (the one we used in this case was SuperLab[2]). As shown in this example, researchers involved in linguistic fieldwork dealing with ethnomathematical activities should be aware of the fact that new technologies are sometimes a necessary tool for understanding what native people think beyond what they say.

14.8 Gestures achieving a complex mathematical transformation

In the quotation from Mauss at the beginning of this chapter, he advised the fieldworker not to use film in recording cat's cradle figures since 'film blurs the figures'. Despite Mauss's recommendation, we will give as the final case study of this chapter an example related to the tableaux of seeds where it appears that film (as video) can be a useful tool for recording the successive steps of a complex formal procedure.

---

[2] http://www.superlab.com/

Fig. 14.8 shows a series of pictures taken from a video shot during fieldwork. If you look carefully, you can see a particular type of transformation applied to the seeds of the mother-*sikidy*. The upper row read from right to left (one, two, two, two) is displaced and oriented in the vertical direction. Then the second row (two, two, one, one) is transformed in the same way and placed as a new column beside the previous one. The same operation is applied to the other rows so that at the end of the process a new mother-*sikidy* is obtained in which rows and columns have been exchanged. The diagram displayed following the series of pictures in Fig. 14.8 summarizes the whole process. Notice that the first two rows are equal to the corresponding columns, since the mother-*sikidy* is partly symmetrical.

This operation creates a new matrix by inverting rows and columns of the initial one. Thus it is similar to the matrix transposition used in linear algebra, except that in mathematics the reflection is done by the main diagonal, which starts from the top left, whereas in *sikidy* divination it is done by the second diagonal, which starts from the top right. Obviously, the properties of a transpose in matrix algebra are not drawn in the context of divination since they are mainly related to the matrix product, which does not seem to be relevant in this context as far as we know. Recall that the transpose is used for defining an 'orthogonal matrix', which is a square matrix whose product with their transpose is equal to the identity matrix. Despites the fact that the function of matrix transposition is different in the context of divination, as we will explain, it is worth mentioning that there exists a close similarity between this transformation and the formal operation used by mathematicians.

Malagasy diviners use a specific word *avaliky* to name this formal transformation in the south of the country. The corresponding verb is *mivaliky*, which means 'to invert'. In official Malagasy it corresponds to the verb *mivadika* because in the dialect of the south words are often derived by replacing the letter 'd' by the letter 'l' (in fact the word for divination itself in the South is *sikily*). For instance, a sentence like '*Mivadika ny akanjoko*' ('inverted-the-shirt') can be translated into 'I put my shirt on the wrong way round'.

What is the function of matrix transposition in *sikidy* divination? The diviner's interest for this formal procedure is related to particular types of tableaux that are of great importance in their practice. One of them is called *fohatse*, and refers to tableaux where the same figure is repeated many times among both its mother-*sikidy* and daughters. Noël Gueunier, a linguist specializing in southwestern Malagasy dialects, noticed that *fohatse* is a variant of the word *vokatse*, which is used in the south with the meaning of 'coming out of the earth' (Chemillier et al. 2007: 28). Lanto Raonizanany, a member of our fieldwork team, observed that the corresponding word in official Malagasy is *vokatra* (with the usual suffix replacement leading to 'tra' instead of 'tse') and that its meaning is 'harvest' so that one can say, for instance, *Vokatra ny katsaka* ('harvest-the-maize') meaning 'the harvest will give a lot of maize'. A possible explanation could be that the repetition of a figure in a tableau called *fohatse* is compared to an abundant harvest of maize ear (or whatever cereal it might be).

The relation between the repetition of a figure in a tableau and the exchange of rows and columns in its mother-*sikidy* relies on the following property. If a figure is repeated at least n times, then the same figure is repeated at least $n-1$ times in the new tableau obtained by transposing the mother-*sikidy*. Indeed, the matrix transposition preserves most of the daughters of the initial *sikidy* tableau. In Fig. 14.9 the daughters are the same in both tableaux except that some of them have been permuted. The three daughters on the right P_{13}, P_{14}, P_{15} have been exchanged with the three daughters on the left P_9, P_{10}, P_{11}; the daughter P_{12} in the middle remains unchanged. The only daughter that can be changed in this process is P_{16}. The tableau *fohatse* on the left is called *adabarà sivy*, which means 'nine occurrences of figure *adabarà* (two, two, one, one)'. One can easily verify that this figure is repeated nine times (namely at position P_2, P_5, P_6, P_9, P_{10}, P_{12}, P_{13}, P_{15}, P_{16}), and that the tableau obtained on the right by transposing the mother-*sikidy* is also *fohatse* with eight occurrences of the same figure (namely at position P_1, P_2, P_3, P_9, P_{11}, P_{12}, P_{13}, P_{14}).

Generally speaking, the *fohatse* property applies to tableaux where the repeated figure occurs at least seven times. It follows that tableaux with at least eight repetitions of the same figure always give a new *fohatse* when their mother-*sikidy* is transposed. Notice that in Fig. 14.9, the second column P_2 is equal to the second row P_6. More generally, as soon as a figure is repeated many times among the positions of a tableau, it is obvious that the rows of the mother-*sikidy* tend to be

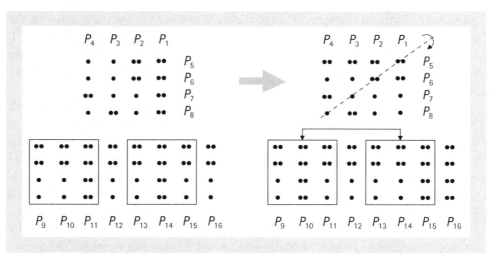

Figure 14.9. The matrix transposition applied to the mother-*sikidy* preserves the daughters by permuting some of them. The *fohatse* tableau on the left with nine repetitions of figure two, two, one, one remains *fohatse* on the right with eight repetitions.

equal to the corresponding columns, so that the mother-*sikidy* becomes partly symmetrical. In most cases, when the number of repetitions of a figure in a tableau takes the greatest possible value, the mother-*sikidy* becomes fully symmetrical, that is to say equal to its transpose. Diviners are aware of these mathematical results, and the function of matrix transposition is clearly to preserve formal properties such as the *fohatse* property, and others of the same kind that are considered as strongly powerful at the symbolic level.

14.9 Conclusion

To sum up the ideas that we have developed in this chapter, it appears that linguistic fieldwork dealing with ethnomathematics has to cope with two kinds of relation between language and mathematical ideas. On the one hand, words for number and measurement are partly based on mathematical constructions more or less related to the theory of congruence, as we have seen in numeration systems with different bases, or measurement systems with various units. These specific lexicons may reflect mathematical ideas from people using them, but their consistency is limited in some way by the conjunction of historical transformations and practical constraints which are not of a mathematical nature. On the other hand, the development of mathematical ideas does not necessarily require a rich lexicon to express them. It also appears that gesture can play an important role in the creation of mathematical ideas, be they geometrical, algebraic, or simply logical. The relatively small size of the set of words involved in this process may be related to the fact that, as opposed to the scientific tradition of literate societies, mathematical activities of non-literate peoples need not be transmitted in a systematic, normalized, and exhaustive way. We have observed during fieldwork on *sikidy* divination that the exploration of their mathematical system by Malagasy diviners was carried out in a quite solitary way. Moreover, part of the knowledge that they develop during their activity is kept secret, as it contributes to their prestige.

How, then, to record ethnomathematical knowledge when doing linguistic fieldwork? The fact that gesture appears to be an essential dimension in the expression of mathematical ideas does not mean that no words are used in this context. On the contrary, we have described in this chapter many examples of already existing words taking on a new meaning when they were adapted to a mathematical context. A first lesson that can be drawn from our observations is that the vocabulary used in these activities must be recorded in close relation to the gestures that express the corresponding ideas with the help of accurate systems of notation. Activities of this type in traditional societies rely on precise procedures and formal rules, which need to be recorded with extreme care if one wants to preserve their consistency and allow subsequent study from a mathematical point of view. It requires from fieldworkers an ability to make use of appropriate diagrammatic records in order to faithfully capture the whole thing (Deacon's notation of the tracing path of sand drawings is a reference example from this point of view).

The second lesson that can be drawn is that video can be a useful tool for recording the successive steps of formal transformations provided that the centring of the image is done properly and that the recording is made of the whole process from beginning to end. Obviously, the ethnographer may note the details of the procedure without a video recording, but the use of media is clearly helpful. Furthermore, as I have shown in this chapter, it happens that important gestures can escape notice, and in this case the ability to play back a video recording is essential to the ethnographer. We have encountered this situation when a diviner moved the seeds on the mat to explain the difference between an even and an odd number of seeds. The same holds for the gesture we have described about the matrix transposition of a mother-*sikidy*. One can even say, in this case, that the advantage of video recording applies to the second situation to a much higher degree, since in the first case, the diviner's purpose was clearly to point out something with his fingers so that the attention of the ethnographer was drawn to his gesture, whereas in the second, his purpose was to make the gesture for himself without any intention of communicating.

Finally, a third lesson can be drawn from this study with the aim of promoting computer experiments during fieldwork (see also Majid, Chapter 2 above). As we have seen in two different situations (basic numerical abilities of Munduruku peoples and complex mental calculation of Malagasy diviners), specific tests using a computer can provide additional information on some aspects of the knowledge of native peoples that are not expressed as a verbal comment on their activity. Moreover, in the case of Malagasy diviners, we have seen that the test situation provides an efficient means for inducing the verbalization of an action. In such situations, the role of video recording is essential in assisting analysis, since the capture of an expert's comments needs to be synchronized with the corresponding screen display, so that the ethnographer can transcribe and analyse them afterwards in order to fully understand the underlying cognitive process.

CHAPTER 15

···

CULTURAL ASTRONOMY FOR LINGUISTS

···

JARITA HOLBROOK

15.1 INTRODUCTION

···

Humans have a long history of watching the sky and incorporating the sky into their culture in the form of art and stories. They developed uses for the sky such as for timekeeping and night navigation. As with other parts of their natural environment, humans continued to watch and learn about the sky to better their lives throughout their history, resulting in an aspect of environmental adaptation that is often overlooked by scholars today. This chapter begins with definitions presented as a first step towards thinking about the many ways that people relate to the sky. This crash course in cultural astronomy should enable the reader to collect relevant information with some rigor and confidence. The interdisciplinary field of cultural astronomy is currently dominated by astronomers, and my personal goal here is to increase linguists' awareness of astronomy as a topic in field research, leading to them attending cultural astronomy meetings and publishing in cultural astronomy journals.

15.2 DEFINITIONS OF CULTURAL ASTRONOMY

Cultural astronomy is broadly defined as the study of the relationship between humans and the sky. There are a couple of working definitions that provide details of this relationship such as that of Campion (1997: 1): 'the use of astronomical knowledge, beliefs or theories to inspire, inform or influence social forms and ideologies, or any aspect of human behaviour.' There are also the very functional concerns of archaeoastronomers set out by Ruggles (1993), rephrased in Bates and Bostwick (2000), and modified here for a linguistic audience:

1. Observation. What do people look at in the sky? Is there a celestial body that they look for repeatedly? Do they make predictions about the next appearance of a celestial body? There is a question as to whether non-academic sky watchers understand the physical forces underlying the celestial motions—the expectation is that they do not. Nonetheless, predictions can be made from long-term repeated observations without physical forces or formulae, and many cultures have done this, for example, predicting when the Pleiades star cluster will appear in the night sky.
2. Perception. What meaning do people attach to that which is observed—what is the cultural significance of the observations? This overlaps with cultural/ethno-classification systems.
3. Use. How do people use the sky? Use of the sky can be entwined with religion, agricultural timings, environmental adaptation, sociopolitical structures, or survival such as navigation by the stars.

Archeoastronomers study the physical remains of earlier societies to understand their observations, perceptions, and use of the sky (simply put, archeoastronomers tend to study dead cultures). Cultural astronomy encompasses these efforts, but cultural astronomers studying contemporary cultures have additional concerns, including:

1. Cosmology. 'In so-called primitive societies, cosmologies help explain the relationship of human beings to the rest of the universe and are therefore closely tied to religious beliefs and practices' (Anon. 2004b). Cosmology is how people tie together their cultural origin story as well as explaining why things are the way they are today. Often the celestial realm is included as part of creation: how the stars got in the sky (which is informative about cultural aspects of knowledge of stars), why the stars are not visible during the day, why the Moon has dark spots, and so on. Similarly, how did the Moon, Milky Way, planets, and meteors (shooting stars) get into the sky? How are the things in the sky related to things on Earth?
2. Stellification. People create asterisms (groups of stars) which they identify with people, animals, and environmental features such as rivers and oceans. How are

these associations chosen—who gets their place in the sky and why? It has been theorized that storytelling plays a major role in what names are created and passed down, especially those reflecting events in local history such as migration stories. The idea is that the groups of stars are mnemonic devices that aid in telling the associated stories. The story of Perseus (below) is an example.

3. Static or evolving sky knowledge. Is their cosmology and resulting sky knowledge static, or are changes and 'evolution' built in? A way to probe this is to ask about transient phenomena such as eclipses, comets, and meteor showers. A related theme is the loss of sky knowledge: do people see their sky knowledge as changing, and what do they see as the future of their sky knowledge? They may hold to the myth of the Golden Age in which people today believe that the generations before them had more knowledge, were more skilled, lived better lives, etc. This is where checking the ethnographic record and other historical documents can be informative.

4. Acquisition and transmission of knowledge. The origins, evolution, and projected future of knowledge concerning the sky. How do people learn about the sky? Who holds what kind of sky knowledge? What is common knowledge and what is specialized knowledge?

5. Cross-cultural sky and formal education. How do people negotiate or reconcile sky knowledge that they learn in school with that of their culture? For example, four planets are easily visible in the night sky (Venus, Mars, Jupiter, and Saturn), yet students are taught there are eight or nine planets in our solar system—two or three cannot be seen with the naked eye. How is this 'correct' yet invisible knowledge handled?

6. Historical remnants. In another twist on the cross-cultural sky, there is the opportunity to investigate if celestial terms are borrowed from neighbours, trade partners, or European languages. For example, the names of the outer planets should all be from European languages, since they were only discovered in the last two centuries and are not visible without the aid of a telescope. Scholars have a detailed understanding of western, Egyptian, Islamic, Babylonian, and Chinese astronomy and astrology and it is possible to tease out elements of these in local cultures, thus revealing the possibility of historical contact. Calendar elements such as the days of the week are common cultural borrowings.

These are the broader issues explored by cultural astronomy researchers. In order to address these issues, data collection methods amount to learning as much as possible about the sky within a culture. In order to identify celestial bodies correctly in the field, researchers first need to learn the sky in their local culture. Learning the sky at home can be a phenomenological experience that aids in both learning the sky in the field and asking better questions about the sky during data collection.

15.3 LEARNING THE NIGHT SKY

Holbrook and Baleisis (2008), a primer aimed at undergraduate students who have no stargazing experience and little astronomy knowledge, includes some simple exercises for learning how to measure distances across the sky. This chapter is aimed at academics who are not used to stargazing yet are very good at learning and processing information and are familiar with astronomy and the names of celestial bodies. In the 1920s, astronomers successfully worked together to standardize the names of celestial bodies and the constellation boundaries, which resulted in the International Astronomical Union (IAU) names used today by astronomers all over the world (cf. Delporte 1930). I will use these IAU names throughout this chapter unless otherwise indicated.

15.3.1 Star charts

A map of the sky at home and at the field site is essential; these maps are called star charts and they can be generated for a particular latitude and longitude, day, hour, and direction. Star charts as well as planispheres (which are round star charts with the North or South Celestial Pole in the centre) can be purchased, or it is possible to create simple charts of black stars on white backgrounds online.[1] The charts can be scaled up or down in angular size and include as much or little detail as desired.

In the Northern Hemisphere the North Celestial Pole is marked by Polaris[2]—the Pole Star. It is part of the constellation Ursa Minor—the Little Dipper. The motion of the stars over the duration of a night is due to the Earth's rotation about its axis: the stars appear to rotate around Polaris and Polaris appears not to move. When learning the night sky in the Northern Hemisphere, Polaris/Ursa Minor and the surrounding constellations are an easy place to start. While there is no convenient star that marks the South Celestial Pole, the Magellanic Clouds and the Southern Cross are often used as starting points for finding constellations in the Southern Hemisphere. Note that the Milky Way (our galaxy) is very bright in the Southern Hemisphere. The Southern Cross lies along the Milky Way with its long axis pointing towards the South Celestial Pole (see Figs 15.5 and 15.6).

Star charts with black stars on white backgrounds are easiest to use at night. A free software program that can be used to study the night sky before going outside is

---

[1] http://www.fourmilab.ch/cgi-bin/Yourhorizon

[2] The names of stars and constellations used here are those adopted by the International Astronomical Union (cf. Delporte 1930), recognizing that, of course, they are entrenched in the western scientific view of the sky.

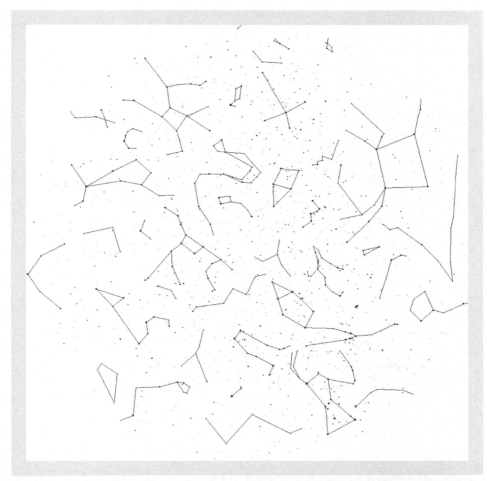

Figure 15.1. Northern Hemisphere star chart with the North Celestial Pole at the centre.

Stellarium.[3] Though there are several other free and commercial night sky software tools (McCool 2009), I find that Stellarium produces the most accurate night sky images. The latitude, longitude, date, and hour can be changed within the program to replicate what can be seen in the sky. In addition, it is possible to pan right/left and up/down. The representation is realistic in that there is daytime, sunset, twilight, and night with progressively fading light over time. Atmospheric effects such as a marine layer haze near the horizon can be added. However, the white stars on black background are very hard to see when working outside at night in the dark, and the night mode, which converts the white to red, is not much better.

[3] http://stellarium.sourceforge.net

Figure 15.2. Northern Hemisphere star chart as in Fig. 15.1, with constellation names added.

Stellarium can generate realistic images of the sky at a particular field site on a particular date, which makes it great for practising learning what constellations are on the eastern or western horizon at sunset or sunrise, which constellations should be visible to the north, etc. It is simple to click the constellation names and boundaries off and on during practice. When actually gathering night sky information with informants, I find that using printouts of individual sections of the sky with black stars on a white background works best.

15.3.2 The legend of Perseus

Learning the legends associated with constellations can be a useful way to learn which constellations are near each other. For example, the classical Greek story of

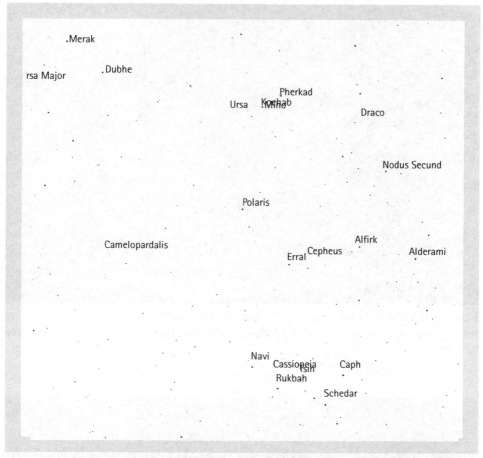

Figure 15.3. The North Celestial Pole with both constellation names and the names of bright stars.

Perseus recounts that Perseus was flying south when he spotted Andromeda chained to a rock. After talking to her, he flew to her parents, the queen and king, Cassiopeia and Cepheus, to learn how to win her freedom. The story goes on, but the point is that Perseus is next to Andromeda which is south of Cassiopeia and Cepheus (as shown in Figure 15.7).

Similarly in the Egyptian story of Osiris and Isis, the Nile River is represented by the Milky Way. Osiris is the constellation Orion and Isis is the star Sirius. The story involves death, life, dismemberment, marriage, and jealousy. Osiris is put back together except for his penis, which is lost in the Nile River—the Milky Way—but Isis, who is his wife, causes the Nile to rise and flood with her appearance. The Egyptian calendar relied upon the appearance of Sirius to mark the year and the beginning of the floods. Again, as with the story of Perseus, Sirius and Orion are next to each other in the sky, with part of the Milky Way nearby.

Figure 15.4. Star Trails showing Polaris at the centre. This picture is taken by leaving the shutter open capturing the Earth's rotation (photo courtesy of Jerry Schad).

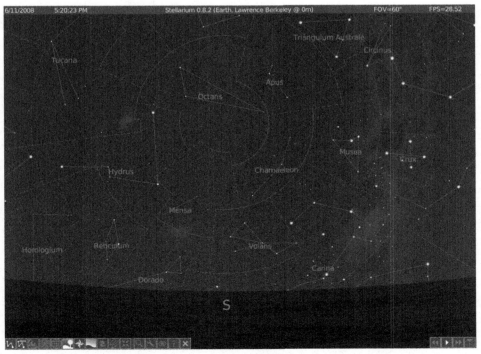

Figure 15.5. Stellarium image of the Magellanic Clouds and the Southern Cross.

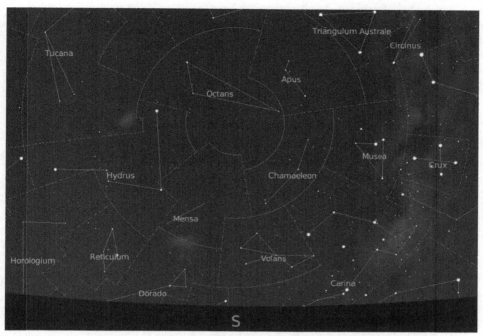

Figure 15.6. Stellarium image as in Fig. 15.5 with constellation names and boundaries.

Table 15.1. Constellations surrounding Polaris/Ursa Minor, the Magellanic Clouds, and the Southern Cross

Celestial object	Formal name	Constellation name	Nearby constellations
The Pole Star	Polaris	Ursa Minor	Ursa Major Draco Cepheus Camelopardalis
Large Magellanic Cloud	LMC	Dorado/Mensa	Volans Pictor Caelum Horologium Reticulum Hydrus Octans Chamaeleon
Small Magellanic Cloud	SMC, NGC 292	Tucana	Octans Hydrus Eridanus Phoenix Grus Indus
The Southern Cross	Crux	Crux	Musca Centaurus

Figure 15.7. Perseus, Andromeda, Cassiopeia, and Cepheus.

Many of the southern hemisphere constellations were not visible to the Greeks and Egyptians and as a result, the modern names do not reflect legends that weave sections of the sky together. This is where indigenous stories from Southern Hemisphere cultures can be helpful (e.g. Johnson 1998).

15.3.3 Practice

Spend as much time as possible studying the night sky before doing fieldwork. Twenty-minute intervals every two to three hours on clear nights is good practice for seeing how the sky changes over the night and learning constellations. The hours spent at home will make it easier to become oriented in the field. Learning how a chart in Stellarium compares to how things really look in the sky is invaluable. Learn the sky in the field in the same manner—before collecting astronomy data. In my experience, as I spent time outside at night learning the sky I attracted informants who were curious as to what I was doing and were extremely helpful later both with providing sky information and with introducing the project to others in their community. Ideally, researchers should be able to orient themselves to the night sky without having any star chart or computer before they start collecting sky information from informants.

15.3.4 Ask an amateur

With star charts, Stellarium, and practice, it still can be difficult to learn the night sky. Amateur astronomers are the best human resource. Local amateur astronomy clubs often have 'star parties' and public viewing nights where they set up their telescopes to show the public the wonders of the night sky. They are experts on naked-eye astronomy—astronomy without telescopes—as well, and are used to interacting with non-experts. In addition, planetariums and university observatories may also host star parties for the public. Star parties are usually advertised on the internet as well as in community-focused weekly newspapers.

15.3.5 Strong laser pointer

One piece of equipment that makes data collection much easier is a laser pointer, a high-powered one with a green beam that is visible for long distances. It makes pointing and identifying stars and asterism with informants very easy because both researcher and informant can see the target as opposed to trying to point with a finger or hand. The laser beam is visible from a great distance, and will attract a crowd that may contain future informants.

15.4 COLLECTING SIMPLE TERMS

Three ways to collect celestial terms are (1) working with informants with a list of terms to be translated, (2) going out at night with informants, and (3) analysing and interpreting terms found in recorded conversations. The problem with working with a list is that it can be like an examination and the answers may be 'school' terms, i.e. standard western terms, rather than local terms. The researcher has to be careful to assess the common usage of each term, and whether informants have heard other people in their community use these terms. The third approach is similar to participant observation in that conversations could be about anything and contain celestial terms about the calendar, time, and duration among other concepts. These three approaches are meant to be suggestive but not exhaustive in relation to the ways of collecting terms.

15.4.1 Daytime

Terms that are associated with the daytime sky should be collected along with associated myths and legends such as for the Sun, Moon, clouds, and rainbows. With weather and climate there is often a predictive aspect associated with terms, such as a ring around the Moon meaning rain is coming, rainbows associated with the end of rain, and cloud colour indicating rain. Cardinal directions (North,

South, East, West), island directions (East, West, towards the ocean, towards the mountains or away from the ocean), and wind directions usually emerge from discussing weather patterns. All these contribute to gaining a broader understanding of people's relationship to both the daytime and nighttime sky.

15.4.2 Bright stars and asterisms

Bright stars are the easiest to identify, and can be collected first. Asterisms are groups of stars that are not official western constellations. For example, the Big Dipper is an asterism of seven bright stars within the constellation Ursa Major. Asterisms tend to represent animals, fish, plants in the local environment, and important historical figures. Asking which stars belong together can begin the dialogue on local asterisms.

15.4.3 Planets

The planets that are visible to the naked eye are Venus, Mars, Jupiter, and Saturn. Mercury is also visible, but because it is very close to the Sun it can only be seen a few

Table 15.2. Twenty brightest stars (note that the larger negative magnitude, the brighter it is, and, conversely, the larger the positive magnitude, the fainter the star)

Star name	Magnitude	Constellation	Visible in which hemisphere
Sirius	−1.46	Canis Major	Both
Canopus	−.72	Carina	Southern
Arcturus	−.04	Bootes	Both
Rigil Kentaurus	−.01	Centarus	Southern
Vega	.03	Lyra	Northern
Capella	.08	Auriga	Both
Rigel	.12	Orion	Both
Procyon	.38	Canis Minor	Both
Achernar	.46	Eridanus	Southern
Betelgeuse	0.3–1.2	Orion	Both
Hadar	.61	Centarus	Southern
Altair	.77	Aquila	Northern
Aldebaran	.85	Taurus	Both
Antares	.96	Scorpio	Both
Spica	.98	Vega	Both
Pollux	1.14	Gemini	Both
Formalhaut	1.16	Piscis Austrinus	Both
Mimosa	1.25	Crux	Southern
Deneb	1.25	Cygnus	Northern

days a year. The best times to see planets are at sunrise and sunset when they are the first and last 'stars' to fade, and they lie along the same path that the Sun and Moon follow in the sky. Stellarium and other night sky software provide the position of planets visible for any date against the background of stars. Venus appears as a very bright star, Mars is red, Jupiter and Saturn are similar in that they are bright and yellowish. One trick for determining planets is that planets appear to twinkle less; another is to learn the bright stars in constellations well enough to recognize the presence of an extra 'star'. It is easiest to create charts before commencing field research that have the planets indicated. Very few researchers have collected detailed information on Mars, Jupiter, Saturn, and Mercury, perhaps due to their own inability to distinguish these from bright stars or the invisibility of Mercury. A pair of binoculars is helpful in positively identifying Mars, Jupiter, and Saturn and for initiating conversations about planets which appear as disks rather than points in binoculars. The moons of Mars and Jupiter lie along a straight line looking like tiny stars near the planet. A good pair of binoculars will show the rings of Saturn.

Venus is the easiest planet to identify and is only visible near sunrise or sunset. Many cultures including Europeans refer to it by two names: the morning star and the evening star. It is very difficult to assess whether people think it is one object or two different objects. In Fiji, for my Moce Island site, I could only conclude that planets were generally referred to by the name for Venus in its evening star mode rather than having individual names, and that Venus was two objects. However, the population I sampled about Venus was small—about five of the thirty interviewees.

15.5 MORE COMPLEX TERMS

15.5.1 Time, duration, past, present, future

Time, duration, past, present, and future may be found as part of grammatical structure rather than existing as independent terms. Equivalents terms for *minutes, seconds, hours, moment, instant, awhile,* and *infinity* are harder to collect while parts of the day connected to the position of the Sun tend to be easier, for example, *sunrise, sunset, morning, midday, afternoon, evening, night, midnight, twilight.* It is possible that some of these do not have indigenous equivalents.

Calendars tend to always have days measured from sunrise to sunset or from midday to midday, whereas the number of days in a week or month may vary. For example, some people have a four day rather than a seven day week (see Chemillier, Chapter 14 above). Months are usually based on observations of the Moon. However, a lunar cycle is 29.5 days rather than an even 30. Many cultures have a lunar calendar, especially those near bodies of water that experience tides. Lunar calendars consist of twelve or thirteen months, neither of which fits the true 365.25 day year, thus, they usually go out of sync with the true year and a correction factor may be built into the calendar. The European tradition of the twelve days of Christmas is an example of the addition of festival days to the lunar calendar to have the days add up to 365 days closer to the true year.

Solar calendars are tied to the annual north–south motion of the Sun on the horizon. They are usually started on spring equinox or sometimes on one of the solstices. This calendar measures what astronomers call the tropical year, which is 20 minutes shorter than the true year; thus solar years make very good calendars.

Stellar calendars measure the true year. Observations are of a particular star or asterism that appears in a certain position at a certain time of night; when that happens again, it is a year later. The Egyptian calendar, which relied on sighting the star Sirius rising in the east just before sunrise, is a classic example of a stellar calendar.

There are also calendars which are mathematically based rather than depending on observations of celestial bodies, but even these seem to have roots in sky observations (Bartle 1978). Many local calendars are a mixture of lunar, solar, and stellar rather than entirely one or another (Turton and Ruggles 1978).

15.5.2 Legends and myths

Collecting stories about celestial bodies is one of the enjoyable aspects of cultural astronomy research. The rescue of Andromeda by Perseus and the story of Osiris and Isis given above are just two of many examples. On a warm night, there is something special about listening to long winding stories about the constellations, stars, and planets overhead. Within a community there may be several variations of the same story, each flavored by the storyteller. Audio recording works well for capturing both the complexity and the variations of each story (see Margetts and Margetts, Chapter 1 above).

15.5.3 Transient phenomena: comets and meteor showers, satellites, eclipses

Comets are transient celestial phenomena in that they are not seen in the night sky every year. As comets get closer to the Sun, their tails get longer, and as they move away from the Sun, their tails get shorter. Whether approaching or retreating, comets tails always point away from the Sun. A comet can be visible in the night sky for several months, but usually only a few comets appear during one lifetime. We are fortunate to have seen three amazing comets in the Northern Hemisphere in the recent past: Halley in 1986, Hayakutake in 1996, and Hale–Bopp in 1997. People

Table 15.3. Dates of annual meteor showers

Shower name	Dates	Shower name	Dates
Quadrantids	Jan 01–Jan 05	Draconids	Oct 06–Oct 10
Alpha Centaurids	Jan 28–Feb 21	Epsilon Geminids	Oct 14–Oct 27
Delta Leonids	Feb 15–Mar 10	Orionids	Oct 02–Nov 07
Gamma Normids	Feb 25–Mar 22	Leo Minorids	Oct 23–Oct 25
Lyrids	Apr 16–Apr 25	Southern Taurids	Oct 01–Nov 25
Pi Puppids	Apr 15–Apr 28	Northern Taurids	Oct 01–Nov 25
Eta Aquarids	Apr 19–May 28	Leonids	Nov 10–Nov 23
Eta Lyrids	May 03–May 12	Alpha Monocerotids	Nov 15–Nov 25
June Bootids	Jun 22–Jul 02	Dec Phoenicids	Nov 28–Dec 09
Piscis Austrinids	Jul 15–Aug 10	Puppid/Velids	Dec 01–Dec 15
Delta Aquarids	Jul 12–Aug 19	Monocerotids	Nov 27–Dec 17
Alpha Capricornids	Jul 03–Aug 15	Sigma Hydrids	Dec 03–Dec 15
Perseids	Jul 17–Aug 24	Geminids	Dec 07–Dec 17
Kappa Cygnids	Aug 03–Aug 25	Coma Berenicids	Dec 12–Jan 23
Alpha Aurigids	Aug 25–Sep 08	Ursids	Dec 17–Dec 26
September Perseids	Sep 05–Sep 16		
Delta Aurigids	Sep 18–Oct 10		

should remember these comets along with Comet McNaught in 2007 in the Southern Hemisphere, and perhaps know the local terms and stories about comets.

The normal rate for shooting stars is around one every ten minutes; this rate increases during meteor showers. Meteor showers occur when the Earth passes through the debris left by a comet. Meteor showers occur several times a year, but they vary in the rate of 'shooting stars'. The Orionids which occur in October (see Table 15.3) have a rate of up to twenty-three meteors per hour.

15.5.4 Artificial satellites

Strangely enough, most sky watchers recognize satellites. Satellites appear in the night sky as small points of light that travel in a line crossing the sky in about 10 minutes. Airplanes are easier to spot because of their blinking lights. In contrast, satellites may brighten and dim as they cross the sky but they will not blink.

15.5.5 Eclipses

Solar eclipses occur when the Moon passes between the Earth and the Sun, casting a shadow on the surface of the Earth. Lunar eclipses occur when the Earth passes between a full Moon and the Sun, placing the Moon in the Earth's shadow. Lunar eclipses, when they occur, can be seen by everyone who can see the Moon. Therefore they are location-dependent in that the Moon has to be visible. In contrast, total solar eclipses are common worldwide but rarely recur in a particular location. For example, Ghana experienced total solar eclipses in 2006 and 1947, but the path of totality through the country was different for each. The best internet source for finding the dates of solar and lunar eclipses is the NASA website[4] and Mr. Eclipse site,[5] both calculated by 'Mr Eclipse', Fred Espanek.

15.6 COMPLICATED TERMS

15.6.1 Faint stars

Bright stars are easy to find, as are their home constellations. However, many cultures have constellations and legends surrounding faint stars as well. Most faint stars do not have 'names' but are simply designated with a Greek letter and the name of the constellation, and a Greek letter is assigned to each star in order of brightness for each constellation (these are known as the Bayer names). There are only twenty-four Greek letters and far more faint stars; once the letters are exhausted the remaining stars are numbered from west to east—these are the Flamsteed names (really numbers!). Fig. 15.8 shows the constellation Sagittarius with star names, while Fig. 15.9 shows Sagittarius with both the Bayer and Flamsteed star names.

Identifying faint stars is often really the researcher's best guess made by first identifying the closest bright stars, then estimating the angular distance and direction from two or three bright stars, and finally sitting down with a star chart and field notes to do a final identification.

15.6.2 Navigation stars

The most common star used for navigation in the Northern Hemisphere is Polaris which is near the North Celestial Pole. It appears to not move and marks North. Many cultures use the Big Dipper to find Polaris, since Polaris is not a bright star. The two stars that make up the leading edge of the Dipper are often called the pointing stars because they point to Polaris. Thus, Ursa Major and Ursa Minor are common constellations used for navigation in the Northern Hemisphere. When Ursa Major is not visible, Cassiopeia is sometimes used to aid in finding Polaris

---

[4] http://eclipse.gsfc.nasa.gov   [5] http://www.mreclipse.com

Figure 15.8. Sirius and Orion setting in the west. These are the Egyptian Isis and Osiris.

(see Figure 15.1). As mentioned earlier, the Southern Hemisphere does not have a star that marks the South Celestial Pole. The Magellanic Clouds and the Southern Cross are often used to locate South (see Figure 15.6).

In the Tropics, the Celestial Poles will be low on the horizon and difficult to use for navigation. People tend to use rising and setting stars and both bright and faint stars. They may use a formal 360-degree 'compass' of stars (Ammarell 1999; Goodenough 1953), or, as I found in Fiji, they just use a convenient star that happens to be in the direction that they are going (Holbrook 2002). Some of these navigation stars may have names, or asterism names, but it is also possible that they have not been named.

Navigation practices are rapidly changing due to a variety of factors, and many traditional techniques have not been recorded. Researchers have used navigation practices to probe human cognitive processes, mental maps, and memorization across cultures. The details of which stars are used when, and the acquisition and transmission of knowledge, are of interest to cultural astronomers.

15.6.3 Calendar markers

In addition to determining if the local calendar is based on observations of the Sun, Moon, stars, or some combination, there may be physical markers on the horizon that are meant to align with certain celestial bodies indicating a special day. The

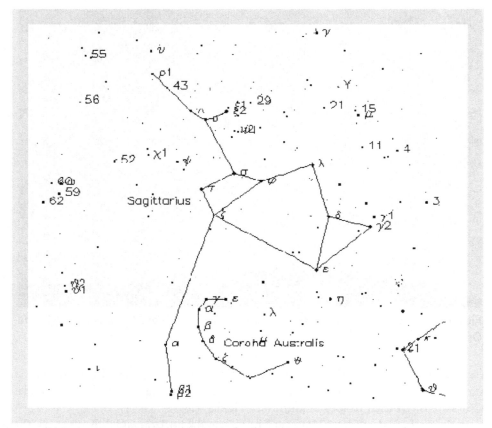

Figure 15.9. Sagittarius with Bayer and Flamsteed names.

Ngas of Nigeria have an observing platform, and notches have been noted in the opposite hillside. Their 'priest' watches for the Moon to rise in line with certain notches to mark the calendar. The film *Cosmic Africa* shows a Dogon 'priest' watching for the Pleiades which would indicate the onset of seasonal rains (Rogers and Rubin 2002). Cultural astronomers are interested in the material remains indicating long-term observations of the sky such as fixed observing locations perhaps marked by a stone or a building and notches on the horizon, or perhaps a second marker building built on the horizon. Such observation sites have to be shifted over time as the heavens shift, which allows cultural astronomers to use old and new alignments to fit astronomical dates.

15.6.4 Weather prediction

Many cultures study the sky to make weather predictions. This touches on cloud watching and knowing from which direction seasonal rains come, but includes observations of the atmosphere by focusing on celestial bodies. For example, in the rhyme 'red skies at night, sailor's delight, red skies at morning, sailor's warning', red skies at sunset or sunrise are marked by clouds but clouds to the west don't indicate a storm, whereas clouds to the east do, perhaps indicating a pattern of storms coming from the east. By observing the Sun at sunrise or sunset, people study its colour, looking for dust and clouds, the turbulence in the atmosphere, and haziness indicating a lot of moisture and/or dust. Each of these can indicate a change in weather. Rings around the Moon or Sun tend to be due to ice particles in the atmosphere or high clouds, and either can indicate freezing weather. If stars twinkle more, this indicates upper-atmosphere turbulence which may mark a storm front moving in. Dust in the atmosphere can change the colour of stars but also cool the atmosphere, indicating cooler weather. Weather is local, so rhymes and sayings about the weather are usually not transferable. It is important to document not only what people are observing about the sky, but what they use to predict weather changes.

15.6.5 Cosmology

Cosmology is concerned with how everything is connected together into a grand narrative. Not all cosmologies begin with the sky, but they usually include accounts of what the sky is and how parts of the sky got up there. As mentioned earlier, typically there are local stories that explain how the stars or the Sun and the Moon got into the sky. Griaule's works with the Dogon of Mali (Griaule 1965; Griaule and Dieterlen 1965) are now classics of African cosmology, and include an examination of the relationships between sounds, numbers, metals, foods, animals, and buildings. The sky is part of the narrative but is of equal importance with many other earthly things like grains. The narrative is explicit about origins and how everything including humans and human relations are part of a cosmological pattern. Cultural astronomers are interested in where the sky fits in, whether the resulting universe is static or evolving, geocentric or heliocentric, the origins of humans are, and the impact of colonization and globalization on these cosmological narratives.

'Origin stories' are used here to focus on both the origin of humans (which may be different from their cosmology) and the origins of those local things that are considered to be from the sky. It is interesting to cultural astronomers if people believe that their ancestors came from the sky and/or return to the sky after they die. Details of where in the sky they came from and how they got to that location before coming to Earth have not typically been recorded. In West Africa, thunder stones were said to have fallen from the sky, though anthropologists identify many as tools used by our ancient ancestors (Balfour 1903). Sky metal or meteorites are also candidates for local objects that truly come from the sky, but other objects may have a magical or functional relationship to the sky that has been solidified by a legend about coming from the sky.

Ocean-going people may have origin stories and cosmologies that revolve around the ocean and deep water rather than the sky, such as mermaid and selkie myths. Comparing the mysteries of the ocean to the mysteries of the sky is of interest to cultural astronomers, as is determining if such marine cosmologies are restricted to proximity to large bodies of water.

15.6.6 Faint asterisms

The term 'faint asterisms' is to some extent a misnomer, since in places where light pollution is minimized the stars appear much brighter, and faint asterisms are easier to see as a result. In Fiji, a young girl identified a constellation that was entirely made up of faint stars which she said was in the shape of a fan. There were no nearby bright stars that I could identify; however, the asterism was made up of a series of pairs of faint stars that made a 'V' in the sky. I memorized that pattern but really had no hope of ever identifying the asterism again, until I saw it one night while I was stargazing back in the United States. I was able to identify the bright star as Fomalhaut in Pisces Austrinis (Fig. 15.10), and the asterism is part of Pisces Austrinus and Grus. Unfortunately, she was the only person to identify this asterism, so it is not publishable.

15.6.7 Path of the planets: Zodiac asterisms

The Sun travels across the sky along a path of stars in the sky called the ecliptic. The Moon and the visible planets which all lie in the plane of the solar system travel close to the ecliptic. The maximum distance of the Moon away from the ecliptic is 5 degrees; Mercury is the planet that travels furthest away, 7 degrees from the ecliptic, and Venus is at a distance of a little over 3 degrees. Venus and Mercury are always close to the Sun, so their distance from the ecliptic is not so important for naked-eye observing. Mars, Jupiter, and Saturn all stay within 2.5 degrees of the ecliptic; thus, knowing the constellations of the ecliptic aids in identifying planets in the night sky. The twelve Zodiac constellations are the constellations along the ecliptic plus an extra constellation named Ophiuchus. The Zodiac asterisms are: Aries, Taurus, Gemini, Leo, Cancer, Libra, Virgo, Sagittarius, Scorpio, Capricorn, Aquarius, and Pisces. The constellation names are the same except for Scorpius and Capricornus. There has not been very much research on local Zodiacs outside of European folk traditions, the Middle East

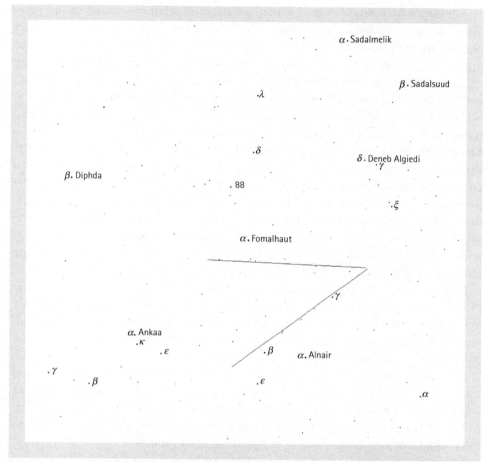

Figure 15.10. The Fan constellation from Fiji, unverified, consisting of very faint lines of stars.

and Muslim trade partners, and Asia, so any new information about people having a local Zodiac would be groundbreaking.

15.7 DIVINATION

Mentioning the Zodiac brings to mind astrology, defined as '[t]he study of the positions and aspects of celestial bodies in the belief that they have an influence on the course of natural earthly occurrences and human affairs' (Anon. 2004a).

Astrologers rely on complicated mathematical calculations related to the positions along the Zodiac of the Sun, Moon, and the visible planets to predict personality, give opinions on decisions, predict the future, etc. Using the sky to predict futures on Earth is not unique, and variations can be found among many cultures around the world. For example, the Chagga of Tanzania have an elaborate system of predicting personality traits based on both the day of the month and the hour of the day in which one is born (Dundas 1926). In the Chagga case, they have a lunar calendar, thus the day of the month is tied to observing the phase of the Moon. Then the hour of the day is marked by the progression of the Sun across the sky as well as routine activities that take place around the same time everyday. In contrast, astrology includes these and adds the position of the planets and the position of the sun and their astrological relationships to each other. In some cases, numerology or the magical properties of numbers may also be evoked. Here the numbers that make up the birth date are combined in some manner to come up with a representative number that can then be used to predict personality, life choices, romance, health, etc.

In Islamic countries, there appears to be a link between astrology and diagnosing illnesses and prescribing medicine that is not common in other present-day astrological traditions, though during the Middle Ages there was such a link among European astrologers with the Zodiac constellations ruling various parts of the body (see Curth 2005 and references therein).

Because of the complexity of observations, the mathematical calculations, and the extensive ways these are said to influence humans, studying divination systems takes a huge time commitment and careful study. Sometimes becoming an apprentice requiring a commitment of several years may be the only way to have access to the divination information and to get permission to publish it.

European astrology in the form of horoscopes has become a standard feature in most daily newspapers, and may now be influencing local divination systems. How people negotiate these two sources of divine influence is of interest to cultural astronomy researchers as part of their study of the globalization of astronomy knowledge.

15.8 RELIGIONS

The connection between the sky, celestial events, and religions has many levels of complexity. Religious calendars are a way to identify important days that correspond with full Moons, solstices, equinoxes, etc. Once these are identified, a researcher can try to make the connection explicit through interviews and archival research. Celestial themes that are found woven into religions include 'twelve' reflecting the classical twelve signs of the Zodiac, 'seven' reflecting the seven visible celestial bodies that move (Sun, Moon, Mercury, Venus, Mars, Jupiter, and Saturn), 'three' days of death with rebirth reflecting the time it takes the Sun to 'turn around' from reaching the solstice to obviously moving again on the horizon. Temples and houses of worship may be aligned such that the Sun's rays enter on religiously significant days. However, the significance may not obviously correspond to solstices and equinoxes; instead it can be when the Sun passes directly overhead (if it is in the tropics), or if dedicated to a particular saint it might be aligned to the Sun's position on the horizon on that saint's day. How to find alignments is beyond the scope of this chapter; instead I recommend that on the day of a proposed alignment the researcher simply take a picture recording the event and thus proving the alignment.

15.9 CONCLUSIONS

Collecting names of celestial bodies requires preparation and uncommon knowledge of the sky, and moving on to collect information on functional relationships and more complex ideas is just as difficult. However, the night sky has enchanted humans throughout time and has served as a source of inspiration as well as being the root of a major branch of science: astronomy. It has been definitively stated again and again that all human cultures have sky knowledge and a relationship to the sky, but as of this millennium, information has not been collected from all human cultures in order to prove or disprove this point.

Linguists can help gather astronomy information and bring new insight that cultural astronomers do not have access to: the linguistic roots of the names of celestial bodies and celestially related objects. Linguists can also show connections between ethnic groups through analysis of astronomy terms that would be missed by cultural astronomers. Finally, cultural astronomers are amenable to collaborations with linguists to mutually benefit both disciplines.

For further reading on cultural astronomy, see Holbrook and Baleisis (2008). On data collection see Fabian (2001), and for more case studies see Chamberlain, Carlson, and Young (2005).

CHAPTER 16

GEOGRAPHY

DOCUMENTING TERMS FOR LANDSCAPE FEATURES

ANDREW G. TURK

DAVID M. MARK

CAROLYN O'MEARA

DAVID STEA

16.1 INTRODUCTION[1]

16.1.1 Motivations

Documentation of a language includes investigation of the semantics of terms in the language. The landscape constitutes an important domain of human experience, which is sometimes inadequately covered in language documentation

[1] Carmelita Topaha facilitated the fieldwork with Navajo language speakers, and Larry King assisted understanding of Navajo landscape terms. Our understanding of the issues discussed in this chapter has been enhanced through interaction with Yindjibarndi, Navajo, and Seri people, and we greatly appreciate their time, assistance, and patience. Permission for the research to be carried out on the Navajo Reservation was provided by the Navajo Nation's Historic Preservation Department under Cultural Resources Investigation Permit No. C0513-E. Funding support by the US National Science Foundation (grants BCS-0423075, BCS-0423023, BCS-0553965 and BCS-0723694), from Murdoch University, and from Microsoft Research is gratefully acknowledged.

activities. By landscape, we mean the larger components of the human environment, composed of very large features and places that often can be best perceived and appreciated from a substantial distance (Granö 1997)—features such as mountains, rivers, valleys, and forests. Voegelin and Voegelin (1957) recognized topography as a fundamental domain for language documentation. We also include large water and vegetation features in our idea of the landscape domain.

While such a physiographic definition of landscape is useful as an initial approach to partitioning off a domain of interest, this definition is not unproblematic. It could be seen to not include emotional and cultural attachment to landscapes, landscape features, and places. To incorporate these considerations into the initial definition would involve a lengthy analysis of relevant issues of cultural geography, phenomenology, semiotics, etc., unfeasible in this context; however, the reader should assume that cultural aspects are included, as discussed further below.

For domains such as zoology and botany, scientific taxonomies can provide a clear etic[2] grid against which indigenous methods of categorization can be recorded. Likewise, the Munsell colour chart (Landa and Fairchild 2005; Munsell 1905) provides an etic grid for recording the semantics of colour terms. For the geographic or landscape domain, however, there is no such grid. One of the reasons that the landscape domain does not have an etic grid is the ontology of landscape— much of the variation of the Earth's surface is more or less continuous, and thus the same region of land can be subdivided into nameable landforms and other landscape features in many ways. Also, geographic objects (mountains, hills, rivers, lakes, etc.) tend to have fuzzy or graded boundaries, and there seems to be considerable variability in what gets delimited and how the objects are categorized and named. Another complication is that geographic objects are almost always very large and in fixed locations, hence it is difficult to elicit terms by showing real examples directly. These characteristics of the landscape domain provide the researcher with a number of methodological challenges regarding the elicitation of landscape terms.

There is some logic in collecting toponyms (place names) during the same field procedures used for investigating generic landscape terms, since the relationship between these two ways of referring to landscape features is an important aspect of understanding conceptualizations of place (see Nash and Simpson, Chapter 17 below). However, there are sometimes complications which make such combined objectives difficult to achieve. For instance, generic landscape terms may be considered as not culturally sensitive, whereas access to placename data might be restricted because of disputes over land tenure rights, or for other reasons.

---

[2] For a definition of 'etic' see the first paragraph of Dousset, Ch. 9 above.

16.1.2 The landscape domain

Since the landscape domain is a key aspect of place, and vice versa, it is an important component of culture and language for all people, especially for those indigenous peoples who have an unbroken intimate association with a particular area of 'country' that has lasted hundreds, perhaps thousands, of generations. However, as mentioned above, the nature of landscape means that there is great potential for different types of classification systems to arise within different languages, even in very similar environments. Hence it is not possible to provide a generic template for investigation of landscape terms.

One option is to base a general landscape classification scheme on the concept of 'affordance' (Gibson 1966), which refers to the characteristics of an object or an environment that relate to its potential for interaction, in this case human interaction. Affordances are likely to play an important role in landscape categorization; things with similar affordances are more likely to be grouped together into some category. The more important aspects of the affordances of natural landscape with respect to human beings includes the domain of topography (landforms) and hydrology (water in the landscape) and then land cover (vegetation). The aspects of landscape considered include:

1. Topography (landforms)
   - Convexities: eminences
   - Concavities 1: longitudinal depressions in the landscape
   - Concavities 2: oval or round openings in the earth
   - Passes (saddle points)
   - Vertical faces (cliffs)
   - Edges of elevated areas
   - Horizontal areas (plains)
2. Hydrology (water in the landscape)
   - Sources of drinking water
   - Bodies of standing water
   - Watercourses
   - Sources and sinks
   - Confluences
   - Parts of large water bodies
   - Shore-bounded land areas (islands etc.)

3. Land cover (vegetation)
   - Vegetation assemblages
   - Enclaves and refugia

This list can serve as a starting point for identifying landscape terms in any particular language, and bears some resemblance to domains recognized by Voegelin and Voegelin (1957). However, the use of this terminology for landforms and hydrology is merely to establish an initial set of categories for tabulating existing dictionary entries for landscape terms. This terminology is not used with the consultants or to describe the terms used in the target language in resulting landscape dictionaries.

It is critical to note that what aspects of landscape are salient for a particular language community depends on their lifestyle, culture, history, and spirituality— their 'lifeworld'. Mohanty (1997: 60) explains this term:

> The lifeworld is a world of **practice** (of action, making and doing) and **praxis** (of social action, of production of goods, and distribution of goods). It would, however, be mistaken to say that these modes of **acting** exhaust the lifeworld in all its dimensions. For example, there are religious, aesthetic, and cultural dimensions. By virtue of these, the world as well as things in the world are presented to subjects inhabiting that world with different sorts of values—as useful, as sacred, as beautiful—all of which can be brought under the general heading 'cultural'.

Affordances can be considered as emergent relations between humans and their physical environment (including landscape). Hence, their categorization (and linguistic terminology) is likely to flow from the everyday actions that the members of any particular language community routinely undertake. Actions determine relationships with our environment, which entail affordances. Heft (2003: 151) puts it thus:

> To experience objects and events of the world most fundamentally as bearing possibilities for our actions, that is, as affordances, is by definition to experience them relationally. Affordances are attributable to the intrinsic properties that features, objects, and events possess by virtue of their makeup, and are delimited or specified in relation to a particular perceiver-actor.

A linguist or ethnographer must therefore seek to understand the lifeworld of the community of speakers of the language in order to determine what sorts of landscape features are likely to have generic terms (or toponyms) and the likely complex sets of meanings that may be attached to individual features or configurations (groups) of landscape elements.

16.1.3 Ethnophysiography

Ethnophysiography is a recently defined field of study that seeks to understand cultural differences in conceptualizations of landscape, via comparisons between the meanings of terms that people from different cultures use to refer to the landscape and its components (Mark and Turk 2003). Landscape is an interesting topic of study because relationships with land are central to many cultures and landscape features pose problems for classification. The basic ethnophysiography hypothesis may be stated as follows: people from different language groups/cultures have different ways of conceptualizing (or cognizing) landscape, as evidenced by different terminology and ways of talking about, and naming, landscape features.

In any effort to document the semantics of terms within some domain of experience, it can prove useful to consult with experts in the domain itself (e.g. geographers for the landscape domain). In some cases, domain experts may take the lead in a domain-specific project. Domain knowledge is useful to language researchers when they try to understand the referents of terms from that domain. A concentrated effort on a specific topic (subject matter domain) is likely to lead to a more comprehensive coverage and better teasing out of referents and definitions of specific words, in the context of detailed understanding of the language community's lifestyle and worldview, including aspects of spirituality.

This can also be seen as implementing an interdisciplinary or transdisciplinary approach to research, which focuses on a knowledge production process less constrained by discipline boundaries and more in touch with the needs of society (Barry, Born, and Weszkalnys 2008). Turk (2007) recommends a transdisciplinary approach to ethnophysiography which includes accountability to language communities and consideration of indigenous knowledges, and the role of phenomenological as well as realist philosophical positions.

Among the authors of this chapter, Carolyn O'Meara is a linguist with a special interest in the geographic domain. The other authors are from other disciplines (geography; information science; psychology; cognitive science; philosophy; etc.); however, they are collaborating with linguists in their ethnophysiography case studies discussed below. For instance, in the Yindjibarndi study the researchers have worked very closely with linguists Vicki Webb, from the Roebourne community cultural organization Juluwarlu, Alan Dench (University of Western Australia), and Eleonora Deak and Sue Hanson from the Pilbara Aboriginal Language Centre (Wangka Maya). In addition, the Australian Institute of Aboriginal and Torres Strait Islander Studies provided material from the Aboriginal Studies Electronic Data Archive (ASEDA).

Obtaining detailed information about any aspect of a language is a very long and difficult task. The experience of Gunter Senft (a linguist from the Max Planck Institute for Psycholinguistics—MPI) emphasizes the need for great patience. He reports that having sought landscape terms and toponyms for twenty-three years from his Kilivila native speaker collaborators (on Kaile'una Island, one of the Trobriand Islands in the Milne Bay Province of Papua New Guinea), a group of men approached him one day and asked if he would like to know about landscape words (Senft 2008). He obtained more information on this topic in one session than during all his previous fieldwork. This also indicates that it is not always easy to obtain words for all language topics, and underlines the virtue of targeted investigations.

16.1.4 Case studies

The methods discussed in this chapter mostly relate to three case studies being carried out by the authors. However, the ideas expressed are also informed by literature and discussions with other researchers active in this field.

The first ethnophysiography case study by Turk, Mark, and Stea is being carried out with the Yindjibarndi people, who are an indigenous (Aboriginal) group living in the state of Western Australia, near the northwestern corner of Australia. Until the nineteenth century, the Yindjibarndi people lived mostly along the middle part of the valley of what Europeans named the Fortescue River, and on adjacent uplands. As part of the European colonization process, Yindjibarndi country was taken over by sheep and cattle stations (ranches) from the 1860s; the Yindjibarndi people were moved off their traditional territory into camps and settlements. Today, most of the Yindjibarndi speakers live in and around Roebourne, in what traditionally was Ngarluma country. Most of the surviving Ngarluma people now speak Yindjibarndi and English in addition to their own language. The Roebourne community is mostly indigenous and people use their own languages and English to differing degrees, depending on the context, sometimes with terms from both languages occurring in the same sentence. Yindjibarndi is a Pama-Nyungan language with about 1,000 remaining speakers, of whom about 500 live in and near Roebourne.

Publications by Mark and Turk (2003) and Mark, Turk, and Stea (2007) present results of the ethnophysiography study of landscape terms and concepts employed by Yindjibarndi-speaking people. A draft photo-illustrated dictionary including about 100 Yindjibarndi landscape terms has been compiled (Turk and Mark 2008). Most of these terms appear to refer to categories that would not be named by a single term in English, and vice versa. For example, if *river* in English makes reference to the riverbed and the water that flows in the riverbed, there is no equivalent term in Yindjibarndi, since riverbeds (*wundu*) and the water that occasionally may flow in those channels are named separately.

The second ethnophysiography case study is with the Navajo people of Arizona, New Mexico, and Utah in the southwestern USA (Mark, Turk, and Stea 2010). The Navajos are reportedly the largest Native American nation in the United States, with about 300,000 members. In 1990, there were about 150,000 speakers of the Navajo language, including about 7,000 monolingual speakers. Considerably more fieldwork and landscape photo response sessions have been carried out with Navajo speakers than we have conducted with Yindjibarndi speakers, but transcription and analysis of the data lag behind. Conceptual systems for many landscape domains appear to be organized differently in the Navajo language than they are in Yindjibarndi or English. For example, the material from which landforms are composed takes a prominent role in landscape terms which, in a templatic language such as Navajo, are often complex. However, full details will have to await completion of the transcription and translation phases.

O'Meara is carrying out an ethnophysiography study with the Comcáac (Seri people) who live along the northeastern coast of the Sea of Cortez in Sonora, Mexico (O'Meara and Bohnemeyer 2008). As of 2000, around 800 Seri people (Gordon 2005) lived in two small coastal villages, Socáaix (Punta Chueca) and Haxöl Iihom (El Desemboque del Río San Ignacio). Seri is their first language, but bilingualism is widespread, with Spanish being the second language. The Seri language is considered to be a language isolate. It has been suggested that it is part of the putative Hokan stock (Kroeber 1915), but there is insufficient evidence to prove or disprove this claim (Marlett 2001). Fieldwork was conducted by O'Meara in collaboration with at least twelve native speakers of Seri between 2004 and 2011 in the village of El Desemboque del Río San Ignacio.[3] Data collection procedures included verification and further exploration of dictionary entries in Moser and Marlett (2005), situated route descriptions conducted during expeditions to areas with geographic entities of interest, including foraging trips with Seri women, landscape diagramming in various locations near El Desemboque del Río San Ignacio, lexical relation elicitation, and general participant observation. In cooperation with native speaker collaborators, O'Meara put together an illustrated workbook for children which is designed to elicit responses containing various landscape terms.

Researchers at the Max Planck Institute in Nijmegen have also been active in this field of investigation. MPI's Language and Cognition Group has concluded a set of case studies of landscape terms (and some placenames) in ten languages (including the work with Seri by O'Meara and Bohnemeyer). These case studies cover a wide variety of geographic locations (although most are in tropical regions) (Burenhult 2008a). This work has extended very significantly the range of ethnophysiography case studies and strengthened its linguistic basis. A systematic cross-linguistic comparison of landscape terms in these languages has not yet been conducted.

Twenty-six participants attended an international workshop on Landscape in Language organized by the authors (in collaboration with the MPI researchers) in Arizona and New Mexico in the southwestern USA in October/November 2008. A book summarizing the proceedings has been published (Mark et al. 2011).

---

[3] O'Meara has worked with more speakers of Seri during her fieldwork seasons, but not necessarily on landscape-related work.

16.2 FIELD METHODS

16.2.1 Methods overview

The methods used by the authors for the three case studies (mentioned above) have varied due to differing physical locations and conditions, numbers of potential native speaker collaborators, etc. However, it is possible to summarize the general method as consisting of the following five stages:

1. dictionary work and photo collection—scoping the domain and preparing 'instruments';
2. field interviews—identifying the set of landscape terms and the distinctions, associations and usage;
3. photo interpretation sessions—clarifying existing terms and collecting new ones (except in the Seri case study);
4. semi-structured follow up—clarifying confusions, probing for extra meanings, evaluating quality of interpretations;
5. reporting the initial results back to community members and getting their feedback.

Of course, the actual fieldwork will also be affected by pragmatic considerations and particular techniques may well be used iteratively. For instance, stage 4 could actually be carried out in two parts, the first after stage 2 and the second after stage 3. Also, the field methods discussed here were adopted for a medium-sized study; smaller, single-researcher postgraduate projects may not have the resources to utilize all of these techniques. Of crucial importance is that any method should be used in a reflective manner, with the fieldworkers continually questioning the validity of their results and ensuring ethical practice (see sections below). Our approach resembles a Grounded Theory methodology (Glaser and Strauss 1967).

A summary of the techniques used in the case studies is provided in the following subsections, each representing a 'stage' in the methodology.

16.2.2 Techniques used in stages of method

16.2.2.1 Dictionary work and photo collection

This stage includes scoping the particular linguistic domain and preparing 'instruments' for use in fieldwork. Specific techniques include:

• Review of existing dictionaries (hardcopy and digital) and word lists; e.g. for Yindjibarndi these included: Anderson (1986), Anderson and Thieberger (2003), von Brandenstein (1992), Wordick (1982). For the Navajo study, bilingual Navajo-English dictionaries, principally Young and Morgan (1992), were used; Moser and Marlett (2005) was used for the Seri project. To compile an initial list of landscape terms for a language, we looked up each term in a long list of English-language landscape terms, in the dictionary of the target language. Also, in one case (Yindjibarndi, in Anderson 1986), the dictionary included 'topic codes' for each term, one of which was 'Geographical features'.

- Review of existing written stories and audio recordings relevant to landscape; e.g. for Yindjibarndi these included von Brandenstein (1970).
- Compilation of lists of all geographic terms from dictionaries, wordlists, etc. For the sake of establishing a starting point for discussions, these can be classified into semantic groups ('landscape domains') according to the usual meanings of their English equivalents, using groups such as water features, land forms (convex and concave), land cover types, etc (as discussed in §16.1.2). It is important, however, that these initial classifications do not inhibit the research-ers from developing a categorization scheme appropriate for the particular language community. The domains are mainly used to help the researchers organize their approach, and are not necessarily a hypothesis regarding how the speakers would group the terms.
- Consultations with linguists familiar with the target language, or at least with closely related languages. This is especially useful to elicit information about the syntax and grammar of the language, for instance, the likely role of parts of speech other than nouns in landscape terms.
- Acquisition of existing images of representative landscape features and/or taking new photographs in the area occupied by the language community and perhaps in adjacent areas.

There are of course also many tasks associated with obtaining background infor-mation about the relevant language community (e.g. history, culture, social struc-tures) and its traditional area of habitation (topography, hydrology, land use, etc.). Appropriate procedures must be used to make contact with the community, to ask permission to conduct fieldwork, as well as obtaining relevant ethical clearances in the case of university-based research projects (see Rice, Chapter 18 below). Some of these issues are discussed further in §16.4 below.

16.2.2.2 *Field interviews*

Field interviews are carried out to identify the set of landscape terms and to clarify their meanings and distinctions, associations, and usage. A variety of different approaches have been used.

An initial approach (used in the Yindjibarndi case study and to a certain extent in the Seri case study) is to discuss the terms collected in the first stage with native speaker collaborators on an individual basis or in pairs or small groups, to see whether the terms are recognized, whether their spellings are correct (if the language has a standard writing system), and whether there are alternative or additional terms for similar features. Terms may be written on a whiteboard and/or discussed verbally, and the sessions may be audio and/or video recorded. General features of the language and history of contact with linguists, or other ethnographers, might also be discussed in these initial sessions.

It is also possible to interact with collaborators directly in the field. For instance, during fieldwork with Navajo speakers, Mark, Stea, Turk, and Topaha spent several hours with each collaborator in the field phase, driving around in the landscape and encouraging them to talk about the particular features encountered. These field trips were in parts of their territory well known to the individual collaborators (Fig. 16.1). The field interviews were exploratory, and the researchers tried to minimize the degree to which they directed the discussion. During the trip, the collaborators were asked to describe the landscape in their language, with the aid of a translator (usually a family member) if necessary, and in English, and to discuss the names of features. This material was audio recorded and photographs of key features that were discussed were taken as the trip progressed. In most cases, a GPS record of the route and locations was taken. A transcript of the

Figure 16.1. Field trip with Navajo collaborators and project consultant, September 2005, at Blue Canyon, Navajo Reservation, Arizona (from left to right, Lorraine Holyan, Andrew Turk, Carmelita Topaha, and Larry King).

field trip description is being made, and will be combined with notes taken by the researchers during the trip and with the photographs and locations. This integrated material can then be examined for landscape terms, compared to the term lists from the dictionaries, and used to provide a more informed understanding of landscape concepts of that language group and how 'generic' landscape terms relate to proper names used for landscape features. Some of the photographs taken during these field interviews were later used in photo interpretation sessions (§16.6.2.2.3).

We also conducted a more structured field interview with some Yindjibarndi speakers. In some cases we asked them to tell us if they saw an example of some landscape term of interest. At other times we stopped near features and asked the speakers to explain to us what they would call the feature, and why. This semi-structured field interview was conducted fairly late in the Yindjibarndi project, when the researchers already felt they had an adequate understanding of many, but not all, terms. Some photographs taken that day were used later with other speakers, to confirm or refine our understanding of the meanings of terms.

The approach used by O'Meara in her work with the Seri has included a variety of types of field interview. Her primary procedure to elicit landscape terms was conducting situated route descriptions with native speaker collaborators. This approach involves going to a particular location that has some cultural significance to the collaborator (which is determined in advance of the trip)—see Fig. 16.2. Once at that location, the collaborator is asked to provide a route description from the location back to the village. The collaborators are reminded

Figure 16.2. Native speaker consultant in the Seri project, Maria Luisa Astorga near the mouth of Rio San Ignacio (the major arroyo near El Desemboque).

that they are providing the route description to somebody who speaks Seri, but does not know the area, in order to increase the likelihood that collaborators will use landscape terms and not placenames. The advantage of this technique is that the elicited material reveals the way that landscape features are used as natural landmarks in spatial description. Such specific interview techniques augment data collected from informal conversations with collaborators and observations of people in the community going about their everyday activities.

O'Meara also collected personal narratives which feature the landscape as a central theme—for example, stories about people gathering food items or getting lost at sea. These personal narratives not only provide additional examples of landscape terms in a natural context, but also allow for further insight into the cultural significance of parts of the Seri landscape which are not made clear through participant observation.

Another method that O'Meara has employed is landscape diagramming. This approach involves going to a location where the researcher and the collaborator both have a good view of a predetermined landscape feature, such as a mountain range, dunes, or a stream. At that point, the collaborator draws the landscape feature or scene that she is observing.[4] The researcher then begins to label the drawing according to the collaborator's instructions. This leads to identifying names and terms for parts of landscape features, as well as names and terms for entire landscape features, visible in the scene. This approach also allows the collaborators to direct the elicitation, such that they determine the way the landscape feature is represented in the diagram and they direct the researcher how to label the diagram.

Finally, O'Meara also looked at what kinds of hierarchical relations hold among landscape terms in Seri, if any—in particular, taxonomical (kind-of) and merony-mical (part-of) relations. To elicit these lexical relations, two different methods are used. The first is to use linguistic frames for the relations being elicited, beginning with examples from various semantic domains, e.g. 'a pear is a kind of fruit'; 'a hawk is a kind of bird'; 'a pond is a kind of water body'. The other method relies on unilateral entailments to elucidate the lexical relations; e.g. *It's a hawk* unilaterally entails *It's a bird*, suggesting that *hawk* is a hyponym of *bird*.

16.2.2.3 Photo interpretation sessions

For the Yindjibarndi and Navajo case studies, the researchers have made extensive use of photo interpretation sessions. The materials used during these sessions were fixed sets of about forty numbered digital colour photographs of landscape features. For some of the Navajo sessions, the photographs were projected onto a screen or

---

[4] In cases where the native speaker consultant does not wish to draw, the researcher can draw the scene slowly in collaboration with the consultant to achieve similar results.

wall where the speakers and researchers could view and discuss them. For all of the Yindjibarndi sessions and the majority of the Navajo sessions, colour prints (approximately 27 × 20 cm; 11 × 8 inches) of the photographs were shown. Each photo was of a landscape scene, and they were chosen (and ordered) to display a good variety of landscape features, without any recognizable sequence in feature type or location. The order of presentation within each language set remained constant. The photographs were almost always shown to groups of speakers, who then discussed and in some cases debated what landscape terms would be appropriate.

The collaborators were asked to discuss the landscape features displayed in the set of photos, with special reference to the landscape terms that were appropriate, in the indigenous language. The interviews were facilitated by one of the researchers, while the other researchers took notes and made occasional contributions to the dialogue (Fig. 16.3). The sessions were audio taped and in some cases were also recorded on video (Fig. 16.4).

Detailed transcriptions of the audio recordings were undertaken and reviewed by the researchers, with reference to their notes and existing dictionaries. In some

Figure 16.3. Navajo collaborators discussing landscape photos at the Sanostee Chapter House, Navajo Reservation, New Mexico, August 17 2006.

Figure 16.4. Juluwarlu staff videotaping interview with Yindjibarndi elder Ned Cheedy at Jirndawurrunha, Western Australia.

cases these transcripts were also reviewed by linguists (e.g. in the Yindjibarndi case study, at the culture/language organizations Juluwarlu and Wangka Maya).

Another approach used is to ask a collaborator, individually, to sort photographs into groups, either an unspecified number of groups, or, often, three groups (triadic sort). Collaborators may then be asked to describe each group and their basis for the grouping. This technique was used with some Navajo speakers and some Anglos at an early stage in the Navajo project, but the researchers found the results difficult to interpret given the small number of collaborators that were available. The sorting protocol did provide insights for reducing a large number of candidate photos to a more manageable set of forty photos for use in the photo interpretation sessions.

16.2.2.4 Semi-structured follow-up

Detailed analysis of the landscape terms used by the collaborators in the second and third stages has allowed the researchers to revise their previous understanding of landscape concepts in the languages studied. However, it has been important to conduct follow-up interviews, photo interpretation sessions, and field excursions to clarify confusions, probe for extra meanings, and evaluate the quality of interpretations. In the Yindjibarndi case study, the whole field research process took seven years and some key understandings emerged only from the most recent fieldwork.

16.2.2.5 *Reporting back and getting feedback*

It is very important for both practical and ethical reasons to report back to native language communities on a regular basis. In the Yindjibarndi case study, an initial version of a photo-illustrated dictionary of landscape terms was distributed to participating individuals and organizations early in the research process to encourage feedback. More recently a full-colour draft dictionary of 100 terms has been distributed, via the Yindjibarndi cultural organization Juluwarlu. The researchers have made a similar commitment to distribute digital copies of a photo-illustrated dictionary of Navajo landscape terms to each of the 100+ chapter houses on the Navajo Reservation. As mentioned earlier, O'Meara and some of the Seri collaborators designed and produced a children's workbook involving various landscape features found in the Seri territory.

16.2.3 Methods not yet implemented

The authors have employed several variants on the use of visual methods in landscape research. Our respondents have been asked to identify, and to provide terms for, landscape features on photographs, or to establish landform categories by sorting large numbers of photographs into groups. Yet another approach would be to have members of the target group take photographs, show them to their elders, and request oral descriptions, which, in some cultural groups may result in extensive stories about the significance of a given landform, relating it to history and/or to traditional stories. The advantage of this emic approach is that it is more culturally sensitive. This approach could provide important contextual information for landscape terms, and enhance understanding of the significance of terms obtained by other means.

A video (or animation) presentation featuring a person (or animal) moving through a series of different sorts of landscape features could be produced. Collaborators could be asked to view this video presentation and provide a verbal narration (in their language) which would later be translated and landscape terms identified.

To the best of our knowledge, three-dimensional relief models have not been used in ethnolinguistic fieldwork for elicitation in the landscape domain. However, such models have been used successfully in participatory community land-use planning in developing countries (e.g. Wisner, Stea, and Kruks 1991; Rambaldi and Callosa-Tarr 2002), and hold promise for elicitation of landscape terms. Virtual reality renderings of terrain might also be used, but would probably only be practical in laboratory settings.

16.2.4 Relevant methods used by other researchers

Researchers at the MPI have very extensive experience in linguistic fieldwork, and have assembled an extensive set of fieldwork materials and apparatus (see Majid, Chapter 2 above), as well as software for data analysis and storage (e.g. ELAN).

For instance, MPI linguists have used a questionnaire which provides a structured tool for eliciting landscape terms and toponyms (Bohnemeyer and Enfield 2002). Data collected through this questionnaire are intended to support the broader MPI project on words for place and space. The developers of the questionnaire suggest three overarching questions:

how to formally identify placenames in the research language (i.e. according to morpho-logical and syntactic criteria); what places placenames are employed to refer to (e.g. human settlements, landscape sites), and how places are semantically construed for this purpose. (p. 55)

Non-verbal stimuli developed by the MPI contain graphics which are used to elicit terms (e.g. for body parts) as well as story books, videos, and 3-D animations. Route descriptions have been especially effective for eliciting landscape terms and toponyms. Collaborators are also sometimes taken to prominent lookout points and asked to name landscape features that they can see.

Researchers at the MPI have also had success with referential communication tasks for collection of landscape terms (e.g. Burenhult 2008b). Two speakers are separated by a visual barrier but communicate by voice. One of them sees a target image or scene, and has to describe it well enough that the other speaker can reconstruct the scene or choose the correct image from a set of landscape images. The resulting dialog produces a good corpus of landscape terms, spatial relations, and directions in the context of natural discourse.

Heyes (2007) has used a number of visual and oral methods that he designed to gain an appreciation of Inuit conceptions of the environment. These included a series of drawing exercises, role-playing scenarios, 'knowledge-trees', memory exercises, genealogical charts, nomenclature exercises, and semi-structured inter-views. He used a Filemaker database to assist with the sorting and coding of the large set of drawings of landscape features (with terms and names) that was obtained from collaborators.

Researchers of the Summer Institute of Linguistics (SIL 2009) have prepared a set of drawings for language elicitation, based on the environments and culture of

Guatemalan regions of humid tropical forest. They provide picture sets for about sixty domains. One of the domains is 'natural phenomena', under which they provide illustrations of about 100 natural phenomena, many of which are of landscape scale or extent. Clearly, drawings have some advantages, and some disadvantages, compared to photographs. Unfortunately, there do not appear to be similar sets of images available for desert, semi-arid, or arctic environments, among others.

16.3 THREATS TO VALIDITY OF CROSS-LANGUAGE INTERPRETATIONS OF LANDSCAPE TERMS

16.3.1 Some specific threats to validity

Some threats to validity of interpretation of landscape terms flow from the nature of ethnophysiography. Work on the ethnophysiography case studies discussed above indicates that definitions of landscape feature types in different languages differ significantly. The following list of potential threats to validity uses Yindjibarndi examples from Turk and Mark (2008), unless otherwise indicated:

a. Terms may relate to fairly equivalent concepts between languages; however the set of examples fitting the concepts might be quite different, e.g. *muji* 'cave': In Yindjibarndi *muji* is the word for a deep hole in *marnda* ('rock face'), with an overhanging roof (a cave), large enough to shelter a person or animal. However, many speakers of English will have experienced a much larger variation of types and sizes of caves than those occurring in Yindjibarndi country. We do not know whether Yindjibarndi speakers would apply the term *muji* to very large caverns. And the word *muji* is also used for smaller holes that would not be called caves by English speakers.

b. What is the extent of any particular landscape feature for which there is a term? E.g. *marnda* refers to an area of *ngurra* ('ground') that stands higher than the country around it—a hill, mountain, ridge, or range. Does *marnda* include surrounding sloping ground or just the steep part of the feature?

c. Terms for sets of landscape features may not match up semantically, e.g. *marnda, bargu, burbaa*—cf. 'mountain', 'hill': *marnda* (see above); *bargu* is a *gubija* ('small') *marnda* made of rock or sand; *burbaa* can refer to a *gubija marnda* that is low, smooth, and rounded—not as steep as a *bargu*. Most instances of the term *marnda* in Yindjibarndi would be called *hill* in English, but features at the southern edge of Yindjibarndi country would probably be called 'mountain' in English but are still an instance of *marnda* to a Yindji-barndi speaker.

d. Different whole-part concepts: e.g. compare the Yindjibarndi terms *wundu, mankurdu,* and *yijirdi* to the English term 'river': A *wundu* is a relatively broad, level channel where water flows or lies after heavy rain. In Yindijibarndi country, there are no *wundu* that flow with water all the time. But the *wundu* is always there. If there is water in a *wundu,* the water is referred to as *mankurdu* if flowing deep and fast, *yijirdi* if flowing gently, and *bawa* if it is just lying there temporarily. Hence, a *wundu* is not really equivalent to a 'river' in English, as it does not include the water. The situation is further complicated by the fact that some *wundu* in Yindjibarndi country bear colonial English proper names ending in 'River', others in 'Creek'.

e. Some terms effectively are defined by shape rather than by topographic objects, e.g. *burbaa* can refer to a *gubija marnda* that is low, smooth, and rounded—not as steep as a *bargu. Burbaa* also refers to a rise in a *yirdiya* ('road', 'track' or 'trail'), especially at the crest. *Burbaa* can also be used to refer to low, rounded areas of higher ground, for instance between *garga* ('gullies'). Here, the term seems to relate more to the shape of the ground, rather than to a particular type of landscape object.

f. Physical point of view may influence conceptualization: e.g. (in Navajo) initial results suggest that *tséyi'* may be preferred for a rock canyon seen from the canyon floor, whereas *tsékooh* would be preferred when the same feature is seen from above the rim. Thus, it is at least possible that there may be more than one term for a particular type of landscape object, depending on the location of the observer. Also, some landscape features are so large that they can only be recognized by viewing from a considerable distance, and others can only be seen when nearby. In Seri, parts of the beach have different names: e.g. *hastoj cnoosc* is the section between low and high water mark.

g. Some terms may refer to spatial locations (places) rather than landscape features, e.g. *wana, wanangga: wana* refers to a hillside (or perhaps a flat area) in the middle distance—where you can still see something (like a kangaroo) but it is much too far away to throw a stone at it (or shoot the kangaroo). *Wanangga* could refer to the location of something in the middle distance. This perhaps is an example of landscape being thought of as a field (for observation and activities) rather than as a set of objects.

h. Spiritual aspects of place, e.g. *yinda* ('permanent pool'): every *yinda* has a *warlu* ('spirit' or 'mythic snake'), that formed and protects the *yinda.* Specific types of landscape features may have spiritual associations, which are part of the meaning of indigenous landscape terms.

i. Groups of places: generic landscape terms, and also toponyms, sometimes refer to groups of landscape features (Hercus and Simpson 2002; also Nash and Simpson, Chapter 17 below).

j. Sets of places, related by spirituality, e.g. *Jirndawurrunha*: During an audio recording session examining photos of landscape features, with the researchers asking for landscape terms, the Yindjibarndi collaborators spontaneously referred to spiritual aspects of the features. The collaborators talked about how the *warlu* ('mythic snake') had come up out of the ocean near Onslow and travelled up the route of the Fortescue River, chasing two boys who broke the Law, until he got to *Jirndawurrunha* (Millstream) (Ieramugadu Group 1995). This is part of an explanation of what Yindjibarndi call the 'learning times' or 'when the world was soft'. This is part of what is also known as 'the dreaming', a translation of indigenous explanations of the formation of the world into its current landscape and ongoing spiritual aspects of landscape. Hence particular places may be part of a set of places linked by a 'dreaming' path.

k. From our discussions, it seems possible that some types of landscape features may be so rare, or even unique, in the territory of the language community that they always have a toponym and there is no generic term used for that type of feature (e.g. prominent mountains).

Other threats are more closely linked to the field methods used and the way data is interpreted. These include:

1. There may be ambiguity of reference leading the linguist to misinterpret the meaning of a term—e.g. previous Yindjibarndi dictionaries (Wordick 1982; Anderson 1986) indicate that *mankurdu* means 'Fortescue River'. However, subsequent fieldwork has shown that *mankurdu* refers to water flow that is deep and fast, and thus has a meaning similar to that of the English word *flood* (Mark and Turk 2003; Mark et al. 2007; Turk and Mark 2008).

2. One potential problem with elicitation in the field is defining and recording the referents of terms (i.e. the particular landscape features). GPS can be used to document the location where the collaborator was standing when he or she used the term, but it is more difficult to record, or even infer, the direction of, and distance to, the referent, although recorded pointing gestures and comments might partly help resolve any confusion.

3. Using landscape photographs can be problematic, as the photo may well contain several landscape features, and great care needs to be taken to ensure that the meaning of terms given are properly interpreted. Also, collaborators may mis-judge the actual sizes of features in photographs, and if their language has two terms, one for larger and the other for smaller features that otherwise are similar, they might choose the 'wrong' term.

4. One problem in photograph-based elicitation is the selection of the photo-graphs or images to be used. Should one use photographs of places or features familiar to the collaborators, or of unfamiliar places but in their traditional environment, or of far-away places? A psychologist likely would

prefer neutral, unfamiliar, or even synthesized examples. But for familiar features, collaborators can bring background knowledge into their choice of terms. Also, Yindjibarndi collaborators were reluctant to give terms for features in photographs of country of their neighbouring language group: 'That's Bunjima country, you should ask Bunjima people.' A similar comment was made by a Navajo collaborator when presented with a photograph of a Western Australian landscape feature.

5. With bilingual collaborators, one can ask for the speaker to give words that mean 'river' or 'hill' in their language, but this has a higher risk of producing a greater cross-language conceptual match than might actually exist.

6. A term may be correctly documented as referring to a particular type of landscape feature, but it may also mean other things as well. In Seri, for example, *xatj* appears to have a more extensive meaning than *reef* in English; additional elicitation might be needed to determine whether the term has a more broad semantic reference than originally thought, or whether it is polysemous.

7. A term may be used for a landscape feature but be in effect a generic term for something of that type (e.g. shape). In Yindjibarndi, *yirra* means the exact edge of a hilltop or a water body but also means 'tooth': is a body part metaphor being employed, or is the core meaning of *yirra* 'sharp edge'?

8. Some languages may have different terms for the same features which are used under different circumstances,—e.g. Navajo speakers use different proper names (toponyms) for the same features in different contexts, and some of these contexts are themselves seasonal. Also, some terms are based on appearance, which may vary with seasons.

9. It is possible to overemphasize lexicalization of concepts in our studies of categorization in ethnophysiography. Are monolexemic terms (i.e. concepts labelled by a specific, simple word) more cognitively salient than concepts that require longer phrases to describe? For instance, O'Meara has found that for Seri, of the 100 landscape terms that have been documented to date, at least 88 have transparent etymologies combining a term for a landscape material (rock, earth, fresh water, or sea water) with a modifier, or are a derived nominal (e.g. a nominalization). Thus at most 12 of the Seri terms for landscape elements are monolexemic. Mark and Stea have observed a similar, though less extreme, trend for the Navajo language, where at least 64 of 163 landscape terms and phrases from published dictionaries (and other sources) begin with a landscape material term followed by shape or position/orientation indicator(s), and are thus clearly multi-morphemic.

16.3.2 Addressing threats to validity

Many of the threats discussed in the previous section are addressed by the fieldwork methods discussed in §16.2. In general terms, threats will be reduced through: use of multiple methods ('triangulation': Webb et al. 2000) and iterative procedures; using a diverse range of collaborators; not 'leading the witness'; being open to alternative interpretations; and becoming as intimate as possible with lifestyle and social structures of the language community.

More specific ways of addressing threats to validity include the following:

- Elicitation can be done using only 'words' or 'language', either oral or (in some cases) written. Requesting formal definitions of terms can seem unnatural to language speakers, but it should not be dismissed as a method. Asking people to explain the meaning of a term may be a more natural way to gain insight on meanings. Asking for differences in the meanings of two or more terms that refer to entities in the same domain, or asking for examples of usage of terms, are especially useful approaches.

- Spelling is something of an issue in this research. For instance, the Yindjibarndi had no written language before European contact, and some of the sounds used in Yindjibarndi are not used in English. Hence, different linguists have decided to interpret and write down particular phonemes in different ways. Standardization of approach is critical to minimizing potential confusion. Where standardized spelling has been agreed upon by linguists it is important to recognize that this may achieve importance among indigenous peoples themselves: one of the authors was criticized by an indigenous Australian at a recent conference for a spelling 'mistake', when he did not follow spelling conventions adopted in a dictionary compiled by Europeans.

- Use of trips through the people's traditional country are very useful, and might produce the most 'authentic' results if one uses traditional modes of transport, such as walking or travel by canoe. However, in the case of endangered languages, while elders are often considered to be the best collaborators, they might have mobility problems due to age. Field travel by modern vehicles may work well in some cultures, especially if the collaborators now normally travel in motor vehicles.

- For some landscape terms in some languages, it seems that observing *actions* in the landscape might better elicit terms that are tightly connected to affordances of landscape. For example, a term for a type of high ground might be coupled to the act of walking to the top of it for a view of surrounding terrain. Sometimes it might be possible to conduct appropriate actions in the field. However, animations or video clips might serve the same purpose and be more practical. They also would facilitate better 'control', since the same clips could be shown to multiple collaborators.

16.4 SOME ETHICAL ISSUES

If ethnophysiography is genuinely to seek to understand the way that landscape is treated in languages across the world, it must do so from a perspective that is not biased towards western concepts of knowledge. In particular, if key case studies of differences between languages are carried out with indigenous peoples, then their worldviews must be reflected in resulting theories.

Such an approach is justified on scientific and ethical bases, but is also necessary to ensure collaboration by indigenous people in ethnophysiography research. Whiteley (1998) discusses what he sees as a crisis in ethnography as it has been practised with Hopi people, and explains why Tribal officials have adopted severe restrictions on research activities. He suggests: 'The reasons for indigenous resistance to cultural commodification by academic ethnography are several . . . but at base they are the result of the social and political estrangement of anthropology as a research-university discipline from the perspectives and situated interests of its subjects' (p. 6). Researchers must not only respect indigenous knowledges but also deliver practical benefits to communities.

Linguists, and others, collecting information about endangered languages may feel that language preservation is their key consideration. However, there is also almost always at least some element of 'appropriation', of 'taking away' things of value from the culture. The usual 'Enlightenment' defence that data collection for research is for the 'good of science' may not carry much weight for indigenous collaborators. Smith (1999: 1–2) put this position very strongly:

From the vantage point of the colonized, a position from which I write, and choose to privilege, the term 'research' is inextricably linked to European imperialism and colonialism. The word itself, 'research', is probably one of the dirtiest words in the indigenous world's vocabulary. When mentioned in many indigenous contexts, it stirs up silence, it conjures up bad memories, it raises a smile that is knowing and distrustful. It is so powerful that indigenous people even write poetry about research. . . . This collective memory of imperialism has been perpetuated through the ways in which knowledge about indigenous peoples was collected, classified and then represented in various ways back to the West, and then, through the eyes of the West, back to those who have been colonized.

Several indigenous participants at the 'Language in Landscape Workshop' in October/November 2008 expressed similar sentiments, arguing strongly that it was essential to understand the worldview of a specific indigenous group before attempting to interpret linguistic data (Turk and Mark 2011). They also emphasized the need for particular language communities to have a strong role in directing linguistic research, especially where the topic is landscape and toponyms, given the centrality of place in indigenous consciousness (Basso 1996). Similar sentiments were expressed by language communities in our own ethnophysiography case studies. For instance, members of the cultural maintenance group Juluwarlu have insisted that they hold the official, definitive copy of the Yindjibarndi language dictionary, rather than a national linguistic organization, or even the regional body, the Pilbara Aboriginal Language Centre (Wangka Maya).

It is important that all linguistic fieldworkers are carefully attuned to the rights of collaborators and language communities. Ethical issues especially important in the field of ethnophysiography include:

- ensuring proper permission is obtained for all fieldwork, through the local cultural organizations (which may have formal or informal approval processes);
- appropriate payments to collaborators to compensate for their time and effort;
- using both male and female researchers to ensure that gender-sensitive issues are appropriately handled;
- permitting the maximum possible community control of the project; its timing, direction, and conclusion;
- not eliciting, recording, storing, or publishing any secret/sacred information not directly relevant to the study;
- obtaining clearance from representatives of the language community for publication of all material and inclusion of culturally appropriate acknowledgement of collaborator contributions;
- providing feedback to the community about the project in a culturally appropriate manner;
- making sure that multiple hard (printed) and soft (CD) copies of all data and resulting publications are left with key people and organizations within the community.

Some of these ethical recommendations may be difficult to adopt for small-scale projects. For instance, it may not be possible for a postgraduate student project to include researchers from both genders and hence to interact with collaborators from both genders. In such circumstances, the research should carefully consider the implications of this constraint on data collection and expressly discuss the matter when reporting the research results.

Carrying out this sort of case study is greatly assisted if it is organized through a key individual and/or organization from the language community. In the case of the Yindjibarndi study, author Turk (and his wife, Dr Kathryn Trees) have a very long-term relationship with the community at Roebourne, and the ethnophysiography fieldwork was facilitated by this relationship and through the collaboration of Juluwarlu. For the Navajo study, the key facilitator role is being carried out by local Navajo consultant Carmelita Topaha. In the case of Seri, O'Meara has been conducting fieldwork on an annual basis in El Desemboque since 2004. Over the years, she has developed a close relationship with her primary native speaker collaborator, Alma Imelda Morales Romero, who has acted as both a local consultant and primary collaborator.

16.5 CONCLUSIONS

This chapter defined and explained the research field of ethnophysiography and its role in documenting aspects of languages relating to landscape. Together with a discussion of key ethical issues, it also summarized methods used in obtaining terms for landscape features and toponyms in a manner which addressed an identified set of threats to the validity of the information. The authors hope that this chapter will assist others undertaking similar work, and would very much welcome enquiries about their efforts. Some relevant papers can be found at: http://www.ncgia.buffalo.edu/ethnophysiography/.

....

CHAPTER 17

TOPONYMY

RECORDING AND ANALYSING PLACENAMES IN A LANGUAGE AREA

....

DAVID NASH

JANE SIMPSON

17.1 INTRODUCTION

....

Placenames are the most direct link between a language and its territory, current or ancestral. For many speech communities, placenames are an important part of their cultural heritage, encapsulating rights to land and recalling events, activities, and knowledge. Coming to grips with the placenames of a speech community involves understanding its landownership system, and the ways in which the people interact with the land (i.e. the practical uses they make of it as well as the ways of talking and thinking about land). Knowing something of the history and prehistory of the area is also important, as placenames may be taken over from earlier inhabitants who spoke a different language; even if the earlier inhabitants spoke an earlier form of the modern language, the relevant vocabulary and morphological structures may have changed since the initial bestowal. This is easy to see in the case of languages with written records, such as English (Cameron 1996), and can sometimes be conjectured in the case of speech communities without written records.

This chapter is directed at the situation of a language as spoken away from an urban area, in rural or more remote landscapes which the speakers have occupied for some generations. Working with speakers of such languages to document the placenames of an area requires working with as many speakers as feasible, since, as Hunn (1996) points out, speakers may vary considerably in the extent of the area they know, and the number of the placenames pertaining to that area. Thus placename documentation implicates variable collective knowledge to a greater extent than general lexical documentation. In many speech communities, place-names may be linked to landownership, and so can be sensitive topics; for example when there are disputes over the extent of an area designated by a placename. Sometimes placenames (as with proper names generally) may be treated as intellectual property, and there may be restrictions on dissemination of information about the place or the placename (Bradley and Kearney 2009).

Toponymy is the study of placenames and their systematic properties within a geographic area or speech community. The need to understand toponymy arises in interdisciplinary and multidisciplinary fieldwork, most obviously in basic location references, whether in biological and physical sciences, or as resonant landmarks in biography and narrative. See also the chapters in this volume on astronomy (Holbrook, Chapter 15), and geography (Turk et al., Chapter 16). Placename documentation relates also to general site recording, cartography, and GIS (Geographic Information Systems: software for storing, managing, and displaying data about places linked to coordinate systems). These related fields are beyond the scope of this chapter.

17.2 LINGUISTIC ASPECTS

Recording the linguistic properties of the name(s) of a place focuses on treating each placename just as any other lexical item in the language. To recognize the placename as a lexeme means first distinguishing it from a description—what makes for example *Bald Mountain* a placename rather than a description of a particular bare mountain. This is not always easy; placenames may have 'descriptive force' (Hunn 1996), in that the name calls to mind some property of the site, or something associated with it. Indeed, descriptions and placenames may merge (Wilkinson, Marika, and Williams 2009), especially for communities in which placenames are created readily for minor places, as Widlok argues is the case for the ≠Akhoe Hai//om people of northern Namibia (Widlok 2008).

Having ascertained that an expression is a placename, we need to describe its denotation, the sense of the name (literal meaning), how the sense relates to the denotation, its etymology if it is not transparent, including any folk etymologies, and its connotations. We also need to find out the grammatical properties of the place-name, both the internal morphological properties and the combinatory properties.

In addition to these usual properties of a lexical item, a placename has further properties to document: the origin of the name (how the name was bestowed and by whom), and the properties of the place denoted: the location of the denotation according to some geographic coordinate system, possibly the social location of the place (e.g. in the land tenure system of the speakers), and associated history, stories, songs, designs, uses, and resources.

A useful general field guide to eliciting placenames and landscape terms has been prepared by researchers at the Max Planck Institute (Nijmegen) (Bohnemeyer et al. 2004; Burenhult 2008a). For work on the placenames of a particular language, a good start is to seek out gazetteers and materials on placenames of the region, and neighbouring groups, because sometimes similar strategies for forming placenames and attitudes towards placenames are found among neighbours (cf. the calquing of morphological properties of placenames in neighbouring but genetically distant languages in northern Australia: McConvell 2009).

17.2.1 Location of the denotation—in the field

With a view to toponymic recording, one can supplement the usual field equip-ment with good maps and a GPS receiver. Basic topographic survey maps can be supplemented by cadastral (land tenure), geological, and vegetation maps. Histor-ical maps can be useful to understand references to past events. In countries that have been colonized, early maps and surveyors' field notes and diaries may contain reference to placenames or variant forms of placenames of the people displaced by the colonizers.

Maps may already be available in digital form, and if not, can be scanned for portability. Digital maps, like any digital graphics, are of two basic kinds: raster and vector, with the latter being more amenable to manipulation by software. Digital maps may constitute interrelated 'layers' within a GIS, including image maps derived from aerial photographs and/or satellite imagery.

Ideally the fieldworker would visit each site with several knowledgeable people, determine with them the area, and maybe photograph or sketch aspects of the site. Even without a site visit, the researcher can have the locals sketch the place in their own terms This may be a map, or it may be a route map locating the place on a track with respect to other places. (*The History of Cartography* (Harley and Wood-ward 1987, 1998) includes coverage of indigenous mapping practices around the world.) With the help of locals, the researcher can locate the area on a survey map and determine its coordinates. Below, we discuss further the kind of information involved in placename documentation.

17.2.2 Denotation

Several senses of the 'meaning' of a placename are to be distinguished. Most basic is its location, part of the denotation of the placename. Understanding the denotation of a placename requires working out what is denoted spatially (including landform, landmark, and built structures). The literal meaning, etymology, and etiology or story behind the name are other aspects (considered below). A place can be conceptualized as having zero (a point), one (linear), or two (areal) dimensions (possibly even three dimensions). For example, a name apparently denoting a river may on inquiry be shown to denote the entire river (and tributaries or possibly its entire catchment), or just a stretch of the channel, or just a pool in the river. The placename may have a narrow (focal) referent and extended referents. What counts as a place worthy of a name will depend on the geographic types recognized by speakers of the language, as well as on the way the speakers use the land, and on historical circumstance.

Each language can be expected to have its own classification of landforms (see Turk et al., Chapter 16 above, and the papers in Burenhult 2008a). At a basic level this depends on the environment, what geographical features are present. But this will be tempered by the ways in which the language's speakers interact with the landscape. For some groups, watercourses are significant places worthy of names; others emphasize the eminences. For some groups, a hill may be a noticeable feature crying out for a name; for others, a well (or rockhole) beside the hill may be much more nameworthy. For some, soil types may be important, determining plants and animal habitats or what crops can be grown.

Hence, the fieldworker needs to work with speakers to document the categorization of landform types in that language, as well as the built structure types (e.g. bridges, aqueducts, irrigation channels), types of habitation (e.g. villages, hamlets, cities, parishes), and farming and forestry types (e.g. paddock, copse, forest, common).

The term 'landform' needs to be considered to include places away from land such as water features; coastal and maritime communities can be expected to have names for sandbars, reefs, currents, fishing grounds, or navigational waypoints. The fieldworker should not expect an equivalence between, say, the category of *mountain* in English, and a category used to denote eminences in the language concerned (Levinson 2008). See also Turk et al. (Chapter 16 above).

It is important to work with consultants to determine good, prototypical examples of particular landform types. This requires paying attention while travelling around the territory. A useful technique can be to ask for guidance on photographing exemplars of each landform type named within the language. This can be cross-checked by photo-matching games in which one speaker is asked to describe a photograph of a landscape to another speaker in such a way that the second speaker can pick out the correct photo from a set.

The contribution of land use varies considerably around the world. Universally, people need fresh water, and so there will be words for sources of water, whether natural (springs, rivers, pools, soakages) or constructed (wells, dams, reservoirs, canals, irrigation channels). Communities living by rivers will have names for crossings or bridges. Communities with well-defined travel routes may have names for paths and trails. Farming communities may have names for fields and grazing land. Sedentary communities can be expected to have names for groups of dwellings. There may be no hard and fast line between landform types and places arising from the inhabitants' interaction with the landscape; for example, a particular tree may be a favourite place to camp, or some bushes may do double duty as a windbreak (Widlok 1996). In some speech communities celestial patterns may be treated as part of the landform categorization (Cablitz 2008), and then may be named in ways which extend placename systems.

Once the landform and built structure categorization has been determined, it can be compared with the kinds of categories used in placenames. They may be the same (e.g. *bridge* and *Cambridge*). Sometimes the placenames may contain landform or built structure names not used in everyday speech, whether archaic as -*ham* in English *Birmingham*, or borrowed from an earlier occupier (e.g. *Lancaster*, which includes Latin *castra* 'camp').

Some places will gain names by virtue of their role as landmarks for travellers, whether by sea or by land. Thus navigation and mapping tasks may be helpful tools in eliciting placenames (Burenhult and Levinson 2008a). Landmarks are part of way-finding, and how people navigate and use the land may affect their place-naming systems. For example, in some communities there are placenames which derive from other placenames because a basic place is taken as a reference point for other places: so *North Sydney, South Sydney*. A similar pattern is evident where a base name repeats in a set of derived toponyms, even though the base is not used as a toponym absolutely, such as *Great Haseley, Little Haseley; Upper Mangrove, Lower Mangrove*.

Placenames live on as landmarks long after the historical circumstance that made them once important. For example, the placename *Charing Cross* in London derives from a Christian cross erected in a former hamlet Charing: the hamlet and the cross no longer exist, but the place where they were is a reference point in London.

17.2.3 Sense, etymology, and etiology

A placename may be transparent; its sense may consist, for example, of a landform type *El Paso* (The Pass), or of a modifier plus landform or built structure type *Red River, Rio Grande*. If such a placename becomes associated with a nearby habitation, then the sense and the denotation diverge, and with time the relation becomes less clear. So *El Paso* is better known as the name of a city. However, it is quite normal in some speech communities for a placename to have no synchronic analysis, whether because the name has been taken over from another language or because the sense has been lost through the generations.

Determining whether a placename is semantically transparent is not easy, since people and communities may well develop folk etymologies for the names of places. It is also difficult if there are concerns about landownership; speakers of language X may be reluctant to admit that a placename in their country is analyzable in language Y if speakers of language Y formerly inhabited that country. Without knowing the circumstances of the bestowal of the name, we can rarely be certain that we have accurately determined the etymological sense of the placename. This is not to discount the importance of recording folk etymologies—the folk etymology of a landform may actually link it into place-name subsystems that have emerged since the initial bestowal. Folk etymologies are useful for understanding how speakers fit the place and the placename into their understandings of the land and its ownership. Ideally, the etymology of a placename is discovered by finding out who bestowed the name, and the circumstances of the bestowal. This is usually impossible for speech communities that do not have written records extending back before oral traditions—indeed, there may be traditions of how all places have been named by ancestral beings (Tamisari 2002). These sometimes competing accounts constitute the etiology of the name.

Once a large body of placenames has been collected, it may be possible to find patterns of placenaming which in turn may help in elucidating the senses of the placenames and the semantic systems of the speech community (Hunn 1996). For example, some speech communities use landform and built structure types as parts of placenames, creating binomial structures or possessive structures, as English speakers do. Others rarely use them. Some communities create placenames from short sentences describing events that happened at the place or that describe characteristic activities at the site. Some communities build the names of people into placenames, whether reflecting some kind of ownership or association or commemoratively, as in the many places in colonized countries named after grandees of the colonizing countries.

Even if a landform or structure is used as part of the sense of the name, the modifier may require exposition. It may be a commemorative modifier (the name *Flinders Island* consists of a landform type and a modifier commemorating the explorer Matthew Flinders), or a metaphor, which describes the landform or something which is associated with the landform (*Pelican Lagoon*), or a modifier which sets a landform as part of a subsystem (*First Creek, Second Creek*).

17.2.4 Social position of the place

Which places get named will be affected by sociocultural practices. Some places may have religious significance. The landownership and governance system of a group will also result in the creation of areas which then are assigned names. The area serviced by a particular church may get a parish name; areas ruled by particular types of people or institutions may be named (County Antrim, Ulster Province, and so on).

Areas of land may be related hierarchically, e.g. farm/parish/region/state. Basso (1984) has described what he calls 'placename partitioning' among the Western Apache, according to which, as population size increases, social differentiation occurs, and a need arises for assigning names to places within named areas. This also results in relations between places being expressed in the names *New X* and *Old X, East X* and *West X, Little X* and *Great X, Upper X* and *Lower X*. The need to differentiate places with the same name may add to this: *Aix-en-Provence, Aix-la-Chapelle (Aachen), Aix-les-Bains* are three French names for places where the base *Aix* derives from the Latin *aqua* 'water', but which are differentiated further (in Provence, 'the chapel', 'the baths'). Places may also be related linearly, as places along a path or trail as in pilgrimages, or more abstractly, as in the Australian 'Dreaming tracks' (the travels of an ancestral being).

17.2.5 Connotations of the placename

Places will have linked to them stories of events that happened at those places, and they may figure as landmarks in biography (Myers 1991) and narrative. The name of the place may be a mnemonic for an event which is believed to have happened at the place (whether in actuality or in mythology) (Merlan 2001), and so placenames may be used allusively in everyday conversation to remind people of those stories (Basso 1996). A placename may evoke a mnemonic network containing it, such as a known travel route, or (as mentioned) a mythic route such as an Australian 'Dreaming track'.

A placename may form the basis of a personal name, from a life event strongly associating a person to a place. In Australia at least, a deceased person may be conventionally referred to by their place of death (e.g. Myers 1991:132, possibly suffixed, as in Warlpiri with -*wana* 'general locative').

Places may have associated songs, dances, or designs, knowledge of which acts in part as signs of landownership, as in central Australia. Styles of cooking, clothing, or craft all may be associated with particular areas and places.

17.3 GRAMMATICAL PROPERTIES OF PLACENAMES

Here we consider the structure of placenames, and the syntactic constraints on the use of placenames. Placenames are proper names and as such may constitute a word class in some languages, with placenames as a subclass. According to the degree of shared properties in morphology, syntax, and semantics, there may also be subclasses within the toponym class.

17.3.1 Morphological structure of placenames

Placenames may be monomorphemic, they may consist of compounds, or they may consist of derived nominals with productive or unproductive suffixes. In many European languages there are binomial placenames, with generics as part of the name (e.g. *Loch Lomond, Lake Windermere, Bodensee*, where *Loch, Lake*, and *See* are generics denoting water features).

In some languages, placenames may consist of reduced clauses, as in some North American and Australian languages (Basso 1996; Baker 2002). Placenames may consist of phrases. These may be synchronically 'transparent, e.g. the French *Côte d'Azur* (coast of blue). A name like *Newcastle* is evidently made up of an adjective and a noun, but the initial stress alerts us to the fact that it is a proper name, and not a compound. Placenames may retain archaisms—for example, *le* in the English placename *Chester-le-Street* is a vestige of Old French *en le* 'in the'. Other examples include the lack of article found in names such as the French *Villefranche-sur-Mer* or the English *Southend-on-Sea*, where *mer* and its counterpart, *sea*, lack articles.

17.3.2. Morphology special to toponyms

Placenames may have special morphological properties. These can consist of derivational affixes which are found only on placenames but they can also relate to allomorphy. For example, in the Australian language Pintupi the augment allomorph *-nga* occurs just on C-final proper name stems, such as in *Narrkalnga* or *Purlpurlnga* (Myers 1991: 132). Other examples include possibilities such as requiring locative case to express static locations on all location nouns except placenames (Harvey 1999; McConvell 2009). The researcher needs to be alert to forms derived from placenames, adjectival or gentilic ('inhabitant of') forms; these may well exhibit irregularities, as in English *Novocastrian, Mancunian, Michigander, Sydney-sider.*

17.3.3 Syntactic properties of placenames

An important syntactic property of placenames is their interaction with definiteness. Any proper name is inherently definite; in a language where definiteness is a grammatical category, placenames can be expected to count as definite, even if not explicitly marked as such. To illustrate: in English, a small fraction of placenames begin with 'The...' (such as *The Briars*, or names of rivers, *the Danube*, the Thames), but rarely if ever begin with the indefinite article *A...*; and note that derived placenames drop the article (*Thames Head, Thames Ditton*).

A second important syntactic property is how placenames behave with respect to the expression of locational relation. Is a placename inherently locational, or must it receive some marking for locational relations such as static location (*at, in, on*) or direction (*to, from*)? In some Australian languages, some placenames are unmarked for static location, but marked for direction (McConvell 2009). In some languages special locational prepositions are used for placenames and nominals viewed as locations, distinct from other nominals (so a difference between *in London* and *in a canoe*) (Cablitz 2008).

17.3.4 Sample dictionary (or gazetteer) entry

Here is an example from central Australia of a placename as it might appear set out as an entry in a dictionary of one of the local languages, Warumungu:

Warupunju. ['waru͵punʸtʸu] Area of Murchison Range, 20°S 13°20'E. Fire Dreaming spread from focal site. Alyawarr equivalent Rwepenty (*Rubuntja*) analysable as *rwe* 'fire', *-penty* 'toponymic suffix'. The name is not analysable in Warumungu. See the Aboriginal Land Commission (1991) report.

The Marshallese–English online dictionary (Abo et al. 2009) lists more than 3,000 placenames, both alphabetically and geographically. Kari (2008) has compiled an exemplary gazetteer of over 2,000 placenames in a part of Alaska. One of the most detailed published gazetteers of an Australian language is the companion to the Bardi dictionary (Aklif 1999).

17.4 WIDER IMPLICATIONS

17.4.1 Alternative names for one place

There may be two or more synonyms for a placename. In some speech communities, the more important a place is deemed to be, the more likely it is to bear more than one name; this may arise from there being an alternative name in a neighbouring language, and can relate to a view that multiple names are an index of importance (Wilkinson et al. 2009). The synonyms might vary according to speech types or register; thus in a song, the form of a placename may be modified. A variant can be used for poetic or humorous effect, such as referring to Edinburgh as *Old Reeky*, or New York City as *The Big Apple*. In Australia and New Zealand many placenames as used in English (especially long ones) have commonly used abbreviations, thus the Sydney suburb *Woolloomooloo* is called by locals *The 'Loo* (Simpson 2001).

Placename synonyms will be encountered in languages spoken in a culture which observes avoidance of the name of a recently deceased person: if a placename derives from, or just sounds similar to, a personal name, and the personal name can no longer be uttered, then the placename can be replaced by a synonym or perhaps by a revealing circumlocution. In Aboriginal Australia, for instance, a proscribed placename might be replaced by a descriptive term based on distinctive flora, or the place's Dreaming affiliation. The use of a particular placename may be proscribed for the whole community or just for a few close relatives, and the proscribed placename can return to general use once the mourning period has passed.

With a complex site, different site elements may not be terminologically distinguished, or else a generic term may be optionally added to the placename to distinguish a site element, such as a hill, well, or claypan at the location. Whether the composite nominal is itself a placename may not be clear.

17.4.2 Language engineering and loans

Not all placenames are necessarily 'old'. There are situations where a new placename is required because there is a new 'place'. Typically this arises from extensions and modifications of the built environment: street names are a common example, or a new centre of habitation, but it might result from a landslide or sinkhole collapse or some such natural change. Placename replacement and revival may arise during upheavals in political history, such as when one colonial power has been replaced by another.

The new placename, as in the rest of the vocabulary, might be a lexical creation, or might result from shifts of meaning. Lexical creations may involve the internal resources of the language, or may involve borrowing. Borrowing of a placename leads to the existence of two separate places with the same name, so that a placename echoes another place with the same or overlapping name. An example is in English *Waterlooville*, which designates an English village that grew up after the decisive battle fought against the French near Waterloo in Belgium. *Waterloo* commemorates the victory; the final descriptor is the French *ville* 'town, city'.

A new name might be imposed by the dominant authority, and may be in a language which dominates the local language; sometimes a more or less sensitive attempt is made to derive a name using the resources of the local language (Amery 2002; Baker 2002). If these new names are to be listed in a dictionary or gazetteer, it is a good idea to flag them as 'introduced'.

Especially in a postcolonial situation, placenames may occur in doublets, one from the traditional land owners and the other bestowed in the historical colonial period. In some jurisdictions this is officially recognized as Dual Naming. An example is the monolith in central Australia known as Uluru and Ayers Rock. There can be disagreement, at times passionate, within the language community over what the 'true' name of a place is—or, even when the name is agreed, the 'true' location of the place.

17.4.3 Extensions of placenames

There are other complex lexemes incorporating a placename: such as *Boston bun*, *Antarctic tern*. These are expected in languages which have spread considerably from their original territory, but are not nearly so common in 'small' languages which are not languages of wider communication. In some Australian languages, the same word can be a placename and the term for a commodity (such as an ochre) sourced from that place—rather like the English word *china* (*chinaware* crockery), from *China*.

17.5 DATA STORAGE AND PRESENTATION

Information collected on placenames can be stored in data files organized like a dictionary. Indeed, each placename can be an entry in the master dictionary file for the language under study. Alternatively, the placenames can be maintained in a dictionary file of their own, effectively a digital gazetteer. A placename entry has fields in common with those of other lexemes (spelling, pronunciation, part of speech, irregular morphology, variant forms, denotation, synonyms, cross-references, etymology), and some special additional fields (location coordinates, corresponding name in other languages). Whether to maintain the placename information in the master dictionary file or in a separate gazetteer is a decision for each project. Relevant considerations would include the extent to which placenames derive from ordinary vocabulary; if quite a lot of placenames derive from other vocabulary items, there can be value in explicitly showing the relationship by way of composite dictionary entries.

If a placenames data file includes geographic coordinates (typically latitude and longitude) for each site, then a Keyhole Markup Language (KML) file can be derived. KML is a file format and associated XML (Extensible Markup Language) specification, which allows interchange of locational data between various software, and in particular allows display by Google Earth. The KML file format also allows the storage of other attributes along with each location, and also allows storage of celestial data (such as stars, constellations, planets). For linguistic research, however, KML would not be an ideal master format, as it is primarily about locations, not about names (as words).

Toponymic data can be combined with other spatial data in a GIS application. Usually this is achieved by inclusion of a placenames layer. In multimedia GIS, each name may be linked to images, sound files, etc. In recent years there have emerged applications tailored for Third World situations, under the headings of Public Participation GIS (PPGIS) and Participatory 3D Modelling (P3DM), and these could offer a framework for detailed research on toponymy. See Chapin, Lamb, and Threlkeld (2005) and the extensive references.

A range of accessible materials can be produced from placename documentation. Maps and gazetteers are obvious and useful reference works for community members and schools, as well as for informing a wider public about local nomenclature. An encyclopedic gazetteer based around geographic knowledge and placename networks is another rewarding way of presenting the information and its wider links. An excellent example is *Shem Pete's Alaska* (Kari, Fall, and Shem Pete 2003), which documents 973 named places in the Upper Cook Inlet area, a brilliant representation and evocation of Dena'ina and Ahtna knowledge. Alongside dictionary-style presentation, graphic representation employing expert cartography enhances accessibility.

17.6 Further reading

Harley, John B. and David Woodward (eds.) 1987–1998. *The history of cartography.* University of Chicago Press.

Koch, Harold and Luise Hercus (eds.) 2009. Aboriginal placenames: Naming and re naming the Australian landscape. (Aboriginal History Monograph 19) Canberra: ANU E Press and Aboriginal History Incorporated. (http://epress.anu.edu.au/ placenames_citation.html Accessed 8 April 2010)

Stewart, George R. 2008 [1945/]. *Names on the land: A historical account of place-naming in the United States.* New York : New York Review Books.

Tobias, Terry N. 2010. *Living Proof: The Essential Data-Collection Guide for Indigenous Use-and-Occupancy Map Surveys.* Ecotrust Canada and the Union of BC Indian Chiefs. http://nativemaps.org/node/3684

http://www.ecotrust.ca/first-nations/new-book-use-and-occupancy-map-surveys-now-available

Also the more popular version *Chief Kerry's Moose,* published in 2000, available at http://www.ubcic.bc.ca/files/PDF/Tobias_whole.pdf

Wikipedia entries (Accessed 8 April 2010):

Participatory 3D Modelling (P3DM): http://en.wikipedia.org/wiki/Participatory_3D_Modelling_(P3DM)

Public Participation GIS: http://en.wikipedia.org/wiki/PPGIS

PART IV

COLLABORATING
WITH THE
COMMUNITY

CHAPTER 18

....

ETHICAL ISSUES IN LINGUISTIC FIELDWORK

....

KEREN RICE

18.1 INTRODUCTION[1]

....

In the past decade or so, there has been a resurgence of attention to ethics in linguistic fieldwork. When I was asked to speak on the subject of ethics in fieldwork in 1999, I was surprised to see how much literature I could find on the scholarly aspects of ethics in fieldwork—namely the imperative for fieldwork on endangered languages in order to have records of the languages. I was equally surprised to learn that, with rare exceptions, very little had been written on the relationships between the linguistic fieldworker and the people with whom she or he engages. Over the past decade there has been an increasing amount written on ethics in fieldwork, focusing on responsibilities not only with respect to languages but also with respect to individuals and communities, and to knowledge systems. This surge of interest around ethics in linguistic fieldwork is likely closely related to the impact of changes in social science research more generally on linguistics, where there has been increased interest in participatory action and community-based research in

[1] Thank you to Nick Thieberger and to two anonymous reviewers for very helpful comments. This work is supported by the Canada Research Chair in Linguistics and Aboriginal Studies held by Keren Rice.

recent years, as well as to the developing influence of indigenous methodologies on linguistic fieldwork. Many linguistic fieldworkers, like others in social science areas, are attempting to move away from an 'expert subject' model to more collaborative types of research. At the same time, the situation of language endangerment, and the development of documentary linguistics as a field, have led to a call for recording and archiving a broad range of language materials, in an attempt to capture the speech of a community. Tensions can arise between these different developments in linguistic fieldwork.

In this chapter, I examine ethics with respect to ethics codes, individuals, communities, languages, and knowledge systems, setting out questions to be considered with respect to each. I begin in §18.2 with a dictionary definition of ethics, and then introduce some ethics codes and how they develop what ethics means with respect to research with people. Following this (§18.3) I narrow the focus, providing an overview of some of the ethics codes that are of relevance to fieldworkers. I then address ethics in linguistic fieldwork, focusing on fairly traditional questions (§18.4). Following this I turn to a different type of question, examining ethics with respect to language (§18.5.1) and ethics with respect to knowledge systems (§18.5.2)—areas that raise additional questions, especially concerning the responsibilities of the linguist in the field.

It is important to note from the start that there are no simple answers to ethical questions. Ethics is the substance of centuries of debate by philosophers and others, and anyone entering a fieldwork setting where they are living in a different culture with different norms will have to think deeply about many issues, many of them with ethics at their core. Different individuals, settings, and times lead to different decisions about these complex issues.

18.2 WHAT IS ETHICS? A BROAD PERSPECTIVE

What is ethics? A dictionary provides the following definition: 'the moral principles by which a person is guided.'[2] This definition includes terms that are not straightforward to understand—what is 'moral'?—and leaves quite open what these moral principles are.

Formal ethics codes attempt to make concrete what is meant by this rather abstract notion of moral principles. An important set of principles is set out in the Belmont Report, a 1979 report from the US Department of Health, Education, and Welfare which attempts to summarize basic ethical principles and guidelines for

---

[2] Oxford English Dictionary on-line; accessed 29 April 2009, http://dictionary.oed.com/

research involving human participants and forms the foundation for many of the ethics codes that have been developed in the social sciences in the United States. The Belmont Report presents three basic principles for ethical research: respect for persons, beneficence, and justice. The first of these principles concerns the protection of the autonomy of all people, treating them with respect and protecting those with limited autonomy. Consequences of this are notions of informed consent, privacy, confidentiality, and protection for vulnerable participants, among others. The second principle states that it is important both to maximize benefits to research and minimize risks to research participants, realized as statements such as 'Do no harm', 'Promote good', and 'Reduce risks'. The third principle, justice, is designed to ensure that procedures be reasonable, non-exploitative, and fairly administered.

Other ethics codes share the core of these principles, developing them in different ways. To take a single example, a recent revised statement on ethical conduct for research with humans by the Canadian Interagency Advisory Panel on Research Ethics (December 2010) takes respect for the value of human dignity as its starting point and identifies three core principles, respect for persons, concern for welfare, and justice. The policy statement acknowledges that these principles must be interpreted in the context of a particular community. It also stresses that concern for welfare includes physical, mental, and spiritual health, involving the quality of life in all its aspects.

Respect for persons, beneficence, justice, and welfare are far-reaching principles that likely receive general agreement cross-culturally, subject to local interpretation, and they frame the discussion that follows in this paper. Building on these principles, many ethics codes have been developed, and I turn to a discussion of some of these.

18.3 UNDERSTANDING ETHICS: ETHICS CODES

In this section, I briefly summarize three ethics protocols, two written by academic societies and one written as a guide for health researchers doing research in Aboriginal communities in Canada.

I begin with the ethics code of the American Anthropological Association which has had an ethics code evolving over time. The paragraph below is the preamble to the latest version, approved in February 2009.

Anthropological researchers, teachers and practitioners are members of many different communities, each with its own moral rules or codes of ethics. Anthropologists have moral obligations as members of other groups, such as the family, religion, and community, as well as the profession. They also have obligations to the scholarly discipline, to the wider society and culture, and to the human species, other species, and the environment. Furthermore, fieldworkers may develop close relationships with persons or animals with whom they work, generating an additional level of ethical considerations. In a field of such complex involvements and obligations, it is inevitable that misunderstandings, conflicts, and the need to make choices among apparently incompatible values will arise. Anthropologists are responsible for grappling with such difficulties and struggling to resolve them in ways compatible with the principles stated here.

This code recognizes that there are different codes of ethics in different groups, and that anthropological researchers have moral obligations to the groups they work with. These responsibilities are developed more fully in later sections of the code: researchers have the responsibility to avoid harm or wrong, to respect the well-being of people, and to consult actively with affected individuals or groups with the goal of establishing a working relationship that can be beneficial to all involved. The preamble also introduces a second type of ethics: in addition to its stress on obligations to people, whatever the group might be, it identifies obligation to the scholarly discipline. This echoes one part of beneficence, as laid out in the Belmont report—the part that focuses on benefits to research.

These different responsibilities are echoed in the recent ethics code developed by the Linguistic Society of America (LSA). The LSA code notes, among other responsibilities, responsibility to both individuals and communities and responsibility to scholarship as key in ethics. It has a number of specific provisions that are applicable to fieldwork, and I cite relevant sections below (Linguistic Society of America ethics statement 2009: 2–3).

Linguists should do everything in their power to ensure that their research poses no threat to the well-being of research participants.

- Research participants have the right to control whether their actions are recorded in such a way that they can be connected with their personal identity. They also have the right to control who will have access to the resulting data, with full knowledge of the potential consequences.
- Linguists are responsible for obtaining the informed consent of those who provide them with data (regardless of whether and how that consent is documented), for maintaining any expected confidentiality in storing data and reporting findings, and for ensuring that any individual's participation in their research is completely voluntary at every stage.
- Linguists should carefully consider whether compensation of some kind is appropriate, be it remuneration for time and effort, or use of their knowledge and expertise to benefit participants or their communities.

While acknowledging that what constitutes the relevant community is a complex issue, we urge linguists to consider how their research affects not only individual research participants, but also the wider community. In general, linguists should strive to determine what will be constructive for all those involved in a research encounter, taking into account the community's cultural norms and values.

Ideal frameworks for interaction with outside researchers vary depending on a community's particular culture and history. In many communities, responsibility for linguistic and cultural knowledge is viewed as corporate, so that individual community members are not in a position to consent to share materials with outsiders, and linguists must try to determine whether there are individuals who can legitimately represent the community in working out the terms of research. Some communities regard language, oral literature, and other forms of cultural knowledge as valuable intellectual property whose ownershp should be respected by outsiders; in such cases linguists should comply with community wishes regarding access, archiving, and distribution of results. Other communities are eager to share such knowledge in the context of a long-term relationship of reciprocity and exchange. In all cases where the community has an investment in language research, the aims of an investigation should be clearly discussed with the community and community involvement sought from the earliest stages of project planning.

Turning from the codes developed by academic associations to those written by groups that have often been the targets of research, generally without directing the research, we find similar principles to those outlined above and some additional principles as well, and I focus here on the latter. The Canadian Institutes of Health Research ethics guidelines for researchers working in Aboriginal health begin by saying that a researcher should understand and respect Aboriginal world views, including responsibilities towards traditional and sacred knowledge. The guidelines address the need to understand and respect the community's jurisdiction over the conduct of research, and the need to provide for an option for participatory research. The guidelines speak to the importance of working with community leaders as well as individuals in gaining free, prior, and informed consent to carry out research involving traditional and sacred knowledge. Other articles address the need to seek guidance from community knowledge holders; the inherent rights of Aboriginal peoples and their communities to cultural knowledge, sacred knowledge, and cultural practices and traditions which are shared with the researcher; intellectual property; the importance that research benefit a community as well as a researcher; the need for a researcher to support education and training; the importance of ongoing communication with the community; and the role of the community in interpretation of data as well as in acknowledgement of community members. Thus this code focuses on responsibilities not just to the individual but also to communities and their practices, and on collaboration in research. We will see many of the principles of this protocol echoed throughout this chapter.

The large-scale picture of ethics that we get through a study of ethics codes is useful—in thinking about ethics, a researcher is thinking about dignity, about respect, about justice, about welfare, about individuals, about communities, about knowledge. We realize these principles through institutionalizing policies that require informed consent, examine confidentiality, and deal with management of data, for instance. While the codes are problematic in numerous ways (see e.g. Rieschild 2003 and the report of the Social Sciences And Humanities Research Ethics Special Working Committee 2004), the codes at their best remind us that ethics is not monolithic but multi-faceted, and that ethics principles must be interpreted relative to societal norms. They nevertheless are framed very broadly. The core ethics principles are sometimes put in other ways that are, perhaps, more easily interpretable—another way of stating them is: 'Do no harm, do some good, and show respect.' Bowern (2008: 148) develops these ideas in her statement of what ethics is: she defines ethics as 'a way of working that you, the research community and the language community think is appropriate'. These more informal notions of ethics, too, require attention in order to understand how they translate into ethical behaviour, and this is especially the case when working with people from a different culture, where the researcher must strive to learn as much as possible about the culture so as to limit the amount of unintended harm, to understand whether actions actually might lead to overall good, and to ensure an appropriate notion of respect. In the next sections I examine some specific questions that a fieldworker might want to think about in terms of linguistic fieldwork with people and communities, languages, and worldviews in hoping to adhere to these principles and understanding what it means to be appropriate.

18.4 ETHICS IN THE FIELD

I will begin again at a broad level—university-based ethics protocols—and then turn to ethics on the ground, organizing the discussion around a series of questions addressing issues that arise out of the various general principles introduced in §18.2. The following are some of the sources on ethics in linguistic fieldwork: textbooks by Bowern (2008), Crowley (2007), and Tsunoda (2005); articles by Austin (2010a), Dwyer (2006), and Rice (2006); and the special issue of *Language and Communication* edited by Innes and Debenport (2010). For some general references on ethics in fieldwork, Cameron et al. (1992), Cameron (1998), Clifford and Marcus (1986), Czaykowska-Higgins (2009), Fluehr-Lobban (1991), Geertz (1968), Shaw (2004), and Yamada (2007) are particularly valuable. See also the appendix to this chapter for some additional references.

18.4.1 What about before the fieldwork begins?

A fieldworker from a university, be they an instructor or a student, will likely have to go through a process within their university to have an ethics protocol approved. While ethics protocols differ somewhat from place to place, the core questions that they ask are similar, and are aimed at meeting the types of principles discussed above—affording dignity, beneficence, respect, showing concern for welfare.

These protocols require that the researcher answer questions in a number of areas. Protocols typically involve questions about the research and how it will be conducted. They ask about how participants will be recruited for the research, and how they will be selected and compensated. They question whether the material to be studied is sensitive or not. They inquire about possible risks to participants in the research, be they physical, psychological/emotional, or social. They query whether deception is involved. They ask about possible harms and benefits of the research to the participants. They inquire about informed consent and how it will be achieved and maintained. They ask about confidentiality, and they inquire about anonymity. They raise questions about what will be done with the materials gathered.

These questions as they are framed in an ethics protocol are often difficult to interpret, and it is important to keep in mind the significance of the general principles that underlie the particular questions that one is asked to answer to have the ethics protocol approved. They can also be difficult to answer. In many cases the questions are not really quite right for linguistic fieldwork, or for qualitative research more generally (see e.g. Social Sciences And Humanities Research Ethics Special Working Committee 2004 for challenges for qualitative research, and Rieschild 2003 for specific challenges in linguistic fieldwork); and in addition, in most cases there is not a single way of behaving ethically, especially in cross-cultural research: what is considered to be not sensitive by one person or one community may be considered to be sensitive by another; what is appropriate methodology in one place is inappropriate in another. Preparing the ethics proto-col thus takes care and thought, and it is important to keep in mind that the basic principles that underlie the complex protocol are actually the end point.

While completing the ethics protocol may be a challenge for someone doing fieldwork, at the same time the protocol helps in reflecting about the types of ethical and moral issues that might arise in fieldwork. The types of questions are likely to be asked in some form or another by any group that you are working with. People generally want to understand research in which they are involved: they need to agree freely to be part of the research, understanding its possible consequences; they need to decide who they want the results of the research made available to, and so on.

It is possible that the unit that reviews an ethics protocol might require addi-tional information beyond the core issues discussed above. For instance, they may want an indication of support from the community or communities that you are planning to go to.[3] It is important to seek this support early on in any case, whether required by the unit that reviews the ethics protocols or not—seeking support from the community leads to engagement with that community beginning early in the process, before actual fieldwork begins. It is the start of the building of a relation-ship. Much of ethics involves building respectful, reciprocal relationships, and

---

[3] It is important to note that the term 'community' is not a straightforward one, as it can be defined in any number of ways. The notion is that there may be a group larger than an individual that is important in the ethics process; it is not necessarily easy to determine just what that group is. I will use the term 'community', recognizing the difficulties inherent in this important word.

engagement with a community from the start is an indication that the researcher understands the importance of these values.

In addition to getting a formal ethics protocol approved, there are other things to be done before the fieldwork actually begins. As a linguist, it is natural to want to learn as much as possible about the language of study or closely related languages and about linguistics. A second type of preparation is probably of even greater importance: read as much as possible about the culture of where you are going and talk with people, as many as possible, who are from the area and who have been involved in work in the area. This type of preparation is invaluble in helping you to avoid unintentional harm, in understanding whether your actions might produce good, and in helping to ensure that respect is not naïve. People familiar with the area can give you invaluable advice about many of the issues raised in the next sections. Some communities are pleased to have researchers, and embrace their presence. In other communities, there is much suspicion of researchers, their goals, and their values. To some degree, how you are received depends on the history of research in a community. Some communities are struggling with their own problems, making it difficult to welcome an outsider; some might say no to researchers at a particular time, but welcome them at another time. Flexibility is important.

A first trip to a community will undoubtedly bring many unexpected things, but at the same time you will have had an opportunity to think in advance about many things if you prepare as fully as possible.

In many cases, completing the university ethics protocol and preparation through reading and talking is not sufficient to begin fieldwork. Some communities require that you have their permission before you can go to the community. Whether your own university requires it or not, it is important to find out if you can simply show up in a community, or if the community might want to review your research plans before giving you permission to carry out your research there.

18.4.2 Getting started in the community

What happens on reaching the field? This is an exciting time, and often a very anxious time as well. Hopefully through the preparation of the ethics protocol for the university, and through talking with people and reading, you are not entering a community cold, with the community having no knowledge of your impending arrival and you having no knowledge of the community beyond the language(s) spoken there. You have support (at least on paper), and you know who to meet when you first get there. What kind of ethical issues must you deal with? I focus here on people who are beginning fieldwork in a particular location, and especially on the novice fieldworker, rather than those who have already been involved in fieldwork in a community.

There are many aspects of fieldwork which at first sight may seem to be practical problems but which nevertheless raise questions of ethics that require careful consideration, and I raise some here, in the form of questions. There are no single, and often no simple, answers to these questions. Not all will be applicable in all circumstances, but overall these are issues that you are likely to face.

There are questions about settling in to a community.

Where should I live? This might seem like an odd question to ask when talking about ethics, but it can be important, if you have a choice. Where you live can affect who you interact with on an informal basis, and can affect what people think of you and how they interpret your goals, making it harder or easier to carry out the work. You might live with a family, in a rented space, in a hotel. There are issues of safety to be taken into account—safety both for you and for community members. For instance, there might be risks to a young woman living alone rather than with a family. There might be political consequences of living with a particular family that could have a detrimental effect on the work. A gay man might be uncomfortable in some settings. Safety issues within a community might suggest that it is preferable to live in a larger community, travelling in to the community to work. Advice is helpful when it is possible to get it, as each of these choices can have consequences for the fieldworker, for relationships with the community, and for the work to be done.

Unless you live on your own and do all your own food preparation, there are other issues you might face. If you are a vegetarian in a community where moose meat is highly valued, you might want to think about whether it would be interpreted as disrespectful for you to refuse moose meat that you are offered. If food considered a delicacy seems disgusting to you, you might consider the consequences of turning it down. While seemingly small, such issues can loom large in how people think of you, and are willing to cooperate with you. Balancing your needs and community expectations can be a challenge, but most find that it is well worth the while for all involved to consider such seemingly small things.

There are questions that relate to an ethics protocol.

Are there any kinds of permissions needed? My ethics protocol was approved in my home university. Can I just get started right away? Often there are other kinds of permissions that are needed, and in some instances, the university-approved ethics protocol, although necessary, can be the least important of all. In some places it is necessary to get a licence from the government in order to do research. This can take some time, and needs to be done before fieldwork can begin. Some communities might have their own written or oral ethics protocol procedures, defined in their terms. Once you arrive in a community, it might be important to meet with a chief or a king or an elder or some other local authority to get support and approval from them for your research. There might be gifts that need to be given. Community protocols are often unwritten, but asking questions and trying to understand these protocols is important to be able to even begin to do research within a community. Again, work in advance can be an enormous asset in getting this 'right.'

There are questions that relate to the fieldwork directly.

Who do I work with? Very often people will be recommended to you, or even arrangements made for you to work with a particular person or people. Sometimes there are people in the community who are regarded as the ones that researchers should work with. Some of these people might be ideal for someone beginning work on the language; others might be better for someone at a more advanced stage. You might not have a choice about who you work with, especially at the beginning, and you may need to find ways of reassessing a working relationship somewhere along the way. Who you work with, just like who you live with, may be political in a way that can be difficult to understand, and this can affect your work. While it is probably best to try to limit your involvement in the politics of a community, often involving very old and complex issues, sometimes it is difficult to know that this is what is going on. Political issues may be stated in a variety of terms; for instance, arguments about choices in orthography may find their roots in differences between groups within a community.

From another perspective, sometimes people who would be good to work with have other jobs. It is important to consider whether it is ethical to draw them away from other work for work that is likely to be of short term.

What do I tell people about my funding? You might have funding to do your research. There may be a perception that as a researcher, you are well off. And this might be true, from the perspective of the community, even if it is not true from your perspective. There may also be negative perceptions about certain funding sources. For instance, in a community where there are tensions with the government, funding from a government agency might make community members associate you with the government, and think that you might be sent to report on their activities. A community may have tried unsuccessfully to get funding for language work and wonder why you, with little or no knowledge of the language or culture, were successful in this while they were not, and this could inhibit the work. Trying to understand what the issues are might help you in finding a way to discuss them.

How do I tell people about what I am doing? What does linguistic work mean? What are people interested in? How can I explain what I do? When people engage in a project, they want to know what they are agreeing to do. It is important to find a way of explaining the work that you hope to do in terms that are accessible, and in ways that people might be able to engage in. In many communities you will need to find plain language in which you explain what you are doing and what your interests are. For instance, suppose that you want to carry out a phonetic study on a particular type of laryngeal contrast and require that people tell you if sounds are the same or different. People might push back, saying that you are trying to change the language or take away the language by asking these questions, and you might need to explain why this work could be important for them. Perhaps the research might relate to language programs that are in the schools, and trying to find a way that those learning the language as a second language are able to pronounce properly. If you are working collaboratively with the community (see later sections), this perhaps becomes easier, while introducing other challenges.

How much should I pay? There may be rates of pay that are generally accepted within a community, and it is likely important that you are in line with those. In some communities, people may be expected to work with a researcher without being paid, especially if the research is deemed to be of value to the community. There might be community standards about how different people are recompensed. Money might not be the most appropriate way of paying—gifts might be considered to be a more appropriate means of recompense, or an exchange of services. Establishing an appropriate means and rate of pay are part of showing respect. Once I was instructed by the band council of a community not to pay people, with the council telling people to give their time freely. When I returned to that community two years later, people told me that they would be happy to work, but only for pay.

It can be complicated within your home university to get funds released from a grant if you have one if you are paying with gifts, or if people are unwilling to sign that they have received payment. You most likely need to meet community standards, so this is something to work out with your university.

What about informed consent? In getting an ethics protocol approved, informed consent is an important issue. It is necessary to think about how you will deal with issues of consent before you begin fieldwork, but this becomes real once you are actually engaged in the fieldwork. While what is most important is probably what underlies informed consent, it is useful to begin with a brief discussion of the mechanics of getting informed consent, as this is not necessarily as straightforward as asking someone to sign a document—the type of informed consent that is often anticipated by ethics boards.

Informed consent can be indicated in various ways. A signature is one way of showing consent, but oral consent is usually possible as well. Some people may not have written literacy, and some may be reluctant to give their signature on what appears to be an official-looking document out of concern for what the consequences might be. In general, people are willing to provide oral consent if they wish to be engaged in the work. Sometimes, where speakers agree to recording, a researcher might record a statement of consent in place of written agreement.

What underlies consent is really what is important: the people who work with you need to understand what they are agreeing to do, and you need to find ways of explaining this clearly, in plain language, as discussed above. In an ongoing project, it is important to revisit issues of consent, as things will likely change over the duration of a project as the kinds of work change, as you become better known in the community.

When you seek informed consent, it is important that people know what they are consenting to. Linguistic fieldwork generally involves recordings, and consent must be sought to record (some people do not wish to be recorded; in some communities recording is not acceptable). This is only a first step, though. People must also be informed about how the materials might be used. At one extreme, will they be made freely available on the internet? At the other extreme, will they be available only to the researcher on a password-protected site? If the latter, what does this mean? Can they be used for commercial purposes? What are potential future uses? Issues of consent need to be negotiated and, generally, renegotiated as the research progresses. (See also Newman, Chapter 19 below.)

And what about confidentiality? In developing your ethics protocol, you had to discuss confidentiality. Many times in linguistic work, individuals want to be recognized by name, generally for stories, and often for elicited material as well. It is important to talk about this with people with whom you work, and to continue to talk about it, as people might change their minds, or want to be acknowledged for some materials but not for others. It is not good to make assumptions, or to generalize from one person, as not everyone will want the same thing, not every community will be the same, and an individual might feel differently about being identified depending on the material involved.

Confidentiality can be viewed in a second way. In addition to an interpretation of confidentiality as anonymity, discussed above, confidentiality can demand that information be kept private. For instance, there might be stories that are not meant for outsiders and that someone is willing to tell you, but does not want you to share with any others. In many Australian cultures, naming and showing pictures of people who have died is taboo, and if someone gives you such information, it may well be done believing that you will not share the knowledge with any others.

The above discussion is based on a model in which the researcher controls the agenda: the researcher determines, in advance, how things like informed consent will be handled, discussing these only later with the participants in the research, the researcher determines what the research agenda is. As mentioned in the introduction, recent years have seen the development of other ways of dong research, namely working with a community to determine common goals and objectives. This shift in paradigms raises a host of other very important ethical issues, and I address some of these next.

What responsibilities do I have as a researcher? What is the role for a researcher in this community at this particular point in time? At one time, a researcher basically set out his or her own approach, recognizing the core ethical principles outlined earlier. This may still be the agenda, with the researcher defining the project and community members participating in it in a traditional way. However, recent years have seen careful thinking about research, taking into account a wide range of issues that are briefly introduced above in the discussion of the Canadian Institute for Health Research guidelines for research with Aboriginal peoples. In discussion of postcolonial and indigenous ethics, there are themes that echo—more symmetric relationships between outside researcher and community; involvement of academic and community researchers in research projects with each serving as active members of a team, when appropriate, working together to determine a common agenda; responsibility of a researcher to help a community meet its own goals if asked. The obligations include working to understand each party's ethical and moral expectations of the other, and responsibilities on both sides. Grenoble and Whaley (2006) provide an overview of responsibilities of linguistics to communities with which they work (some recent works that address this topic include Amery 2006; Austin 2010a; Berardo and Yamamoto 2007; Czaykowska-Higgins 2009; Dobrin 2008; Dorian 2010; Grenoble 2009; Grinevald 2007; Hale and Hinton 2001; Himmelmann 1998; 2008; some papers in Innes and Debenport 2010; Otsuka and Wong 2007; Rice 2009; Shaw 2004; Speas 2009; Thieberger and Musgrave 2006; and Yamada 2007).

It is important to understand the role that you are able to play in a community at a particular point in time and what is expected of you. You might be expected to do something for the community. This could be a task like cooking for someone, or cleaning roads, or helping people with their income tax forms. In some cases, linguists are asked to help to develop orthographies, to participate in training people to make practical dictionaries, or to assist in creating language surveys or to provide language awareness workshops for teachers in the school. You might be asked to teach people how to digitize tapes, or how to use a video recorder, or to transcribe placenames. It is important to keep in mind what is realistic. Are you in the community for a month? What knowledge of the language and culture do you have? For instance, if you are just beginning fieldwork on a language that you know nothing about, the chances are good that work on developing an orthography is not realistic, while teaching how to archive materials may well be possible if you have that knowledge.

Researchers and communities do not always share perceptions about what their work is: communities may often have expectations of researchers that are not shared by the researchers, and vice versa. For instance, the linguist may expect to do linguistic fieldwork, with elicitation and recording of various genres of speech and gathering of some sociolinguistic material, while the community may expect curriculum materials; the community may expect the linguist to learn to speak the language, while the linguist may expect to learn about the language. Your role needs to be discussed, and negotiated.

If a more equitable research model is the goal, how are the responsibilities determined? What is the responsibility of the researcher to train community members, and of community members to train the researcher? There is no simple or straightforward answer to these questions. Basically, be open to talking, and to thinking as a team, negotiating and dividing up responsibilities, recognizing strengths; be open to reconsidering responsibilities as time goes on. Such a model takes time to develop—it can thrive when people have built up relationships with each other and there is some trust and understanding. Research unfolds differently in different communities, and is different at different times. Where you are in your own career can have an effect, as can the state of things in the community. These questions are further addressed in §18.5.

The above are some of the ethical issues that you will need to think about in relating to people and communities. As already discussed, there are no single answers: different communities, different researchers, different contexts within a community, different times, and changing external forces all have a great effect on fieldwork (see Holton 2009 for a comparison of how different he found the notion of ethical fieldwork in two different communities; see also Dobrin 2008). Early fieldwork is a type of adaptation to a new situation. As in any change, it is a challenge for an outsider to build a place for him- or herself within a new community, and the challenges are probably enhanced when the outsider seeks to control or is not really able to 'hear' a community.

18.5 Ethics with respect to scholarship

The principles identified in the ethics codes target not only people, both individuals and communities, but also scholarship, and I now turn to this. In linguistic work, it is worth thinking about ethics with respect to scholarship in two different ways: ethics with respect to languages and ethics with respect to knowledge systems.

18.5.1 Ethics and languages

As discussed in the introduction, the realization of the previously unforeseen rate of language endangerment led to a call to linguists to work with speakers of languages that were disappearing. Much of the early discussion about the necessity for research on endangered languages is framed in terms of moral responsibility, with statements of the following types: a linguist has a responsibility to record a language because each language is a storehouse of knowledge, an encoding of a peoples' culture and history; language diversity is to be valued (see e.g. Hale et al. 1992; Crystal 2000; Nettle and Romaine 2000; Harrison 2007). Such reasons for research on languages are clear in statements found for various programs that support research on endangered languages that were developed in the later part of the previous century and the earliest years of this one. For instance, the following quotation about the Documenting Endangered Languages program, sponsored by the National Science Foundation and the National Endowment for the Humanities in the United Sates of America, talks to the need to rescue languages:

'This is a rescue mission to save endangered languages,' said NEH Chairman Bruce Cole. 'Language is the DNA of a culture, and it is the vehicle for the traditions, customs, stories, history, and beliefs of a people. A lost language is a lost culture. Fortunately, with the aid of modern technology and these federal funds, linguistic scholars can document and record these languages before they become extinct.'[4]

The website for the Hans Rausing Endangered Languages Documentation Program includes the following statement, 'Because every lost word means another lost world',[5] speaking to the tragedy of language loss. The concern in these quotations is with languages and the moral responsibility to study languages: this is ethics with respect to scholarship and knowledge systems, as outlined in the ethics codes discussed in §18.5.2.

The recognition of the extent of language endangerment at the end of the twentieth century, coupled with enormous advances in technology in terms of ability to record both audio and video and to store vast amounts of data, has led to the establishment of a field that has come to be known as documentary linguistics (e.g. Himmelmann 1998; 2008; Woodbury 2003; 2011; articles in Gippert, Himmelmann, and Mosel 2006). Language documentation involves data collection, transcription, and translation. The products of language documentation include edited fieldnotes and, more fundamentally, text collections, with the aim of recording the linguistic practices and traditions of a speech community. Texts of all genres, representing all types of major communicative events (exclamative, directive, conversational, monological, ritual) gathered through participant observation, elicitation, and recording, are the focus, with texts transcribed and translated.

Many ethical issues arise with documentation of languages, both technological and human. Technology allows for easy recording, both audio and video, and for archiving of materials. Again I ask a series of questions, beginning with issues that are largely technical, and moving to those that are more human.

What kind of equipment should I use to record? While technology might not be obvious as an ethical issue, brief discussion is worthwhile. You want to make recordings that are of the highest quality and that will be of lasting duration. This means using equipment that is appropriate for this, and also appropriate for the particular circumstances in which you are living. While audio recordings are

---

[4] http://www.neh.gov/grants/guidelines/del.html, accessed 7 May 2009.
[5] http://www.hrelp.org/, accessed 7 May 2009.

often sufficient, in many cases video recordings provide fuller information about communicative events, including gesture systems and non-verbal interactions between participants, that enhances the understanding of the language.

Yet what if an individual or a community is not keen to be recorded? What if audio recordings are acceptable, but video recordings are considered taboo? Best practice in language documentation and what is acceptable in a community may be in conflict, and your recording equipment may be left to languish, at least for a while, as surreptitious recording is not acceptable.

Who can I record? Recall from earlier discussion that it is necessary to have consent of speakers to record; recording should not be done illicitly. Some people might be fine with audio recording but not video recording, but not vice versa; some might not welcome any recording, at least not at the beginning, although they will still be willing to work with you. You, working with community members, will have to decide how to handle each of the types of situations that might arise.

In some communities it might not be acceptable for a woman to work with men, or for a man to work with women. In some places it might be appropriate to work with groups, at least at certain stages.

Again, as with other aspects of scholarship, there might be conflicts between what the field of linguistics considers to be best practice and what is acceptable in a community.

What do I need to record? In order to create what might be called an ethical corpus from the perspective of linguistics, you want to aim at a corpus that is diverse in terms of communicative events, gathered in ways appropriate to the particular materials, and carefully checked with speakers (see Himmelmann 1998; 2008; Woodbury 2003; 2011).

A corpus should consist of a range of materials. What if people are not interested in having this kind of range of communicative events documented? Your ability to develop such a corpus will depend to a large degree on your relationship with people in the community—as noted already, human issues and technological issues cannot be separated, but rather intersect with each other in complex ways.

For someone new to a community, it may be very difficult to meet the demands of documentary linguistics as described above. From the viewpoint of members of the community, people do not know you, and may well not understand just what your goals are or what you will do with the materials that you collect. They do not know what, if anything, you know of the language, of the culture, of cultural constraints. From your viewpoint, if this is a language you have never studied, this will be obvious to people. In order to build up the type of varied corpus that you might like to have, time is needed. Creating the corpus involves the time required to do the recordings and for you to become reasonably familiar with the materials—for instance, with many forms of speech and even elicitation, it may be that the material given in early days of fieldwork is simplified, taking into account that the speakers realize that you as the listener are not knowledgeable about the language, or the culture. Creating the corpus also involves the time needed for you and people you work with to develop a relationship where there is some degree of trust about what you are doing and what you will do with the materials.

Even when you are familiar in a community, there might be people who do not want to tell stories, but may well be happy to be involved with elicitation, and vice versa. Some people might willingly engage in conversations that are recorded; others might reject this. People might change what they are willing to do over time. There are some types of texts that people might not wish to share, or might be willing to share but not have recorded, or have recorded but only with restricted access conditions. This is particularly the case with sacred texts, which often are not to be shared with outsiders. What is considered sacred requires an understanding—it might not be what you think. For instance, there are historical events that are not told to outsiders in some communities. Once a researcher has developed a strong relationship with a community, it might be possible to record this type of speech, with consent and agreement on accessibility.

There might be other reasons why people are reluctant to share texts. That reluctance might be due to many factors. The particular speaker might question his or her competence in the language. They might feel that they are not a storyteller, or that the particular story you would like to record is not their story to tell. They might feel that the content is not appropriate to tell an outsider. And there might be other reasons as well. For instance, in many North American communities, there are stories that can be told only in the winter: it is inappropriate for the storyteller to tell those stories at other times of the year. An understanding of cultural norms might help you to understand why there is a reluctance to engage in what you hoped you could do.

It is imperative to respect the rights and decisions of people in the community even if you disagree, as discussed already. If you do not have permission to record material, be it audio recording or notes on paper or a computer, it is unethical to do so, no matter how much you think that the material would be a wonderful addition to your corpus. If someone is willing to be recorded and have their tapes archived but does not want their language to be included in research products, whether those products be stories for children in the community, a dictionary, a grammar, or a research article or book, this is to be respected. And if individuals and a community are keen to have materials made public and published, issues of authorship and copyright also require discussion.

How about archiving the data that I record? Language documentation requires that data be archived safely and securely, with the best attempts you can make to store the data permanently (see e.g. Himmelmann 1998; Bird and Simons 2003; Austin 2006; Aristar-Dry 2009; Nathan 2010). This is complex: data needs to be digitized; it needs to be archived; it needs to be migrated to new formats as they arise so that it continues to be accessible. It is important to have data archived in more than one place in case something happens to one of the copies. There are a number of places that archive linguistic data now, and talking with them in advance of fieldwork will help sort out these complex questions, leading to an understanding of current practices.

Where to archive can be an issue. A community might want material archived with them, and not elsewhere; a local museum may be an appropriate place to archive rather than a specific linguistic archive. Again, these alternatives need to be discussed.

Once the data is archived, can anyone access it? If best practices are to archive data and make it accessible, one might think that this should take priority. However, as discussed earlier, permissions for access are very important. Individual speakers or communities may choose to make all data accessible, or may place very severe restrictions on what is accessible. Someone might choose to make available some types of stories, but block access to other types such as sacred stories. Certain types of information might be available only to family, or only to women; recordings might be made available only after a time delay.

The ethical issues around recording at first appear to be quite simple—kinds of equipment to use, necessity to gather a varied and rich corpus, obligation to archive following best practices. These are part of ethical conduct with respect to scholarship in the field. Yet these technological issues cannot be viewed in isolation from the individuals and communities involved, and what might appear to be straightforward is actually part of the process of working together and building respect.

What if people do not want recordings archived at all? As discussed earlier, it is up to an individual and a community to decide what they want done with recordings that are made of them. While from the perspective of linguistics as a science there is a mandate to record and archive, this may well not be the goal of the community.

What about ownership of the research findings? Questions of intellectual property can loom large in fieldwork; see Dwyer (2006) and Austin (2010a) for some discussion, as well as Newman (2007, and in Chapter 19 below) on copyright. Who owns the data, the recordings, the content? In some cases individuals and communities might freely allow you to use any data; in other communities they might ask that you get permission for each sentence that you would like to use in an article that you write. You also need to consider authorship on articles—when you have worked extensively with someone, should they be a co-author on work where you have done the analysis? Independent of such questions, best practice in linguistic research is to acknowledge the contributions of speakers if they desire it.

18.5.2 Ethics and knowledge systems

Many of the languages that are endangered today are spoken by peoples who have been deeply affected by colonization. Recent years have seen the development of indigenous research, with an attempt to shift the focus of research paradigms involving indigenous peoples towards areas such as traditional knowledge and ways of knowing, recognizing different epistemological traditions and systems and, as discussed earlier, developing ethical standards for research (for work in this area, see e.g. Bach 2003; Battiste and Henderson 2000; Brown and Strega 2005; Cyr 1999; Gil 2001; Manatowa-Bailey 2007; Nevins 2004; Smith 1999; Wilson 2008). There is a focus on respect and responsibility in research, and on reciprocity, as outlined in the earlier discussion of the Canadian Institutes for Health Research ethics guidelines for work with Aboriginal peoples.

As the value of different knowledge systems has come to be recognized, it has also become evident that different knowledge systems may make different demands. Thus, what is considered to be scientific, what is considered to be important to study, what is recognized as interesting or important, may well differ between you and members of a community in which you are working when you are raised in different systems of knowledge. The purposes of serving scholarship narrowly defined as university-driven, western-tradition scholarship, and those of the community are not necessarily one and the same. Two distinct worldviews can be in conflict with one another, with different types of knowledge valued or privileged by different intellectual traditions. For instance, the linguist might feel that recording as large a corpus as possible is important not only for science, but for the community itself down the road, if it ever wants to work to revitalize its language. That language revitalization projects depend on having excellent documentation of a language is clear: the well-known revitalization projects with the Wampanoag (Ash, Fermino, and Hale 2001) and Myaamia (Leonard 2007) communities in the United States of America and the Kaurna community (Amery 2000) in Australia, for instance, depend on the quality of materials available. However, a community might feel that the time for the language is past, and it is not interested in participating in this endeavor—or is perhaps even actively opposed to this (e.g. Manatowa-Bailey 2007), while others might view languages as sleeping, to be awakened at the appropriate moment (e.g. Leonard 2008). As a less radical example, a linguist may feel that the highest priority in creating a dictionary is to produce the most comprehensive, detailed dictionary possible. A community might want to have a more encyclopedic dictionary, with less coverage but giving priority to cultural information that is considered to be important. A linguist might feel that the detailed documentation described above must be privileged above all else; a community might feel that certain types of cultural knowledge are most important, and aim to focus narrowly on what they would like to record. From a more core linguistic perspective, views on what is important about language may differ. You may think that what is important about a language is its morphology, syntax, semantics, and pragmatics, while members of the community might value knowledge of its phonetics and lexicon.

Recognition that there are different knowledge systems leads to a number of questions.

What if the goals of the community and the goals of the researcher do not mesh? Is it appropriate for the researcher to try to persuade the community that his/her goals are the right ones? Is it appropriate for the community to insist on its goals? Is it possible for the two to work together to discover where there are overlapping goals and work from these together, respecting the needs of each to work on their own goals as well? What is my accountability to the community? There are extremes in how linguists undertake fieldwork. At one extreme, there is the linguist who flies into a community and collects their data. For someone who has already developed a relationship with a community, this likely does not raise any danger signals. But for someone going to a community without having already developed a relationship with people there, this will often create problems. Such a type of fieldwork might be helpful in terms of getting a particular type of data. However, it takes a while of working with people for each of you to figure out what the other is all about, what each of your strengths are, and so on. So quick trips simply to get data probably do not result in the best-quality data. And fly-in/fly-out fieldwork will not work in most communities because there is not an opportunity to develop the relationships that help to make ongoing fieldwork possible for you or for those who might follow you.

At another extreme, in some cases the community has had control of the research agenda. Wilkins (1992) addresses his work in Australia, identifying advantages to this type of research—personal growth, academic growth in learning things that he would not have learned otherwise. At the same time, the time to complete a degree is longer, he did not work on the questions that he originally brought with him, and he lost his scholarship funding.

Different kinds of balances exist. Czaykowska-Higgins (2009) outlines different ways of working with different communities in a community-based research project, and Holton (2009) details his very different experiences in Alaska and Indonesia, pointing to the local nature of ethical responsibilities.

The questions that introduce this section have no single answers, but many linguists and communities have found ways, over time, of defining common goals and respecting those that are not in common; people who have engaged in such work generally report that it is for the better for all. Often as linguists work with speakers, they come to find the fundamental similarities that exist in their goals, and work through the differences. Again, this takes time and patience. Working together often allows for common goals to be found. As a simple example, suppose that you want to record autobiographies because you are interested in getting first person forms, and the community wants stories in the language for the school. It might be possible to accomplish both of these, with you working together with teachers to do your part of creating the school materials while they work together with you to assist you in obtaining the recordings that you want.

18.6 SUMMARY

I have surveyed some of the ethical issues that arise in fieldwork, framing them in terms of individuals, communities, and scholarship with respect to languages and knowledge systems. To talk in generalities, ethical behaviour can be said to be based in a number of 'r' words—respect, relationships, reciprocity, and responsibility. Being ethical means thinking about these. It involves people from different cultures, often with quite different ways of viewing the world, working together to try to understand one another, recognizing that what is considered appropriate for one may not be for the other.

In a paper on ethics in cooperative fieldwork, Dwyer (2006) sets out what she calls ethical principles for language documentation that summarize much of what I have written:

> Do no harm (including unintentional harm).
> > Harm must be specified in the local context.
> Reciprocity and equity.
> > Establish consultative, continuously negotiated, respectful relationships.
> Do some good (for the community as well as for science).
> Obtain informed consent before initiating research.
> Archive and disseminate your data and results.
> > (One might add to this final statement 'if this is approved by relevant people'.)

Doing ethical research is a challenge. It involves thinking and learning and being willing to adapt and to change. It involves not just treating people well, but also respecting their knowledge and learning to see something where you might have thought that there was nothing. It involves reconceptualizing ways of viewing the world. In many ways engaging in long-term fieldwork is like engaging in a long-term relationship such as a marriage. There are good times and difficult times; there are times when one or the other is ready to give up. There is a difference, however, in that the researcher is often an outsider to a community (there are, as one might imagine, many ethical issues that arise for a researcher who is an insider in a community), and generally from a dominant culture in global terms. This places a responsibility on the researcher to try to understand the different ethical systems, and to respect and honor the cultural values in the broadest of senses. When there have traditionally been major power differences between the culture of the community of the researcher and that of the community where the research is being done, there may be sensitive issues, and trying to understand what those are and find ways of working to overcome the power differentials is very important—part of what equal moral status is all about. For both parties involved, there can be struggles in overcoming the historical imbalances, and reconfiguring them. Fieldwork is not for everyone; among those who take it on, especially in a cooperative framework, many find it to be highly rewarding, and engaging with the complex ethical issues is one of the rewards.

18.7 APPENDIX

This appendix collects a number of references of interest for their discussion of various aspects of ethics in linguistics fieldwork.

General sources on ethics in linguistic fieldwork include textbooks on field methods, ranging from the older books by Bouquiaux and Thomas (1992), Kibrik (1977), and Samarin (1967) to the recent texts including Bowern (2008), Chelliah and de Reuse (2010), Crowley (2007), and Tsunoda (2005), this last one on language revitalization. The collection by Newman and Ratliff (2001) includes general information about ethics in fieldwork. Some articles provide an overview of ethics in linguistic fieldwork, including Austin (2010a), Dwyer (2006), and Rice (2006). A recent issue of *Language and Communication*, edited by Innes and Debenport (2010), addresses ethical dimensions of language documentation, with articles on legacy resources, responsibility in documentation, informed consent, privacy, and cultural property, among others.

For detailed discussion of documentary linguistics, see Himmelmann (1998; 2008), Woodbury (2003; 2011), Austin (2010b), and the articles in Gippert, Himmelmann, and Mosel (2006).

There is recent literature on the responsibility of linguists towards communities. Grenoble and Whaley (2006) provide an overview; see also Amery (2006), Austin (2010a), Berardo and Yamamoto (2007), Bobaljik (1998), Comrie (2007), Craig (1992; 1993; 1997), Czaykowska-Higgins (2009), Dimmendaal (2001), Dobrin (2008), Dorian (2010), England (1992), Gerdts (1998; 2010), Grenoble (2009), Grinevald (1998; 2007), Hale and Hinton (2001), Hale (1965), Himmelmann (1998; 2008), Holton (2009), Labov (1972c; 1982), Nagy (2000), articles in Ostler (2007), Otsuka and Wong (2007), Rice (2009), Shaw (2004), Speas (2009), Sutton and Walsh (1979), Thieberger and Musgrave (2006), Valiquette (1998), Wilkins (1992), Wolfram (1993), Wolfram and Shilling-Estes (1995), and Yamada (2007), among others.

For general work on social science paradigms and ethical responsibilities, see Cameron et al. (1992) and Cameron (1998) as well as Clifford and Marcus (1986), Fluehr-Lobban (1991; 2003) and Geertz (1968).

Works on decolonizing and indigenous research methodologies include Brown and Strega (2005), Smith (1999), and Wilson (2008), among many others.

On different paradigms of knowledge, from different perspectives, see Assembly of First Nations (1990; 1992; 2000), Bach (2003), Battiste and Henderson (2000), Collins (1998), Cree School Board (n.d.), Cyr (1999), Gil (2001), Hale and Hinton (2001), Hale (1972), Harrison (2007), Manatowa-Bailey (2007), Nevins (2004), Report of the Royal Commission on Aboriginal Peoples (1996), Smith (2000), and Smith (1999), as well as discussion in other sources.

Ethics codes with respect to linguistics are discussed in Rieschild (2003). See also Social Sciences And Humanities Research Ethics Special Working Committee (2004).

Crystal (2000) introduces language endangerment with discussion about the value of linguistic diversity; see also Hale et al. (1992) and papers in Grenoble and Whaley (1998) and Nettle and Romaine (2000), among many others.

Differing perspectives on language revitalization are given in Grenoble and Whaley (2006), Ash, Fermino, and Hale (2001), Leonard (2007), and Manatowa-Bailey (2007), among many others.

Technical issues are discussed in Bird and Simons (2003), some articles in Gippert et al. (2006), and Aristar-Dry (2009) as well as many other sources.

For a recent presentation on archiving, see Nathan (2010) (http://www.ailla. utexas.org/site/lsa_archiving10.html; accessed 4 June 2010)

For work on language reclamation, see Amery (2000) on Kaurna, Baldwin (2003) and Leonard (2007; 2008) on Miami, and Ash et al. (2001) on Wampanoag. See Hinton (2001) for general discussion.

C H A P T E R   1 9

··

COPYRIGHT AND OTHER LEGAL CONCERNS

··

P A U L   N E W M A N

19.1 INTRODUCTION[1]

··

Fieldworkers normally think of copyright as something that they will have to deal with later when they have returned home and are involved in writing up and publishing, and not something to worry about when they are busy in the field with data and text collection, participant observation, or controlled experiments. At one time this may have been the case, de facto if not legally. But nowadays, when people are sensitive to the reach of copyright and the protection of indigenous intellectual property rights, failure by the linguist to pay attention to copyright concerns in the field could create unpleasant complications later, cause frictions for future researchers, and even present obstacles to using one's own research materials. That

[1] In preparing this chapter, I was extremely fortunate to have received detailed comments and constructive suggestions from Ms Brigitte Vézina, an intellectual property expert who works with the World Intellectual Property Organization (WIPO). I would like to express my utmost gratitude to her for her careful reading of my paper and her incisive observations. Nevertheless, the opinions, interpretations, and substantive statements about copyright law expressed in this chapter are my own. Neither Ms Vézina nor WIPO endorses nor should be held responsible for anything said here.

is why it was deemed important for this volume to contain a chapter on copyright and related intellectual property issues.

19.2 COPYRIGHT BASICS

The key to being able to appreciate the application of copyright law to field situations is to have a basic understanding of copyright law, namely what it is and how it operates. Although a full explanation of copyright could take upwards of a thousand pages, it is possible to cut through the details and boil matters down to a manageable number of essential concepts and principles. Note that for the purposes of this chapter, I shall limit myself essentially to US law, which has a special status throughout the world due to the dominant role that the US plays in the production of intellectual property, with the understanding that its principles can serve as a guide to copyright requirements and operation wherever one is working.

19.2.1

Copyright deals with intangible mental products and not with the physical objects in which they are manifested. For example, suppose you buy a hardcover book consisting of five short stories by five different authors. As the purchaser you own the book. You can lend it to a friend, sell it to a used bookstore, donate it to a public library, or put it in the shredder. You can do these things because you own the book *per se*. But you do not own the copyright; and thus you cannot photocopy the book as a whole or any of the stories in it, nor can you make an inexpensive paperback version of the book for your class, nor translate the Spanish stories in the book into English (or the English stories into Spanish), nor do a public reading of one of the stories for your book club, nor turn one of the stories into a play for your amateur theatre group. Although you own the physical object, the book, the copyright in the stories belongs to others, and without their permission, you may not do the kinds of things just mentioned. The copyright to the individual stories belongs to the individual authors (at least initially), the copyright to the introduction belongs to the compiler(s)/editor(s), and the copyright to the book as a whole, which probably has its own copyright apart from the content, belongs to the compiler(s)/editor(s) or perhaps to the publisher (see §19.3.5 below). Only they, the copyright holders, have the right to exploit the content of the book, not you, the owner of the book in your hand.

19.2.2

Copyright covers artistic and literary creations in the broadest sense of the term, including but not limited to literature, non-fiction writing, painting, sculpture, photography, motion pictures, dance, music, and sound recordings. It does not apply to ideas, scientific principles, inventions, procedures and methods, discoveries, facts, or real world historical or current-day incidents. Natural languages are not copyrightable. As far as intellectual property is concerned, languages are not owned by the communities that speak them, and thus native speakers have no legal basis for restricting access by others to materials written in or about their languages.[2]

Copyright also covers the organization, manipulation, and adaptation of pre-existing materials, whether those materials are copyrighted or not. For example, a translation of a work from one language into another has copyright even if it is of an old work that itself has no copyright protection. Similarly, an anthology or collection of poems or short stories or scholarly articles can have its own copyright, independent of the copyright status of the works included. For example, if you or your field assistants collect a large number of proverbs and organize them in some coherent fashion, that collection will be covered by copyright even though the individual proverbs themselves presumably are not. What this means is that other scholars can freely make use of any or all of the proverbs for their purposes without needing your permission, although they cannot copy or (re)publish the collection as a whole.

19.2.3

Copyright provides copyright holders with exclusive (monopolistic) control over their works, i.e. it encases works in shackles whether the author intends this or not. Although usually described as an affirmative right, copyright is better thought of in the negative, i.e. as a set of rules on what others may *not* do. Works not covered by copyright, either because they never qualified for copyright in the first place or because the copyright has expired (or occasionally has been abandoned) are said to be in the *public domain*. These works are free for all to use as they wish.

---

[2] This does not prevent native speakers or well-intentioned linguists (e.g. Maxwell 2004) from making such claims, nor does it prevent fearful publishers from giving in to threats and pressures from language-speaking communities; see e.g. the unfortunate story in Hill (2002). But from the perspective of American copyright law, these claimed rights are more accurately characterized as social *interests* and cultural *concerns*, and not legal rights. Of course traditional peoples do have a valid interest in protecting their 'intangible cultural heritage' from exploitation by the rich and the powerful, but that is a different story. A proper discussion of issues involving respect for and protection of traditional knowledge (TK) and traditional cultural expression (TCE) would require a full chapter on its own at the very least, see Brown (2003); UNESCO (2003); Story, Darch, and Halbert (2006); WIPO (2010b; 2010c).

19.2.4

The supposedly monopolistic rights that copyright holders control are in fact subject to various limitations that are intended to alleviate copyright bottleneck and allow for socially desirable uses, such as the special provisions for libraries and for the blind. One of the most significant of these limitations is what in the US is called 'Fair Use', a provision that allows reasonable use of a work without requiring permission from the copyright holder when obtaining permission would pose an undue and pointless burden on the person wanting to make use of the copyrighted work without commensurate benefit for the copyright holder. A scholar writing a book review, for example, would naturally want to quote passages from the book being reviewed. To insist that the reviewer go to the trouble and expense of seeking permission for every sentence or paragraph quoted in writing the review, which may likely help promote sales of the book, makes no sense. The essence of the 'fair use' limitation, which began as a judge-made rule of common sense, is now incorporated in US copyright law (17 US Code 107): '[T]he fair use of a copyrighted work...for purposes such as criticism, comment, news reporting, teaching (including multiple copies for classroom use), scholarship, or research is not an infringement of copyright.' In determining whether a use is 'fair use', courts look to factors such as whether the use is commercial or not, whether the copyrighted work is factual or creative, how much of the work is being used, and the impact of the use on the potential market for the copyrighted work. These are rough measures and no guidelines are provided as to how to weigh one criterion versus another. In the final analysis, fair use is a determination that the use was reasonable under the circumstances. The practical application of the fair use doctrine is thus fraught with uncertainty, but the principle, which is that limitations on the rights of copyright holders are built into the law to encourage creativity and scholarship, remains an important component of copyright law and not an odd exception thereto.

19.2.5

Copyright has characteristics of tangible property, which is why it is referred to as 'intellectual property'.[3] Among these property-like features, the most significant for our purposes is the ability to be transferred, whether by sale or rent or gift or

---

[3] The term 'intellectual property' is strongly disliked by progressive scholars who decry what they view as the commodification of culture (see e.g. Lessig 2004; Porsdam 2006; Vaidhyanathan 2001). In this spirit it would be preferable to refer to the person having a copyright as the copyright *holder* rather than the copyright *owner*; nevertheless, the phrase 'copyright owner' is so well established and commonly used that it makes no sense to go out of one's way to avoid it if the alternative creates stylistic infelicities. The other thing to keep in mind about intellectual property is that the scope of this concept is much broader than merely copyright. Copyright is a subcategory within intellectual property, which also includes, patent, trademark, trade secrets, etc.

inheritance. When one sees a book with a notice such as '© Oxford University Press 2005', it is almost always the case that the publisher acquired the copyright by transfer from the then owner, i.e. the work's author or some subsequent copyright holder. It is rarely the case that OUP or any other publisher actually wrote the books whose copyrights it holds. Moreover, given that the duration of copyright is typically a person's life plus a certain number of years (see §19.3.4 below), it follows that the copyright holder(s) is/are eventually going to be someone or some ones other than the person who created the work, such as the author's widow or widower, the author's child or children or nieces or nephews, or some charitable institution to which the author left his/her estate.

19.2.6

The initial copyright holder is the creator, namely the person who wrote the article, composed the music, painted the picture, sculpted the statue, etc. In American copyright law this person is referred to as the 'Author' regardless of the medium.

If more than one author is involved, the result is a joint work, where each author has equal rights with all of the others. There may be, and often is, unequal contribution to a work—one person effectively did two-thirds of the work and the other person did one-third (or one did a half, one did a quarter, and two others each did an eighth)—but from the perspective of American copyright law, each author has equal rights. What this means is that each author, even the one with the minimal 1/8th input, has full right to use the work to its fullest, including publishing it, without needing permission from the other co-authors. What a joint author may not do on his or her own is transfer the copyright to someone else or give it up entirely, which is to say, put the work in the public domain.

The copyright laws of some countries, particularly the US, allow an employer, whether an individual or a large corporation, to stand in the shoes of a creative employee and be treated as the initial Author. In US law, this is referred to as the Work Made for Hire doctrine (often shortened to the Work for Hire doctrine), a terribly inapt and misleading term. Other countries reject this legal fiction of employer as Author, but find other ways to allow the employer to benefit from the creative activities of his/her/their employees, notably by contract or by 'shop right' type rules.[4] Nevertheless, the essential thing to keep in mind is that the default rule everywhere is that the individual creator is the Author, and that payment in and of itself does not necessarily change that fact. For the Work for Hire rule to apply, the person whose creative product is claimed by someone else must count as a real employee, narrowly defined, and not as a freelance worker

---

[4] 'Shop right' is a doctrine in patent law that grants employers a non-exclusive licence to make use of employees' inventions created on the job without requiring extra payment or special permission.

commissioned to prepare the work. Thus, if you (for example) hire someone to write an anniversary song to celebrate that occasion, for which you pay a large sum, that does not make you the Author and thus copyright holder of the song. Given the essential property nature of copyright, you of course can contract to buy the copyright to the song if the composer is willing to sell it, but that is totally independent of the Work for Hire rule. Similarly, a granting agency, such as the National Science Foundation (NSF), that provides funds for your research, including perhaps your summer salary, does not thereby become the copyright holder of your creative products. As the source of funds, NSF or any other agency can impose contractual restrictions, requirements, and conditions on what you may or may not or must do with your research materials, such as insisting that results of the research be deposited in an open-access archive; but it cannot override copyright law as such, which says that as the creative party you are the Author and thereby the initial copyright holder.

19.2.7

Copyright is divisible. One normally uses the term copyright in the singular, but in reality copyright represents a bundle of rights, such as the right to copy, distribute, display, perform, or make derivative works (such as abridgements, adaptations, or translations). Each of these rights can be controlled, exploited, or transferred separately of the others.

19.2.8

Copyright comes from national law and not from international law nor from some universal natural law. Who is the copyright holder and what rights that person has and for how long come from specific laws of specific countries. The rights that creators have are limited to what the laws of that person's country say they have: no more and no less. In these days of globalization, it may seem surprising, but there is no such thing as international copyright law *per se*. There are international treaties, the most significant being the Berne Convention,[5] which is adhered to by over 160 countries; but although Berne sets out detailed guidelines and minimum conditions

[5] The International Convention for the Protection of Literary and Artistic Works, usually referred to as the Berne Convention, was created back in 1886. Original signatories included Belgium, France, Germany, Italy, Spain, Switzerland, Tunisia, and the United Kingdom. Remarkably, the US didn't join until 1989, and even now does not adhere to all of the terms of the Berne Convention, US law, for example, still not fully enforcing the principle of authors' 'Moral Rights' as spelled out in Article 6bis, and discussed here in §19.2.9. The full text of the Berne Convention can be found on the website of the World Intellectual Property Organization (WIPO), see <http://www.wipo.int/treaties/en/ip/berne>, a specialized agency of the United Nations which has the responsibility of promoting and developing a

and principles that member countries are required to adhere to, it is not international law as such. All copyright actions take place within a specific country in terms of the laws of that country including its treaty obligations.

The unfortunate consequence of the above is that one cannot provide a common set of copyright rules applicable to all field linguists. A German linguist doing research in Kenya whose results are published by SOAS in London would potentially be subject to German, Kenyan, and British copyright law—and where would one find an expert on all three?—and if infringement occurred in the US, the resulting legal case would be covered by American law.[6] However, in reality, the copyright laws in different countries are essentially the same. They are not identical, i.e. they do differ in details, but generally speaking they are similar enough and have a sufficiently common starting point such that the description of one can serve as a basis for all of the others.[7] Thus, although my discussion of copyright issues draws primarily on US law, my intention is that it will serve the needs of scholars whatever their nationality and wherever they may be conducting their research.

19.2.9

Copyright tends to be thought of first and foremost in terms of economic rights—a perception that is encouraged by the widespread use of the term 'intellectual *property*'. However, there also exist significant non-commercial interests and concerns relating to the honor and reputation of the author or artist and the integrity

---

'balanced and accessible international intellectual property (IP) system' covering patent, trademark, and other types of IP in addition to copyright.

  [6] The way the Berne Convention works is that a country generally must give protection to copyright holders of all member countries on at least the same terms it accords its own citizens. It does not have to enforce the laws of the source country and normally does not. Let me illustrate with reference to the complex matter of duration. Copyright protection in Mexico lasts for the life of the author plus 100 years; in the US it is life plus 70 years. An American court adjudicating an infringement case involving a Mexican copyright will thus limit the copyright's validity to the US prescribed life plus 70 and ignore the life plus 100 duration specified under Mexican law. Similarly, under American law, a Jordanian work will have a term of life plus 70 even though the copyright term in Jordan is life plus 50. However, in both of these cases, the Berne Convention permits the US to apply the original country's duration if it wanted to do so, which would result in giving more protection to the Mexican copyright and less protection to the Jordanian copyright than the US accords its own citizens. In fact, the US has chosen to ignore the different durations of foreign countries and has opted to apply life plus 70 across the board.

  [7] Having an essentially common copyright regime throughout the world presents many advantages. However, members of the CopySouth group, see <http://www.copysouth.org>, take the position that the copyright laws of most developing countries of Africa, southeast Asia, and Latin America were taken over uncritically from the laws of European, particularly formerly colonial, countries even though these laws as written appear to be contrary to the best social and economic interests of these poorer countries (Story 2009; Story et al. 2006).

of the work. These non-economic interests are referred to as 'Moral Rights' (see Berne Convention, Article 6bis). Unlike economic rights, which are freely transferable, moral rights are treated as an extension of the author's personality and are inalienable.

Although this chapter is grounded in US copyright law, which has only recently incorporated moral rights and only to a limited extent in the case of the visual arts (see 17 US Code 106A), there are two good reasons for including a treatment of moral rights here. The first is that this is a case where the US is out of step with the rest of the world. Most countries of the world treat moral rights as an integral part of their copyright laws—a perspective that has become part of the Berne Convention. Thus non-American scholars and American scholars working abroad need to understand what obligations moral rights entail. Second, from the point of view of professional ethics, the rights included under moral rights seem to be fundamental and to deserve adherence. Even if US copyright law does not require it, one could argue that field linguists and other scholars have an ethical duty to respect authors' moral rights.

As with general copyright rights, the scope and specifics of moral rights vary from country to country, but generally speaking, moral rights contain two components. These are (1) the right of attribution (or paternity), and (2) the right of integrity.

The right of attribution essentially means that the creator of a work has a right to be acknowledged as its author. If, for example, a traditional poet dictates poems in his own language and the field linguist later publishes the poems or significant parts thereof in a scholarly paper on tone or rhyme or what have you, the poet has a moral right to be mentioned by name. A corollary of the right of attribution is the right not to have one's name attached to a work if one didn't actually create it, or if the work has been so changed by others owning the copyright (e.g. an editor or a translator) that association with the work would be detrimental to one's reputation and professional standing.

The right of integrity protects works from distortion, mutilation, or destruction. For example, abridgements or editorial cleansing (e.g. removing profanity or sexual references or religious criticism) that changed the essential character of a work would constitute distortions that moral rights are intended to prevent. Similarly, the right of integrity would prohibit an individual or company from shredding the only extant copy of a potentially competing dictionary even if the copyright holder had bought the copy itself at a fair price and had paid handsomely for the copyright.

In sum, in conducting linguistic fieldwork one should be vigilant in looking out for the moral rights of the people with whom one works and treat these rights as if there were required by copyright law. The simple test in all cases is this: if I were the author and this were my work, how would I like to be treated?

19.3 BASICS OF US COPYRIGHT LAW

The current US copyright law, which was adopted in 1976 and went into effect in 1978 (and subsequently expanded and modified by various amendments), is found in US Code 17.[8] Rather than go over this step by step, I shall focus on essential matters that fieldworkers need to know to ensure that they personally have full use of research materials that they have collected and that they are in a position to make their materials available to others, whether through archiving, informal sharing, or publication.

19.3.1

Copyright is automatic. Although one often comes across the active verb 'to copyright', one in fact does not copyright a work. Rather a work becomes copyrighted (the stylistically despised passive being required), i.e. it acquires copyright protection whether one wants it or not. There are no formalities required, neither with regard to notice nor registration. One does not have to put © (or 'copyright') and one's name and date on a work for it to be copyrighted, nor must one register the work with the US copyright office.[9] Formerly, US copyright law required explicit copyright notice on all published works or the copyright would be forfeited—quite a draconian system—but this requirement was dropped in 1989 when the US joined the Berne Convention, which states the principle of formality-free protection. It is still good practice to put a copyright notice on works. It is an explicit statement that you have an interest in protecting your copyright and it makes it clear to the world who the copyright holder is (at least at the time) and who can be contacted for necessary permission. Most major publishers do in fact put a copyright notice in their books on what is still referred to as the copyright page, namely the back of the title page, but lack of the notice does not invalidate the copyright or weaken its force.

---

[8] This copyright code is available in full at the United States Copyright Office website <http://www.copyright.gov> or at the Cornell University Law School website <http://www.law.cornell.edu/uscode/17>.

[9] Formal registration actually bestows numerous legal benefits, registration, for example, being a precondition to filing suit for copyright infringement; nevertheless, it is not a condition of copyright *per se*. Moreover, registration is always possible at some later date and need not take place when a work is first produced or first published. This schizoid approach to registration—it is not required, but you had better do it!—reflects a far from satisfactory compromise between the US tradition of (and strong preference for) registration and the Berne Convention principles which forbid formalities as a requirement for copyright.

19.3.2

Copyright applies equally to unpublished works and to published works. If traditional poets have composed yet-unpublished poems, these poets have copyright over their poems (subject to one proviso discussed in the section below) even if they do not know it. Prior to 1978, the US had totally different legal regimes for published works (covered by federal copyright law) and unpublished works (covered by individual state laws), but this distinction has been eliminated, with all of the benefits and problems that this entails.

19.3.3

Copyright attaches to creative works the moment that they are *fixed*, i.e. reduced to 'tangible form'. If poems are in someone's head, they are not copyrighted. This is true even if the compositions are complete from the poet's point of view, even if the poet recites them publicly, even if other people know the poems by heart, and even if everyone knows whose poems they are. But if a linguist were to take down the poems by hand, or record them on tape, or have the poet write them out, the poems would suddenly become copyrighted. At that point, without explicit or implied permission from the poets, who might have no idea that their works were now copyrighted, the linguist would have no right to translate them into English (or any other language) or to reproduce them in the original language in scholarly works that the linguist might prepare.

19.3.4

Under US law, copyright for works created in 1978 or thereafter lasts for the life of the author (or last surviving author in the case of joint works) plus 70 years—an incredibly long time.[10] In some countries, e.g. Jordan, it is life plus 50, in others, e.g. Mexico, it is life plus 100, but for all practical purposes, the copyright lasts so long, whichever country's laws are controlling, that it can be thought of as

---

[10] The initial author remains the measuring life for duration purposes even if, as is normally the case, the copyright has been transferred to someone else, either during the author's lifetime or later. With works where the author's life cannot be determined, e.g. anonymous items or works where a company counts as author under the Work for Hire doctrine, copyright duration is specified in terms of a set number of years, which in the US is currently 95 years from the date of publication or 120 years from the date of creation, whichever comes earlier. Some countries have different copyright durations for different classes of works, e.g. one duration for books and another for motion pictures. In the US, the duration is the same regardless of the medium or type of work.

perpetual. The issue of duration is thus essentially irrelevant when it comes to the primary materials that a field linguist normally collects.[11]

19.3.5

Copyright attaches to original creations.[12] To begin with, the work must be that of the putative Author and not something copied from someone or something else or something passed down through the generations. Folktales, traditional tunes, proverbs, or centuries-old aphorisms are not copyrightable. Second, a work must exhibit a modicum of creativity. The author doesn't have to be an e. e. cummings or Thelonious Monk or Stephen Jay Gould, but something more than trivial creativity is required. Thus simple conversations or a shopping list or an alphabetical list of the students in one's class would not qualify. Unfortunately there is no clear measure on how much creativity is required. Presumably a single dictionary entry, such as Hausa 'kàrée' = English 'dog', wouldn't qualify whereas a 10,000 word Hausa–English dictionary would; but how about a 100-word Swadesh list with simple equivalents in some previously undocumented endangered language? One presumably could view this as copyrightable creativity, but one could equally argue that such a list is empirical fact not qualifying for copyright even though collecting the list involved travel to some difficult location and the expenditure of considerable funds.[13] Or consider the matter of folktales. Folktales, being part of a culture's shared tradition and not the composition of some identifiable human author, would appear to be excluded from copyright protection (but see WIPO 2010b). On the other hand, a creative rendition of a tale by a master storyteller could qualify for copyright. And even if the folktale itself or the performance of the folktale did not qualify for copyright protection, a sound recording of someone reciting the tale would be copyrighted and subject to standard rules regarding permissions, transfers, etc.

[11] The issue of copyright duration, however, remains a factor if the linguist wants to make use of handwritten manuscripts or other older sources. The basic term for pre-1978 publications is 28 years potentially renewable for another 67, with different duration rules applying to foreign works and to unpublished works. Determining whether older works are still covered by copyright or are in the public domain and thus available for free use turns out to be an extremely complicated question; for such matters the linguist is well advised to seek the help of a copyright professional.

[12] There exist categories of works that do involve originality and creativity, but which under US law have been explicitly excluded from copyright coverage, e.g. brief phrases, titles of works, and typefaces (but not computer fonts, which are copyrightable). Also excluded are all works of the US Government and state constitutions, statutes, and judicial opinions.

[13] The amount of time and effort involved in creating something is irrelevant in American law, which rejects the concept of copyright based on the 'sweat of the brow' (see *Feist* 1991). It seems counterintuitive, but data that required a year's worth of hard work to amass might not be copyrightable whereas a letter to the editor of a scholarly journal that took an hour to write would be copyrighted.

19.3.6

Copyright conveyances are of two major types, which have related procedural requirements. For purposes of convenience, I shall call one 'transfer' and the other 'non-exclusive licence'. The prototypical transfer is the transfer of a full copyright from one person to another. This is what happens when, for example, Abel, an author and copyright owner, conveys his copyright to Baker, who thereupon becomes the copyright holder with all related rights and privileges, none remaining with Abel. A typical example is when a scholar assigns the copyright to her book or article to the publisher, whereupon a notice such as © 2000 Oxford University Press will appear on the copyright page and the scholar will later discover, much to her chagrin, that she needs permission from the Press to use her own book or article in her own research and teaching.

A lesser but still powerful transfer is the granting of an exclusive licence. The copyright holder retains the copyright as such (which may be an essentially empty shell), but gives someone else the exclusive right to exploit the work fully or in specific ways. For example, a copyright holder may give a publisher the exclusive right to exploit a work in every possible way, thereby retaining no rights although nominally remaining as the vacuous copyright holder, or the copyright holder can give some organization the exclusive right to publish Spanish translations of the work throughout the world, or give some company the right to distribute the work in particular countries or parts of the world, e.g. the Far East or Latin America. What is essential here is not the extent of the rights conveyed—they can be quite general or very specific and limited—but whether the rights are exclusive or not.

The other type of conveyance is the 'non-exclusive licence', which is just a fancy term for 'permission to use'. Here the copyright holder gives someone (or some group of people) permission to use the work, either without restriction or in some limited manner, but this permission is not exclusive. For example, Cable, a copyright holder, may give three different colleagues permission to use his article in a course packet, where this licence does not preclude Cable from allowing other people to use the same article in their course packets or from using the work himself. Unlike copyright transfer, which always involves a specified recipient who is then the exclusive holder of the rights that were transferred, a non-exclusive licence can be offered to unnamed or unknown people or to everyone. If a scholar posts a draft paper on his personal website with an accompanying statement that anyone is free to download it or copy it for teaching or research purposes, that would be an example of a recipient-unspecified non-exclusive licence. This would allow anyone in the world to use the posted paper, but none of these people would thereby obtain a copyright interest in the work such that they would have the right or power to prevent anyone else from using the paper. Other frequently encountered non-exclusive licences with unspecified recipients are Creative

Commons licences (see Garlick 2005), which are issued by copyright holders who want to share their work with others without limiting or specifying who these 'others' are.

The two kinds of conveyances have a couple of very important procedural differences. To begin with, non-exclusive licences (i.e. permissions to use) need not be in writing. They can be oral or they can even be implied from a situation. For example, if someone dictates a text for you in connection with your linguistic research, the person normally understands that you are going to translate the text into English and therefore permission to do so is implied. Similarly, if you submit a book review to a journal, even in the absence of a contract or cover letter, the clear implication is that you have given the journal permission to publish the review in accordance with its normal publishing practice. Second, non-exclusive licences can be granted by any of the copyright holders, without the agreement or even the knowledge of the other copyright holders. If two scholars writes a joint paper, either can post it on a website so as to allow friends and colleagues to copy it, make use of it, and incorporate it in their works without consulting or informing the co-author. From a professional point of view, this behaviour would be frowned upon, but from a copyright point of view, such actions are allowed.[14]

By contrast a transfer (= assignment of the copyright as such or an exclusive licence) must be in writing and signed by the copyright holder(s). One doesn't have to have a formal legal-looking printed form on velum or other elegant paper—courts have accepted rough memos on paper napkins or on the back of envelopes—and one doesn't have to have witnesses or guarantees by notaries or other officials, but there must be a writing accompanied by a signature. No exceptions or excuses are allowed. Second, the transfer must be agreed to and signed by all of the copyright holders. One person could sign on behalf of others if there were indisputable evidence that the person was authorized to do so, but, unlike in the case of non-exclusive licences, all of the copyright holders must agree to the transfer. The problem is that when field linguists get ready to publish a work and are dealing with a publisher who requires copyright assignment, as many do, if they haven't made proper arrangements in advance, they may find that they cannot get a proper response from fieldwork assistants who qualify as copyright-holding co-authors and thus cannot meet the publisher's contractual demands.

---

[14] The only legal requirement is that if monies are involved, e.g. someone pays one of the co-authors for permission to include the joint article in a collected volume, the co-copyright holder who is operating unilaterally must provide an accounting and sharing of proceeds with the other copyright holders on an equal basis.

19.4 Co-workers in the field:
who owns what?

Field linguists depend on the good graces and assistance of speakers of the languages they study in order to conduct their research (see Newman and Ratliff 2001: esp. 2–4). The question is: what copyright interests do these people have in their contributions to the linguistic study, and what must linguists do to ensure that they have all the legal rights necessary to use the materials fully, to publish books and articles based on the research, and to archive basic data for use at a later time and by other scholars? Let us separate out five categories of native speakers involved in the fieldwork phase of a research project, with the understanding that one person often fills more than one role and that the roles themselves inevitably overlap with one another. I shall call these people (1) informants, (2) subjects, (3) text providers, (4) assistants, and (5) consultants.

19.4.1

Linguistic informants (often referred to euphemistically by the semantically inaccurate term 'consultant') are people who provide natural samples of their language and raw data about the language, involving things ranging from simple translation equivalents to transformational-manipulative processes to grammaticality judgements. The informant could be someone whose contribution is limited to a one-time ad hoc description of the names of musical instruments and their parts or someone who works with the linguist over an extended period of time. To the extent that the informant is providing facts about the language and examples thereof, i.e. is helping to amass facts, the informant has no copyright interest in or legal rights to the work. Copyright protects the expression of facts and ideas, not facts and ideas in and of themselves. As a matter of politeness and professional courtesy, the linguist ought to acknowledge the informant's contributions and give credit where credit is due, but this is divorced from intellectual property issues. From a copyright point of view, the linguist is free to utilize all of the data that he obtained from the informant, analyse them, put them in archives, publish them in scholarly articles or commercial trade books, etc., all without worrying about intellectual property rights that the informant might have.

19.4.2

Subjects are people whom the linguist studies by such means as sociolinguistic observation or phonetic/psycholinguistic experiment. If the linguist sprays someone's mouth with chocolate powder to make a palatogram, that person is a subject; if the linguist measures teenage students' reactions to colour charts in relation to their colour terminology, those students are subjects; and if the linguist sits quietly in the waiting room of a driver's licence bureau carefully jotting down observations regarding the frequency, manner, and situation of language shifting among the workers behind the counter and the many multi-lingual individuals coming in and out, those people are subjects. These subjects have no copyright claims on the notes and other materials that the linguist has amassed. If the linguist were to make an audio recording of the people's speech or to videotape their social and linguistic interactions, copyright issues still would not arise. The linguist still would have full control over the materials and full freedom to use them for her scholarly purposes. There very well could be privacy issues, especially where videos or photos are concerned, and the re-search would have to take into account rules and agreements with and obliga-tions to the researcher's Institutional Review Board that handles Human Subjects Review, but copyright wouldn't present a problem.

19.4.3

By contrast, individuals who provide texts, whether simple narratives, oral history, folktales, modern poetry, letters written in the native orthography, or what have you, will in most cases qualify as the authors of those works and thus, as soon as they are written down, or fixed in any other tangible form, acquire copyright on those works. As indicated earlier, it is the author who obtains the copyright—without asking for it—even if the researcher commissioned the work and paid a considerable amount for it. The only question is whether that author's work is an original creative work that qualifies for copyright. If the text provider is simply repeating a traditional poem verbatim or has done no more than spoken a few lines of conversation, then the text might not meet the very minimal standards required for copyright protection. But if the work qualifies for copyright, the question of who initially owns the copyright to the work is usually straightforward, namely the text provider.

How then can researchers assure themselves of the ability to use and publish these texts, which they may have gone to a lot of trouble and expense to collect because of their potential linguistic, cultural, or literary value? There are two main possibilities, which relate to the two kinds of conveyances discussed above. One approach would be for the linguist to have the text provider make a written transfer of his or her copyright to the linguist so that, from that time forward, the linguist would be the copyright holder. In the case of mundane texts provided for linguistic purposes, this seems reasonable and the text provider might be fully willing to do so given that the texts have no real value apart from the linguist's project. Placing the copyright in the researcher's hands so that the texts then had the same legal status as the rest of the linguist's corpus of materials would appear to be the most effective strategy. If convenient, the linguist could explain this arrangement to the test provider before the texts were collected, but the transfer could equally be done after the fact. In either case, a written document signed by the text provider would be needed.

In the case of stories, oral history, poetry, songs, etc., i.e. works that have some intrinsic literary or artistic value, the question is whether it really would be appropriate for the linguist to encourage the copyright holder to transfer the copyright leaving the person with no proprietary rights whatsoever. Even with the best of intentions, the idea of a linguist going to a field site as a guest and walking away as the owner of the copyright to the creative works of local poets and storytellers feels dishonest and exploitative. Moreover, the linguist has a duty to ensure that if such a transfer were to happen it would be made with informed consent, and, depending on the level of education and sophistication of the text provider, this could be problematic. The linguist could, of course, buy the copyright, which in some cases would leave everyone happy, but determining the fair value of intellectual property in an unequal power rela-tionship involving individuals from distant countries and disparate cultures is not so easy.

The best solution in most situations when dealing with works having intrin-sic literary or artistic value is for the linguist to get a broad non-exclusive licence from the text providers/copyright holders. Since, as we now know, a non-exclusive licence is nothing more than permission-to-use, this satisfies the researcher's needs while leaving the text providers with the copyright to which they are entitled. With written texts, the copyright holder could simply add a note at the bottom of a particular text or on a separate sheet of paper covering a number of texts giving the linguist permission to use. The statement could be formal sounding, e.g. 'I, Gorko Mbukulu, give Ms Sarah Smith, an American lady studying our language, permission to use my poem/story/parable/etc. in her work in whatever way she finds helpful'; or it could be as little as 'Sara, do with this what you want, [signed] Mbu.' (Sample permission letters are provided in the appendix to this chapter.) Note that even though the texts are written, the permission could be oral, e.g. a call to one's cellphone or a simple face-to-face conversation, although it is helpful if you have some means of demonstrating that the permission was actually given just in case a dispute were to arise. With recorded materials, the easiest and best practice is to have the text provider give permission on the tape itself, either at the beginning or the end of the audio or video recording. This way the text and the permission do not get separated and possibly lost.

19.4.4

The irony when it comes to research assistants, the fourth category of native speaker identified, is that the better and more effective they are, the more likely it is for copyright problems to arise. To the extent that they are simply involved in data collection or target language elicitation or tape transcription or secretarial-type services (such as making and filing 3 × 5 cards), their work does not reach the level that would legally qualify as copyrightable. But as they get more involved in producing linguistic works and not just helping with data, such as pulling together a proverb collection or in the compilation of a dictionary, they begin to metamorphose into joint authors with all of the legal copyright entitlements and claims that that entails. As mentioned earlier, someone who, for example, contributes 15 per cent to the preparation of a work, would still count as co-author with a half copyright interest in the work. The linguist does not (or should not) want to deny her assistant his due, neither in terms of recognition nor decision-making nor money. On the other hand, owning a copyright jointly with someone half way around the world is far from ideal, and is sure to create practical difficulties and potentially hard feelings. Much more sensible is to have the full legal copyright in the hands of the person who is best situated to exploit the work from a scholarly point of view, including activities such as archiving and publishing, which would normally be the linguist and not her field assistant. This can be accomplished in two ways, only the second of which I recommend.

If the assistant works for the linguist on a regular salaried basis for a set period of time, let's say six months or more, then the assistant's authorship would accrue to the linguist under the Work for Hire doctrine. That is, from a legal point of view the assistant would not count as an author and the problem of joint authorship would not arise. This seemingly simple solution turns out not to be as attractive as it appears. In the first place, not all countries have something in their copyright laws comparable to the US Work for Hire rule and so, depending on the linguist's nationality and the place where the research is being carried out, this provision might not be applicable. But even if the Work for Hire rule is in place, it is not so easy to establish that the assistant is an *employee*. Only employees are covered by the rule, not freelance individuals who are hired to do specific tasks of one sort or another. In the US, employees are easily identified as such by formal hiring processes, tax deductions, personnel office record-keeping, etc. But when a single linguist, not a big corporation, informally asks someone in a village to serve as an assistant, often on flexible terms, it's not so clear that the person providing the linguistic services is really an employee rather than a freelance contractor. Finally, even if one has a true Work for Hire situation, i.e. the linguist as employer is entitled to be considered the legal author of the assistant's work products, a publisher—or archivists with whom the linguist is dealing—might not be satisfied with the legal explanation and want to see relevant paperwork, which might not exist.

The prudent step, therefore, is to eschew use of the Work for Hire doctrine and, operating as if the assistant were a joint author with a partial interest in the copyright, arrange for the assistant to provide a straightforward copyright transfer.[15] As described earlier, this is not complicated: all that one has to do is make sure that the assistant's transfer of the copyright to you the linguist is in writing and signed. The easiest way to do this is to have the assistant sign a paper at the time he is hired stating that he thereby assigns any and all copyright to materials produced in the conduct of his work with you to you. Nothing fancy or formal is required, although it's probably a good idea to have more than a note on the back of a vocabulary card. This is not because that casual note wouldn't suffice, but because one has an obligation to make it clear to the assistant that what he is signing is serious and has legal consequences.

In the same way that you as author want to preserve rights when you transfer copyright to a publisher, your assistant's interests as joint author should be protected when that person transfers his or her copyright to you. Protection of the assistants' legitimate rights should be taken into account and incorporated into the transfer agreement if done at the end of the research period, or by means of an addendum if the copyright transfer were covered in at the beginning when the assistant was hired, and one really had no idea how extensive that person's contribution would turn out to be. In the written memo or note or form specifying the copyright transfer, one definitely should spell out how financial proceeds are to be shared should one publish something involving single payment of royalties. You may think that the likelihood of ever earning anything of significance from your scholarly works is small, but it is good practice, and good personal and public relations, to officially acknowledge your assistant's claims to a portion of what you earn. For you, a $200 check from a publisher for a book chapter drawing on your field research might not seem that much given the time and effort (rewriting and proofing, etc.) that preparation of the chapter required; but sending half of that to your assistant instead of pocketing it all yourself could have both symbolic and practical significance at the receiving end.

19.4.5

The input of consultants is unlikely to present copyright ownership problems, whether one is talking about native speaker PhD linguists at a local university, expatriates with years of residence in the country, or elders in the community

---

[15] There are actually legal consequences of getting the copyright initially as employer-Author under the Work for Hire doctrine and getting the copyright from the initial author by copyright assignment, different advantages accruing in the different cases. Although this would make a challenging question in a final examination in a law school copyright course, the differences are inconsequential for most purposes and we need not go into them here.

whose input and advice has proved particularly valuable. The role of consultants is to provide ideas, information, insight, leads, questions, and criticism. In so doing they are unlikely to contribute materials that would qualify for copyright protection. However, people who fill these roles as consultants have all experienced (or have heard stories about others) being 'exploited' and having had their ideas stolen by visiting American or European researchers; thus one should be extremely sensitive about perceptions, and be meticulous about meeting rules of social reciprocity and explicit or implicit financial obligations.

19.4.6

Before concluding this section, I need to reiterate that it has been restricted to copyright matters. Linguists in the field also have to be attune to social norms, personal expectations, and customary laws relating to traditional knowledge (e.g. ancient traditions, beliefs, and values) and aspects of traditional culture, whether language-based (e.g. folktales, word games, epic poetry), or not (e.g. signs and symbols, rituals, drawings, paintings, jewellry, designs, handicrafts), or both (e.g. vocal music or dramatic performances). The handling of secret, spiritual, and sacred materials raises questions of cultural sensitivity and professional responsibilities that go far beyond the confines of copyright law.

19.5 GETTING MATERIALS BACK TO THE FIELD

Nowadays, most professionally responsible field linguists appreciate the need to make the results of their research available to the individuals with whom they worked and to members of the communities and countries where they lived. Whether this was an explicit condition of a visa or research permission, and whether the materials are to go back to the field site itself or to a university or research centre somewhere else in the country, we can assume that field linguists recognize the obligation to send something back. The linguist may send back actual copies of notes, reports, articles, or books, not to mention copies of sound or video recordings, or may make the results of the research trip widely available by other means. As anyone who has conducted field research knows, this seemingly simple professional imperative raises all kinds of practical, social, and ethical issues. I shall sidestep these sensitive matters here and leave others to deal with them. What I want to focus on are the copyright issues, so that at least that dimension can be taken into account. For convenience, I shall treat published works and unpublished works apart.

19.5.1

Generally speaking there are no copyright problems with regard to making copies of unpublished materials available to others. Either your works are not copyrighted, as in the case of rough field notes or data sets, or else you are the copyright holder and thus may freely make copies at your discretion. Even if you worked jointly with someone else who has a copyright interest in the works in question, e.g. a colleague, research associate, or field assistant, as *a* copyright holder, you may make copies of the work available to others without needing the permission of any of the other copyright holders. There are, however, two factors that you must keep in mind.

First, although you are free to behave as you want with regard to materials for which you have the sole copyright (or for which there is no copyright), your ability to share other people's works, where the copyright is not yours, or not solely yours, e.g. stories, poetry, or songs, depends on what copyright law applies and what agreements you have in place. If you recorded poetry by an indigenous poet, followed by transcription and translation, in the absence of a copyright assignment, the poet would own the copyright. Surprisingly, you could own the copyright to the translation but still not be able to make full use of it because someone else owned the copyright to the underlying work in the original language. You might have an explicit or implicit licence to use the poetry or story in your scholarly work, but you might not have obtained the right to make copies to send back and distribute in multiple form to the author's community or country. This could prove to be an unpleasant oversight where the researcher finds himself caught in the middle between local scholars, librarians, and archivists, on the one hand, who expect to have access to the full panoply of research materials, and indigenous poets, praise singers, and storytellers, on the other hand, who demand control over their artistic output in the home setting.

Second, even if there are no copyright problems to deal with, there may be contractual issues. For example, the research lab under whose auspices you did the research might have rules or embargoes on the external sharing of the materials, or the organization that funded the research might have archiving requirements and related conditions covering the distribution of field materials. These requirements are independent of copyright issues and have to be adhered to on their own terms.

19.5.2

The main difficulty with published works is that the publisher typically demands a transfer of rights as a condition of publication, such that the field researcher often relinquishes his or her ability to make full and free use of the work. The fieldworker may have been the initial author, and thus the initial copyright holder, but after publication may discover that she lacks the right to make copies to send back to the people where she worked, clearly an embarrassing situation. The solution is to anticipate the bottleneck before it happens and take steps in advance to alleviate the problem.

In the case of journal articles and chapters in edited volumes, the author needs to understand that he does not have to sign the preprinted contract but rather can preserve desired rights through sensible negotiation. Although publishers typically ask for copyright assignment pure and simple, they are becoming increasingly aware that they do not need all of these rights and that they can function just as well by being author-friendly. For example, *Language*, the flagship journal of the Linguistic Society of America (LSA), has a very progressive Author's Agreement which allows authors to retain a large number of important rights.[16] However— and this was probably an oversight—the agreement does not include a provision allowing fieldworkers to make copies of their articles to send back to their field sites. Fortunately, even if the publisher hasn't anticipated authors' needs in the boilerplate agreement, most are now open to contractual adjustments on an ad hoc basis. Thus, if the author writes and says, 'I would like to be able to make copies of my article in paper or electronic form (e.g. PDF or Word) to share with field assistants and colleagues and educational institutions in country X', the request will often be granted without great fuss. Adjustments are sometimes more difficult in the case of journals than with edited volumes because the publisher may have a fixed policy and set legal document for all of its journals, which it does not want to play with, but even here reasonable requests often result in contract modifications.

---

[16] Section 4 of LSA's 'Publication Agreement and Transfer of Copyright' for *Language*, which I helped draft, provides considerable protection for authors' rights:

'4. The AUTHOR of a work published in *Language* shall retain the following rights: a. the right to include the Work in a thesis or dissertation; b. the right to expand the Work into book-length form for publication; c. the right to include the Work in a compilation edited by the AUTHOR or in a collection of the AUTHOR's own writings, whether edited by the AUTHOR or by someone else; d. the right to reproduce and distribute the Work to students in a course taught by the AUTHOR; e. the right to present the Work at a conference and to hand out copies of the paper to persons attending the conference; f. the right to deposit the Work in the AUTHOR's institutional repository or other noncommercial scholarly archive subject to a two-year embargo from the time of publication.'

[The perceptive reader may ask on what basis could someone writing this chapter (in this case me) include the long quotation just presented? To this question, which can serve as a test to see whether readers of this chapter have captured the essence of US copyright law, there are at least three possible answers. The first is that I might have sought and received permission from the LSA, permission always being a good solution when one wants to use copyrighted materials. The second is that since I helped draft LSA's Publication Agreement, I qualified as a joint author, and thus co-copyright holder, who thereby had the right to use the material as I pleased (see §2.6 above). The third is that citing a standard author's agreement for a scholarly article falls within the range of 'fair use', for which permission from LSA was unnecessary (see §19.1.4 above).]

In recent years there has been a movement, led by library organizations such as SPARC[17] and followed by university consortia, to encourage authors to use a preset, institutionally endorsed Author's Addendum, which presents publishers with wide-ranging demands, usually phrased in an unnecessarily hostile manner. Not surprisingly, the results have been far from successful, although the movement has captured the attention of publishers who have sometimes made pre-emptive changes in their copyright policies to forestall conflicts with their authors. Although the idea of having a common Author's Addendum drawn up by copyright specialists may sound good, in my view, better practical results have been achieved by authors acting on their own who have made reasonable requests which they are able to justify on the basis of concrete circumstances and real scholarly needs. In the final analysis, the protection of the legitimate rights of authors will depend on concerted action by professional societies, not by individual scholars working on their own.

Most often, the Author's Agreement (= publishing contract) that scholars receive when their papers are accepted for publication comes from the business office rather than from the academic editor(s). Nevertheless, it is useful to contact the editor(s) and seek their support and intervention in requests for contract adjustments. This is especially recommended in the case of edited volumes, where many of the contributors may be junior scholars without much power, whereas the editors may be senior scholars with international reputations with whom the publisher has a business incentive to want to remain on good terms.

The previous discussion relates to traditional journals (and edited volumes). Nowadays, there is another option which may make some of these problems moot. Here I am talking about Open Access journals. These journals, which are increasing in number and reputation and professional significance, are distributed on-line on the web and made available worldwide without subscription fees. This means that people in the field site country who have computers and internet connection, which is increasingly becoming the norm, and who wouldn't have had access to subscription-based print journals, can immediately get hold of a researcher's writings—in fact at exactly the same time and as easily as people in America, Europe, or Japan. Thus the field researcher is able to satisfy his professional obligation to get information back to the field without any extra effort or negotiation and possible conflict with the publisher. It may be that a scholar has other, well-founded reasons for choosing to publish in a traditional journal, but all things

---

[17] SPARC is the acronym for The Scholarly Publishing and Academic Resources Coalition, see <http://www.arl.org/sparc/>. Although SPARC undoubtedly means well and cares about the welfare of scholars and academic institutions, my personal view is that its aggressive activism and distorted propaganda has shown it to be naïve and wrongheaded when it comes to important political and policy matters affecting academia.

being equal, the field researcher concerned about making materials maximally available needs to keep relevant Open Access journals in mind.[18]

When it comes to publishing results in book form, the approach has to be somewhat different. There are two good ways to try to make your book maximally available in the country (or countries) where the field research was done. One technique is to retain publishing rights in that country and not give them to your publisher. For example, if you did your research in Tanzania, you could give your American or European or Australian publisher full rights *except for* Tanzania, whereupon you could arrange with a local publisher to put out the work in an inexpensive paperback format. Although an established press might insist that they always get world rights for the books they publish, you can easily convince them that they don't know how to sell books in Tanzania, for example—which is to say, they financially would lose nothing by acceding to your wishes.

The other thing that you can do is make a better arrangement for buying books to give away to deserving people in your field site or country. For example, whereas most publishers allow authors a 30 per cent or 40 per cent discount on books purchased for personal use, you could try to negotiate a discount of, let's say 50 per cent for a specific number of books intended to be donated to people and institutions in the field research country. Even at a 50 per cent discount, the amounts can add up—ideally, funds for buying books to give back should be built into field research grants—but this is a small price to pay for the generosity of the people with whom you worked.

19.5.3

The PhD dissertation has a special status, which doctoral student researchers should be aware of and think about. Most American universities require that dissertations be submitted to University Microfilms International (UMI), now part of a large information company called ProQuest, which handles public sale and distribution of theses. UMI does not, however, require assignment of copyright, which remains with the author. Thus if the author wants to make his work freely accessible to anyone and everyone, he can upload the dissertation on a

---

[18] The Directory of Open Access Journals <http://www.doaj.org> currently lists close to 7,000 open access journals in existence. Since the DOAJ is not aware of all journals that are published on an open access basis, and since open access journals continue to be launched at a rapid rate, their listing could be off by as much as 100%: the number of such journals could easily be in the 8,000 journal range. Good peer-reviewed open access journals differ from traditional journals only in the means of production and distribution and not in matters of editorial policy or in scholarly standards. As a result, the initial resistance by scholars to publish in unproven open access journals is wilting away. In the case of field linguistics, what is arguably the top journal in the field, *Language Documentation & Conservation* (<http://www.nflrc.hawaii.edu/ldc/>), is an open access journal.

personal or departmental website. Moreover, many universities around the world now have open-access digital repositories which will house PDF versions of their students' PhD dissertations and make them discoverable, and this is often a sensible way to make this information available. Alternatively, if the author is willing to pay a small fee, UMI offers an open access option that allows interested readers to get hold of the dissertation for free through UMI itself. Another possibility, if the author would like to make the thesis available in the host country, but not necessarily to everyone without restriction throughout the world, would be to make copies of the dissertation to send back on computer disk, with the idea that some enterprising person in the field site country could print out copies on demand.

Finally, given the traditional idea that a dissertation is supposed to be an academic product that contributes to human knowledge, and not a student's personal property, one could argue that all dissertations should be in the public domain. That is, when it comes to dissertations, there should be a policy not only of open access but also open use. Since it is the student and not UMI/ProQuest who owns the copyright, there is nothing stopping a new PhD copyright holder from dedicating the copyright on the thesis to the public. There could be a brief delay, of let's say seven years, during which time only the student would have the opportunity to exploit the material in the thesis in whole or in part, but thereafter, the work would enter the public domain and be available for anyone to enjoy and benefit from. That is, using the oft-cited words of US Supreme Court Justice Louis Brandeis, the thesis would then be 'as free as the air to common use' (*International* 1918: 250).

19.6 CONCLUSION

Linguistic fieldworkers are not trained to know copyright law any more than copyright lawyers are trained to do phonetic transcription or carry out sophisticated morphophonemic analysis. Nevertheless, copyright and other intellectual property matters do impinge on the ability of linguists to carry out their research fully and to meet professional and ethical obligations, and thus some degree of familiarity with the principles of copyright is essential. Providing that basic exposure to copyright principles and practice has been the goal of this chapter. No field linguist can be expected to understand or solve every intellectual property difficulty that might come along, but the hope is that this overview will alert linguistic fieldworkers to the nature of copyright so that they can anticipate problems, make necessary preparations, and have a good idea as to when they need to seek legal help.

19.7 FURTHER READING

Useful brochures about copyright law can be found on the website of the US Copyright Office <http://www.copyright.gov>. A number of American universities, especially Cornell, Duke, Maryland, and Stanford, have extremely helpful copyright web pages, but the one that I would recommend most is that of the Copyright Advisory Office of Columbia University <http://copyright.columbia. edu/copyright/>. Another good source of information is WIPO's web page *Basic Notions of Copyright and Related Rights* (WIPO 2010a). The best comprehensive one-volume treatment of copyright law is Leaffer (2010). Strong (1999) is less detailed and now somewhat out of date, but it is still very reliable and, for the non-lawyer interested in the subject, much easier to read than Leaffer. Useful works focusing on copyright in an academic setting are Crews (2006) and Lindsey (2003). A discussion of copyright with specific reference to issues that confront linguists is found in Newman (2007). Information regarding the important Creative Commons organization can be obtained from their website (http://www.creative commons.org) and from the informative article by Garlick (2005).

19.8 APPENDIX. SAMPLE FORMS

[Disclaimer: The following are examples of the *kinds* of consent forms that one could use in a fieldwork setting. These are not legal documents and should not be interpreted as such. Whether they are suitable or not will depend on the nationality of the researcher, the laws of the country in which he or she is working, and the specific circumstances involved.]

I. Copyright assignments/transfers (Must be in writing and signed.)

a. Research assistant

My name is _____. I have been [or will be] working as a paid research assistant for Amy Apfel, who is doing a study of the X language. I hereby assign to Ms Apfel any copyright interest that I may have in lexical, grammatical, textual, or other materials produced in connection with this research project. She agrees to acknowledge my participation in the project as professionally appropriate in any of her published works. Signed _____ Date _____

b. *Occasional freelance worker*

My name is _____. I am a teacher in the XYZ Advanced Teachers College. During vacation times, I helped Baron Barker, who is doing a study of the Y language. Specifically, I translated eleven folktales and fifty proverbs from our language into English. I hereby assign my copyright in these translations to Mr Barker so that he can use them for scholarly purposes. [Optional: However, if he should earn money from works containing these translations, he agrees that I am entitled to 50 per cent of whatever he gets.]

Signed _____ Date _____

c. *Poet*

My name is _____. I am the author of the following poems written in the Z language: [list by title]. I hereby give Cathy Cantor the exclusive right to translate these poems into English, to publish the English translations, to post them on the web, or to use them for other educational or scholarly purposes. I also give Ms Cantor permission to use the language Z originals of my poems in scholarly works, but only if they are accompanied by the English translations. I hereby acknowledge receipt of $200 as payment for the transfer of these rights.

Note that I retain copyright in these poems and that this transfer of rights only belongs to translations into English. I reserve rights over translation into Spanish or other languages, and I also reserve full rights to publish or perform my original poems in language Z here in Peru or anywhere else in the world.

Signed _____ Date _____

II. Copyright Permission (non-exclusive licence) (can be oral, e.g. on a tape recorder, or can be written)

d. *Traditional storyteller (oral permission)*

My name is _____. I am a tailor by trade. I live in psq quarter in abc town. I am about to recite [or I have just recited] a number of stories into a tape recorder for Donald Deutsch. I hereby give Mr Deutsch permission to write these stories down, to translate them into any other foreign language, and to make use of the stories in the original or in translation in his studies of our language.

[If this statement is made in the original language, it is best to have a translation provided on the tape, although a separate translation note added later will do.]

e. *Educated friend (informal written permission)*

To Evelyn Edwards from your friend Jacques Junaidu. As a former classmate at UCLA, I am happy to allow you to use my autobiography written in language G in your PhD dissertation and in any other studies of the language that you might write. However, (a) I do not want you to deposit the autobiography in any archive since I may want to do that here in Yaoundé; and (b) in exchange, if you should translate the autobiography into English, I would expect you to provide me with a copy of the translation and allow me to attach it to my original version for my own scholarly and personal uses.

Signed: Jack

CHAPTER 20

···

TRAINING LINGUISTICS STUDENTS FOR THE REALITIES OF FIELDWORK

···

MONICA MACAULAY

This chapter uses examples from the author's first fieldwork experience to illustrate the need for better training of graduate students in linguistics on the subject of fieldwork, especially in the personal and practical aspects. This very personal account also points out the need for the development of a better and more extensive literature on linguistic fieldwork, and makes suggestions about issues that should be covered in such a literature.[1]

[1] Thanks to Colleen Cotter, Megan Crowhurst, Miriam Meyerhoff, Marianne Mithun, Joe Salmons, Peggy Speas, Sara Trechter, Tony Woodbury, and many others for their feedback on this paper. Thanks also to my professors (especially Leanne Hinton) for doing their best to bring me along as a linguist and fieldworker. Thanks are most especially due, though, to the many Mixtec speakers who led me towards a greater understanding of the appropriate place of a linguist among native peoples. I realize now that I was an especially slow learner. [Editor's note: This text of this chapter was first published in *Anthropological Linguistics* (Summer 2004, Vol. 46 Issue 2: 194–209) and is reproduced here (without revision of content or style) with the kind permission of the author and of the editors of *Anthropological Linguistics*.]

20.1 INTRODUCTION

The goal of this chapter is to make a very simple point: that we, as linguists, need to rethink our training of graduate students for fieldwork. While we generally do a very thorough job of teaching them how to elicit and analyse data, we often forget to tell them that there is a personal and practical side to fieldwork that can very well derail their research if they are not prepared for it.

A case in point is my first field trip to work with Mixtec speakers in Chalcatongo, a remote village in the mountains of Oaxaca, Mexico. The account I present here is quite personal, in order to provide the reader with an example of just how unprepared *this* student was for the practical and psychological aspects of being a fieldworker in another culture.

The anthropological and sociological literature on fieldwork is vast. Yet as a graduate student in theoretical linguistics, it never occurred to me that such a literature would exist, nor that such a thing would be useful to me. We might well ask why this literature on fieldwork has been so invisible to (at least some) field linguists. I think the answer lies in the history of our field. With the generative revolution we cast off the Structuralists, and with them, our ties to anthropology. For someone like me, raised in the generative tradition, those ties were simply a part of history. In the generative tradition, language, of course, is studied apart from culture and society. This is feasible for those whose data come from their own native speaker intuitions, but it can lead to an odd schizophrenic existence for those who believe in the generative approach yet gather their data in the field.

On my first field trip, in my ignorance, I thought that since I was just studying language I had no need for any of that anthropological 'stuff.' I had no interest in Mixtec culture: I wanted to know about Mixtec morphology and syntax. But this attitude, I now realize, was the cause of many of my problems on that first trip.

In fact, I still think that I was right that I could do morphological analysis without knowing anything about Mixtec culture. But this is not the issue. The issue is that there I was, living among a group of people that I knew very little about. My awkwardness and confusion would have been greatly lessened if I had simply taken the time to learn more about them. At the same time, had I read up on what fieldwork is like for the fieldworker, I might not have felt so much like I was losing my mind while I was there, nor that I was a complete failure for not loving every second of it.

Now, obviously different fieldworkers have different backgrounds, different training, and different personalities. I am sure that many linguists have gone into the field for the first time with a solid knowledge of both the cultures they were visiting and what the fieldwork experience might be like. But plenty of stories indicate that others of us go into the field for the first time without such preparation.[2]

This chapter provides an example of how such ignorance can result in a miserable (even if productive) first field trip. It is designed to provide the reader with three things: a feel for the environment that I found myself in; a sense of the practical things I dealt with on my first field trip and my reactions to them; and finally, some suggestions on how we can make the experience somewhat easier for others. To accomplish this, I include some artifacts from my trip, primarily excerpts from my field journal and quotes from the anthropological and (limited) linguistics literature illustrating the ordinary and almost predictable nature of my experiences and reactions.[3] These are set off from the text in boxes, such as the one immediately below.

Fieldwork is a deeply emotional experience for those who undertake it ... (Wengle 1988: xiv)

7/8/82: [First journal entry]

WHAT AM I DOING HERE?

Made it to Oaxaca. I'm sitting in a cafe drinking café con leche trying to calm down. I'm almost hysterical again. I feel so awful. I'm constantly on the verge of tears.

Why am I here? I don't want to be here. I don't want to do this. It's 6 weeks staring me in the face. Will I feel like this for 6 weeks? I'll die. If I still feel like this in 2 weeks I guess I could go home. I don't know quite what it is that's so awful. I just want to be home ... Oh god. Six weeks. I can't do it.

This is unreal. How did this happen? How did I let this happen?

Young women fieldworkers—and by young I mean women in their twenties—appear to have the most difficult time in the field. This is particularly so if they enter the field alone. (Wax 1979: 518)

---

[2] Newman (1992) apparently shares my view of the training linguistics graduate students get (or do not get) before they go out into the field: 'the position of [field methods] in the training of our graduate students is indeed marginal and is likely to remain so. This combined with the fact that publications by linguists on FM have essentially ceased to appear and relevant books and articles by anthropologists and sociologists are generally ignored means that the number of new field workers will remain small and many scholars undertaking fieldwork for the first time will be untrained and unprepared' (1992: 6).

[3] The excerpts from my field journal are very personal and somewhat melodramatic (I was in my 20s, after all). They are not the kind of thing I would normally put in a paper, yet I think they communicate almost better than my description what I went through in my first experience with fieldwork.

20.2 'Monica, Hell'

I should preface the description of my first field trip with two points: first, I was quite fluent in Spanish, which I used as a contact language with the Mixtec speakers in Chalcatongo (virtually all of whom are bilingual). Second, I had spent a great deal of time in South America (a year and a half in Chile, with travels throughout most of the continent), and had made numerous trips to Mexico and Guatemala. So my problems were not due to any language barrier, nor to a general lack of knowledge about cultures south of the US border. My ignorance was far more specific than that.

> The so-called 'field manuals' that exist for the student are little more than vast recipe books, good on methodological concerns but nearly silent on matters of psychological adjustment. The student is also under tremendous pressure to justify his existence in the field—to the natives, to himself, and to the funding agencies and faculty judging his performance. His reputation and career are dependent, in some (probably large) measure, on his performance in the field. In all likelihood, the fieldworker is far less than fluent in the natives' language, and certainly he is ignorant about his place and behavioural responsibilities. (Wengle 1988: 9)

I had decided to go to Mexico to do fieldwork on the Otomanguean language Mixtec after working on it for about two years with a speaker in Berkeley, California. As my departure date got closer, I began to have a sense that events were sweeping me along towards a trip I had never really intended to go on. Although *I* had been the one who made the plans, suddenly I realized that what had sounded good in theory was terrifying in fact.

When the day came, I got on the plane, in hysterics. I made it to Mexico, and I made it to Oaxaca City. Eventually I found the buses I needed to get to Chalcatongo. Upon arrival, I found myself deposited on a dusty, deserted street. I had been told that there was a house that rented rooms, and I managed to find it. I was in luck—they actually had a room available. I got inside, closed the door, and cried some more.

> 7/12 [in Tlaxiaco, on the way to Chalcatongo]: So I'm sitting here getting drunk. I'm on my second beer. This one is a warm Tres Xs. Mmm. I had to get drunk because I fell apart again tonight. I cried & cried.
>
> [A man had been harassing me the night before]: So I came home and became hysterical. I wanted someone real to talk to. Same old shit. When I'm like that I can't imagine making it through this. I really am thinking seriously about just going home

early. Six weeks just seems insurmountable. I dunno, I just want to have the option. But it scares me to contemplate doing it—face-losing...

[From a brief description of a graduate student's first day in the field]: *And he cannot leave, for his entire career, his prestige ranking within the discipline of anthropology, his professors' respect—and much else—depend on his maintaining a stiff upper lip, on organizing this chaos into a Ph.D. thesis.* (Wengle 1988: 3–4)

7/31: Eighteen more days—it's a lot ... When this nightmare is over it'll seem so petty. I'll think, heck, what's six weeks? No one will understand why I was so miserable, and I probably won't either. When I was talking to that Israeli woman in Oaxaca [who was travelling around the world for a year] about being alone I said something about how I didn't know how she could stand it—I was flipping out just from 6 weeks. She said 'yeah, but you're probably more alone than I am.' True, true. This is like the fucking isolation ward ... Lost in space. I'll say.

8/7: I keep thinking how long each day is. Eleven [more] of 'em. When I get back will I even remember this feeling of wanting to push time along? Please, time, go by quickly. In the evenings I say to myself 'only two hours till bedtime' because bedtime signifies another day over, signifies another morning to come, where I can cross another day off.

This really is like being in jail. Or in the isolation ward. Or on the moon.

I spent six weeks in Chalcatongo that first time, and quickly found two consultants. They were both knowledgeable, careful, and caring, and I was very lucky to find them.

Nonetheless, my bouts of hysterical crying continued. There was no phone in the village, so I wrote incessantly—in my journal, and in my letters home. As my return address, I wrote 'Monica, Hell.' I lived for mail, which only rarely came, and read my few books over and over again. I know now that these are classic signs of culture shock—but at the time I just thought I was going crazy.

Diaries and letters to and from the field are apt to be excellent sources in aiding the maintenance of one's sense of identity. One of the more important functions of diaries is to translate otherwise chaotic events into some order that makes sense to the individual in terms of his own lived past. (Wengle 1988: 24)

Let me describe some of the things I was dealing with.

First, I had trouble finding food. Eventually I was able to establish a routine where I had a noon meal at a restaurant, and otherwise ate bananas and tomato sandwiches. But bananas, tomatoes and bread were all things I could only buy twice a week, on the two market days. If I didn't buy enough, and ran out of food, sometimes I could buy little packaged pastries at one of the stores, but that was about it. I lost a lot of weight.

7/17: Food is such a problem here. Yesterday I went to the one restaurant I know of and had: a small plate of greasy rice, tortillas (homemade wheat ones, not good at all), a main dish of—get this—breaded pork knuckle? They told me it was pata de puerco. Well, all it was was bone and gristle with breading over it, and red sauce of some questionable origin. Oh yeah and a tiny plate of beans. Not even black beans—pinto beans. Maybe today I'll get up my nerve and go see if that other place I spotted really is a restaurant. It's sort of hard to tell. No sign, nothing painted outside on the wall.

7/18: Today was mini-market day. On Sunday, there's a small market—about 1/2 the size of Thursday's. I bought bread and tomatoes and mangos and bananas. So I don't have to eat at the foul restaurants. Actually yesterday I did try the other restaurant and it was better. I just had eggs and beans (black beans—yay!) and tortillas. That was a hell of a lot better than breaded pig's knuckles. I'm glad I had eggs—I don't think I'm getting any protein.

7/24: Today I had the first good food I've had [here]—at my eggs & beans restaurant. It was mole verde [green sauce]—with chicken, potatoes, and squash floating around in it. I asked if it was real hot, knowing full well it was a stupid question, & they said no, no. Of course I almost died it was so hot. But it was good.

Malnutrition . . . is produced by failure to consume adequate food. This can be related to the availability of food in the fieldwork environment, and also sometimes to the difficulty of transporting food supplies from outside sources to the research site. (Howell 1990: 75)

[The other side of the coin—a fieldworker who gained 30 pounds]: *In the face of extreme isolation from familiar social and intellectual sources of emotional satisfaction . . . an intensification of dependency needs was inevitable. Since it was essential that she not openly express her frustration and anger . . . , she attempted to relieve her insecurity by eating.* (Wintrob 1969: 66)

Second, it was the rainy season, and I was at an altitude of about 9,000 feet. It was extremely cold, and I was not prepared for it. I wore layers and layers of clothes, and froze when I had to wash something. We did have electricity in the house I lived in—most houses in the village had it. But of course there was no heat, and often when it rained the lights would go out.

7/13: I'm sitting here with my down vest on over my thermal shirt, shortsleeve shirt and sweatshirt. It's fucking cold in this place.

7/18: Well, it's pouring and the lights are out and if I leave my door open for light the rain comes in. It's 5:45 so it's gonna be dark soon anyway. What, may I ask, am I going to do in the dark? I asked the señora if she had a candle but apparently she doesn't—she never came back. This is swell. It's thundering . . .

7/19: Well, the lights are flickering again and my tape deck is operating at varying speeds so I guess I just have to quit working for a while. I bought a bunch of candles today so when the lights go I'll be able to see. At least dimly.

8/4: I'm freezing. Today I washed my thermal shirt—I wear it 24 hours a day so it gets sorta filthy. I wear it every day and then to bed too. I sure shoulda brought more warm clothes.

I almost immediately became covered in little red bites from invisible insects. No bug spray or lotion helped, and this continued for the entire time I was there. My room was also filled with flies. I got very good at killing them, and it became one of my favourite forms of entertainment. My record was 41 in one evening.

> 7/15: I'm all covered in red bumps. They hardly itch at all. I wonder what it is. I guess I should spray my bed.
>
> 7/17: Now they itch. They keep me awake at night. I sprayed my bed. I cover myself in insect repellent twice a day, to no avail. Ugh.
>
> 7/23: My bites kept me up all night. I kept waking up scratching. And I woke up with a bunch of new ones. I even put [the] super-repellent on before I went to bed. I put it on again this morning. I don't know why, it doesn't seem to work. Nothing does . . . 26 more days . . .
>
> 8/3: I just killed 15 flies—there are easily twice as many again in my room. [Later]: And I have now killed 34 flies in my room. Lots left.
>
> 8/4: I woke up yesterday morning with a line of 12 bites going up from my knee. My legs, below the knee, are just completely polka-dotted . . . But the big problem is sleeping. They keep me awake at night. And then I wake up scratching sometimes— ugh. It's so awful. They're mainly on my legs. I got three on my stomach, and a couple of weeks ago a bunch on one arm but other than that it's been the legs only. These fleas are leg-men. Assuming they're fleas. That's what everyone tells me. Invisible fleas, though.

I did manage to find consultants fairly easily, but they stood me up all the time.[4] Of course the notion of scheduling appointments was not quite the same to the people I was dealing with as it was to me, with my Midwestern expectations of promptness and politeness. If the consultant wasn't available, the day was shot for me—it was very hard to get people to agree to work without at least a day's notice.

> 7/19: I worked with C again this morning and have been working all day since on transcribing and also going through my data. I don't believe how much I work. I guess when there's nothing else to do . . . If I ever want to write a dissertation, I know where to come.
>
> 7/23: Oh shit. C stood me up again. I haven't done any eliciting in days and I'm getting bored. Besides, I have so much planned that I want to do.
>
> 7/24: Now I've got a lot to write about. But no time, since I have my hot date at 2:00, and it's 1:45 . . . I was sitting here working (C stood me up again) and M came and knocked on the door and asked if I wanted to do some work. How wonderful. I was just

---

[4] Apparently being stood up is not uncommon. Henry (1969: 43) describes the same problem with government officials in Trinidad, and Saberwal (1969: 50–52) describes it in his work with the Embu of Kenya.

feeling upset about not doing enough eliciting. So now I have tons of tape to go over ...
and of course I'm just writing in here.

*The fieldworker finds himself writing letters of a length and intensity of feeling that is not
at all characteristic of him. Or the fieldworker finds that he is spending most of his time
dictating into his tape recorder and typing it up in field notes.* (Wintrob 1969: 67)

Then there was my work itself: the more I worked on the language, the more
incompetent I felt. I had terrible fears that I was putting myself through this torture
for nothing—that there would be no results to show for it when I returned home.

7/17: God, I went a whole day without writing in here. Amazing. That's because I worked
all day yesterday. I worked with C a couple of hours in the morning and then spent about
six hours in the afternoon and evening working on the data. Jesus. I never work like this.
It's a little frustrating ... I'm having trouble getting verb tenses and stuff out of him. He
doesn't get the idea of paradigms at all ...
    I don't know what I'm doing. Face it.
    7/18: I also feel like I don't know what I'm doing, in terms of my work here. I feel so at
sea. What am I investigating? How do I do it? I haven't the vaguest.

*During the early period of fieldwork, anxiety that builds up tends to be free floating. It
relates to environmental stresses, health concerns, and self-image, with fears of rejection by
the community, feelings of inadequacy in collecting essential data, and fears of failure in
completing the planned research.* (Wintrob 1969:67)

One thing that I expected that I actually did *not* find was unwanted attention
from men. I had been in enough big cities in Mexico to know what to expect along
those lines, but it did not happen in Chalcatongo, at least not from the locals. They
watched me, certainly, but it was more like being an animal in a zoo than a woman
being ogled by men.

Unfortunately, there were a few men there from bigger cities, and they did give
me some trouble. One in particular was a real problem. He would get drunk and
pound on my door, and say strange things to me. At times I felt completely
confined to my room—that it simply was not safe to go out. This was especially
problematic since of course the bathroom was across the courtyard.

7/31: God I hate this [place]. I went out to go to the bathroom & this guy who lives in one
of the rooms here accosted me. He's drunk off his ass, mumbling, making gestures with
his hands while looking at me meaningfully. I tried & tried to listen & understand—
finally I started trying to leave. He kept saying no, no, mumble mumble. Finally I just
told him I can't understand drunk men, and walked off. Came into my room & just
pounded the walls. Now he's 'singing.' I hate drunks ... I can't stop crying. I hate this

[place] and I want to go home. NOW. TODAY. Goddamn it. I was going to go out for a walk but now I feel like I'm a prisoner in this room. I guess I could go out & make a beeline for the front door—ignore him. Besides, I can't go out till I stop crying . . . I hate this [place].

8/1: The drunk guy came and knocked on my door late last night. He kept mumbling 'Préstame revista' [loan me a magazine]. I kept telling him I didn't have any revistas. Finally he said, then a book. I told him I only had books in English & he said to give him one of those. So I gave him 'The Groves of Academe' by Mary McCarthy. I thought it was hilarious. So this morning he brought it back . . . He was still drunk, said, 'mumble mumble'—I'm sure telling me how much he enjoyed the book. He's been drunk all day today, too—singing obnoxiously, staggering around. UGH. He's been hanging out some with [the neighbour], who's probably drunk too, although luckily I haven't seen him up close enough to tell. They make me ill. It's not the fact of drunkenness—shit, I like to get smashed, myself, sometimes. It's just the way they get. The way the asshole has been drunk for 2 days now . . . I hate 'em.

Most of the time, though, I was simply a curiosity. Occasionally there was ridicule that I was aware of, but usually they just stared at me. And they had good reason to stare! Take a look at Fig. 20.1.

Figure 20.1 The author with a member of the community and her sons.

Note the sheer difference in scale between the two adults. Although it is really a very embarrassing picture, I include it to show how my mere physical presence affected how I must have been perceived. It was clear the whole time that I was there that I was regarded as an alien from outer space. I was an unmarried woman by herself, twice as tall as most people, with short hair, and wearing jeans.

> *The fieldworker's marital status is of particular significance to anthropological informants, since most 'primitive' cultures take kinship bonds as the fundamental source of social structure and social order... But an unmarried, childless adult woman has no fully legitimate social place in most cultures.* (Warren 1988: 13)

A further idea of just how sore-thumb-like I was can be seen in the following anecdote: shortly before I left the village someone asked me if I had ever noticed that children ran screaming from me when I walked down the street. Of course I *had* noticed that. She told me that it was because the women had taken to telling their children to be good—*or the gringa would take them.*

I had become the bogeyman.

Although it is a funny story—and I tell it as a funny story—it also just sums up perfectly how alien I felt, and how alien they regarded me as being.

> 7/31: So I got on the bus to Chalcatongo & this time it left at 5:30 [a.m.]. These 2 obnoxious women got on a little after 5 & proceeded to make all sorts of noise—screaming & giggling in the front of the bus (they were friends of the drivers). Imagine my (unpleasant) surprise when the louder of the two started talking about me. The first clue was something about 'la muchacha que parece a un muchacho' [the girl who looks like a guy]. I couldn't hear or understand all of what she said and I was really getting down on myself for being so paranoid, but then they went through this thing about 'entró'—'she got on the bus', obviously. This was all in whispers, with glances to the back of the bus—it was too dark for her to see me. Then they got into this simply hilarious joke which consisted of Miss Obnoxious saying 'Do you speak English' in a bad accent—they repeated that one about five times. That was when I knew for sure I wasn't being paranoid. Later, on the road, when it got light, they would every now & then whisper something & turn & look at me... I fantasized all sorts of things to say to her but of course didn't say anything. She got off at Chalcatongo too—maybe I'll see her in town & can trip her or something.
>
> 8/4: [M and I] were talking about the United States, and she said that she had heard—she didn't know if it was true—she couldn't believe it was (lots of hemming and hawing) but that she had heard that when Americans didn't want their children they killed them. I tried to set her straight.
>
> [In a discussion of what fieldwork may/may not be like]: *catastrophic identity fragmentation ... a searing and traumatic attack against his or her sense of identity ...* (Wengle 1988: x)

20.3 How did this happen
and what can we do about it?

I have already suggested that at least part of the reason that I could go to the field so unprepared for what daily life would be like is that—at least for many of us—there is no place in our curriculum for training students in the practical aspects of doing fieldwork. Another factor plays a role, though, which is that the mystique of fieldwork remains very strong in our field.

A passage in the 'Editor's Introduction' to *Emotions and Fieldwork* (Kleinman and Copp 1993) sums this up quite nicely:

> Fieldwork is supposed to be fun . . . Anger, boredom, confusion, disgust, self-doubt, depression, lust, despair, frustration, and embarrassment are perhaps more than occasionally associated with fieldwork, but they are not often discussed—at least not in print—because such sentiments violate the pleasure principle so often associated with model practice . . . This curious policing of socially correct feeling within the fieldwork community can lead to a rather bizarre slanting of research reports wherein the fieldworker is represented as wallowing in an almost unmitigated delight while engaged in the research process. This is quite possibly one reason why the actual experience of fieldwork can come as such a shock to the neophyte. (1993: vii)

Consider the explicit example of this in Samarin's 1967 book on linguistic fieldwork:

> Here and elsewhere in this volume I may give the impression that field work is more awesome than it really is. A field worker should take his work seriously, but he need not do it lugubriously, for an exciting and life-enriching experience awaits him. Field work is characterized in one word—at least for me; it is *fun*. (Samarin 1967: vii)[5]

So, although until very recently linguists have rarely discussed their fieldwork experiences in print—we just write about our data—the 'pleasure principle' message does get communicated. I do not know exactly where I learned it, but I *knew* that I was a failure because I hated my fieldwork so incredibly much.

---

[5] There is one note I am obliged to make here: while working on this chapter, I went back to the small number of works that were available on the subject of linguistic fieldwork in 1982. To my chagrin, I discovered that Samarin (1967) does have some warnings I wish I had paid attention to, for example: 'In his preoccupation with data . . . the linguist can very easily forget the human factors in his investigation of language. His collection and analysis of language phenomena are dependent on and in some way influenced by the people among whom he works and by his own personality and training. Without some understanding of himself, the language community, and the informant the linguistic investigator goes ill-prepared to the field' (Samarin 1967: 7). But aside from a short section addressing such issues, most of Samarin is dedicated to linguistic analysis.

> Berreman [1962: 4] laments the dearth of information on 'the practical problems' of carrying out fieldwork, such that 'the person facing fieldwork for the first time ... may suspect ethnographers of having established a conspiracy of silence on these matters... As a result of the rules of the game which kept others from communicating their experience to him, he may feel that his own difficulties of morale and rapport ... were unique and perhaps signs of weakness or incompetence. Consequently, these are concealed or minimized. (Wintrob 1969: 64)

Now, I realize that for some people fieldwork really is unproblematic, not to mention fun. In fact, *I* actually enjoyed myself on two subsequent trips to Chalcatongo, in 1985 and 1992. This is not to say that there were no difficult moments, or that every minute was bliss. But on these trips I knew the territory, and, perhaps most importantly, I had company. I now understand that a great deal of what I experienced on that first trip was simply due to being alone under a difficult set of circumstances.

In subsequent years I have done fieldwork with two North American tribes, the Karuk and the Menominee, and have had quite different experiences from that first trip to Chalcatongo. Although I always have (and probably always will have) some difficulty with the awkward social situation that fieldwork imposes, my abilities have steadily improved. I attribute this improvement both to age and to having learned (through bitter experience!) that indeed it *is* important to learn about a culture before one becomes involved with it, even if one really is only interested in how reduplication or plural marking works. I have focused on my negative experiences in this chapter, however, because we need to be reminded that they can happen, and that some students may not be naturals at this undertaking.

> Research courses and methodological texts only teach students how research ought to go, rather than how it does go in the real world. As social scientists, we have an obligation to share experiences with other researchers in order to develop our research skills and enterprise. (Easterday et al. 1977: 346)

In anthropology and sociology, it has now become standard to talk about any and all aspects of the fieldwork experience. We need to start doing this in linguistics as well. Obviously there is no way to come up with an exhaustive list of prescriptions for successful fieldwork, since each situation is different—yet there *is* one very simple thing we can do to help our graduate students approach fieldwork more intelligently: we can describe for them a range of possibilities of what they might encounter.

> *Fieldwork itself is unquestionably that aspect of qualitative inquiry in which one can assert the least control. One can be prepared, but that does not necessarily entail formal 'training' of any kind. How one has learned to cope with all the other exigencies to be confronted in the course of everyday life surely has more predictive power for fieldwork success than how many courses one has taken, manuals one has read, or ethnographers one has known. (Wolcott 1995: 146)*

Some initial suggestions on things that we should address in training our students for linguistic fieldwork appear, then, below.

(i) Mechanics

- Getting into the community: the necessity of a letter of introduction ('one of the cardinal rules of fieldwork procedure': Henry 1969:36).
- Finding someone to work with: I was told that finding consultants would not be a problem—that they would probably find me. This was in fact exactly what happened.
- Consultant compensation: is it necessary? If so, how much is required?

(ii) Going alone vs. going with company.

This is something that can only be decided on an individual basis. A prospective fieldworker should think carefully about their own personality— their feelings about being alone, their ability to deal with awkward social encounters and so on—and make a decision based on that.

> *While a few standardized formulas for the success of a fieldwork project exist (the do's and don'ts of fieldwork), in the final analysis, the skills and experience of each researcher in relation to the situation in which he undertakes to work seem to be the more crucial factors. The success of fieldwork is largely the result of the unique interaction between the personality of the fieldworker, the nature of the research problem, and the socio-cultural environment in which research is undertaken. (Henry 1969: 46)*
>
> *I realized how much the process of field work would be enriched, and the psychological health of the field worker supported by the opportunity of working in the field with another person who was undergoing parallel experiences. I would recommend that field work by solitary investigators of either sex be discouraged whenever possible. (Golde 1970: 78)*
>
> *To minimize the distress, we can recognize that mental stress can be very great in the field, and that we will vary as individuals and at different times in our lives in our ability to accept and cope with these stresses. We need to entertain the possibilities of our own limits in deciding what fieldwork we can and cannot do. There is an endless array of researchable problems, and no one has to go work on leech-infested jungle trails, on high altitude mountains, or in urban slums if that is beyond their own psychic capacity. 'Know thyself', we are advised, and that seems to be particularly wise advice in the case of someone planning fieldwork. (Howell 1990: 162)*

(iii) Practical matters

- Health and safety: note that the issue of going into the field alone arises under this heading as well, and should be considered carefully.

> No matter how knowledgeable you are in theoretical linguistics, no matter how skilled you are in techniques of description and analysis, you're not going to achieve what you set out to do if you are sick or dead. (Newman 1992: 3)

- Food: the anthropological literature on fieldwork tends to assume that food will be plentiful, and instead focuses on things like hiring someone to do shopping and food preparation. This was out of the question for me, since I had no access to cooking facilities, and was not in Chalcatongo long enough to make any such arrangements. The lack of cooking facilities also meant that I could only buy ready-to-eat foods, which severely limited the possibilities.

> Health in the field, as anywhere, depends in part on the diet available. Researchers typically have to balance their desire for a supply of fresh and attractive foods of the kinds they enjoy with their desire to avoid spending a large portion of their time cooking, shopping, or even growing food or hunting and gathering it... We note that the single most frequently mentioned arrangement for food preparation is to hire a local cook and have that person do the cooking (and usually the shopping as well). (Howell 1990: 57)

(iv) Gender and sex. Clearly a woman—especially a single woman—going into the field has to be prepared to face what the anthropological literature quaintly calls 'hustling'.

(v) Emotional reactions and culture shock. Frank discussions of individual's experiences and a good reading list would be invaluable. Students should be familiar with the concept of culture shock and its many manifestations. I know now that things like uncontrollable crying and loss of self-confidence in one's work are commonplace. Although knowing such things intellectually may not provide complete protection from feeling them, it does usually help to know one is not alone in one's reactions.

> ... one characteristic does seem to stand out in all the accounts of fieldwork that I am familiar with. I am referring to the associated problems of disorientation, worry, depression, fatigue, loneliness, stress, and the like. (Wengle 1988: xviii)

(vi) Missionaries. No matter what one's religious beliefs are, and no matter what one thinks about the goals and methods of missionary organizations, a non-missionary fieldworker may have to deal with the issue of missionary linguists who have preceded him or her. For me this was a real problem, since I encountered attitudes ranging from mild suspicion to downright hostility based on the assumption that all linguists are missionaries. During a later field trip, my companion and I were even denied permission to work in a neighbouring town because the authorities assumed (and could not be convinced otherwise) that we were missionaries. My point here is simply to emphasize that a beginning fieldworker should be forewarned about the potential problems that they might face due to the prior presence of missionaries, and should understand the religious politics of the place that they go to.

> 7/14: [A neighbour] told me one interesting thing—he knew some SIL linguists who were here. He didn't remember their names, unfortunately. He went on a long tirade about how [evil] they were. He said the people here already have their own religion and these people came in and 'treated us like a lower form of life and tried to shove their religion down our throats.' I explained that I knew about them and that I was not in any way connected with them. He seemed reassured and said he could tell I wasn't one of them. But that's the first I've heard of SIL. Some people have mentioned that there have been other gringos here, studying Mixtec, but they haven't said anything about them being missionaries.

As I said, this list is only a beginning, and is designed simply to get us thinking about publishing more specifically on linguistic fieldwork. Although the anthropological literature can be immensely helpful, there are significant differences in the ways that we approach the field. Among other things, linguists generally do not stay as long as anthropologists do, and many of us do not even try to integrate ourselves into the community in the same way that an anthropologist would. This of course means that our experiences will be very different. Until recently, however, there has been very little published on linguistic fieldwork (except for a few things like Dixon's 1984 book and Newman's 1992 article). This is now starting to change, with, for example, the publication of Vaux and Cooper (1999) and Newman and Ratliff (2001), but there is still surprisingly little.[6]

---

[6] I have recently heard of three in-progress field guides for linguists, so this situation may be changing shortly after publication of this article. [Recall that this chapter was originally published in 2004.]

> *For most young people a first field experience is an educational adventure, but it is usually difficult and it can be painful, discouraging, depressing and sometimes even agonizing. Some of these discomforts might be avoided if young fieldworkers and their research supervisors were made more aware of the fact that young persons in the field have certain inescapable disadvantages. There are some things that they simply cannot be expected to do. On the other hand, ... young people have certain distinct advantages and they can do certain kinds of research which are out of bounds for older persons. (Wax 1979: 517)*

20.4 CONCLUSION

I have used my own first experience with fieldwork as an illustration of just how naïve a young linguist can be about all aspects of the fieldwork experience. Although embarrassing to admit to, the experiences that I had serve to highlight a gaping hole in the training that we give our students.

Usually the only discussion of such issues that a student gets is in a linguistics field methods course (if they take one). But even there, the personal and psychological aspects of fieldwork often get short shrift. I know that when I teach field methods, I am often overcome by the need for more time for elicitation. This can lead to a shrinking of the time spent in the classroom *without* the consultant; time where the students and instructor get a chance to talk about the fieldwork experience, rather than perform it. We need to remind ourselves that learning through doing is not the only goal of a field methods course, and should be sure to reserve time to talk about the many personal, political, and practical issues that can arise. That is, instead of treating field methods simply as a class where students learn to apply their analytical skills to a real language, we should reconceive it as a class in which we also prepare students to go out into the 'real' field to work, with all the complications that that can entail.

A second way to approach this is to develop a literature which specifically addresses the field experiences of linguists, especially issues like the ones I have mentioned here. It is only by developing a cumulative body of work on our widely differing fieldwork experiences—and reactions to fieldwork—that we can adequately get across to novice linguistic fieldworkers some idea of what they are getting themselves into. The present chapter is my contribution to that nascent body of literature.

REFERENCES

ABBI, ANVITA, 2001. *A Manual of Linguistic Fieldwork and Structures of Indian Languages.* Munich: Lincom Europa.

ABO, TAKAJI, BYRON W. BENDER, ALFRED CAPELLE, and TONY DEBRUM, 2009. Place names of the Marshall Islands. In the *Marshallese–English Online Dictionary* (*MOD*) (http://www.trussel2.com/MOD/), accessed 21 February 2010.

Aboriginal land commission, 1991. *Warumungu Land Claim. Report by the Aboriginal Land Commissioner to the Minister for Aboriginal Affairs and to the Administrator of the Northern Territory.* Report no. 31. Canberra: AGPS.

ABRS, 1981–. *Flora of Australia. Australian Biological Resources Study*; accessed 2 Sept. 2009 at: http://www. environment. gov. au/biodiversity/abrs/publications/flora-of-australia/index.html

ADACHI, CHIE, 2011. A sociolinguistic investigation of compliments and compliment responses among young Japanese. PhD dissertation, University of Edinburgh.

AGOO, E. MARIBEL G., ANDRÉ SCHUITEMAN, and EDUARD F DE VOGEL, 2003. *Flora Malesiana: Orchids of the Philippines,* vol. 1: *Illustrated Checklist and Genera.* Leiden: National Herbarium of the Netherlands.

AIKHENVALD, ALEXANDRA, 2007. Typological distinctions in word-formation. In Shopen (2007: 3.1–65).

AKERMAN, KIM, 2007. Contemporary knowledge of Iwaidja material culture: Cobourg Peninsula, Arnhem Land, Northern Territory 2005–2006. MS.

AKLIF, GEDDA, 1999. *Ardiyooloon Bardi Ngaanka: One Arm Point Bardi Dictionary.* Hall's Creek: Kimberley Language Resource Centre.

ALEXIADES, MIGUEL N. (ed.), 1996. *Selected Guidelines for Ethnobotanical Research: A Field Manual.* New York: New York Botanical Garden Press.

ALI-SHTAYEH, MOHAMMED S., et al., 2008. Traditional knowledge of wild edible plants used in Palestine (Northern West bank): a comparative study. *Journal of Ethnobiology and Ethnomedicine* 4: 13.

ALTMAN, JON, 1981. An inventory of flora and fauna utilized by Eastern Gunwinggu in the Mann/Liverpool Region, North/Central Arnhem Land. MS, ANU Department of Prehistory and Anthropology.

AMERICAN ANTHROPOLOGICAL ASSOCIATION. AAA Code of ethics. Accessed 10 May 2009 at: http://www.aaanet.org/issues/policy-advocacy/Code-of-Ethics.cfm

AMERY, ROB, 2000. *Warrabarna Kaurna! Reclaiming an Australian Language.* Lisse: Swets & Zeitlinger.

——2002. Reclaiming through renaming: the reinstatement of Kaurna toponyms in Adelaide and the Adelaide plains. In Luise Hercus, Flavia Hodges, and Jane Simpson (eds), *The Land is a Map: Placenames of Indigenous Origin in Australia.* Canberra: Pacific Linguistics and Pandanus Press, 255–76.

——2006. Directions for linguistic research: forging partnerships in language development and expansion of the domains of use of Australia's indigenous languages. In Denis Cunningham, David E. Ingram, and Kenneth Sumbuk (eds), *Language Diversity in the Pacific: Endangerment and Survival*. Clevedon: Multilingual Matters, 162–79.

AMMARELL, GENE, 1999. *Bugis Navigation*. New Haven, Conn.: Yale University Southeast Asia Studies.

ANDERSON, BRUCE, 1986. *Yindjibarndi Dictionary*. Darwin: Summer Institute of Linguistics.

——and NICHOLAS THIEBERGER, 2003. *Yindjibarndi Dictionary*. Document 0297 of the Aboriginal Studies Electronic Data Archive (ASEDA), Australian Institute of Aboriginal and Torres Strait Islander Studies, Canberra. [This archive was accessed in 2003 for use in research by Mark, Turk, and Stea.]

ANDERSON, M. KAT, 2005. *Tending the Wild: Native American Knowledge and the Management of California's Natural Resources*. Berkeley: University of California Press.

ANDROUTSOPOULOS, JANNIS (ed.), 2006. Sociolinguistics and computer mediated communication. Special edn of *Journal of Sociolinguistics*, 10.4: 419–38.

ANON., 2001–. World Wide Wattle. Accessed 8 August 2009 at: http://www.worldwidewattle. com/

ANON., 2004a. Astrology. In *The American Heritage New Dictionary of Cultural Literacy*. Boston, Mass.: Houghton Mifflin.

ANON., 2004b. Cosmology. In *The American Heritage New Dictionary of Cultural Literacy*. Boston, Mass.: Houghton Mifflin.

ANTWORTH, EVAN, and RANDOLPH J. VALENTINE, 1998. Software for doing field linguistics. In John Lawler and Helen Aristar-Dry (eds), *Using Computers in Linguistics: A Practical Guide*. London: Routledge, 170–96.

APPADURAI, ARJUN (ed.), 1986. *The Social Life of Things: Commodities in Cultural Perspective*. Cambridge: Cambridge University Press.

——1996. *Modernity at Large: Cultural Dimensions of Globalization*. Minneapolis: University of Minnesota Press.

APTED, MEIKI, 2010. Songs from the Inyjalarrku: the use of a non-translatable spirit language in a song set from North-West Arnhem Land, Australia. *Australian Journal of Linguistics* 30.1: 93–103.

ARISTAR-DRY, HELEN, 2009. Preserving digital language materials: some considerations for community initiatives. In Wayne Harbert, Sally McConnell-Ginet, Amanda Miller, and John Whitman (eds), *Language and Poverty*. Clevedon: Multilingual Matters, 202–22.

ARONOFF, MARK, and KIRSTEN FUDEMAN, 2005. *What is Morphology?* Oxford: Blackwell.

AROUET, FRANÇOIS-MARIE (Voltaire), 1877. *Dictionnaire philosophique* I. In *Œuvres complètes de Voltaire*. Paris: Garnier.

ASCHER, MARCIA, 1991. *Ethnomathematics: A Multicultural View of Mathematical Ideas*. New York: Chapman & Hall.

——1997. Malagasy Sikidy: a case in ethnomathematics. *Historia Mathematica* 24: 376–95. (Repr. in Ascher 2002.)

——2002. *Mathematics Elsewhere: An Exploration of Ideas Across Cultures*. Princeton, NJ: Princeton University Press.

——and ROBERT ASCHER, 1986. Ethnomathematics. *History of Science* 24: 125–44.

ASH, ANNA, JESSIE LITTLE DOE FERMINO, and KEN HALE, 2001. Diversity in local language maintenance and restoration: a reason for optimism. In Leanne Hinton and Ken Hale (eds), *The Green Book of Language Revitalization in Practice*. San Diego, Calif.: Academic Press, 19–35.

ASHMORE, LOUISE, 2008. The role of digital video in language documentation. In Austin (2003–10: 5).

ASSEMBLY OF FIRST NATIONS, 1990. *Towards Linguistic Justice for First Nations*. Ottawa.

——1992. *Towards Rebirth of First Nations Languages*. Ottawa.

——2000. *A Time to Listen and the Time to Act*. Ottawa.

ATRAN, SCOTT, 1990. *Cognitive Foundations of Natural History*. Cambridge: Cambridge University Press.

——1998. Folk biology and the anthropology of science: cognitive universals and cultural particulars. *Behavioural and Brain Sciences* 21: 547–69.

AUSTIN, PETER K. (ed.), 2003–10. *Language Documentation & Description*, vols 1–7. London: Hans Rausing Endangered Languages Project, SOAS.

——2006. Data and linguistic documentation. In Gippert et al. (2006: 87–112).

——2010a. Communities, ethics and rights in language documentation. In Austin (2003–10: 7.34–54).

——2010b. Current issues in language documentation. In Austin (2003–10: 7.12–33).

BACH, EMMON, 2003. Postcolonial (?) linguistic fieldwork. *Massachusetts Review* 44.1 and 2: 167–81.

BAKER, BRETT, 2002. 'I'm going to where-her-brisket-is': placenames in the Roper. In Luise Hercus, Flavia Hodges, and Jane Simpson (eds), *The Land is a Map: Placenames of Indigenous Origin in Australia*. Canberra: Pacific Linguistics and Pandanus Press, 103–29.

BAKER, WILLIAM J., and JOHN DRANSFIELD, 2006. *Field Guide to Palms of New Guinea*. Kew: Royal Botanic Gardens.

BALDWIN, DARYL, 2003. Miami language reclamation: from ground zero. Accessed 12 September 2009 at: http://writing.umn.edu/docs/speakerseries_pubs/baldwin.pdf

BALÉE, WILLIAM, 1994. *Footprints of the Forest: Ka'apor Ethnobotany: The Historical Ecology of Plant Utilization by an Amazonian People*. New York: Columbia University Press.

BALFET, HÉLÈNE, 1975. La technologie. In Robert Cresswell (ed.), *Éléments d'ethnologie*, vol 2. Paris: Colin, 44–7.

——(ed.), 1991. *Observer l'action technique: des chaînes opératoires pour quoi faire?* Paris: CNRS.

BALFOUR, HENRY, 1903. 'Thunderbolt' Celts from Benin. *Man* 3: 182–3.

BALGOOY, MAX M. J. VAN, 1997. *Malesian Seed Plants*, vol. 1: *Spot Characters: An Aid for Identification of Families and Genera*. Leiden: Nationaal Herbarium Nederlands.

——1998. *Malesian Seed Plants*, vol. 2: *Portraits of Tree Families*. Leiden: Nationaal Herbarium Nederlands.

——2001. *Malesian Seed Plants*, vol. 3: *Portraits of Non-Tree Families*. Leiden: Nationaal Herbarium Nederlands.

BALICK, MICHAEL J., et al., 2000. Medicinal plants used by Latino healers for women's health conditions in New York City. *Economic Botany* 54: 344–57.

BANACK, SANDRA A., 1991. Plants and Polynesian voyaging. In Paul A. Cox and Sandra A. Banack (eds), *Islands, Plants and Polynesians: An Introduction to Polynesian Ethnobotany*. Portland, Ore.: Dioscorides Press, 25–40.

BARAKAT, ROBERT A., 1975. *Cistercian Sign Language*. Kalamazoo, Mich.: Cistercian Publications.

——1976. Arabic gestures. *Journal of Popular Culture* 6: 749–92.

BARKER, JOHN, 2005. Kawo and Sabu: perceptions of traditional leadership among the Maisin of Papua New Guinea. In Claudia Gross, Harriet D. Lyons, and Dorothy A. Counts (eds), *A Polymath Anthropologist: Essays in honour of Anne Chowning*. Auckland: University of Auckland, Research in Anthropology and Linguistics, 131–7.

BARNES, JOHN, 1980. *Who Should Know What? Social Science, Privacy and Ethics*. Cambridge: Cambridge University Press.

BARRY, ANDREW, GEORGINA BORN, and GISA WESZKALNYS, 2008. Logics of interdisciplinarity. *Economy and Society* 37.1: 20–49.

BARTHES, ROLAND, 1997. Toward a psychosociology of contemporary food consumption. In Counihan and Van Esterik (1997: 20–27).

BARTIS, PETER, 2002. *Folklife and Fieldwork: An Introduction to Field Techniques*. Washington, DC: Library of Congress.

BARTLE, PHILIP F. W., 1978. Forty days: the Akan calendar. *Africa* 48.1: 80–84.

BARWICK, LINDA, 2000. Song as an indigenous art. In Margo Neale and Sylvia Kleinert (eds), *The Oxford Companion to Aboriginal Art and Culture*. Melbourne: Oxford University Press, 328–35.

——2006. A musicologist's wishlist: some issues, practices and practicalities in musical aspects of language documentation. *Language Documentation & Description* 3: 53–62.

——BRUCE BIRCH, and NICHOLAS EVANS, 2007. Iwaidja Jurtbirrk songs: bringing language and music together. *Australian Aboriginal Studies* 2: 6–34.

————and JOY WILLIAMS, 2005. *Jurtbirrk Love Songs of Northwestern Arnhem Land* [audio CD of research recordings with accompanying scholarly booklet]. Batchelor, NT: Batchelor Press.

——ALLAN MARETT, MICHAEL WALSH, NICHOLAS REID, and LYSBETH FORD, 2005. Communities of interest: issues in establishing a digital resource on Murrinh-patha song at Wadeye (Port Keats), NT. *Literary and Linguistic Computing* 20.4: 383–97.

——and NICHOLAS THIEBERGER, 2006. Cybraries in paradise: new technologies and ethnographic repositories. In Cushla Kapitzke and Bertram C. Bruce (eds), *Libr@ries: Changing information space and practice*. Mahwah, NJ: Erlbaum. 133–49.

——et al., 2006. *Murriny Patha Song Project Website*. Retrieved 16 January 2007 from: http://azoulay.arts.usyd.edu.au/mpsong/

——et al., 2010. *Wadeye Song Database* [multimedia database]. Retrieved 17 January 2011 from: http://sydney.edu.au/wadeyesong/

BARZ, GREGORY F., and TIMOTHY J. COOLEY (eds), 1997. *Shadows in the Field: New Perspectives for Fieldwork in Ethnomusicology*. New York: Oxford University Press.

BASSET, YVES, VOJTECH NOVOTNY, SCOTT E. MILLER, and RICHARD PYLE, 2000. Quantifying biodiversity: experience with parataxonomists and digital photography in Papua New Guinea and Guyana. *Bioscience* 50: 899.

————————GEORGE D. WEIBLEN OLIVIER MISSA, and ALAN J. A. STEWART, 2004. Conservation and biological monitoring of tropical forests: the role of parataxonomists. *Journal of Applied Ecology* 41: 163–74.

BASSO, KEITH H., 1984. Western Apache place-name hierarchies. In Elisabeth Tooker (ed.), *Naming Systems: 1980 Proceedings of the American Ethnological Society*. Washington, DC: American Ethnological Society, 78–94.

——1996. *Wisdom Sits in Places: Landscape and Language Among the Western Apache*. Albuquerque: University of New Mexico Press.

BATES, BRYAN, and TODD BOSTWICK, 2000. Issues in archaeoastronomy methodology. In César Esteban and Juan Belmonte (eds), *Astronomy and Cultural Diversity.* Tenerife: Organismo Autónomo de Museos y Centros, Cabildo de Tenerife.

BATTISTE, MARIE, and JAMES (SA'KE'J) YOUNGBLOOD HENDERSON, 2000. *Protecting Indigenous Knowledge and Heritage: A Global Challenge.* Saskatoon: Purich.

BAUDRILLARD, JEAN, 1968. *Le Système des objets.* Paris: Gallimard.

BAUER, LAURIE, 2003. *Introducing Linguistic Morphology,* 2nd edn. Edinburgh: Edinburgh University Press.

BAUGH, JOHN, 2000. *Beyond Ebonics: Linguistic Pride and Racial Prejudice.* Oxford: Oxford University Press.

BAVELAS, JANET. B., NICOLE CHOVIL, DOUGLAS A. LAWRIE, and ALLAN WADE, 1992. Interactive gestures. *Discourse Processes* 15.4: 469–89.

BEARD, JOHN S, 1968. Drying specimens in humid weather. *Taxon* 17: 744.

BECKMAN, MARY E., and JULIA HIRSCHBERG, 1994. *The ToBI Annotation Conventions*: http://www.ling.ohio-state.edu/~tobi/ame_tobi/annotation_conventions.html

BELASCO, WARREN, 2008. *Food: The Key Concepts.* New York: Berg.

BELMONT REPORT, 1979. *Ethical Principles and Guidelines for the Protection of Human Subjects of Research,* National Commission for the Protection of Human Subjects of Biomedical and Behavioural Research (18 April).

BENVENISTE, ÉMILE, 1971. *Problems in General Linguistics* (trans. Mary Elizabeth Meek). University of Miami Press.

BERARDO, MARCELLINO, and AKIRA YAMAMOTO, 2007. Endangered language communities and linguists: listening to the voices of indigenous peoples and working toward a linguistics of language revitalization. In Osahito Miyaoka, Osamu Sakiyama, and Michael E. Krauss (eds), *The Vanishing Languages of the Pacific Rim.* Oxford: Oxford University Press, 107–62.

BEREZ, ANDREA L., 2007. Review of EUDICO Linguistic Annotator (ELAN). *Language Documentation & Conservation* 1.2: 283–9; available at: http://hdl.handle.net/10125/1718

BERKES, FIKRET, 1999. *Sacred Ecology: Traditional Ecological Knowledge and Resource Management.* Philadelphia: Taylor & Francis.

——and CARL FOLKE (eds), 2001. *Linking Social and Ecological Systems.* Cambridge: Cambridge University Press.

BERLIN, BRENT, 1992. *Ethnobiological Classification: Principles of Categorization of Plants and Animals in Traditional Societies.* Princeton, NJ: Princeton University Press.

——DENNIS E. BREEDLOVE, and PETER H. RAVEN, 1973. General principles of classification and nomenclature in folk biology. *American Anthopologist* 75: 214–42.

——and PAUL KAY, 1969. *Basic Colour Terms: Their Universality and Evolution.* Berkeley: University of California Press.

BERMAN, RUTH ARONSON, and DAN ISAAC SLOBIN (eds), 1994. *Relating Events in Narrative: A Crosslinguistic Developmental Study.* Hillsdale, NJ: Erlbaum.

BERNARD, H. RUSSELL, 2002. *Research Methods in Anthropology: Qualitative and Quantitative approaches,* 3rd edn. Walnut Creek, Calif.: AltaMira Press.

BERREMAN, GERALD D., 1962. *Behind Many Masks.* Ithaca, NY: Society for Applied Anthropology.

BESNIER, NIKO, 2009. *Gossip and the Everyday Production of Politics.* Honolulu: University of Hawai'i Press.

BEVER, THOMAS G., 1970. The cognitive basis for linguistic structures. In John R. Hayes (ed.), *Cognition and the Development of Language.* New York: Wiley, 279–362.

BIBER, DOUGLAS, and SUSAN CONRAD, 2009. *Register, Genre and Style*. Cambridge: Cambridge University Press.

————and GEOFFREY LEECH, 2002. *Longman Student Grammar of Spoken and Written English*. Harlow: Pearson Education.

BIJKER, WIEBE, and JAMES LAW (eds), 1992. *Shaping Technology, Building Society: Studies in Sociotechnical Change*. Cambridge, Mass.: MIT Press.

BIRCH, BRUCE, 2006. Nawangardi understands about rope: providing an intelligent audience for endangered knowledge. Presentation at 2006 DoBeS Workshop, Nijmegen.

————and NICHOLAS EVANS, 2008–. Draft Iwaidja electronic dictionary. MS.

————JOY WILLIAMS MALWAGAG, and SABINE HOENG, 2005. *Kalkbirr burdan Mangkuldalkuj: Sea Shells from Croker Island*. Poster published by Batchelor Press, Batchelor, NT.

————2006a. *Mangambuk: Plant Medicine of Croker Island 1*. Poster published by Iwaidja Inyman, Jabiru Town Council.

————2006b. *Burdan ldalha, Burdan Wubaj: Saltwater and Freshwater Fish from Croker Island*. Poster published by Iwaidja Inyman, Jabiru Town Council.

————2007. *Mangambuk: Plant Medicine of Croker Island 2*. Poster published by Iwaidja Inyman, Jabiru Town Council.

BIRD, STEVEN, and GARY SIMONS, 2003. Seven dimensions of portability for language documentation and description. *Language* 79: 557–82.

BISPHAM, JOHN, 2006. Rhythm in music: what is it? who has it? and why? *Music Perception* 24.2: 125–34.

BLACK, H. ANDREW, and GARY F. SIMONS, 2009. Third wave writing and publishing. SIL Forum for Language Fieldwork 2009–005; available at: http://www.sil.org/silepubs/abstract.asp?id=52287)

BLACKING, JOHN, 1973. *How Musical is Man?* Seattle: University of Washington Press.

BLAKE, BARRY, 2008. *All About Language*. Oxford: Oxford University Press.

BLOCH, MAURICE, 1998. *How We Think They Think*. Boulder, Colo.: Westview Press.

BLOM, JAN-PETTER, and JOHN J. GUMPERZ, 1972. Social meaning in linguistic structure: codeswitching in Norway. In John J. Gumperz and Dell Hymes (eds), *Directions in Sociolinguistics*. New York: Holt, Rinehart & Winston, 407–34.

BLONDEAU, HÉLÈNE, 2001. Real-time changes in the paradigm of personal pronouns in Montreal French. *Journal of Sociolinguistics* 5.4: 453–74.

————and NAOMI NAGY, 2008. Subordinate clause marking in Montreal Anglophone French and English. In Miriam Meyerhoff and Naomi Nagy (eds), *Social Lives in Language: The Sociolinguistics of Multilingual Speech Communities*. Amsterdam: Benjamins, 273–314.

BLOOD, ANNE J., and ROBERT J. ZATORRE, 2001. Intensely pleasurable responses to music correlate with activity in brain regions implicated in reward and emotion. *Proceedings of the National Academy of Sciences of the United States of America* 98.20: 11818–23.

BOAS, FRANZ, 1911. Introduction. In *Handbook of American Indian Languages*, vol. 1. Washington, DC: Government Printing Office.

BOBALJIK, JONATHAN, 1998. Visions and realities: researcher–activist–indigenous collaborations in indigenous language maintenance. In Erich Kasten (ed.), *Bicultural Education in the North*. Münster: Waxmann, 13–28.

BOGATYREV, PIOTR, 1971[1937]. *The Function of Folk Costume in Moravian Slovakia*. The Hague: Mouton.

BOHNEMEYER, JÜRGEN, MELISSA BOWERMAN, and PENELOPE BROWN, 2001. Cut and break clips. In Stephen C. Levinson and Nicholas J. Enfield (eds), *Manual for the Field Season 2001*.

Nijmegen: Max Planck Institute for Psycholinguistics, 90–96; available at: http://fieldman-uals.mpi.nl/volumes/2001/cut-and-break-clips/

——Niclas Burenhult, Nicholas J. Enfield, and Stephen C. Levinson, 2004. Landscape terms and place names elicitation guide. In Asifa Majid (ed.), *Field Manual*, vol. 9. Nijmegen: Max Planck Institute for Psycholinguistics, 75–9. http://fieldmanuals.mpi.nl/volumes/2004/landscape-terms-and-place-names/

——and Martijn Caelen, 1999. The ECOM clips: a stimulus for the linguistic coding of event complexity. In David Wilkins (ed.), *Manual for the 1999 Field Season*. Nijmegen: Max Planck Institute for Psycholinguistics, 74–86.

——and Nicholas J. Enfield, 2002. Toponyms questionnaire. In Stephen C. Levinson and Nicholas J. Enfield (eds), *'Manual' for the Field Season 2001*. Nijmegen: Max Planck Institute for Psycholinguistics, 55–61.

——Nicholas J. Enfield, James Essegbey, Iraide Ibarretxe-Antuñano, Sotaro Kita, Friedrike Lüpke, and Felix K. Ameka, 2007. Principles of event segmentation in language: the case of motion events. *Language* 83.3: 495–532.

Bolinger, Dwight, 1968. Judgements of grammaticality. *Lingua* 21.1: 34–40. doi: 10. 1016/ 0024–3841(68)90036–3.

Bonnemère, Pascale, 1996. *Le Pandanus rouge: corps, différence des sexes et parenté chez les Ankave-Anga (PNG)*. Paris: CNRS/MSH.

——1998. Trees and people: some vital links. Tree products and other agents in the life cycle of the Ankave-Anga of Papua New Guinea. In Laura Rival (ed.), *The Social Life of Trees: Anthropological Perspectives on Tree Symbolism*. Oxford: Berg, 113–31.

——and Pierre Lemonnier, 2007. *Les Tambours de l'oubli. Drumming to Forget*. Papeete, Au Vent des Îles, Paris: Musée du quai Branly.

Booij, Geert, 2007. *The Grammar of Words*, 2nd edn. Oxford: Oxford University Press.

——Christian Lehmann, and Joachim Mugdan (eds), 2000 and 2004. *Morphology: An International Handbook of Inflection and Word Formation*, vols 1 and 2. Berlin: de Gruyter.

Borgman, Christine L., 2007. *Scholarship in the Digital Age: Information, Infrastructure, and the Internet*. Cambridge, Mass.: MIT Press.

Boroditsky, Lera, 2000. Metaphoric structuring: understanding time through spatial metaphors. *Cognition* 75.1: 1–28.

——and Alice Gaby, 2010. Remembrances of times east: absolute spatial representations of time in an Australian Aboriginal community. *Psychological Science* 21.11: 1635–9.

Boster, James, 1987. Agreement between biological classification systems is not dependent on cultural transmission. *American Anthropologist*, n.s. 89: 914–20.

——and Jeffrey C. Johnson, 1989. Form or function: a comparison of expert and novice judgements of similarity among fish. *American Anthropologist* 91.4: 866–89.

Bouquiaux Luc, and Jacqueline Thomas (eds), 1976. *Enquête et description des langues à tradition orale: l'enquête des terrain et l'analyse grammaticale*, 2nd edn. (vol. 1: *L'enquête de terrain et l'analyse grammaticale*; vol. 2: *Approche linguistique*; vol. 3: *Approche thématique*). Paris: Société d'Etudes Linguistiques et Anthropologiques de France.

————(eds), 1992. *Studying and Describing Unwritten Languages*, trans. James Roberts. Dallas, Tex.: Summer Institute of Linguistics.

Bourdieu, Pierre, 1984. *Distinction: A Social Critique of the Judgement of Taste*, trans. Richard Nice. Cambridge, Mass.: Harvard University Press.

——1990. *Language and Symbolic Power*, trans. Gino Raymond and Matthew Adamson. Cambridge: Polity Press.

BOWERMAN, MELISSA, and ERIC PEDERSON, 1992. Topological relations picture series. In Stephen C. Levinson (ed.), *Space Stimuli Kit 1.2: November 1992, 51.* Nijmegen: Max Planck Institute for Psycholinguistics.

BOWERN, CLAIRE, 2008. *Linguistic Fieldwork: A Practical Guide.* New York: Palgrave Macmillan.

BOYNTON, ROBERT M., 1997. Insights gained from naming the OSA colours. In Clyde L. Hardin and Luisa Maffi (eds), *Colour Categories in Thought and Language.* Cambridge: Cambridge University Press, 135–50.

BRADLEY, JOHN J., and A. KEARNEY, 2009. Manankurra: what's in a name? In Harold Koch and Luise Hercus (eds), *Aboriginal Placenames: Naming and Re-naming the Australian Landscape.* Canberra: ANU E Press and Aboriginal History Incorporated, 463–79.

BRAUE, DAVID, 2004. Preserving our musical heritage. *Australasian Wheels for the Mind* 14.1: 7.

BREMMER, JAN, and HERMAN ROODENBURG (eds), 1991. *A Cultural History of Gesture.* Cambridge: Polity Press.

BREWER, DEVON D., 1995. Cognitive indicators of knowledge in semantic domains. *Journal of Quantitative Anthropology* 5: 109–28.

BRIDGES, KENT W., and WILL C. McCLATCHEY, 2009. Living on the margin: ethnoecological insights from Marshall Islanders at Rongelap atoll. *Global Environmental Change* 19: 140–46.

BRIDSON, DIANE, and LEONARD FORMAN, 1998. *The Herbarium Handbook,* 3rd edn. London: Royal Botanic Gardens, Kew.

BRIGGS, CHARLES L., 1986. *Learning How to Ask: A Sociolinguistic Appraisal of the Role of the Interview in Social Science Research.* Cambridge: Cambridge University Press.

BRIGHT, WILLIAM, 2007. Contextualizing a grammar. In Thomas E. Payne and David J. Weber (eds), *Perspectives on Grammar Writing.* Amsterdam: Benjamins, 11–17.

BRILLAT-SAVARIN, JEAN-ANTHELME, 1970[1825]. *The Philosopher in the Kitchen,* trans. Anne Drayton. Harmondsworth: Penguin.

BROOKER, M. IAN H., 2006. *Eucalyptus—Australia—Identification.* Melbourne: CSIRO.

BROOKES, HEATHER J., 2004. A repertoire of South African quotable gestures. *Journal of Linguistic Anthropology* 14.2: 186–224.

——2005. What gestures do: some communicative functions of quotable gestures in conversations among Black urban South Africans. *Journal of Pragmatics* 37.12: 2044–85.

BROSI, BERRY J., et al., 2007. Cultural erosion and biodiversity: canoe-making knowledge in Pohnpei, Micronesia. *Conservation Biology* 21.3: 875–9.

BROWN, KEITH, and SARAH OGILVIE, 2009. *Languages of the World.* Oxford: Elsevier.

BROWN, LESLIE, and SUSAN STREGA (eds), 2005. *Research as Resistance: Critical, Indigenous, and Anti-Oppressive Approaches.* Toronto: Canadian Scholars Press.

BROWN, MICHAEL F., 2003. *Who Owns Native Culture?* Cambridge, Mass.: Harvard University Press.

BRUN, THEODORE, 1969. *The International Dictionary of Sign Language.* London: Wolfe.

BUCHOLTZ, MARY, 1999. Why be normal? Language and identity practices in a community of nerd girls. *Language in Society* 28.2: 203–23.

BUCHSTALLER, ISABELLE, and ALEXANDRA D'ARCY, 2009. 'Localized globalization: a multi-local, multivariate investigation of quotative *be like*', *Journal of Sociolinguistics* 13.3: 291–331.

BULMER, RALPH N. H., 1974. Folk biology in the New Guinea Highlands. *Social Science Information* 13: 9–28.

——and MICHAEL J. TYLER, 1968. Karam classification of frogs. *Journal of the Polynesian Society* 77: 333–85.

BURENHULT, NICLAS (ed.), 2008a. Language and landscape: a cross-linguistic perspective. *Language Sciences* 30.2–3.

——2008b. Streams of words: hydrological lexicon in Jahai. *Language Sciences* 30.2–3: 192–9.

——and STEPHEN LEVINSON, 2008a. Language and landscape: a cross-linguistic perspective. *Language Sciences* 30.2–3: 135–50.

————2008b. Semplates: a new concept in lexical semantics? MS.

BURLING, ROBBINS, 1984. *Learning a Field Language*. Ann Arbor: University of Michigan Press.

BUTTERS, RONALD, 2000. Conversational anomalies in eliciting danger-of-death narratives. *Southern Journal of Linguistics* 24: 69–81.

BYE, ROBERT A., 1986. Voucher specimens in ethnobiological studies and publications. *Journal of Ethnobiology* 6: 1–8.

CABLITZ, GABRIELE H., 2008. When 'what' is 'where': a linguistic analysis of landscape terms, place names and body part terms in Marquesan (Oceanic, French Polynesia). *Language Sciences* 30.2–3: 200–226.

CALBRIS, GENEVIEVE, 1990. *The Semiotics of French Gesture*. Bloomington: Indiana University Press.

CAMERON, DEBORAH, 1998. Problems of empowerment in linguistic research. *Cahiers de l'ILSL* 10: 23–38.

——ELIZABETH FRAZER, PENELOPE HARVEY, BEN RAMPTON, and KAY RICHARDSON, 1992. *Researching Language: Issues of Power and Method*. London: Routledge.

CAMERON, KEITH, 1996. *English Place Names*. London: Batsford.

CAMPBELL, PATRICIA SHEHAN, 1997. Music, the universal language: fact or fallacy? *International Journal of Music Education* 29: 32–39.

CAMPION, NICHOLAS, 1997. Editorial. *Culture and Cosmos* 1.1: 1–2.

CANADIAN INSTITUTE OF HEALTH RESEARCH, 2007. *CIHR Guidelines for Health Research Involving Aboriginal People*. Accessed 10 May 1009 at: http://www.cihr-irsc.gc.ca/e/29134.html

CAPELL, ARTHUR, 1962. *A New Approach to Australian Linguistics*. Sydney: Oceania Linguistic Monographs.

CAPELL, ARTHUR, and HEATHER HINCH, 1970. *Maung Grammar*. The Hague: Mouton.

CAPRILE, JEAN-PIERRE, JEAN-CLAUDE RIVIERRE, and JACQUELINE M. C. THOMAS, 1992. Oral tradition. In Luc Bouquiaux and Jacqueline Thomas (eds), *Studying and Describing Unwritten Languages*. Dallas, Tex.: Summer Institute of Linguistics, 689–91.

CARSTEN, JANET (ed.), 2000. *Cultures of Relatedness: New Approaches to the Study of Kinship*. Cambridge: Cambridge University Press.

CASTANEDA, HÉCTOR, and JOHN RICK STEPP, 2007. Ethnoecological Importance Value (EIV) methodology: assessing the cultural importance of ecosystems as sources of useful plants for the Guaymi people of Costa Rica. *Ethnobotany Research and Applications* 5: 249–57.

CBD, 1993–. Convention on Biological Diversity. Accessed 2 Sept. 2009 at: http://www.cbd.int/

CESKA, ADOLF, and OLDRISKA CESKA, 1986. More on the techniques for collecting aquatic and marsh plants. *Annals of the Missouri Botanical Garden* 73: 825–7.

CHALOUPKA, GEORGE, and PINA GIULIANI, 1984. *Gundulk Abel Gundalg: Mayali Flora*. Darwin, NT: Museum of Arts and Sciences.

CHAMBERLAIN, VON DEL, JOHN CARLSON, and M. JANE YOUNG, 2005. *Songs from the Sky: Indigenous Astronomical and Cosmological Traditions of the World*. Austin and Leicester: University of Texas Press and Ocarina.

CHANG, ECHA, CHU-REN HUANG, SUE-JIN KER, and CHANG-HUA YANG, 2002. Induction of classification from lexicon expansion: assigning domain tags to WordNet Entries. In *Proceedings of the Coling 2002 Workshop 'SemaNet'02: Building and Using Semantic Networks*, Taipei, August.

CHANG, KWANG-CHIH (ed.), 1977. *Food in Chinese Culture*. New Haven, Conn.: Yale University Press.

CHAPIN, MAC, ZACHARY LAMB, and BILL THRELKELD, 2005. Mapping indigenous lands. *Annual Review of Anthropology* 34: 619–38. doi:10.1146/annurev.anthro.34.081804.120429

CHARTERS, MICHAEL L., 2003–. *Flora of Southern Africa*. Accessed 1 Oct. 2009 at: http://www.calflora.net/southafrica/index.html

CHELLIAH, SHOBHANA L., 2001. The role of text collection and elicitation in linguistic fieldwork. In Newman and Ratliff (2001: 152–64).

——and WILLEM J. DE REUSE, 2010. *Handbook of Descriptive Linguistic Fieldwork*. Dordrecht: Springer

CHEMILLIER, MARC, 2002. Ethnomusicology, ethnomathematics: the logic underlying orally transmitted artistic practices. In Gérard Assayag, Hans Georg Feichtinger, and Jose Francisco Rodrigues (eds), *Mathematics and Music: A Diderot Mathematical Forum*. Berlin: Springer, 162–83.

——2007. *Les Mathématiques naturelles*. Paris: Jacob.

——2009. The development of mathematical knowledge in traditional societies: a study of Malagasy divination. *Human Evolution* 24.4: 287–99.

——DENIS JACQUET, VICTOR RANDRIANARY, and MARC ZABALIA, 2007. Aspects mathématiques et cognitifs de la divination sikidy à Madagascar. *L'Homme* 182: 7–40.

CHESHIRE, JENNY, 1982. *Variations in an English Dialect: A Sociolinguistic Study*. Cambridge: Cambridge University Press.

CHMIELEWSKI, JERRY G., and GORDON S. RINGIUS, 1986. Polyurethane foam: an alternative plant pressing material especially suitable for population-based studies. *Taxon* 35: 106–7.

CIENKI, ALAN, and CORNELIA MÜLLER (eds), 2008. *Metaphor and Gesture*. Amsterdam: Benjamins.

CLARK, HERBERT H., 1996. *Using Language*. Cambridge: Cambridge University Press.

——and DEANNA WILKES-GIBBS, 1986. Referring as a collaborative process. *Cognition*. 22.1: 1–39.

CLARK, ROSS, 2009. **Leo Tuai: A Comparative Lexical Study of North and Central Vanuatu Languages*. Canberra: Pacific Linguistics.

CLAYTON, MARTIN, REBECCA SAGER, and UDO WILL, 2005. In time with the music: the concept of entrainment and its significance for ethnomusicology. *European Meetings in Ethnomusicology* 11: 3–142.

CLIFFORD, JAMES, 1990. Notes on (field)notes. In Roger Sanjek (ed.), *Fieldnotes: The Makings of Anthropology*. Ithaca, NY: Cornell University Press, 47–70.

——and GEORGE E. MARCUS, 1986. *Writing Culture: The Poetics and Politics of Ethnography*. Berkeley: University of California Press.

COCHRANE, ANNE, ANDREW D. CRAWFORD, and CATHERINE A. OFFORD, 2009. Seed and vegetative material collection. In Offord and Meagher (2009).

COLLETT, PETER, 2004. Problems and procedures in the study of gestures. In Roland Posner and Cornelia Müller (eds), *The Semantics and Pragmatics of Everyday Gesture*. Berlin: Weidler, 173–93.

COLLINS, JAMES, 1998. Our ideologies and theirs. In Bambi B. Schieffelin, Kathryn A. Woolard, and Paul V. Kroskrity (eds), *Language Ideologies: Practice and Theory*. New York: Oxford University Press, 256–70. (Originally published in *Pragmatics* 2–3 (1992): 405–15.)

COMRIE, BERNARD, 1989. *Language Universals and Linguistic Typology*. Oxford: Blackwell.

——(ed.), 1990a. *The Major Languages of Western Europe*. London: Routledge.

——(ed.), 1990b. *The Major Languages of Eastern Europe*. London: Routledge.

——(ed.), 1990c. *The Major Languages of South Asia, the Middle East and Africa*. London: Routledge.

——(ed.), 1990d. *The Major Languages of East and South-East Asia*. London: Routledge.

——2007. Documenting and/or preserving endangered languages. In Osahito Miyaoka, Osamu Sakiyama, and Michael E. Krauss (eds), *The Vanishing Languages of the Pacific Rim*. Oxford: Oxford University Press, 25–34.

——and NORVAL SMITH, 1977. Lingua descriptive series questionnaire. *Lingua* 42: 1–72; available at: http://www.ling.udel.edu/pcole/Linguistic_Questionnaires/LinguaQ.htm

CONKLIN, HAROLD C., 1955. Hanunóo colour categories. *Southwestern Journal of Anthropology* 11.4: 339–44.

——1967. The relation of Hanunoo culture to the plant world. PhD dissertation, Yale University.

CONN, BARRY J., 1994. Documentation of the flora of New Guinea. In C.-I. Peng and C. H. Chou (eds), *Biodiversity and Terrestrial Ecosystems, Institute of Botany*. Academia Sinica Monographs Series No. 14, 123–56.

——1996. HISPID3: Herbarium Information Standards and Protocols for Interchange of Data, version 3. Accessed 2 Sept. 2009 at: http://hiscom.chah.org.au/wiki/HISPID#HISPID_3

——and KIPIRO Q. DAMAS, 2006–. *Guide to Trees of Papua New Guinea*.Accessed 15 Aug. 2009 at: http://www.pngplants.org/PNGtrees

——KENNETH HILL, and LINN LINN LEE, 2004–. PlantNET: The Plant Information Network System of Botanic Gardens Trust, Sydney, Australia, version 2.0. Accessed 2 Sept. 2009 at: http://plantnet.rbgsyd.nsw.gov.au

COOK, FRANCES E. M., and HEW D. V. PRENDERGAST, 1995. *Economic Botany Data Collection Standard*. Kew: Royal Botanic Gardens Press.

CORDER, PITT, 1973. *Introducing Applied Linguistics*. Harmondsworth: Penguin.

COUNIHAN, CAROLE, and PENNY VAN ESTERIK (eds), 1997. *Food and Culture: A Reader*. New York: Routledge.

COUPAYE, LUDOVIC, 2009. What's the matter with technology? Long (and short) yams: materialisation and technology in Nyamikum village, Maprik district, East Papua New Guinea. *Australian Journal of Anthropology* 20: 93–111.

COUPLAND, NIKOLAS, 1984. Accomodation at work: some phonological data and their implications. *International Journal of the Sociology of Language* 46: 49–70.

——2007. *Style, Language Variation and Identity*. Cambridge: Cambridge University Press.

COURT, DOREEN, 2000. *Succulent Flora of Southern Africa*. Brookfield, Vt.: Balkema.

COX, PAUL A., 1982. Cordyline ovens (Umu Ti) in Samoa. *Economic Botany* 36: 389–96.

COYNE, TERRY, JACQUI BADCOCK, and RICHARD TAYLOR, 1984. *The Effect of Urbanization and Western Diet on the Health of Pacific Island Populations.* SPC Technical Paper 186, Noumea.

CRAIG, COLETTE, 1992. A constitutional response to language endangerment: the case of Nicaragua. *Language* 68: 17–24.

——1993. Fieldwork on endangered languages: a forward look at ethical issues. *Proceedings of the XVth International Congress of Linguists/Actes Du XVᴇ Congrès International des Linguistes.* Sainte-Foy, Quebec: Presses de l'Université Laval.

——1997. Language contact and language degeneration. In Florian Coulmas (ed.), *The Handbook of Sociolinguistics.* Oxford: Blackwell, 257–70.

CREE SCHOOL BOARD, n.d. http://www.%20cscree.%20qc.%20ca/about/philo.%20htm. Accessed 10 May 2009 (no longer active).

CREIDER, CHET, 1977. Towards a description of East African gestures. *Sign Language Studies* 14: 1–20.

CRESSWELL, ROBERT, 1972. Les Trois Sources d'une technologie nouvelle. In Jacqueline M. C. Thomas and Lucien Bernot (eds), *Langues et techniques, nature et société*, II: *Approche ethnologique, approche naturaliste.* Paris: Klincksieck, 21–7.

CREWS, KENNETH D., 2006. *Copyright Law for Librarians and Educators: Creative Strategies and Practical Solutions*, 2nd edn. Chicago: American Library Association.

CRIPPEN, JAMES, 2009. Studying grandmother's tongue: heritage language and linguistics. Paper presented at the First International Conference for Language Documentation and Conservation 2009, University of Hawai'i at Manoa, 12–14 Mar.; available at: http://hdl.handle.net/10125/5097

CROAT, THOMAS B., 1979. Use of a portable propane gas oven for field drying plants. *Taxon* 28: 573–80.

——1985. Collecting and preparing specimens of Araceae. *Annals of the Missouri Botanical Garden* 72: 252–8.

CROFT, WILLIAM, 2001. *Radical Construction Grammar: Syntactic Theory in Typological Perspective.* Oxford: Oxford University Press.

——and KEITH T. POOLE, 2008. Inferring universals from grammatical variation: multidimensional scaling for typological analysis. *Theoretical Linguistics* 34.1: 1–37.

CROSS, IAN, 2003. Music as a biocultural phenomenon. *Annals of the New York Academy of Sciences.* 999: 106–11.

——2007. Music and cognitive evolution. In Robin Dunbar and Louise Barrett (eds), *Oxford Handbook of Evolutionary Psychology.* Oxford: Oxford University Press, 649–68.

——2008. Musicality and the human capacity for culture. *Musicae Scientiae*, special issue 2008: 147–67.

——2009. The evolutionary nature of musical meaning. *Musicae Scientiae*, special issue 2009–10: 179–200.

CROWLEY, TERRY, 2007. *Field Linguistics: A Beginner's Guide.* Oxford: Oxford University Press.

CRUMP, THOMAS, 1990. *The Anthropology of Numbers.* New York: Cambridge University Press.

CRUSE, D. ALAN, 1986. *Lexical Semantics.* Cambridge: Cambridge University Press.

CRYSTAL, DAVID, 2000. *Language Death.* Cambridge: Cambridge University Press.

CUKOR-AVILA, PATRICIA, and GUY BAILEY, 2001. The effects of the race of the interviewer on sociolinguistic fieldwork. *Journal of Sociolinguistics* 5.2: 254–70.

CUNNINGHAM, ANTHONY B., 2001. *Applied Ethnobotany: People, Wild Plant Use and Conservation*. London: Earthscan.

CURTH, LOUISE, 2005. Astrological medicine and the popular press in early modern England. *Culture and Cosmos* 9.1: 73–94.

CYR, DANIELLE, 1999. Metalanguage awareness: a matter of scientific ethics. *Journal of Sociolinguistics* 3.2: 283–6.

CZAYKOWSKA-HIGGINS, EWA, 2009. Research models, community engagement, and linguistic fieldwork: reflections on working within Canadian Indigenous communities. *Language Documentation and Conservation* 3.1: 15–50.

DAHL, ÖSTEN, 1985. *Tense and Aspect Systems*. Oxford: Blackwell.

DAI QINGXIA, LUO RENDI (RANDY J. LAPOLLA), and WANG FENG (eds), 2009. *Dao Tianye qu: Yuyanxue Tianye Diaocha de Fangfa yu Shijian* [To the Field: The Method and Experience of Linguistic Fieldwork]. Beijing: Minzu Chubanshe. (In Chinese.)

DALE, IAN R. H., 1978. Beyond intuition: the use of questionnaires in linguistic investigation. *Anthropological Linguistics* 20.4: 158–66.

DALESZYŃSKA, AGATA, 2011. Changes in past temporal marking in Bequia English. PhD dissertation, University of Edinburgh.

DAMON, FREDERICK, 2008. On the ideas of a boat: from forest patches to cybernetic structures in the outrigger sailing craft of the eastern kula ring, Papua New Guinea. In Sather Clifford and Timo Kaartinen (eds), *Beyond the Horizon: Essays on Myth, History, Travel and Society in Honor of Jukka Siikala*. Helsinki: Finnish Literature Society, 123–144.

DAVIDSON-HUNT, IAIN J., PHYLLIS JACK, EDWARD MANDAMIN, and BRENNAN WAPIOKE, 2005. Iskatewizaagegan (Shoal Lake) plant knowledge: an Anishinaabe (Ojibway) ethnobotany of Northwestern Ontario. *Journal of Ethnobiology* 25: 189–227.

DE VRIES, LOURENS, 2007. Some remarks on the use of Bible translations as parallel texts in linguistic research. *Sprachtypologie und Universalienforschung* 60.2: 148–57.

DEACON, BERNARD, 1934. Geometrical drawings from Malekula and other islands of the New Hebrides. *Journal of the Royal Anthropological Institute* 64: 129–75.

DEHAENE, STANISLAS, VÉRONIQUE IZARD, PIERRE PICA, and ELIZABETH SPELKE, 2006. Core knowledge of geometry in an Amazonian indigene group. *Science* 311.5759: 381–4.

DE LANGHE, J. EDMOND, 1972. Preparation of thick or succulent plants for the herbarium. *Bulletin du Jardin Botanique Nationale de Belgique* 53: 508–9.

DELAPORTE, YVES, 1988. Les costumes du sud de la Laponie: organisation et désorganisation d'un système symbolique. *Techniques et culture* 12: 1–19.

——2002. *Le Regard de l'éleveur de rennes (Laponie norvégienne): essai d'anthropologie cognitive*. Louvain and Sterling, Va.: Peeters and SELAF.

DELPORTE, EUGÈNE, 1930. *Délimitation scientifique des constellations*. Cambridge: Cambridge University Press.

DESCOLA, PHILIPPE, 2006. Introduction. In Salvatore D'Onofrio and Frédéric Joulian (eds), *Dire le savoir-faire: gestes, techniques, objets*. Paris: L'Herne, 9–12.

DEWIT, HENDRIK C. D., 1980. Drying herbarium specimens in moist tropical conditions. *Boletim da Sociedade Broteriana*, ser. 2, 53: 549–53.

DIAMOND, JARED M., 1966. Zoological classification system of a primitive people. *Science* 151: 1102–4.

——1991. Interview techniques in ethnobiology. In Andrew M. Pawley (ed.), *Man and a Half: Essays in Pacific Anthropology and Ethnobiology in Honour of Ralph Bulmer*. Auckland: Polynesian Society, 83–6.

DIMMENDAAL, GERRIT J., 2001. Places and people: field sites and informants. In Newman and Ratliff (2001: 55–75).

DIXON, ROBERT M. W., 1980. *The Languages of Australia*. Cambridge: Cambridge University Press.

——1982. *Where Have All the Adjectives Gone? and Other Essays in Semantics and Syntax*. Berlin: Mouton.

——1984. *Searching for Aboriginal Languages*. Chicago: University of Chicago Press.

——2010. *Basic Linguistic Theory*, vol. 1: *Methodology*. Oxford: Oxford University Press.

——and ALEXANDRA AIKHENVALD, 2000. *Changing Valency: Case Studies in Transitivity*. Cambridge: Cambridge University Press.

————2006. *Complementation*. Oxford: Oxford University Press.

DOBRIN, LISE M., 2008. From linguistic elicitation to eliciting the linguist: lessons in community empowerment from Melanesia. *Language* 84.2: 300–324.

DORIAN, NANCY, 2010. Documentation and responsibility. *Language and Communication* 30.3: 179–85.

DOUGLAS, MARY, 1975. *Implicit Meanings*. London: Routledge & Kegan Paul.

——1982. *In the Active Voice*. London: Routledge & Kegan Paul.

——and BARON ISHERWOOD, 1979. *The World of Goods: Towards an Anthropology of Consumption*. New York: Basic Books.

DOUGLAS-COWIE, ELLEN, 1978. Linguistic code-switching in a Northern Irish village: social interaction and social ambition. In Peter Trudgill (ed.), *Sociolinguistic Patterns in British English*. London: Arnold, 37–51.

DOUNY, LAURENCE, 2007. The materiality of domestic waste. *Journal of Material Culture* 12.3: 309–31.

DOUSSET, LAURENT, 2003. On the misinterpretation of the Aluridja kinship system type (Australian Western Desert). *Social Anthropology* 11.1: 43–61.

——2005. Structure and substance: combining 'classic' and 'modern' kinship studies in the Australian Western Desert. *Australian Journal of Anthropology* 16.1: 18–30.

——2007. There never has been such a thing as a kin-based society: a review article. *Anthropological Forum* 17.1: 61–9.

——2008. The 'global' versus the 'local': cognitive processes of kin determination in Aboriginal Australia. *Oceania* 78.3: 260–79.

DRANSFIELD, JOHN, 1986. A guide to collecting palms. *Annals of the Missouri Botanical Garden* 73: 166–76.

DRETTAS, GEORGES, 1980. *La Mère et l'outil: contribution à l'étude sémantique du tissage rural dans la Bulgarie actuelle*. Paris: SELAF.

DREW, PAUL, and JOHN HERITAGE (eds), 1992. *Talk at Work*. Cambridge: Cambridge University Press.

DREYFUS, SIMONE, 1993. Systèmes dravidiens à filiation cognatique en Amazonie. *L'Homme* 33.2–4: 121–40.

DU BOIS, JOHN W., 1980. Introduction: the search for a cultural niche. Showing the pear film in a Mayan community. In Wallace L. Chafe (ed.), *The Pear Stories: Cognitive, Cultural, and Linguistic Aspects of Narrative Production*. Norwood, NJ: Ablex, 1–8.

——1991. Transcription design principles for spoken discourse research. *Pragmatics* 1: 71–106.

——SUSANNA CUMMING, STEPHAN SCHUETZE-COBURN, and DANAE PAOLINO, 1992. *Discourse Transcription*. Santa Barbara: University of California, Dept of Linguistics.

——Stephan Schuetze-Coburn, Susanna Cumming, and Danae Paolino, 1993. Outline of discourse transcription. In Jane A. Edwards and Martin D. Lampert (eds), *Talking Data: Transcription and Coding in Discourse Research*. Hillsdale, NJ: Erlbaum, 45–90.

Dubois, Sylvie, and Barbara Horvath, 1999. When the music changes, you change too: gender and language change in Cajun English. *Language Variation and Change* 11: 287–313.

Dumont, Louis, 1968[1957]. The marriage alliance. In Paul Bohannan and John Middleton (eds), *Marriage, Family and Residence*. New York: Natural History Press, 203–11.

Dundas, Charles, 1926. Chagga time-reckoning. *Man* 26: 140–43.

Dunlop, Fuchsia, 2008. *Shark's Fin and Sichuan Pepper*. London: Norton.

Duranti, Alessandro, 1997. *Anthropological Linguistics*. Cambridge: Cambridge University Press.

Dwyer, Arienne, 2006. Ethics and practicalities of cooperative fieldwork and analysis. In Gippert et al. (2006: 31–66).

Dwyer, Peter D., 2005. Ethnoclassification, ethnoecology and the imagination. *Journal de la Société des Océanistes* 120–21(1–2): 11–25.

Easterday, Lois, Diana Papademas, Laura Schorr, and Catherine Valentine, 1977. The making of a female researcher. *Urban Life* 6.3: 333–48.

Eckert, Penelope, 2000. *Linguistic Variation as Social Practice*. Oxford: Blackwell.

——and Sally McConnell-Ginet, 1992. Think practically and look locally: language and gender as community-based practice. *Annual Review of Anthropology* 21: 461–90.

Edwards, Jane A., 2003. The transcription of discourse. In Deborah Schiffrin, Deborah Cameron, and Heide Hamilton (eds), *The Handbook of Discourse Analysis*. Oxford: Blackwell, 321–48.

——and Martin D. Lampert (eds), 1993. *Talking Data: Transcription and Coding of Spoken Discourse*. Hillsdale, NJ: Erlbaum.

eFloras, 2009. Missouri Botanical Garden, St. Louis, MO and Harvard University Herbaria, Cambridge, MA: accessed 20 Sept. 2009 at: http://www.efloras.org/

Efron, David, 1941/1972. *Gestures, Race and Culture: Approaches to Semiotics*. The Hague: Mouton.

Ekman, Paul, and Wallace V. Friesen, 1969. The repertoire of nonverbal behaviour: categories, origins, usage, and coding. *Semiotica* 1.1: 49–98.

Ellen, Roy (ed.), 1984. *Ethnographic Research: A Guide to General Conduct*. Orlando, Fla.: Academic Press.

——1996. Putting plants in their place: anthropological approaches to understanding the ethnobotanical knowledge of rainforest populations. In David S. Edwards, Webber E. Booth, and Satish C. Choy (eds), *Tropical Rainforest Research: Current Issues*. Dordecht: Kluwer, 457–65.

——2003a. Arbitrariness and necessity in ethnobiological classification: notes on some persisting issues. In Glauco Sanga and Gherardo Ortalli (eds), *Nature Knowledge: Ethnoscience, Cognition, and Utility*. Oxford: Berghahn, 47–56.

——2003b. Variation and uniformity in the construction of biological knowledge across cultures. In Helaine Selin (ed.), *Nature across Cultures: Views of Nature and the Environment in Non-Western Cultures*. Dordrecht: Kluwer, 47–76.

——2006. *The Categorical Impulse: Essays in the Anthropology of Classifying Behaviour*. Oxford: Berghahn.

——2007. Local and scientific understandings of forest diversity on Seram, Eastern Indonesia. In Paul Sillitoe (ed.), *Global Science vs Local Science: Approaches to Indigenous Knowledge in International Development*. Oxford: Berghahn, 41–74.

ELLIS, CATHERINE, 1985. *Aboriginal Music: Education for Living*. St Lucia: University of Queensland Press.

——and LINDA BARWICK, 1988. Singers, songs and knowledge. In Andrew McCredie (ed.), *Conspectus Carminis: Essays for David Galliver*. Adelaide: University of Adelaide, 284–301.

EMMOREY, KAREN, 2002. *Language, Cognition, and the Brain: Insights from Sign Language Research*. Mahwah, NJ: Erlbaum.

ENFIELD, NICHOLAS, 2007. Tolerable friends: multilingualism and fieldwork. *Proceedings of the 33rd Annual Meeting of the Berkeley Linguistics Society*, vol. 33. Berkeley, Calif.: Berkeley Linguistics Society.

——2009. *The Anatomy of Meaning*. Cambridge: Cambridge University Press.

——in press. Tolerable friends. In *Multilingualism and Fieldwork: Proceedings of the 33rd Annual Meeting of the Berkeley Linguistics Society*. Berkeley, Calif.: BLS.

——SOTARO KITA, and JAN PETER DE RUITER, 2007. Primary and secondary pragmatic functions of pointing gestures. *Journal of Pragmatics* 39.10: 1722–41.

ENGLAND, NORA, 1992. Doing Mayan linguistics in Guatemala. *Language* 68: 29–35.

ENTWISLE, TIMOTHY J., and NICK YEE, 2000–. *AFA: Australian Freshwater Algae*; accessed 2 Sept. 2009 at: http://www.rbgsyd.nsw.gov.au/science/current_research/australian_freshwater_algae2)

ETKIN, NINA, 1993. Anthropological methods in ethnopharmacology. *Journal of Ethnopharmacology*. 38: 93–104.

EVANS, NICHOLAS, 1995. *A Grammar of Kayardild*. Berlin: Mouton de Gruyter.

——1998. Iwaidja mutation and its origins. In Anna Siewierska and Jae Jung Song (eds), *Case, Typology and Grammar: In honour of Barry J. Blake*. Amsterdam: Benjamins, 115–49.

——2000a. Iwaidjan, a very un-Australian language family. *Linguistic Typology* 4.2: 91–142.

——2000b. Kinship verbs. In Petra M. Vogel and Bernard Comrie (eds), *Approaches to the Typology of Word Classes*. Berlin: Mouton de Gruyter, 103–72.

——2001. The last speaker is dead—long live the last speaker! In Newman and Ratliff (2001: 250–81).

——2002a. Country and the word: linguistic evidence in the Croker Sea Claim. In John Henderson and David Nash (eds), *Language in Native Title*. Canberra: Aboriginal Studies Press, 51–98.

——2002b. The true status of grammatical object affixes: evidence from Bininj Gun-wok. In Nicholas Evans and Hans-Jürgen Sasse (eds), *Problems of Polysynthesis*. Berlin: Akademie, 15–50.

——2003. *Bininj Gun-wok: A Pan-Dialectal Grammar of Mayali, Kunwinjku and Kune* (2 vols). Canberra: Pacific Linguistics.

——2004. Experiencer objects in Iwaidjan languages. In Bhaskararao Peri and Subbarao Karumuri Venkata (eds), *Non-Nominative Subjects*, vol. 1. Amsterdam: Benjamins, 169–92.

——2006a. Verbos de parentesco en Ilgar y Iwaidja. In Zarina Estrada Fernandez (ed.), *Octavo Encuentro Internacional de Lingüística en el Noroeste, Memorias*, vol. 1. Hermosillo: Editorial Unison, 11–49.

——2006b. Some roots are a bit too short: a puzzle in Iwaidja internal reconstruction. Paper presented at Australianist Workshop, Somlo, April.

——2007. Pseudo-argument affixes in Iwaidja and Ilgar: a case of deponent subject and object agreement. In Matthew Baerman, Greville G. Corbett, Dunstan Brown, and Andrew Hippisley (eds), *Deponency and Morphological Mismatches: Proceedings of the British Academy* 145: 271–96.

——2010. *Dying Words: Endangered Languages and What They Have to Tell Us.* Maldon, Mass.: Wiley-Blackwell.

——ALICE GABY, STEPHEN C. LEVINSON, and ASIFA MAJID (eds), 2011. *Reciprocals and Semantic Typology.* Amsterdam: Benjamins.

——STEPHEN C. LEVINSON, NICHOLAS J. ENFIELD, ALICE GABY, and ASIFA MAJID, 2004. Reciprocal constructions and situation type. In Asifa Majid (ed.), *Field Manual Volume 9.* Nijmegen: Max Planck Institute for Psycholinguistics, 25–30; available at: http://fieldmanuals.mpi.nl/volumes/2004/reciprocals/

——and HANS-JÜRGEN SASSE, 2007. Searching for meaning in the library of Babel: field semantics and problems of digital archiving. In Austin (2003–10: 4.58–99).

EVANS-PRITCHARD, EDWARD E., 1940. *The Nuer.* Oxford: Clarendon Press.

EVERETT, DANIEL L., 2001. Monolingual field research. In Newman and Ratliff (2001: 166–88).

——2005. Cultural constraints on grammar and cognition in Pirahã. *Current Anthropology* 46.4: 621–46.

FABIAN, STEPHEN MICHAEL, 2001. *Patterns in the Sky: An Introduction to Ethnoastronomy.* Long Grove, Ill.: Waveland Press.

FARNELL, BRENDA, 1995. *Do You See What I Mean? Plains Indian Sign Talk and the Embodiment of Action.* Austin: University of Texas Press.

FEAGIN, CRAWFORD, 2004. Entering the community: fieldwork. In Jack. K. Chambers, Peter Trudgill, and Natalie Schilling-Estes (eds), *The Handbook of Language Variation and Change.* Oxford: Blackwell, 20–39.

Feist 1991 = Feist Publications, Inc. v. Rural Tel. Serv. Co. 499 U. S. 340, 1991.

FERREIRA, EMMANOELA N., JOSÉ DA S MOURÃO, POLLYANA D. ROCHA, DOUGLAS M. NASCIMENTO, and DANDARA DA S. Q. BEZERRA, 2009. Folk classification of the crab and swimming crab (Crustacea Brachyura) of the Mamanguape river estuary, North-eastern Brazil. *Journal of Ethnobiology and Ethnomedicine* 5: 22.

FIRTH, RAYMOND, 1936. *We, the Tikopia.* London: Allen &Unwin.

——1939. *Primitive Polynesian Economy.* London: Routledge.

——1957. A note on descent groups in Polynesia. *Man* 57: 4–8.

——1973. *Symbols, Public and Private.* Ithaca, NY: Cornell University Press.

FISHER, MARY F. K., 1954. *The Art of Eating.* New York: World.

——1997. Foreword from *The Gastronomical Me*, repr. in Counihan and Van Esterik (1997).

FITCH, W. TECUMSEH, 2006. The biology and evolution of music: a comparative perspective. *Cognition* 100: 173–215.

FLORA OF CHINA, 1994–. Flora of China: continuing series; accessed 20 Sept. 2009 at: http://hua.huh.harvard.edu/china/

——n.d. Dictionaries and Glossaries; accessed 2 Oct. 2009 at: http://hua. huh. harvard. edu/china/mss/related_data.htm#dictionaries

FLORA OF THE GUIANAS, 1985–. Kew and Königstein: Royal Botanic Gardens and Koeltz Scientific Books.

FLUEHR-LOBBAN, CAROLYN (ed.), 1991. *Ethics and the Profession of Anthropology: Dialogue for a New Era*. Philadelphia: University of Pennsylvania Press.

——(ed.), 2003. *Ethics and the Profession of Anthropology: Dialogue for Ethically Conscious Practice*. Walnut Creek, Calif.: AltaMira Press.

FOLEY, WILLIAM A., 1986. *The Papuan Languages of New Guinea*. Cambridge: Cambridge University Press.

——2003. Genre, register and language documentation in literate and preliterate communities. In Austin (2003–10: 1.85–98).

FORNEL, MICHEL DE, 1991. De la pertinence du geste dans les séquences de réparation et d'interruption. In Bernard Conein, Michel de Fornel, and Louis Quéré (eds), *Les Formes de la conversation*, vol. 2. Paris: Résaux, 119–53.

FORTES, MEYER, 1959. Descent, filiation and affinity: a rejoinder to Dr. Leach. *Man* 59.309, 331: 193–7, 206–12.

FOSBERG, FRANCIS R., 1960. Plant collecting as an anthropological field method. *El Palacio* 67.4.

——and MARIE-HÉLÈNE SACHET, 1965. Manual for tropical herbaria. *Regnum Vegetabile* 39: 1–132 (Utrecht).

FOSTER, GEORGE M., 1948. *Empire's Children: The People of Tzintzuntzuan*. Washington, DC: Smithsonian Institution Institute of Social Anthropology.

FOX, ROBERT B., 1953. The Pinatubo Negritos: their useful plants and material culture. *Philippine Journal of Science* 81: 173–414.

FOX, ROBIN, 1996[1967]. *Kinship and Marriage*. Cambridge: Cambridge University Press.

FRANCHETTO, BRUNA, 2006. Ethnography in language documentation. In Gippert et al. (2006: 183–211).

FRIEDL, JEFFREY E. F., 2006. *Mastering Regular Expressions*, 3rd edn. Sebastopol, Calif.: O'Reilly Media.

FRODIN, DAVID G., 2001. *Guide to Standard Floras of the World*, 2nd edn. Cambridge: Cambridge University Press.

FULLER, TOM C., and G. DOUGLAS BARBE, 1981. Drying herbarium specimens in moist tropical conditions. *Boletim da Sociedade Broteriana*, ser. 2, 53: 549–53.

GAFARANGA, JOSEPH, 2007. *Talk in Two Languages*. Basingstoke: Palgrave Macmillan.

GARDE, MURRAY, 1997. *Kuninjku (Eastern Kunwinjku): A Dictionary Based on Semantic Fields*. ASEDA item 282. Canberra: Aboriginal Studies Electronic Data Archive.

——2002. Social deixis in Bininj Kun-wok conversation. PhD thesis, University of Queensland.

——and KEVIN DJIMARR, 2007. *Wurrurrumi kun-borrk: Songs from Western Arnhem Land by Kevin Djimarr*. On *The Indigenous Music of Australia CD 1* [audio CD with scholarly notes]. Sydney: Sydney University Press.

GARIBAY-ORIJEL, ROBERTO, JAVIER CABALLERO, ARTURO ESTRADA-TORRES, and JOAQUÍN CIFUENTES, 2007. Understanding cultural significance: the edible mushroom case. *Journal of Ethnobiology and Ethnomedicine* 3: 4.

GARLICK, MIA, 2005. A review of creative commons and science commons. *Educause*: http://www.educause.edu/ir/library/pdf/ERM05510.pdf

GARRETT, PAUL B., 2005. What a language is good for: language socialization, language shift, and the persistence of code-specific genres in St. Lucia. *Language in Society* 34.3: 327–61.

GARRY, JANE, and CARL RUBINO, 2001. *Facts about the World's Languages: An Encyclopedia of the World's Major Languages, Past and Present.* New York: Wilson.

GATES, B. N., 1950. An electrical drier for herbarium specimens. *Rhodora* 52: 129–34.

GAVIN, MICHAEL C., and GREGORY J. ANDERSON, 2005. Testing a rapid quantitative ethnobiological technique: first steps towards developing a critical conservation tool. *Economic Botany* 59: 112–21.

GEERTZ, CLIFFORD, 1968. Thinking as a moral act: ethical dimensions of anthropological fieldwork in new states. *Antioch Review* 28: 139–58.

GELL, ALFRED, 1992. The technology of enchantment and the enchantment of technology. In Jeremy Coote and Anthony Shelton (eds), *Anthropology, Art, and Aesthetics.* Oxford: Oxford University Press, 40–63.

——1996. Vogel's net: traps as artworks and artworks as traps. *Journal of Material Culture* 1.1: 15–38.

——1998. *Art and Agency: An Anthropological Theory.* Oxford: Clarendon Press.

GENTNER, DEDRE, 1982. Why nouns are learned before verbs: linguistic relativity versus natural partitioning. In Stan Kuczaj II (ed.), *Language Development*, vol. 2: *Language, Thought and Culture.* Hillsdale, NJ: Erlbaum, 301–34.

GERDES, PAULUS, 1995. *Une tradition géométrique en Afrique: les dessins sur le sable* (3 vols). Paris: L'Harmattan.

——2006. *Sona Geometry from Angola: Mathematics of an African Tradition.* Monza: Polimetrica.

GERDTS, DONNA, 1998. The linguist in language revitalization programmes. In Nicholas Ostler (ed.), *Endangered Languages: What Role for the Specialist?* Bath: Foundation for Endangered Languages, 13–22.

——2010. Beyond expertise: the role of the linguist in language revitalization programs. In Lenore A. Grenoble and N. Louanna Furbee (eds), *Language Documentation. Practice and Values.* Amsterdam/Philadelphia: John Benjamins Publishing Company, 173–92.

GERWING, JENNIFER, and JANET BAVELAS, 2005. Linguistic influences on gesture's form. *Gesture* 4.2: 157–95.

GIBBON, DAFYDD, 2006. Fieldwork computing: PDA applications. Paper presented at 2006 E-MELD Workshop on Digital Language Documentation, Lansing, Mich., 20–22 June: http://linguistlist.org/cfdocs/emeld/workshop/2006/papers/gibbon.pdf

GIBSON, JAMES J., 1966. *Senses Considered as Perceptual Systems.* Boston, Mass.: Hougton Mifflin.

GIL, DAVID, 2001. Escaping Eurocentrism: fieldwork as a process of unlearning. In Newman and Ratliff (2001: 102–32).

GILLE, BERTRAND, 1978. *Histoire générale des techniques.* Paris: Gallimard.

GIPPERT, JOST, NIKOLAUS HIMMELMANN, and ULRIKE MOSEL (eds), 2006. *Essentials of Language Documentation.* Berlin: Mouton de Gruyter.

GIVÓN, TALMY, 2001. *Syntax* (2 vols). Amsterdam: Benjamins.

GLADWIN, THOMAS, 1970. *East is a Big Bird: Navigation and Logic on Puluwat Atoll.* Cambridge, Mass.: Harvard University Press.

GLASER, BARNEY G., and ANSELM L. STRAUSS, 1967. *The Discovery of Grounded Theory.* New York: Aldine de Gruyter.

GODELIER, MAURICE, 1982. *La Production des grands hommes: pouvoir et domination masculine chez les Baruya de Nouvelle-Guinée.* Paris: Fayard.

——1986. *The Making of Great Men: Male Domination and Power among the New Guinea Baruya*. Cambridge: Cambridge University Press.

——1998. Afterword: transformation and lines of evolution. In Godelier et al. (1998: 386–413).

——2004. *Métamorphoses de la parenté*. Paris: Fayard.

——THOMAS R. TRAUTMANN, and FRANKLIN E. TJON SIE FAT (eds), 1998. *Transformations of Kinship*. Washington, DC: Smithsonian Institution Press.

GOFFMAN, ERVING, 1959. *The Presentation of Self in Everyday Life*. New York: Doubleday.

——1971. *Relations in Public*. New York: Basic Books.

GOLDE, PEGGY, 1970. Odyssey of encounter. In Peggy Golde (ed.), *Women in the Field: Anthropological Experiences*. Chicago: Aldine, 67–93.

GOLDIN-MEADOW, SUSAN, 2003. *The Resilience of Language: Essays in Developmental Psychology*. New York: Psychology Press.

——and JODY SALTZMAN, 2000. The cultural bounds of maternal accommodation: how Chinese and American mothers communicate with deaf and hearing children. *Psychological Science* 11.4: 307–14.

GOODENOUGH, WARD H., 1953. *Native Astronomy in the Central Carolines*. Philadelphia: University Museum.

GOODWIN, CHARLES, 1986. Gestures as a resource for the organization of mutual orientation. *Semiotica* 62.1–2: 29–49.

GOODWIN, MAJORIE H., and CHARLES GOODWIN, 1986. Gesture and coparticipation in the activity of searching for a word. *Semiotica* 62.1–2: 51–75.

GORDON, RAYMOND G., JR, 2005. *Ethnologue: Languages of The World*, 15th edn. Dallas, Tex.: SIL International. Online version: http://www.ethnologue.com/

GOSSELAIN, OLIVIER, 1999. In pots we trust: the processing of clay and symbols in sub-Saharan Africa. *Journal of Material Culture* 4.2: 205–30.

——2010. De l'art d'accommoder les pâtes et de s'accommoder d'autrui au sud du Niger. In Claire Manen, Fabien Convertini, Didier Binder, and Ingrid Sénépart (eds), *Premières Sociétés paysannes de Méditerranée occidentale: structures des productions céramiques*. Paris: Mémoire de la Société préhistorique française 51, 249–64.

GRANÖ, JOHANNES G., 1997. *Pure Geography*. Baltimore, Md.: Johns Hopkins University Press.

GREEN, JENNY, 2009. Between the earth and the air: multimodality in Arandic sand stories. PhD dissertation, University of Melbourne.

GREENBAUM, SIDNEY, and RANDOLPH QUIRK, 1970. *Elicitation Experiments in English: Linguistic Studies in Use and Attitude*. Coral Gables, Fla.: University of Miami.

GRENOBLE, LENORE A., 2009. Linguistic cages and the limits of linguistics. In John Reyhner and Louise Lockhard (eds), *Indigenous Language Revitalization: Encouragement, Guidance, and Lessons Learned*. Flagstaff: Northern Arizona University, 61–9.

——and LINDSAY J. WHALEY (eds), 1998. *Endangered Languages: Language Loss and Community Response*. Cambridge: Cambridge University Press.

———2006. *Saving Languages*. Cambridge; Cambridge University Press.

GRIAULE, MARCEL, 1965. *Conversation with Ogotemmeli*. London: Oxford University Press.

——and GERMAINE DIETERLEN, 1965. *Le Renard pâle*. Paris: Institut d'ethnologie.

GRIES, STEFAN T., 2009. *Quantitative Corpus Linguistics with R: A Practical Introduction*. London: Routledge.

GRIFFITHS, D., 1907. Preparation of specimens of *Opuntia*. *Plant World* 9: 278–84.

GRIMM, LAURENCE G., and PAUL R. YARNOLD, 1995. *Reading and Understanding Multivariate Statistics*. Washington, DC: American Psychological Association.

GRINEVALD, COLETTE, 1998. Language endangerment in South America: a programmatic approach. In Lenore A. Grenoble and Lindsay J. Whaley (eds), *Endangered Languages: Language Loss and Community Response*. Cambridge: Cambridge University Press, 124–59.

——2003. Speakers and documentation of endangered languages. In Austin (2003–10: 1.52–72).

——2007. Linguistic fieldwork among speakers of endangered languages. In Osahito Miyaoka, Osamu Sakiyama, and Michael E. Krauss (eds), *The Vanishing Languages of the Pacific Rim*. Oxford: Oxford University Press, 35–76.

GUEST, ANN HUTCHINSON, 1989. *Choreo-graphics: A Comparison of Dance Notation Systems from the Fifteenth Century to the Present*. New York: Gordon & Breach.

GUMPERZ, JOHN J., 1982. *Discourse Strategies*. Cambridge: Cambridge University Press.

GUNN, BRIAN, et al., 2004. *Seed Handling and Propagation of Papua New Guinea Tree Species*. Canberra: CSIRO Forestry and Forest Products.

GUY, GREGORY R., 1980. Variation in the group and the individual: the case of final stop deletion. In William Labov (ed.), *Locating Language in Time and Space*. New York: Academic Press, 1–36.

HAERI, NILOOFAR, 1994. A linguistic innovation of women in Cairo. *Language Variation and Change* 6: 87–112.

——2003. *Sacred Language, Ordinary People: Dilemmas of Culture and Politics in Egypt*. Basingstoke: Palgrave Macmillan.

HALE A. M., 1976. A portable electric herbarium dryer. *Rhodora* 78: 135–40.

HALE, KENNETH, 1965. On the use of informants in fieldwork. *Canadian Journal of Linguistics* 10. 108–19.

——1972. Some questions about anthropological linguistics: the role of native knowledge. In Dell Hymes (ed.), *Reinventing Anthropology*. New York: Pantheon, 382–400.

——2001. Ulwa (Southern Sumu): the beginning of a language research project. In Newman and Ratliff (2001: 76–101).

——et al., 1992. Endangered languages. *Language* 68: 1–42.

HALLE, NICOLAS, 1961. Un séchoir à gas butane pour la preparation des herbiers. *Journal de l'Agriculture Tropicale et Botanique Appliquée* 8: 70–71.

HAMILTON, KIM N., SHANE R. TURNER, and SARAH E. ASHMORE, 2009. Cryopreservation. In Offord and Meagher (2009).

HANNA, JUDITH LYNNE, 2001. Dance. In Helen Myers (ed.), *Ethnomusicology: An Introduction*, vol. 1. London: Macmillan, 315–26.

HARDEN, GWEN, WILLIAM McDONALD, and JOHN WILLIAMS, 2006. *Rainforest Trees and Shrubs: A Field Guide to the Rainforest Trees and Shrubs of Victoria, NSW and Sub-tropical Queensland using Vegetative Characters*. Nambucca: Gwen Harden.

HARLEY, JOHN B., and DAVID WOODWARD, 1987, 1998. *The History of Cartography*, vols 1 and 2. Chicago: University of Chicago Press.

HARRINGTON, JAN L., 2009. *Relational Database Design and Implementation*, 3rd edn. Burlington, Mass.: Morgan Kaufman.

HARRIS, MARVIN, 1985. *The Sacred Cow and the Abominable Pig*. New York: Simon & Schuster.

HARRISON, K. DAVID, 2007. *When Languages Die: The Extinction of the World's Languages and the Erosion of Human Knowledge*. Oxford: Oxford University Press.

——2010. *The Last Speakers: The Quest to Save the World's Most Endangered Languages*. Washington, DC: National Geographic.

HARVEY, MARK, 1999. Place names and land-language associations in the western Top End. *Australian Journal of Linguistics* 19.2: 161–95.

HARWOOD, DALE, 1976. Universals in music: a perspective from cognitive psychology. *Ethnomusicology* 20.3: 521–33.

HASPELMATH, MARTIN, 1997. *Indefinite Pronouns*. Oxford: Clarendon Press.

——2002. *Understanding Morphology*. London: Arnold.

——(ed.), 2004. *Coordinating Constructions*. Amsterdam: Benjamins.

——2007. Pre-established categories don't exist: consequences for language description and typology. *Linguistic Typology* 11.1(7): 119–32. doi: 10. 1515/LINGTY, 2007. 011.

——MATTHEW S. DRYER, DAVID GIL, and BERNARD COMRIE (eds), 2008. *The World Atlas of Language Structure Online*. Munich: Max Planck Digital Library: http://wals.info

——EKKEHARD KÖNIG, WULF OESTERREICHER, and WOLFGANG RAIBLE, 2001. *Language Typology and Language Universals: An International Handbook* (2 vols). Berlin: de Gruyter.

HAUDRICOURT, ANDRÉ-GEORGES, 1988. *La Technologie, science humaine*. Paris: Maison des sciences de l'Homme.

HAVILAND, JOHN B., 1993. Anchoring, iconicity, and orientation in Guugu Yimithirr pointing gestures. *Journal of Linguistic Anthropology* 3.1: 3–45.

——2003. How to point in Zinacantán. In Kita (2003: 139–70).

——2006. Documenting lexical knowledge. In Gippert et al. (2006: 129–62).

HAYASHI, MAKOTO, 2003. Language and the body as a resource for collaborative action: a study of word searches in Japanese conversation. *Research on Language and Social Interaction* 36: 109–41.

HAYNES, ROBERT R, 1984. Techniques for collecting aquatic and marsh plants. *Annals of the Missouri Botanical Garden* 71: 229–31.

HAZEN, KIRK, 2000. *Identity and Ethnicity in the Rural South: A Sociolinguistic View through Past and Present* Be. Durham, NC: Duke University Press.

——2002. Identity and language variation in a rural community. *Language* 78: 240–57.

HEALEY, ALAN (ed.), 1975. *Language Learner's Fieldguide*. Ukarumpa: Summer Institute for Linguistics.

HEATH, JEFFREY, 1984. *Functional Grammar of Nunggubuyu*. Canberra: Australian Institute of Aboriginal Studies.

HEATH, SHIRLEY B., 1983. *Ways with Words: Language, Life, and Work in Communities and Classrooms*. Cambridge: Cambridge University Press.

HEFT, HARRY, 2003. Affordances, dynamic experience, and the challenge of reification. *Ecological Psychology* 15.2: 149–80.

HEIDER, FRITZ, and MARIANNE SIMMEL, 1944. An experimental study of apparent behaviour. *American Journal of Psychology* 57.2: 243–59.

HEIMER, MARIA, and STIG THØGERSEN, 2006. *Doing Fieldwork in China*. Copenhagen: Nias.

HELLWIG, BIRGIT, 2006. Field semantics and grammar-writing: stimuli-based techniques and the study of locative verbs. In Felix K. Ameka, Alan Dench, and Nicholas Evans (eds), *Catching Language: The Standing Challenge of Grammar Writing*. Berlin: Mouton de Gruyter, 321–58.

——and DIETER VAN UYTVANCK, 2007. *EUDICO Linguistic Annotator (ELAN) version 3.9.0 manual*: http://www.lat-mpi.eu/tools/elan/manual

HENRY, FRANCES, 1969. Stress and strategy in three field situations. In Frances Henry and Satish Saberwal (eds), *Stress and Response in Fieldwork*. New York: Holt, Rinehart, &Winston, 35–46.

HERCUS, LUISE, and GRACE KOCH, 1995. Song styles from near Poeppel's Corner. In Linda Barwick, Allan Marett, and Guy Tunstill (eds), *The Essence of Singing and the Substance of Song: Recent Responses to the Aboriginal Performing Arts and other essays in honour of Catherine Ellis*. Sydney: Oceania Publications, University of Sydney, 106–20.

——and JANE SIMPSON, 2002. Indigenous placenames: an introduction. In Luise Hercus, Flavia Hodges, and Jane Simpson (eds), *The Land is a Map: Placenames of Indigenous Origin in Australia*. Canberra: Australian National University and Pandanus Press.

HERDT, GILBERT, 1981. *Guardians of the Flutes: Idioms of Masculinity*. New York: McGraw-Hill.

HERRING, SUSAN C. (ed.), 1996. *Computer-Mediated Communication: Linguistic, Social and Cross-Cultural Perspectives*. Amsterdam: Benjamins.

HEWITT, HEATHER, LUCY McCLOUGHAN, and BRIAN McKINSTRY, 2009. Front desk talk: discourse analysis of receptionist–patient interaction. *British Journal of General Practice* 59: e260–e266.

HEYES, SCOTT, 2007. Inuit knowledge and perceptions of the land–water interface. PhD thesis, McGill University.

HICKERSON, NANCY P., 1975. Two studies of colour: implications for cross-cultural comparability of semantic categories. In M. Dale Kinkade, Kenneth Hale, and Oswald Werner (eds), *Linguistics and Anthropology: In Honor of C. F. Voegelin*. Lisse: de Ridder, 317–30.

HICKSON, IAN, 2011. *HTML 5: A Vocabulary and Associated APIs for HTML and XHTML*. W3C Working Draft 13 January 2011; accessed 17 January 2011 at: http://www.w3.org/TR/html5/

HILL, JANE H., 2006. The ethnography of language and language documentation. In Gippert et al. (2006: 112–28).

HILL, KENNETH C., 2002. On publishing the *Hopi Dictionary*. In William Frawley, Kenneth C. Hill, and Pamela Munro (eds), *Making Dictionaries: Preserving Indigenous Languages of the Americas*. Berkeley: University of California Press, 299–311.

HIMMELMANN, NIKOLAUS, 1998. Documentary and descriptive linguistics. *Linguistics* 36: 161–95.

——2006a. Language documentation: what is it and what is it good for? In Gippert et al. (2006: 1–30).

——2006b. The challenges of segmenting spoken language. In Gippert et al. (2006: 253–74).

——2008. Reproduction and preservation of linguistic knowledge: linguistics' response to language endangerment. *Annual Review of Anthropology* 37: 337–50.

HINDLE, DONALD, 1979. The social and situational conditioning of phonetic variation. PhD dissertation, University of Pennsylvania.

HINTON, LEANNE, 2001. Sleeping languages: can they be awakened? In Hinton and Hale (2001: 413–17).

——and KENNETH HALE (eds), 2001. *The Green Book of Language Revitalization in Practice*. San Diego, Calif.: Academic Press.

HISPID, 2007–. Herbarium Information Standards and Protocols for Interchange of Data; accessed 2 Sept. 2009 at: http://hiscom.chah.org.au/wiki/HISPID

HOCKETT, CHARLES F., 1962. Preface to *The Menomini Language*, by Leonard Bloomfield. New Haven, Conn.: Yale University Press.

HOFFMAN, BRUCE, 2009. Drums and arrows: ethnobotanical classification and use of tropical forest plants by a Maroon and Amerindian community in Suriname, with implications for biocultural conservation. PhD dissertation, University of Hawai'i at Manoa.

——and TIMOTHY GALLAHER, 2007. Importance indices in ethnobotany. *Ethnobotany Research and Application* 5: 201–18.

HÖFT, MARTINA, SAROJ K. BARIK, and ANNE METTE LYKKE, 1999. Quantitative ethnobotany: applications of multivariate and statistical analyses in ethnobotany. *People and Plants* 6.

HOLBROOK, JARITA C., 2002. Celestial navigation and technological change on Moce island. Berlin: Max Planck Institute for the History of Science. http://www.mpiwg-berlin.mpg.de/Preprints/P216pdf

——and AUDRA BALEISIS, 2008. Naked-eye astronomy for cultural astronomers. In Jarita C. Holbrook, Rodney Medupe, and Johnson O. Urama (eds), *African Cultural Astronomy: Current Archaeoastronomy and Ethnoastronomy Research in Africa*. Amsterdam: Springer.

HOLMAN, ERIC W., 2005. Domain-specific and general properties of folk classifications. *Journal of Ethnobiology* 25.1: 71–91.

HOLMES, JANET, 2006. *Gendered Talk at Work: Constructing Gender Identity Through Workplace Discourse*. Oxford: Blackwell.

HOLTON, GARY, 2009. Relatively ethical: a comparison of linguistic research paradigms in Alaska and Indonesia. *Language Documentation and Conservation* 3.2: 161–75; available at: http://hdl.handle.net/10125/4424

HOLY, LADISLAV, 1996. *Anthropological Perspectives on Kinship*. London: Pluto Press.

HONEYMAN, TOM, and LAURA C. ROBINSON, 2007. Solar power for the digital fieldworker. *Language Documentation and Conservation* 1.1: 17–27; available at: http://hdl.handle.net/10125/1722

HOPPER, PAUL J., and SANDRA A. THOMPSON, 1984. The discourse basis for lexical categories in universal grammar. *Language* 60.4: 703–52.

HORNE, CLARE E., 2000. *Geometric Symmetry in Patterns and Tilings*. Cambridge: Woodhead.

HOWELL, NANCY, 1990. *Surviving Fieldwork: A Report of the Advisory Panel on Health and Safety in Fieldwork*. Washington, DC: American Anthropological Association.

HUA, CAI, 2000. *Une société sans père ni mari: les na de Chine*. Paris: PUF.

HUGHES, THOMAS, 1986. The seamless web: technology, science, etcetera, etcetera. *Social Studies of Science* 16: 281–92.

HUNN, EUGENE, 1996. Columbia Plateau Indian place names: what can they teach us? *Journal of Linguistic Anthropology* 6.1: 3–26.

HURON, DAVID, 2001. Is music an evolutionary adaptation? In Robert J. Zatorre and Isabelle Peretz (eds), *The Biological Foundations of Music*. New York: New York Academy of Sciences, 43–61.

HUTTON, IAN, 2008. *A Guide to World Heritage, Lord Howe Island*. Lord Howe Island: Ian Hutton.

HYLAND, BERNIE P. M., 1972. A technique for collecting botanical specimens in rain forest. *Flora Malesiana Bulletin* 26: 2038–40.

——TREVOR WHIFFIN, DAVID C. CHRISTOPHEL, BRUCE GRAY, and REBEL W. ELICK, 2003. *Australian Tropical Rain Forest Plants: Trees, Shrubs and Vines*. Melbourne: CSIRO.

HYMES, DELL, 1974. *Foundations in Sociolinguistics: An Ethnographic Approach.* Philadelphia: University of Pennsylvania Press.

IERAMUGADU GROUP, 1995. *Know the Song, Know the Country: The Ngarda-Ngali Story of Culture and History in the Roebourne District.* Roebourne: Ieramugadu Group.

INGOLD, TIMOTHY, 1997. Eight themes in the anthropology of technology. *Social Analysis* (special issue, *Technology as Skilled Practice*, ed. P. Harvey): 106–38.

——1999. 'Tools for the hand, language for the face': an appreciation of Leroi-Gourhan's 'Gesture and Speech', *Studies in the History and Philosophy of Biological and Biomedical Science* 30.4: 411–53.

——2000. *The Perception of the Environment: Essays on Livelihood, Dwelling and Skill.* London: Routledge.

——2004. Culture on the ground: the world perceived through the feet. *Journal of Material Culture* 9.3: 315–40.

——2007. Materials against materiality. *Archaeological Dialogues* 14.1: 1–16.

INNES, PAMELA, and ERIN DEBENPORT (eds), 2010. Ethical dimensions of language documentation. *Language and Communication,* special issue, 30.3.

INTERAGENCY ADVISORY PANEL ON RESEARCH ETHICS, 2010. Tri-Council Policy Statement: Ethical Conduct for Research Involving Humans, 2nd edn, Dec. 2010. Accessed 10 January 2011 at: http://www.pre.ethics.gc.ca/eng/policy-politique/initiatives/tcps2-eptc2/Default/

International 1918. = *International News Service v. Associated Press,* 248 U.S. 215, 1918.

INTERNATIONAL SOCIETY OF ETHNOBIOLOGY CODE OF ETHICS, 2006. *ISE Code of Ethics (with 2008 additions)*; available at: http://ise.arts.ubc.ca/global_coalition/ethics.php

JAFFE, ALEXANDRA, 2009. *Stance: Sociolinguistic Perspectives.* Oxford: Oxford University Press.

JANKE, TERRI, and ROBYNNE QUIGGIN, 2006. *Indigenous Cultural and Intellectual Property: The Main Issues for the Indigenous Arts Industry in 2006.* Sydney: Australia Council for the Arts.

JANZEN, DANIEL, 2004. Setting up tropical biodiversity for conservation through non-damaging use: participation by parataxonomists. *Journal of Applied Ecology* 41: 181–7.

JENNE, GERTRUDE E., 1968. A portable forced air plant dryer. *Taxon* 17: 184–5.

JERNIGAN, KEVIN, 2006. An ethnobotanical investigation of tree identification by the Aguaruna Jivaro of the Peruvian Amazon. *Journal of Ethnobiology* 26: 107–25.

JEROME, NORGE, 1980. *Nutritional Anthropology: Contemporary Approaches to Diet and Culture.* Pleasantville, NY: Redgrave.

JINXIU, WANG, LIU HONGMAO, HU HUABIN, and GAO LEI, 2004. Participatory approach for rapid assessment of plant diversity through a folk classification system in a tropical rainforest: case study in Xishuangbanna, China. *Conservation Biology* 18: 1139–42.

JOHANNES, ROBERT E., 1981. *Words of the Lagoon: Fishing and Marine Lore in the Palau District of Micronesia.* Berkeley: University of California Press.

JOHNSON, CATHERINE J., and ALLEGRA FULLER SNYDER, 1999. *Securing Our Dance Heritage: Issues in the Documentation and Preservation of Dance.* Washington, DC: Council on Library and Information Resources.

JOHNSON, DIANE, 1998. *Night Skies of Aboriginal Australia: A Noctuary.* Sydney: University of Sydney.

JOHNSTON, E. CLAY, 1995. Computer software to assist linguistic field work. *Cahiers des sciences humaines* 31.7: 103–29.

JOHNSTON, TREVOR, MYRIAM VERMEERBERGEN, ADAM SCHEMBRI, and LORRAINE LEESON, 2007. Real data are messy: considering cross-linguistic analysis of constituent ordering in Australian Sign Language (Auslan), Vlamse Gebarantaal (VGT), and Irish Sign Language (ISL). In Pamela Perniss, Roland Pfau, and Michael Steinbach (eds), *Visible Variation: Comparative Studies on Sign Language Structure.* Berlin: Mouton de Gruyter, 163–208.

JOHNSTONE, BARBARA, 2000. *Qualitative Methods in Sociolinguistics.* Oxford: Oxford University Press.

JONES, DAVID L., et al., 2006. *Australian Orchid Genera: An Information and Identification System.* Melbourne: CSIRO.

JORGENSEN, VICTORIA, 1972. The preparing, pressing and mounting of bromeliads. *Journal of Bromeliad Society* 23: 211–14.

JUSLIN, PATRIK N., and PETRI LAUKKA, 2003. Communication of emotions in vocal expression and music performance: different channels, same code? *Psychological Bulletin* 129.5: 770–814.

KA'ILI, TEVITA, 2005. Tauhi va: nurturing Tongan sociospatial ties in Maui and beyond. *Contemporary Pacific* 17.1: 83–117.

KAJEWSKI, S. FRANK, 1933. Botanical collecting in the tropics. *Contributions Arnold Arboretum* 4: 103–8.

KARI, JAMES, 2008. *Ahtna Place Names List.* 2nd edn revised. Fairbanks: Alaska Native Language Centre.

——JAMES FALL, and SHEM PETE, 2003. *Shem Pete's Alaska: The Territory of the Upper Cook Inlet.* Fairbanks: University of Alaska Press.

KAY, PAUL, 2006. Methodological issues in cross-language colour naming. In Christine Jourdan and Kevin Tuite (eds), *Language, Culture, and Society: Key Topics in Linguistic Anthropology.* Cambridge: Cambridge University Press, 115–34.

——BRENT BERLIN, LUISA MAFFI, WILLIAM R. MERRIFIELD, and RICHARD COOK, 2009. *The World Colour Survey.* Stanford, Calif.: CSLI.

——and TERRY REGIER, 2003. Resolving the question of colour naming universals. *Proceedings of the National Academy of Sciences of the United States of America* 100.15: 9085–9.

KEANE, WEBB, 2006a. Subjects and objects. In Tilley et al. (2006: 197–202).

——2006b. Signs are not the garb of meaning: on the social analysis of material things. In Daniel Miller (ed.), *Materiality.* Durham, NC: Duke University Press, 182–205.

KENDON, ADAM, 1981. Geography of gesture: a critical review of Morris et al. *Semiotica* 37.1–2: 129–63.

——1982. The study of gesture: some observations on its history. *Recherches sémiotiques/ Semiotic Inquiry* 2.1: 45–62.

——1984a. Knowledge of Sign Language in an Australian Aboriginal community. *Journal of Anthropological Research* 40.4: 556–76.

——1984b. Did gestures have the happiness to escape the confusion at Babel? In Aaron Wolfgang (ed.), *Nonverbal Behaviour: Perspectives, Applications, Intercultural Insights.* Lewiston, NY: Hogrefe, 75–114.

——1986a. Some reasons for studying gesture. *Semiotica* 62.1–2: 3–28.

——1986b. Iconicity in Warlpiri sign language. In Paul Bouissac, Michael Herzfeld, and Roland Posner (eds), *Iconicity: Essays on the Nature of Culture.* Tübingen: Stauffenburg, 437–46.

——1988a. How gestures can become like words. In Fernando Poyatos (ed.), *Crosscultural Perspectives in Nonverbal Communication.* Toronto: Hogrefe, 131–41.

——1988b. *Sign Languages of Aboriginal Australia: Cultural, Semiotic, and Communicative Perspectives*. Cambridge: Cambridge University Press.

——1990. Signs in the cloister and elsewhere. *Semiotica* 79.3–4: 307–29.

——1992. Some recent work from Italy on quotable gestures ('emblems'). *Journal of Linguistic Anthropology* 2.1: 92–108.

——1995. Gestures as illocutionary and discourse structure markers in southern Italian conversation. *Journal of Pragmatics* 23.3: 247–79.

——2004a. *Gesture: Visible Action as Utterance*. Cambridge: Cambridge University Press.

——2004b. Some contrasts in gesticulation in Neapolitan speakers and speakers in North-amptonshire. In Cornelia Müller and Roland Posner (eds), *The Semantics and Pragmatics of Everyday Gesture*. Berlin: Weidler, 173–93.

——2007. Some topics in gesture studies. In Anna Esposito, Marcos Bratanić, Eric Keller, and Maria Marinaro (eds), *Fundamentals of Verbal and Nonverbal Communication and the Biometric Issue*. Amsterdam: IOS Press, 3–19.

——2008. Some reflections on the relationship between 'gesture' and 'sign'. *Gesture* 8.3: 348–66.

——and LAURA VERSANTE, 2003. Pointing by hand in Neapolitan. In Kita (2003: 109–37).

KERSWILL, PAUL, and ANN WILLIAMS, 2000. Creating a new town koine: children and language change in Milton Keynes. *Language in Society* 29: 65–115.

KHASBAGAN, CHEN, and SOYOLT, 2008. Indigenous knowledge for plant species diversity: a case study of wild plants' folk names used by the Mongolians in Ejina desert area, Inner Mongolia, P. R. China. *Journal of Ethnobiology and Ethnomedicine* 4: 2.

KHETARPAL, NAVEEN, ASIFA MAJID, BARBARA C. MALT, STEVEN A. SLOMAN, and TERRY REGIER, 2010. Similarity judgements reflect both language and cross-language tendencies: evidence from two semantic domains. In Stellan Ohlsson and Richard Catrambone (eds), *Proceedings of the Thirty-Second Annual Conference of the Cognitive Science Society*. Austin, Tex.: Cognitive Science Society, 358–63.

KIBRIK, ALEKSANDR E., 1977. *The Methodology of Field Investigations in Linguistics: Setting Up the Problem*. The Hague: Mouton.

KITA, SOTARO (ed.), 2003. *Pointing: Where Language Culture and Cognition Meet*. Hillsdale, NJ: Erlbaum.

——2009. Cross-cultural variation of speech-accompanying gesture: a review. *Language and Cognitive Processes* 24.2: 145–67.

——EVE DANZIGER, and CHRISTEL STOLZ, 2001. Cultural specificity of spatial schemas, as manifested in spontaneous gestures. In Meredith Gattis (ed.), *Spatial Schemas and Abstract Thought*. Cambridge, Mass.: MIT Press, 115–46.

——and JAMES ESSEGBEY, 2001. Pointing left in Ghana: how a taboo on the use of the left hand influences gestural practice. *Gesture* 1.1: 73–95.

——and ASLI ÖZYÜREK, 2003. What does cross-linguistic variation in semantic coordination of speech and gesture reveal? Evidence for an interface representation of spatial thinking and speaking. *Journal of Memory and Language* 48.1: 16–32.

————SHANLEY ALLEN, AMANDA BROWN, REYHAN FURMAN, and TOMOKO ISHIZUKA, 2007. Relations between syntactic encoding and co-speech gestures: implications for a model of speech and gesture production. *Language and Cognitive Processes* 22.8: 1212–36.

——INGEBORG VAN GIJN, and HARRY VAN DER HULST, 1998. Movement phases in signs and co-speech gestures, and their transcription by human coders. In Ipke Wachsmuth and

Martin Fröhlich (eds), *Gesture and Sign Language in Human–Computer Interaction.* Berlin: Springer, 23–35.

KLEINMAN, SHERRYL, and MARTHA A. COPP, 1993. *Emotions and Fieldwork.* Newbury Park, Calif.: Sage.

KOCH, GRACE, and MYFANY TURPIN, 2008. The language of Aboriginal songs. In Claire Bowern, Bethwyn Evans, and Luisa Miceli (eds), *Morphology and Language History in honour of Harold Koch.* Amsterdam: Benjamins, 167–83.

KOLO, FINAU, 1990. Historiography: the myth of indigenous authenticity. In Phyllis Herda, John Terrell, and Neil Gunson (eds), *Tongan Culture and History.* Canberra: Australian National University, 1–11.

KOLOVOS, ANDY, 2010. *Vermont Folklife Centre audio field recording equipment guide*; accesssed 10 January 2011 at: http://www.vermontfolklifecentre.org/res_audioequip.htm

KOPYTOFF, IGOR, 1986. The cultural biography of things. In Arjun Appadurai (ed.), *The Social Life of Things: Commodities in Cultural Perspective.* Cambridge: Cambridge University Press, 64–91.

KROEBER, ALFRED L., 1915. Serian, Tequistlatecan, and Hokan. *University of California Publications in American Archaeology and Ethnology* 11: 279–90.

KROEGER, PAUL R., 2005. *Analyzing Grammar: An Introduction.* Cambridge: Cambridge University Press.

KRONENFELD, DAVID B., 1991. Fanti kinship: language, inheritance, and kin groups. *Anthropos* 86.1–3: 19–31.

KULICK, DON, and MARGARET WILLSON, 1995. *Taboo: Sex, Identity, and Erotic Subjectivity in Anthropological Fieldwork.* London: Routledge.

LABOV, WILLIAM, 1972a. *Sociolinguistic Patterns.* Philadelphia: University of Pennsylvania Press.

——1972b. *Language in the Inner City: Studies in the Black English Vernacular.* Philadelphia: University of Pennsylvania Press.

——1972c. Some principles of linguistic methodology. *Language in Society* 1: 97–120.

——1978. Denotational structure. In Donka Farkas, Wesley M. Jacobsen, and Karol W. Todrys (eds), *Papers from the Parasession on the Lexicon.* Chicago: Chicago Linguistics Society, 220–60.

——1982. Objectivity and commitment in linguistic science: the case of the Black English trial in Ann Arbor. *Language in Society* 11: 165–201.

——1984. Field methods of the project on linguistic change and variation. In John Baugh and Joel Sherzer (eds), *Language in Use: Readings in Sociolinguistics.* Englewood Cliffs, NJ: Prentice-Hall, 28–53.

——2001. *Principles of Linguistic Change: Social Factors.* Oxford: Blackwell.

——PAUL COHEN, CLARENCE ROBINS, and JOHN LEWIS, 1968. *A Study of the Non-Standard English of Negro and Puerto Rican Speakers in New York City.* Final report, Cooperative Research Project 3288. 2 vols. Philadelphia: U.S. Regional Survey.

LAIRD, SARAH A. (ed.), 2002. *Biodiversity and Traditional Knowledge: Equitable Partnerships in Practice.* London: Earthscan.

LAMPHERE, LOUISE, 2001. What happened to kinship studies? Reflections of a feminist anthropologist. In Linda Stone (ed.), *New Directions in Anthropological Kinship.* Lanham, Md.: Rowman & Littlefield, 21–47.

LAMPMAN, AARON M., 2007. General principles of ethnomycological classification among the Tzeltal Maya of Chiapas, Mexico. *Journal of Ethnobiology* 27: 11–27.

LANDA, EDWARD R., and MARK D. FAIRCHILD, 2005. Charting colour from the eye of the beholder. *American Scientist* 93.5: 436–43.

LAPPE, FRANCES MOORE, and JOSEPH COLLINS, 1986. *World Hunger: Twelve Myths*. New York: Grove Press.

LASCARIDIS, ALEX, and MATTHEW STONE, 2009. Discourse coherence and gesture interpretation. *Gesture* 9.2: 147–80.

LATOUR, BRUNO, 1996. *Aramis, or the Love of Technology*. Cambridge, Mass.: Harvard University Press.

——2005. *Reassembling the Social*. Oxford: Oxford University Press.

LAUGHREN, MARY, 1982. Warlpiri kinship structure. In Jeffrey Heath, Francesca Merlan, and Alan Rumsey (eds), *Languages of Kinship in Aboriginal Australia*. Sydney: Oceania Linguistic Monographs, 72–85.

LAWLER, JOHN, and HELEN ARISTAR-DRY (eds), 1998. *Using Computers in Linguistics: A Practical Guide*. London: Routledge.

LE GUEN, OLIVIER, 2011. Speech and gesture in spatial language and cognition among the Yucatec Mayas. *Cognitive Science* 35.5: 905–38.

LEA, VANESSA, 2004. Aguçando o entendimento dos termos triádicos Mebengôkre via aborígines australianos: dialogando com Merlan e outros. *Liames* 4: 29–42.

LEACH, EDMUND R., 1965. Unilateral cross-cousin marriage. *Man* 65.11–114, article 12: 25.

LEACH, GREG J., and PATRICK L. OSBORNE, 1985. *Freshwater Plants of Papua New Guinea*. Port Moresby: University of Papua New Guinea Press.

LEAFFER, MARSHALL A., 2010. *Understanding Copyright Law*, 5th edn. New Providence, NJ: LexisNexis/Matthew Bender.

LEE, RICHARD, and IRVEN DEVORE, 1968. *Man the Hunter*. New York: Wenner Gren Foundation and Aldine de Gruyter.

LEFÉBURE, CLAUDE, 1978. Linguistique et technologie culturelle: l'exemple du métier à tisser vertical berbère. *Techniques et culture*, 1st ser., 3: 84–148.

——1983. Linguistique et technologie culturelle, quelques remarques. *Techniques et culture*, 2nd ser., 1: 121–7.

LEMONNIER, PIERRE, 1984. L'écorce battue chez les Anga de Nouvelle-Guinée. *Techniques et culture*, 2nd ser., 4: 127–75.

——1989. Bark capes, arrowheads and Concorde: on social representations of technology. In Ian Hodder (ed.), *The Meaning of Things: Material Culture and Symbolic Expression*. London: Unwin Hyman, 156–71.

——1992. *Elements for an Anthropology of Technology*. Ann Arbor, Mich.: Museum of Anthropology.

——(ed.), 1993a. *Technological Choices: Transformation in Material Cultures since the Neolithic*. London: Routledge.

——1993b. The eel and the ankave-anga of Papua New Guinea: material and symbolic aspects of trapping. In Claude Marcel Hladik et al. (eds), *Tropical Forests, People and Foods: Biocultural Interactions and Applications to Development*. Paris: UNESCO, 673–82.

——2005. Mythiques chaînes opératoires. *Techniques et culture* 43–4: 25–43.

——2006. *Le sabbat des lucioles: sorcellerie, chamanisme et imaginaire cannibale en Nouvelle-Guinée*. Paris: Stock.

LEONARD, WESLEY Y., 2007. Miami language reclamation in the home: a case study. PhD dissertation, University of California, Berkeley.

——2008. When is an 'extinct' language not extinct? Miami, a formerly sleeping language. In Kendall A. King, Natalie Shilling-Estes, Lyn Fogle, Jia Jackie Lou, and Barbara Soukup (eds), *Sustaining Linguistic Diversity. Endangered and Minority Languages and Language Varieties.* Washington, DC: Georgetown University Press, 23–33.

LEPP, HEINO, 2008–. The bryophyte groups: what is a moss? Accessed 1 Oct. 2009 at: http://www.anbg.gov.au/bryophyte/what-is-moss.html

LEROI-GOURHAN, ANDRÉ, 1971[1943]. *Evolution et techniques: l'homme et la matière.* Paris: Albin Michel.

——1973[1945]. *Evolution et techniques: milieu et technique.* Paris: Albin Michel.

——1993[1964]. *Gesture and Speech*, trans. Anna Bostock Berger. Cambridge, Mass.: MIT Press.

LESSIG, LAWRENCE, 2004. *Free Culture.* New York: Penguin.

LETTE, KATHY, 1989. *Girls' Night Out.* London: Bloomsbury.

LEUENBERGER, BEAT E., 1982. Microwaves: a modern aid in preparing herbarium specimens of succulents. *Cactus and Succulent Journal* (Great Britain) 44: 42–3.

LÉVI-STRAUSS, CLAUDE, 1967[1947]. *Les Structures élémentaires de la parenté.* Paris: Mouton.

——1987[1950]. *Introduction to the Work of Marcel Mauss.* London: Routledge & Kegan Paul.

——1990[1968]. *The Origin of Table Manners: Mythologiques*, vol. 3, trans. John Weightman. Chicago: University of Chicago Press.

——1997. The culinary triangle. In Counihan and Van Esterik (1997: 28–35).

LEVINSON, STEPHEN, 2008. Landscape, seascape and the ontology of places on Rossel Island, Papua New Guinea. *Language Sciences* 30.2–3: 256–90.

——SÉRGIO MEIRA, and The Language and Cognition Group, 2003. 'Natural concepts' in the spatial topological domain-adpositional meanings in crosslinguistic perspective: an exercise in semantic typology. *Language* 79.3: 485–516.

——and DAVID WILKINS (eds), 2006. *Grammars of Space: Explorations in Cognitive Diversity.* Cambridge: Cambridge University Press.

LIBERMAN, MARK, 2009. The Journal of Experimental Linguistics. Paper presented at the American Association for Corpus Linguistics 2009 conference, University of Alberta, 8–11 October; available at: http://www.ualberta.ca/~aacl2009/PDFs/Liberman2009AACL. pdf

LIDDELL, SCOTT, and MELANIE METZGER, 1998. Gesture in sign language discourse. *Journal of Pragmatics* 30.6: 657–97.

LINDSEY, MARC, 2003. *Copyright Law on Campus.* Pullman: Washington State University Press.

LINGUISTIC SOCIETY OF AMERICA, 2009. Ethics statement; accessed 5 May 2010 at: http://www.lsadc.org/info/lsa-comm-ethics-more.cfm#projects

LOGAN, JAMES, 1986. A pre-pressing treatment for Begonia species and succulents. *Taxon* 35.4: 671.

LONGACRE, ROBERT, 1964. *Grammar Discovery Procedures: A Field Manual.* The Hague: Mouton.

LUCY, JOHN A., 1994. The role of semantic value in lexical comparison: motion and position roots in Yucatec Maya. *Linguistics* 32.4: 623–56.

———1997. The linguistics of 'colour'. In Clyde L. Hardin and Maffi Luisa (eds), *Colour Categories in Thought and Language*. Cambridge: Cambridge University Press, 320–46.

LYNE, ANDREW, n.d. Botanical Glossaries; accessed 1 Oct. 2009 at: http://www.anbg.gov.au/glossary/glossary.html

LYONS, JOHN, 1968. *Introduction to Theoretical Linguistics*. Cambridge: Cambridge University Press.

MACAULAY, MONICA, 2004. Training linguistics students for the realities of fieldwork. *Anthropological Linguistics* 46.2: 194–209.

MACAULAY, RONALD, 2002. Extremely interesting, very interesting, or only quite interesting? Adverbs and social class. *Journal of Sociolinguistics* 6.3: 398–417.

MACDOUGALL, THOMAS, 1947. A method for pressing cactus flowers. *Cactus and Succulent Journal*, 19: 188.

MÂCHE, FRANÇOIS BERNARD, 2000. Necessity of and problems with a universal musicology. In Nils L. Wallin, Björn Merker, and Steven Brown (eds), *The Origins of Music*. Cambridge, Mass.: MIT Press. 473–9.

MADDIESON, IAN, 2001. Phonetic fieldwork. In Newman and Ratliff (2001:211–29).

MAFFI, LUISA, 2005. Linguistic, cultural, and biological diversity. *Annual Review of Anthropology* 34: 599–617.

MAHIAS, MARIE-CLAUDE, 1993. Pottery techniques in India: technical variants and social choice. In Pierre Lemonnier (ed.), *Technological Choices: Transformation in Material Culture since the Neolithic*. London: Routledge, 157–80.

———2002. *Le Barattage du monde: essais d'anthropologie des techniques en Inde*. Paris: Maison des sciences de l'homme.

MAJID, ASIFA, 2007. *Field Manual Volume 10*. Nijmegen: Max Planck Institute for Psycholinguistics.

———JAMES S. BOSTER, and MELISSA BOWERMAN, 2008. The cross-linguistic categorization of everyday events: a study of cutting and breaking. *Cognition* 109.2: 235–50.

———and MELISSA BOWERMAN (eds), 2007. *Cutting and Breaking Events: A Crosslinguistic Perspective*. Special issue of *Cognitive Linguistics*, 18.

———MIRIAM VAN STADEN, and JAMES S. BOSTER, 2007. The semantic categories of cutting and breaking events: a crosslinguistic perspective. *Cognitive Linguistics* 18.2: 133–52.

———NICHOLAS EVANS, ALICE GABY, and STEPHEN LEVINSON, 2011. The grammar of exchange: a comparative study of reciprocal constructions across languages. *Frontiers in Cultural Psychology* 2.34; doi: 10.3389/fpsyg.2011.00034

———MARIANNE GULLBERG, MIRIAM VAN STADEN, and MELISSA BOWERMAN, 2007. How similar are semantic categories in closely related languages? A comparison of cutting and breaking in four Germanic languages. *Cognitive Linguistics* 18.2(9): 179–94; doi: 10. 1515/COG, 2007. 007

———and STEPHEN LEVINSON (eds), 2011. The senses in language and culture. *The Senses and Society*, special issue, 6.

MAJOR, ALAN P., 1975. *Collecting and Studying Mushrooms, Toadstools and Fungi*. Edinburgh: Bartholomew.

MAKIHARA, MIKI, 2004. Linguistic syncretism and language ideologies: transforming sociolinguistic hierarchy on Rapa Nui (Easter Island). *American Anthropologist* 106: 529–40.

——2005. Being Rapa Nui, speaking Spanish: children's voices on Easter Island. *Anthropological Theory* 5: 117–34.

MALCHUKOV, ANDREJ, and ANDREW SPENCER (eds), 2008. *The Oxford Handbook of Case.* Oxford: Oxford University Press.

MALINOWSKI, BRONISLAW, 1921. *Coral Gardens and their Magic* (2 vols). London: Allen & Unwin.

——1922. *Argonauts of the Western Pacific: An Account of Native Enterprise and Adventure in the Archipelagoes of Melanesian New Guinea.* London: Routledge & Kegan Paul.

MALLERY, GEORGE, 1987[1880]. A collection of gesture-signs and signals of the North American Indians with some comparisons. In Umiker-Sebeok and Sebeok (1987: 77–406).

MALLINSON, CHRISTINE, and CHILDS, BECKY, 2007. Communities of practice in sociolinguistic description: analyzing language and identity practices among Black Women in Appalachia. *Gender and Language* 1: 173–206.

MALT, BARBARA C., et al., 2008. Talking about walking. *Psychological Science* 19.3: 232–40.

MALTHUS, THOMAS ROBERT, 1999[1798]. *An Essay on the Principle of Population*, ed. Geoffrey Gilbert. Oxford: Oxford University Pres

MANATOWA-BAILEY, JACOB, 2007. On the brink. *Cultural Survival Quarterly* 31.2.

MANMURULU, DAVID, MEIKI APTED, and LINDA BARWICK, 2008. Songs from the Inyjalarrku: the use of non-decipherable, non-translatable, non-interpretable language in a set of spirit songs from North-West Arnhem Land. Paper presented at the 2008 Symposium on Indigenous Music and Dance, Charles Darwin University, Darwin, NT.

MARCUS, GEORGE E., 2009. Notes toward an ethnographic memoir of supervising graduate research through anthropology's decades of transformation. In James D. Faubion and George E. Marcus (eds), *Fieldwork Is Not What It Used To Be: Learning Anthropology's Method in a Time of Transition*. Ithaca, NY: Cornell University Press, 1–34.

MARETT, ALLAN, 2000. Ghostly voices: some observations on song-creation, ceremony and being in northwest Australia. *Oceania* 71.1: 18–29.

——2010. Vanishing songs: how musical extinctions threaten the planet. *Ethnomusicology Forum*, 19.2: 249–62.

——and LINDA BARWICK, 2003. Endangered songs and endangered languages. In Joe Blythe and R. McKenna Brown (eds), *Maintaining the Links: Language Identity and the Land.* Bath: Foundation for Endangered Languages, 144–51.

——et al., 2006. The National Recording Project for Indigenous Performance in Australia: year one in review *Backing Our Creativity: the National Education and the Arts Symposium, 12–14 September 2005.* Surry Hills, NSW: Australia Council for the Arts, 84–90.

MARGETTS, ANNA, 2009. Data processing and its impact on linguistic analysis. *Language Documentation and Conservation* 3.1: 87–99.

——2011. Filming with native speaker commentary. Presentation at the Second International Conference on Language Documentation and Conservation, University of Hawai'i.

MARK, DAVID M., and ANDREW G. TURK, 2003. Landscape categories in Yindjibarndi: ontology, environment, and language. In Werner Kuhn, Michael F. Worboys, and Sabine Timpf (eds), *Spatial Information Theory: Foundations of Geographic Information Science*, vol. 2825, *Lecture Notes in Computer Science.* Berlin: Springer, 28–45.

————and DAVID STEA, 2007. Progress on Yindjibarndi ethnophysiography. In Stephan Winter, Matt Duckham, Lars Kulik, and Benjamin Kuipers (eds), *Spatial Information Theory: Lecture Notes in Computer Science* No. 4736. Berlin: Springer, 1–19.

————Niclas Burenhult and David Stea (eds), 2011. *Landscape in Language: Transdisciplinary perspectives*. Benjamins.

————————2010. Ethnophysiography of arid lands: categories for landscape features. In Leslie Main Johnson and Eugene S. Hunn (eds), *Landscape Ethnoecology: Concepts of Physical and Biotic Space*. Oxford: Berghahn, 27–45.

MARLETT, STEPHEN A., 2001. La relación entre las lenguas 'hokanas' en México: ¿Cuál es la evidencia? Presentation at the third Swadesh conference, México, DF.

MARRALA, KHAKI, et al., 2008. *Nganduka Angmaju? Where Does it Hurt? A Guide for Health Professionals*. Jabiru: Iwaidja Inyman.

MARTIN, GARY J., 2004. *Ethnobotany: A Methods Manual*, 2nd edn (1st edn 1995). London: Earthscan.

MARTINELLI, BRUNO, 1996. Sous le regard de l'apprenti. *Techniques et culture* 28: 9–47.

————(ed.), 2005. *L'Interrogation du style: anthropologie, technique et esthétique*. Marseille: Presses de l'Université de Provence.

MASLIN, BRUCE R., 2001. *Wattle: Acacias of Australia*. Melbourne: CSIRO.

MAUSS, MARCEL, 1954[1923–4]. *The Gift: The Form and Reason for Exchange in Archaic Societies*. London: Cohen & West.

————1967[1926]. *Manuel d'ethnographie*. Paris: Editions sociales.

————2006[1935]. Techniques of the body. In Marcel Mauss and Nathan Schlanger (eds), *Techniques, Technology and Civilisation*. Oxford: Berghahn, 77–95.

————2007[1947]. *The Manual of Ethnology* (trans. Dominique Lussier). New York and Oxford: Durkheim Press and Berghahn.

MAXWELL, JUDITH M., 2004. Ownership of indigenous language: a case study from Guatemala. In Mary Riley (ed.), *Indigenous Intellectual Property Rights: Legal Obstacles and Innovative Solutions*. Walnut Creek, Calif.: AltaMira Press, 173–217.

MAYER, MERCER, 1969. *Frog, Where Are You?* New York: Dial Press.

McALLESTER, DAVID P., 1971. Some thoughts on 'universals' in music. *Ethnomusicology* 15.3: 379–80.

McCLATCHEY, WILL C., MYKNEE Q. B. SIRIKOLO, LAZARUS KALEVEKE, and CAREFREE PITANAPI, 2006. Differential conservation of two species of *Canarium* (Burseraceae) among the Babatana and Ririo of Lauru (Choiseul), Solomon Islands. *Economic Botany* 60: 212–26.

————RANDALL THAMAN, and SONYA JUVIK, 2008. Ethnobiodiversity surveys of human/ecosystem relationships. In Dieter Mueller Dombois, Kent W. Bridges, and Curt C. Daehler (eds), *Biodiversity Assessment of Tropical Island Ecosystems: PABITRA Manual for Interactive Ecology and Management*. Honolulu: B. P. Bishop Museum Press, 159–96. Available at: www.botany.hawaii.edu/pabitra/biodiversity/

McCONVELL, PATRICK, 1982. Neutralisation and degrees of respect in Gurindji. In Jeffrey Heath, Francesca Merlan, and Alan Rumsey (eds), *Languages of Kinship in Aboriginal Australia*. Sydney: Oceania Linguistic Monographs, 86–106.

————2009. 'Where the spear sticks up': the variety of locatives in placenames in the Victoria River District, Northern Territory. In Harold Koch and Luise Hercus (eds), *Aboriginal Placenames: Naming and Re-naming the Australian Landscape*. Canberra: ANU E Press and Aboriginal History Incorporated, 359–402.

McCOOL, MATTHEW, 2009. Touring the cosmos through your computer: a guide to free desktop planetarium software. *Communicating Astronomy to the Public* 7: 21–3.

McDermott, Josh, and Marc D. Hauser, 2005. The origins of music: innateness, uniqueness and evolution. *Music Perception* 23.1: 29–59.

——2006. Thoughts on an empirical approach to the evolutionary origins of music. *Music Perception* 24.1: 111–16.

McGill, Stuart, and Sophie Salffner, n.d. Power solutions in the field: solar power for laptop computers [ELAR advice document 3]: available at: http://www.hrelp.org/archive/advice/solar.html)

McGregor, William B., 2009. *Linguistics: An Introduction.* London: Continuum.

McKenzie, Donald, 1990. *Inventing Accuracy: A Historical Sociology of Nuclear Missile Guidance.* Cambridge, Mass.: MIT Press.

McNeill, David, 1992. *Hand and Mind: What the Hands Reveal about Thought.* Chicago: University of Chicago Press.

——2005. *Gesture and Thought.* Chicago: University of Chicago Press.

Meigs, Anna, 1984. *Food, Sex and Pollution: A New Guinea Religion.* New Brunswick, NJ: Rutgers University Press.

——1997. *Food as a Cultural Construction.* In Carole Counihan and Penny Van Esterik (eds), *Food and Culture.* New York: Routledge, 95–106.

Meir, Irit, Wendy Sandler, Carol Padden, and Mark Aronoff (2010). *Emerging Sign Languages.* In Mark Marschark and Patricia Spencer (eds), *Oxford Handbook of Deaf Studies, Language, and Education,* vol. 2. Oxford: Oxford University Press.

Meissner, Martin, and Stuart. B. Philpott, 1975. The sign language of sawmill workers in British Columbia. *Sign Language Studies* 9: 291–308.

Mekbib, Firew, 2007. Infra-specific folk taxonomy in sorghum (*Sorghum bicolor* (L.) Moench) in Ethiopia: folk nomenclature, classification, and criteria. *Ethnobiology and Ethnomedicine* 3: 38.

Mendes dos Santos, Gilton, and Yasmine Antonini, 2008. The traditional knowledge of stingless bees (Apidae: Meliponina) used by the Enawena-Nawe tribe in western Brazil. *Journal of Ethnobiology and Ethnomedicine* 4: 19.

Mendoza-Denton, Norma, 2008. *Homegirls: Language and Cultural Practice Among Latina Youth Gangs.* Malden, Mass.: Wiley-Blackwell.

Mennell, Stephen, 1985. *All Manners of Food.* Oxford: Blackwell.

Merlan, Francesca, 1989. Jawoyn relationship terms: interactional dimensions of Australian kin classification. *Anthropological Linguistics* 31.3–4: 227–63.

——2001. Form and context in Jawoyn placenames. In Jane Simpson, David Nash, Mary Laughren, Peter Austin, and Barry Alpher (eds), 2001. *Forty Years On: Ken Hale and Australian Languages.* Canberra: Pacific Linguistics, 367–83.

——and Jeffrey Heath, 1982. Dyadic kinship terms. In Jeffrey Heath, Francesca Merlan, and Alan Rumsey (eds), *Languages of Kinship in Aboriginal Australia.* Sydney: University of Sydney, 107–24.

Meyerhoff, Miriam, 2001. Dynamics of differentiation: on social psychology and cases of language variation. In Nikolas Coupland, Christopher Candlin, and Srikant Sarangi (eds), *Sociolinguistics and Social Theory.* London: Longman, 61–87.

——2006. *Introducing Sociolinguistics.* London: Routledge.

——2009. Replication, transfer and calquing: using variation as a tool in the study of language contact. *Language Variation and Change* 21: 1–21.

——and Naomi Nagy (eds), 2008. *Social Lives in Language: The Sociolinguistics of Multilingual Speech Communities.* Amsterdam: Benjamins.

——and JAMES A. WALKER, 2007. The persistence of variation in individual grammars: copula absence in 'urban sojourners' and their stay-at-home peers, Bequia (St Vincent and the Grenadines). *Journal of Sociolinguistics* 11.3: 346–66.

MILLAR, Alan J. K., 1999–. Aussie algae; accessed 2 Sept. 2009 at: http://www.aussiealgae.org/

MILLER, DANIEL, 1995. *Acknowledging Consumption: A Review of New Studies*. London: Routledge.

——2005. *Materiality*. Durham, NC: Duke University Press.

——2006. Consumption. In Tilley et al. (2006: 341–54).

MILLER, ROBERT J., 1973. Cross-cultural research in the perception of pictorial materials. *Psychological Bulletin* 80.2: 135–50. doi: 10. 1037/h0034739

MILROY, JAMES, and LESLEY MILROY, 1978. Belfast: change and variation in an urban vernacular. In Peter Trudgill (ed.), *Sociolinguistic Patterns in British English*. London: Arnold, 19–36.

MILROY, LESLEY, 1980. *Language and Social Networks*. Oxford: Blackwell.

——and MATTHEW GORDON, 2003. *Sociolinguistics: Method and Interpretation*. Oxford: Blackwell.

MINTZ, SIDNEY, 1985. *Sweetness and Power*. New York: Penguin.

MITHUN, MARIANNE, 2001. Who shapes the record: the speaker and the linguist. In Newman and Ratliff (2001: 34–54).

——2007a. Grammars and the community. In Thomas E. Payne and David J. Weber (eds), *Perspectives on Grammar Writing*. Amsterdam: Bejamins, 45–69.

——2007b. Linguistics in the face of language endangerment. In W. Leo Wetzels (ed.), *Language Endangerment and Endangered Languages: Linguistics and Anthropological Studies with Special Emphasis on the Languages and Cultures of the Andean–Amazonian Border Area*. Leiden: Research School of Asian, African and Amerindian Studies, 15–34.

MITTELBERG, IRENE, 2002. The visual memory of grammar: iconographical and metaphorical insights: available at: http://www.metaphorik.de/02/mittelberg.htm

——2007. Methodology for multimodality: one way of working with speech and gesture data. In Monica Gonzalez-Marquez, Irene Mittelberg, Seana Coulson, and Michael J. Spivey (eds), *Methods in Cognitive Linguistics*. Amsterdam: Benjamins, 225–248.

MOHANTY, JITENDRA N., 1997. *Phenomenology: Between Essentialism and Transcendental Philosophy*. Evanston, Ill.: Northwestern University Press.

MONDADA, LORENZA, 2007. Multimodal resources for turn-taking: pointing and the emergence of possible next speakers. *Discourse Studies* 9.2: 194–225.

MOORE, DAVID, 1993. *Flora Europaea*, vol. 1 (revised): *Lycopodiaceae to Platanaceae*. Cambridge: Cambridge University Press.

MOREY, STEPHEN, 2004. *The Tai Languages of Assam: A Grammar and Texts*. Canberra: Pacific Linguistics, Research School of Pacific and Asian Studies.

MORGAN, LEWIS H., 1997[1871]. *Systems of Consanguinity and Affinity of the Human Family*. Lincoln: University of Nebraska Press. [Originally published by the Smithsonian Institution.]

MORI, SCOTT A., 1984. Use of 'swiss tree grippers' for making botanical collections of tropical trees. *Biotropica* 16: 79–80.

MORRIS, DESMOND, PETER COLLETT, PETER MARSH, and MARIE O'SHAUGHNESSY, 1979. *Gestures: Their Origins and Distribution*. London: Cape.

MORRIS, MICHAEL W., and KAIPING PENG, 1994. Culture and cause: American and Chinese attributions for social and physical events. *Journal of Personality and Social Psychology* 67.6: 949–71. doi: 10. 1037/0022–3514. 67. 6. 949

MOSEL, ULRIKE, 2006a. Fieldwork and community language work. In Gippert et al. (2006: 67–85).

——2006b. The art and craft of writing grammars. In Felix Ameka, Alan Dench, and Nicholas Evans (eds), *Catching Language: The Standing Challenge of Grammar Writing.* Berlin: Mouton de Gruyter, 41–68.

——2008. Putting oral narratives into writing: experiences from a language documentation project in Bouganville, Papua New Guinea. Paper presented at the Simposio Internacional Contacto de lenguas y documentación, August, Buenos Aires, CAIYT; available at: http://www.linguistik.uni-kiel.de/mosel_publikationen.htm#download

MOSER, MARY B., and STEPHEN A. MARLETT, 2005. *Comcáac Quih Yaza Quih Hant Ihíip Hac: Dictionary Seri–Spanish–English.* Mexico City: Universidad de Sonora, Hermosillo Plaza y Valdés.

MUELLER-DOMBOIS, DIETER, KENT W. BRIDGES, and CURT C. DAEHLER (eds), 2008. *Biodiversity Assessment of Tropical Island Ecosystems: PABITRA Manual for Interactive Ecology and Management.* Honolulu: B. P. Bishop Museum Press; available at: www. botany.hawaii.edu/pabitra/biodiversity/

MÜLLER, CORNELIA, 1998. *Redebegleitende Gesten. Kulturgeschichte—Theorie—Sprachvergleich.* Berlin: Berlin Verlag A. Spitz.

——2004. The palm-up-open-hand: a case of a gesture family? In Cornelia Müller and Roland Posner (eds), *The Semantics and Pragmatics of Everyday Gestures.* Berlin: Weidler, 233–56.

MULLER, JOCELYN and ASTIER M. ALMEDOM, 2008. What is 'famine food'? Distinguishing between traditional vegetables and special foods for times of hunger/scarcity (Boumba, Niger). *Human Ecology* 36: 599–607.

MUNN, NANCY, 1970. The transformation of subjects into objects in Walbiri and Pitjantatjara myth. In Ronald Berndt (ed.), *Australian Aboriginal Anthropology.* Nedlands: Australian Institute of Aboriginal Studies, University of Western Australia Press, 141–63.

MUNSELL, ALBERT H., 1905. *A Colour Notation.* Boston, Mass.: G. H. Ellis Co.

MURDOCK, GEORGE P., 1949. *Social Structure.* New York: Macmillan.

MURRAY, LAURA J., and KEREN RICE (eds), 1996. *Talking on the Page: Editing Aboriginal Oral Texts.* Toronto: University of Toronto Press.

MYERS, FRED R., 1991. *Pintupi Country, Pintupi Self: Sentiment, Place, and Politics among Western Desert Aborigines.* Berkeley: University of California Press.

MYERS, HELEN, 1992. *Ethnomusicology: An Introduction.* London: Macmillan.

NAGY, NAOMI, 2000. What I didn't know about working in an endangered language community: some fieldwork issues. *International Journal of the Sociology of Language* 144: 143–60.

NAKATA, MARTIN, and MARCIA LANGTON (eds), 2005. *Australian Indigenous Knowledge and Libraries.* Canberra: Australian Academic and Research Libraries.

NANBAKHSH, GOLNAZ, 2010. Persian pronouns of politeness. PhD dissertation, University of Edinburgh.

NATHAN, DAVID, 2004. Sound recording: microphones. *Language Archive Newsletter* 1.3: 6–9.

NATIONAL TAIWAN MUSEUM, 2006. Collection and observation of sea weeds; accessed 2 Sept. 2009 at: http://www.ntm.gov.tw/seaweeds/english/study/study1_01_3.asp

NEE, MICHAEL H., 2004. *Flora de la región del Parque Nacional Amboró, Bolivia*, vol. 2. Santa Cruz de la Sierra, Bolivia: Editorial FAN.

———2008. *Flora de la región del Parque Nacional Amboró, Bolivia*, vol. 3. Santa Cruz de la Sierra, Bolivia: Editorial FAN.

NEEDHAM, RODNEY, 1973. Prescription. *Oceania* 43.3: 166–81.

NETTL, BRUNO, 1983. *The Study of Ethnomusicology: Twenty-Nine Issues and Concepts*. Urbana: University of Illinois Press.

———2000. An ethnomusicologist contemplates universals in musical sound and musical culture. In Nils L. Wallin, Björn Merker, and Steven Brown (eds), *The Origins of Music*. Cambridge, Mass.: MIT Press, 463–72.

NETTLE, DANIEL, and SUZANNE ROMAINE, 2000. *Vanishing Voices: The Extinction of the World's Languages*. New York: Oxford University Press.

NEUMANN, RAGNHILD, 2004. The conventionalization of the ring gesture in German discourse. In Cornelia Müller and Roland Posner (eds), *The Semantics and Pragmatics of Everyday Gestures*. Berlin: Weidler, 217–24.

NEVINS, MARYBETH ELEANOR, 2004. Learning to listen: confronting two meanings of 'language loss' in the contemporary White Mountain speech community. *Journal of Linguistic Anthropology* 14.2: 269–88.

NEWMAN, PAUL, 1992. Fieldwork and field methods in linguistics. *California Linguistic Notes* 23.2: 1, 3–8. (Reprinted with a new introduction in *Language Documentation & Conservation* 3: 113-25 (2009).)

———2007. Copyright essentials for linguists. *Language Documentation & Conservation* 1. 1: 28–43; http://hdl.handle.net/10125/1724

———and MARTHA RATLIFF (eds), 2001. *Linguistic Fieldwork*. Cambridge: Cambridge University Press.

NGUYEN, MYLIEN L. T., 2003. Comparison of food plant knowledge between urban Vietnamese living in Vietnam and in Hawai'i. *Economic Botany* 57: 472–80.

———2006. Insertions and deletions: evolution in the assemblages of Vietnamese food plants. *Ethnobotany Research and Applications* 4: 175–201.

———JULIA WIETING, and KATHERINE T. DOHERTY, 2008. Vegetation analysis of urban ethnic markets shows supermarket generalists and Chinatown ethnic-specialist vendors. *Ethnobotany Research and Applications* 6: 63–85.

NICHOLS, G. S., and H. ST. JOHN, 1918. Pressing plants with double-faced corrugated paper boards. *Rhodora* 20: 153–60.

NICKUM, MARK, 2008. Ethnobotany and construction of a Tongan voyaging canoe: the Kalia mileniume. *Ethnobotany Research and Applications* 6: 129–253.

NOLAN, JUSTIN M., KATLIN E. JONES, KENNETH W. McDOUGAL, MATTHEW J. McFARLIN and MICHAEL K. WARD, 2006. The lovable, the loathsome, and the luminal: emotionality in ethnozoological cognition. *Journal of Ethnobiology* 26: 126–38.

NOONAN, MICHAEL, 2007. Complementation. In Shopen (2007: 2.52–150).

NUNEZ, RAPHAEL E., and EVE SWEETSER, 2006. With the future behind them: convergent evidence from Aymara language and gesture in the cross-linguistic comparison of spatial construals of time. *Cognitive Science* 30.3: 401–50.

O'KEEFFE, ISABEL, 2010. Kaddikkaddik ka-wokdjanganj 'Kaddikkaddik spoke': language and music of the Kun-barlang Kaddikkaddik songs from Western Arnhem Land. *Australian Journal of Linguistics* 30: 35–51.

O'MEARA, CAROLYN, and JUERGEN BOHNEMEYER, 2008. Complex landscape terms in Seri. *Language Sciences* 30: 2–3, 316–39.

OCHS, ELINOR, 1979. Transcription as theory. In Elinor Ochs and Bambi B. Schieffelin (eds), *Developmental Pragmatics*. New York: Academic Press, 43–72.

——1992. Indexing gender. In Alessandro Duranti and Charles Goodwin (eds), *Rethinking Context: Language as an Interactive Phenomenon*. Cambridge: Cambridge University Press, 335–58.

——and CAROLYN TAYLOR, 1995. The 'Father knows best' dynamic in dinnertime narratives. In Mary Bucholtz and Kira Hall (eds), *Gender Articulated: Language and the Socially Constructed Self*. London: Routledge, 99–122.

OFFORD, CATHERINE A., and PATRICIA F. MEAGHER (eds), 2009. *Plant Germplasm Conservation in Australia*. Canberra: Australian Network for Plant Conservation.

——and THOMAS G. NORTH, 2009. Living plant collections. In Offord and Meagher (2009: 149–61).

OKAMOTO, SHIGEKO, 1997. Social context, linguistic ideology, and indexical expressions in Japanese. *Journal of Pragmatics* 28.6: 795–817.

OLIVER, IAN, and ANDREW J. BEATTIE, 1993. A possible method for the rapid assessment of biodiversity. *Conservation Biology* 7: 562–8.

OSTLER, NICHOLAS (ed.), 2007. *Proceedings of FEL XI. Working Together for Endangered Languages: Research Challenges and Social Impacts*. Bath: Foundation for Endangered Languages.

OSTRAFF, MELINDA, 2006. Limu: edible seaweed in Tonga, an ethnobotanical study. *Journal of Ethnobiology* 26: 208–27.

OTSUKA, YUKO, and ANDREW WONG, 2007. Fostering the growth of budding community initiatives: the role of linguists in Tokelauan maintenance in Hawai'i. *Language Documentation and Conservation* 1.2: 240–56.

OTTENBERG, SIMON, 1990. Thirty years of fieldnotes: changing relationships to the text. In Roger Sanjek (ed.), *Fieldnotes: The Makings of Anthropology*. Ithaca, NY: Cornell University Press, 139–60.

ÖZYÜREK, ASLI, 2002. Do speakers design their co-speech gestures for their addressees? The effects of addressee location on representational gestures. *Journal of Memory and Language* 46.4: 688–704.

——et al., 2008. Development of cross-linguistic variation in speech and gesture: motion events in English and Turkish. *Developmental Psychology* 44.4: 1040–54.

PAPULU APPARR-KARI ABORIGINAL LANGUAGE AND CULTURE CENTRE, and BARWICK, LINDA, 2000. *Yawulyu Mungamunga: Dreaming Songs of Warumungu Women, Tennant Creek, Central Australia* [audio CD with scholarly booklet]. Sydney: Festival Records D139686.

PARDO-DE-SANTAYANA, MANUEL, et al., 2007. Traditional knowledge of wild edible plants used in the northwest of the Iberian Peninsula (Spain and Portugal): a comparative study. *Journal of Ethnobiology and Ethnomedicine* 3: 27.

PASCAL, BLAISE, 2008[1660]. *Pensées*, trans. William Finlayson Trotter. Charleston, SC: BiblioBazaar.

PATEL, ANIRUDDH D., 2006. Musical rhythm, linguistic rhythm and evolution. *Music Perception* 24.1: 99–104.

——JOHN R. IVERSEN, YANQING CHEN, and BRUNO H. REPP, 2005. The influence of metricality and modality on synchronization with a beat. *Experimental Brain Research* 163: 226–38.

PAWLEY, ANDREW, 1993. A language which defies description by ordinary means. In WILLIAM A. FOLEY (ed.), *The Role of Theory in Language Description*. Berlin: Mouton de Gruyter, 87-129.

PAYNE, THOMAS E., 1997. *Describing Morphosyntax: A Guide for Field Linguists*. Cambridge: Cambridge University Press.

——2006. *Exploring Language Structure: A Student's Guide*. Cambridge: Cambridge University Press.

PELTO, GRETEL, PERTTI J. PELTO, and ELLEN MESSER (eds), 1989. *Research Methods in Nutritional Anthropology*. New York: United Nations University Press.

PERETZ, ISABELLE, and ROBERT J. ZATORRE 2005. Brain organization for music processing. *Annual Review of Psychology* 56: 89–114.

PFEIFFER, JEANINE, and YEREMIAS URIL, 2003. The role of indigenous parataxonomists in botanical inventory: from Herbarium Amboinense to Herbarium Floresense. *Telopea* 10: 61–72.

PHILLIPS, OLIVER, and ALWIN GENTRY, 1993a. The useful plants of Tambopata, Peru, I: Statistical hypotheses tests with a new quantitative technique. *Economic Botany* 47: 15–32.

——1993b. The useful plants of Tambopata, Peru, II: Additional hypothesis testing in quantitative ethnobotany. *Economic Botany* 47: 33–43.

PIATTELLI-PALMARINI, MASSIMO, 1994. *Inevitable Illusions: How Mistakes of Reason Rule Our Minds*. New York: Wiley.

PICA, PIERRE, CATHY LEMER, VÉRONIQUE IZARD, and STANISLAS DEHAENE, 2004. Exact and approximate arithmetic in an Amazonian indigene group. *Science* 306.5695: 499–503.

PICKERING, MARTIN J., and VICTOR S. FERREIRA, 2008. Structural priming: a critical review. *Psychological Bulletin* 134.3: 427–59. doi: 10.1037/0033-2909.134.3.427

PIKE, KENNETH LEE, 1967. *Language in Relation to a Unified Theory of the Structure of Human Behaviour*, 2nd edn. The Hague: Mouton.

PINKER, STEVEN, 1997. *How the Mind Works*. New York: Norton.

PITT-RIVERS, JULIAN, 1973. The kith and the kin. In JACK R. GOODY (ed.), *The Character of Kinship*. Cambridge: Cambridge University Press, 89–105.

PLANK, FRANS (ed.), 1985. *Relational Typology*. Berlin: Mouton.

——(ed.), 1995. *Double Case: Agreement by Suffixaufnahme*. Oxford: Oxford University Press.

POGGI, ISABELLA, 1983. La mano a borsa: analisi semantica di un gesto emblematico holofrastico. In Grazia Attilli and Pio E. Ricci-Bitti (eds), *Communicare senza parole*. Rome: Bulzoni, 219–38.

POLLAN, MICHAEL, 2006. *The Omnivore's Dilemma: A Natural History of Four Meals*. New York: Penguin Press.

POLLOCK, NANCY J., 1984. Breadfruit fermentation. *Journal de la Societé des Océanistes* 40.79: 151–64.

——1986. Food classification in Fiji, Hawaii, Tahiti. *Ethnology* 25.2: 107–18.

——1992. *These Roots Remain*. Hawai'i: Institute of Polynesian Studies, and University of Hawai'i Press.

——1995. Introduction. In Igor De Garine and Nancy Pollock (eds), *Social Aspects of Obesity*. New York: Taylor & Francis, xiii–xxxiii.

——2007. Nutrition and anthropology: cooperation and convergences. *Ecology of Food and Nutrition* 46.3: 245.

——2009. Food and transnationalism. In Helen Lee and Steve Francis (eds), *Migration and Transnationalism*. Canberra: ANU E Press, 103–14.

——Debbie Dixon, and Jackie Ann Leota (eds), 1996. *Food Decisions in Wellington Low Income Households*. Report to Dept of Social Welfare, Wellington, NZ.

Porsdam, Helle (ed.), 2006. *Copyright and Other Fairy Tales: Hans Christian Andersen and the Commodification of Culture*. Cheltenham: Elgar.

Posey, Darrel A., and William L. Balée, 1989. *Resource Management in Amazonia: Indigenous and Folk Strategies*. New York: New York Botanical Garden Press.

Post, Jennifer, 2004. *Ethnomusicology: A Research and Information Guide*. New York: Routledge.

Press, J. Robert, Krishna K. Shrestha, and David A. Sutton, 2000–. *Annotated Checklist of the Flowering Plants of Nepal*. London: Natural History Museum; accessed 1 Oct. 2009 at: http://www.efloras.org/flora_page.aspx?flora_id=110

Pym, Noreen, and Bonnie Larrimore, 1979. *Papers on Iwaidja Phonology and Grammar*. Darwin: SIL-AAB, series A, vol. 2.

————n.d. Draft Iwaidja dictionary file. Electronic data file lodged at Aboriginal Studies Electronic Data Archive, Canberra.

Radford, Albert E., William C. Dickinson, Jimmy R. Massey, and C. Richie Bell, 1998. *Vascular Plant Systematics*. New York: Harper & Row. Accessed 1 Oct. 2009 at: http://www.ibiblio.org/botnet/glossary/

Rambaldi, Giacomo, and Jasmine Callosa-Tarr, 2002. *Participatory 3-dimensional Modelling: Guiding Principles and Applications*. Los Baños: ASEAN Regional Centre for Biodiversity Conservation.

Rampton, Ben, 2005. *Crossing: Language and Ethnicity Among Adolescents*, 2nd edn. Manchester: St Jerome Press.

Regier, Terry, Paul Kay, and Naveen Khetarpal, 2007. Colour naming reflects optimal partitions of colour space. *Proceedings of the National Academy of Sciences* 104.4: 1436–41.

Report of the Royal Commission on Aboriginal Peoples, 1996. Accessed 15 May 2009 at: http://www.ainc-inac.gc.ca/ch/rcap/index_e.html

Revolon, Sandra, 2007. The dead are looking at us: place and role of the *apira ni farunga* ('ceremonial bowls') in post-funeral wakes in Aorigi (Eastern Solomon islands). *Journal de la Société des Océanistes* 124.1: 59–67.

Reyes-García, Victoria, Neus Martí, Thomas McDade, Susan Tanner, and Vincent Vadez, 2007. Concepts and methods in studies measuring individual ethnobotanical knowledge. *Journal of Ethnobiology* 27: 182–203.

——Vincent Vadez, Tomás Huanca, William Leonard, and David Wilkie, 2005. Knowledge and consumption of wild plants: a comparative study in two Tsimane villages in the Bolivian Amazon. *Ethnobotany Research and Applications* 3: 201–7.

Rice, Keren, 2001. Learning as one goes. In Newman and Ratliff (2001: 230–49).

——2006. Ethical issues in linguistic fieldwork: an overview. *Journal of Academic Ethics* 4: 123–55.

——2009. Must there be two solitudes? Language activists and linguists working together. In John Reyhner and Louise Lockard (eds), *Indigenous Language Revitalization: Encouragement, Guidance, and Lessons Learned*. Flagstaff: Northern Arizona University, 37–60.

RICHES, DAVID, 1978. On the presentation of the Tiv segmentary lineage system, or, speculations on Tiv social organisation. *Queen's University Papers in Social Anthropology* 3: 55–81.

RICKARD, RICHARD P., and PAUL A. COX, 1984. Custom umbrellas (Poro) from *Pandanus* in Solomon Islands. *Economic Botany* 38: 314–21.

RICKFORD, JOHN R., 1997. Unequal partnership: sociolinguistics and the African-American speech community. *Language in Society* 26.2: 161–97.

——and FAYE MCNAIR-KNOX, 1994. Addressee and topic-influence style shift: a quantitative sociolinguistics study. In Douglas Biber and Edward Finegan (eds), *Sociolinguistic Perspectives on Register*. New York: Oxford University Press, 235–76.

——and RUSSELL J. RICKFORD, 2000. *Spoken Soul: The Story of Black English*. Oxford: Wiley.

RIESCHILD, VERNA ROBERTSON, 2003. Origami in a hurricane: current challenges to linguistic research. *Australian Journal of Linguistics* 23.1: 71–98.

RILEY, KATHLEEN, 2007. To tangle or not to tangle: shifting language ideologies and the socialization of Charabia in the Marquesas, F.P. In Miki Makihara and Bambi B. Schieffelin (eds), *Consequences of Contact: Language Ideologies and Sociocultural Transformations in Pacific Societies*. Oxford: Oxford University Press, 70–95.

RIVERS, WILLIAM H. R., 1910. The genealogical method of anthropological inquiry. *Sociological Review* 3: 1–12.

RIVIERRE, JEAN CLAUDE, 1992. Text collection. In Luc Bouquiaux and Jacqueline Thomas (eds), *Studying and Describing Unwritten Languages*. Dallas, Tex.: SIL, 56–63.

ROGERS, ANNE, and CARINA RUBIN, 2002. *Cosmic Africa* [film]. Druyan Ann: Cosmos Studios.

ROSSI-WILCOX, SUSAN M., n.d. *Chinese–English Glossary of Botanical Terms*. Accessed 2 Oct. 2009 at: http://flora.huh.harvard.edu/Glossary/index.html

ROYAL ANTHROPOLOGICAL INSTITUTE OF GREAT BRITAIN AND IRELAND, 1951. *Notes and Queries on Anthropology*, 6th edn. London: Routledge & Kegan Paul.

RUDDER, JOHN, n.d. Introduction to website *Ethnomathematics in Australia*. Canberra: Australian Institute of Aboriginal and Torres Strait Islander Studies: http://www1.aiatsis.gov.au/exhibitions/ethnomathmatics/ethno_intro.htm

RUGGLES, CLIVE L. N., 1993. The study of cultural astronomy. In Clive L. N. Ruggles and Nicholas Saunders (eds), *Astronomies and Cultures*. Niwot: University Press of Colorado, 1–31.

RUSSELL-SMITH, JEREMY, 1985. Studies in the jungle: people, fire and monsoon forest. In Rhys Jones (ed.), *Archaeological Research in Kakadu National Park*. Canberra: ANPWS, 241–67.

SABERWAL, SATISH, 1969. Rapport and resistance among the Embu of Central Kenya (1963–1964). In Frances Henry and Satish Saberwal (eds), *Stress and Response in Fieldwork*. New York: Holt, Rinehart, & Winston, 47–62.

SACKS, HARVEY, EMANUAL A. SCHEGLOFF, and GAIL JEFFERSON, 1974. A simplest systematics for the organization of turn-taking for conversation. *Language* 50: 696–735.

SAEMANE, GEORGE, 1999. *Vegetation Classification and Plant Resource Utilization and Management: A Discussion of the Traditional Knowledge of the People of Savo Island, Solomon Islands*. Washington, DC: Terralingua.

SAHAGÚN, FRAY BERNADINO DE, 1970. *Florentine Codex: General History of the Things of New Spain*. Translated from the Aztec into English by Arthur J. O. Anderson and Charles E. Dibble. Salt Lake City: University of Utah Press.

SALICK, JAN, et al., 2003. *Intellectual Imperatives in Ethnobiology: NSF Biocomplexity Workshop Report*. St. Louis: Missouri Botanical Gardens.

——et al., 2007. Tibetan sacred sites conserve old growth trees in the Eastern Himalayas. *Biodiversity and Conservation* 16.3: 693–706.

SALZMANN, ZDENEK, 1950. A method for analyzing numerical systems. *Word* 6.1: 78–83.

SAMARIN, WILLIAM J., 1967. *Field Linguistics: A Guide to Linguistic Field Work*. New York: Holt, Rinehart, & Winston.

SANJEK, ROGER, 1990. The secret life of fieldnotes. In ROGER SANJEK (ed.), *Fieldnotes: The Makings of Anthropology*. Ithaca, NY: Cornell University Press, 187–271.

SANKOFF, GILLIAN, 2004. Adolescents, young adults and the critical period: two case studies from 'Seven Up'. In CARMEN FOUGHT (ed.), *Sociolinguistic Variation: Critical Reflections*. Oxford: Oxford University Press, 121–39.

——and HÉLÈNE BLONDEAU, 2007. Language change across the lifespan: /r/ in Montreal French. *Language* 83.3: 560–88.

SAPIR, EDWARD, 1921. *Language: An Introduction to the Study of Speech*. New York: Harcourt, Brace.

SASSE, HANS-JÜRGEN, 1988. Der irokesische Sprachtyp. *Zeitschrift für Sprachwissenschaft* 7.2: 173–213.

SAUSSURE, F. DE, 1966[1916]. *Course in General Linguistics*, ed. Charles Bally, Albert Sechehaye, and Albert Riedlinger; trans. Wade Baskin. New York: McGraw-Hill.

SAVILLE-TROIKE, MURIEL, 2003. *The Ethnography of Communication: An Introduction*, 3rd edn. Oxford: Blackwell.

SCHACHNER, ADENA, TIMOTHY F. BRADY, IRENE PEPPERBERG, and MARC D. HAUSER, 2009. Spontaneous motor entrainment to music in multiple vocal mimicking species. *Current Biology* 19.10: 831–6.

SCHEGLOFF, EMANUEL A., 1980. Preliminaries to preliminaries: can I ask you a question? *Sociological Inquiry* 50.3–4: 104–52.

——1984. On some gestures' relation to talk. In J. MAXWELL ATKINSON and JOHN HERITAGE (eds), *Structures of Social Action*. Cambridge: Cambridge University Press, 266–96.

——2007. *Sequence Organization in Interaction: A Primer in Conversation Analysis*, vol. 1. Cambridge: Cambridge University Press.

SCHIEFFELIN, BAMBI, 1990. *The Give and Take of Everyday Life: Language Socialization of Kaluli Children*. New York: Cambridge University Press.

——and ELINOR OCHS (eds), 1986. *Language Socialization Across Cultures*. Cambridge: Cambridge University Press.

SCHILLING-ESTES, NATALIE, 2007. Sociolinguistic fieldwork. In Robert Bayley and Ceil Lucas (eds), *Sociolinguistic Variation: Theories, Methods, and Applications*. Cambridge: Cambridge University Press, 165–89.

SCHLANGER, NATHAN, 1991. Le fait technique total: la raison pratique et les raisons de la pratique dans l'œuvre de Marcel Mauss. *Terrain* 16: 114–30.

——2006. Introduction. Technological commitments: Marcel Mauss and the study of techniques in the French social sciences. In MARCEL MAUSS and NATHAN SCHLANGER (eds), *Techniques, Technology and Civilisation.* Oxford: Berghahn, 1–29.

SCHLEEF, ERIK, and MIRIAM MEYERHOFF, 2010. Sociolinguistic methods for data collection and interpretation. In Miriam Meyerhoff and Erik Schleef (eds), *The Routledge Sociolinguistics Reader.* London: Routledge, 1–26.

SCHLEGEL, JENNIFER, 1998. Finding words, finding meanings: collaborative learning and distributed cognition. In Susan Hoyle and Carolyn Temple Adger (eds), *Kids Talk: Strategic Language Use in Later Childhood.* New York: Oxford University Press, 187–204.

SCHMIDL, MARIANNE, 1915. Zahl und Zählen in Afrika. *Mitteilungen der Anthropologischen Gesellschaft in Wien* 35: 165–209.

SCHMIDT, LARS, 2000. *Guide to Handling of Tropical and Subtropical Forest Seed.* Humlebaek: Danida Forest Seed Centre.

SCHMIDT, PETER, 1996. Reconfiguring the Barongo: reproductive symbolism and reproduction among a work association of iron smelters. In Peter R. Schmidt (ed.), *The Culture and Technology of African Iron Production.* Gainesville: University Press of Florida, 74–127.

SCHNEIDER, CYNTHIA, 2011. Why field linguists should pay more attention to research in second language acquisition and teaching. *Australian Journal of Linguistics* 31.2.

SCHROETER, RONALD, and NICHOLAS THIEBERGER, 2006. EOPAS, the EthnoER online representation of interlinear text. In Linda Barwick and Nicholas Thieberger (eds), *Sustainable Data from Digital Fieldwork: Proceedings of the Conference Held at the University of Sydney, 4–6 December 2006.* Sydney: Sydney University Press, 99–124.

SCHUBERT, TIMOTHY S., LISA L. BREMAN, and SARAH E. WALKER, 1999. Basic concepts of plant disease and how to collect a sample for disease diagnosis. *Plant Pathology Circular* 307: 1–8; accessed 2 Sept. 2009 at: http://www.doacs.state.fl.us/pi/enpp/pathology/pathcirc/pp307.pdf

SCHUITEMAN, ANDRÉ, and EDUARD F. DE. VOGEL, 2001. *Orchids of New Guinea,* vol. I: *Illustrated Checklist and Genera.* Leiden: National Herbarium of the Netherlands.

————2002. *Flora Malesiana: Orchids of New Guinea,* vol. II: *Dendrobium and Allied Genera.* Leiden: National Herbarium of the Netherlands.

————2005. *Flora Malesiana: Orchids of New Guinea,* vol. III: *Genera* Acanthephippium *to* Hymenorchis *(excluding* Dendrobiinae *s. l.).* Leiden: National Herbarium of the Netherlands.

————2006. *Flora Malesiana: Orchids of New Guinea,* vol. IV: *Genera* Kuhlhasseltia *to* Ophioglossella. Leiden: National Herbarium of the Netherlands.

————2008. *Flora Malesiana: Orchids of New Guinea,* vol. V: *Genera* Pachystoma *to* Zeuxine *(excluding* Dendrobiinae *s. l.).* Leiden: National Herbarium of the Netherlands.

——JAAP J. VERMEULEN, and EDUARD F DE. VOGEL, 2008. *Flora Malesiana: Orchids of New Guinea,* vol. VI: Bulbophyllum *and allied genera.* Leiden: National Herbarium of the Netherlands.

SCHULTZE-BERNDT, EVA, 2006. Linguistic annotation. In Gippert et al. (2006: 213–51).

SCHWEITZER, PETER P. (ed.), 2000. *Dividends of Kinship.* London: Routledge.

SEEGER, ANTHONY, 1992. Ethnomusicology and music law. *Ethnomusicology* 36.3: 345–60.

——2001. Intellectual property and audio visual archives and collections. In *Folk Heritage Collections in Crisis*. Washington, DC: Council on Library and Information Resources, 36–47.

——2005. New technology requires new collaborations: changing ourselves to better shape the future. *Musicology Australia* 27 (2004–5): 94–111.

SEGALL, MARSHALL H., DONALD THOMAS CAMPBELL, and MELVILLE J. HERSKOVITS, 1966. *The Influence of Culture on Visual Perception*. Indianapolis: Bobbs-Merrill.

SEIFART, FRANK, 2006. Orthography development. In Gippert et al. (2006: 275–99).

——2008. On the representativeness of language documentations. In Austin (2003–10: 5.60–76).

SEN, AMARTYA, 1999. *Development as Freedom*. London: Oxford University Press.

SENFT, GUNTER, 1986. *Kilivila: The Language of the Trobriand Islanders*. Berlin: Mouton de Gruyter.

——2000. *Systems of Nominal Classification*. Cambridge: Cambridge University Press.

——2008. Landscape terms and place names in the Trobriand Islands: the Kaile'una subset. In Niclas Burenhult (ed.), *Language and Landscape: A Cross-Linguistic Perspective*, special issue of *Language Sciences* 30.2–3: 340–61.

——2009. Fieldwork. In Gunter Senft, Jan-Ola Östman, and Jef Verschueren (eds), *Culture and Language Use*. Amsterdam: Benjamins, 131–9.

SERZISKO, FRITZ, 1983. Über Verwandtschaftsbezeichnung in Somali. In Rainer Voßen and Ulrike Claudi (eds), *Sprache, Geschichte und Kultur in Afrika: Vorträge, gehalten auf dem III Afrikanistentag, Köln, 14/15 Oktober 1982*. Hamburg: Buske, 125–44.

SEYFEDDINIPUR, MANDANA, 2004. Meta-discursive gestures from Iran: some uses of the 'pistolhand'. In Cornelia Müller and Roland Posner (eds), *The Semantics and Pragmatics of Everyday Gestures*. Berlin: Weidler, 205–16.

——2006. *Disfluency: Interrupting Speech and Gesture*. Nijmegen: Max Planck Institute, Dept of Linguistics.

SHACK, DOROTHY N., 1997. Nutritional processes and personality development among the Gurage of Ethiopia. In Counihan and Van Esterik (1997: 117–24).

SHACK, WILLIAM, 1966. *The Gurage, a People of the Ensete Culture*. London: Oxford University Press.

SHAW, PATRICIA, 2004. Negotiating against loss: responsibility, reciprocity, and respect in endangered language research. In Osamu Sakiyama, Fubito Endo, Honoré Watanabe, and Fumiko Sasama (eds), *Lectures on Endangered Languages 4: From Kyoto Conference 2001*. Kyoto: Endangered Languages of the Pacific Rim, 181–94.

SHEPARD, J. GLENN, DOUGLAS W. YU, and BRUCE W. NELSON, 2004. Ethnobotanical ground-truthing and forest diversity in the western Amazon. In Thomas J. S. Carlson, and Luisa Maffi (eds), *Ethnobotany and Conservation of Biocultural Diversity*. New York: New York Botanical Garden Press, 133–74.

SHERZER, JOEL, 1991. The Brazilian thumbs-up gesture. *Journal of Linguistic Anthropology* 1.2: 189–97.

——1993. Pointed lips, thumbs up, and cheek puffs: some emblematic gestures in social interactional and ethnographic context. In Robin Queen and Rusty Barret (eds), *SALSA I: Austin Proceedings of the First Annual Symposium about Language and Society*. Austin: University of Texas, Dept of Linguistics, 197–212.

SHOPEN, TIMOTHY (ed.), 2007. *Language Typology and Syntactic Description*, vols 1–3. Cambridge: Cambridge University Press.

SIEWIERSKA, ANNA, 2008. Passive constructions. In Haspelmath et al. (2008). Accessed 12 February 2010 at: http://wals.info/feature/107

SIL (SUMMER INSTITUTE OF LINGUISTICS), 2009. Pictures for language learning: Guatemala artwork. Web document; accessed 17 Mar. 2009 at: http://www.sil.org/lglearning/artwork/index.htm

SILLAR, BILL, 1996. The dead and the drying: techniques for transforming people and things in the Andes. *Journal of Material Culture* 1: 259–89.

SILLITOE, PAUL, 1998. An ethnobotanical account of the vegetation communities of the Wola region, Southern Highlands Province, Papua New Guinea. *Journal of Ethnobiology* 18: 103–28.

——2007. Local science vs. global science: an overview. In Paul Sillitoe (ed.), *Local Science vs. Global Science: Approaches to Indigenous Knowledge in International Development. Journal of the Royal Anthropological Institute* Special Issue no. 1. Oxford: Berghahn, 1–22.

SIMPSON, JANE, 2001. Hypocoristics of place-names in Australian English. In Peter Collins and David Blair (eds), *Varieties of English: Australian English*. Amsterdam: Benjamins, 89–112.

SINGER, RUTH, 2007. Agreement in Mawng. Doctoral dissertation, University of Melbourne; available at: http://eprints.infodiv.unimelb.edu.au/archive/00003242/

SIO, BRENDA, 1995. *Food Pyramid: Samoa*. Noumea: South Pacific Commission.

SKLAR, DEIDRE, 2000. Reprise: on dance ethnography. *Dance Research Journal* 32.1: 70–77.

SLAMA-CAZACU, TATJANA, 1976. Nonverbal components in message sequence: 'mixed syntax'. In William C. McCormack and Stephen A. Wurm (eds), *Language and Man: Anthropological Issues*. The Hague: Mouton, 217–27.

SLOBIN, DAN I., 1996. From 'thought and language' to 'thinking for speaking'. In John J. Gumperz and Stephen C. Levinson (eds), *Rethinking Linguistic Relativity*. Cambridge: Cambridge University Press, 70–96.

SMIL, VADISLAV, 2002. Eating meat: evolution, patterns, and consequences. *Population and Development Review* 28: 599–639.

——2005. Feeding the world: how much more rice do we need? In K. Toriyama K. L. Heong, and B. Hardy (eds), *Rice is Life: Scientific Perspectives for the 21st Century*. Los Baños: International Rice Research Institute, 21–3.

SMITH, GRAHAM HINGANGAROA, 2000. Protecting and respecting Indigenous knowledge. In MARIE BATTISTE (ed.), *Reclaiming Indigenous Voice and Vision*. Vancouver: University of British Columbia Press, 209–24.

SMITH, J. JEROME, 1993. Using ANTHRPAC 3.5 and a spreadsheet to compute a free-list salience index. *Cultural Anthropology Methods Newsletter* 5: 1–3.

SMITH, LINDA TUHIWAI, 1999. *Decolonizing Methodologies: Research and Indigenous Peoples*. London: Zed Books.

SOBAL, JEFFREY, 1991. Obesity and socio-economic status. *Medical Anthropology* 13: 231–47.

——1999. Food system globalization, eating transformations and nutrition transitions. In RAYMOND GREW (ed.), *Food in Global History*. Boulder, Colo.: Westview Press, 171–93.

SOCIAL SCIENCES AND HUMANITIES RESEARCH ETHICS SPECIAL WORKING COMMITTEE, 2004. *Giving Voice to the Spectrum: Report to the Interagency Panel on Research Ethics*. Ottawa.

SODERSTROM, THOMAS R., and STEPHEN M. YOUNG, 1983. A guide to collecting bamboos. *Annals of the Missouri Botanical Garden* 70: 128–36.

SONG, JAE JUNG, 2001. *Linguistic Typology: Morphology and Syntax*. Harlow: Pearson Education.

SOUZA, SHIRLEY P., and ALPINIA BEGOSSI, 2007. Whales, dolphins or fishes? The ethnotaxonomy of cetaceans in São Sebastião, Brazil. *Journal of Ethnobiology and Ethnomedicine* 3: 9.

SPARHAWK, CAROL M., 1981. Contrastive-identificational features of Persian gesture. In Adam Kendon (ed.), *Nonverbal Communication, Interaction, and Gesture*. The Hague: Mouton, 421–58.

SPEAS, MARGARET, 2009. Someone else's language: on the role of linguists in language revitalization. In John Reyhner and Louise Lockhard (eds), *Indigenous Language Revitalization: Encouragement, Guidance, and Lessons Learned*. Flagstaff: Northern Arizona University, 23–36.

SPENCER, ANDREW, and ARNOLD M. ZWICKY, 2001. *The Handbook of Morphology*. Oxford: Blackwell.

SPERBER, DAN, and LAWRENCE HIRSCHFIELD, 1999. Culture, cognition and evolution. In Robert A. Wilson and Frank C. Keil (eds), *The MIT Encyclopedia of Cognitive Sciences*. Cambridge, Mass.: MIT Press, cxi–cxxxii.

STANNARD, BRIAN L., 1995. *Flora of the Pico das Almas, Chapada Diamantina: Bahia, Brazil*. Kew: Royal Botanic Gardens.

STEELE, ORLO C., 2006. Natural and anthropogenic biogeography of mangroves in the Southwest Pacific. PhD dissertation, University of Hawai'i at Manoa.

STEENIS, CORNELIS G. G. J. van, 1949–. *Flora Malesiana* series 1, vol. 4. Leyden: Noordhoff, continuing series, plus series 2 (ferns), by various authors.

STEINHOFF, PATRICIA G., THEODORE C. BESTOR, and VICTORIA LYON-BESTOR, 2003. *Doing Fieldwork in Japan*. Honolulu: University of Hawai'i Press.

STEPP, JOHN R., et al., 2004. Development of a GIS for global biocultural diversity. *Policy Matters* 13: 267–70.

STEVENS, FRANK L., 1926. Corrugated aluminium sheets for the botanists press. *Botanical Gazette* 82: 104–6.

STEVENS, KENNETH N., 1998. *Acoustic Phonetics*. Cambridge, Mass.: MIT Press.

STEVENS, PETER S., 1981. *Handbook of Regular Patterns: An Introduction to Symmetry in Two Dimensions*. Cambridge, Mass.: MIT Press.

STEWART, IAN, 1997. Cat's cradles, calculus challenge. *Scientific American* (June): 90–92.

STIGLITZ, JOSEPH, 2006. *Making Globalisation Work*. New York: Norton.

STOKOE, WILLIAM C., 1960. *Sign Language Structure*. Buffalo: State University of New York at Buffalo.

——1987. Sign languages and the monastic use of lexical gestures. In Umiker-Sebeok and Sebeok (1987: 325–38).

STONE, BENJAMIN C., 1983. A guide to collecting Pandanaceae (*Pandanus, Freycinetia*, and *Sararanga*). *Annals of the Missouri Botanical Garden* 70: 137–45.

STONE, LINDA (ed.), 2001. *New Directions in Anthropological Kinship*. Lanham, Md.: Rowman & Littlefield.

STORY, ALAN, 2009. *An Alternative Primer on National and International Copyright Law in the Global South: Eighteen Questions and Answers*. Canterbury: CopySouth Research Group; available at: http://copysouth.org/portal/copyright-primer

——COLIN DARCH, and DEBORAH HALBERT (eds), 2006. *The Copy/South Dossier*. Canterbury: Copy/South Research Group.

STRATHERN, MARILYN, 1988. *The Gender of the Gift: Problems with Women and Problems with Society in Melanesia*. Berkeley: University of California Press.

——2004. *Commons and Borderlands: Working Papers on Interdisciplinarity, Accountability and the Flow of Knowledge*. Oxford: Sean Kingston.

STREECK, JÜRGEN, 1993. Gesture as communication I: Its coordination with gaze and speech. *Communication Monographs* 60.4: 275–99.

——1994. Gesture as communication II: The audience as co-author. *Research on Language and Social Interaction* 27.3: 239–67.

——2009a. Forward-gesturing. *Discourse Processes* 46.2–3: 161–79.

——2009b. *Gesturecraft: The Manufacture of Meaning*. Amsterdam: Benjamins.

STRONG, WILLIAM S., 1999. *The Copyright Book: A Practical Guide*, 5th edn. Cambridge, Mass.: MIT Press.

STRYCHARZ, ANNA, 2011. Indexing social meaning through the (non) use of honorifics. In Chie Adachi, Agata Daleszynska, and Anna Strycharz (eds), *Proceedings of the Summer School of Sociolinguistics 2010*. Edinburgh: University of Edinburgh.

——forthcoming. Social factors in the obsolescence of local honorifics: the case of Osaka Japanese. *Journal of Sociolinguistics*.

SUNDBERG, JOHAN, 1987. *The Science of the Singing Voice*. DeKalb: Northern Illinois University Press.

SUTTON, PETER, and MICHAEL WALSH, 1979. *Revised Linguistic Fieldwork Manual for Australia*. Canberra: Australian Institute of Aboriginal Studies.

TAGLIAMONTE, SALLY, 2006. *Analysing Sociolinguistic Variation*. Cambridge: Cambridge University Press.

TAI, 2003–. Flora of Taiwan, database version; accessed 1 Oct. 2009 at: http://tai2.ntu.edu.tw/fotdv/fotmain.htm

TAMISARI, FRANCA, 2002. Names and naming: speaking forms into place. In Luise Hercus, Flavia Hodges, and Jane Simpson (eds), 2002. *The Land is a Map: Placenames of Indigenous Origin in Australia*. Canberra: Pacific Linguistics and Pandanus Press, 87–102.

TANNEN, DEBORAH, 1984. *Conversational Style: Analyzing Talk among Friends*. Oxford: Oxford University Press.

TAYLOR, ALLAN R., 1978. Nonverbal communication in aboriginal North America: the Plains Sign Language. In Jean Umiker-Sebeok and Thomas A. Sebeok (eds), *Aboriginal Sign Languages of the Americas and Australia*, vol. 2. New York: Plenum Press, 223–44.

Taylor, Mary S., 1990. Field techniques used by Missouri Botanical Garden: recommended reading; accessed 2 Sept. 2009 at: http://www.mobot.org/mobot/molib/fieldtechbook/reading.shtml

TEO, AMOS, 2007. Breaking up is hard to do: teasing apart morphological complexity in Iwaidja and Maung. Honours thesis, University of Melbourne; available at: http://eprints.infodiv.unimelb.edu.au/archive/00003816/

TERSIS, NICOLE, 1992. The noun and the noun phrase. In Luc Bouquiaux and Jacqueline Thomas (eds), *Studying and Describing Unwritten Languages*. Dallas, Tex.: SIL, 275–301.

THIEBERGER, NICHOLAS, 2004. Documentation in practice: developing a linked media corpus of South Efate. In Austin (2003–10: 2.169–78). (http://repository.unimelb.edu.au/10187/2199)

——2006. *A Grammar of South Efate: An Oceanic Language of Vanuatu*. Honolulu: University of Hawai'i Press.

——2009. Steps toward a grammar embedded in data. In Patricia Epps and Alexandre Arkhipov (eds), *New Challenges in Typology: Transcending the Borders and Refining the Distinctions.* Berlin: Mouton de Gruyter, 389–408; available at: http://repository.unimelb.edu.au/10187/4864

——and Simon Musgrave, 2006. Documentary linguistics and ethical issues. In Austin (2003–10: 4. 26–36).

THIELE, KEVIN R., and LAWRENCE G. ADAMS, 2002. *The Families of Flowering Plants of Australia: An Interactive Identification Guide.* Melbourne: CSIRO.

THIERS, BARBARA, 1997–. *Index Herbariorum: A Global Directory of Public Herbaria and Associated Staff;* available at: http://sciweb.nybg.org/science2/IndexHerbariorum.asp

THOMAS, EVERT, et al., 2007. What works in the field? A comparison of different interviewing methods in ethnobotany with special reference to the use of photographs. *Economic Botany* 61: 376–84.

THOMAS, JULIAN, 1998. The socio-semiotics of material culture. *Journal of Material Culture* 3.1: 97–108.

TICKTIN, TAMARA, NAMAKA WHITEHEAD, and HOALA FRAIOLA, 2006. Traditional gathering of native hula plants in alien-invaded Hawaiian forests: adaptive practices, impacts on alien invasive species, and conservation implications. *Environmental Conservation* 33.3: 185–94.

TILLEY, CHRISTOPHER, WEBB KEANE, SUZANNE KÜCHLER, MICHAEL ROWLANDS, and PATRICIA SPYER (eds), 2006. *Handbook of Material Culture.* London: Sage.

TONKINSON, ROBERT, 1991[1978]. *The Mardu Aborigines: Living the Dream in Australia's Desert.* New York: Holt, Rinehart & Winston.

TOPP FARGION, JANET (ed.), 2001. *A Manual for Documentation, Fieldwork and Preservation for Ethnomusicologists,* 2nd edn. Bloomington, Ind.: Society for Ethnomusicology.

TORRE-CUADROS, MARIA DE LOS ANGELES LA, and NORBERT ROSS, 2003. Secondary-biodiversity: local perceptions of forest habitats among the Maya of Solferino, Quintana Roo, México. *Journal of Ethnobiology* 23: 287–308.

TREHUB, SANDRA E., 2003. Musical predispositions in infancy: an update. In Isabelle Peretz and Robert J. Zatorre (eds), *The Cognitive Neuroscience of Music.* Oxford: Oxford University Press, 3–20.

TRUDGILL, PETER, 2000. *Sociolinguistics: An Introduction to Language and Society.* London: Penguin.

TSUNODA, TASAKU, 2005. *Language Endangerment and Language Revitalization.* Berlin: Mouton de Gruyter.

TURK, ANDREW G., 2007. A phenomenology basis for trans-disciplinary research in ethnophysiography. In *Proceedings of the 26th International Human Science Research Conference.* Trento: University of Trento [CD-ROM].

——and DAVID M. MARK, 2008. *Illustrated Dictionary of Yindjibarndi Landscape Terms.* (Informal publication) Perth, WA: Murdoch University.

————2011. Perspectives on the ethical conduct of landscape in language research. In David M. Mark, Andrew G. Turk, Niclas Burenhult and David Stea (eds) *Landscape in Language: Transdisciplinary perspectives.* Benjamins, 411–34.

TURNER, NANCY J., 2009. 'It's so different today': climate change and indigenous lifeways in British Columbia, Canada. *Global Environmental Change* 19: 180–90.

TURPIN, MYFANY, 2005. Form and meaning of Akwelye: a Kaytetye women's song series from Central Australia. PhD thesis, University of Sydney.

——2007a. Artfully hidden: text and rhythm in a Central Australian Aboriginal song series. *Musicology Australia* 29: 93–108.

——2007b. The poetics of Central Australian song. In Allan Marett and Linda Barwick (eds), *Studies in Aboriginal Song: A Special Issue of Australian Aboriginal Studies*. Canberra: Aboriginal Studies Press, 100–115.

——and Tonya Stebbins, 2010. The language of song: some recent approaches in description and analysis. *Australian Journal of Linguistics* 30.1: 1–17.

Turton, David, and Clive Ruggles, 1978. Agreeing to disagree: the measurement of duration in a southwestern Ethiopian community. *Current Anthropology* 19.3: 585–600.

Tutin, Thomas, Vernon Heywood, Alan Burges, and David Valentine, 1964. *Flora Europaea*, vol. 1. Cambridge: Cambridge University Press.

——————1968. *Flora Europaea*, vol. 2: *Rosaceae to Umbelliferae*. Cambridge: Cambridge University Press.

——————1972. *Flora Europaea*, vol. 3: *Diapensiaceae to Myoporaceae*. Cambridge: Cambridge University Press.

——————1976. *Flora Europaea*, vol. 4: *Plantaginaceae to Compositae (and Rubiaceae)*. Cambridge: Cambridge University Press.

——————1980. *Flora Europaea*, vol. 5: *Alismataceae to Orchidaceae*. Cambridge: Cambridge University Press.

Tuzin, Donald, 2002. Art, ritual and the crafting of illusion. *Asia Pacific Journal of Anthropology* 3.1: 1–23.

Ulloa, Maria del Carmen U., and Per M. Jørgensen, 2004–. *Arboles y arbustos de los Andes del Eucador*; accessed 20 Sept. 2009 at: http://www.efloras.org/flora_page.aspx? flora_id=201

Umiker-Sebeok, Jean, and Thomas A. Sebeok (eds), 1987. *Monastic Sign Languages*. Berlin: Mouton de Gruyter.

UNESCO, 2003. *Convention for the Safeguarding of the Intangible Cultural Heritage*; available at: http://www.unesco.org/culture/ich/index.php?pg=00006

United Nations, 2000. United Nations Millennium Development Goals. Accessed 13 April 2011 at: http://www.un.org/millenniumgoals/

Urry, James, 1972. Notes and queries on anthropology and the development of field methods in British anthropology, 1870–1920. *Proceedings of the Royal Anthropological Institute for 1972*: 45–57.

Vaidhyanathan, Siva, 2001. *Copyrights and Copywrongs: The Rise of Intellectual Property and How It Threatens Creativity*. New York: New York University Press.

Valiquette, Hilaire Paul, 1998. Community, professionals, and language preservation: first things first. In Nicholas Ostler (ed.), *Endangered Languages: What Role for the Specialist?* Bath: Foundation for Endangered Languages, 107–12.

Van der Merwe, Phillip, and P. J. Grobler, 1969. Electric drying press for herbarium specimens. *Plant Life* 25: 132–5.

Vandendriessche, Éric, 2007. Les Jeux de ficelle: une activité mathématique dans certaines sociétés traditionnelles. *Revue d'histoire des mathématiques* 13.1: 7–84.

Varela, Francisco, Eleanor Rosh, and Evan Thompson, 1993. *L'Inscription corporelle de l'esprit, sciences cognitives et expérience humaine*. Paris: Le Seuil.

Vaux, Bert, and Justin Cooper, 1999. *Introduction to Linguistic Field Methods*. Munich: Lincom Europa.

——————and Emily Tucker, 2007. *Linguistic Field Methods*. Eugene, Ore.: Wipf & Stock.

Vérin, Pierre, and Narivelo Rajaonarimanana, 1991. Divination in Madagascar, the antemoro case and the diffusion of divination. In Philip Peek (ed.), *African Divination Systems*. Bloomington: Indiana University Press, 53–68.

Verpoorte, Rob, 2009. Voucher specimens. *Journal of Ethnopharmacology Newsletter* 6.

Victor, Janine, Marinda Koekemoer, Lyn Fish, Shirley Smithies, and Marthina Mössmer, 2004. *Herbarium Essentials: The Southern African Herbarium User Manual*. Pretoria: South African Botanical Diversity Network.

Virolle-Souibès, Marie, 1989. Pétrir la pâte, malaxer du sens: exemples kabyles. *Techniques et culture* 13: 73–101.

Voegelin, Charles F., and Florence M. Voegelin, 1957. *Hopi Domains: A Lexical Approach to the Problem of Selection*. Baltimore: Waverly Press.

Vogl-Lukasser, Brigitte, and Christian R. Vogl, 2004. Ethnobotanical research in homegardens of small farmers in the alpine region of Osttirol (Austria): an example for bridges built and building bridges. *Ethnobotany Research and Applications* 2: 111–37.

von Brandenstein, Carl G., 1970. *Narratives from the North-West of Western Australia in the Ngarluma and Jindjiparndi Languages*. Canberra: AIAS.

——1992. *Wordlist from Narratives from the North-West of Western Australia in the Ngarluma and Jindjiparndi Languages*. Canberra: AIATSIS, ASEDA.

Wagner, Roy, 1987. Figure–ground reversal among the Barok. In Louise Lincoln (ed.), *Assemblage of Spirits: Idea and Image in New-Ireland*. New York: Braziller, 56–62.

Walsh, Michael, 1991. Conversational styles and inter-cultural communication: an example from Northern Australia. *Australian Journal of Communication* 18.1: 1–12.

——1997. *Cross Cultural Communication Problems in Aboriginal Australia*. Darwin, NT: North Australia Research Unit.

——2007. Australian Aboriginal song language: so many questions, so little to work with. *Australian Aboriginal Studies* 2: 128–44.

——2010. A polytropical approach to the 'Floating Pelican' song: an exercise in rich interpretation of a Murriny Patha (Northern Australia) song. *Australian Journal of Linguistics* 30.1: 117–30.

Walters, Max, and David Webb, 2001. *Flora Europaea*, vols 1–5 and CD-ROM pack. Cambridge: Cambridge University Press.

Warnier, Jean-Pierre, 2001. A praxeological approach to subjectivation in a material world. *Journal of Material Culture* 6.1: 5–24.

——2007. *The Pot-King: The Body and Technologies of Power*. Leiden: Brill.

Warren, Carol A. B., 1988/86. *Gender Issues in Field Research*. Newbury Park, Calif.: Sage.

Washington Native Plant Society, 2007. *Policy on Collection and Sale of Native Plants*; accessed 6 Oct. 2009 at: http://www.wnps.org/about_wnps/administration/policies/collection_policy.htm

Wax, Rosalie H., 1979. Gender and age in fieldwork and fieldwork education: no good thing is done by any man alone. *Social Problems* 26.5: 509–22.

Webb, Eugene J., Donald T. Campbell, Richard D. Schwartz, and Lee Sechrest, 2000. *Unobtrusive Measures*, revised edn. Thousand Oaks, Calif.: Sage.

Weber, David J., 2007. The linguistic example. In Thomas E. Payne and David J. Weber (eds), *Perspectives on Grammar Writing*. Amsterdam: Bejamins, 199–213.

WEGENER, CLAUDIA, 2008. A grammar of Savosavo: a Papuan language of the Solomon Islands. PhD dissertation, Radboud University.

WEHR, JOHN D., and ROBERT G. SHEATH, 2003. *Freshwater Algae of North America: Ecology and Classification.* San Diego, Calif.: Elsevier Science.

WEINER, ANNETTE, 1976. *Women of Value, Men of Renown: New Perspectives.* Austin: University of Texas Press.

WEINREICH, LOTTE, 1992. *Verbale und nonverbale Strategien in Fernsehgesprächen.* Tübingen: Niemeyer.

WENGER, ETINENNE, 1998. *Communities of Practice: Learning, Meaning, and Identity.* Cambridge: Cambridge University Press.

WENGLE, JOHN L., 1988. *Ethnographers in the Field: The Psychology of Research.* Tuscaloosa: University of Alabama Press.

WESTERN AUSTRALIAN HERBARIUM, 1998–. *FloraBase: The Western Australian Flora*; accessed 8 Sept. 2009 at: http://florabase.dec.wa.gov.au/

WHALEY, LINDSAY, 1997. *An Introduction to Language Typology: The Unity and Diversity of Language.* Thousand Oaks, Calif.: Sage.

WHITELEY, PETER M., 1998. *Rethinking Hopi Ethnography.* Washington, DC: Smithsonian Institute Press.

WIDLOK, THOMAS, 1996. *Topographical Gossip and the Indexicality of Haiǁom environmental knowledge.* Nijmegen: Cognitive Anthropology Research Group, Max Planck Institute.

——1997. Orientation in the wild: the shared cognition of Haiǁ om bushpeople. *Journal of the Royal Anthropological Institute.* 317–332.

——2008. Landscape unbounded: space, place, and orientation in ≠Akhoe Haiǁom and beyond. *Language Sciences* 30.2–3: 362–80.

WIERZBICKA, ANNA, 2005. There are no 'colour universals' but there are universals of visual semantics. *Anthropological Linguistics* 47.2: 217–44.

——2007. Bodies and their parts: an NSM approach to semantic typology. *Language Sciences.* 29.1: 14–65.

——2009. 'Reciprocity': an NSM approach to linguistic typology and social universals. *Studies in Language* 33.1.1: 103–74. doi: 10.1075/sl.33.1.05wie

WILKINS, DAVID, 1992. Linguistic research under Aboriginal control: a personal account of fieldwork in Central Australia. *Australian Journal of Linguistics* 12: 171–200.

——1999. Spatial deixis in Arrernte speech and gesture: on the analysis of a species of composite signal as used by a Central Australian Aboriginal group. In ELISABETH ANDRÉ, MASSIMO POESIO, and HANNES RIESER (eds), *Deixis, Demonstration and Deictic Belief.* Utrecht University, 30–42.

——2003. Why pointing with the index finger is not a universal (in socio-cultural and semiotic terms). In Kita (2003: 171–215).

——2006. Review of 'Gesture: visible action as utterance' by Adam Kendon. *Gesture* 6.2: 119–44.

WILKINSON, MELANIE, R. MARIKA, and NANCY M. WILLIAMS, 2009. This place already has a name. In Harold Koch and Luise Hercus (eds), *Aboriginal Placenames: Naming and Renaming the Australian Landscape.* Canberra: ANU E Press and Aboriginal History Incorporated, 403–62.

WILMÉ, LUCIENNE, 2002. Glossary of botanical terms in French and English; accessed 25 Sept. 2009 at: http://www.mobot.org/mobot/glossary/

WILSON, SHAWN, 2008. *Research is Ceremony: Indigenous Research Methods*. Halifax, NS: Fernwood.

WINTROB, RONALD M., 1969. An inward focus: a consideration of psychological stress in fieldwork. In Frances Henry and Satish Saberwal (eds), *Stress and Response in Fieldwork*. New York: Holt, Rinehart, & Winston, 63–79.

WIPO (WORLD INTELLECTUAL PROPERTY ORGANIZATION), 2010a. *Basic Notions of Copyright and Related Rights*: available at: http://www.wipo.int/export/sites/www/copyright/en/activities/pdf/basic_notions.pdf

——2010b. *Traditional Cultural Expressions (Folklore)*; available at: http://www.wipo.int/tk/en/folklore/

——2010c. *Traditional Knowledge, Genetic Resources and Traditional Cultural Expressions/Folklore*; available at: http://www.wipo.int/tk/en/

WISNER, BEN, DAVID STEA, and SONIA KRUKS, 1991. Participatory and action research methods. In Ervin H. Zube and Gary T. Moore (eds), *Advances in Environment, Behaviour, and Design*, vol. 3. New York: Plenum.

WOBST, MARTIN, 1977. Stylistic behaviour and information exchange. In Charles E. Cleland (ed.), *Papers for the Director: Research Essays in Honor of James B. Griffin*. Ann Arbor: University of Michigan Museum of Anthropology, 317–42.

WOLCOTT, HARRY F., 1995. *The Art of Fieldwork*. Walnut Creek, Calif.: AltaMira Press.

WOLFRAM, WALT, 1993. Ethical considerations in language awareness programs. *Issues in Applied Linguistics* 4.2: 225–55.

——1998. Scrutinizing linguistic gratuity: issues from the field. *Journal of Sociolinguistics* 2.2: 271–9.

——and NATALIE SHILLING-ESTES, 1995. Moribund dialects and the endangerment canon: the case of the Ocracoke brogue. *Language* 71: 696–721.

WOMERSLEY, JOHN S., 1976. *Plant Collecting for Anthropologists, Geographers and Ecologists in Papua New Guinea*. Botany Bulletin No. 2, Office of Forests, Division of Botany, Lae: Papua New Guinea Government Press.

WOODBURY, ANTHONY C., 2003. Defining documentary linguistics. In Austin (2003–10: 35–51).

——2011. Language documentation. In Peter K. Austin and Julia Sallabank (eds), *The Cambridge Handbook of Endangered Languages*. Cambridge: Cambridge University Press, 159–86.

WORDICK, FRANK J. F., 1982. *The Yindjibarndi Language*. Canberra: Dept of Linguistics, Research School of Pacific Studies, Australian University.

WROBEL, EMILIA (forthcoming). What can you get from a media-sharing website that is of sociolinguistic relevance? *Journal of Pidgin and Creole Languages*.

WUNDT, WILHELM, 1973[1921]. *The Language of Gestures*, ed. Thomas A. Seboek; trans. J. S. Thayer, C. M. Greenlauf, and M. D. Silberman from *Völkerpsychologie* (Stuttgart: Kröner, 1921). The Hague: Mouton.

WURM, S. A., 1967. *Linguistic Fieldwork Methods in Australia*. Canberra: Australian Institute of Aboriginal Studies.

YAMADA, MASASHI, BURDIATO RAHMAT, ITOH HIDENORI, and SEKI HIROHISA, 1997. Topology of cat's cradle diagrams and its characterization using knot polynomials. *Transaction of Information Processing Society of Japan* 38.8: 1573–82.

YAMADA, RACQUEL-MARÍA, 2007. Collaborative linguistic fieldwork: practical application of the empowerment model. *Language Documentation and Conservation* 1.2: 257–82.

YOUNG, ROBERT M., and WILLIAM MORGAN, 1992. *Analytical Lexicon of Navajo.* Albuquerque: University of New Mexico Press.

ZASLAVSKY, CLAUDIA, 1973. *Africa Counts: Number and Pattern in African Culture.* Boston, Mass.: Prindle, Weber, & Schmidt.

ZAVALA, ROBERTO, 2000. Multiple classifier systems in Akatek (Mayan). In Gunter Senft (ed.), *Systems of Nominal Classifications.* Cambridge: Cambridge University Press, 114–46.

ZEMP, HUGO, 1979. Aspects of 'Are'are musical theory. *Ethnomusicology.* 23.1: 5–48.

——1994. *'Are'are Music and Shaping Bamboo.* Bloomington, Ind.: Society for Ethnomusicology.

ZENT, STANFORD, 2001. Acculturation and ethnobotanical knowledge loss among the Piaroa of Venezuela: demonstration of a quantitative method for the empirical study of traditional ecological knowledge change. In Luisa Maffi (ed.), *On Biocultural Diversity: Linking Language, Knowledge, and the Environment.* Washington, DC: Smithsonian Institution Press, 190–211.

——2005. Transmission, loss and persistence of traditional ecological knowledge. *Encyclopedia of Life Support Systems (EOLSS) Ethnobiology* unit 5. Washington, DC: American Anthropological Association: available at: http://www.eolss.net/outlinecomponents/Ethnobiology.aspx

——and EGLEE LÓPEZ-ZENT, 2004. Ethnobotanical convergence, divergence, and change among the Hotï of the Venezuelan Guayana. In Thomas J. S. Carlson and Luisa Maffi (eds), *Ethnobotany and Conservation of Biocultural Diversity: Advances in Economic Botany.* New York: New York Botanical Garden Press, 79–112.

Index of Names

Index of Topics

Made in the USA
Coppell, TX
02 February 2021

49454067R00308